People Funny Boy

Also by David Katz

Solid Foundation: An Oral History of Reggae

People Funny Boy

The Genius of Lee 'Scratch' Perry

David Katz

WHITE
RABBIT

First published in Great Britain in 2000 by Payback Press
This updated edition published in 2021 by White Rabbit,
an imprint of The Orion Publishing Group Ltd
Carmelite House, 50 Victoria Embankment
London EC4Y 0DZ

An Hachette UK Company

1 3 5 7 9 10 8 6 4 2

A CIP catalogue record for this book is
available from the British Library.

ISBN (Hardback) 978 1 3996 0154 2
ISBN (Export Trade Paperback) 978 1 4746 2253 0
ISBN (eBook) 978 1 4746 2255 4
ISBN (Audio) 978 1 4746 2256 1

Typeset by Born Group
Printed and bound in Great Britain by Clays Ltd, Elcograf S.p.A.

MIX
Paper from
responsible sources
FSC® C104740
FSC
www.fsc.org

www.whiterabbitbooks.co.uk
www.orionbooks.co.uk

To Scratch, for the music, wisdom and direction, and to Claudia for the enduring bond

'I am the book, and I am the half – the half that's never been told'

— Lee 'Scratch' Perry

Contents

A Blessing

By Rainford Hugh Lee 'Scratch' Perry

Thank you David Katz
You have my blessings on this special book.
The future facts of life, reality knocks.
God bless you
Good luck
Success
From President £ee £eo $cratch Perry ABC Love.
Mr Ghost Writer
The buyer will be very pleased with this book of Reinford
King Hugh Perry rain all over the Globe.
Park to parks
Streets to streets
Lane to lane
Black Ark rain.
I rain facts of life
$un of £ord Thunder
Black Ark God Zadkiel
X29, 1999.
Kids God
Kids King
Kids Lord,
Lord Jesus Christ God
INRI.
One Love
X INRI
Jah Love
Enjoy this.

FOREWORD

The Upsetter

British reggae pioneer Dennis Bovell, one of the 'Cricklewood 12', once told me about the circumstances that led to him being arrested and charged with incitement to riot in 1974. He was playing Sufferer's sound system in a sound clash against Lord Koos and Count Nick's at a venue called Burtons. Lee 'Scratch' Perry was in attendance, supplying him with dub plates. The police entered the venue and tried to make an arrest just as one of the selectors began playing Junior Byles' 'Beat Down Babylon', produced by Perry. Fighting broke out between the revellers and the police. According to Bovell, Perry declared, 'I am the Upsetter', turned up his collar and made a speedy exit.

I once described Lee 'Scratch' Perry, the Upsetter, as the Salvador Dalí of reggae. I wasn't thinking so much about their art, but more about the audacity of their public image. In my youth I was a big fan of Perry's music, especially his instrumental productions. Having met him on a few occasions over the years, beginning in 1977, hearing several anecdotes from people who had encountered him, and seeing him briefly in performance, I have been left with the impression that he was a man with an impish sense of humour and Anancy-like attributes. Eventually an octogenarian, the phenomenal Jamaican music maker and performer lived a roller-coaster life of epic proportions. Renowned for his creative wizardry in the world of reggae music, Perry had already become a legend by the age of fifty. What makes his story so extraordinary is the fact that he has never been proficient on any musical instrument, and yet the cream of his prolific output of recordings belong to the reggae canon. His innate gift for music, rooted in his Jamaican rural background where he was grounded in Afro-Jamaican folk culture, first found expression in his talent as a dancer. Musicians, vocalists and producers alike have all spoken about the magical power of Perry's creativity and his sonic genius in the recording studio. He had a talented pool of session musicians to draw from. Moreover, he soon found access to the growing market for reggae music in Britain.

Perry served his apprenticeship under the tutelage of pioneering record producer Clement 'Sir Coxsone' Dodd, learning every aspect of the music business, and became his right-hand man before branching out on his own. One of his early songs, 'People Funny Boy', signalled the arrival of the reggae beat in the late 1960s and Perry's rise to fame as a songwriter, arranger, producer, recording engineer and entrepreneur. Not blessed with a great singing voice, it was as a producer that Perry soon established a reputation as the man with the Midas touch. What set him apart from his competitors was his unique creativity, his idiosyncratic approach to music making and his peculiar sonic sensibility.

It was during the late 1960s and early '70s that Perry established his reputation as a hit-maker, with tunes like Susan Cadogan's 'Hurt So Good' and The Upsetters' 'Return of Django'; he also worked with Bob Marley on some of the

Wailers' classic tunes. He reached the apotheosis of his creativity during the Black Ark years when, with the convenience
of his own studio, he was able to give free rein to his creative
imagination, producing his own unique sound, enhancing
his credentials as the undisputed master of the sonic art of
dub with the classic album, *Super Ape*. With success came
enormous pressures. The Black Ark Studio became a magnet,
not only for singers and players of instruments, but also
undesirables, leading to its eventual demise by fire. It was all
too much for the Upsetter, who at the time appeared to have
undergone some kind of nervous breakdown and assumed
the new persona of Pipecock Jackxon. His utterances were
sometimes outrageous, his behaviour bizarre.

Perry's newly acquired reputation as a madman enhanced
his notoriety, magnified his mystique. The last two decades
of the twentieth century were a remarkably productive time
for him in the studio and on the road. It was during this
period that Perry realised his ambition as a solo artist and
performer. With Britain as his new base, he was able to make
forays into Europe and further afield. Moreover, he embraced
opportunities for engagement with the new musical forms
of the digital age. By the end of the last millennium, he had
settled in Switzerland, continuing his musical journey.

People Funny Boy, David Katz's critically acclaimed biography of Perry, a work of keen scholarship, is truly a labour of
love. Meticulously researched, it maps Perry's journey from his
Jamaican peasant roots to his cult status as reggae guru on the
global stage. In the telling of Perry's story, Katz's main focus
is on his career in music, but we also learn something about
his personal life. It is a book not just for fans of Lee 'Scratch'
Perry, but also reggae scholars in general, as it illuminates
the history of reggae and its impact on other popular musical

genres. This new edition allows the author to deal with a few inaccuracies and omissions in the first edition whilst bringing us up to date with the first two decades of the twenty-first century. The Lee 'Scratch' Perry of his later years was the old warrior of yesterday who, having conquered his demons and slain the dragons, continued to chart his own course. May his sounds continue to vibrate on.

Linton Kwesi Johnson
8 September 2021

Introduction

I first met Lee 'Scratch' Perry in January 1987 at Dingwalls nightclub in Camden, a few weeks after I left the relative tranquillity of San Francisco to complete my studies in the grey chaos of London. Captivated by his music during my teens through the many reggae radio programmes broadcast on Bay Area community stations, I had already written an article about him for underground magazine *Wiring Department* and hoped to conduct an interview, but Perry had little inclination, spending most of the evening performing obscure rituals, blowing herb smoke through a wooden recorder placed in alternate nostrils while standing on one leg, grabbing illuminated lightbulbs with his bare hands and blowing a whistle at regular intervals. He did, however, take home the article I had written and a few days later summoned me to a southeast London studio, where he was filming himself with a tripod-mounted video camera, voicing a new version of Bob Marley's 'Exodus'. Perry asked me to bring him thirteen stones from the banks of the Thames, which he placed inside the video monitor, and when the engineer later told him the song was thirteen minutes and five seconds long, he found 'the other five' stones evidently missing from his video set.

Before the day was done, he presented me with a silver ring adorned with a winged death's head, which I was to wear every time I put pen to paper; Lee Perry thus appointed me his 'Ghost Writer', bestowing the highest of honours and heaviest of burdens on a journalist decidedly green. Perry had apparently been seeking someone to help with a book about his life and was taken with my comments on his auto-biographical 'Introducing Myself', in which he challenged Ronald Reagan, Margaret Thatcher, Queen Elizabeth II and the Pope. Though other journalists were bemoaning him as a lost cause whose career was over, Perry understood that his message was reaching me and took my arrival as a sign, and despite my ongoing protests that others were more suited to the task, he insisted that the choice had been made.

I then held – and continue to hold – Lee Perry's music paramount as the most striking, inspirational, and original I have ever encountered, and it was long clear that his unique vision made him one of the major creative figures of the twentieth century, but it took many months for me to even consider attempting the task; meanwhile, through the perpetual contact he initiated, I found myself being drawn into what can only be described as another world – a whimsical and pre-ordained universe laden with spiritual significance and symbolic truths, where retribution awaits the unsuspecting and unseen forces are constantly at work, where there is no such thing as an accident and everything happens for a reason.

I spent the majority of the next two years in Perry's company, spending time with him nearly every day. London then ceased to be his home base, though it has continued to be mine, so we have since inevitably spent less time together, but continued to meet regularly in diverse locations and frequently spoke by telephone.

Once Perry was no longer a London resident, I began an early longhand draft of this book, but grappled with major gaps in my knowledge. I thus concentrated on interviewing collaborators and associates, ceaselessly gathering data, and constructing other drafts over the years before finally bringing the first edition of the book into print at the dawning of the new millennium.

Then, during the next twenty years, I conducted dozens of other interviews with important figures, as well as longer formal interviews with Perry himself, and have spent much more time in Jamaica and other global locations where Perry has worked, furthering my understanding of his life and output, as well as the context of his lived environments. The intervening years have allowed me to correct many errors in the original text and to pose new questions to Perry and his associates, yielding a story that is more complete, accurate, nuanced, and up to date, and I have done my best to remove the worst instances of purple prose to yield a more satisfying and approachable read for a general audience.

Nevertheless, in many ways, this book remains something other than what either of us originally conceived. Perry once requested a comic book format, and at one point was more concerned with the number of pages than what was written on them, but the biggest obstacle was that Perry seemed to think the book would write itself, early on responding to questions with an endless series of riddles or blank replies. Thankfully, he opened up over time, especially during the years when he stopped drinking alcohol and smoking weed, though the abstinence was not to last, and in more recent times, as the halcyon days became more distant and the focus more esoteric, memories were harder to dredge up.

In any case, the only truly predictable thing about Perry was his unpredictability, and perpetual moodiness often rendered direct questioning out of the question. The Perry I came to know typically wove a constant, conflated stream of parables and enigmas, speaking in rapid, abstract sequences that are not easily translated, the verbal conflagration of a mind on fire.

Some life events have proven too traumatic for Perry and his family to confront; consider, for example, the following typical early exchange:

'What about this book you're writing,' Perry would often glare at me.

'But Scratch,' I once protested, 'there are still many things I need to know to make a proper start.'

'Anything you want to know, just ask me,' he insisted.

'OK, tell me about your parents,' I suggested, not knowing that he had been denounced by his mother and had not spoken to her for many years, his father having long abandoned him. 'Were they farming people, or . . .'

'*Blood claat*, David, you no see it? Me dead already, me is a ghost.'

End of story.

Additionally, different happenings from diverse eras became blurred in a mind that perpetually worked overtime, making a muddled and often misrepresented history all the more confused; for example, he once spoke of the destruction of some of his studio equipment in the early 1980s as being partially motivated by King Tubby's murder, which occurred in 1989, problematising the chronology.

On the other hand, Perry was always perfectly frank when ready to describe a situation to me or when he had something specific to relate, even dictating exact passages for verbatim inclusion, and the shifting nature of our relationship over the years inevitably resulted in the texture of this book, which mixes the testimony of others along with Perry's own, his connection to everyone of significance in Jamaican music and other major figures outside it precipitating the inclusion of other voices.

Those familiar with the vengeful punning of Perry's proclamations may already be prepared for baffling and contradictory statements, and testimony from associates may add to the confusion rather than alleviate it. I was often presented with differing accounts of significant events, particularly regarding recording sessions, as well as personal relationships. I am aware of misleading information deliberately stated to justify unauthorised releases and dubious song-writing claims, or to further a longstanding grudge; more often, respondents simply had difficulty remembering the circumstances of sessions or events from decades ago. Human memory has its limitations and statements given in good faith are not necessarily accurate; habitual ganja smoking has been associated with short- and long-term memory loss (as well as possible psychosis). Furthermore, those who have delved into the murky waters of Jamaican vinyl releases will already know just how little data was available until relatively recently, the lack of precise dates yielding a chronology that may not seem entirely logical.

Despite my best efforts to improve this edition, as with other texts on Jamaican music, this book is bound to have errors and omissions that will later be brought to light, and I apologise for them in advance and claim full ownership, though certain lesser creations are purposefully omitted, due to the volume of Perry's work.

Ultimately, the greatest source of fact-checking of the first edition came from Perry himself, whose stringent scrutiny of a draft in May 1999 resulted in significant alterations; Mr Perry has my supreme gratitude for his willingness to listen to and comment on the entire text, which I read to him over the course of a few days in Düsseldorf. Other substantial amendments were made before the publication of the second edition, particularly during a week spent with Perry in Switzerland in January 2006, as well as the formal interviews I have since conducted for this present expanded edition.

In seeking to chart the particular life journey of Lee 'Scratch' Perry, this book attempts to illuminate the endless creativity that has marked his incredibly complex body of work while exploring the mass of contradictions that lurk behind his legend. Perry was so far ahead of his time for so long that a broader recognition came late, and this book is partly concerned with making clear precisely why so many have attested to his genius – a word that is grossly overused in popular music, but entirely justified in Perry's case.

Lee Perry was concretely involved with every significant phase of Jamaican music, from the pre-ska years of the early 1960s to the proto-dancehall of the 1980s and '90s, and his creative innovations have found a broader resonance in a range of other genres, from rap and hip-hop to punk, jungle, ambient and trip-hop, from electronica to avant-garde, stretching across six continents. Though Perry is now a hip name for pop stars to drop, his individuality and unpredictability saw him reap fewer rewards than some of his students – most notably Bob Marley, Jamaica's most famous son, whose career was largely shaped by creative interaction with Perry. It is through the exploration of such links that this book attempts to show the importance of Perry's vision and trace its lasting impact on various music styles.

At the same time, I have tried to make sense of the complicated alternate space created for Perry's curious spiritual vision whilst simultaneously detailing the particulars of an invariably unique lifestyle. If the mysteries of Rastafari are often confounding to outsiders, then Perry's particular cosmology is doubly so; though often baffling and far from simple, I have done my best to explain its significance in his life and work.

To be relatively objective, I have consciously left key points open to the interpretation of the reader. Perry remains an enigmatic figure, partly of his own design, and many of his actions, as with his work, are debatable. Though several describe him as a genius, others degrade him as a madman, accuse him of being a *ginal* (crook) or dismiss him as a charlatan; the reader must ultimately make their own impression. Similarly, I offer no claim of gospel truths in my depiction of Perry's music. Though I have tried to be as accurate as possible in my contextual explanations, readers will have to draw their own conclusions about the worthiness of the records themselves.

Accounts of Jamaican music have often tended towards the mythical, with depictions of Marley as a saint or deity particularly troubling. Though mysticism has played an important role in Perry's life (as it has to some degree with the majority of the island's musical figures), I have consciously avoided an overdramatised or eulogised portrait. Perry may have been one of the most original and inspired men to ever walk the face of this earth, but he was only a man, despite a creative vision that rendered him beyond the constraints of ordinary mortals. Similarly, Perry has been likened to free-form jazz pioneer Sun Ra, wacky funk star George Clinton and eccentric artist Salvador Dalí, but such comparisons are ultimately futile in the face of Perry's singular trajectory.

I am also aware of the limitations I have brought to this text through my situation as an outsider, younger than many who appear in its pages; I have spent far less time on the blessed island of Jamaica than I would have liked, and a portion of the music described in this book was recorded before I was born. Perry has noted that he came before his time, and he certainly came before *mine*, which has influenced the narrative framing through the testimony of those who were present at the events described, aided by minimal contextual commentary. I feel that the best historical portions of this book lie in the words of the true experts of Jamaican music who are quoted throughout it: the musicians, singers, producers and engineers who have themselves created it, and Perry's own words, of course, speak for themselves.

As with other writers, I have found that the printed word does not do justice to the essence of Jamaica's spoken patois, but I have not attempted to Jamaicanise nor Anglicise quotations. Instead, I have tried to reproduce spoken statements as accurately as possible, in keeping with each speaker's use of language.

This book is also the culmination of my own long and difficult journey in an adopted land, the quest for accurate information taking me to far-flung locations. My ultimate motivation in following through has been to help Perry achieve the greater glory he was due while he was still alive to benefit from it. Lee 'Scratch' Perry is one of the few who truly deserved the title of living legend; the foolhardy speculations on his sanity detract from the creativity that has resulted in some of the most inspiring and visionary sounds to yet grace the ears of the human race. Above all, I hope this biography has helped to clarify the importance of his creations.

CHAPTER ONE

Introducing Myself:
From Kendal to Kingston

'I'm an artist, a musician, a magician, a writer, a singer. I'm everything. My name is Lee from the African jungle, originally from West Africa. I'm a man from somewhere else, but my origin is from Africa, straight to Jamaica through reincarnation, reborn in Jamaica. Superman comes to earth cos him sick and tired. I'm not sick and tired because I'm learning what goes on, so when we get frustrated, that is when the music come down by raindrops to support all here with a broken heart and don't know what to do. I have been programmed. Many people who born again must come back to learn a lesson. Have you heard of E.T.? I am E.T., savvy? Savvy?'

Lee Perry has spoken of his origins in contradictory ways. He claimed to come from Jupiter, once said he was born in the sky, often named Africa as his true birthplace, and suggested that his empty body was commandeered by space aliens after an undocumented death. According to family members, his earthbound arrival came in the rural district of Kendal in northwest Jamaica, the third of four children born to Henry Perry and

Lilian Davis during the 1930s. Like rural peasants the world over, he was raised in an environment marked by centuries of exploitation and neglect, the remoteness of the region contributing to the lack of information about his early life, perhaps fitting for a man who kept himself shrouded in mystery.

His first name was Rainford — sometimes spelt Reinford — his middle name Hugh, but in keeping with the customs of his West African ancestors, once an individual personality began to manifest, he was given the pet name Leeburn by his mother, shortened to Lee. Incorrect citations and Perry's habit of adding a year to his age when speaking of it publicly have contributed to confusion about his date of birth, but official records indicate that Lee Perry was born on Friday, 20 March 1936, entering the world on a payday under the star sign of Pisces.

Hanover Parish lies at the northwest tip of Jamaica, about the farthest point from Kingston on the island, and Kendal is a cluster of rudimentary dwellings buried deep in its interior, the terrain marked by inhospitable land and the stifling humidity of the untamed bush. Most inhabitants descended from the slaves that toiled on the nearby Saxham sugarcane estate, which remained the focal point for local employment after emancipation, and bananas were later established as a second plantation crop, but before he was born, most had succumbed to a disease.

During the time of Perry's great-grandparents, many locals could still remember when Busha Aide was the overseer. A sadistic brute who took perverse pleasure in publicly denigrating his workforce, Aide and his wife Mary ruled Kendal and the surrounding estates of Grange, Prospect and Cauldwell with an iron fist. The slaves he controlled cultivated and harvested cane that was exported from the nearby port of

Lucea as part of an endemic system that was a primary driver of economic growth in Britain, and since Jamaica was the largest sugar exporter in the Empire, her plantations were lynchpins of British capitalism and imperialism.

Lilian Davis, known as Ina, was born in Kendal in 1915 from an informal liaison between Jane Ann Horton and Jonathan Davis; her parents never married, and each had children from previous relationships. Ina's father died when she was young, so her mother raised her in the harshness of poverty with half-siblings Philippe, Mary, Celeste, Sammy and Gussie, and she also came to know some of her father's children, including Essie, Sue, Amy, Man-Man, and a boy called Ira who died young. Ina's mother farmed staple crops on a nearby ridge, struggling to grow enough to feed the family, so when Ina came of age, she took up sewing to contribute to the family's welfare. In later years, she would be universally addressed as Miss Ina.

At age sixteen, she began a relationship with Henry Perry, an eighteen-year-old from the same village, sometimes referred to as Cornel Perry.

'I did know him from school days when me is a small girl,' said Miss Ina. 'He come from the same place, Kendal.'

Henry was a roadwork contractor whose quarter-Indian blood made him stand out. Their first child, Beryl, was born in September 1932 and given the pet name Dulcie; Lesbert was born two years later, known as Sonny as the couple's firstborn son, and a second daughter, Icelyn, was born in February 1938 and given the nickname Sitta.

Shortly thereafter, when Lee was only two years old, Henry Perry left the family home, taking up with a woman called Miss Tad in another part of Kendal. Although the rest of the children stayed with Miss Ina, young Lee was placed in his father's care, but life with Henry Perry was unbearable, the regular beatings causing Lee to shelter at the home of a family friend, who brought him back to his mother.

'Growing up, it was really a rough life,' said Perry. 'My mother have four of us and when she and my father part, she take three and leave me alone with my father because my father like me most and want to keep me, but it's not much me father could do for me because he didn't learn anything about how to have feelings for somebody. Maybe he just wanted me to be his slave. I didn't stay with him much because I couldn't take the treatment, because it wasn't any love treatment or anything. He wasn't the type that have feelings for children like me, so I decide to run away to me mother.'

Henry Perry maintained little contact with Lee and his siblings and later moved to England with his new wife. Miss Ina and the children were left to struggle on their own, the next few years particularly trying.

'For my mother, things was always hard because she's just like an ordinary woman, with no education or something like that – like a sufferer, a suffering woman. The house that we were sharing, I don't think it was much bigger than this room. We had to sleep in one bed, and she was trying to send us to school, but couldn't afford it much.'

Growing up in Kendal, Lee was just another barefoot country boy that would walk up the hill to Kendal School with empty pockets and a hungry belly. Two meals a day was standard and sometimes the children would have to make do with one, supplemented by whatever scraps they could find to share with friends.

'When we go to school we was very, very poor,' said Sonny. 'Sometimes a penny a day we get to carry to school, so we have to take it easy, buy cool drink and patty and bread, and all ten of we eat the one.'

His mother remembered Lee as a lively little boy that was well liked by his peers, though prone to mischief-making when older. He and Sonny had a natural affinity in younger days, since they resembled each other physically, were closest in age and the only male children in the household.

'When we were growing up, we used to love each other and never war,' said Sonny. 'In the early days, all 'bout, anywhere is me and him. Me never left him, me always be like a bodyguard for me smaller brother. We never bow, nor trouble no one, as we are very honest.'

Apart from school, the children were sometimes recruited to help their mother to make ends meet.

'My mother used to be involved in farming, planting yams and everything,' said Perry. 'Certain times, when she's not doing her own planting, she go to the estate and cut cane to make some money, and then some weekends, or Thursday or Friday, me might go and help my mother cut some cane, too, because my mother was living alone with four of us, and my father was living with another woman and wouldn't pay us any mind.'

'We mother did poor, and we daddy did poor, so we just help out,' said Sonny.

They attended the Anglican church in nearby Rock Spring, though it was not a central focus; instead, Ettu was a cornerstone. Passed down to Ina by her mother, the express purpose of this ritualistic form of West African dance is to invoke ancestral spirits for atonement, especially after the death of a member of the community or if an ancestor appears in a dream. The word derives from the Yoruba *etutu*, meaning appeasement or reconciliation, connoting a rite that placates ancestral spirits through reverence.

Practitioners of Ettu are normally of Yoruba origin, a minority population that arrived in Jamaica by a circuitous route as indentured labourers in the period immediately following the abolition of the slave trade; many endured the Middle Passage twice, having first been deposited in Sierra Leone after being liberated from blockaded slave ships. Unique to a handful of communities established in western Jamaica, Ettu dancing is accompanied by a large kerosene pan that is beaten with both hands to provide a rattling sound, along with the beats of a smaller goatskin drum, with call-and-response chants utilising Yoruba language; the ritual is usually begun by the sacrifice of an animal, its blood used to mark the foreheads of participants with the sign of a cross, with grated kola nut distributed and white rum poured on the ground in libation. Though Jamaica's colonial rulers were intent on wiping out all cultural practices Africans had brought from their homeland, a proliferation of underground activities saw certain customs retained and adapted. Ettu thus thrived in remote bush communities, allowing Miss Ina to retain a link with her ancestors, preserving traditions from before the forced migration of her forebears to a hostile land. Eventually, she would emerge as an Ettu Queen, the elder in her community that leads the dance.

'It's an ancient order from Africa,' said Perry. 'It has something to do with chanting spirits, keeping ancient spirits together. Even when our people are getting old, they still show respect and holler out for them. They drink rum, so you put rum on the earth, cook rice without salt, make porridge without sugar and throw it on the earth for the spirits to eat, then start playing drums and start to do the culture dance. My mother happens to be one of the Ettu Queens, and her mother before was an Ettu Queen, so it pass on along the family line, and when them dance, them barefoot and make connection with the earth, dancing to the drum and connecting the soul. Those people beat them foot on the earth, making sound and making communication, like telepathic sound to the earth. So she do the culture dance and talk to the spirits and the spirits tell them what goes on. The ancient spirit who was here before, those that are dead and gone, they talk to those people and those people talk to them.'

A related African custom with pervasive influence was belief in the broader spirit world, the existence of benign and malevolent spirits and their corresponding powers to assist or harm viewed with absolute gravity. Such beliefs continue to be the norm throughout much of Jamaica, despite a majority adherence to Christianity.

Around six years after the end of her relationship with Henry Perry, Miss Ina was courted by Granville Blythe, a kind soul that was 'Head Man' at the Saxham sugarcane estate, in charge of the employment of workers and transportation of the cane. When the couple married, the family moved into his home in the small settlement of Grange, about a mile and a half west of Kendal, where the children were embraced by their stepfather.

'He did like them, he took them as him own,' said Miss Ina. 'They get on all right, no problem.'

Ina and Granville soon began to have children of their own, beginning with Veta Aneta, born in August 1949 and given the pet name Girlie. The family began attending the local Church of God, one of the African-influenced evangelical churches where hats were worn and the Lord was praised through song, accompanied by rhythmic clapping and the banging of tambourines, though religion still played a peripheral role in their lives. Sonny, Lee and Sitta were then attending Green Island School, a good three-mile walk away (where future prime minister P. J. Patterson was a fellow student), while

Dulcie had gone in search of work to Negril, a fishing village some twenty miles west.

Though other family members refute it, Perry said he found school a pointless exercise, the archaic instruction forcing conformity to an alien European model; the language of his lessons was incomprehensible, and the experience marked by cruelty. His small size and quick mouth made him an easy target for the teacher's cane and the bullying of older students, like his cousin, Sissy Davis, who used to torment one of his closest friends, until the wily Perry struck back with a razor blade.

'We did have a good friend named Manzie, but one girl, big and coarse, she did fight the guy and the guy afraid,' said Sonny. 'One day when the gal start to fight Manzie, Lee come up and give around three slashes, and it's under Saxham bridge he go hide. When him come out, him get flogged still – the old lady beat him.'

'Manzie didn't have much time with him own brother because you always have to find somebody who think like you when you're growing up,' said Perry. 'So he find me, but he wasn't a fighter. Sissy pick a fight with him and beat him to show off to her friends and I didn't like it, so I take my razor blade and start to do the doctor job on the girl's hand, cut her up and bite her. It was a surprise because they never expect that me could be so small and carry a weapon to school. Then me used to beat long nails like ten-penny nail, hot it with iron on the fire and beat it out, sharpen it and make our own knife.'

After the incident with his cousin, Lee began to carry a weapon with him everywhere, which he would sharpen with a stone kept in his pocket. The bullies stopped troubling him, but the oppressive and alien nature of school continued to be anathema. He dropped out, aged fifteen, at the start of the 1950s.

'I had to leave school at Fourth Form, and I didn't learn anything in school,' said Perry. 'It was like a joke, like wasting time. We didn't learn to write, and we didn't learn to add anything. It's when me leave school me start to learn to write, without a teacher.'

Perry later insisted his knowledge came entirely from nature, and another kind of lesson came when he was in the hills, minding the family animals.

'He used to tend the goats and one Sunday morning he go and buck him big toe and have to go to the hospital in Lucea – he never wear shoes in those days,' chuckled Sonny. 'The nurses them love him, doctor and everybody.'

'I was loving animals, so I have to feed the goats early in the morning and feed the rabbits,' said Perry. 'I used to run the goats for energy and the next thing I know, I end up in Lucea Hospital for six months because the head of the toe come off.'

Not long after the toe healed, in October 1952, Miss Ina gave birth to Desmond, who was given the pet name Lloyd.

Coming of age, Perry felt increasingly constrained by his environment. There was little to keep him in Grange, and his only solace came through music, which inspired him to do the wild dance moves that yielded an early reputation.

'The crossroads is where the dancehall used to be, and he couldn't pass it,' said Sonny. 'He have a crowd of gal and boy around him, and every one of them are friends.'

But rousing his peers at the dancehall was not enough to keep him in the area, and as soon as an opportunity arose, he was gone.

Lee Perry spent much of his teens and early twenties ambling around the west and south of Jamaica, motivated by an unseen spiritual force. As he later explained, 'People who deal with spiritual vibration like me, the spirit tell me exactly what to do.'

The youth he spent in Kendal and Grange was defined by impoverishment; slavery had been banished for over a century, but Jamaica's Black majority continued to bear the brunt of colonial oppression. As the young Rainford contemplated the ceaseless drudgery, he questioned whether this was to be his lowly purpose. Older family members and most of his peers had endured back-breaking labour in the cane fields for a pittance, but even those jobs were in short supply in Kendal and the wages substandard. Instead, he took the first step towards a long and winding path of non-conformity by answering the call of the domino game.

As a domino champion, Perry learned more than just how to slap the tiles and which numbers to play first; he would study the faces of the other players while keeping his own expressionless, trying to use unseen senses to determine what move to make next, conveying subtle gestures to make silent communication with teammates. Mastering the art of unspoken communication and the sizing up of his opponents, he retained the skills for use in other contexts.

'Dominoes, it's like a mental thing,' said Perry. 'If you are playing with a partner, you might show him a hand code and him shake him head, then he don't have to tell you anything more. So it's a mental thing, a telepathic thing.'

A friend named Dougie, who everyone called Bogus, had gone to work in distant Clarendon Parish and come back with a bicycle, so Lee and Sonny followed Dougie's lead and travelled 100 miles to the southeast by truck to reach the Race Course estate, near the town of Hayes, where they cultivated and harvested sugarcane for several months, lodging at basic shared digs the estate provided.

'Dougie was going to Clarendon every year, so we decide to go with him one of the years,' said Perry. 'He know when the truck going, and we catch the truck.'

'Him carry we down and we no have no money,' said Sonny. 'He take care of we until we start work.'

'Dougie showed me what to do because me no know much about cultivating and cutting cane, so him was teaching me how to survive,' Perry continued. 'Me was young and have lots of energy, so me was enjoying it because me wasn't doing anything in Hanover. He had a bicycle and me did want to buy a bicycle, but me couldn't cut enough cane in Saxham to buy a bicycle, so I go to Clarendon.'

Back in Grange, the bicycle enabled him to reach dances in the surrounding area more easily. During the sugarcane cropping season, he attended many competitions held in the neighbouring parish of Westmoreland, where his reputation began to soar as a virtuoso of the latest moves during a time when he was known as the Neat Little Man.

'They would have dance contests in Grange Hill, Little London, Savanna La Mar, and I was the champion all the time. I was the best boogie-woogie dancer, then it come into Yanking and I become the best Yanker, and then things change to the Mashed Potato and I was still winning.'

The dance contests were fuelled by the sound systems, mobile pieces of public address equipment that had huge sets of speaker boxes, powerful amplifiers and a turntable that could be set up to blast pre-recorded music anywhere. New Orleans artists always made a strong impression, with Louis Jordan a favourite for boogie-woogie and Fats Domino's forlorn 'Going To The River' his preferred song for the Yank's drastic disjointedness, Perry feinting his partner into a false backwards fall in time to the rhythm, then catching her at the last moment.

19

'When him come ah Grange Hill and have dance round ah Mint Road and all them places, crowd come gather waiting to see him,' said Perry's cousin, Stainton Moore, known as Archie after the American boxer. 'He used to dance with Amy, the daughter of a musician named Smith who used to have an orchestra band in Grange Hill, and when them dance, everybody just hold on and watch them.'

While Perry was dancing his way towards glory, his mother gave birth to Milton in October 1956, nicknamed Poppa Son, or P-Son for short.

Lee and his siblings spent their formative years during a fraught time in Jamaican history. The Great Depression had hit Jamaica hard, resulting in high unemployment, poor wages for the working and a dire lack of civil and political rights, leading to the widespread labour disputes that rocked the island in May 1938, first at the Kingston wharves, where United Fruit Company workers staged a strike, and then at Tate and Lyle's sugarcane estate in Frome, about eight miles southeast of Kendal, where police shot three protestors dead, bayoneted a fourth and jailed 109; farmworkers also downed tools in St Mary. With thousands on strike across the country, a State of Emergency was declared, resulting in hundreds of arrests and forty-six deaths.

The bitter struggle for decent working conditions led to the emergence of two charismatic trade union leaders who lobbied Jamaica's colonial rulers to implement a basic living wage: Norman Manley was a Rhodes scholar who became a leading criminal barrister, and his gregarious second cousin, Alexander Bustamante, a plantation overseer's son who achieved little formal education. Born William Alexander Clarke, Bustamante was a moneylender with self-mytholo-gising tendencies who adopted the surname after mysterious travels in Panama, Cuba and the USA, where he reportedly made a fortune on the stock market. These key figures of the independence movement had visions for Jamaica that were diametrically opposed, since Manley was a Fabian socialist and Bustamante a free-market champion. Manley was invited to lead the People's National Party (PNP) when the accountant and independence campaigner Osmond Theodore Fairclough founded it in 1938 as a pro-independence vehicle, and the PNP maintained Bustamante's trade union following his internment in 1940, but on his release in 1942, Bustamante quit the party to form the right-wing Jamaica Labour Party (JLP), which swept to power by a wide margin in the island's first general elections in 1944, making Bustamante the leader of Jamaica's first democratically elected Executive Council, though the election had been marred by stabbings and stone-throwing incidents amongst party supporters. The JLP narrowly clung to power in the 1949 election but lost to the PNP in 1955, establishing a pervasive pattern of two-term reigns.

The government then earmarked a new tourist development in Negril, eventually opening an isolated fishing village to international visitors. The project began in earnest in mid-1959 with the construction of a highway to Orange Bay in Hanover, ultimately allowing direct access from Montego Bay, where a new airport for international visitors was situated, and despite having no formal qualifications, Perry got a job bulldozing roads in the early stages of the project.

'While I was in Kendal, I met a guy named Jenkins who drive a tractor,' said Perry. 'I stick with him and start to copy everything him do, buts he never know that I was learning what he was doing. Then I heard that there is construction in Negril and they're looking for tractor drivers, so I go and get a job when the woods and all just start to cut, and I start to drive a TD9 tractor. I find out that everything I try to do, it just happens, so I don't even have to try. I see that I'm lucky, and people who can't get the job are wondering how me can get it.'

'He even dynamite rocks with electric dynamite,' said Sonny. 'He like those things, but it's dangerous!'

While concentrating on the task at hand, Perry tuned into the sounds generated by the construction, focusing on the energies of the machines as they clashed with nature from the seat of a yellow Caterpillar bulldozer. On the job, time passed with its own rhythm; back in Kendal, sister Lorna, later known as Miss Nell, was born in January 1960.

During the project, Perry rented a spartan room in a large tenement in the town of Little London, located between Negril and Savanna La Mar, where he became romantically involved with teenaged Ruby Williams, who used to visit her friend at the tenement. Affectionately known as Tootsie, she was an enchanting beauty of part-Indian descent with long, wavy hair that mesmerised him during their courtship: 'I wanted to have kids with Indian hair, and that was it.'

Eventually, as things became more serious, the pair were jointly baptised at the local Church of God, where the pastor convinced them to marry; their wedding took place on 7 January 1961, when he was twenty-four and she sixteen, but was hastily arranged and sparsely attended, a portent that the marriage would soon falter.

'We lived together for about eighteen months, then we wanted a change and the pastor suggested we get married, but after the marriage we only lived together for six months,' said Perry. 'It could not work because the girl was from a poor family and we were getting short of money because the programme in Negril was closing. The money wasn't coming in to make it like you could run a married house, so she run away to Montego Bay. When you just met somebody, the vibration you get off a new love is nice, so it take a time until we find we weren't living cooperatively because she never show what she is like at the beginning, that she only love silver and gold and money. She could do sewing but never wanted to work by it, so she go to Montego Bay to try to live off others. Then I went to Kingston because that was my destiny and where destiny call you, you have to go. I was in Negril heaping up stone and trench-stone with tractor, and after a while, me go up to Kingston and fling rock-stone after Goliath.'

He later explained that mysterious events, 'miracle gifts' and 'blessings from God' occurred during the time of his construction work, directing him to Kingston.

'I get an overload from throwing stones down there. I started making positive connection with stones, by throwing stones to stones I start to hear sounds. When the stones clash I hear the thunder clash, and I hear lightning flash, and I hear words, and I don't know where the words them coming from. These words send me to King's Stone: to Kingston. Kingston means King's Stone, the son of the King. That's where the music's coming from, so I go up to King's Stone because the stone that I was throwing in Negril send me to King's Stone for my graduation.'[1]

Perry's independent spirit and impulsive nature ensured he would never remain stagnant for long, despite his impoverished beginnings and the little formal education he received. Possessed by creative urges in his teens and early twenties, the life of wandering he began was largely a search for the means to express himself; indeed, most of his life would constitute exploratory journeys to better interpret the world through song. With a strong desire to make it as a singer, he heeded the wisdom of his guiding spirit and made the journey to Kingston.

Perry arrived in the capital during a time of significant musical change, as leading sound system proprietors began releasing records by local performers. Heated rivalries spurred inventiveness, as Perry soon understood, and though no one took him seriously at first, important figures would come to recognise his talent after witnessing the creativity he was capable of harnessing, a peculiar ingenuity that was entirely beneficial to musical entrepreneurs. He may have been nothing more than a little man fresh from the country with some curious ideas, but the big sound men would soon learn that Perry's ears heard things that theirs could not, and his very strangeness would see him become a key player in the creation of a distinctly Jamaican music.

CHAPTER TWO

Chicken Scratch:
The Studio One Years

Perry left Westmoreland as the Jamaican independence movement was gathering steam, though not in a unified fashion. There were significant developments in the island's popular music too, as a local recording industry was established.

In 1958, Jamaica joined the twelve other English-speaking Caribbean islands to form the ill-fated Federation of the West Indies in what was meant to be a new multi-island nation, with joint independence scheduled for 1963 and central governance based in Trinidad. However, Bustamante began a vociferous campaign against the Federation in 1961, arguing that Jamaica should go it alone, and he thus became the first prime minister of independent Jamaica on 6 August 1962.

Perry arrived in Kingston in the midst of these independence struggles.[1] His aunt Essie, a milliner, could not accommodate him at her home in overcrowded Jones Town, so he spent his nights at a tailor's shop run by a man from Hanover named Lawrence at 45 Spanish Town Road, jostling with other fresh arrivals for floor space.

'It reach a stage where him have one suit 'pon him back and him go and buy himself a T-shirt so that him could

25

change him shirt,' said Perry's cousin Archie, a useful ally who knew his way around. 'But when him go out, them thief the T-shirt and him have to put on back the same shirt that he did have on before.'

Spanish Town Road is the main artery that reaches downtown Kingston from the west, and Perry's patch was an area known as Dog Park because of the many canine strays that congregated there. It bordered the massive, sprawling slum of Back-O-Wall, one of the largest shanty towns in the entire Caribbean region, where thousands of people shared three standpipes, disconnected from the grid and sanitation services, sheltering in makeshift dwellings patched from abandoned vehicles, discarded wood and whatever else could be scavenged from a nearby municipal garbage dump, known as the Dungle or dunghill.

As well as being political flashpoints that influenced the Jamaican music scene, Back-O-Wall, the Dungle and the adjoining community of Ackee Walk were Rastafari bastions. The movement emerged after the coronation of Prince Tafari Makonnen in 1930 as Haile Selassie, Emperor of Ethiopia, which seemed to validate the proclamation, 'Look to Africa, when a black king shall be crowned, for the day of deliverance is at hand', attributed to Jamaican activist Marcus Garvey, but possibly proclaimed first by his African American deputy, Reverend James Morris Webb.

Campaigning for Black self-determination through the Universal Negro Improvement Association (UNIA), Garvey sought to establish voluntary repatriation to Africa through the Black Star Line steamship corporation. Hounded out of Jamaica by the authorities in 1916, he moved to Harlem, New York City, but was imprisoned for fraud when the Black Star Line collapsed, dying in London in 1940 with few of his goals realised. Yet, his revolutionary ideals had wide-ranging effect, influencing the US civil rights movement and Kwame Nkrumah's revolution in Ghana, as well as social struggles in Jamaica.

In a series of eloquent and fiery speeches, Garvey made frequent reference to the biblical Ethiopia as the 'land of our fathers' and expressed a belief in 'the God of Ethiopia'. As Garvey enjoyed widespread support among the Jamaican poor, the downtrodden of the island took note when Selassie was crowned, the notion of his divinity boosted by Bible passages such as 'Princes shall come out of Egypt, Ethiopia shall soon stretch out her hands unto God' in Psalm 68 and 'Behold, the Lion of the tribe of Judah, the Root of David has triumphed. He is able to open the scroll and its seven seals' in Revelation 5, validating Selassie's royal title, the Conquering Lion of the Tribe of Judah, and his claim of Solomonic lineage. New Jamaican religious leaders such as Leonard Howell, Joseph Hibbert, Claudius Henry, Robert Hinds and Prince Emmanuel Edwards began to galvanise support for the faith by proclaiming that God was Black and Africa the rightful place for Black Jamaicans.

Different strands emerged in the ghettos of western Kingston, where a fertile intermingling took place amongst the Rastafari and the Burru, the latter a lowly community of criminal outcasts from rural Clarendon that were at the very bottom of Jamaican society. The Burru retained the drumming traditions of their Ashanti ancestors and had a long history of rebellion and criminality that stretched back to slavery days. Burru music revolves around a trio of hand drums: the large bass drum (pounded with a stick) and the *funde* hold the rhythm, while the smaller *kette* or repeater drum takes the melodic lead. The Burru used music as a powerful means to express defiance. Derived from a fertility ceremony that accompanied a masquerade dance, Burru drumming greeted prisoners returning home and was used to boost the morale of the incarcerated. Although the Burru played an important role in fomenting insurrection during slavery, their propagation of African traditions was seen as backward in the Eurocentric aftermath of emancipation. But the Burru held immense appeal for the Rastafari, the groups exchanging music and spiritual doctrine which would each eventually permeate Jamaican music, despite their strictly underground beginnings.

Rastafari drumming also has precedents in Kumina, a ritual practice involving spirit possession brought by indentured labourers from the Congo, and various forms of Revival Christianity, which incorporated similar practice within a Christian milieu. But the radical Rastafari subset known as the Youth Black Faith made a concerted effort to distance Rastafari from Revivalism, wearing dreadlocks in emulation of Mau Mau warriors to mark themselves apart, using symbolic reconfigured language to transcend potentially negative words or syllables and transforming Burru drumming into Nyabinghi from 1952, enacting rituals with drumming, dancing and fire to target oppressive forces. The Nyabinghi appellation was introduced by a dubious *Jamaica Times* article of 1935, reprinting an Austrian news report that sought to justify Italy's invasion of Ethiopia by claiming that Selassie was the head of a secret society waging war against Europeans, whose name meant 'Death to the Whites', though the term actually referenced an East African queen of the 1500s whose spiritual reincarnation, Muhumusa, spearheaded anticolonial struggles in the early 1900s. Later, the Youth Black Faith became known as the Nyabinghi Theocracy, officially the Theocratic Government of Emperor Haile Selassie I, holding Nyabinghi 'groundations' as ceremonial gatherings where the drums are beaten, and spiritual and social matters debated and discussed.

Rastafari consciousness, Nyabinghi drumming, and the Nyabinghi Theocracy would all be embraced by Perry in time, but for now, as a long-standing devotee of dance music, he was fixated on the pervasive sound system culture in Kingston and the sheer power of the bigger sets. Yet, things were far more competitive here, with shifting allegiances and rivalries. Open confrontations took the form of the 'sound clash', where two systems would battle against each other in downtown civic venues such as Forester's Hall and outdoor spaces like King's Lawn and Chocomo Lawn, as well as the Pioneer Club in Jones Town. At such events, the dancers were egged on by over-the-top microphone commentary from deejays that revelled in comic exhortations of verbal wit, outrageously exaggerated imitations of the hepcat jive-talk employed by Black American radio disc jockeys, such as Jocko Henderson.

In the early days, operators relied on exclusive records brought back from America, with vintage obscurities often more popular than current hits. But as rock 'n' roll supplanted rhythm and blues, the kind of music that Jamaican dance fans craved became harder to find, so the more enterprising sound system proprietors began recording a local variant of rhythm and blues, first cut on hard shellac acetates or demonstration discs for their own exclusive use (ironically called 'soft wax', and later known as dub plates), followed by general releases. Through this process, by the start of the 1960s, early innovators such as Tom the Great Sebastian, Sir Nick the Champ and Count Smith the Blues Blaster had given way to three towering entities that successfully branched into record production: Duke Reid the Trojan, King Edwards the Giant, and Sir Coxsone's Downbeat.

The Duke, born Arthur Reid, was a flamboyant and intimidating figure who bludgeoned his way to the top of the sound system circuit. His decade in the police force yielded a fondness for firearms and close association with the street-wise underclass, often appearing with a rifle, a .45 magnum at his waist and a pistol in his vest for good measure. A hefty man who liked to throw his weight around, Reid had a legion of henchmen who were always willing to lend a heavy hand against the competition, like Whoppi King, a notorious criminal known as Public Enemy Number One for his ruthlessness. The occult rings worn on every finger, obtained from the De Laurence Company of Chicago, despite being contraband in Jamaica, added to the sense that Reid was untouchable.

King Edwards the Giant, run by PNP activist Vincent Edwards and his brother George from the liquor store and record shop they ran at 161 Spanish Town Road, controlled a sizeable area further west. Vincent was renowned for tracking down impossible finds in the States, while George oversaw their local record productions.

As a schoolboy, Clement Dodd was known as Coxsone after English cricketer, Alec Coxon. Dodd's father was a successful masonry contractor who helped build the landmark Carib Theatre and other theatres in rural parishes; his mother, of Maroon heritage, ran the restaurant Nanny's Corner, which later became a liquor store, at the intersection of Laws Street and Ladd Lane, about twelve blocks east of Reid's headquarters. After working as a cabinetmaker and training as an automobile mechanic, Dodd undertook seasonal work picking crops in the American South, returning with a stack of records that he delivered to Reid, who was close to Dodd's parents. Then, after making successful guest appearances on Reid's sound system, Dodd was determined to give the Duke a run for his money by starting a sound of his own.

Dodd began visiting Rainbow Records in Harlem in 1954 to purchase jazz and rhythm and blues. Returning with an impressively powerful amplifier, he established the Downbeat sound system with the help of his mother at a newer branch of the family liquor store on the corner of Beeston Street and Love Lane, where he also sold imported records.

Although these innovators started from the ground up, some of the earliest record producers came from the mercantile class and a few were establishment figures, and the Jamaican recording industry really began with mento, the indigenous folk form that shared common ground with calypso through bawdy satire, but which used distinctive instrumentation, such as a banjo, bamboo saxophone and 'rhumba box' (an oversized thumb piano, used for bass notes). By December 1950, Jewish-Jamaican businessman Stanley Motta was already issuing mento 78s from his electrical goods store on Harbour Street, recording Lord Fly, Lord Power and Count Lasher in a tiny makeshift studio around the corner. Ken Khouri, whose father was a Lebanese immigrant and his mother of Cuban heritage, worked in furniture before releasing Lord Flea and Hubert Porter 78s by the summer of 1951, first using a portable disc recorder he acquired in Miami, and later a monophonic studio he built himself at 129 King Street, with rudimentary record pressing ability. Then, in October 1957, he opened a large, modern recording facility called Federal on the industrial Foreshore Road, about three miles west of downtown, which was to become the focal point of the local record industry, introducing large-scale record manufacturing there a few months later. Some early records were also cut clandestinely at Radio Jamaica Rediffusion (RJR), a cable subscription broadcaster that had sprung from the ashes of the government wartime station, ZQI.

The mento produced by Motta, Khouri and other pioneers was partly a reaction to imported calypso releases, and after Harry Belafonte broke records with his million-selling *Calypso* LP, their mento output was partly aimed at the overseas calypso craze. Nevertheless, airplay on RJR inspired sound system proprietors and other entrepreneurs to begin recording local performers, with rhythm and blues their preferred template.

In September 1959, the Jamaica Broadcasting Corporation (JBC) was established to counter RJR's monopoly. As the sound system bosses increased the number of their official releases, both stations began upping Jamaican content. Weekly talent shows held at Kingston theatres were another part of the process, especially those staged by the journalist and actor Vere Johns, which were broadcast on RJR as *Opportunity Knocks*.

Laurel Aitken's 'Boogie Rock', released in September 1959 by Dada Tewari, a prominent dry goods businessman of Indian extraction who owned the Tivoli Theatre, was the first locally recorded release to top the Jamaican radio charts. Aitken continued to rule with hits like 'Boogie In My Bones' and 'Little Sheila', both recorded for a young Chris Blackwell, then just getting his start in the music industry.

Blackwell spent his formative years in Jamaica and was educated at Harrow, an elite English public school, from which he was expelled for selling alcohol and cigarettes to fellow students. His mother, Blanche Lindo, descended from a high-flying mercantile, financier and planter family that had renounced their Judaism in the mid-nineteenth century, while his father, Joe Blackwell, was an officer in the Irish Guards and a distant relative of the family behind the hugely successful Crosse and Blackwell foods company.

Blackwell chose a non-conformist path at an early age. Sent to England to train as an accountant at Price Waterhouse, he abandoned the apprenticeship for a stab at professional gambling. Returning to Jamaica in 1955, Blackwell served briefly as aide-de-camp to the governor general, Sir Hugh Foot, but disliked Foot's successor, Kenneth Blackman, so tried his hand at real estate, renting motor scooters to tourists in Ocho Rios, and operating the waterskiing concession at the Half Moon Hotel. Then, in the winter of 1958, a quartet led by blind Bermudan pianist Lance Hayward came to play at the hotel, leading Blackwell to issue the album *At The Half Moon*, recorded at Federal, with guitarist Ernest Ranglin featured on the B-side, officially inaugurating Island Records.

Edward Seaga also had important involvement in the island's fledgling music industry, in tandem with his early political career. Of Lebanese, Scottish, Indian and African parentage, Seaga's prominent family was bolstered by his father's lucrative travel agency. After studying anthropology at Harvard, Seaga supervised the earliest known recordings of African-inspired religious folk music in Jamaica, embedding himself in a Revivalist community in Buxton Town, St Catherine, as well as Salt Lane and Denham Town in west Kingston, where African cultural practices involving spirit possession were retained, the recordings released by Ethnic Folkways as *Folk Music Of Jamaica* in 1956. Seaga started importing records from the USA shortly thereafter, and later began releasing popular Jamaican 45s through the West Indies Records Limited (WIRL) label. He scored a big hit with 'Manny Oh' by Trench Town duo Higgs and Wilson, which reached the Jamaican top ten in May 1960 (recorded at RJR prior to the construction of WIRL's own studio on Bell Road, close to Federal), but Seaga had already been appointed to the Legislative Council by Bustamante, so he released music only sporadically. A cousin ran the studio after Seaga became more active in politics, until control passed to Guyanese businessman George Benson and his Jamaican associate Clifford Rae, and when Seaga began representing the volatile Kingston Western constituency in April 1962, he continued to hold district meetings at Chocomo Lawn as a means of maintaining core support, proof that music and politics were never far from each other in Kingston, as Perry would soon understand.

By the time Perry arrived in the capital, Duke Reid had already produced sizeable hits with the Jiving Juniors and the duo of Derrick Morgan and Patsy Todd, who modelled themselves after American sweetheart duo Shirley and Lee, as well as rhythm and blues instrumentals like 'What Makes Honey', 'Joker' and 'Duke's Cookies'. Since the sound system scene had always thrived on competition, Reid was also producing censorious songs where artists threw coded barbs at their rivals, as heard on Morgan's 'Leave Earth', as well as the series of contentious hits he and Prince Buster later recorded, aiming boastful insults at each other on songs like 'Black Head Chinaman' and 'Blazing Fire', once Morgan began recording for Chinese-Jamaican producer Leslie Kong. Perry was captivated by this kind of vinyl jousting and was toying with the concept in lyrics he had formulated before travelling to Kingston, but when Perry offered something similar to the Duke, the response was not entirely positive.

'Before me come to Kingston, me used to like those records where you call it "tracing", passing on hot words,' said Perry. 'Like a sound want to prove which sound is the tougher and man want to prove which man is tougher, which man have more lyrics than the other. That is the type of thing that inspire me to come, and I want to be a part of that, but me never even want to talk about those days because it was ugly. Me go to Duke and him say him like me songs, but me is a country boy, me can't sing.'

Perry said he was probably in Duke Reid's camp for around six months, but Reid refused to record him. The rupture came one day at Federal after Reid relegated the lyrics of Perry's rebuking 'Rough And Tough' to Stranger Cole, an upcoming hopeful whose brother Leroy was a selector on Reid's sound system. Though Cole insists he wrote the song after being challenged by a romantic rival, the incident saw Perry aligning himself with Sir Coxsone's camp, after a heated confrontation, in which Perry was walloped by the Duke.

'Scratch came from country and was hearing all these local musics,' said Dodd. 'He wanted to get into the business, so he used to hang out by Duke's session or my session. How we really get together that first time, Perry come by Federal and he and Duke in the focus. He explained to me that the song that going to record in there is a song that steal from him. He did sing it and rehearse fe him and Duke go record it over. So seeing he and Duke and some of the guys clash, I came in and pacify it, and realising he was outnumbered, I took him away from whatever was happening. I said, "In future, don't sing your song to let people hear it, cos sometimes they will have a better voice and *they'll* sing the song." We had a good talk, then he went back to the country and when he came back, he stop visiting Duke and then started by me and in no time I created a little job for him.'

'We join forces to drop a bigger guy who said he was the biggest guy in town, and we small guys, the little got big and make him feel it,' said Perry. 'The pressure with Duke, you couldn't take it because Duke never have no sense about humanity, him just figure that him is a bully. You would be

35

afraid of his gun. Though he's not going to shoot you, he have his gun like a whip, and he can skin you. He thinks he's the boss, but him have no feelings that you could go with him and enjoy yourself, and Mr Dodd, he's always like a kid. So you can go to the people and share their thoughts and laugh, make your own entertainment. I think me was trailing the sound system too, that's how I really reach to Coxsone. I come to reach Downbeat sound system and then me was with him all the while cause me like people who smart, and me was his sidekick. Me was driving with him everywhere, so when him have food, me have food. Me always have an angel who guide me, so my guardian angel always make sure that him find where me going to stay.'

After Dodd took 'Little Lee' under his wing, Perry found more acceptable digs in Vineyard Town, east Kingston, one of the middling working-class districts that formed a buffer zone between the cramped warrens of the downtown trouble spots and the exclusive residences uptown. In the distant shadow of Long Mountain, it was a considerable improvement on Dog Park, though still well below the uptown dividing line.

Although Perry began at the bottom in Dodd's stable, running errands and fulfilling whatever odd jobs he was allocated, Dodd could see Perry's potential in ways that Reid could not, and Perry liked the fact that Sir Coxsone's Downbeat was the underdog.

'Duke Reid was bigger than Coxsone in sound system. Coxsone was like a little chicken and Duke Reid was like a big dog, but me discover it was easier to deal with Coxsone than to deal with Duke, so me start up a thing with Coxsone, saying, "Make we beat him down like a David and Goliath affair", and that's what we do to Duke Reid: mash him up, hit him with an invisible rock.'

Dodd described Perry as a handyman, though Perry saw himself as a gopher, tasked with the delivery and collection of recorded material that was pressed at Federal, and other mundanities, but his contributions would soon become more important.

'I was getting his records pressed and getting them delivered to the shop, going to the shop and take orders, go to the record factory, get the labels, and order the amount of records that me think can sell.'

Releasing music officially since 1959, Dodd began with the hard blues of Jackie Estick's 'My Baby', the sentimental 'I Love You' by Bunny and Skitter, and a rousing shuffle take of Glenn Miller's 'Little Brown Jug' (as 'Shufflin Jug'), the latter by Clue J and the Blues Blasters, who provided backing on Dodd's early sessions. Later, Theophilus Beckford's 'Easy Snappin' prefaced a new direction by shifting emphasis to the afterbeat. With such material, after Dodd had spent years building up the Downbeat sound, now Perry furthered the process by delivering vinyl, fresh off the press, and observing which new tunes were popular when aired at sound system events. He was neither selector nor operator of the sound, as has been reported elsewhere, and was not involved in transporting or setting up the sound equipment.

'I might go at certain times to see what was happening or bring new songs to give to the selector to play,' said Perry. 'I would check the direction of the people: if it's this cut we want or that cut we want, or if you like this one, maybe we should make another cut of it.'

As part of Dodd's entourage, Perry made many important musical and social connections, sparking a friendship with the singer and tailor Clancy Eccles, and the sound system 'box boy' George Phillips, who would help string up the set at Downbeat's dances, later producing records under the alias Phil Pratt.

One day, Dodd acquainted Perry with Back-O-Wall, where he first smoked marijuana, the 'wisdom weed', known locally as ganja, which he would later use habitually, with dramatic effects.

'When me first smoke herb is when me did come to Kingston when I was twenty-five and it make me feel like I wasn't on this earth anymore, take me into a higher heights that me think me gone crazy. Me go with Coxsone to Back-O-Wall, there was a guy named Frankie round there, one of Coxsone's friends, so we visit every Sunday, and it was there me smoke herb, the first time, as a spliff. I wasn't here anymore for maybe half an hour until I come back on planet earth. I don't know where I went, but if I would even try to walk, maybe I would be stepping high.'

A few weeks after bagging his newfound employment, Perry auditioned at the shop and rehearsal space Dodd ran near the Ward Theatre, performing a song called 'Chicken Scratch', inspired by a dance step that mimicked the movements of a chicken foraging for food, which was a popular move in Jamaica.

'He auditioned with a song called "Chicken Scratch" and that's how he got the name, but they didn't take him because Coxsone said he wasn't any good, and we were all laughing because we didn't think he could sing,' said future Gaylads leader B. B. Seaton, who would later become one of Dodd's most trusted pair of ears as auditions supervisor. 'We started calling him "Chicken Scratch" until it come down to "Scratch", but he stayed with Coxsone and started to be like a handyman.'

Despite the rejection, Dodd tested Perry's ability in the studio shortly thereafter, cutting 'Chicken Scratch' at a Federal session using the core musicians who would later form the

Skatalites. Though not released on vinyl at the time, it was a popular sound system special.

Perry moved to 1¾ Water Street in Allman Town, another modest midtown neighbourhood a bit further west, where the streets were narrower and more immediately urban, renting a room that was conveniently located near Clement Dodd's home; his estranged wife Tootsie briefly joined him there, but the relationship could not be rekindled.

'I was expecting her to come back. I did love her, definitely, and I say, "I going to wait and see if she want to come back", but when she come back, it could not work,' said Perry. 'We were waiting to get the truth, then we don't have to wait anymore.'

Now Perry was firmly in the lines of Dodd's defenders, men who were employed not only to protect the Downbeat sound from rival sabotage, but to ensure that it stayed at the forefront by learning which songs were popular on other sounds, just as Prince Buster had done for Dodd before setting up his rival Voice of the People outfit, and Perry quickly understood that observing the action undetected was a necessary skill.

'You go to the dance where other people playing and listen to the songs, what the people like more, so you know exactly what goes down or what you're supposed to throw. Like you had King Edwards' big sound system, then you pass by and listen to what he's playing that you don't have, and if me know a song that the people like, me just tell Coxsone, "They like this one", so that we can version it somehow.'

One night a Downbeat dance at Forester's Hall had been infiltrated by Duke Reid's heavies. A fight broke out that soon turned ugly, so Dodd fled the premises while Perry was given a knockout punch. Prince Buster, Dodd's mutinous former ally, appeared just in time, dragging the unconscious Perry to safety after a considerable battle with his attackers.

'Even now, them call me Friend of the Underdog,' said Buster. 'It was their dance, but I wasn't with Coxsone anymore. I really helped Perry out there and I guess that must have brought me and him closer. People in Jamaica will tell you that most of the fights or problems I get into wasn't from me. I'm always defending somebody.'

Born Cecil Bustamante Campbell, Buster was a downtown street tough from a staunch JLP-supporting family. Dodd made an initial approach after seeing him chase a notorious gangster called Mean Stick down Luke Lane with his knife drawn. As a follower of Tom the Great Sebastian, Buster held vengeful feelings against Duke Reid since Reid's thugs had chased Tom out of the downtown area. Trained as a professional boxer, he helped fend off the saboteurs and was adept at spying, venturing into rival territory to identify what the competition was playing, but once he broke away from Dodd, Buster provided serious opposition himself.

Tired of taking repeated blows and knife wounds for a man that kept himself far from danger and was not always known for fair payment, Buster planned a record-buying trip to the US in 1959 but moved into record production after Dodd's father-in-law, a trade union official, had him deselected from the work gang, recording 'Little Honey' and Rico Rodriguez's trombone instrumental 'Luke Lane Shuffle' at JBC. Based at 36 Charles Street, below Orange Street, he would later give Reid a helping hand by producing songs for him like Rico's 'Let George Do It'.

Buster's first hit, the Folkes Brothers' 'Oh Carolina', was a truly monumental recording. With the lyrics of a love song and the music in shuffle mode, Buster's masterstroke was the inclusion of Count Ossie's drumming troupe, which really set the song apart, their Nyabinghi drumming carrying forgotten echoes of an African past.

When Buster first visited Ossie's encampment in the Wareika Hills above east Kingston, the master drummer is said to have feared that Buster was trying to ridicule him, so deep was society's prejudice against the Rastafari, or any Jamaican expressing awareness of an African identity, but Buster persisted and recorded the Count, despite Reid's best efforts to sabotage the recording session by double-booking JBC. Through exposure at sound system dances, popular demand for the song grew so great that both RJR and JBC had to overturn their airtime bans.

After fulfilling Buster's abandoned role as an infiltrator of rival sound systems, Perry began slowly rising in the ranks and was soon conducting auditions for Dodd himself every Sunday, though Perry said noteworthy talent could be spotted anytime.

'If on a Monday we see a guy on the street, we go and arrest him on the street and bring him in.'

One of Perry's greatest finds was the Maytals, the vocal trio that Toots Hibbert, Jerry Matthias and Raleigh Gordon formed after meeting in a Trench Town barbershop, where Toots worked. As a trio, they were distinguished by the emotional gospel underpinning of Toots' lead, since both his parents were preachers back in his hometown of May Pen, Clarendon. The sound was so powerful and striking that when the group auditioned at Dodd's shop on Orange Street one Sunday, Perry told Dodd to record them right away and they were soon belting out the hits.

'Scratch always work for these people,' said Toots. 'He tell them, "Go listen what Toots have, go listen what the other guy have." That's what he have to do with it.'

Debut single 'Hallelujah' and follow-up 'Fever' were size-able hits, as was the later 'Six And Seven Books Of Moses', a song referencing mysterious occult texts which Perry said he earmarked, but it turned out to be their last hit for Dodd, since they left his stable in 1964 to record for Prince Buster.

By then, Jamaican music was moving away from the pervasive influence of rhythm and blues. During the struggle for independence and its immediate aftermath, Jamaican musicians and record producers were striving to create a form of music they could truly claim as their own.

The wake-up call came in ska, an infectious new beat that was harder, faster and generally more Jamaican than the local variant of rhythm and blues that dominated in the late 1950s and early '60s. Although most early ska vocal songs retained echoes of rhythm and blues beneath the quirky beat, ska gradually became more uptempo, characterised by wild drumming and full horn sections utilising adventurous jazz arrangements, and a number of important players came to the fore in the process. On upright bass, Clue J was superseded by Lloyd Brevett, a tall young man from Jones Town, taught to play by his father David, the bassist of a big jazz band. Drummer Arkland 'Drumbago' Parks gave way to Portland-born Lloyd Knibb, a hugely inspired player that punctuated his patterns with furious rimshots and even adapted Burru rhythms on his drum kit. The gifted guitarist Ernest Ranglin acted as Federal's musical arranger, his expressive lead lines gracing many a tune, while his understudy Jerome Haynes, known as Jah Jerry, was more reliable on rhythm guitar. Keyboardists Cecil Lloyd and Aubrey Adams were part of the old guard that were being supplanted by Theophilus Beckford, Aubrey's nephew Gladstone Anderson and the teenaged Jackie Mittoo, the latter an organ specialist who would prove a gifted arranger too.

Saxophonists Tommy McCook and Roland Alphonso were both extremely talented, as was Carl 'Cannonball' Bryan and the young Lester Sterling. Trombonist Don Drummond was a major creative force whose minor-key melodies pointed to his troubled emotional state, and his protégé, Rico Rodriguez, built a solid reputation playing in the Rastafari community. Baba Brooks and Johnny Moore were the trumpeters most in demand, and Charles Cameron an expressive harmonica player, known as Charlie Organaire. Most of the horn players learned their craft at the Alpha Boys School, a Catholic reform institution for children whose parents could not care for them, located on South Camp Road, a strict training ground for the island's leading jazz musicians under Sister Ignatius, a jazz fan who ran her own sound system.

In different configurations, these musicians recorded for all the leading producers, being variously credited as the Baba Brooks Band, the King Edwards All Stars, Drumbago's Band, and so on, but their work for Clement Dodd was arguably the most important, and once he convinced Tommy McCook to lead an all-star group, officially christened the Skatalites in June 1964, they became the band that defined the genre. Centred on the nucleus of Knibb, Brevett, Jah Jerry, Mittoo, McCook, Alphonso and Drummond, other members drifted in and out of the group.

By the time Perry began working for Dodd, he had plenty of material of his own, some dating from before his arrival in Kingston. He was fond of grafting lyrics onto adapted folksongs and traditional melodies, but Dodd was still hesitant to record him, fearing Perry's voice lacked training and sounded too provincial.

Instead, Dodd felt more confident in Perry's songwriting ability, especially his combative work, and thus began using

43

Perry's lyrics for other upcoming artists, Perry occasionally playing the odd bit of percussion on Dodd's productions too.

Delroy Wilson was Jamaica's first child star, recording for Dodd in the high-pitched voice of adolescence when he was only thirteen years old. Perry wrote 'Joe Lieges', which Wilson recorded, as a direct reply to Prince Buster's 'They Got To Come', which lamented bad-minded people who wanted to see him fail; as Buster was trying to steal Dodd's *lieges* or glory from him, Perry came up with the scathing lyrics, which he later said were about 'people who just want to take and don't want to give'. Similarly, 'I Shall Not Remove', based on a spiritual, was also aimed at Buster, while 'Spit In The Sky', which B. B. Seaton said he co-wrote with Perry, reprimanded through the use of proverbs.

'Buster was trying a little thing. At that time he was looking like a personal fight, so Mr Dodd have to use Delroy Wilson to trace him back,' said Perry. 'It was a little joke fight because when it comes to battling, Mr Dodd always have a thing to do with words. He sees words as funny and I see words funny as well, so we always want to add another word to it to make it match and rhyme, and we become a battle-axe. That is the way him is: when he say, "One," I say, "Two," and we build up on it.'

There was also 'Lion Of Judah', which Wilson recorded. Similar to Jimmy Cliff's 'King Of Kings' and an unrelated Laurel Aitken song with the same title, 'Lion Of Judah' adapted a Christian hymn, making coded reference to the growing importance of Rastafari; Perry said he brought the concept to Dodd and wanted to record it himself, but Dodd gave the song to Wilson and failed to acknowledged Perry as the songwriter.

Shenley Duffus, an accomplished tenor with a broad vocal range, was heavily influenced by American blues and soul singers like Big Joe Turner, Louis Jordan and Ben E. King. Arriving at Dodd's camp in late 1962, he and Perry began collaborating too, beginning a lasting friendship and musical association. Perry had a hand in Duffus' debut success for Dodd, 'What A Disaster', which addressed the vinyl feud between Prince Buster and Derrick Morgan. 'Fret Man Fret' was another joint creation aimed at Buster, 'Doreen' took aim at a girlfriend and 'Give To Get' reminded that you reap what you sow.

'Lee Perry was one of the best "banton" writers in Jamaica,' said Duffus. 'He give you all kinds of ideas: rhythmic, lyric. When Perry's around, you can look for hit songs.'

Perry also wrote the broken-hearted 'Leticia', but Dodd changed the title to 'Lolita' and had popular singer Roy Panton voice it instead. The constant rejection was tiring, especially when Dodd's name appeared in songwriting credits.

When Dodd finally allowed Perry to record some songs himself in 1963, his first efforts continued to attack the competition, especially Prince Buster. 'Mad Head' was a parody of Buster's 'Madness'; 'Prince Is In The Back' used proverbs to suggest that the Prince's break with Dodd was hasty; 'Don't Copy' accused him of plagiarism, labelled him a Judas Priest and derisively referenced the feud with Morgan; 'Prince And The Duke' said that he copied Duke Reid, and 'Royalty' claimed that Reid rescued Buster from the gutter. In contrast, 'Old For New', which Perry said was the first to be recorded, used proverbs to warn against hastily ending relationships, the lyrics broken by understated saxophone solos, and 'Bad Minded People' a general warning against maliciousness with a plaintive harmonica break. Similarly, the spirited 'Never Get Weary' was a ska hymn proclaiming determination, and the moralism of 'Can't Be Wrong' was introduced by a horn pastiche of the 'London Bridge' nursery rhyme, while 'Man And Wife' was a half-sung tale of familial infidelity and 'Chatty Chatty Woman' dissed a blabbermouth.

Each of these early sorties was marked by the slow shuffle of Jamaican rhythm and blues as it edged closer to full-blown ska, typically backed by restrained drum patterns and loping acoustic basslines, with harmonica, saxophone or trumpet solos breaking things up. There was an innocence about the music and Perry's vocals were decidedly rough-hewn, justifying Dodd's wariness in places, but his wit made up for the occasional lapse during tense recording sessions where everything was captured live by one microphone. Most of the songs were issued abroad on the R&B and Ska Beat labels that Rita and Benny Izons ran from their record shop in London's Stamford Hill, and a few surfaced on Island, which Chris Blackwell moved to London following Jamaica's independence.

Then, in October 1963, the opening of the Jamaica Recording and Publishing Studio Limited, popularly known as Studio One, allowed Clement Dodd better control of his output and the ability to increase the production schedule. Located at 13 Brentford Road, near the Carib Theatre in the Cross Roads business district, at the site of a former nightclub called The End, it was very much a family operation, with Dodd's father assisting with its creation and cousin Sid Bucknor installing the recording equipment, including Federal's original mono-phonic machine.

The arrival of the Wailers soon increased Dodd's fortunes and Perry was a significant part of the process. Mentored in vocal harmony by Joe Higgs of Higgs and Wilson, the Trench Town-based group came to Studio One as the unruly five-piece of Bob Marley, Peter Tosh, Neville Livingston, Junior Braithwaite and Cherry Green, who alternated with

Beverley Kelso on early recordings. Perry was tasked with promoting singles of theirs, such as 'It Hurts To Be Alone', which he distributed to other sound systems as a blank label pre-release, stimulating serious demand. The group joined the growing roster of Studio One success stories, making a swift impact on the scene under Dodd's tutelage, and Dodd acted as a surrogate father to Marley for a time, housing him in a small room adjoining the studio.

The years 1964 and '65 constituted a period of refinement for both Perry and the Wailers at Studio One, which now had a two-track recorder. The group was strengthening their output, becoming more competent as songwriters, and clarifying their direction through an unbeatable series of hits. After Junior Braithwaite joined his family in Chicago in September 1964, Beverley Kelso and Cherry Green drifted away, leaving the robust core of Marley, Tosh and Livingston (the latter better known as Bunny Wailer).

As the ska pace picked up, Perry's recorded output showed significant progression. Now recording and performing as King Perry or King Scratch, 'Mother In Law' was one of the first he tried to the faster ska beat, howling frenziedly as he implored his mother-in-law to mind her own business. The song became a highlight of his guest spots with the Skatalites at the popular Sunday afternoon sessions Dodd held at the Gold Coast Beach in Bull Bay, about eight miles east of Kingston, where Perry also played percussion with the group; he was also part of the revue they backed at the Success Club in July 1964, along with Delroy Wilson, Doreen Shaefer and Barbadian singer Jackie Opel, who was then in high demand.

Songs like 'Help The Weak' and 'Wishes Of The Wicked' attacked social injustice rather than Dodd's rivals; other singles, featuring the vocal backing of female duo the Dynamites, showed an emerging individuality as Perry became more comfortable in the studio environment. For instance, 'John Tom' described a visit to a traditional healer to cure an aching back, 'Trial And Crosses' was another ska hymn, 'Gumma' used proverbs to warn of life's hardships, and 'By Saint Peter' related Bible stories to a bouncing ska beat, using a call-and-response framework with the Dynamites, broken up by an energetic trumpet solo.

Perry also recorded with the Soulettes, a popular trio comprised of Bob Marley's future wife, Rita Anderson, her cousin Constantine 'Vision' Walker, and their friend, Merlene 'Precious' Gifford. They are credited on the popular 'Please Don't Go', where Perry refuted an errant lover's pleas, and are present on 'Roast Duck', its title a slang term connoting rear-entry sex, from a glut of rude records he began voicing in late 1964.

On New Year's Day 1965, the music world was rocked by the news that Don Drummond had murdered his girlfriend, the rhumba dancer Margarita Mahfood, and was incarcerated at Bellevue, Jamaica's psychiatric hospital. The Skatalites tried to soldier on without him, backing the Wailers, the Soulettes, the Maytals, Joe Higgs, Delroy Wilson and other artists at an Ash Wednesday gala held at the Ward Theatre on 3 March, where King Scratch made a hapless guest appearance, performing a rendition of 'Roast Duck' with the Soulettes that totally bombed.

'Scratch was just a right-hand [man] for Coxsone when he had auditions. One day he said he had a song to do and everybody was amused by it, so we sing the background on it,' said Rita Marley. 'We did a concert with him at the Ward Theatre, singing "Roast Duck", but were stoned off stage because nobody knew Lee Perry as a singer. It was his first appearance and everyone said, "Get off the stage!"'

'The audience never like it because Jamaican people never like my music until foreign people start to like it,' said Perry. 'I know these people wasn't ready for me, but I still have to test them.'

Similarly suggestive work of the period includes 'Hold Down', the first of many to use food as a metaphor for sex – in this case, Perry sang of a woman who had eaten too much 'honey' – and 'Open Up (Cook Book)', which used more blatant innuendo. By the time Perry recorded the despicable 'Rape Bait', reconfiguring folk song 'Jane Ann And The Pumpkin' to nefarious ends, he was steadily gaining a reputation as one of the slackest singers on the island.

Thankfully, Perry was never one to be stuck in the same groove for too long, and not all the material he created in this period was slack. For instance, his version of Dee Clarke's pop-tinged rhythm and blues hit 'Just Keep It Up' was a mournful tirade by a heartbroken lover. In contrast, 'Deacon Johnson' and 'Tackoo' evidenced Perry's backwoods origins, his lead vocal and the Dynamites' harmonies steeped in the expressions of countryfolk; the latter title was a patois term for fool, the song directed at an errant girlfriend. 'Hand To Hand', with the Wailers on harmony, again had a spiritual feel, another ode to the determination that would lead to the vanquishing of his enemies; infused with hidden meanings, it hinted at the dramatic potential of the musical connection between Perry and the group.

Following the break-up of the Skatalites in August 1965, Roland Alphonso formed the Soul Brothers with Jackie Mittoo at Studio One, and Tommy McCook defected to Duke Reid, forming the Supersonics with Lloyd Knibb as the house band for Reid's newly opened Treasure Isle studio, heightening their rivalry.

At the end of September, Perry enjoyed top billing at the grand reopening of the Brown Jug club in Ocho Rios, backed by the Soul Brothers along with Marcia Griffiths and Delroy Wilson, but such on-stage elevation was not sustained. Although he would continue to make guest spots with the Soul Brothers at Dodd's regular Sunday live events, Perry was having greater success behind the scenes, helping to shape Dodd's recording sessions and continuing to audition artists with Jackie Mittoo, such as future Ethiopians lead singer Leonard Dillon, another artist Perry greenlighted after Peter Tosh brought him for an audition.

Other vinyl efforts that surfaced in late 1965 and early '66 include a forgotten dance number called 'Do The Push Push', heavily laden with sensual imagery that lingered on every note, and 'Sugar Bag', alluding to the hidden sweetness of a woman. Yet, like so much of his work at Studio One, these songs made little impact.

Somewhere along the way, Pauline Morrison came into Perry's life. He had often seen the enticing and secretive young woman from Trench Town loitering outside the Gold Coast, looking for a way to sneak in, her high cheekbones and mysterious air impossible to resist. On a particular Sunday in 1965, Perry thus enabled her entry, beginning their relationship at a time when she was a teenager and he was approaching 30, and she soon moved into his rented room at Water Street.

Pauline was an underprivileged girl from the ghetto, already hardened by Kingston life. Perry learned that her family came from a village on the Portland side of the Blue Mountains in eastern Jamaica, where her grandmother, Miss Hilda, was a domestic worker for wealthy white landowners. Pauline had a young son named Derrick, but the relationship with his father did not last and the boy was mostly cared for by her older sister; much later, Perry would understand that, even at this tender age, Pauline had been romantically involved with other singers before him.

When Pauline gave birth to a daughter named Michelle at Jubilee Public Hospital on 17 January 1966, Perry accepted the task of raising her as though she was his own, despite not knowing who the biological father was.

'I don't know if the child is for Toots or Lord Tanamo or for who. Later on I find out that she was Toots' girlfriend in Trench Town and Lord Tanamo was Pauline's boyfriend too.'

Perry sent for his younger sister Girlie to help care for the newborn, so she stayed at Water Street for about three months before returning to Hanover, and it was already obvious that Perry's relationship with Pauline was as volatile as it was passionate. Though they quickly grew close to one another in the fiery confines of their love, they would also endure stormy periods of problematic unrest.

Perry continued working closely with the Wailers and the Soulettes at this time, strengthening a bond that would bear all manner of fruit in years to come. They performed together at the upscale Bournemouth Club at Bournemouth Beach in east Kingston on 30 January as the Wailers enjoyed the continued success of 'I'm Gonna Put It On', a rousing ska underpinned by raw spiritual energy, which was reportedly spun repeatedly at Bob and Rita's wedding on 11 February. Since advances in multi-track technology allowed for rhythm tracks to be reused for different purposes, Perry manipulated the 'Put It On' rhythm for 'Rub And Squeeze', another risqué number backed by the Soulettes. His 'Doctor Dick' made Lord Kitchener's innuendo-laden calypso 'Doctor Kitch' even more blatant in a ska arrangement, and the popular 'Pussy Galore' was similarly slack, a paean to the heroine of *Goldfinger* (the character reportedly inspired by Blanche Lindo); the latter featured the Wailers on backing vocals and made use of an alternate take of their ska medley, titled 'Rude Boy', another of the songs Perry helped arrange, its unusual structure placing an adapted line from the Impressions' 'I've Got To Keep On Moving' in the middle of a string of Jamaican proverbs.

'Rude Boy' was named in reference to the growing problem of hoodlums perpetrating wanton violence in Kingston, though the track was more coded than overt. In contrast, Perry's 'Run Rudie Run', with the Gaylads on backing vocals, was one of the first to directly comment on the phenomenon in song.

These disenfranchised citizens had crept forth from the ghettos since the late 1950s to form fearsome gangs that terrorised the city. Inspired by hyper-real displays of cinematic violence regularly screened at downtown cinemas like the Rialto and the Majestic, the rude boys sought to emulate their movie heroes by bashing, slashing and shooting their way to the glory of a short-lived retribution, taking what society had denied them by the most direct and brutal means. Some rudies were recruited by sound system proprietors as 'dance crashers'; they would smash up a rival dance, destroy the equipment and beat, knife or rape audience members. Others began to commit random crimes just for the hell of it.

By the mid-1960s, larger gangs with an evident hierarchy had formed. Most began through the bonds of loose kinship in overcrowded communities with few employment opportunities and little state support, taking on territorialised dimensions through political patronage.

When Edward Seaga began bulldozing Back-O-Wall in February 1966 as Minister of Development and Welfare, he turned to the Phoenix gang of neighbouring Denham Town for support because Back-O-Wall was then a PNP stronghold with the Spanglers gang at the heart of it. Thousands of people were displaced to build Tivoli Gardens, Jamaica's first government-backed housing scheme, which was subsequently populated by JLP supporters, kept loyal to the party by the 'enforcers' of the Phoenix gang (later known as the Shower Posse); the Spanglers moved half a dozen blocks east, to Mathews Lane, where they acted as PNP enforcers. The result was a steady escalation of violence, culminating in the declaration of a month-long State of Emergency in October, making life all the more challenging in the capital.

Shortly after his wedding to Rita, Bob Marley travelled to Delaware, where his mother had settled. He was thus absent when Haile Selassie made an official state visit to Jamaica on 21 April 1966, which had profound effects on the Rastafari faithful, as well as both Rita and Perry. Tens of thousands were present when the imperial plane landed at Kingston's Palisadoes Airport, and although Perry only glimpsed Selassie when the imperial motorcade passed along Windward Road, he was greatly struck by the magnitude of the event.

'I saw him when he came to Kingston in 1966. 12,000 Rastas were waiting for him at the airport. The prophecy said that one morning a single white dove would fly over the assembled Rastas, followed by a short shower of benediction. His plane came from the East, coming out of the dawn and it rained when the plane landed. The chalices were being passed around and people were smoking herb with our flags, our rockets, our spliffs and our music, and above all the Abeng horn that was the rallying instrument of the Maroons in the bush two centuries ago.'[2]

Rita Marley said that when Selassie's motorcade passed, she saw the stigmata on his waving hand and converted on the spot. Although Perry had not yet embraced the faith outwardly, the Emperor's visit made a deep impression, and he began to listen to Rastafari reasoning with greater interest. Inwardly, he recognised something in Selassie, whom he resembled physically.

'When His Majesty come, I was living at Water Street and I just see it,' said Perry. 'Me stay in the back and see him pass and everything, but I know that it's not the first time that I see this man. Me see this man long, long time and know who this man is from ever since, so me no have to worry. Me just look exactly like the man me think me should look like.'

Since his arrival in Kingston, Perry had undertaken much personal growth and his social status had slowly risen, but he resented the glory that Dodd reaped by the sweat of his brow. He thus took some time out to look into himself and understood that the state of affairs could not continue. A breeze of change was blowing in his direction, and as he pondered on that breeze, he realised that he needed to move on.

CHAPTER THREE
Give Me Justice: The Upsetter Emerges

In the latter half of 1966, Lee Perry was increasingly frustrated by his situation at Studio One. He had been instrumental in facilitating Dodd's rise from underrated challenger to virtual ruler and was a crucial force in shaping his recorded output, as well as helping Sir Coxsone's Downbeat to maintain its dominance. Once Dodd began recording local artists in earnest, Perry's ear for talent often brought the biggest-selling acts, and although Dodd managed groups like the Maytals and the Wailers, their growing popularity owed much to Perry's largely unseen efforts.

Perry had voiced over thirty tunes for Dodd, but some were left in the can. Dodd thought nothing of giving Perry's lyrics to younger singers and did not always credit him properly, the lack of proper financial reward irksome, the irregular acknowledgement a deeper sting.

'He think me can't sing neither,' Perry lamented. 'Me have a lot of songs that they take from me and not even my name was written as the writer. They just take them because me is a country boy and me can't say anything, otherwise they would beat me up. They respect the words and respect the sounds, but not me.'

55

Another bone of contention was Dodd's initial disapproval of music expressing Rastafari sentiment. Most of the musicians and a growing number of singers adhered to the faith, and although Dodd was not as anti-Rasta as Duke Reid, who retained a blanket policy against Rastafari music for the whole of his career, Dodd was also against songs openly expressing such beliefs because of a strong Christian orientation, and marijuana was taboo in the studio when Dodd was around, though he would later soften on both issues.

'He don't smoke ganja and don't like people who smoke ganja,' said Perry, 'and those people that sing about Rastafari, he don't want to have anything to do with them.'

Perry said that he and Jackie Mittoo were responsible for much of the music coming out of Studio One in this phase. They had become close friends and drinking buddies, but their input was not adequately acknowledged by the increasingly absent Dodd.

'Jackie and me was friends and we was travelling together like pals. Him was addicted to white rum and me actually was addicted to it too, so we becomes partners: me not going to go home without him and he's not going to go home without me. Most of the time, when Coxsone's away, he don't know that it's mostly me and Mittoo making music.'

Already over thirty years of age, Perry felt worsening resentment at the lack of recognition and repayment. Thinking back over his meandering teen years, he remembered the joy of being in the limelight at the domino games and dance tournaments, where he received due recognition, but now there was a quietly seething bitterness. The unseen spirit that had guided Perry to Kingston was gently urging him to step away from Dodd, despite their friendship and close working relationship.

'The payment that he was giving me wasn't no great payment that could pay the rent or even support me, much less to have a girlfriend, so I wasn't really getting any justice. Through we are friends, we go out together. Him wake me every morning and him not going to travel without me, and at night, sometimes we come back at four o'clock and him drop me, as we live at the same street. Him was just a friend, so I don't think him think that the friend need any money, cos if me go to his home, me can have dinner and tea and everything there. The little pocket money was OK, but him didn't think that me needed anything more than that, so that's where him make a mistake and that's why me leave him. He was a lovely person, but he was actually too mean. Then me decide that me going to upset him, so me tell him that me gone to visit my mother, but I didn't go to my mother, I go to the studio to upset him.'

Recorded clandestinely at Studio One, 'Give Me Justice' was an impassioned plea for the fair dealing denied him, the first of several songs aimed directly at Dodd's head. 'Why take advantage of the innocent ones?' Perry sang forcefully over the bouncing ska rhythm, 'soon it will be a change of plan . . . Give me justice!'

The song marked his departure from Studio One, but Perry never forgot that Dodd agreed to record him before anyone else.

'I don't have a reason to hate Mr Dodd. What I do is upset him and teach him a lesson, and I did really even forgive him as well. Duke Reid didn't give me no chance – he take all me tunes – but even if Coxsone only give me one pound a week, it doesn't matter. I was just giving Mr Dodd my service and he was giving me some food because me didn't have any at the time. Me get to that me not sleeping in the tailor shop anymore. I could afford to rent a place, whatsoever little money he give me and what little me can achieve for my side, me can make it and me live. If I was waiting on Duke Reid I would still be in the tailor shop, so though it was one little money Mr Dodd was giving me, my word was going out on record.'

'Give Me Justice' was relegated to the B-side of 'Such A Good Wood Man', Perry's innuendo-laden tale about an unfaithful wife, notable for recurrent, out-of-tune piano chords. Credited to Lee King Perry, it was one of the first releases on the Sir JJ label, run by jukebox supplier Karl Johnson from his record shop on Orange Street. Johnson came from a prominent, if atypical, family: his father, Bromley, was a self-made man who worked his way up from humble beginnings as a butcher and shopkeeper to run the successful Magnet Bus Company; his brother Copley opened the popular Johnson's Drive Inn restaurant and entertainment venue in Half Way Tree in the 1950s, where Teenage Dance Party was held; and another brother, Millard, attempted to revive Marcus Garvey's radical People's Political Party or PPP in 1960, but relocated to Africa following the party's thorough defeat in 1962.

The Sir JJ single was licenced to Ska Beat in England (as 'The Woodman') but had little impact in either territory, and although Perry never worked with Johnson again, it indicated the kind of freedom that was being denied him under Dodd's thumb, both in the musical experimentation of 'Such A Good Wood Man' and the frank admonishments of 'Give Me Justice'.

Towards the end of 1966, a new style was ruling the Jamaican charts as the frantic pace of the ska era gave way to the slower, more spacious rock steady, with singers such as Hopeton Lewis, Alton Ellis and Roy Shirley backed by smaller, studio-based ensembles rather than the big-band jazz of ska. Rock steady increased emphasis on lead guitar and keyboards as horn sections were diminished or dismissed, rendering a less cluttered sound influenced by soul groups like the Impressions, as heard in the exquisite harmony of the Melodians, the Techniques, the Paragons, and the Jamaicans.

A small coterie of interrelated players maintained rock steady's core: at Treasure Isle, Tommy McCook's recruitment of the young Jackie Jackson helped define the new style, his melodic basslines drawing on the methods of James Jamerson at Motown; at Studio One, Roland Alphonso was working with understated bassist Brian Atkinson and drummer Joe Isaacs in the Soul Brothers. Other important groups included the Jets, led by Trinidadian guitarist Lynn Taitt, and the Caribbeats, led by guitarist Bobby Aitken, the younger brother of Laurel.

Taitt arrived in Jamaica to back Lord Melody and other calypso singers at Jamaica's independence celebrations and remained on the island after the tour manager disappeared with the wages. Playing and recording with leading ska groups, Taitt formed the Comets, and later, the Jets, with Atkinson, Isaacs, Treasure Isle pianist Gladdy Anderson, and organ specialist Winston 'Brubeck' Wright. Contracted to Federal, they played on Hopeton Lewis' 'Take It Easy', a huge hit that helped inaugurate the rock steady genre, marked out by Taitt's intricate picking style, which was influenced by the steel pan melodies he played in Trinidad before picking up the guitar.

Guitarist Linford 'Hux' Brown passed through the Soul Brothers and the Supersonics before joining Taitt's studio band as a rhythm guitarist. Adept at lead as well as rhythm guitar, his Hofner was ubiquitous, especially after Taitt taught him how to ska with all six strings, and how the use of heavier strings would give a deeper, more resonant tone for solos.

Drummer Winston Grennan was an important part of the Caribbeats, his patterns retaining dramatic tension despite rock steady's slower pace, informed by religious and folkloric forms. He also played in the Supersonics and at Studio One, meeting Lee Perry at Dodd's Muzik City premises.

Hugh Malcolm was a rival drummer with a unique style, active since the ska days. While Grennan's idiosyncrasy was to place his cymbals behind his drum kit, Malcolm sometimes wound furious drumrolls to impart a sense of urgency.

With the rock steady beat creating new buoyancy, Perry was anxious to return to the studio, but did not have much money to hand, nor an outlet for his product, leading to new alliances and freelance projects throughout 1967 as he sought to find his feet away from Studio One. Financial considerations were becoming more concretely important too, as his domestic responsibilities were increasing. He had moved his family to a larger place on Johnson Terrace in Rollington Town, another midtown neighbourhood of modest homes in east Kingston, to make way for a new family member: Pauline gave birth to Marvin Hugh, Lee Perry's first child, on 11 April 1967. Initially nicknamed Django after the antihero of Sergio Corbucci's bloody spaghetti western, Pauline later gave Marvin the pet name Sean, after Sean Connery of James Bond fame.

Despite dissing him repeatedly on the early vinyl sorties for Dodd, Perry then began collaborating closely with Prince Buster, basing himself for a time at Buster's Record Shack on Charles Street. Buster brought Perry to Federal to voice two languorous love songs, 'Give It To Me' and 'Call On Me', the latter featuring a driving horn fanfare and a wistful harmonica break, but both failed to hit, as did the Prince's 'Bitter With The Sweet', a rollicking rock steady addressing life's ups and downs, with Perry on backing vocals. However, a trio of collaborations addressing the ongoing 'Rude Boy' issue were more artistically and commercially successful, the most far-reaching being the epic courtroom drama, 'Judge Dread'.

The Prince had already made an oblique reference to the problem on 'Rude Rude Rudee' (aka 'Don't Throw Stones') and consigned the rudies to the slammer on 'Shanty Town', but escalating violence by politically aligned gangs had significantly worsened in western Kingston, resulting in October's State of Emergency. In response, on 'Judge Dread' Buster appears as a saviour from Ethiopia that condemns the rude boys to 400 years in prison for their acts of senseless violence. Over an arresting rock steady rhythm with a prominent Jackie Jackson bassline and repeated horn fanfare, Buster reels off a list of terrible crimes and worse punishments. Perry, alongside Buster's brother Fitzroy, appear as the defendants Adolphus James, George Grab-and-Flee and Emmanuel Zachariah Zackypon, and proffer a series of unconvincing denials, collapsing in tears as the sentences are pronounced. The song made veiled references to actual rudies, such as PNP supporter George Phillips and JLP supporter Rudolph Lewis, the latter known as Zacky the High Priest, who was shot dead by four members of the Vikings gang in October 1966 and so valued by Seaga that a street was named after him in Tivoli Gardens.

'That time the gun had just come to Jamaica, and the police were so afraid they wouldn't arrest certain people,' said Buster. 'The court was too lenient on wrongdoers through fear of repercussions, and it had gotten out of hand. So I went to Scratch and said, "I don't like this!" and Scratch said, "But you can't do this". Him was a little bit nervy because if him name go 'pon it, he might even get killed out ah street. All them who turn gun men, we all went to school together, so

61

we not exactly friends, but we know each other, but what cause "Judge Dread" fe make is when they shut down Denham Town School and rape kids in the school and the teacher have to run with her panty – that was enough for me. The whole west was under fire that time because the gun just panic the whole society. It wasn't functioning as it should, so I decide to put back some teeth in the judicial system at the risk of my own life. If somebody was going to that studio and make that record, the first time it play, they would have to run and hide somewhere, cos it was going against people who are evil, gangsters. I tell Scratch, "Come", and just give him the part and we go into it. Inspectors of police, about two judges and all decent respectful people come down ah me shop and shake me hand because they hear that play on the radio. Nobody dared to speak out, but I am entitled "Voice of the People", so I must.'

According to engineer Sylvan Morris, 'Judge Dread' was partly shaped by Perry, who came up with spontaneous dialogue at WIRL.

'Scratch was the one who instigated it,' said Morris. 'Him make a suggestion and him and Buster just go about it. Scratch is an extraordinary individual. He creates things which is abnormal and unusual.'

'I was saying, if him think it might be a war, me would be like the accused, so it just come out of his mouth that I am Emmanuel Zachariah Zackypon,' said Perry. 'I don't think even now he know the meaning of Emmanuel, but it all come back because it was a revolution: Emmanuel means "God amongst his people" and he give me the name because he look into a book, see it there and just think it was a movie. If you are an artist you are open, and Prince Buster have open ears: he can hear words too.'

The immediate and broad success of the song spawned many imitations and sequels, including some by Buster himself, the original making such an indelible impression that the *Gleaner* newspaper even lauded Buster for it publicly in June 1967.

Perry's backing vocals also graced Buster's eerie 'Ghost Dance', which saluted prominent fallen rudies as they tried to hold a sound system dance in the afterlife, putting a lighter spin on a serious issue. Those mentioned include Zacky the High Priest, Nyah Keith (born Loban Campbell, alias Keith Anderson), believed to have been one of Zacky's assailants and killed by police a few days after Zacky's death, and Carlton 'Busby' Butler, the protagonist of Alton Ellis' 'Cry Tough' and Derrick Morgan's 'Tougher Than Tough', shot dead at a dance in January 1967.

Perry and Buster also collaborated on 'Johnny Cool', a two-part rock steady medley whose title referenced a 1963 film about a mobster's vendetta, adapting popular songs such as the Jamaicans' 'Ba Ba Boom' and the Impressions' 'Minstrel And Queen', as Buster again took vengeance on the rude boys in his lyrics.

'When you go out in the night-time, you have a set of man in Jamaica who just rape and because they were so bad, people used to get scared to say they raped them,' Buster explained. 'They stop a girl by Trench Town late one night and I go after them at a dance, so in the song I say, "Them mess with my girls, sometimes I become a icebox man, Johnny Cool." Sometimes you don't have to cuss a lot of bad word and all that, all you have to do is just cool.'

The song entered the Jamaican hit parade in November 1967 and remained in the top ten for two months, peaking at the number two position in early December. The artistic success was vindicating, and Perry felt that Buster treated him fairly too. Above all, they maintained mutual respect – a rare thing in the Jamaican music industry.

After Buster left Jamaica to tour the UK, Perry returned to freelance operations. Falling back on useful industry connections, he arranged with WIRL's manager, Clifford Rae, to record now and pay later; WIRL would take care of the session and pressing fees, until revenue was raised through record sales, while Perry would supervise other recording sessions for the company and distribute their records on the second-hand Honda 50 he acquired. Perry thus took another swipe at Dodd with the playfully scathing 'Run For Cover', warning of the volley of musical blows that would result from his superior output. With the Sensations on harmony and Lynn Taitt's supreme picking in the bridge, 'Run For Cover' was a formidable rock steady attack. Released as a WIRL single, the B-side was a fairly faithful rendering of 'Something You Got', a 1961 hit for New Orleans singer-songwriter Chris Kenner (which was successfully covered by Fats Domino in 1964). At the same session, Perry cut 'Whup Whop Man', advancing his outlook as that of a free spirit, not to be interfered with by friend, lover, nor foe; on 'Wind Up Doll' he offered himself to a prospective lover, leaving space for a sublime Taitt guitar solo in the bridge.

Seeking to squeeze the maximum mileage out of a potential hit, Perry reused the 'Run For Cover' rhythm for two alternate songs, 'Set Them Free' and 'Don't Blame The Children', this time endorsing the rude boys. Credited to the Defenders, 'Set Them Free' cast Perry as Lord Defend, informing the judge that the rudies were forced into violent crime by a crooked system that upheld the racially divisive values of colonial Jamaica. In a relaxed, rhyming testimony, Perry posits that a true understanding of the situation must overturn their convictions by right:

They are from a poor generation
Having no education, no qualification
So they are driven to desperation
Can't get a job, they have been forced to rob
I'm not suggesting that they should, but as you know
A hungry man is an angry one . . .
Your Honour, as you already know,
That robbery was from creation
For it was robbery that befall the Black nation.
Our ancestors once ruled this world and all its gold
But now they are poor
Who stole the gold?
Your Honour, could you answer me that question?
If you can't, then there must be silent thief
As well as violent thief . . .

'Don't Blame The Children' continued this defence, allotting the true blame to poor parental role models and the widespread promotion of films glorifying crime and violence; perhaps, Lord Defend suggested, the older generation was really at fault.

Clancy Eccles also began working with Perry at WIRL in 1967, just as Eccles was launching his own label. Debut single 'What Will Your Mama Say' was a rock steady adaptation of an obscure soul-styled love song (first recorded by harmony group the Zodiacs at Federal), Clancy's pared-down version featuring Lynn Taitt's band, and the B-side, 'Darling Don't Do That', a song of regretful heartbreak. The combination of Eccles and Perry was a powerful one, and 'What Will Your Mama Say' a lasting hit.

'Scratch was like my A&R man then,' said Eccles. 'I knew Scratch from he came from the country. I was about leaving

Coxsone and Scratch and I get on very well. I believe Scratch is a great songwriter and top A&R man. For the recording sessions, I would give Scratch my panel to help on a session because Scratch understand sounds very, very well. He's a self-taught sound person, but I believe he has a little more than the ordinary. When we start getting very close, he and Pauline was living in Rollington Town and he was working with West Indies Records.'

The collaborative work took place just as new avenues were opening for Jamaican producers to licence product overseas. Chris Blackwell and Lee Gopthal formed Trojan Records in July 1967, initially to issue Duke Reid's material in Britain; Gopthal, an Indian-Jamaican accountant, was the landlord of Island's headquarters in Kilburn, northwest London, and the proprietor of the Beat & Commercial distribution company, which handled Jamaican and American material. Expanding its roster to house the work of any producer (followed by producer-specific subsidiaries), Trojan would become Britain's leading label for Jamaican music under Gopthal's direction once Blackwell shifted Island's focus to rock.

Pama Records was established by three Black Jamaican entrepreneurs as competition to Blackwell and Gopthal's concern; Harry Palmer was in charge of licencing, brother Carl took care of the books, and Jeffrey ran the London Apollo Club in nearby Willesden. When Harry Palmer travelled to Jamaica seeking product to licence, Eccles was one of the first producers he signed up, bringing the material he produced with Perry to Pama, which would soon become an important outlet for Perry's own work.

The tale of Perry's one-off single with the Gaylets, 'How Come You Come', echoed the 'Roast Duck' saga. The female harmony trio of Judy Mowatt, Beryl Lawson and Merle

Clemenson began working with Linford Anderson, WIRL's chief recording and mastering engineer, when he started producing music clandestinely during downtime, persuading musicians to work for free at the end of a recording session; known as Andy Capp after the English comic strip character, he and Clemenson began a romance while working together. One night at WIRL, Perry convinced the group to back his new rude tune, recorded with Lynn Taitt and the Jets; starting with a squeaky door and embellished by plenty of sighing harmonies, 'How Come' was more light-hearted Perry sleaze, employing clunky innuendo in a duet executed with Lawson.

'That was one of the worst things I have ever done, as my self-esteem was not as it is today,' said Mowatt. 'As a young girl, you would like to hear yourself on radio. We really wanted popularity and Scratch was kind of moulding us. We had so much respect for Scratch and nobody much was in the studio, so we went in and covered our shame with the darkness and did the song, hoping that he would not let anybody know that it is us. Then, Christmas morning they had the stage show at the Ward Theatre. Scratch was dressed like a magician and he asked us to come and perform the song with him. We were so ashamed, but we didn't want to lose face. But God was so good that riot broke out before Scratch went on and the show mashed up.'

When 'How Come' was issued on Pama, it was somehow miscredited to Lloyd Terrel, a misspelling of the given name of Lloyd Charmers, who produced risqué material for the company, and WIRL had licenced Perry's vocal singles to Doctor Bird, the label that former Federal and Studio One engineer Graeme Goodall established in London after breaking away from Island. However, as with so much of Perry's output to date, these singles made little impact on either side of the

Atlantic, and although the sessions at WIRL did not cost anything upfront, the work was not earning him much either.

In the end, Clifford Rae terminated Perry's brief in-house position due to a lack of hit material, his shoes temporarily filled by Bunny 'Striker' Lee, a record plugger from the gritty Greenwich Farm district, bordering an industrial zone at the western edge of downtown, who was just moving into record production himself. Lee's first session at Treasure Isle yielded Roy Shirley's surreal 'Music Field' and Lloyd and the Groovers' 'Do It To Me Baby', but the widespread popularity of the work he recorded with the Uniques at WIRL brought him to another level.

'I was doing a session, "Let Me Go Girl" with Slim Smith and the Uniques, and Scratch was the producer for WIRL at the time, but he didn't know Mr Rae did give me permission to run the session and Scratch tell the musicians the session shouldn't go on,' said Lee. 'So, Scratch lose him work, and then the tune come out and was a big hit. But when Mr Rae fire Scratch, Scratch come back, and I make him get studio time and everything.'

'Scratch was just a guy who earmark some records,' said Roy Shirley. 'Like when you have a tune to record, Scratch take that man in the studio and Scratch arrange out that thing, but he didn't have the contacts that Bunny Lee have, so the company would have seen it more beneficial to get rid of him and bring on Bunny Lee.'

But according to the deejay Dennis 'Alcapone' Smith, who would launch the El Paso sound system in 1969, Perry understood that Lee was a useful ally, the connection leading to close collaboration.

'Perry was Coxsone's right-hand man,' said Alcapone. 'Anywhere you see one, you see the other and when him and

Coxsone parted company, him and Bunny Lee becomes good friends. Scratch see Bunny as a shoulder to lean on because him and Downbeat is not friends anymore. You have to have somebody in your corner because Downbeat is a man who thump you down. You can't go against that man because he is heavy, so Scratch was friends with Striker, them used to go in the studio and make rhythms, give each other rhythms and so forth.'

After his dismissal from WIRL, Perry began working with Joel Gibson – popularly known as Joe Gibbs – another record shop proprietor then entering music production. A native son of Salt Spring, located on the outskirts of Montego Bay, Gibbs had worked on the US naval base in Guantanamo Bay, Cuba, training as an electronic technician, and on his return to Jamaica in the mid-1960s after working for the engineering firm Stone & Webster, he began selling records from his television repair shop on Beeston Street, launching the Amalgamated label from the premises. Like Perry, he lacked ready cash but knew there was money in producing. Roy Shirley's 'Hold Them' was Gibbs' spectacular entry point, the enduring hit driven by Shirley's peculiar delivery, thin and quivering one moment, deep and gravelly the next, the off-kilter Jets rhythm inspired by a local Salvation Army band that Shirley had seen on Orange Street; Bunny Lee helped establish the song's popularity, prior to his arrival at WIRL.

Now that Gibbs was gradually staking a claim in the music industry, Perry became an increasingly important force in his operation, acting as the producer while Gibbs took the hands-off role of executive producer, allowing him to concentrate on the business side of things.

'He was like the producer,' said bassist Jackie Jackson of Perry's work with Gibbs. 'Scratch would come into the studio and say, "Play this for me", or he might say, "The drum, give me this beat." He's not a musician, but he can relate to you what he wants.'

Before Perry's appearance, Gibbs had scored a hit with a loose rock steady adaptation of Barbara Lynn's defiant 1962 rhythm and blues release 'You're Gonna Need Me', recorded by the Denham Town-based singer Errol Dunkley, Jamaica's second child star. The follow-up, 'Please Stop Your Lying', was one of the first songs Perry arranged for Gibbs and an even bigger hit than its predecessor.

'Scratch was a freelance producer, he's got a good hearing for sound,' said Dunkley. 'Joe Gibbs was just the guy who's spending the money, but Lee Perry's the guy who could compare with the musicians. When Gibbs tried to tell them what to do, they just laughed because him couldn't talk to them in the term of music.'

Then Perry brought Stranger Cole and Gladdy Anderson's 'Just Like A River' to Gibbs' attention. Cole had been recording popular duets with Ken Boothe and Patsy Todd, among others, and recorded lilting love song 'Just Like A River' with Anderson, along with 'Seeing Is Knowing', which warned of a pending heartbreak, but when the producer and record distributor Sonia Pottinger refused to pay an advance to handle the self-produced single, Cole brought it to Perry, who convinced Gibbs to issue it; the resulting hit vied with 'Johnny Cool' for the top spot on the Jamaican charts in December 1967 and the single became the first release of the UK branch of Amalgamated, one of Trojan Records' earliest producer-designated subsidiaries.

Ever willing to make further use of a good rhythm, Perry dramatically reworked 'Seeing Is Knowing' for a song called 'Kimble', credited to the Creators, casting himself as the protagonist of *The Fugitive* television series that was then gripping Jamaican viewers. With breaking bottles, cracking whips and other sound effects bringing the tale audibly to life, 'Kimble' showed Perry's tendency to embrace an alter-ego to the absolute fullness, actually *becoming* the character for the song's duration.

For the rest of the year and part of 1968, Perry recorded a range of artists for Gibbs: the deejay Cool Sticky (Uziah Thompson, whom he knew from Studio One), the Overtakers, led by a young singer from Trelawny named Leo Graham, who employed a high tenor, the Mellotones, led by Winston Francis, and the Versatiles, led by Junior Byles (Keith Byles Junior), a six-foot-tall mechanic from Jones Town with a distinctive tenor lead that formed the group with Dudley Earl and future Morwells member, Louis Davis.

Under Perry's direction, the Versatiles cut 'The Time Has Come', a heartfelt plea for unity based around Jamaica's national motto, 'Out of many, one people', which was entered in the annual Festival Song Competition, held in the summer as a component of independence celebrations; Edward Seaga had launched the contest the year before as a means of stimulating cultural pride, and although the song fared poorly in the competition, it spawned a series of performances by the group around the island and marked the start of a long working relationship with Perry.

With Gibbs' releases gaining greater currency, Perry was determined to send another message to Clement Dodd and did so with 'I Am The Upsetter', heralding his latest antagonistic persona. Over a jaunty rhythm on which Lynn Taitt was doubled-tracked to play two different guitar lines, Perry queried Dodd's *gravalicious* covetousness; he was greedy, *red-eye* and could not be satisfied, Perry proclaimed, but the avenging Upsetter was on the musical rise, overpowering Dodd with a vinyl uppercut, and the song's aggressive structure made it a sound system favourite in Britain too.

According to Lynn Taitt, the musicians structured the overall composition of 'The Upsetter' in the studio after Perry sang the lyrics he had written.

'He was going to have a recording session with Gladdy Anderson and Jackie Jackson and Drumbago on drums,' said Taitt. 'I arranged the song in the studio. He sing the song, we listened to it and then Gladdy said, "Taitt, you have any introduction?" and we work it up together. If Scratch don't like it, he say, "No, no, no, change that!"'

The single's B-side, 'Thank You Baby', exposed the Upsetter's more loving side, making the most of another superb rhythm arranged by Taitt, Anderson and company.

In the same period, Perry was moonlighting for Deltone, a record shop and short-lived label based at 111 Orange Street, run by Mrs Edel Barnett (known as Del). In addition to arranging a few inconsequential tunes by the Versatiles, the biggest hit Perry produced for the label was 'Combination', voiced by Theophilus Beckford's teenaged nephew Keeling, loosely adapting the melody and structure of the Temptations' 'Since I Lost My Baby'. The song was recorded at the same session as the Tennors' 'Ride Yu Donkey', a massive hit that Perry also had a hand in, and the B-side of Beckford's single reused the 'Combination' rhythm for the Versatiles' 'Action Line', which parodied a radio phone-in to poke fun at producers that copied the work of their rivals.

The most commercially successful material Gibbs released while working with Perry was recorded with the Pioneers, then the duo of Sidney Crooks and Jackie Robinson. Crooks formed the first version of the group in Trench Town in

August 1966 with his brother, Derrick, and Winston Hewitt, which split when Hewitt migrated to Canada. Then, in the spring of 1967, a chance encounter with Gibbs on Beeston Street led Crooks to form a new Pioneers for 'Give Me Little Loving', recorded one fateful night at WIRL. The problem was that Crooks needed a competent lead singer, so he randomly recruited the teenaged Robinson who was loitering outside the studio, trying to steel his nerves for the recording of his own solo effort. According to Robinson, 'Give Me Little Loving' reached the number two position on the Jamaican charts, starting the new group off with a bang and making him their permanent lead vocalist.

Although absent for 'Give Me Little Loving', Perry was involved with a couple of spectacular Pioneers hits during his brief time with Gibbs, using alternate takes of the same rhythm. The first was 'Long Shot', which decried the failures of a racehorse that 'busted the bet' of a gambling protagonist who lost his money when the horse failed to 'bust the tape' at the finish line. Introduced by a trumpeted 'Call To Post' as heard at the racetrack, the song's minimal musical backing used a disjointed rhythm that mimicked the trots of a racehorse, given further demarcation by repetitive steel pan beats, played by the noted Trinidadian pannist and percussionist Mackie Burnette, then based in Jamaica; alternate voicing 'Jackpot' reversed the tale by celebrating a racetrack victory, with 'sweet music, rice and chicken' for the protagonist, though the victorious horse is not named. Both songs reached the number four position on the Jamaican charts ('Jackpot' peaking in mid-June), and both were popular in Britain, particularly with the white working-class skinheads that were emulating Jamaican popular culture through dance steps, bravado and sharp dress. According to a 1969 *Gleaner* article, 'Long Shot' and 'Jackpot' sold over 20,000 copies in Jamaica and over 6,000 copies in their first week of release in the UK.

But as Gibbs reaped the spoils, Perry found himself in a familiar position. Despite his best efforts, the financial recompense and recognition were far from evident, and after a heated argument, Perry stopped working for Gibbs, his departure making space for Winston 'Niney' Holness, whose nickname stemmed from the missing thumb that was severed in a welding accident. He and Perry knew each other from Perry's dancing days in Hanover, since Niney spent part of his teens in Lucea, working with a high-school band featuring future Studio One session guitarist Eric Frater; like Perry, he became a record salesman and general assistant in Kingston who moved into freelance music production, working closely with Bunny Lee and other producers.

After the rupture with Gibbs, Perry cut more important work with Clancy Eccles and Linford Anderson, this time contributing to a dramatic shift in the predominant rhythm. Perry brought Monty Morris to Eccles' attention, resulting in the sizeable hit 'Say What You're Saying', recorded at Treasure Isle, its chugging rhythm broken by melodic organ hooks. Eccles and Perry revisited the rhythm for 'CN Express', a deejay cut by Cool Sticky, referencing Jamaican travellers to London, with a blown bottle emulating a train whistle; on the B-side, Perry's solo alternate 'You Were Meant For Me' was a straightforward plea to an absent lover. The songs were arranged by Ernest Ranglin, who was drafted in when Lynn Taitt made upfront payment demands.

Perry and Linford Anderson then formed a brief partnership with trainee engineer Barrington Lambert to issue singles on the Upset label, the name coined from an advertising billboard. As Anderson explained, 'I was driving along one day and I just see a commercial, "Are you having upset stomach?" And I say, "Oh, that's a damn good name for a label!" At the time, Lee Perry didn't have a label.'

According to Anderson and Perry's cousin Archie, the first song Perry proposed to the Upset team was 'Honey Love', an innocuous cover of a Drifters doo-wop hit by an unknown adenoidal crooner called Burt Walters, who Perry discovered singing barefoot on the street in Rockfort, east Kingston.

'Perry came to us and said, "I have some ideas to produce a song", cost about thirty pounds each,' said Anderson. 'Barry and me put the money up because Perry didn't have any.'

The song was recorded hurriedly in the middle of the night to keep costs to a minimum and issued on a single with a blank label, rubber-stamped Upset Records. The A-side of the 45 had little to differentiate it, but the B-side was a shocker: 'Evol Yenoh' was the same song with the entire vocal track played backwards, Walters' saccharine sentiment the fervent pleas of glossolalia, the sweet banality of pop turned on its head to produce something startling and alien. Such a radical representation of a singer's voice was virtually unheard of; even the Beatles had only reversed half a vocal line on their experimental B-side 'Rain', while some of pop's more bizarre novelty records such as Napoleon XIV's 'They're Coming To Take Me Away, Ha-Haaa' and Ohio Express's bubble-gum hit 'Yummy Yummy Yummy' reversed the entire song on the B-side, but these were apparently done in a deliberate ploy of reaping publishing royalties rather than in the spirit of avant-garde experimentation.

When Anderson pressed 300 copies of 'Honey Love', Perry was only able to find half the money required, so he and cousin Archie hopped on the Honda to hustle some funds with available stock: the electrical goods store and record shop KG's, located on Slipe Road at Cross Roads, took some on consignment; Harry J paid cash to stock his Orange Street record shop, and Patricia Chin of Randy's Records gave Perry a hefty cheque for the remainder, freeing up the rest of the impounded stock, which they peddled to other Kingston record outlets.

'Honey Love' sold poorly in Jamaica, but at least allowed Walters to buy a pair of shoes, and after Anderson licenced the single to Trojan, the team recouped their initial investment; Perry was ready for more, but his partners were reluctant.

'We did the song in about an hour, and it was not a big hit,' said Anderson. 'We sold the song for £100, at that time it was a lot of money. He said he wanted to continue with the business, I said whatever he wanted to do was fine. Then Barry said he figured he should get more. Barry said, "I'll take my money now", so I said, "OK, I'll take mine too." Barry and I went straight to the racetrack with thirty-three pounds each and we lost the money! Lee Perry, he's not working, so he doesn't gamble.'

Perry was determined to persevere and make his mark, aiming for the kind of success Sir JJ enjoyed with the Ethiopians, Sonia Pottinger with the Melodians, and Bunny Lee with the Uniques, and he wanted to burst Gibbs' bubble too. He began pressing small quantities of new material on Upset that he would sell from a corner of Clancy Eccles' shop, the Mellotones' 'Nonesuch' another song about a racehorse that 'busted' the bet of the protagonist, paired with Val Bennett's reggae rendering of Acker Bilk's anodyne trad-jazz TV theme, 'Stranger On The Shore.' Then came a prodigious record, aimed at Gibbs, its inspiration stemming from a most unsuspected source.

'One night he say, "Let me buy you a drink", so we stopped at this bar close to my house and there was a church there, doing Revival stuff,' said Anderson. 'When we left, Scratch starting rocking. They had this band with drum and bass and guitar and everything. The next day Lee Perry came and said, "I've got the idea for a song".'

Perry said the inspiration came from 'touring the night': 'At them time, me used to go out in town and stay late, drink one or two little beer, things like that. And one night me walking past a Pocomania church and hear the people inside a wail. And me catch the vibration and say boy! Let's make a sound fe catch the vibration of them people! Them was in spirit and them tune me in spiritually. That's where the whole thing come from, cos them Poco people getting sweet.'[1]

Pocomania church services retain powerful vestiges of African culture, despite attempts at erasure during slavery. Through singing, dancing, drumming and the rhythmic 'trumping' of breath, ancestral spirits are evoked, as in Ettu; congregants may be possessed by the Holy Spirit or saints, cleansed through the spiritual truths imparted during the experience.

Tapping into the unknown memories of a distant land, the midnight mass Perry stumbled upon reached somewhere into the depths of his soul. The following evening, he made his way down to WIRL a bit later than usual, hoping to find the musicians already warmed up and in a more receptive mood. He explained what he wanted to Gladdy, Jackie Jackson, Hux Brown and the other musicians, and then the tape was rolling; the vibe was right, the band was tight, and the session was getting hot. Perry was behind the mixing console while the rhythm was laid, Clancy Eccles providing a guide vocal until the musicians captured the feeling Perry was after. Once the rhythm track was delivered satisfactorily, Perry went into the voicing booth and performed his lyrics with electrifying speed. With the Pocomania session of the night

77

before in mind, he kept his voice gruff and unrestrained in the choruses.

The resultant sound was startling, the beat frenetic. It contained an unfettered urgency and frustrated clamour that went against the relaxed pace of the waning rock steady, but instead of hankering back to the jazz underpinning of ska, this crazy, pounding beat went in another direction, with Perry's interpretation of the midnight Pocomania expressing the transmogrified trauma of Africans transported to a hostile, alien environment.

The melody reconfigured that of the Pioneers' 'Longshot', Gladdy's piano chords here with gospel undertones, Hux's guitar spun in rapid bursts of aggressive energy and Winston Wright's organ relayed an unusual melody beneath Perry's angry snarl. Between the repeated refrains of 'Why, why, people funny boy', Perry lashed out at Gibbs, reminding how the executive producer had turned his back on him after reaping rewards from Perry's creativity; now that Gibbs had his jackpot of hits from the Pioneers and other artists developed by Perry, he was stuffing his belly full of rice and peas, the song proclaimed, while Perry and his family were starving. To further emphasise this point, Perry overdubbed the famished bawling of an infant, taken from a sound effects record at Linford Anderson's suggestion.

'Andy at West Indies was the best thing we ever have in the music business,' said Perry. 'He had total experience, just like a little scientist. It's even he hear the baby bawling and it was his idea to put it in the song. He listen to funny things and hear this record with this baby crying, bring it to me and me listen to it and say, "But fuck this, man! We fe put it in the song" and bam! It's coming like a real natural thing. Everybody saying it was some baby in Jamaica crying, but we didn't know where the baby come from. He was something special in the record business – Andy unleash a goldmine.'

Perry emphasised the song's rooting in personal experience: 'They say word is the wind and words is a weapon, so because me know what me had done for these people, giving them free energy, I said, "What I've done for you, you don't remember that. When you was down and out, I help you out with my spiritual vibration, and now you're rich, you have money and a big car and build studio and all them things, you don't remember that", so I was using that like a sword to cut up those people because it was reality. They use me to get famous and get rich, and them say they are the producer and the promoter, and they do it by themselves, which was a lie.'

Preparing to issue the song as a single, he paired it with Burt Walters' unremarkable rendition of Bob Dylan's 'Blowin' In The Wind', recorded at the 'Honey Love' session and embellished by wind sound effects. Perry designed an Upset label bearing a scarlet, blood-dripping machete, the symbol suggesting the magic arts of Obeah or 'Science', its practitioners believed capable of providing protection from enemies or inflicting harm on a foe. But as Perry lacked the money to press the record, he approached Neville Chow-Fung at KG's, who would often help smaller producers that were unable to release potential hits without financial support.

'He didn't have any money to press or nothing, so he told KG about it,' said Linford Anderson. 'Them print a thousand and put it out, the radio play it a couple of times and they said, "OK, print ten thousand." It became a big hit, and them take it to England [where it was issued on Doctor Bird]. KG press the record and he sell it to KG at a price!'

The song entered the Jamaican charts in July 1968, just as 'Jackpot' faded from it. The ubiquitous hit sold 60,000 copies and was popular for eight or nine months, according to Perry, allowing him to purchase a Ford Escort. At last, he was reaping directly from his work, and getting all the credit for it too.

Gibbs tried a dual counter-attack on an Amalgamated single: 'People Grudgeful', credited to Sir Gibbs, mimicked the melody and reversed the lyrics of 'People Funny Boy' to aim it back at Perry; the Pioneers' B-side 'Pan Ya Machete' warned 'Mr Upsetter' that 'little sins can lead to big things', dissing Scratch for having 'too much chat' and further berating him with the sound of a whining puppy, a meandering violin adding to the ridicule. Yet, compared to the hard-hitting 'People Funny Boy' this was feeble mockery, the vinyl jousts ultimately emphasizing that the Upsetter was a force to be reckoned with.

Clancy Eccles' 'Feel The Rhythm', recorded with Perry, entered the Jamaican top ten in September. Like 'People Funny Boy', which Eccles said was recorded later, the song was something else entirely, utilising an urgent beat that was totally new and so intense that Eccles spent much of the song describing its effects: you either danced the rhythm or you 'upset' the rhythm, even as false friends tried to take advantage and rivals sought to steal your thunder.

Both songs heralded the arrival of a new style, as yet unnamed, which would come to be identified as reggae, a fast-paced dance music that swept Jamaica in the latter half of 1968. Clancy Eccles said he coined the term, which Perry disliked as it was too close to 'streggae', a derogatory slang connoting a loose woman, or something worn out and worthy of discarding.

'Scratch was fighting us,' said Niney. 'Streggae is some careless girl that walk the streets, so it was nothing good, but those days reggae wasn't in the dictionary. Clancy Eccles is the only one who go with it and said, "This is reggae".'

Musicians, producers and historians are still arguing over which was the first reggae record, with many claims staked for different reasons. For instance, Alva Lewis claimed his rhythm guitar made Stranger Cole and Lester Sterling's 'Bangarang' the first reggae, while Gladdy Anderson said it was his organ shuffle on the Melodians' 'Everybody Bawling'. Bunny Lee agreed that 'Bangarang' was the first reggae song, but claimed it was down to Glen Adams' organ riffs. Larry Marshall's 'Nanny Goat' and the Cables' 'Baby Why' are also cited, and Toots' 'Do The Regay' as the first record to mention it by name. But even if 'Nanny Goat' ruled the charts longer than any other hit, each of these songs was released after 'People Funny Boy', as was 'Feel The Rhythm' (although the latter may have been recorded first).

'We were the first people who did reggae music, with a tune by Clancy Eccles named "Feel The Rhythm" and a next one by Monty Morris, "Say What You're Saying",' suggested Ernest Ranglin. 'Scratch and Clancy were the producers, and I was the arranger.'

'"Say What You're Saying" had been the first crossover moving away from the rock steady to the reggae, and "Feel The Rhythm" strengthened the whole thing, a totally different thing than the average,' said Eccles. 'Scratch is supposed to be a part of it because he was there with me. He helped and did the A&R work.'

'People say it's "People Funny Boy", and if they see it that way, it's true,' countered Perry, 'because after me leave Coxsone, me want a different music, then me did go back to the church and listen the energy and the vibration of the fire and the shouting of the people. That was something different from dancehall business, something like them want to fly. So that's really where it was coming from.'

'People Funny Boy' held a furious, pent-up energy, expressing the frustration that resulted not just from Perry's immediate circumstances but which followed on from centuries of inequality and injustice. The Upsetter had inaugurated a different beat that would lead Jamaican music to become synonymous with reggae, regardless of the fact that he would never be happy with the term.

CHAPTER FOUR
The Return of Django: International Success

After the tremendous success of 'People Funny Boy', Perry had far more cash at his disposal, and finding appropriate housing for his family was top priority. They briefly occupied a rental property off Molynes Road, bordering the compact, congested Drewsland district of northwest Kingston, before renting another home at 2 Caenwood Crescent in the suburb of Washington Gardens, just off the main through road, Weymouth Drive.

Located at Kingston's western edge, Washington Gardens is composed of some two-dozen broad streets, formed in a half-oval grid that was laid out in the late 1950s as part of the city's expansion. The neighbourhood sits below the broad expanse of Washington Boulevard and above the top end of Spanish Town Road, both busy thoroughfares feeding the highway to Spanish Town, with sewerage gullies forming an eastern barrier to the more densely populated district of Waterhouse, the limited entry points contributing to an isolated feel. The houses were newer, bigger and further apart from each other here, and the additional breathing space was certainly welcome. He was in good company, too, since Prince Buster lived a few streets away on Whitney

Drive, enabling a close friendship to form between Pauline and Buster's wife, Blossom.

Perry's base of operations was now the Upsetter Record Shop, located at 36 Charles Street, the former site of Buster's original Record Shack. Archie Moore became the manager there after injuring his hand at a shoemaking factory, and was later assisted by Delroy Phillips, a downtown bad boy known as Jubie, who Perry tried to steer away from violence. An audition room was set up at the back of the shop and, later, there was the adjacent Green Door Saloon, where ranking toughs like Claudie Massop of the Phoenix gang would while away the hours drinking beer, and a herb vendor named Dizzy sold weed and *ital* meals from a shack that backed onto the shop, offering a menu of freshly cooked wholefoods and strong spliffs. A popular downtown hangout spot, it would later be frequented by industry personnel and sound system proprietors such as Winston Blake of Merritone, who featured Perry's productions at their residency at the fashionable Peyton Place in Jack's Hill, an exclusive enclave overlooking Kingston.

The new Upsetter label reworked the old Upset design, its red and white lettering flanked by curved daggers dripping blood and a menacing scorpion, so Perry naturally began crediting his band as the Upsetters, or sometimes the Upsetter All Stars, the mainstays including Jackie Jackson, Gladdy Anderson, Winston Wright, Hux Brown and Hugh Malcolm or Winston Grennan on drums, though other players were often featured.

Perry began holding regular recording sessions at WIRL several days a week. Working late into the night, the perfectionist producer recorded repeated takes of each song, until the musicians played everything precisely as he pictured it.

Despite being unable to read music, Perry always knew exactly what he wanted and was typically dictatorial at work.

For the rest of 1968, Perry worked mostly with rising talent, plus a few veterans he knew from before, sometimes experimenting with multiple uses of the same rhythm in the process. Early issues included the Mellotones' 'Uncle Charley', in which the protagonist was dubbed 'King of the Bottle' through his repeated bouts of drunkenness, with Perry and the group making retching noises of alcoholic excess, and its agreeable, bouncing rhythm was reused for 'Uncle Desmond', in which Charley counters the insalubrious claims, again with booze-infused spluttering.

There was Val Bennett's saxophone take of Ben E. King's 'Spanish Harlem' and a reworking of the 'Nonesuch' rhythm with a steel pan pastiche of the 'People Funny Boy' melody, titled 'Handy Cap' as a further racetrack reference; the Ethiopians, then the duo of Leonard Dillon and Stephen Taylor, recorded 'Cut Down (On Your Speed)' and 'Not Me', chugging reggae songs that both scorned a lover, which surfaced on Doctor Bird in England; and there was the defiant 'Sentence', which was about avoiding a prison-term frame-up, credited to Danny and Lee, as well as a tasteful rendition of Jerry Butler's 'He Don't Love You' by the Silvertones harmony trio.

Thirteen of Perry's earliest independent productions were issued on Trojan and two on their Duke subsidiary in 1968, and for British audiences, 'Tighten Up' was the standout. Credited overseas to the Untouchables, the song featured the Inspirations, a duo formed by Trevor Shaw, later known as Jimmy London, and Ransford White, later known as Billy Dyce, whose brother Doraney was a member of the Techniques. Early work for Sir JJ failed to impact, and after Roy Shirley brought the duo to Perry, they recorded 'Tighten

Up' at WIRL, re-recording the vocals at Studio One for greater precision. The dance-oriented song was inspired by the recent success of Archie Bell and the Drells' funk hit of the same name, and following its widespread popularity with the growing British reggae audience, Trojan made 'Tighten Up' the title of its longstanding cut-price compilation series, the track a main selling point of the first volume.

Another Inspirations session yielded the suggestive 'You Know What I Mean' and a spirited original called 'Stand By Me', and later, there was the ballad 'Love Oh Love', which made the most of their well-balanced harmonies, but the group felt Perry was not giving them adequate attention and soon began working for Joe Gibbs.

Then, in late September, David Isaacs' emotional rendition of Stevie Wonder's 'A Place In The Sun' entered the Jamaican top ten; the young singer from Denham Town had joined the Comets in the late rock steady phase, which ultimately led to this first solo hit.

'I said to Lynn Taitt, "I would like to cover this tune because it is a favourite of mine", and he said that I would have to check a producer, so I came down Orange Street one evening and went to Clancy Eccles with it,' said Isaacs. 'Clancy was doing tailoring at that time. He said that he liked the song, but why don't I try and give Upsetter it? The two of them had a shop side-by-side, Upsetter on Charles Street and Luke Lane corner and Clancy on Orange Street corner, so I went to Upsetter with it and right away, he took me in Coxsone's studio.'

'I was running a session by West Indies Records and Scratch was there with me and didn't have any hit record,' said Clancy Eccles, who named Perry's perfectionism as the defining element of the song's success. 'At the end of the day Scratch said to me, "Boy, David Isaac's tune sound good", so

I said, "Hear what happen: you deal with that song", so he took the song from me, went to Coxsone and did the voice over, and it took him a very long time to get the voice the way he wanted it. He turned it into a very good song, better than what I would have gotten, cos I probably wouldn't have put in so much time. I believe it took around sixteen hours to do it. He went there around three days till he got it right.'

Keyboardist Grub Cooper of the popular showband Fabulous Five devised a new introduction using chord changes to build dramatic tension, which helped the song to hit.

'Scratch used him on the session and right away, it was a hit,' said Isaacs. 'It did well in London too and Harry Palmer came down and offered me a contract, but I couldn't go to London at that time. Because I was new in the business I didn't really want to take the gamble. I wanted to be more mature, so I stick with Upsetter and keep recording with him.'

A trio of songs co-written by Perry hinted at overriding preoccupations: the Mellotones' 'What A Botheration' spoke of hard times with no money, playing the lottery as a last resort; on Perry's own vocal recording, also called 'What A Botheration', he sang of meeting the approaching Christmas with torn pants, empty pockets and a dead car battery, with even the racetrack off-limits. Slim Smith's haunting 'What A Situation' (aka 'Give Me'), voiced at a joint session shared between Perry and Bunny Lee, also spoke of the debilitating confusion brought on by the stress of ghetto life.

There were other grudgeful jousts too, such as Perry's 'Hey Mama', voiced with Eccles, reworking the mento 'Chambolina' to take aim at the Eurocentric views of a certain 'white Black man'; 'You Crummy' was aimed at Eccles himself, a former pal lambasted as envious of Perry's growing success, prompting Eccles to respond in kind with 'Bag-A-Boo', proclaiming himself 'King of the Reggae' and questioning Perry's musical credibility.

Unusually, Perry had saxophonist Val Bennett voice a couple of rhythm and blues numbers in 1968, adapting Ruth Brown's 1952 hit '5-10-15 Hours' as 'Baby Baby', and the original 'Barbara' had Bennett decrying bad treatment from a 'wicked, brown-skinned gal' that was drugging and two-timing him.

Sir Lord Comic's 'Django Shoots First' (aka 'Bronco') was the first of many songs to reference the spaghetti western underdog, its keyboard melody vamping on the 'Old Man River' Broadway showtune theme as Comic's slow drawl and imitation gunshots emulated Django's bloody cinematic exploits; the song fleetingly entered the Jamaican top ten in late October, helped by an extended run of the film at the King's Theatre.

'Eight For Eight' transposed Zimbabwean saxophonist Augustine Musarurwa's oft-versioned 'Skokiaan' as a reggae instrumental; the first of many Upsetter hits led by a prominent organ, it briefly reached the Jamaican top ten the following January.

In late 1968, at Studio One, during the same session in which Max Romeo voiced 'Wet Dream' for Bunny Lee on a rhythm laid earlier at Treasure Isle, Perry tried to voice a cover version of 'Sick And Tired', a Chris Kenner original that became an incredible success for Fats Domino in 1958. The rhythm was centred on Jackie Jackson's relaxed bassline, with bluesy guitar riffs from Hux Brown and Bobby Aitken, choppy piano chords from Theophilus Beckford and a dual horn vamp from Bennett and trumpeter Johnny Moore, as well as an off-kilter drum pattern from Hugh Malcolm with tight snare fills in the breaks. But Perry was displeased by the vocal and shelved the song for a time. It was eventually released as the instrumental 'Return Of Django', with Bennett's searing saxophone solo a defining element, but the song made little impact in Jamaica, unlike in Britain, where it would be the sleeper that belatedly changed everything, though not until late in the following year.

As Perry began notching up the hits with greater regularity, there was a new arrival in the family: on 30 December, Pauline gave birth to a son named Mark Anthony, later known as Omar after film star Omar Sharif, bringing much joy to the Perry household; shortly thereafter, his divorce from Ruby Williams was finalised.

1969 would prove to be a prolific breakthrough year, in which Perry would unleash around fifty singles in Jamaica, many of which were also issued overseas, and there were Upsetter album releases too, the increased output and greater artistic success partly due to developments at Kingston's recording studios, better licencing deals, and a new set of backing musicians, resulting in a change of direction midway through the year.

Following a mysterious fire and the subsequent liquidation of the company, the bass player and Dragonaires bandleader Byron Lee, of mixed Chinese and African ancestry, acquired West Indies Records, which he upgraded to eight tracks and renamed Dynamic Sounds; the new equipment resulted in greater sonic clarity, and there were higher-capacity pressing facilities too, all fully operational by June 1969.

There was also Randy's, the smaller and more affordable recording studio opened by the Chinese-Jamaican producer and retailer Vincent Chin, who had run the Randy's label since the ska years. Conveniently located upstairs from the massive record shop and distribution service he and his wife Patricia ran at 17 North Parade in downtown Kingston, Perry would use the facility with greater frequency the following year, especially since the Chins allowed him to record without upfront payment, making up the balance through record sales.

'When we didn't have the money to pay for studio time, him give us time free, and when we could pay, we pay him,' said Perry. 'Those were the people who give people a chance. Me could do any amount of things me want to do at the studio, and Miss Pat just put it 'pon a bill for me, and when me give her records, they subtract that from what me owe them. So there was a free credit for me there all the while, no care what it is.'

The Chins had relatives in New York acting as overseas affiliates: brother Victor launched an American branch of Randy's at his electronics shop in Brooklyn's Crown Heights, which became a prime stateside channel for Perry's productions, and another brother, Keith, also issued product on his own eponymous imprint.

But Perry's most important overseas market was Britain, where Trojan and Pama handled key outlets for his work. There was now a designated UK branch of the Upsetter label, established as a Trojan subsidiary, and some twenty-five singles would be released on it between March and December; Trojan scheduled a debut album, *The Upsetter*, for release in the summer, which would be delayed by several months. At the same time, Pama issued the first dozen Perry-produced singles on their Camel, Crab and Punch subsidiaries, and occasionally, the same songs were licenced to both companies, whether by accident or design.

The Pama connection was forged by Bunny Lee during a trip to London in 1968; obtaining a sizeable advance for his own productions, he cut Perry in on the deal, enabling him to begin producing for the company too.

'Me and Scratch really go back a long way,' said Lee. 'We used to check girls together, do a lot of things together. If anything, me carry Scratch, me is the first man come and take £500 from Pama and bring come give Scratch, and Scratch luckier than me: Pama give him a job after that.'

'The deal with Scratch sort of arrived out of the Bunny Lee thing,' confirmed Harry Palmer, who would open a branch of Pama Records on Orange Street in the summer. 'I arrived in Jamaica a second or third time, and I was introduced to Scratch by Bunny at Randy's studio, and we started going out together, drinking, eating fish. I had a girl that I wanted him to produce, but it didn't work out, and Scratch became a good friend. I used to go to his home in Washington Gardens, and we used to go out and get drunk in the night, and then I used to have to drive him back – me alone, with a drunk man in the car.'

Perry made his first trip to London in time for Bunny Lee's wedding to Marva Leigh, which took place in Lambeth, south London, in June 1969; Harry Palmer arranged for Perry's airline ticket, and he and Perry acted as joint best men. Although Lee already had a place of his own in Forest Gate, east London, where the newlyweds were based before returning to Jamaica, Palmer arranged for Perry to stay close to Pama's headquarters in Harlesden, northwest London, at the home of aspiring singer Tony Owens, which often served as a resting place for visiting artists and associates because Owens' mother was an old friend of the family; Tony had joined his mother in London in 1967 and had recently won a talent contest at the London Apollo with 'Telephone Line', co-written by Alton Ellis.

Despite the brevity of the trip, Perry was enticed by his first glimpse of London's reggae underbelly, which made clear there were ample opportunities. He got a sense of which tunes were making waves too, with 'Israelites' and 'Wet Dream' both still very present in the pop charts, and the Pama link had valuable fringe benefits, since Carl Palmer helped Perry acquire a second-hand Jaguar S, which added to his kudos on the music scene once he shipped it to Kingston.

Back in Jamaica, Perry was working with diverse talent that was exploring myriad subject matter, the weekly, hour-long *Upsetter Presents* radio show he sponsored on JBC helping his productions to gain local currency; recording sessions were often shared with Bunny Lee, and Niney was acting as the chief record salesman for both of them (as well as Clancy Eccles) and helping with musical arrangements when required. Perry recorded plenty of standard vocals in this phase, but the organ instrumentals and rough-edged deejay cuts had greater impact, this time on both sides of the Atlantic.

Of the vocal tracks, Monty Morris' 'Can't Get No Peace' complained of persistent home hauntings by malevolent spirits, known as duppies; Ernest Wilson of the Clarendonians offered a civil rights theme on the soulful 'Freedom Train', and the Termites duo voiced 'I'll Be Waiting', an odd number set in Paris. Upcoming trio the West Indians, led by the idiosyncratic falsetto of Eric Donaldson, recorded a number of impressive songs for Perry, including the forlorn 'Oh Lord', the broken-hearted 'Strange Whispering' and the determined lover's plea, 'Never Get Away', but none of them hit, leading the group to disband. 'Mini Dress', by former Flames member Winston Jarrett, saluted the appeal of his girlfriend's skimpy evening wear, but sales were disappointing and Perry reluctant to pay, according to Jarrett: 'I get thirty pounds in cheque, but I have a hard time to get it changed – sometimes it bounce.'

Perry continued sporadically cutting his own vocal songs, including 'People Funny Fi True', which updated the 'People Funny Boy' theme. 'Mad House' was something else entirely, Perry's scat-vocal gibberish and clattering sound effects – achieved by banging a spring reverb unit – acting as an abstract aural representation of a psychiatric ward, cluttering a rollicking reggae rhythm that was led by Val Bennett's saxophone; as the first record to question Perry's sanity, it was a theatrical precursor of things to come.

In a more conventional format, former Mellotones Wesley Martin and Sammy Lowe were now working as the Bleechers, fronted by the distinctive high tenor of Leo Graham, who became their leader following Winston Francis' migration to Canada. Of the handful of songs they recorded for Perry in 1969, 'Check Him Out' was an infectious number advertising the sweet music to be found at the Upsetter Record Shop, complete with directions to 36 Charles Street; 'Everything For Fun' wooed a woman to a dance; 'Farmer In The Den' adapted nursery rhyme 'Farmer In The Dell'; 'Ram You Hard' was a slack track, oddly credited abroad to John Lennon and the Bleechers; and love songs 'Ease Up' and 'You're Gonna Feel It' were recorded at Dynamic and credited as Byron Lee productions, but actually produced by Perry, who received a songwriting credit.

Confusingly, 'Pound Get A Blow' credited the Bleechers on its UK release but featured Jimmy Nelson and Derrick 'Watty' Burnett, young hopefuls from Portland who performed at the 1968 Festival Song Competition as Jimmy and Derrick, alternately known as the Soul Twins. Voiced at Treasure Isle, where a hug from Toots helped Burnett to overcome his nervousness, the song was written in reaction to Jamaica's coming decimalisation in September, replacing pounds, shillings and pence with dollars and cents, ultimately resulting in devaluation.

There was general fluidity where credit was concerned, and sometimes rhythms or even songs were swapped, especially on releases culled from the many sessions Perry shared with Bunny Lee. For instance, Lee released Pat Kelly's take of James Carr's 'Dark End Of The Street' with the equally popular 'Since You Are Gone' on the B-side, both credited as Bunny Lee productions (with Kelly renamed Little Boy Blue), but Perry said he produced them; 'Since You Are Gone' was also a cover, which David Isaacs took a stab at for an Upsetter single, Kelly's rendition borrowing a refrain from Delroy Wilson's 'Give Love A Try'. Then, Perry released organ instrumental 'Night Doctor' on an Upsetter single, credited as one of his productions, but the song was produced by keyboardist Ansel Collins a full year before he licenced it to Perry.

Collins got his start as a singer with the Caribbeats and moved to drums after tutoring from Winston Grennan, who subsequently suggested he switch to keyboards. After playing on Uniques hits for Bunny Lee (including 'Beatitude'), Collins joined the RHT Invincibles with drummer Sly Dunbar, guitarist Ranchie McLean and a bassist called Baba as the resident band at the Rainbow Healing Temple, a Rastafari bakery on Spanish Town Road, producing 'Night Doctor' and three vocal songs at their initial recording session at Federal. Unable to release the material himself, he sold the vocal tracks to Clement Dodd and other producers and approached Perry with 'Night Doctor' on an acetate, mindful of the success he was having with organ instrumentals like 'Eight For Eight'.

'In those days, I could only record and wait for somebody else to do the releasing for me,' said Collins. 'It's easy to find studio time, but to release songs, you have to have money. I do "Night Doctor" and I have it there for one year. I gave it to Scratch on dub plate and someone stole it. Then he found it back and said that he wanted the song, so he release it and give me money.'

The song would later make a powerful impact in Britain, in part because of Dunbar's unusual drum pattern and Collins' bubbling organ lines, which incorporated the sol-fa scale in the bridges.

'It went in the British chart, sell like hot bread, and after a while, he give me some more money,' said Collins. 'He's the best one out of all of them for me [financially]. He remember me.'

Perry loved reworking foreign hits in reggae, his 1969 releases including David Isaacs' take of Jim Reeves' broken-hearted country favourite, 'He'll Have To Go' and an over-the-top, double-time rendition of Ben E. King's 'Til I Can't Take It Anymore'; Carl Dawkins made an affecting cover of Otis Redding's 'Too Hot To Handle' (as 'Hard To Handle') and Perry slowed the Coasters' 'Yakety Yak' for his own percussion-laden rendition, which had a squeaking toy hammer buried in the mix; and there was Pat Satchmo's unremarkable take of 'Hello Dolly', his 'Boss Society' emulating Louis Armstrong too. Hotel circuit mainstay Busty Brown tackled the Bee Gees' 'To Love Somebody' (patterned after Al Green's soulful rendition) and offered a faithful cover of Clarence Carter's forlorn rhythm and blues number 'I Can't See Myself' (re-titled 'Crying About You'), while the Silvertones delivered their take of Brook Benton's cheery love song 'Kiddio', with lead singer Delroy Denton's baritone a defining feature.

Other originals addressed serious topics head on. Busty Brown's 'King Of The Trombone' lamented the terrible death of Don Drummond in a Kingston psychiatric ward on 6 May; 'No Bread And Butter' was an anguished cry of debilitating hunger by former Leaders member Milton Henry (credited to Milton Morris), and the Gaylads' 'If You Don't Mind' (aka 'I Wear My Slanders') used tight pop harmonies to refute discrimination.

'In those days, people used to look down on the dreadlocks,' said B. B. Seaton. 'I'm just trying to say to them, "Don't watch the clothes and the hair." As long as your heart is clean, everything is cool.'

Perry followed up 'Night Doctor' with 'A Live Injection', which hit in Britain towards the end of the year; using the rhythm of 'Babam Bam' by the Ravers, Winston Wright let loose on the organ, churning out furious scales and rapid chord bursts from one end of the keyboard to the other.

The final instalment of the series came in 'Medical Operation'. Based loosely on the relaxed groove of 'Sophisticated Sissy' by New Orleans funk act the Meters, but with a faster pace and tighter arrangement, 'Medical Operation' was the first recording Perry made with the Hippy Boys, who would play an increasingly important role in his creations from the latter half of 1969. The group was recommended to Perry by Bunny Lee, with whom they had already established a close working relationship; though he still considered Gladdy's All Stars to be the Upsetters, the Hippy Boys would gradually fill their shoes, eventually supplanting them.

Spinning off from the Gaylads backing band, the Hippy Boys provided live support for the Reggae Boys, led by former Emotions frontman, Max Romeo. Bassist Aston Barrett, known as Family Man because of his many children, and his drumming brother Carlton, known as Carly, spent much of their youth in the same downtown tenement yard as Val Bennett; self-taught musicians who made their own instruments from disused pots and a discarded broomstick, they joined the group after Lloyd Charmers arranged for Family Man to play on the Uniques' 'Watch This Sound' (an adaptation of Buffalo Springfield's 'For What It's Worth'), starting his professional career on the right foot. Both gifted musicians, Family Man's instinctive command of the bass offered the raw meatiness of funk riffs, coupled with a judicious use of rest stops, while Carly's drumming was marked by precision timing, his tightly wound drumrolls punctuated by off-beat pulses and accented rimshots. Lorraine Williams, known as Ronnie Bop, was an understated lead guitarist with a blues influence, his chops offset by the Greenwich Farm-based rhythm guitarist Alva Lewis (known as Reggie after popular Jamaican broadcaster and actor, Reggie Carter), who brought an aggressive, unfiltered approach. Keyboardist Glen 'Capo' Adams was a tailor from Jones Town who had worked as musical arranger for Duke Reid during the ska years (notably on Margarita Mahfood's 'Woman A Come'), singing in early iterations of the Heptones and the Pioneers before recording rock steady and reggae singles for Bunny Lee, Leslie Kong and Joe Gibbs; he had recently become a session organist following his successful contributions to Stranger Cole and Lester Sterling's 'Bangarang' and Slim Smith's 'Everybody Needs Love', both recorded for Bunny Lee, and had known Perry since his early days in Kingston, when Adams recorded 'Wonder Thirst' for Clement Dodd.

The Hippy Boys played on many landmarks in late 1968 and throughout '69, including the Reggae Boys' 'Mama Look Deh', a spectacular Jamaican hit, and Max Romeo's ribald 'Wet Dream', which topped the British charts despite a BBC ban for its rude lyrics. They also charted in Jamaica with Romeo's reggae rendition of the spiritual 'Swing Low Sweet Chariot' and with their own 'Dr No Go', the latter a funky instrumental with incidental deejay patter, recorded for Sonia Pottinger shortly before they first collaborated with Perry. They also backed the Scorchers' 'Ugly Man' for Lloyd 'the Matador' Daley, the Beltones' 'No More Heartaches' for Harry J, and Lloyd Charmers' 'Five To Five', as well as 'The Liquidator', another tremendous hit on both sides of the Atlantic.

Perry began working with the Hippy Boys because he wanted to keep his sound different from the rest, and his harnessing of the group would have all kinds of important repercussions. He approached them because his regular Upsetters were providing hits for all the other leading producers, rendering standardisation across the board.

'In them days, Mrs Pottinger, Leslie Kong, Scratch, everybody wanted their own sound, so everybody approached us and said, "We want you to record for us exclusively", but we said, "No, we can't do that!"' said Jackie Jackson. 'So Scratch went and found Family Man and his brother Carly, and Reggie and Glen, and that's the birth of the Upsetters, but the Upsetters was never a band of musicians. Scratch and his label is the Upsetter, and whoever went and played, the end product is the Upsetters.'

According to Perry, the naming of his group fit with wider ideas about the function his music was serving, the change in backing musicians taking place so that the sound would not become too predictable.

'Those days, any musicians me use, me used to call them the Upsetters. That was the image in me mind, the group that me want to have. Whether now or the other generation, me must name them the Upsetters because whatever set of musicians, me want to *upset* – like upset politicians, upset government, upset parson, upset Pope and people like those, and me music me can use to upset them – so me have to have a set of people working with me as musicians named the Upsetters. At them time me used to have Jackie Jackson, Hux Brown, Hugh Malcolm and then after a while it becomes, play it fe everybody, everybody music sound the same way. So then me want a different set of musicians or a different set of music, so Barrett them come. Them was young and they wanted to do something, so me let them do something how me wanted to do it and it sound different from the set of musicians me used to use before. So, me call the Barretts now the Upsetters, cos them was with me now.'

Despite numerous requests from other leading producers, the Hippy Boys chose to concentrate on working for Perry and Bunny Lee, due to their practical approaches to business and their grounding in the downtown music scene.

'Lee "Scratch" Perry and Bunny Lee was the more kind of ghetto promoters, what you call down to earth,' said Family Man. 'We like a little down to earth thing, so we play for anyone, but we're mostly with Lee "Scratch" Perry and Bunny Lee.'

The Reggae Boys' 'Ba Ba' (aka 'What Is This'), produced by Adams, was the platform for wild organ cut 'Cold Sweat' (aka 'Power Cut'); their 'Selassie' sounded like a pop song, but was in fact a warning to the heathen about the powers of the true and living God of Rastafari.

Family Man, Carly, Reggie, Glen Adams and Max Romeo had all accepted the manifestation of Rastafari in their lives by then, while Perry was grappling with its messages and meanings, both liberating and disturbing. The fashion-conscious Perry ostensibly bore the trappings of a 'soul man' with a finely combed mini-Afro and manicured moustache, yet some say Perry was already taking the Rasta message seriously and he had clearly been pondering its veracity since Selassie's visit, though Romeo remembered him as a Rasta sympathiser who respected the faith but did not yet fully share its religious beliefs, a view supported by several family members. Perry has said that although he was 'a soul man from ever since', he also held Rasta beliefs in his heart 'from ever since'; he suggested that, regardless of his appearance, he may have inwardly accepted the faith without yet acknowledging it outwardly.

Always keen to exploit the full potential of a solid rhythm, Perry stripped 'Selassie' to its core for a stunning alternate underscored by religious orthodoxy. 'Rightful Ruler' was one of the singles Peter Tosh recorded while Bob Marley was visiting his mother in Delaware; Tosh gave a spoken benediction in Amharic at the beginning of the song and played Nyabinghi drums throughout, along with Ras Michael, one of the prime exponents of the form; at the centre, Psalm 1 was chanted by U Roy, the toaster who was shortly to change the face of Jamaican music through a fluid rapping style that shifted the role of the deejay from incidental commentator and noisemaker to that of a lyrical sage whose contribution was as valid and important as that of any singer.

'Peter Tosh was not a professional drum player, but him have an idea, so we listen to what him have and get an original drummer, Ras Michael, to play what him have in mind,' said Perry. 'Me did like it — it was very hypnotising.'

Ras Michael Henry came from a Rastafari community in St Mary, where he learned to play the repeater drum in his youth. Moving to Kingston in his teens, he began frequenting the yard of an elder drummer named Solomon Wolfe in Waterhouse, joining respected funde players such as I Jack and I Marts, with the bass drum beaten by Sidney Wolfe, Solomon's oldest son; Lloyd Brevett and Tommy McCook often gave musical coaching. In the mid-1960s Ras Michael formed his group, the Sons of Negus, launched the Zion Disc label, and was also a session player at Studio One, using the proceeds to fund *Lion Of Judah Time*, a Rastafari radio programme broadcast on JBC.

'Rightful Ruler' was ground-breaking on several levels. The most bass-heavy version of a song yet produced, it was a thunderous work of majestic proportions that heralded Rastafari, entirely undisguised and without apology, at a time when adherence to the faith could result in a beating, imprisonment or worse; intriguingly, the song's introduction was grafted from the start of Ras Michael's self-produced 'Ethiopian National Anthem', a Zion Disc single based on the anthem of the UNIA. 'Rightful Ruler' thus shows Perry reshaping his creations through the new application of cut-ups, placing the deejay in central focus, while heightening the primacy of the bass.

When Perry and Bunny Lee arranged for U Roy to voice 'Rightful Ruler' at Randy's in the summer of 1969, the toaster, born Ewart Beckford, had already recorded a couple of other songs for Keith Hudson, a producer and dental technician that had scored a big hit with Ken Boothe's 'Old Fashioned Way'. Like Perry, Hudson understood that the deejay needed to be given proper space to express himself, and 'Dynamic Fashion Way' left plenty of room for U Roy's message, but radio stations refused to play test pressings. Travelling to New York shortly thereafter, Hudson shelved the song temporarily, making 'Rightful Ruler' the toaster's vinyl debut, despite its later recording date.

'My first tune I ever do was "Dynamic Fashion Way" with Keith Hudson,' said U Roy. 'Then, Bunny Lee and Scratch Perry check me about doing a song with Peter Tosh, so we did "Earth's Rightful Ruler", but those tunes didn't get very far. Them sell a couple hundred because the Jamaican crowd does not recognise deejay music at the time.'

U Roy later recorded 'OK Corral' for Perry, perhaps the most surreal deejay record then issued, on which the toaster croaks the law of the urban jungle: 'An eye for an eye, a tooth for a tooth, if you want I, don't argue, just shoot.' Over another inordinately bass-heavy rhythm informed by funk, augmented by breaking glass and rapid machine-gun fire, U Roy barks a fierce warning to those who dare insult the Rastafari, be they rude boy, gunman, dubious record producer or politician.

As evidenced by the Upsetter singles issued by Pama, 'Return Of The Ugly', 'For A Few Dollars More' and 'Taste Of Killing' all revealed the pervasive influence of westerns, and there were more standard deejay cuts by Cool Sticky, including 'Dry Acid', a boastful song adapting radio jive-talk, and 'I've Caught You', on which the deejay barks incomprehensible slogans over an organ cut of 'Can't Take It Anymore'; Niney voiced a spirited take of Eddie Floyd's Stax classic 'I've Never Found A Girl (To Love Me Like You Do)', retitled 'Ain't No Love', and 'My Mob' was a beautiful organ transposition of the Inspirations' 'Love Oh Love'.

The reworked instrumentals continued to provide the biggest hits, and they would fly thick and fast in the autumn months, the shift made on the instruction of his spirit guide, according to Perry.

'There was too much vocalists and it was getting boring with everybody copying each other, so me want to try to make something that didn't have anything to do with something that you hear every day,' said Perry. 'So same like how me hear the guide come to me and say to write these songs and write these words, tell the artists how fi sing it, same way the spirit come to me and say me fi choose this song and do

it with the organ, or sometimes it have to do with the trombone, trumpet, saxophone.'

The next to hit was 'Soulful I', an organ interpretation of
'Since You Are Gone' that paralleled the lyrics through intricate keyboard trilling, which entered the Jamaican charts in
late August and remained in the top ten a full two months;
inspired by Young Holt Unlimited's 'Soulful Strut' (a piano
reworking of Barbara Acklin's 'Am I The Same Girl'), the
title 'Soulful I' made coded reference to Rastafari consciousness, placing primacy on 'I' rather than 'me' to connote one's
adherence to the faith.

The saxophone and organ instrumental 'Drugs And Poison'
briefly hit the lower reaches of the Jamaican top ten in October.
It was one of the first to feature the skills of young downtown
drummer Lloyd Adams, known on the scene as 'Tin Legs';
tutored by Winston Grennan, his style was characterised by
furiously fraught drumrolls that often arrived off-beat, adding
a distinctive dynamism.

'Clint Eastwood' then entered the Jamaican charts, where
it remained to the end of the year, and it was also popular in
Britain when issued on a Punch 45. A skeletal cut of 'Yakety
Yak' with a spoken introduction announcing that Eastwood
was tougher than Lee Van Cleef (his co-star in *The Good, The
Bad and the Ugly*), 'Clint Eastwood' was a quirky instrumental
led by a throbbing cowbell and punctuated by the squeaking
of a plastic toy hammer, and B-side 'The Tackro' furthered
the themes on an augmented cut of the same rhythm, using
echoing shouts and an Ennio Morricone-styled keyboard riff
to drive home the cinematic references.

According to Clancy Eccles, 'Clint Eastwood' was made in
answer to King Stitt's 'Lee Van Cleef', one of Eccles' biggest
western-themed hits.

103

'When I did "Van Cleef", Scratch did "Clint Eastwood",' said Eccles. 'He go on my record changer and played "Clint Eastwood" and make me hear "Clint Eastwood tougher than Lee Van Cleef". It was just a joke.'

'Clint Eastwood was my favourite star, my favourite cowboy,' said Perry. 'I like when he used to smoke his cigar and bite it, draw his gun and shoot the guy, just like that, with one shot. Stitt claim that Lee Van Cleef is a better gunman than Clint Eastwood and I know that Clint Eastwood was the top gunman at the time, so I say, "Clint Eastwood is boss for Lee Van Cleef", and it vanquished Stitt and Clancy.'

Then came Dave Barker's 'Prisoner Of Love', a runaway hit borrowing the title of a James Brown ballad for a fast reggae number with a soul backbone, voiced on the uptempo rhythm originally laid for Slim Smith's 'Slip Away' (recorded on another joint Perry/Bunny Lee session); Busty Brown's cut, 'Soul Juice', was popular with Black audiences in Britain but 'Prisoner Of Love' stormed into the Jamaican charts in November and became a strong seller in Britain too, Barker tailoring his voice to sound like Brown, leading local audiences to believe he was American.

Born David Crooks in Franklyn Town, east Kingston, the vocalist who became Dave Barker began his career singing with Glen Brown in the duo Glen and Dave, before Brown brought him to Perry's attention, resulting in the new artist name and solo career.

'One night we were walking past Randy's recording studio,' said Barker. 'At that time Scratch had a green and black Jag, which he transported from London. This car drop this short, slim guy, with fancy-dress business and a whole heap of guys behind him, and it was all excitement. Everybody was just, "Scratch, Scratch, Scratch!" Randy's door open and we find ourselves in with the crowd. We go upstairs, Busty Brown was amongst the lot, and the booze and the weed was flowing, and I was in the corner, checking out everything. Scratch put this tape on and Busty tried and tried, but him just couldn't connect with that track. Then Glen Brown say to Scratch, "Try Dave, man, Dave would touch this track now", and Scratch say, "Who named Dave? Dave! Come round the mike, man. You feel you can tackle this tune here?" We put on the headphones and Scratch run the track and me just start sing, "Baby, baby, yeah, you made me a prisoner . . ." and me go right through, me sing non-stop.

'From I did "Prisoner of Love", there was this excited buzz and Scratch could not control himself. Then him start to drink and smoke. Then him look 'pon me and him say, "Now you want a stage name. Give me your full name." I say, "David Crooks". Him say, "No man, Dave Crooks can't work, that no sound showbiz at all. Barker! Dave Barker, man!" And the Dave Barker stick. Everybody come out of the studio buzzed! I felt so excited because when they played the track back, I'm saying to myself, "Wait, is *me* do that?" The next day, Scratch go to the pressing plant and the music just start to tear down the whole of Jamaica, and the whole buzz about me is that I am an American star.'

The fruitful working relationship soon yielded another hit, but this time for Duke Reid: stopping by Treasure Isle one afternoon, Perry had Barker voice an American-styled toast for Reid called 'Lock Jaw', which he arranged, resulting in another lasting chart success that seriously revived the Duke's flagging career.

'I got an inkling he probably was going flat businesswise, and that tune make him surface back,' said Barker. 'Serious thing: everywhere you go, it's "Lock Jaw".'

Although he was concentrating on instrumentals, Perry continued working closely with Barker in late 1969 and early 1970, cutting further hits that would reach the Jamaican top ten midway through the yar.

In London, Trojan finally issued *The Upsetter* as a debut Lee Perry album, the cover showing the dapper producer wearing green velveteen, flanked by two beauties in a green space. Seven of the twelve songs were organ instrumentals: 'Tidal Wave' transposed 'He'll Have To Go' and 'Heat Proof' reworked 'Hard To Handle'; there was 'Soulful I' and 'Night Doctor', as well as a new version of the same rhythm, titled 'Thunderball', delivered as a saxophone and organ duet, a similar format employed for a song called 'Big Noise'; 'Man From MI5' betrayed a heavy Meters influence and 'Wolfman' was a spacey keyboard cut of the Bleechers' 'Everything For Fun'. Along with Busty Brown's 'To Love Somebody' and 'Crying About You', there was 'Kiddio', the Silvertones here credited as the Muskyteers.

But the real breakthrough came when 'Return of Django' entered the top fifty of the British pop charts in late September, thanks to its use in a surreal Cadbury's Fruit and Nut chocolate bar advertisement, directed by Terry Gilliam (just before the debut of *Monty Python's Flying Circus*), using an unusual mix of animation and live acting figures, moving in time to the quirky reggae beat. The radio version of the Fruit and Nut campaign sparked a lot of interest too, with listeners apparently phoning the BBC to request that the song be aired in full after hearing the portion used in the advert.

'I heard it at one of the clubs I used to go to and bought it at a record shop in North Finchley,' said film editor Alan Bates, who suggested the song to Gilliam. 'We needed something that was jocular in feel, that had beats you could cut to and had sufficient phrase repetition, so I thought this could work, apart from the fact that reggae and ska were pretty hot at the time, and it did go well with the ad. In fact, it became quite talked about, and so they re-released it.'

The song hit the top twenty the second week in October, and as Trojan and their associates scrambled to organise a brief British tour, Perry opted to bring the Hippy Boys rather than the original Upsetters that played on the song.

'It just didn't happen,' said Jackie Jackson. 'We heard about it and everyone was excited, and then it just petered out.'

'It was Jackie them that played the tune,' said Perry, 'but me wanted to do Family Man them a favour.'

Lead guitarist Ronnie Bop had other engagements with the Supersonics, so Lloyd 'Gitsy' Willis was considered as an alternate rhythm player, with Reggie slated for lead, but in the end, Willis was dropped from the line-up, as well as Val Bennett, which caused bitter resentment since his saxophone solo was a key part of the hit. But the real problem was Perry's chaotic personal life. His embroilment in an affair with a short, light-skinned beauty named Melanie Jonas delayed the tour at a crucial moment, which meant that when 'Return Of Django' was broadcast on *Top of the Pops* on 23 October, there were only the resident Pan's People dancers on screen, since the new Upsetters were still in Jamaica, where Perry was nursing a serious wound.

'When we were to come on tour to carry it to number one, Scratch have an accident,' said Family Man. 'He get a stab in his arm from one of his ladies, so we have to wait two months, so by the time we come, we could only reach it to number five.'

With a one-track mind Perry's default mode, fidelity was an alien virtue. His longstanding reputation as a ladies' man was heightened through growing fame on the music scene and by the trappings of visible wealth.

'When Scratch go in a woman's house for the first time and him want to drink ice water and she no have no fridge, Scratch just phone for a fridge,' suggested Bunny Lee. 'Him used to have a big, four-ply chequebook.'

Perry had an air of excitement and prosperity about him: always immaculately dressed, his goatee and moustache groomed, and with gaudy gold rings shining on his pinkie fingers, many women found him irresistible, and the feeling was often mutual.

An early side relationship was struck up with a woman of Chinese extraction called Lou who eventually left the island, and after a brief affair with a woman called Junie, a son was produced whom she christened Delano Perry, though Perry insisted the child was not his and had little contact with either of them after the birth.

Then Perry met Melanie Jonas through Judy Mowatt, her co-worker at Colgate Palmolive. Jonas also had ambitions to be a singer, despite being less obviously talented, and she and Perry were often spotted together in town, so when Pauline inevitably discovered the affair, she attacked Perry with a knife, inflicting a deep arm wound that required several stitches.

While Perry was in hospital, a panic-stricken Pauline brought the children to Miss Ina's home in Hanover, where she said nothing of the incident, until a telegram arrived, blowing her cover. Pauline decamped to Rollington Town for a time, and Perry continued his liaison with Jonas, even taking her to Hanover to meet his mother.

During the time of this affair, Perry was involved in a serious car accident on east Kingston's Windward Road, near the island's chief cement works. As Perry held no driver's licence, his Jaguar was normally chauffeur-driven by Val Bennett, until an argument ended the arrangement; one evening, Perry and Jonas had been drinking with a Bermudan that worked at JBC, along with a certain Frankie, a run-around man for Clancy Eccles, and a man named Justin, who worked in a similar capacity for Perry. Hearing of a function at Port Royal, past the airport, the five sped off into the night: Perry and Jonas were in the Jaguar with the Bermudan at the wheel, and Justin was riding a motorbike with Frankie a pillion passenger. In a show of machismo, the drivers began to race each other, until someone lost control along the way and the car collided with the bike, killing Frankie and seriously injuring Justin.

'They was drinking, and they was riding careless, riding to see who can ride faster, and go in front of the car and get knocked off,' said Perry. 'Justin was riding the bike and him get crippled, and the other guy dead. Me wasn't driving, me have the small islander driving and give the police my statement.'

The Bermudan is said to have served a long jail sentence after being convicted of drunk driving. Malicious rumours later surfaced that the bike was intentionally hit after Perry accused the men of stealing his records, or because Pauline was said to be having an affair with one of the men. Certain foes even alleged that Perry himself was at the wheel, driving drunk, but Perry has flatly denied such suggestions, citing the police statement as proof of his innocence.

'Anything what look very nasty, is me that,' said Perry, 'but I'm not nasty enough to kill Frankie and scupper Justin.'

After the accident, Perry left the Jaguar at a garage and despite the damage, Clancy Eccles purchased it while Perry was on tour, leading him to later acquire a Chrysler.

Perry finally arrived at Heathrow on 22 November with Family Man, Carly, Reggie, Glen Adams and Melanie Jonas, as well as the Pioneers, now a trio with George Agard (alias George Dekker), who were scheduled to complete a separate tour of their own (backed by local act, Noel and the Fireballs), since their epithet to the Long Shot saga, 'Long Shot Kick The Bucket', was also riding high in the charts, vying for space with 'Return Of Django', 'The Liquidator' and Jimmy Cliff's orchestrated 'Wonderful World, Beautiful People'. On arrival, both groups were housed at hotels in Praed Street, Paddington, a bustling, transient area of west London.

The Upsetters began their tour at Crewe's Up The Junction club on 28 November, and over the course of the next six weeks, they would hit some thirty venues, playing at ballrooms, cinemas, youth clubs and schools across the country, travelling in a clapped-out van. The second night of the tour, they played to a largely skinhead audience at Manchester's New Century Hall, a strong contrast to the majority Black audience at their London debut, held on 7 December at the ABC cinema in Kensal Rise at a multi-artist gala billed as 'Reggae Steady Go', with the Pioneers, Max Romeo, Desmond Dekker and Pat Kelly. Christmas Eve found them at Torquay's 400 Club and, two days later, they were special guests at Dalston's Four Aces, a longstanding site of sound system activity in east London; there was a New Year's Day set at Coventry's Chesterford Grange and a three-night run at Birmingham's Rainbow Suite from 8 January, the final date of the initial tour taking place at the East Sheen Bull on 11 January.

According to Family Man, they were also flown to Holland for an appearance on a television special: 'The show was called *Shoo Be Doo* and I remember we fly over just to do the TV show. It was just one cut, one take, and we did it like we were professionals. We were all in different colours. It's a beautiful show and they show it on *Top of the Pops*.'

The band was reportedly featured at a 'Soul vs Reggae' event in Kent, with Percy Sledge, and they also travelled to Cardiff for a BBC interview, where the 'Cockney Sinatra' Mat Monro was present, helping to introduce the band and reggae to a wider audience.

'I think Tom Jones was there,' said Reggie. 'They were asking us, "What about this reggae?" and them play the "Return Of Django".'

The tour was arranged by Commercial Entertainment, run by Bruce White and Tony Cousins (the latter born Anthony Bautista, to Gibraltarian parents), who had organised earlier tours for the Ethiopians, Desmond Dekker, and the Maytals, after approaching Leslie Kong through Graeme Goodall; Larry Lawrence, a Jamaican immigrant who would soon move into record production, acted as unofficial road manager.

'Lee Perry came over here with the Hippy Boys when "Return Of Django" was in the charts to do a tour and I used to have to take them around,' said Lawrence. 'Daytime, he would want to go shopping, and in the evenings, we'd go to nightclubs and rave together.'

After the first set of dates, Commercial Entertainment scheduled a six-week national tour package with Desmond Dekker, Jimmy Cliff, Max Romeo, the Upsetters, the Pioneers and the Harry J. All Stars, to commence in late January 1970 with a gala event at the Royal Albert Hall, but the tour was scrapped after skinhead disturbances elsewhere resulted in widespread cancellations. Instead, the Upsetters performed with Dekker, the Pioneers, skinhead favourites Symarip, and Noel and the Fireballs at the Purley Orchid on 13 January and at the Ilford Palais the next day (without Symarip), followed by Upsetters performances in south London, Kent, Norfolk and Gloucestershire to the end of the month.

Conditions on both tour legs were extremely basic, with substandard digs and, according to the band, chronic under-payment; they unfolded chaotically, being prone to last-minute changes, and made more difficult, according to White, by Perry's unpredictable whims.

'Scratch was running his own thing and really cherry-picked what he wanted to do. One night he decided he was going onstage, the next night he decided he wasn't. One time he decided he'll play a triangle, that was probably somewhere like Birmingham. He's a great talent, but he's got a mind of his own – whatever took his fancy, you had to do it.'

Nevertheless, the tour's success helped 'Night Doctor' and 'A Live Injection' to hit, paving the way for a *Return Of Django* album, billed as the Upsetters' 'debut' LP. Released by Trojan in a gatefold sleeve in early January, this collection of organ instrumentals had a bigger proportion of hits than *The Upsetter*, including 'Eight For Eight', 'Drugs And Poison', 'Soulful I', 'Night Doctor', 'Live Injection', 'Man From MI5' and 'Medical Operation', as well as the title track, duplicating some of the roster from *The Upsetter* in the process.

In contrast, Pama's *Clint Eastwood* compilation felt harder, largely filled with the aggressive Perry-produced singles they issued that featured the Hippy Boys and whose titles bore cinematic references, including 'Return Of The Ugly', 'For A Few Dollars More', 'Dry Acid', 'Taste Of Killing' and 'My Mob', as well as the title track, issued along with 'Prisoner Of Love', 'Selassie', 'Rightful Ruler', 'I've Caught You' and 'Ain't No Love'. It all helped make the Upsetters one of the hottest reggae acts on the market in Britain, despite the enigmatic nature of their largely absent ringleader.

Though the tour unfolded during a consistently icy winter, Perry was fascinated by what he experienced in the UK; buoyed by his growing popularity, he began to consider relocating to London.

Yet, as the tour ground to a halt, the Upsetters found themselves cast adrift. Business and personal matters saw Perry flitting between Kingston and London for much of the winter, leaving the band largely to fend for themselves, and with accommodation and food costs mounting, they were forced to begin working under their own steam.

'They finished the tour, and they wasn't actually signed to Scratch or nothing like that, so they were trying to do their own thing,' said Larry Lawrence. 'I actually end up with the band because Scratch had to go back and forth to Jamaica, so he's left them with me to take care of. They had to move out of the hotels and everywhere that they was living when the tour was finished. They had to start finding digs for themselves, so they had to work sessions for other people.'

Bruce White and Tony Cousins were just starting to produce records themselves, having sold half the shares of their booking agency to Trojan, and thus persuaded the Upsetters to record an album's worth of instrumentals in London, which Trojan would release in August 1970 as *The Good, The Bad And The Upsetters* after a planned deal with President Records fell through.

Although it bore the Upsetter name, Perry was not involved with the project and was out of the country when most of it was recorded. Production credit was given to Bruce Anthony, a pseudonym used by White and Cousins on records that they financed. Largely leaden compared to their authentic Jamaican recordings, the LP's frigid atmosphere and obviously hurried completion failed to find favour, and Perry was furious when he found out about the album, resenting its illegitimate titling.

113

'I didn't know anything about that,' said Perry. 'That was after they want to play their own game, so I leave them on their own. I was not involved, and I've never heard that album yet.'

He would eventually get his own back by issuing an alternate album in Jamaica with the same title, but not for some considerable time.

The year 1969 was in many ways a turning point for Lee Perry. He had moved away from the conventional vocal in favour of instrumental reinventions of previously recorded rhythms and had continued his sonic experimentation therein. His chart successes enabled him to provide a better home for his family on the outskirts of the city, to import a flash car and to maintain a mistress as well. His record shop was becoming a focal point for the burgeoning talent of the area, his productions so sought after that he had to hire help with sales and distribution, and his tour of the UK caused more than just a flicker of interest from the British press, who were normally dismissive of Jamaican music. 1969 had finally brought the Upsetter to the attention of a broader overseas audience, but 1970 would herald events that were to rock the very foundations of the music world.

CHAPTER FIVE

Soul Rebels:
The Upsetter and the Wailers

As a new decade was dawning, Lee Perry continued the experimentation that had brought him to the attention of the outside world. Consumed by music for the whole of the 1960s, with all else in life taking second place, he got his first glimpse of fame and fortune after struggling to establish himself as an independent production force. Now that Perry had more solid avenues allowing the greater distribution of his product, he sought to make the most of such opportunities by delving further into uncharted sonic territory to test the limits of his creative urges. Always aware of the power exerted by his secret spirit guide, he pondered what form the next exciting sound would take, how it would come to him and what significance it would bring to his life. As he began to mature as a musical creator, he again sought to change the focus of Jamaican popular music through sounds and ideas that were challenging and different.

Recordings from early 1970 showed that Melanie Jonas was still in the picture. Archie Moore described the affair as a mere stopgap dalliance, yet Perry gave her prominence on a version of Blue Mink's 'Melting Pot', credited to the Heaters, and recorded a version of Blood, Sweat and Tears' 'Spinning Wheel' as a duet between Jonas and Dave Barker.

Jonas' emigration finally ended their affair, enabling reconciliation with Pauline. Yet, to provide further financial support for Jonas, Perry established the Spinning Wheel label as a Trojan subsidiary, crediting her as the producer of four singles, issued in the summer, most of which were recorded on 13 January at the session where the 'Spinning Wheel' rhythm was laid, including O'Neil Hall's 'This Man', 'Penny Wise' and 'Do It Madly' by singer Chuck Josephs (alias Chuck Berry Junior), and further organ cuts of the 'Spinning Wheel' rhythm, 'Haunted House' and 'Double Wheel' crediting Jonas as songwriter.

'A big chance was there to give her some money because I did like her,' said Perry. 'She wasn't looking the type that rough: she was clean skin, looking nice. She give me a good vibration, so why shouldn't I give her a start?'

Down at 36 Charles Street, the Upsetter sound system was now holding sway. The equipment that powered it was passed on to Perry's crew by Bunny Lee, who had acquired it from Lloyd the Matador to challenge Harry Mudie to a sound clash (where Mudie reigned triumphant because his set was far more powerful). Perry's security man and general assistant Jubie thus took control of the Upsetter sound, with Cool Sticky on the mike in the early days, and though the set was small and operated sporadically, it was a popular downtown fixture for a number of years.

In late February, Trojan released *Scratch The Upsetter Again*, which had nine instrumentals, including organ cuts of 'Return Of The Ugly' as 'Bad Tooth' and 'King Of The Trombone' as 'Outer Space', while 'Take One' was a version of 'Medical Operation' with the organ removed. The three vocal numbers were Dave Barker's version of the Shirelles' 'Will You Still

Love Me Tomorrow', Reggie's dejected take of Ben E. King's 'She Is Gone Again' and Count Prince Miller's rendition of Frankie Laine's oft-versioned cowboy opus 'Mule Train', complete with zoological sound effects.

As Perry increased the amount of reverb on his overdubbed instruments, he also began a thematic shift with his titles, referencing the poor state of his dental health on 'Bad Tooth' and 'The Dentist', and in response to the fierce competition between Kingston's upcoming producers, Perry proclaimed himself the winner instrumentally on 'The Result', answering records such as Lloyd Charmers' 'Vengeance', on which Charmers claimed he would usurp the Upsetter's throne with a superior beat, and send Niney packing along with him.

Pama's *Many Moods Of The Upsetters* had been conceived during Harry Palmer's visit to Jamaica in August 1969 but was not realised until early the following year, and its title aptly suggested the range of influences Perry was drawing on to reflect his different dispositions. The surreal album cover emphasised the point through photos taken at sunrise on the beach one Sunday morning, showing Perry in various moods, ranging from the suave 'detective' to the unseen 'invisible', the presence of bikini-clad beauties underlining that his swinger credentials were intact, and for the 'greeting mood' image, Perry straddled the Jaguar's roof to shake Glen Adams' hand.

'I came to Jamaica knowing we wanted to make *Many Moods* after *Clint Eastwood*,' said Palmer. 'Scratch is a man of many moods, so some little psychologist in me tells me this man could be an artist in his own right because up until then, there was no such thing as Lee Perry being an artist, so I got a photographer and we went out on St Thomas Road, gave him an overcoat, briefcase and hat, and did this fantastic photo session. I went back with tapes as well, then Scratch came over and we sat down in Jeff's office and went through all these shots and had to say, "This is his silent mood and that is his detective mood", so it was a collaboration of ideas. I think even Bunny Lee had some say in the matter because people used to live good then. If one of them had a dollar, everybody else would eat off of it.'

Mostly cut at Randy's with the Hippy Boys, including Ronnie Bop and Lloyd Charmers, the album had 'Can't Take It Anymore', 'Boss Society' and Pat Satchmo's serene reworking of the rude 'Goosy' calypso as though it too was a Louis Armstrong song, and Carl Dawkins gave the Temptations' 'Cloud Nine' a fairly faithful run through. The transfigured instrumentals included an organ augmentation of 'Selassie' titled 'Ex Ray Vision', a heavily overdubbed cut of 'Check Him Out' called 'Soul Stew', a sombre organ take of 'I'll Be Waiting' as 'Low Lights', and an organ version of 'Taste Of Killing' called 'Beware'. There was also a manic piano and organ duet called 'Prove It', reworking the 'Uncle Charley' rhythm (first attempted with Val Bennett's saxophone, which was dropped), while 'Mean And Dangerous' was a cut of 'Stand By Me' using overdubbed piano, organ and sax, and a Mackie Burnette steel pan version of Joe South's 'Games People Play' concluded the British pressing, with a lilting bonus steel pan track included on Jamaican pressings (suitably titled 'Extra'), the album on sale at the Upsetter Record Shop by April.

In the studio, Perry continued the western themes on 'Son Of Thunder', his drawling vocal inspired by an episode of television drama *Death Valley Days* that was based on the historic exploits of Orrin Porter Rockwell (known as the Destroying Angel of Mormondom); 'Sipreano' saw Perry assume the role of Don Cipriano, the Mexican governor in the 1959 Robert Mitchum vehicle, *The Wonderful Country* (Perry's half-spoken vocal complete with cod-Mexican accent); and 'Kill Them All' was an abstract audio collage with a filmic introduction, mixing the rhythms of 'Clint Eastwood', 'Melting Pot' and 'Dollar In The Teeth', the latter with a new organ line.

Perry was generally neglecting singers to concentrate on instrumentals, but Dave Barker was an exception and recorded fairly steadily for him as both singer and deejay from late 1969 to early 1971. Barker's next hit, 'Shocks Of Mighty', was recorded early in the year, reaching the Jamaican top ten in May. Voiced on a cut of the Inspirations' 'Bhutto Girl' that Perry obtained from Bunny Lee, Barker delivered his minimal lyrics in exorbitant yelps, emulating Soul Brother Number One.

'He picked up this line of James Brown slang, it sounded like, and he did it so good,' said former Uniques member Jimmy Riley, who helped Barker voice the song for Perry at Randy's. 'He used to tell people that he was born in Mississippi, talking like he was a Yankie.'

'Scratch played the track and I found it hard to respond, and Scratch could not understand that it's not all the time a certain vibe comes to you,' said Barker. 'If the vibe isn't there, don't care how you force and force, it won't come. He got very upset and stormed out of the studio, which made me very upset too. Imagine the first time I go into the studio and gave him "Prisoner Of Love" and everything was nice and sweet, but this time we go in and the vibe was not there, and the man go get upset. I started saying to myself, this man kind of lack understanding.'

'Dave used to be up and down, and he couldn't manage it, so I was teaching him to ride the rhythm, giving him the slurs,' said Riley. 'He's a good singer, he just didn't know what to do, so I was kind of singing it for him and tell him, "Follow after me".'

Two weeks after the abortive first take, Barker had another go with the same rhythm, this time adapting the Temptations' 'Born To Love You' for a song called 'Set Me Free', with more instantaneous success.

'We went back into the studio with the same track, and can you believe, from the man play the track, one cut again, and the man start him excitement, jumping up and down, that cut there done, and Scratch can't contain himself,' said Barker. 'Then him say, "The flipside is a version. Wha'ppen, you feel you can do a talking?" Him play the rhythm, and me deh-deh, "This is . . . Shocks of mighty! This is a bad, bad . . ." Him say, "All right, you have 'Shocks of mighty', suppose before you say, 'Shocks of mighty,' you say, 'This is upsetting!'" So I go round the mike and me say, "This is upsetting! Shocks of mighty! Hit me back!" Right into it, and just one cut again! And Scratch was just dancing all over again, come out of the studio, couldn't walk!'

Perry aired an acetate of 'Shocks Of Mighty' at a prestigious uptown venue that same evening, the crowd response confirming he had a hit on his hands.

'Randy's had a cutting machine, same place in the studio, so Scratch cut a disk there immediately and we jump in Scratch's car and go to the clubs, uptown by Half Way Tree, to check the people's response to the music. From Scratch put on the slate and we start, "This is upsetting!" the people them shocked because it's the first time they hear something like that. It's a club where everybody's in tables and chairs, sort of a groovy spot where everybody sits down, and from Scratch put on the slate and them hear, "This is upsetting! Shocks of mighty! Hit me back!" slowly, the people start to get on the dancefloor − everybody start move.'

'Me did want to make another James Brown out of Dave

Barker and I always clean my tape machine heads with a special thing called acetone,' said Perry. 'It give the machine a different tone and a different sound, so one day him decide to drink some of that, cos him want to know why the machine sound so good. So that's where he get his voice, from a chemical called acetone.'

In the midst of the work with Barker, there was a break-in at the Upsetter Record Shop, where sixty-three dollars' worth of records were stolen – mostly stock of Barker's latest hit – along with a transistor radio, an electric shaver and a travelling holdall, after someone used a ratchet knife to force entry at the rear.

Making his way to the shop on the morning of 7 March, Archie Moore knew something was not right when he found shop frequenter Lloyd Michael, known as Darkie, near some of their empty record boxes in the street.

'Somebody tear off the back door,' said Archie. 'Me see the record boxes there right in the morning, and something drop from them going down Princess Street, but when Darkie come up, he was looking suspicious. Talking to him, I realise him was the culprit, so we lock him up.'

Nevertheless, when the trial took place at Sutton Street Court the following month, Darkie laid the blame on a rough-neck called Skinner and was released with a caution, and the stolen goods were never retrieved.

After this momentary setback, Archie ultimately stepped away from Upsetter Records to concentrate on his Cavemen sound system following a contentious meeting with industry associates regarding the overseas success of rude number 'Self Control', which Jimmy Riley produced with Val Bennett's daughter Fay, and licenced to Perry, bringing it onto the UK Upsetter label.

'Because I used to hang with Bunny Lee, I was always on the street,' said Riley. 'At that time, Slim Smith used to live at the back of Muzik City, at the apartment upstairs, and Scratch's record shop, Upsetter, was across the street on the lane. We used to smoke herb chalice a lot in the big yard besides Scratch, so going between the house and the shop we always saw Scratch, just run into each other like that.'

Archie let Riley know that 'Self Control' was popular in Britain, despite selling poorly in Jamaica. He confidentially suggested that Riley ask Trojan for payment, which Riley received with his assistance, but when his role in the ruse was revealed, it sparked a brawl in which he and Perry were injured.

'I had a sister named Rosie who worked at an office and I told her to ask one of them lawyer man to write a letter and scare them, and them send some money come give him,' said Archie. 'One day a meeting called between everybody, discussing who make Jimmy know, and from one argument to the other, a fight started. Me fight with a guy that was working with Bunny Lee and Scratch run right between us, him get a severe lick in him ears and couldn't hear. The guy break a bottle and cut me, so me draw me ratchet and run him down, cut him right by Charles Street. They sew him up at Kingston Public Hospital, and them sew up my arm. Then basically me break ranks with them. Anywhere you see trouble, you try and get out of it. Scratch was upset over it too, so me see the cold shoulder and leave, but me never leave immediately after the incident.'

Since it attracted too many freeloaders, Perry gradually made himself scarce at the Upsetter Record Shop, leaving Jubie to run it for a time, until Pauline took over.

'Me don't want to go to the shop because too much guys always want to beg,' said Perry. 'So me just collect the money at weekends, or when they want records, me go and give it to them.'

Distancing himself from the record shop was part of the move towards greater stability, grounding and focus, and in the spring of 1970, Perry was in the process of purchasing a three-bedroomed house of his own from a mechanic named Graham, located a few streets away from the Caenwood Street rental at 5 Cardiff Crescent. Situated behind high gates in a compound with a sizeable backyard, it cost JMD$11,000 (then worth US$13,200), and Perry would complete the purchase in July, saddling himself with a JMD$6,300 mortgage.

The Upsetter label was really thriving in this period. In addition to Al and the Vibrators' 'Water More Than Flour', a song addressing rising food prices and labour shortages that made the finals of the Festival Song Competition (but lost out to Hopeton Lewis' 'Boom Shacka Lacka'), there was the grudging 'The Thanks We Get' from the Versatiles, and later, a stunning song of social protest, 'What's The World Coming To', recorded by Junior Byles under the alias King Chubby, which Harry Palmer had such high hopes for that he engaged Stan Butcher to score an orchestral arrangement, overdubbed at Pye in the vain hopes of following Bob and Marcia's 'Young, Gifted And Black' into the pop charts. Perry was also stockpiling backing tracks, enabling him to select particular rhythms whenever a specific idea came to mind. He continued covering foreign pop hits, too, but was not content with merely licking them over; most were thoroughly mutated, especially on the version B-sides.

'I did have a collection of songs that did mean something to me, all pop hit records,' said Perry. 'Most of them, we used to put the tracks down until me see somebody who might look like them can do it, then run the track and give them the words.'

Thus, two different renditions of 'Groove Me', a recent smash for New Orleans soul singer King Floyd, were voiced by Dave Barker for a back-to-back single, the A-side fairly faithful to the original, the B-side a slow and sensuous reggae cut. Busty Brown tackled Eddie Floyd's 'Consider Me' and the Inspirations adapted Otis Redding's 'Same Thing All Over'; in contrast, Steam's 'Na Na Hey Hey (Kiss Him Goodbye)' was subjected to Upsetter kinks, the melody played by an organ subjected to heavy wah-wah effects, and Hank Lochlin's country favourite 'Send Me The Pillow' became a messy, spaced-out organ instrumental.

As Perry put together such odd innovations in instrumental sound, the Wailers were seeking a way forward. They left Studio One not long after Perry split with Dodd, equally frustrated by the financial arrangements, but with the exception of 'Nice Time', a considerable hit in 1967, the few releases on their Wail'n Soul'm label were largely unheard. The future looked brighter after the group met Black Texan pop singer Johnny Nash, his manager Danny Sims, and the keyboardist and arranger Arthur Jenkins, who were producing a series of Nash hits in Jamaica for their JAD label; struck by the obvious ability of Marley and his cohorts, they presented the group with an exclusive song-writing and publishing contract.

JAD began recording demos in the hopes of breaking the Wailers into lucrative overseas markets, but in June 1967, Bunny Wailer was arrested for marijuana possession and jailed for fourteen months, making Rita Marley his temporary replacement. The 1968 JAD single 'Bend Down Low'/'Mellow Mood' was issued in France and Canada, credited to Bob, Rita and Peter, but everything else was on ice. Then, during the summer of 1969, Bob and Rita spent some months with

Marley's mother in Delaware, resulting in the group's most definitive withdrawal from the music scene.

After Marley was sent registration papers for the US military draft, he returned to Jamaica eager to record and approached Perry on his own with an adaptation of James Brown's heartbroken 'I Guess I'll Have To Cry, Cry, Cry', not knowing it was a favourite of the producer; Perry heard Marley's interpretation as a confession, speaking to the disappointments he faced with Dodd and Sims, and unable to deny an approach of such open honesty, Perry agreed to record the song, for just as the Hippy Boys had been drawn to the Upsetter sound, so too was Marley.

'Bob heard what we were doing, and our rhythm was taking the town by storm,' said Glen Adams. 'The rhythm section was just happening, and Bob was doing stuff, but he wasn't getting anywhere, so he comes amongst us and he approached Scratch because they were at Coxsone together.'

'That's why Bob came when he come into it because I was creating that sound and the young musicians, Family Man and Reggie, them hear the sound and they wanted to join it, so them come by me and decide they want to play some music for me – they was ready to play that kinky, funny type of idea that I had,' Perry once explained. 'Bob was with Coxsone. After I left Coxsone, the thing wasn't strong with Coxsone anymore and even Bob's thing was shaking – the Wailers thing was shaking, everything shake. When me leave Coxsone, everything gone reggae, so Bob went away, maybe to America, wherever him going him hear that funny sound that I had. He go to England and he hear it and he come back to Jamaica and say, "Scratch, you have a sound and honestly, I really want to work with you." I say, "I don't really want to work with no singer at the moment" because I was just making instrumentals. I was really burned and bitter after the Coxsone treatment and I decide to upset. When I look 'pon Bob, it was like somebody sent him. From inside, I didn't want to do it, definitely, cos I didn't need no help from Bob or nobody. I did have an upsetting vibration and it was good enough for me, but Bob hear it and want to join it. I said, "OK then", but when I look I see that someone really sent him because he need help somewhere. I say, "Let me hear the songs that you have to sing". He sing this "My cup is overflowing, I don't know what to do." I said to myself, as a producer listening to an artist's inspiration, this is a true confession, it's the truth! His cup run over and don't know what to do, so he need help. I didn't say that to him, but I think about it. I listen. I didn't want to take him on because I didn't need no help and I didn't want to use any singers, cos them was behaving so stink and so rude that I didn't want to get involved, just wanted to do instrumentals. But then, I looked, and I hear somebody's inside dark, and I want to hear what the person say, so I tell him to let me hear what song him have to sing and him say his cup overflowing and he don't know what to do.'[1]

Marley considered going solo with 'My Cup', but Perry counselled him to continue working with Peter Tosh and Bunny Wailer on material they deemed revolutionary soul, initiating what many feel is the greatest work of their respective careers.

As Perry once explained, 'I was working with Bob and Bob didn't want to go back with the Bunny and Peter thing. I say, "Well, I think you should do it with this soul revolution for special reason because the three of your voices blend very good like an angel, to manifest your work on this soul revolution." That was a revolution – a spiritual revolution, fighting against government pressure and things like that, so he say, "I'll take your advice and call 'em back", otherwise there would be no more Peter and Wailer when the Coxsone thing break up. It was my idea to put them back together, he alone didn't want to do it. Bob wanted to sing with me alone without them, but I said, "No, you need them for special work."'[2]

And so it was that one of the greatest musical partnerships the world has ever known came to fruition: the incredible combination of Lee 'Scratch' Perry and the Wailers. Lee Perry transformed the Wailers sound by paring it down and aiming it more towards Jamaican ears as opposed to simply aping the styles of their American soul heroes. He spent weeks rehearsing the group behind the Upsetter Record Shop, restoring confidence in their creative abilities, and persuading them to reach higher heights through a more honest expression of their true selves, though the partnership took time to solidify, and in the beginning was not absolute.

'My Cup' surfaced in Jamaica early in the year, but only in small quantities on a blank label pre-release, to little effect; Perry placed the group's unrestrained harmony on Carl Dawkins' 'Cloud Nine' for *Many Moods Of The Upsetter* and on a Dawkins original called 'True Love', recorded at the same session, which was relegated to a Punch B-side. Then, as Perry and the Wailers put together the *Soul Rebels* LP in a short space of time, singles were trickling out from other producers in the interim, along with self-produced work.

For instance, there was the radical funk of 'Black Progress', adapting James Brown's 'Say It Loud – I'm Black And I'm Proud' with Fams and Carly (issued on a short-lived Wail'n Soul'm subsidiary called Power), followed by a Tosh-led cover of the Box Tops' 'The Letter' (issued on another called Tempa), as well as a reggae adaptation of the Archies' 'Sugar

Sugar' for Vincent Chin. The pop-reggae gospel single 'Adam And Eve' was recorded for Ted Powder (born Theo Kruijt), a Dutch trombonist/bassist and bandleader who was working with Byron Lee, and then, in late April to mid-May 1970, the group recorded an album's worth of material for Leslie Kong, backed by Jackie Jackson, Gladdy Anderson and company; Kong issued four singles in quick succession, beginning with 'Soul Shakedown Party' (which borrowed some lines from James Brown's 'Licking Stick'), but none of this material made much impact, paving the way for a more exclusive Upsetter/ Wailers partnership.

Working solidly together for the rest of 1970 and part of '71, they recorded a body of timeless work, since the Wailers were the hardest and most original vocal trio on the island and the Upsetters were creating the toughest rhythms under Perry's limitless artistic vision. Just as he had crafted something new with 'People Funny Boy', Perry was now in the process of changing the reggae beat, with the Wailers realising the new direction.

'When the people hear what I-man do, them hear a different beat, a slower beat, a waxy beat – like you stepping in glue,' said Perry in an oft-quoted 1977 interview. 'Them hear a different bass, a rebel bass, coming at you like sticking a gun.'[3]

Although Perry coaxed brilliant performances from each of the Wailers, his special relationship with Marley yielded much of the strongest material, so future releases credited Bob Marley and the Wailers rather than the more egalitarian Wailers appellation of before. Perry's greatest gift was his ability to teach, and many have testified to the changes his coaching brought, especially with Marley's approach to singing.

As Clancy Eccles noted, 'Perry was always a fan of Bob Marley. He loved Bob. He feel like Bob is the best singer in the world, but Bob Marley never used to sing like how he sings now. Then he used to sing a different way, but Perry used to sing that way how Bob Marley sounds now.'[4]

'He was the one who taught Bob Marley to sing, really, that's the honest-to-God truth,' said Jimmy Riley. 'The way Bob Marley sing is the way Scratch sing, for real. Bob Marley used to sing a different way before he start singing with Scratch. If you listen to Studio One Bob Marley and when he start working with Scratch, it's a different way. Scratch is not really a singer, but Scratch can express himself. He's slower in a different kind of way. That style is effective because you hear what he's saying more, so Bob Marley pick up that style and work with him.'

'The man is a real scientist, same thing with the Wailers too,' said guitarist Earl 'Chinna' Smith. 'It's like they no give him the rating whe' he supposed to get. The man do 'nuff, hold out Bob with a style of singing.'

Recording at Randy's with the engineer Errol Thompson over several months, the group cut over two albums' worth of material with Perry which helped change the direction of reggae, their socially relevant lyrics delivered in a more distinctly Jamaican vocal style, atop music with rougher edges.

Cool Sticky became an important part of the picture after Perry directed him to percussion, effectively ending his career as a deejay but ultimately revealing his true calling, his percussion lending a subtle African feel, the unobtrusive licks and skilful timing forming delicate enhancements. Errol Thompson's perceptive engineering also greatly helped to shape the work, and he and Perry became close friends, Thompson often visiting him at home on Sundays.

Once *Soul Rebels* was committed to tape, Glen Adams travelled to London on 1 May to deliver it to Lee Gopthal and

Graham Walker at Trojan, mastering the album at Pye in July while Perry remained in Jamaica, busy with his house purchase and other matters.

Mixing love songs and unadulterated protest music, *Soul Rebels* showed how far the Wailers had come since leaving Studio One, and it was conceived as an album rather than a collection of singles, which was still a novel concept in Jamaica. Issued in a garish sleeve incongruously showing a bare-breasted model with a submachine gun before an idyllic waterfall, the opening title track, with former Termite Lloyd Parks on bass, set the tone as a declaration of intent that went beyond mere macho posturing, Marley dismissing the malicious gossip aimed at him, declaring himself a man with a greater purpose and the determination to see it through. The group had made a half-hearted attempt at the song for JAD, which was flattened out through cheesy horns and a doo-wop vocal arrangement, but Perry's version fully restored its raw power, and even the stammer that Bob had been cultivating was stripped down, allowing the singer to better express his proud optimism.

In contrast, 'Try Me' was a love song that would have been generic, if not for the adaptation of the biblical line 'I am black and comely' from the Song of Solomon towards the end, while 'It's Alright' recounted Bob's late-night work at a Chrysler assembly plant in Newark, Delaware, and 'No Sympathy' (issued in limited quantities as a blank label pre-release single) was a trudging number from the tortured soul of Peter Tosh, who would always be misunderstood as a Rastafarian in Eurocentric Jamaica. 'My Cup' was the James Brown adaptation that got the whole ball rolling (which Trojan issued as a single in August, without much impact), and 'Soul Almighty' saluted the dances of yesteryear (like the Funky

Chicken, Mashed Potato and Alligator), again with a strong James Brown influence.

On side two, 'Rebel's Hop' updated the 'Rude Boy Ska' medley the group cut at Studio One, here with a fuzzy wah-wah guitar and Sticky's driving percussive licks, incorporating a few lines from 'Cloud Nine', a favourite of both the Wailers and Perry. 'Cornerstone' used a passage from Psalm 118 to lend a serious air to a cheeky plea for love, and '400 Years', again with Parks on bass, was the most revolutionary statement yet to come from Peter Tosh's critical pen, an anguished cry imploring Black people to internally liberate themselves from the legacies of slavery and its post-colonial aftermath. 'No Water' was Bob's titillating request for a wet nurse to quench his sexual thirst, while 'Reaction' was a prophetic bit of grainy urban soul that spoke of the impact their music would have on the world, rocking and shocking unsuspecting listeners from their rough and tenuous existence in a Jamaican shanty town. Closing out the album was an instrumental version of '400 Years', confusingly titled 'My Sympathy'.

As Perry began working more concertedly with the group, Bob Marley became part of the Perry household, lodging in the front room of 5 Cardiff Crescent so that he, Perry and the spirits could commune. Just as Dodd had acted as a surrogate father to Marley in the ska years, now Perry was fulfilling a similar role, but he and Marley were closer in age and shared a similar outlook. They were non-conformist rebels who smoked herb, venerated Rastafari and had burning desires to challenge the status quo.

'It was great to have Bob Marley in my house because there was so much message delivering that I alone could not take on the message, and if he wasn't there, some of the messages that the people hearing now, they would not hear it,' said Perry. 'I think of him like my brother, and I didn't put him in my back room, I live in the back room and put him in my front room, so he was hearing what I could not hear at the moment. He was visioning what's happening in the East and I was visioning what's happening in the West, so that's why we were so strong and other people didn't like it. Coxsone give Bob a back room in Studio One, maybe that's why Bob couldn't reach any further, whereas I give him my front room, so him go to the front. So him become like me brother and me see me are more responsible for him.'

Marley and Perry worked on several songs together at Cardiff Crescent, strengthening their creative bonds. They would later travel to Miss Ina's in Hanover, soaking up the vibrations of the countryside as stimulus for new works and drawing energy from the massive boulder that jutted from the earth behind her home, which provided a unique source of natural inspiration.

But the intense fusion of the Wailers and Upsetters was not without friction, especially where money matters were concerned, and financial conflicts soon led Perry to the Soul Syndicate, based at the house next door to Bunny Lee in Greenwich Farm. They had worked a marathon recording session for Lee for a mere $200 and had backed John Holt's massive hit 'My Heart Is Gone' for Phil Pratt too, so Perry approached them when working on a quiet and introspective number Marley had written called 'Sun Is Shining'.

The nucleus of the group included bassist George 'Fully' Fullwood, rhythm guitarist Tony Chin, drummer Carlton 'Santa' Davis and lead guitarist Cleon Douglas, who was later replaced by Chinna Smith, and numerous keyboard players and vocalists drifted in and out of the group. Soul Syndicate would soon be the band of choice for Niney the Observer and Keith Hudson, but when Perry cut 'Sun Is Shining' they were still largely unknown.

'Even though Scratch used to have the Upsetters, Scratch always want a different sound, so he tune into Soul Syndicate, come down and hear the band,' said Chinna. 'The word go out that Soul Syndicate wicked, so Scratch come in and draw them fe do "Sun Is Shining".'

'The first thing for Scratch was a song with Bob Marley called "Sun Is Shining" and the first time I ever be in the studio with Scratch, it was an experience – this guy's head is full of ideas,' said Santa Davis. 'People like Scratch and even Niney, they shaped sound in a new way, to make a music that had never been played in Jamaica in that time. They used to come up with ideas that other producers wouldn't have, and they would actually arrange the music, would show you things. Scratch wanted a particular type of mood in the song. He didn't want any eight beat or anything going on, as it would distract from the rhythm. I was playing and he took away the high-hat. He said, "You play this song without the high-hat." I said, in my mind, "How am I going to do that?" But then, as a musician, you have a challenge, so we play the song without the high-hat, and that's why it sounds open.'

Though Fams, Carly and company remained Perry's house band, the next time there was a quarrel about money, he drew for Soul Syndicate again, this time the more problematic circumstances yielding a spectacular result, since 'Duppy Conqueror' was one of the most original and striking songs the Wailers had ever recorded. A duppy is a malignant spirit, forced to roam between the spirit land and our visible world if the body it inhabited in life was given an incomplete burial or lay in a grave that was desecrated, and when captured by a worker of Obeah, a duppy is believed able to cause serious harm to the living. Co-written by Marley and Perry at the Green Door Saloon, 'Duppy Conqueror' boasted of Marley's strength and prowess as the 'Tuff Gong' that had returned to shake up the Kingston music scene, but the recording of the song was convoluted due to financial disputes.

'There was a session Scratch was planning after they write the song "Duppy Conqueror", but at the time, I didn't have the cash to pay my rent,' said Family Man. 'So I says, "Scratch, I need some money!" He says, "You ah come to the session?" I says, "Well, I better go somewhere else to look some cash. If I don't make it, I'll feel better trying."'

For the first attempt at 'Duppy Conqueror', made with the Soul Syndicate at Randy's, Tony Chin played lead guitar and Cleon Douglas handled rhythm, with Fully and Santa, and Glen Adams on Wurlitzer organ, as well as Peter Tosh on overdubbed organ parts.

'He bring in the Soul Syndicate and they do the rhythm for "Duppy Conqueror" and he cut a dub,' said Family Man. 'When he see me, he called me in the record shop and said, "You didn't come . . . what you think?" I say, "It's nice, it's good, but that's not 'Conqueror' rhythm. You have to book a different time, that's not what we started out." So that rhythm end up being "Mr Brown", and we went back, and we do the proper rhythm for "Duppy Conqueror" – that was special!'

Perry agreed with Family Man: the Soul Syndicate rhythm was good, but not fit for 'Duppy Conqueror'. He thus arranged to rebuild the rhythm at Randy's with the Wailers, Family Man, Carly, Reggie, Glen Adams and Sticky, with Vincent Chin engineering, the resultant 'Duppy Conqueror' all the rage when it hit the street a few days later on a blank label pre-release.

'Duppy Conqueror' would enter the Jamaican top ten at the end of August and remain there for a couple of months as the breakthrough single that finally re-established their dominance, topping the chart in late September, when the Wailers stole the show at a gala Derrick Harriott staged at the VIP club. Overseas, both Trojan and Pama handled it in the UK, and the following year it surfaced in the US on Shelter, a Capitol Records subsidiary.

As the song continued its inexorable rise in Jamaica, Perry had Dave Barker voice the alternate 'Upsetting Station' (aka 'Conqueror Version 3') on the same rhythm, a semi-sung, semi-toasted take that drew on the lyrics of the Temptations' 'Runaway Child', and Joe Gibbs sought to cash in with an instrumental recut called 'Ghost Capturer', but Perry got his own back by re-pressing Gibbs' version as 'Bigger Joke', with added mechanical laughter effects.

'Man To Man', which Marley and Perry co-wrote, was a one-off Wailers single to surface on the Jamaican Upsetter label in the wake of 'Duppy Conqueror'. Re-recorded by Marley years later as 'Who The Cap Fit', the song used proverbs to warn of duplicitous friends, its version side, titled 'Nicoteen', revealing the sharp edges of musical accompaniment that lay beneath the trio's ethereal harmonies. It was another of the releases enabled by an advance from retail record mogul KG, and shortly thereafter, Perry struck a distribution deal with Sonia Pottinger to free up his release schedule.

Then, on 28 October, as 'Duppy Conqueror' continued making waves across Jamaica, downtown Kingston was gripped by the terrifying phenomenon of a duppy that was said to be speeding through the land on a three-wheeled coffin, with three coat-wearing 'John Crows' or vultures perched on top, one of which was asking for a certain John Brown. It was

135

first sighted in Mandeville, reappeared in Sligoville, was shot at by a policeman in Spanish Town and arrived in Kingston by the Old Harbour Road, so when Glen Adams appeared on Charles Street that morning, he found a sizeable crowd searching for the coffin right in front of the Upsetter Record Shop and quickly put together some lyrics.

The origins of the tale remain obscure and conflicting accounts point to diverse beginnings. Adams said it stemmed from a murder case in Mandeville, while the *Gleaner* cited a case of petty theft in the same town and Bunny Wailer pointed to a publicity drive by Brown's Funeral Parlour on North Street. Several songs referencing the tale were released in quick succession, the Wailers' 'Who Is Mr Brown' the most successful.

Adams went to voice the song the same afternoon at Randy's, using the original 'Duppy Conqueror' rhythm that Soul Syndicate had recorded, but Perry suggested that the Wailers voice it instead; to emphasise the ghoulish nature of the tale, Bunny Wailer supplied maniacal laughter, worthy of a Hammer horror film, and both Adams and Peter Tosh overdubbed spooky organ parts. The song is said to have sold 15,000 copies in Jamaica, its overseas release on UK Upsetter as 'Mr Brown' helping to bring the group to the attention of a wider audience in Britain.

Soul Rebels was one of a trio of Perry-produced albums issued by Trojan records in the latter months of 1970, and after their stampers were cut in the UK, Perry also pressed copies in Jamaica for the local market.

The first to surface, *Eastwood Rides Again*, followed the typical Trojan formula by mixing older singles like 'Dollar In The Teeth', 'Baby Baby' and 'Django Shoots First' with newer instrumentals, most of which were heavily influenced by funk. 'Popcorn' was a drum-and-bass workout, drawing on James Brown's 'Mother Popcorn', and 'Catch This' had a similar framework to the output of his JB's backing band; 'Power Pack' stripped 'Rebel's Hop' to its raw rhythm, and there was an instrumental rendition of Eddie Floyd's 'Knock On Wood', which the Inspirations had covered for Perry. 'Red Hot' was the most extreme reworking on the set, with all other instruments removed except the rhythmic bedrock provided by Fams and Carly; pared down to quasi-dub form, it pointed the way towards evolving sounds of the future, along with 'Tight Spot', an eerie Upsetter stomp featuring Dave Barker, whose minimal vocal input helped update the western theme.

Dave Barker's *Prisoner Of Love* had some of his most popular releases, including the title track 'Shocks Of Mighty' and 'Set Me Free', as well as another 'Runaway Child' adaptation (voiced on the 'Rebel's Hop' rhythm), his take of 'My Cup' and a rendition of 'Blowing In The Wind', but Barker felt the album was compiled hastily, with under-par work.

'I was annoyed with him for doing that because some tracks were good, and some tracks were bad,' said Barker. 'I said, "Why not let us concentrate on doing a proper album?" Songs that were done spontaneously and didn't work out right, which he had ditched, he brought them together for the album which displeased me immensely. At that time, it was putting a blot on my ability as an artist. As far as I'm concerned, that isn't an album.'

Barker's fortunes would shortly change for the better: after voicing 'Double Barrell' for producer Winston Riley, he would find himself in London in the spring of 1971, summoned to *Top of the Pops* as half of the duo Dave and Ansel Collins.

Just before the Christmas of 1970, Niney the Observer clashed with Perry and the Wailers over his prophetic 'Blood

And Fire'. The spectacular hit would be crowned 'Song of the Year' in 1971, but when it was still in acetate form and Perry and the group first got wind of it, Niney was accused of copying the staggered organ chords of the Wailers' newly issued 'Love Light' (a sensual song with a spiritual framework, pressed on both Upsetter and the Wailers' Tuff Gong label), resulting in a physical attack from Glen Adams, who drew blood.

There had been another dig at Niney earlier in the year when the Wailers updated their ska track 'Mr Talkative' for Bunny Lee as 'Mr Chatterbox', with Perry overdubbing a spoken introduction to imply that Niney was their intended target, though Niney said the original request from Lee was simply for the group to re-record the ska hit rather than to aim it at anyone.

In the midst of all the ups and downs, on 4 February 1971, Pauline gave birth to Marsha Rachel Perry, who would grow to be her father's favourite, the presence of Bob and Rita Marley at St Joseph's Hospital for her arrival a testament to Marley and Perry's connectedness.

Under Perry's guidance, the Wailers continued to go from strength to strength. Medley fever was soon to grip the nation through singles by the Gaylads, Errol Dunkley, the Heptones and others, and Perry was among the first to set the trend. He had the Wailers lay a combination track called 'All In One', reworking previous hits such as 'Bend Down Low', 'Nice Time', 'One Love', 'Simmer Down', 'It Hurts To Be Alone', 'Love And Affection' and 'Put It On' (plus a few bars of 'Duppy Conqueror' on British pressings).

At the same time, as part of Perry's camp, Peter Tosh played guitar and Bunny Wailer played the kette drum on Little Roy's 'All Africans' (aka 'Don't Cross The Nation'), a song tackling the outdated terminology applied to Black people, harmonised by Ewen 'Ian' Gardiner.

'From [when] I was going to school, Lee Perry lived about three houses from me in Washington Gardens, so some evenings I go to his record shop and I usually come home with him and Pauline,' said Little Roy, born Earl Lowe. 'I did "Don't Cross The Nation" because I was reading a Marcus Garvey book and certain things he was explaining, like the word "Negro": we are not Negroes because it's a downgrading word. A lot of Black people don't know that, so that's why I had to sing a song like that. All Wailers was there because they was Lee Perry's crew at the time.'

Similarly, Perry wrote 'What A Confusion' with the Wailers in mind, but gave it to Dave Barker instead, roping Bunny Wailer in to harmonise with Barker as a defining element of the work.

Then, Bunny's 'Dreamland' was a significant hit that became his signature tune. Adapted from obscure soul ballad 'My Dream Island' by the Pennsylvania-based El Tempos, the Wailers first covered the song at Studio One, but Perry's version was far superior. Bunny's melodious tenor remained clear and expressive throughout, complemented by a spacious rhythm featuring Tony Chin's expressive picking guitar line, and although ostensibly a love song, its heady imagery was infused with a subtle spiritual content, conjuring images of an idyllic distant land, far from Babylon, and the just rewards that the faithful knew they would receive in Zion.

'Kaya' was also highly significant as the first song Perry released in praise of marijuana, and the first by the Wailers to address the subject too, written during one of Perry and Marley's visits to Hanover, where Perry's brother Sonny sped off on a bicycle, trying to replenish the herb supply before being caught out by the approaching rain. Released on Upsetter in Jamaica and Trojan in Britain, it also surfaced as the B-side of 'All In One' on the short-lived Black Heart in the US, the label name an ironic appropriation of a derogatory term that equated Rastafari with devil-worshippers that ate the hearts of abducted children.

At the same time, Perry was really fretting over the power exerted by the three biggest recording studios in Jamaica: Ken Khouri's Federal, Clement Dodd's Studio One and Byron Lee's Dynamic Sounds. In many ways, he and his peers were at the mercy of these industry giants, particularly Federal and Dynamic, who controlled the manufacturing of local product as well as its recording, and their proprietors were also known to be closely aligned with the nation's political and economic powerholders, particularly Lee, who had been brought into the business by Edward Seaga, the rising star of the JLP. If an independent producer got too big for their britches, the giants would not hesitate to make things difficult, so Perry responded with 'Small Axe', one of the few Wailers songs he produced with a full horn section.

Recorded at Dynamic with Jackie Jackson, Hux Brown and other first generation Upsetters, 'Small Axe' pointed to the emerging roots reggae style that would become increasingly popular later in the decade, with vibrant hand-drumming and a scalding wah-wah lead guitar heightening this scathing admonishment's agitation.

As Perry once explained: 'One Sunday morning I get up and sort of think over the whole thing and I got this idea. I said, "well if they are the big three we are the small axe." And I started to write that song. Then I got stuck at a certain part so I bring it to Bob. Bob read it and started to sing a melody. Bob created the melody for that. We were stuck for about three quarters of an hour and I went for a Bible . . . we saw it there, "Why boasteth thyself oh evil men", that come from the Bible. That was when the beat change again.'[5]

'Many of these songs was written at my place,' said Clancy Eccles. 'Although Scratch was around the road, Scratch use my toilet at my record shop. Scratch would pass me with a roll of toilet paper and a piece of cement bag, and when him coming back, it was a song written on the cement bag. Sometimes I don't even remember he was there because him round there all two or three hours, sitting on the toilet and writing the songs. I remember "Small Axe", when him coming back, him say, "Why boasteth thyself oh evil men . . ."'

The song was an immediate and lasting hit, reaching the top ten in March and remaining there for several months, holding the number one spot in June. To make the most of the hit, Perry reused the rhythm for an alternate Wailers vocal, 'More Axe', issued with 'The Axe Man', a Nyabinghi drumming version featuring Bongo Herman and Les, and Dave Barker and Charlie Ace voiced the deejay version, 'Shocks '71'. Similarly, U Roy voiced a version of 'Dreamland' called 'Rhythm Land', which appeared in limited quantities on a blank label pre-release, and the 'What A Confusion' rhythm was reused for U Roy's 'Earthquake', another startling piece of Perry innovation with double-tracked vocals, as though the toaster was in conversation with himself.

Another Carl Dawkins single also surfaced with the Wailers on harmony, this time a furious rendition of Freddie McKay's 'Picture On The Wall' (credited to Ras Dawkins and the Wailers), evincing his longstanding links with the group.

'I grew up in east Kingston but I inna the west with Bob all the while, so all of the Wailers is dear friends,' said Dawkins.

'We did have such a nice relationship, and Perry always deh-deh to help we along, inspirational and spiritual and heavy.'

More importantly, a later set of recording sessions at Randy's yielded another crop of exceptional Wailers material, much of which was issued in Jamaica as the album *Soul Revolution* in June 1971. Even stronger than *Soul Rebels*, *Soul Revolution* marked a turning point for the Wailers, evidencing a new maturity. The hits they had crafted with Perry helped ferment a clearer vision, and their closeness to the Upsetters rhythm team made their sound more distinctive, with a newfound strength in their fiery vocals.

'Keep On Moving' was a full reworking of the Impressions' 'I've Got To Keep On Moving' that the group had tried with Perry at Studio One, here featuring Bunny's shrill imitation of Curtis Mayfield in the bridge. Reworking a Wail'n Soul'm single, 'Don't Rock My Boat' was a stunning proclamation of romantic concord with sparse musical backing, voiced by Marley alone. At Studio One, the message of the original 'Put It On' had been easy to miss in the frantic jump-up of a crowded ska arrangement, so Perry completely restructured the song to emphasise its spiritual nature: guiding the trio of vocalists in unison through a slow and balanced rhythm track, Perry procured a powerful delivery radiant with religious undercurrents, culminating in the furious drumrolls and excited exclamations worthy of a Revivalist prayer session. Next, 'Fussing And Fighting' was an urgent plea for unity in the streets, followed by 'Duppy Conqueror (Version 4)', a version of the outstanding hit with half the vocals dropped out. 'Memphis' was a funky instrumental led by Peter Tosh on melodica, the toy keyboard's chords and melody line meandering curiously, and traces of a guide vocal can be heard faintly in the background, indicating a previous attempt to voice the rhythm.

Side two opens with Bunny Wailer's lead on 'Riding High', singing of an elusive lover over a choppy rhythm with an elaborate organ line, followed by herb anthem 'Kaya'. 'African Herbman' slowed Ritchie Havens' 'Indian Rope Man' to a becalmed trickle, a quiet and less cluttered arrangement that placed emphasis on the exceptional vocal arrangement, changing the sense of Havens' obscure, imagistic lyrics towards the Rastafari as African descendants that made ritual use of herb, and 'Stand Alone' was a tale of love's treachery given an emotive work through by Marley. 'Sun Is Shining' was another Marley solo vocal, nicely complemented by the pleasant strains of Tosh's melodica, echoing the cadence of his voice atop a smooth Soul Syndicate rhythm. Bunny Wailer's 'Brain Washing' closed out the set in a dash of righteous anger, indicting the education system by refuting the nonsense of nursery rhymes.

The album demonstrated a new level of excellence, but would take time to surface in Jamaica, enduring a problematic release that saw it unjustly overlooked. Perry brought the *Soul Revolution* master tapes to London along with a companion volume that was totally instrumental, and although both sets were mastered, and stampers were cut, along with test pressings, Trojan declined to issue either LP.

According to Perry: 'We made *Soul Revolution* because *Soul Rebels* was so successful. I asked Trojan to push these guys. They said I'm wasting my time because they can't make it because they can only sell to the West Indian market. And *Soul Rebels* did well here but through lack of promotion it didn't do what we expected. And then he [Lee Gopthal] wasn't interested in *Soul Revolution*. And then it was like he was trying to tell me to forget these guys because they'll never make it. I said man you're crazy.'[6]

In Jamaica, Perry issued the vocal album in a blue sleeve, confusingly bearing the title *Soul Revolution II*, its photographs, taken by Glen Adams in Perry's yard, showing the Wailers as rebel outlaws brandishing pistols, rifles and automatic weaponry, with Perry as the ringleader, doling out the guns. Bob and Peter were dressed in overcoats and Bunny in a Mexican poncho, placing them between the radical chic of the Black Panthers and the gratuitous violence of Al Capone or Django. But lest we take the scenes too seriously, a photo reveals that the guns were the plastic toys of Perry's children, harmless as his son's miniature dumper truck.

The instrumental companion album was released in small quantities on an Upsetter label in a blank sleeve, bearing the title *Soul Revolution Rhythm Part 2* on the A-side and *Soul Revolution Rhythm Part 3* on the flip. Regardless of the confused titles and mislabelled sleeves, the instrumental album was another first, presenting the entire *Soul Revolution* with the vocals removed to lay bare its rhythmic foundations. Though dub albums would later become commonplace, presenting remixed songs with disappearing and reappearing vocals, bathed in delay or other effects with the equilibrium of the mix radically altered, this version of *Soul Revolution* presented the pure, unadulterated rhythms, plain and simple. Another of Perry's unequalled innovations, no one else had issued an album quite like it.

Casting the songs in a completely different light, the voiceless rhythms revealed hidden musical flourishes previously buried in the mix. 'Keep On Moving' here featured dynamic interplay between piano and organ, and between rhythm and lead guitar; the blues underpinning of the lead was heightened, as was intricate tapping on the cymbals and high-hat. 'Don't Rock My Boat' placed the bass in front, with subtle percussion an integral accompaniment. 'Put It On' and

'Fussing And Fighting' were now led by the plaintive saxophone line that was a mere flicker on the originals, and the
organ mingled with the fancy trilling of the piano on each.
'Duppy Conqueror (Version 4)' was driven by bursts of organ,
a ghostly guitar and that subtle but vital percussion, while
'Memphis', sans melodica, was a fast-paced slice of Upsetter
blues. Piano and organ interplay was again exposed on 'Riding
High', the loose guitar strumming that drove 'Kaya' placing
it between flamenco and merengue. The guitar and organ
of 'African Herbman' kept its mournful quality intact, and
'Stand Alone' revealed the melancholy strains of a ghostly
melodica. In contrast, the skeletal form of 'Sun Is Shining',
with the melodica removed, became a shuffling organ rhythm
in stop-start time, and the guitar picking that lay beneath
'Brain Washing' reminded listeners how closely the music was
related to rhythm and blues. The Wailers were undoubtedly
the best vocal trio on the island, but this companion volume
showed that the Upsetters were the hottest session musicians,
and with or without the vocals, *Soul Revolution* was music of
an unbeatable standard.

During the same trip to London, Perry mastered his alternate edition of *The Good, The Bad And The Upsetters*, bringing
back stickered album sleeves with the new track listing.
Similar in feel to *Soul Revolution*'s companion volume and
also issued in June, the album had instrumental cuts of fourteen of Perry's recent productions, including 'Soul Rebel',
'Mr Brown', 'Man To Man' and 'It's Alright', along with two
cuts of the Inspirations' 'Same Thing All Over' (the second
featuring deejay Teddy), plus a steel pan rendition of 'If You
Don't Mind' and various raw Upsetter rhythms. The album
was released in very small numbers, rendering it among the
most obscure of all his early 1970s output.

Back in Jamaica, changes were afoot in Perry's camp, as members of the Wailers and Upsetters pursued opportunities off the island.

'Ever since I travelled to London, my outlook on life was kind of different,' said Glen Adams, who was in the process of emigrating to New York in the spring of 1971. 'It was hard to settle for what was coming, and as I was looking at it, I was seeing a dead end. Bob travelled out to Sweden, and then I travelled to the US.'

Marley was summoned to Sweden in March 1971 to work on the soundtrack of *Love Is Not A Game*, an unlikely cinematic venture casting Johnny Nash as a dance instructor that begins an ill-fated romance with a Swedish air stewardess. The project was problematic from the start, especially where financial matters were concerned, and the weeks that Marley spent in the country were bewildering.

During Marley's absence, Perry continued working with the other Wailers, cutting noteworthy material with Peter Tosh, with whom he had built a strong rapport in the studio. The first single to surface was 'Downpresser', a version of the African-American spiritual 'Sinner Man', inspired by the Book of Exodus, that the Wailers first recorded at Studio One following Nina Simone's popular rendition. As with 'Put It On', this version for Perry was stronger, the pace of the rhythm and its general edginess intensifying the ominous message of the lyrics, now directed at the oppressors, renamed 'down-pressers' in Rastafari dialect, with Bunny Wailer providing a falsetto counterbalance to Tosh's deep tones.

In contrast, Tosh's dejected 'Secondhand' (aka 'Brand New Secondhand') was a jaded, sour-grapes statement from a jilted lover that flaunted the range of Tosh's baritone. It was issued in Jamaica on a new label called Justice League, bearing the legend 'Produced and Directed by Upsetter – Wonder Man', placing Perry between comic book hero and the audio equivalent of a self-financed film director.

Perry was also instrumental in furthering Tosh's solo career by recommending him to Joe Gibbs, who subsequently recorded significant hits with the singer, such as the chart-topping 'Maga Dog' and 'Them A Fi Get A Beaten', and employed him as a session musician.

'Peter Tosh was an artist by himself,' said Perry. 'He didn't see himself as an artist to sing harmony, so me tell Joe Gibbs to use him and him play guitar and all them things because he have a star quality. At the moment, I didn't big enough. I could record with Bob Marley and Peter Tosh and the Wailers, but it did need somebody else to put out Peter Tosh's message because Bob is in my house and if I promote the two of them, it would be a big jealousy. Because Bob was in my house, Bob was hearing what I was hearing, he was feeling what I was feeling, then I have to concentrate on him and they need somebody else to concentrate on Peter, so I give him to Joe Gibbs.'

In truth, there was all kinds of tension behind the music, and while Perry and the Wailers were perfecting their creations, resentment was building on both sides. Eyewitnesses have said that Perry and Bunny Wailer never got on, their distrust of one another later blossoming into full-blown animosity. Bunny's incarceration had hardened him, and his reputation as something of a loose cannon meant that people tended to stay out of his way; a profoundly religious person, Bunny tended to retreat so deeply into his faith as to become uncommunicative, and even he and Bob were said to go for long periods without speaking.

In 1975, Perry recounted Bunny's strengths and foibles in *Black Music*: 'Bunny is a good singer, I like Bunny's voice very much. The "message" that Bunny writes is not so easy to understand, like Bob and Peter would write. See Bunny is a man who believes in a thing [the doctrine of Rastafari] so much that he gives himself less time to think. He would do great if he give himself more time to think . . . See, he's a guy that don't like you to rough him. If you cool with Bunny, you can get anything out of Bunny.'[7]

Perry's close bond with Marley also ruffled Peter Tosh, who felt that the dictatorial producer was destroying what little democracy was left in the group; Bob was touted as the star and was Perry's confidant, so the others felt slighted. Nevertheless, it was obvious that the Wailers were transforming through their work with Perry.

When contemplating the trio in retrospect, Perry suggested a hierarchy: 'Bob have unlimited talent and Peter is a superstar. Him just come on brave and say what him want to say and no care who vexed, and Bunny seem like a good harmony singer who could sound clearly like Curtis Mayfield, him have one of those good falsetto voices that can do things too.'

Marley's absence stoked the tension, and his time in Sweden was ultimately counterproductive since the Johnny Nash film was a critical failure that would fold one week after its release in September, the soundtrack left unissued. Danny Sims and his entourage had blown a lot of money, notably in a high-stakes card game, and Marley's promised wealth and fame did not materialise.

Regrouping once more in Jamaica, the Wailers mooted their thorough disillusionment with the producers they had worked with, and Peter Tosh and Bunny Wailer were eager to sever ties with Perry. Marley's friend, the footballer Allan 'Skill' Cole, had assumed management of the group and, by August 1971, was suggesting they make a clean break. During the time that they operated the Soul Shack, selling records, Tosh's hand-carved combs and freshly cooked food at 127 King Street in the heart of downtown Kingston.

Although everyone agrees that the split was traumatic, there are many contentious claims and counterclaims as to what caused the rupture.

'Me put all my energy into it for Bob to go out on top, so that is why Bunny Wailer hates me because me and him was friends before Bob, and me give Bob the fair go,' said Perry, suggesting that Bunny's envy played a part. 'Bob was a little easy to get jealous, but not that type of jealousy like Bunny.'

'We had combined our resourcefulness with the likes of Lee Perry, intending on benefiting from the UK market, only it didn't turn out as we planned,' countered Bunny Wailer, who said that money was the bottom line. 'Lee Perry run around because he can't play music. He called himself a producer, but at the end of the day, he took away all the money that was made from those recordings.'

Bunny Lee claimed that the Wailers gave Perry a severe beating when they discovered John Holt received a Ford Cortina when 'Stick By Me' hit, the attack supposedly resulting in Perry's hospitalisation, but Perry has flatly denied such questionable claims and, furthermore, insisted that he bought a Volkswagen Beetle for Marley and another vehicle for his bassist.

'Me buy Bob the first car, a Love Bug,' said Perry. 'Me buy Family Man car, and who me no buy car, me have to pay them rent.'

'The Wailers didn't have Scratch as a beating stick,' said Glen Adams. 'Nobody couldn't beat Scratch, but you would have a disagreement, just like anything else.'

In Roger Steffens' *So Much Things To Say*, Bunny Wailer claimed that Perry and the Wailers had a verbal agreement in place for a 50/50 profit share, which Perry reneged on, though such an agreement would have been highly unusual; no other established producer was offering terms remotely similar, nor was Perry offering those terms to any other artist. In any case, according to Bunny, things came to a head one Friday night at the Sombrero Club on Molynes Road, when the group confronted him about monies owing and a tipsy Perry suggested a ten-cent-per-record royalty rate as the correct calculation; Bunny lost his temper and assaulted Perry, causing some tables and chairs to topple in the fracas, humiliating him before Claudie Massop and other assembled onlookers.

A few days later, there was a tense meeting at the back of the Upsetter Record Shop, where demands for payment by Tosh and Wailer were met by a determined, if nervous, resistance; Bunny said he realised that a bottle on the table contained acid that Perry intended to hurl at him, though the notion was dismissed by Perry.

'That was his suspicion, but there was no acid there, that come out of his thoughts,' said Perry. 'They always think me have something to do them something, but it was only in their thoughts because they know I wasn't a chicken.'

Bob Marley later met with Perry to go through the accounts, bringing Michael Gordon-Martin (alias Mikey Faith), a computer salesman who ran the Emperor Faith sound system on the side, to help him review everything; according to Bunny Wailer, the paperwork showed that Rita Marley had been receiving records from Perry to resell in lieu of payment – 'thousands of records', Bunny claimed in *So Much Things To Say* – negating any royalties due.

In 1973, Perry told *Blues and Soul*'s Chris Lane that the Wailers had 'no cause for complaint': 'They signed all the papers, contracts, etc., and I gave them their money when they signed',[8] going on to highlight that artists' expectations did not always square with the agreements they entered into.

In his book *Bob Marley: The Untold Story*, Chris Salewicz stated that Perry received £18,000 advance for *Soul Rebels* and *Soul Revolution*, but Perry said he received a total of £2,000– 3,000 for the material, in keeping with Trojan's standard practice, which was to offer a low advance against the promise of future royalties, which were never paid.

Yet, regardless of the financial particulars, when the Wailers severed their links with Perry, they robbed him of his rhythm section in the process. The true break was demonstrated by 'Trench Town Rock', an exclamatory Tuff Gong tour-de-force, celebrating the power of their ghetto music, which reached the Jamaican top ten in August, where it remained for three months straight, unseating John Holt's 'Stick By Me' from the number one position and instigating a self-determined success they had never seen before. With the Barrett brothers now officially accepted members of the group, the Wailers would never let themselves be at the mercy of Jamaican producers again.

'The producers in Jamaica, upfront, them never too really overstand the business,' said Family Man. 'We get to under- stand that as time goes by, so them make little mistakes for themselves too. And then the Wailers were as forceful, and we [the Barrett brothers] were as forceful too, so we decided to do something on our own. We said that we're going to let these promoters sing and play for themselves.'

'Scratch used to take credit for everything,' said Glen Adams. 'We didn't know what credit was all about, why we should get credit, and that we should really put our name here in parentheses. And he didn't know either.'

We will probably never know the exact circumstances of the Wailers' departure, but what remains overwhelmingly clear is that the work they did together changed the face of Jamaican popular music, with the new vocal phrasing and Jamaicanised structure of their rebel music preparing the Wailers for the international stardom they were soon to achieve upon signing to Island Records.

The Wailers had progressed dramatically with Perry, the close tutoring strengthening Marley's resolve and radically altering his approach to singing. The intonation and phrasing introduced by Perry had overtaken Jamaica and, in time, would move audiences the world over, and although Tosh and Livingston were happy to distance themselves, Marley retained respect for the troublesome craftsman and would return to Perry's side at crucial moments throughout his career. The rift between the Wailers and the Upsetter was insurmountable, but the deep bond shared by Marley and Perry was too strong to be severed because of mere cash or ambition.

Perry has since made a series of confusing and contradictory statements about the Wailers, and they continued to stimulate the most extreme reactions from him when brought up in conversation or at interviews, but regardless of the odd statement to the contrary, Perry upheld his love and respect for Bob Marley, an artist whose work he consistently valued for the whole of his career.

In 1975, Perry made this perfectly clear to Carl Gayle of *Black Music*: 'Every song that Bob Marley sing is good. That is the only artist in Jamaica that I really admire and nothing Bob can do can be wrong as far as I'm concerned. I just like the way he's professional. I think he's the best. I and him can even quarrel cos there are certain things between me and Bob that no one understand. We work together, we have ideas and in Jamaica, professionally and musically we are blood brothers man so there's nothing he can do wrong for me. You see I believe in originality and Bob is an original . . . Most of the time I have a pen writing while he's singing. And I write and he sings it. I don't tell no lie, Bob Marley great man!'[9]

In the same article, he acknowledged the contributions of Peter Tosh and Bunny Wailer, stating: 'There's no harmony in Jamaica can sound as good as Wailers' harmony.'

Although the Wailers had broken away, Bob Marley would never keep himself far for long, and if the Wailers thought they had other fish to fry, so did Perry, who was happy to devote more time to instrumentals, and there was still a wealth of vocal talent seeking his input too. But the work he and the Wailers created together is simply some of the greatest music ever recorded on the island of Jamaica, and many consider it far superior to the Wailers' subsequent releases.

Lee Perry echoed the sentiment of a legion of fans around the world when he later described the work as their perpetual best: 'The records will continue to live forever – those recordings can't die.'[10]

CHAPTER SIX

Beat Down Babylon: Building the Ark

As the Wailers aimed for full self-sufficiency through Tuff Gong, Lee Perry continued scouring the field for outstanding talent, resulting in notable one-off recordings with a range of artists. Much of his output now addressed weighty matters of social protest and Rastafari consciousness, the militant Wailers helping to redefine his work even as he had helped redefine theirs, though there was humour too, as well as cover versions.

Travelling frequently between Kingston and London, Perry would often bring rhythm tracks from Jamaica for voicing at Chalk Farm, the studio that engineer Vic Keary ran at a former dairy near Camden Market, sometimes recording for Pama at Tony Pike's studio in Tooting.

Perry's early 1970s productions weave a convoluted trail, since there were many recordings with lesser-known artists, some renamed or miscredited. For instance, Rastafari vocal duo the Faithful Brothers, led by Lloyd DaCosta, recorded a warning to Obeah practitioners called 'Iniquity Worker', issued on an Upsetter single in Jamaica, but their repatriation call, 'Mount Zion', was credited to the Righteous Souls on a Supreme 45 in the UK; the Supreme B-side, 'All Over', was attributed to Eccles and Neville, and to further confuse matters, Perry Marvin was the credited producer, inverting his firstborn son's given name.

Similarly, some Righteous Flames singles credited the Hurricanes, including the ballad 'Got To Be Mine', led by Winston Jarrett, and 'You Can Run', led by Danny Clarke, the latter a warning to evildoers atop a foreboding rhythm punctuated by fiery brass. Clarke was a singer from Trench Town who had recently joined the Flames, along with future Jays member Lloyd Forrester; his devotional 'Zion' credited the Flames, while 'Run Up Your Mouth', a warning to loose-lipped informers, credited the Hurricanes on a Spinning Wheel single in Jamaica and Rob Walker on UK Upsetter, but featured Stranger Cole on lead vocals; and 'Run To The Rock', led by Jarrett, was produced by Perry and licenced to Sonia Pottinger, who assumed production credits.

Alton Ellis' sister Hortense cut some covers for Perry under the alias Mahalia Saunders (grafting gospel singer Mahalia Jackson's first name onto her married surname), namely Erma Franklin's 'Piece Of My Heart', Brenda and the Tabulations' 'Tip Of My Tongue', and 'Suspicious Minds', which had been a big hit for Elvis.

Other adaptations included David Isaacs' implausible reggae take of Tony Orlando's 'Knock Three Times' and a delicate rendering of Solomon Burke's 'Just Enough', his emotive vocal enhanced by Glen Adams' organ accompaniment; shortly before he left Jamaica, Adams made a convincing cover of Stevie Wonder's 'Never Had A Dream', harmonised by Milton Henry, with a free-form organ interpretation on the B-side; Lloyd Parks tackled B. J. Thomas' 'Mighty Clouds Of Joy' with considerable feeling, transforming the country-pop gospel into a meditative reggae dance track.

An old calypso, 'Stone Cold Dead In The Market', was the platform for Max Romeo's 'Ginalship', which had political overtones, addressing crooked politicians who were destroying the island through corruption and deceit.

'It was a new beat, so the rhythms and melodies can't all be new: you have to be as close to traditional as you can, in order for them to get that taste,' said Romeo, born Maxwell Smith. 'In those times, the political pressure was brewing up: the *ginal* is the politicians who are hiking prices every day, not doing anything for the people, but they're reaping a lot. Ginalship is the act of being a crook. "Crookedness mash up the country", that's what I'm really saying in that song.'

The Stingers' 'Give Me Power', led by Leroy Tibby, was one of the more striking originals of 1971. It benefitted from an exceptional arrangement highlighting piano and organ interplay, as Tibby sang of the need to embrace all of humanity, as ordained by God; its version side, 'More Power', stripped the rhythm down to its core elements, elevating the bass and drum, and a later deejay cut by Roy Lee as King Iwah the First had alternate Stingers vocal lines and fresh organ overdubs.

There was also 'The Creeper', a plodding rhythm with zany jive-talk from deejay Charlie Ace, while Winston Wright's soulful organ gave the instrumental 'Example' its groove. 'All Combine' was an unprecedented muzak medley, skirting elevator music through adaptations of Perry's 'Yakety Yak', Andy Capp's 'Pop A Top', Max Romeo's 'Maccabee Version', Neil Diamond's 'Holly Holy' (covered by the Fabulous Flames for Clancy Eccles), and on 'Part Two', Derrick Harriott's 'Solomon' and the Wailers' 'Mr Brown', 'Duppy Conqueror' and 'Sun Is Shining', as well as Keeling Beckford's 'Combination', the horn overdubs overseen by Harry Palmer in London. As reggae medleys go, 'All Combine' was one of the most unique, marking another first for the Upsetter in his unabashed fusion of raw rhythm and instrumental schmaltz, a theme later explored in greater detail by producers such as Harry Mudie.

During the same trip to London that delivered 'All Combine', Perry made his first recording with Denzil 'D. D.' Dennis, a Kingston native who was brought to London by Melodisc Records in 1963. Impressed by Dennis' strings-laden take of Frank Sinatra's 'My Way', Perry recorded a reggae rendition of the Monkees' 'I'm A Believer' with session players in Jamaica, voicing Dennis on the rhythm at Chalk Farm with a trio of white English girls, known as the Carols, on backing vocals; strings were later overdubbed by Richard Hartley at Tony King's studio in Hammersmith, and there were prominent strings on an instrumental version of the Temptations' 'My Girl', cut for Pama at the same time and pressed in limited numbers on an Upsetter blank.

Dennis was also a member of the Classics, with future Third World frontman Milton Hamilton, who had recorded the popular 'History Of Africa' for Laurel Aitken in 1970, along with 'Sex Education', which Perry licenced for pressing on Upsetter in Jamaica. In London, Perry had the group record a version of Eric Donaldson's Festival-winning 'Cherry Oh Baby' as 'Cheerio Baby', confusingly released on a 45 with a more striking Jamaican recording called 'Civilization', also credited to the Classics but featuring the duo of Anthony Doyley, a Trench Town schoolboy who would later lead the group Knowledge, and his school friend, Norman Edwards. According to Doyley, Bob Marley brought the duo to Perry, who recorded their song at Randy's one afternoon, but they received only two school uniforms as payment and were unaware their song had been released. Owen Gray's 'You Gonna Miss Me' was another song that Perry then licenced for release in Jamaica,

Pama's pressing crediting Sydney Crooks as producer.

Perry had an ear for deejay talent and his releases helped the form gain currency during the early 1970s. Some of the best examples were recorded with Dennis Alcapone, whose deejay cut of 'Cherry Oh Baby' was a big hit for Bunny Lee; Perry tried voicing Alcapone's deejay partner, Lizzy, on a further cut of the rhythm with a prominent trombone overdub and new keyboard chords, but Alcapone ended up voicing it instead as 'Well Dread'.

'Lizzy couldn't get the basic idea of what they wanted, so I was trying to direct Lizzy from behind the glass,' said Alcapone. 'Bunny said, "Dennis, go in and tell him", so me actually go in and illustrate to Lizzy, and Scratch said, "What you did on the rhythm, we'll have that", but I didn't want that. For a start, I just did "Ripe Cherry" on the same rhythm and I didn't want two songs on the same rhythm, but that's how "Well Dread" come about.'

Alcapone said working with Perry was easy but getting paid was less straightforward.

'I can't remember Scratch giving me any money, honestly. I can remember Scratch telling me to come for my money and me keep going . . . Pauline tell me Scratch not there, or some shit.'

Yet, other deejays were always willing to step up to the plate. Through the Upsetter sound system, Perry began working with Winston Thompson, a young deejay variously known as Winston Prince, Winston Cool or Youth Winston, who would later come to prominence as Doctor Alimantado. He was one of a number of street urchins that took shelter at 112 Princess Street, the home of Tippertone sound system, in the heart of Spanglers gang territory.

'Upsetter was one of the up-and-coming producers at that time,' said Alimantado. 'He was very outstanding in his work and everybody knew that. I used to deejay on a sound that was *the* sound in Jamaica at that time, and the Upsetter came to one of the dances. The next day I was by a shop looking at some records and he said I should come and do some songs for him, but I didn't really take it up at the time. Then he used to have a sound named Upsetter too, and one of my friends, Jah Stitch, and a youth named Jubie used to play Upsetter sound, so when his sound was playing, we used to go and listen. That's how it came about, really.'

Their first collaboration yielded 'Maccabee The Third', a toasting cut of Max Romeo's 'Maccabee Version' that called for the burning of the King James Version of the Bible, replaced by a forbidden text that had been removed, allegedly revealing the true supremacy of Black people. Some said that Perry had a copy of the Maccabee Bible, and either way, 'Maccabee The Third' is one of the many songs of the era showing Perry's overt support of Rastafari and its doctrine.

The definitive rupture with the Wailers robbed Perry of more than just his most successful vocal trio: the Barrett brothers became bona fide members of the Wailers band, and Glen Adams and Ronnie Bop had both emigrated. Perry thus recruited the 'third generation' Upsetters: on bass, there was Lloyd Parks, Val Douglas of the Now Generation band, and Ranchie McLean, who also played rhythm guitar, as well as Family Man on the odd occasion; drum duties were split between Tin Legs, Hugh Malcolm and Leroy 'Horsemouth' Wallace; Winston Wright, Gladdy Anderson and Theophilus Beckford were still there on keyboards, with Ossie Hibbert sometimes on organ, and Ron Wilson was trombonist of choice, along with trumpeter Bobby Ellis and saxophonist Tommy McCook, who arranged much of the material.

But the greatest difference was the absence of Bob Marley in his daily life, leaving a void both personal and professional.

Perry was thus searching for an artist of a similar calibre who was just as serious, determined and personable. He sought an artist whose talents he could cultivate as an inspired challenger with notions of their own, a singer-songwriter adaptable enough to handle the peculiar rhythms he was fashioning, receptive to his guidance, but whose outlook would be different enough to cause Perry himself to take note. By the end of 1971, Perry realised he had found the answer in Junior Byles.

Then working as a bus driver, Byles had a distinctive voice and solid songwriting ability, capable of producing songs of weight and gravitas, as well as works with a wry humour, and he even excelled at the slack. Yet, Byles' concern with the plight of humanity would see him subject to repeated arrests and later bouts of mental illness, and once Byles demonstrated a commitment to the Rastafari faith, there was conflict with his parents, resulting in longstanding familial estrangement.

'Junior Byles is something different, something special,' said Perry, who forged a sound working bond with the singer, though it took time to come to fruition. 'You know why most people can't record Byles? He's really a confusing artist if you don't know how to get with it and he's one of the best artists to come. He has a sweet voice, but he's not easy to control, though it was not difficult for me. He had good thoughts, very good ideas and to get it, you have to have patience.'

After the orchestrated 'What's The World Coming To' failed to find favour overseas, Perry took a gambit on Byles' Festival Song Competition entry, 'Rub Up Festival '71', but the song was disqualified in June after radio stations refused to play it, due to its bacchanalian content, which drew letters of complaints in the press when Byles performed it at the finals. The winner, 'Cherry Oh Baby', may have been suggestive, but Byles' lyrics about a drunkard seeking 'a gal who is fat and juicy' and a tourist who goes into a bar 'to rub up with a big ugly man' were deemed beyond the limits of public decency.

Recorded circa February 1971, at the same session as 'Dreamland' according to Tony Chin, 'Place Called Africa' was the first to hint at the dramatic potential of Byles' partnership with Perry, a moving portrait of a young Jamaican grappling with his African heritage:

> There's a place called Africa far, far away
> There's a place called Africa many miles away
> Mom says that's where I'm from
> And I know she can't be wrong
> Take me back to Africa
> Mama how did I get here?

Recorded around the same time, 'Got The Tip' was another saga of losing bets at the racetrack, issued on Punch as the B-side to Tosh's 'Downpresser', but this enjoyable dance number failed to impact.

Once the Wailers were out of the picture, Perry had the time and inclination to give Byles more concerted attention, the extraordinary 'Beat Down Babylon' an instant success and one of the year's defining hits. It was written by Byles' friend Harold Meikle, who recorded his own version in Canada as 'Righteous Rastaman' for a grassroots label called Tropical, and now Perry tinkered with the lyrics to better fit the rhythm he constructed, punctuated by the startling sounds of a cracking whip to drive home that the Rastafari would whip the oppressive forces of Babylon into submission, aided by the Almighty. According to Byles, the song was aimed at 'the forces whose principles seek to destroy the unity of Mankind'.[1]

Said me no like them kinda Babylon
Said me no dig them kinda wicked men
For I'm a righteous Rastaman
And I am a dread, dread one-high man
I and I going beat down Babylon
I and I must whip them wicked men . . .

'Beat Down Babylon' was one of the first studio recordings to feature the Now Generation, whose drummer, Tin Legs, brought them to Perry's attention when they were the house band at the Stables Club on Red Hills Road. Val Douglas' meaty bass gave 'Beat Down Babylon' its melodic anchor, complemented by Mikey Chung's understated guitar, and Earl 'Wire' Lindo's organ melody lent a spiritual feel.

'Beat Down Babylon' made its mark in the latter months of 1971, leaping to the top of the Jamaican charts just after Christmas, and it remained in the top ten until the following February, its continued popularity sparking a series of versions voiced on the same rhythm. The original B-side, 'Ital Version', was another aural experiment using reverb to enhance rhythmic peps made by mouth, an uncredited toast unfolding in the background. Next came Dennis Alcapone's 'Alpha And Omega', with chanted biblical proverbs between Byles' disappearing verses; Shenley Duffus' 'Bet You Don't Know' adapted an earlier ska ballad, now with a few lines in Amharic. 'Ring Of Fire' was an absurd instrumental centred on Ron Wilson's phased trombone, adapting the melody of Johnny Cash's original before collapsing into anarchic ad-libbing.

Further cuts brought the song back to its initial theme: On 'Babylon's Burning', Max Romeo sang of the inevitable retribution facing the wicked over a bass-heavy cut of the rhythm punctuated by thunderclaps and a percussive shaker, with choral voices from Niney, Earl Morgan and Barry Llewellyn of the Heptones, and toaster Jah T furthered the biblical attack on the ominous flipside, 'Lion Of Judah'. Junior Byles voiced the alternate 'Informer Men', railing against police informants, while Jah T reached from beyond the Seven Seas of Galilee to spur Byles on to higher heights. 'Outformer Version', the final cut Perry issued in 1972, kept snatches of Byles' new vocal drifting rhythmically in and out of the mix as part of his endless quest to test the limits of conventional recording.

The popularity of 'Beat Down Babylon' was so great that producers such as Keith Hudson, Clement Dodd, Joe Gibbs and Blacka Morwell all fashioned their own recuts, though none significantly challenged the original. Perry would continue focusing on Byles, with much fruitful work to come.

Africa's Blood and *Battle Axe* were the latest LPs Perry compiled for Trojan, also issued on Upsetter in Jamaica. Indicative of his present direction, *Africa's Blood* only had two standard vocal songs, the Hurricanes' broken-hearted 'Isn't It Wrong' and Dave Barker's soulful groove 'Do Your Thing', complemented by 'Place Called Africa Version 3', Winston Prince's competent deejay version. The other twelve instrumentals mixed older rhythms with new creations, including many adapted soul hits. There was Winston Wright's organ cut of 'Dreamland', Glen Adams' organ take of Byles' autobiographical 'Poor Chubby' (appropriately titled 'Long Sentence', since the vocal mentions time spent in jail), and 'Well Dread Version 3', credited to the Addis Ababa Children, was a Nyabinghi cut of 'Well Dread'. The derivative soul material included an instrumental take of Otis Redding's 'My Girl', with prominent melodica chords, and a sped-up version of 'Groove Me' titled 'Move Me'; 'Saw Dust', 'Not Guilty' and 'Bad Luck' (an instrumental take of 'Run Up Your Mouth') also betrayed a strong soul influence, playfully recast to better suit Jamaican palates.

The soul and funk aesthetic also influenced the album cover image: unlike the velveteen chic of *Return Of Django* or the polyester of *Scratch The Upsetter Again*, on *Africa's Blood*, Perry wore little more than his jewellery, and his woman an African headdress, displaying themselves for all the world to see as regal beings, proudly aware of their African heritage, the album a statement of Black pride, according to Perry.

'That LP is really based on being black . . . just a feeling, telling the people this is the blood of Africa. So once it's done, black and white have to appreciate everything in it cos I love black, I love white, I love everyone.'[2]

Battle Axe was another hodgepodge, joining peculiar instrumentals with the occasional unaltered vocal, though now Perry was making use of what would later be commonplace practices in dub by playfully remixing the vocal tracks. For instance, Delroy Wilson's hits 'Cool Operator' and 'I'm Yours', cuts of which Perry obtained from Bunny Lee, were remixed as quasi-dubs to include only a fraction of their vocals, placing the songs in an entirely different context; Little Roy's 'Don't Cross The Nation' (credited to Mark and Luke), underwent a similar transformation. Dave Barker's 'Groove Me' and a Clancy Eccles recut of Theophilus Beckford's 'Easy Snapping' were both stripped of their vocals entirely, while 'Knock Three Times' had a swirling organ and phased horns in place of David Isaacs' voice, turning a cheesy love song into a psychedelic instrumental oddity. The 'Cherry Oh Baby' rhythm here became the raw rhythm of 'Cheerio', while the rhythm of Andy Capp's 'Pop A Top' was faded jerkily in and out of the mix (as 'Pop A Pop'). Only 'Place Called Africa' and 'Picture On The Wall' kept their vocals intact, while 'Rough And

Smooth' allowed Stranger Cole to update 'Rough And Tough' with a benediction to Jah midway through. The remaining instrumentals were 'Earthquake', the title track (a 'Small Axe' variant), and 'Dark Moon', which was a saxophone version of 'Blue Moon'.

Perry was creating this music during another key moment in Jamaican history. As 1971 gave way to 1972, Jamaica endured a fraught election campaign that would see the JLP's Hugh Shearer ousted by Norman Manley's son Michael at the end of February, beginning a new era of Jamaican politics. The JLP had ruled since independence, and although there was relative economic prosperity for much of the 1960s, the global recession of the early 1970s had drastic consequences for Jamaica. A quarter of the overall population was unemployed, imported goods were at a premium, and the gap between rich and poor was clearly worsening. Some felt that the JLP served a wealthy minority at the expense of the poor majority, and a decisive moment that shifted public opinion against Shearer came in October 1968, when he prevented the Guyanese academic and activist, Walter Rodney, a socialist that taught African history at the University of the West Indies, from re-entering Jamaica on his return from a Black writers' conference in Montreal, precipitating widespread rioting (though Norman Manley initially supported Shearer's ban). After Michael Manley became leader of the PNP in 1969, he appealed to the people in a populist campaign, casting himself as the biblical Joshua, who led the Israelites into the Promised Land after the death of Moses, while Shearer was likened to the Egyptian Pharaoh in the Book of Exodus, who enslaved the Israelites and killed their children.

The PNP used music to their advantage in the campaign, co-opting Delroy Wilson's 'Better Must Come' as their theme song (just as Bustamante had used Clancy Eccles' 'Freedom' against the Federation of the West Indies), though Wilson said the song was not written in support of either party. Manley toured the country with a musical bandwagon featuring Clancy Eccles, Max Romeo, the Wailers, and other artists, sporting a 'Rod of Correction' said to have been given to him by Haile Selassie, the Rastafari symbolism increasing his popularity amongst the poor, despite family origins that placed him firmly within the reigning elite he claimed to challenge. Yet, after a solid decade of JLP rule, the country was clearly ripe for change and Manley's platform offered many the scope for greater agency.

In recording 'Pharaoh Hiding', Junior Byles sanctioned Manley's campaign, adapting a traditional spiritual in which Pharaoh and his army are drowned in the Red Sea. The song was issued on a new Perry label called Wizzdom, decorated by an obscure Hermes-like symbol, and it briefly graced the Jamaican top ten in late March 1972.

Similarly, on 'King Of Babylon' Byles likened Shearer to the evil Nebuchadnezzar, labelled an enemy of God and his chosen people in the Bible, with Lloyd Parks' distinctive bass pattern an outstanding element.

'Scratch was one of the greatest producers that Jamaica has ever seen,' said Parks. 'He get things out of me that I didn't even know I had inside of me as a bass player. I did "Mighty Clouds Of Joy" and that is the time he could identify my talent as a bass player, and when I play on "Nebuchadnezzar", the man say, "Boy, what's making that sound? It's just something different."'

'King Of Babylon' was recorded at Randy's and released on Vincent Chin's Impact label, but most of Perry's work was now undertaken at Dynamic Sounds, then Jamaica's leading recording studio, with top-of-the-range equipment. In November 1972, Byron Lee would make a further quantum leap towards the future by installing the first sixteen-track recorder on the island in its immaculate Studio A, where overseas artists worked. Dynamic's superior gear allowed a broader, cleaner and more complex arrangement of sound, and Perry became very comfortable in its well-equipped environment, typically working in Studio B (which began as a four-track).

Perry's arrangement at Dynamic was similar to that which he established at WIRL, acting as an A&R supervisor and in-house producer in exchange for studio time and record manufacturing. Lee had already issued some of Perry's Bleechers material and made use of Perry's talents on albums like *Many Moods Of Lee Volume Two*, and after the recording of 'Small Axe', he engaged Perry to earmark potential hits.

'When Leslie Kong was alive, you had Bob Marley, Toots and the Maytals, the Maytones, the Gaylads, the Melodians, all those groups coming in,' said Lee. 'After that era you had Johnny Nash coming down to record and then Lee Perry was one of the producers we had. When Lee Perry first come, what attract us to him was that he had tremendous talent. He could recognise a hit. Out of all the producers we had worked with, his ear for a hit before it was actually recorded, he had that gift in his head. A lot of producers have to hear the song first to say it could be a hit, but he could generate the hit from day one. I remember he brought Junior Byles and he brought "Small Axe" with Bob Marley. He was a tremendous producer that we were very happy to be associated with.'

Perry's work at Dynamic was based on informal bartering that suited both their needs, according to Lee.

'We had four A&R people working as in-house production for us: Lee Perry, Bunny Lee, Tommy Cowan and Boris

Gardiner. We had a kind of joint production deal where Perry would do stuff for us, we would release some of it under our label, some under his, and he would get production royalties, or sometimes he would waive his production fees for facilities we have, like studio time, stamper pressing or distribution. Then he never had the cash to finance his operations, so we would take his talent in the studio and in return, give him cash to counter the production costs. He would go and make another record with somebody else, and he would press them here – we call it third-party licencing.'

But since his time with the Wailers, Perry was determined to start a studio of his own, increasingly constrained by having to rely on the facilities of others. Every aspect of record production in Jamaica was in the hands of a select few and Perry resented their control. His muse was cramming so many ideas into his head that he really needed a rightful place where he could freely pursue the eclectic paths of his creativity, without the pressure of time constraints. And since studio time was expensive, it made sense in the long run too.

Perry had been scouring Kingston for a suitable location without success, until a vision finally showed him the way in the spring of 1972: in the yard behind his house was a large *Lignum vitae*, an evergreen tree whose flowers release a distinct scent at Christmas time; said to be the heaviest and densest wood in the world, the *Lignum vitae*, or Tree of Life, is exceptionally hardy, and its resin was used by the Arawak for medicinal purposes. According to Pauline Morrison, it was while half-dozing beneath the tree that the spirits spoke again to Perry, making it clear that he was resting at the exact spot on which his studio was to be built.

Although he had salted away some funds with the express determination to build a studio, the stash was not sufficient, so in April 1972, he remortgaged the house at Cardiff Crescent, freeing up another JMD$2,000, and as the work began, he conceived a fourth bedroom and extra bathroom to be installed at the house, and for a veranda to be constructed. In time, Bobby Aitken would become the chief contractor who erected much of the masonry, while Leonard Dillon of the Ethiopians did the patterning on the cement walls of the surrounding compound and a handyman known as Django provided general assistance. The building of the studio was a long, slow process that was ultimately expensive, reportedly costing £12,000, and the work would stretch right through to late 1973.

While the studio was being built, Perry's brother P-Son transplanted himself from rural Hanover to the unfamiliar ways of Cardiff Crescent. Then just fifteen, much of his future would be spent assisting with the day-to-day happenings in the Perry family yard.

Meanwhile, Perry continued the experimentation that set his work apart. When Junior Byles entered the 1972 Festival Song Competition with the nonsensical dance track 'Da Da', harmonised by the Jamaicans, it placed third, yielding another hit during the summer.

In contrast to the innocuous original, alternate version 'Come Da Da' was a Perry/Byles duet with several noteworthy differences. Introduced by some studio dialogue, where Byles asks that reverb be applied to his voice, the song had Perry proclaiming that Jah would increase his righteous marijuana plant, and there was one of his favourite sayings buried in the mix too: 'Matthew, Mark, Luke and John, drop the knife and spoon and *nyam* with your hand', referencing the gospels of the New Testament and suggesting an abandonment of European table etiquette in favour of African customs, a concept adapted from the Bible, according to Perry.

'It said before the fork and knife was here, you had to eat,' said Perry. 'You're not going to *not* eat because you don't have any. These hands are your fork and knife, originally.'

The B-side of the UK Upsetter pressing of this single also began with a revealing proclamation: 'In thee oh Jah I put my trust, deliver I from confusion.'

Now Perry was openly proclaiming a belief in Rastafari in his work and using the I-words of Rastafari dialect as part of a concerted effort to convert 'word-sound' into power through the selective reshaping of Jamaican English, substituting syllables deemed negative with the more uplifting 'I', suggesting all things 'high' and therefore closer to God. Thus, the syllable 'ban' of the word 'banana' must be removed, for as a natural life-giving fruit, the item cannot be 'banned'; the word 'I-yana' is seen as preferable. Marijuana was brought to Jamaica from India by indentured labourers and the strong weed became known as 'collie' through a corruption of Kali, the potent Hindu goddess of destruction and rebirth, but as 'collie' can also be a lowly dog that pisses against the walls of Babylon, Perry used 'I-lee' in 'Come Da Da' instead.

Though some had him down as a mere Rasta sympathiser for his 'soul man' Afro and trimmed facial hair, others recognised him as already having embraced the faith, and even if he retained the physical countenance of a 'baldhead', at least the beard he sported was a nod to the Rasta dress code. Such issues were dealt with on 'Hail To Power', the version side of 'Pharaoh Hiding' in which a disguised voice asks, 'Well sir, do you think it's right for a baldhead man to claim that he's a Rasta?', the answer being, 'It all depends on his heart.'

'Beat Down Babylon', 'Place Called Africa' and 'Da Da' made Junior Byles a star. He worked solidly with Perry for the rest of 1972 and, by the time of the Festival, they had already recorded over a dozen tracks, ten of the best being selected for Byles' debut LP, titled *Beat Down Babylon* after the phenomenal hit. Dynamic Sounds released the album in Jamaica at the end of July, and Trojan issued it in the UK in November, as well as in Canada through Montreal's Trans World Records. Except for the opening Festival hit, each song allowed Byles to convey the depth of his feelings, and most of the album dealt with issues affecting the wider society. 'I've Got A Feeling' decried racial injustice, male harmonic chants emphasising the gravity; 'I Don't Know Why' addressed the inherent difficulty in keeping a woman satisfied, and a pared-down 'What's The World Coming To' as 'Demonstration And Protest' had more obvious power without the strings, the less-cluttered instrumentation allowing Byles' tenor to shine; 'Coming Again' had machine-gun blasts between the horns and intricate piano trills, reminding of Jamaican volatility in the aftermath of a fiercely fought election. After 'Beat Down Babylon', 'A Place Called Africa' and 'Joshua's Desire', 'A Matter Of Time' was a coming-of-age tale, describing a teen's conflict with her father, and the autobiographical 'Poor Chubby' reminded that Byles walked a thin tightrope, making him vulnerable to unemployment, incarceration and homeless-ness, as well as being misunderstood by his peers. With every song a winner, *Beat Down Babylon* remains the finest album of Byles' career, as well as one of the strongest albums Perry produced with a solo singer.

The pair enjoyed a further hit with Byles' rendition of 'Fever', Little Willie John's oft-covered rhythm and blues hit that was also a tremendous success for Peggy Lee, here with a false start and a heavily reverberating mix.

According to Milton Henry, the rhythm of 'Fever' was recorded at Randy's with Lloyd Parks and Reggie for Henry's original song 'This World', with Byles on harmony, the popular single credited to King Medious on release in Jamaica, while 'Fever' may only have been issued in the UK on a Pama 45. Further cuts include Jah T's deejay piece 'Lick The Pipe Peter', as well as 'Hot And Cold', a typically expressive melodica version by Augustus Pablo, the gifted session musician of part-Indian parentage, born Horace Swaby, who scored 'Instrumental of the Year' with 'Java'.

Shenley Duffus' fine rendition of William Bell's soul ballad 'I Forgot To Be Your Lover' was the best of a batch of songs he voiced for Perry in 1972. Issued as 'To Be A Lover', the song's non-standard construction came courtesy of Horsemouth, Lloyd Parks and Tommy McCook on keyboards, whose chords lent an unusual melodic cadence, with Duffus' brother Kenneth and cousin Keith on harmonies. Duffus' renditions of the Moonglows' 'Sincerely', Jesse Belvin's 'Goodnight My Love' and Earl Grant's 'At The End Of A Rainbow' failed to impact (all three voiced on a rhythm Ansel Collins built for Perry at Federal), but when Duffus voiced 'To Be A Lover', everyone present knew it would hit. Duffus said it was the most popular song he ever recorded, though he would soon concentrate on stage performances, where payment was more reliable.

Perry said the song's success caused friction between himself, Ken Khouri and Clement Dodd, who knocked him down during an altercation at Federal; Claudie Massop and his lieutenant, Carl 'Biah' Mitchell, offered violent retribution, which Perry declined.

'Coxsone was vexed when we were making "To Be A Lover", he was jealous,' said Perry. 'He think that me was with him, and me and Mr Khouri making hit tune and he was making none, so him get mad, come and start to fight. Mr Dodd wanted to make war with me and some of those guys did want me to employ them to discipline him, but that would cost me a lot of money so I wouldn't agree to anything like that and if anything go wrong, it's going to be a problem too. He also have a gun and those guys have unlicenced guns, so we don't know who would shoot. When one producer on top, then all rude boys want to join him and the other producer who is not the boss anymore always want to get rid of you because you take away their power. So me did have all those Denham Town guys on my side, like Flux, Claudie Massop and Biah, the whole set of them, but me did say, "All right, just cool off, keep cool and don't do that" because it's not nice.'

Perry's close association with Max Romeo and Niney also continued to yield notable efforts, including 'Rasta Band Wagon' and 'Public Enemy Number One', songs that reflected strong friendships as well as close working relationships. Romeo and Niney had been living in the same house, close to Perry's home in Washington Gardens, so the three were often around each other in the studio, improvising and sharing ideas.

Issued on Niney's Observer label, 'Rasta Band Wagon' addressed the changing face of Rastafari, which now attracted uptown folk and non-Black Jamaicans through the inclusive efforts of the Twelve Tribes of Israel, founded in Trench Town in 1968 by juice vendor Vernon Carrington, alias the Prophet Gad; the lyrics are delivered, tongue-in-cheek, over a minimal rhythm with a Nyabinghi bass drum marking its unhurried beat.

On the B-side, credited to Murt, Turt and Purt, Perry's lead characterised the Almighty's wrath, proclaiming in an ominous voice that Jah would kill, cramp and paralyse His enemies, Romeo and Niney giving choral emphasis at key points.

'Public Enemy Number One' was the first of many to vilify the Devil, Romeo fingering Satan for a variety of social ills on another sparse rhythm with a wobbling bass line, and its version side, 'John Public' (aka 'I Know Something'), had distorted murmuring, an accentuated kick drum and a prominent organ riff straight out of a sci-fi horror soundtrack.

With such a high volume of material, it was inevitable that some releases would not sell as much as they deserved, though there was no disputing the quality. Still feeling the loss of the Wailers, Perry recycled 'Keep On Moving' for Dennis Alcapone's 'Rasta Dub', complete with cock-crowing noises, and there was 'Moving Version', an exuberant take from Tippertone's star deejay, Big Youth, who Marley once named as his favourite toaster. The Stingers' 'Preacher Man' attacked hypocritical men of the cloth, their 'Forward Up' a song of weed dealing with a revving motorcycle adding to the aural realism. Reggie Lewis' 'Natty Natty' was autobiographical, relating the disapproval expressed by his girlfriend's parents of his budding dreadlocks and empty pockets; built on tightly wound drumrolls from Tin Legs and a rumbling bassline, the song had a series of false endings, adding to the feeling of dejected disappointment. There was also the Melodians' 'Round And Round', pondering the cyclical nature of life through exceptional harmony, and on 'Professor Ironside', Lloyd Parks saluted the wheelchair-bound television detective in a gruff voice. The Heptones cut a likeable cover of Billy Stewart's 'I Do Love You' for Perry with the Soul Syndicate at Randy's, which Earl Morgan said was popular in Jamaica. Neville Grant's militant 'Black Man's Time' called for Black equality and self-determination amidst a repeated 'Pop Goes The Weasel' saxophone phrase, its rhythm reused for the slack innuendo of 'Puss See Hole', voiced by Perry over the raw drum and bass; 'Whiplash' by Wesley Martin of the Bleechers (credited as Wesley Germs) recounted streetwise sexual peccadillos, and 'Water Pump' was Perry at his slackest, a graphic boast of sexual exploits that equated his ejaculating phallus with the pump of the title. Perry also cut an updated version of 'People Funny Boy' that he voiced himself as 'People Sokup Boy', which may have been left unissued until the late 1990s, though the rhythm was reused for Dennis Alcapone's 'Backbiter' (Perry also issued Winston Groovy's 'Want To Be Loved' in Jamaica, but the song was produced by Groovy in London without his involvement).

Pat Francis' devotional 'King Of Kings' was not especially popular, but it brought Perry his new chief record salesman. The young man from Trench Town got his start at Studio One in rock steady group the Eagles, later forming the Mediators, who recorded the popular 'Look Who A Bust Style' for Rupie Edward, and Francis was selling records for Edwards too, helping songs like Dobby Dobson's take of Tom Jones' 'That Wonderful Sound', Joe Higgs' 'Burning Fire' and the Gaylads' 'My Jamaican Girl' to hit. Then, after cutting a few solo sides under his given name, he approached Perry with 'King Of Kings'.

'I always know him at Studio One but never really get to do work with him until we meet at 36 Charles Street,' said Francis. 'Then we rehearse, and I do a song named "King Of Kings" and when I do that song, he said I seem to be a lucky man. Then after I would be a salesman for Lee Perry too. You'd have to go from shop to shop and try to put out the record to the people, make them know that it's a good record, try to get it off the ground.'

'French Connection' was another Upsetter oddity, obviously inspired by the cinematic thriller, though the lyrics are largely nonsensical, Perry spurring dancers on over a chugging rhythm led by a sprightly organ line, and later referencing obscure personae. The song is noteworthy as among the first that Perry mixed at King Tubby's studio, the B-side richly bathed in delay, the mix spotlighting a wooden fish, kick drum and organ in turn, a fully fledged dub that pointed towards the masterworks of the future.

Osbourne Ruddock, alias King Tubby, was an enigmatic jazz head, soul buff and electrical technician who ran a popular sound system in Waterhouse. In addition to supplying electrical transformers to hotels and other businesses, he built amplifiers and serviced the machines at Treasure Isle, before he built his own mixing console to tinker with recordings in a converted bedroom of his mother's home at 18 Dromilly Avenue. Then, through Bunny Lee's assistance, he acquired an obsolete MCI mixing desk from Dynamic Sounds and changed the bathroom into a voicing booth, making King Tubby's studio the main site of dub innovation from late 1971. It was a tiny space with minimal equipment, but it became the premier place for mixing dub version B-sides, and many producers began voicing their A-sides there too, with Bunny Lee in near-permanent residence. Tubby revolutionised Jamaican music through the dubs that came out of his studio, his application of reverb, delay and other effects turning the subgenre into an art form; as Perry began to use the facility with increasing frequency, his version sides were transformed throughout 1973 and he and Tubby became fast friends, despite the latter's antisocial tendencies.

Some of the material Perry recorded in late 1972 would not surface until the following year, including the Gatherers' landmark 'Words Of My Mouth', one of Perry's most moving and enduring productions. This short-lived harmony group, first called the Gatherlites after the Skatalites, had formed on a Trench Town street corner with Anthony 'Sangie' Davis, Barrington Daley and Earl 'Bagga' Walker (alias Errol Walker), three teenaged singers who had performed with nightclub acts such as the Graduates and the Melody Enchanters. In 1972, around the time that the group first entered the studio with producer Jimmy Radway, Sangie joined the Twelve Tribes of Israel, whose teachings profoundly influenced his lyrics.

'I was just learning to play guitar then, and that was about the same time me write a tune that say, "A man can live for a hundred years or more, for umpteen years and a score, not only by the words of him mouth, but the meditation of him heart . . . bring righteous praises to the King",' said Sangie. 'That song "Words", it's me and Barry really write it and it was an inspiration that stem from amongst the whole of us, our actual trodding through life.'

When a neighbourhood friend suggested the group approach Perry, they went to Dynamic with a number of acquaintances, and Perry was so taken by the strength of their delivery that he recorded everyone on the spot.

'About fourteen people did that song. Through you there in Trench Town them times, when you go studio, a lot of people come, so all who can sing, we just say, "Come in man, sing some harmony" and them sing the background part, "doobie doobie wah wah". Me play rhythm guitar and Barrington Daley play lead, Bagga play bass, Touter Harvey play keyboards and the drums I think was Benbow.'

There was a ghostly melodica from Augustus Pablo too, playing a mournful refrain to chilling effect, the rhythm so striking, durable and popular that Perry would reuse it on several occasions. Alternate cuts were issued shortly there-after, including one with just the harmonies alone, as well as 'Hot Tip', a searing deejay cut, credited to Prince Django, with a false start allowing for an argument between Perry and an auditioning hopeful.

At the same session, the group cut the optimistic 'Start Over', led by Barrington Daley and propelled by rapid snare drumrolls and rim shots, but the group never recorded again. They received JMD$1,400 from Perry for their efforts, Sangie later collaborating with Bob Marley and becoming a leading record producer, with Bagga Walker a prominent bassist (notably at Studio One).

Perry also recorded his latest deejay discovery in late 1972, the material surfacing throughout the following year: Lester Bullock was a protégé of Dennis Alcapone who began his career on El Paso as Young Alcapone, but was renamed Dillinger by Perry, one of the first to take a gamble on his talents. Since he was primed and ready to go, Perry voiced him on an endless stream of rhythm tracks, including vintage songs like 'Tighten Up' and 'Stranger On The Shore', as well as more recent creations like 'You Can Run', 'French Connection' and 'Words Of My Mouth'.

'I had a lot of songs that I did want to get on the market, so I went to Dynamic Sounds and Scratch was there recording,' said Dillinger. 'He let me do about two LPs that night, straight through. Due to you're young and greedy, you have a lot of inspiration and stress and anxiety to get it all out.'

As the studio construction continued at Cardiff Crescent, Lee Perry's work was becoming noticeably more radical in both content and form, with references to Black Power, Rastafari and social activism increasing as his instrumental versions moved further into the realm of dub. He was undertaking more transatlantic travel, too, in an effort to broaden his reach and to render his output different from the rest.

In the autumn of 1972, Perry flew to London, having brokered an album deal with Creole, though he almost did not make the journey.

'I can remember in the ninth hour, when he's supposed to be flying in tomorrow, if we didn't send him another ticket for Pauline, then the whole thing was off,' said Bruce White.

Two versions of the *Cloak And Dagger* album were mastered in London on this trip, one for release in the UK on Creole's Rhino subsidiary, distributed by EMI, and the other for its Jamaican Upsetter issue. The British edition surfaced in 1973 and its cover showed Pauline emerging from Perry's open leather cloak, the pair appearing as a sort of Black Avengers team. There were horn instrumentals arranged by Tommy McCook, including the title track (based on Burning Spear's 'He Prayed'), 'Rude Walking' (based on Horace Andy's 'Skylarking'), 'Sunshine Rock' (a horns cut of 'My Girl') and 'Iron Claw', along with some Winston Wright organ pieces, such as 'Liquid Serenade' (based on 'The Liquidator'), 'Hail Stone', 'Retail Love' and 'Creation'; 'Musical Transplant' was an instrumental adaptation of Ernie Smith's easy listening hit 'Pitta Patta', and 'Wakey Wakey' was the closest thing to a dub track, being a pared-down cut of 'Son Of Thunder'. The odd song out was 'Caveman Skank', an experimental dance number toasted by Perry atop a bass-heavy rhythm with running water, crashing cars and a Native American reading a portion of the Bible in Cherokee, lifted from a sound effects record; some of the live street sounds were recorded in the area surrounding Chalk Farm studio, an animated Perry bouncing around in an effort to get a reaction from the public.

If the Rhino issue of the album saw Perry leaning more towards the outer limits of instrumental sound, the Jamaican Upsetter issue took things one step further by skating the fine line between instrumental and dub. 'Retail Love', 'Creation', 'Sunshine Rock' and 'Wakey Wakey' were removed to make room for 'Sharp Razor' (a dub of 'Cloak And Dagger'), 'Side

Gate' (a dub of 'Professor Ironside'), 'Version Ironside' (a dub of 'Iron Claw') and 'Bad Walking' (a dub of 'Rude Walking'). The Jamaican *Cloak And Dagger* thus contained another exclusive Upsetter experiment: it was the first album to have instrumentals followed immediately by dub versions of the same rhythm, in what would later be known as the 'showcase' style (though that format typically had vocal tracks immediately followed by dubs). Both editions of the album were mixed in split stereo, with the lead instrument and voice overdubs in one channel and the unaltered rhythm in the other.

Available in Jamaica from late October 1972, *Cloak And Dagger* sold rapidly to local music fans, but the British edition achieved little success. Perry attributed the failure to record company disinterest, the absence of strings and unpolished rawness resulting in a lack of promotion.

'I gave that album to Rhino but at the time they were doing little things in reggae which the people didn't really like so they weren't really buying their records like they should then. A big company like EMI can't handle reggae people because they have so much at stake, they can't worry to go through that.'[3]

'When it came to *Cloak And Dagger*, I don't think Scratch can say EMI didn't understand reggae,' said Bruce White. 'Maybe they didn't, but we were always there to push it in the areas where it needed pushing, and the main thing about having a company like EMI was their distribution. I think *Cloak And Dagger* might have been a bit before its time – perhaps the people weren't ready for it.'

Crossing paths with Dave Barker, who was working with Creole under Larry Lawrence's supervision, Perry had him deliver another Yankee-style soul toast for the Rhino single 'Sunshine Rock', credited to Dave Collins, and the Dave and

Ansel Collins B-side 'Hot Line', recorded for Winston Riley, benefitted from an overdubbed introduction, with Perry and Pauline emulating a radio phone-in.

Larry Lawrence continued to help out as a run-around man, just as he was setting up the Ethnic label, which would later be an important outlet for Perry's work, and he helped Perry equip his studio too.

'We become such good friends that when he comes to the airport, I'll have to go and pick him up and I would take them to their meetings and everything,' said Lawrence. 'If they want a good studio they ask me which are the best. Then we start getting into the studios and start making records with a girl called Silky Davis and some of the Trojan artists like Dandy Livingston. We used to take them into the studio with Scratch and make records for them.'

Before heading to New York to conduct more business, Perry delivered the *Rhythm Shower* album to Trojan, though they declined to issue it, probably fearing it was too abstract for British audiences. Perry thus brought the stamper down to Jamaica at the end of the trip, along with that of *Cloak And Dagger*, issuing both on Upsetter in late October 1972.

Rhythm Shower was another mishmash, but this time with proto-dubs, deejay tracks and standard instrumentals. Most of the set was very current, except for 'Django Shoots First' and a new mix of 'Uncle Charley' with only half the vocals intact. There was Winston Wright's 'Double Power' (an organ cut of 'Give Me Power'), 'Rumplesteelkin [sic]', another instrumental without dub enhancements, and a standard Dillinger toast called 'Skanking', but everything else was heavily dubbed: 'Connection' censored Dillinger's toasting cut of 'French Connection', interrupting his flow with some studio dialogue, and there were fine dub cuts of 'To Be A Lover' and Dillinger's

'Bring The Kuchy Come', his salute to the marijuana waterpipe that was voiced on the 'Words' rhythm. 'Operation' was the album's tour-de-force, a dub medley splicing stripped-down cuts of 'Whiplash', 'Fever' and a melodica cut of 'Give Me Power', here with blaring sirens and winding master tapes.

Although *Rhythm Shower* languished in obscurity, Perry continued to score with Junior Byles. 'Rasta No Pickpocket' attacked false Rastas that used dreadlocks as a cover for their crimes; 'Auntie Lulu' drew on the wisdom of proverbs, the rhythm propelled by Tin Legs' furious rolls; 'Education Rock' was one of many songs using the alphabet as the basis of a reggae dance tune; and 'When Will Better Come' was aimed at Michael Manley's failure to provide real change, inverting the message of the Delroy Wilson hit that the PNP had appropriated.

One of Perry's most outstanding singles of 1973 was 'Better Days' by Carlton and the Shoes (credited to the Carltons), a trio formed in the mid-1960s by Carlton Manning and his brothers Donald and Linford, the latter two also members of the Abyssinians. Known for their love songs at Studio One, 'Better Days' presented a harder, more spiritual side; singing in unison of the betterment coming to the Black race, their voices soared to choral heights over a typically solid Upsetter rhythm with vibrant kette drumming and piercing horns.

Stranger and Gladdy's boastful 'Conqueror' was another Wizzdom gem, reworking a song they recorded for Duke Reid in ska; Spanish Town-based deejay I Roy (Roy Reid) turned 'Medical Operation' into 'Doctor Who', a relaxed toasting homage to the British television time traveller. Perry also revisited the 'Return Of Django' rhythm for Neville Grant's rendition of 'Sick And Tired.' He voiced a wild duet on the 'Retail Love' rhythm with JBC disc jockey Jerry Lewis for

'Burning Wire', and I Roy voiced the similarly excessive 'Space Flight' on a cut of 'French Connection' with hefty Moog over-dubs; using a barebones cut of 'Give Me Power', there was Perry's own 'Sunshine Showdown', recounting the famous boxing match between George Foreman and Joe Frazier, held at Kingston's National Stadium in January 1973.

The King Tubby connection continued to yield exceptional material. Perry's 'Black IPA' (Rasta slang for pepper) and its version, 'IPA Skank', both featured horn sections so phased and mutated as to sound virtually unrecognisable, an under-water quality blurring the brass. With Ernest Ranglin on lead guitar and Hux Brown on rhythm, 'Jungle Lion' transformed Al Green's 'Love And Happiness' into a funky reggae jaunt, Perry growling out a warning to his enemies through symbolic Rastafari codes, and its version, 'Freak Out Skank', gave more excessive phasing to the horns.

Similarly, 'Bucky Skank' drew on a riff from the Temptations' 'Poppa Was A Rolling Stone' for a disjointed dance track that gave a frowning nod to the trigger-happy gunmen on the corner, since bucky is patois for a homemade gun. Driven by Tin Legs' pounding, off-beat rolls and subjecting Perry's shouted slogans and odd vocal peps to heavy doses of delay, it was another record totally unlike anything released by his contemporaries, and unbeknownst to Perry, it had far-reaching effects, helping Brian Eno to reconsider his approach to recorded sound, just as he was exiting Roxy Music.

'I was living in Notting Hill where you were always hearing reggae and ska on the streets and walking down the road one morning I heard this extraordinary thing, like nothing I'd ever heard before,' said Eno. 'Since when I was a student, studying painting and sculpture, I had become aware that the recording studio was really a way of painting with sound, but when I heard "Bucky Skank", I thought, that is the closest thing to sculpture I've ever heard in music and I could imagine how he'd done it, taken a track that was already recorded and just chopped stuff out of it, made these big holes where there were otherwise consistent things running through. He was taking a block of sonic stone, chopping bits out of it and making something of the spaces. So this was a radical thought at the time because every advance in recording had been to do with addition, being able to put more and more on, and then along comes this guy doing exactly the opposite. So for me it was the discovery of a new idea in making electronic music.'

As a non-musician whose main role came through the use of studio technology, 'Bucky Skank' validated Eno's evolving unorthodox methods.

'I don't really play anything, so the material that I worked with was the recording studio and it became clear to me that effects were actually a big part of the vocabulary of music, so to hear Lee Perry foregrounding those things was another important message for me as it confirmed my drive towards minimalism. By that time I was already sick of the overindulgence of most pop recording, with bloody orchestras and horn sections and percussionists and everything filling up, and to have somebody doing exactly the opposite made me think, "Yeah, this is the way to go, taking stuff away is as important as anything else." It just made me feel like I had company because when I first started recording even overdubbing was considered to be cheating. There was a really strong feeling that the serious job of being a musician was the craft part of it, the chops, getting everything right, and then there was all this decoration that you added on at the end, like effects, and that was trivial, and it was becoming more and more obvious that was a historical separation that really had no value at all. And "Bucky Skank" was the first definitive proof of it.'

If 'Bucky Skank', 'Freak Out Skank' and 'IPA Skank' were unusual, 'Cow Thief Skank' was something else entirely. The lyrics of this duet between Perry and Charlie Ace were aimed at Niney, referred to as Moccasin for his preference for cheap shoes, and the song suggests his missing thumb came from retribution for the attempted theft of a cow, Ace taunting Niney as the one to 'take out the shitty-shitty pail' when incarcerated, as Perry bellows, 'Go back to Lucea!' with absurd mooing sounds heightening the insults, though Niney took it all in his stride.

'In those days we used to have "musters", but at the end of the day we is friends,' Niney emphasised. 'I used to sometimes stay far from Scratch and Bunny and move around Joe Gibbs, and they will come and pick a fight with me: those times Bunny Lee gave me a bike and I left my bike at Bunny's. Scratch take the bike and lock it up in the shop and drive away, so it's just like a muster those days and we used to make songs off each other. Like Bunny Lee make a tune Bob Marley sing, say, "Hey! See the one Niney there, Mr Chatterbox!" In those days, we laugh at those things and if we want to make back a song on each other we make it, but nowadays youth can't do that. They want to fire their gun in your face.'

The insults notwithstanding, 'Cow Thief Skank' marks another Perry first in the history of recorded sound. As is more readily apparent on the version side, '7¾ Skank', 'Cow Thief Skank' is a composite creation, splicing together three different Upsetter rhythms to create something unique. A few bars of the Staples Singers' 'This Old Town', surreptitiously lifted from their record, prefaces a bit of the Inspirations' 'Stand By Me', the remainder of the song alternating between dubbed-out portions of the 'Better Days' rhythm and a cut of

'Musical Transplant'. Again, this cut-up technique was not adapted by others in reggae and it pre-dates similar techniques used in new wave and hip-hop by many years, despite the technical limitations of the equipment at Perry's disposal.

Then, 'Dub Organiser' was Dillinger's salute to King Tubby on the 'Cloak And Dagger' rhythm, acknowledging his importance as a dub pioneer, voiced at Tubby's studio for Perry one evening with a considerably improved delivery.

'In that era you find sounds like Emperor Faith, Tippertone and Ruddy's, a lot of sounds used to go to King Tubby for dub because he got the best dub in those days,' said Dillinger. 'Everybody have to see Tubby, so the idea come: Tubby's supposed to be the dub organiser, for everybody come to him for dub.'

By May 1973, Perry had issued the first of a spate of singles with former Bleecher Leo Graham. Although 'Three Blind Mice' merely set lines from nursery rhymes to an enjoyable reggae backdrop with a bright horn section, 'News Flash' (the last of the UK Upsetter 45s) spoke of food shortages, rising prices and other present calamities unfolding under Michael Manley's reign, and dub B-side 'Flashing Echo' was one of a flurry of exemplary creations made at Tubby's studio, here with astute application of delay. The rhythm was reused for 'Station Underground News', recasting the song as a virtual news broadcast, with Perry as a roving reporter (credited as King Koba on the Jamaican release), splicing in a line from the Chi-Lites '(For God's Sake) Give More Power To The People' to better emphasise the point. Perry also cut his own adaptation of the Chi-Lites song as 'Justice To The People', reconfigured as a slow and heavy reggae, with bawling babies, wailing adults and rocking guitar lines, incongruously introducing the dub B-side with a lewd gag about a doctor screwing his

186

wife, parodying the mores of polite society before allowing the listener to be enveloped by audio sound effects.

When the Hoo-Kim brothers opened Channel One on Maxfield Avenue in western Kingston, Perry was among the first to take up their offer of a session of free studio time and would use the facility fleetingly, though Dynamic continued to be his main base. Future Congos member Roydel Johnson, an old friend from Kendal, tried to voice 'Standing On The Hill' at Channel One, but Perry was displeased with the result and re-recorded it with Shenley Duffus for a Pama 45, voicing an alternate himself that was left unissued.

In July 1973, Perry and Pauline were back in London, joining Clancy Eccles, Bunny Lee and Alvin Ranglin, who were all doing business in the capital. The Wailers had released *Catch A Fire* on Island and now Trojan tried to capitalise on the hype by issuing *African Herbsman*, which had all of *Soul Revolution* except 'Memphis', along with '400 Years', 'Small Axe' and two self-produced tracks, 'Lively Up Yourself' and 'Trench Town Rock'. The Wailers were furious, blaming Perry for the issue of their material without permission, though Perry suggested that Trojan had acted improperly, claiming he had nothing to do with the track selection and laying the blame on Lee Gopthal, who had rejected *Soul Revolution* in the first place.

Towards the end of the month, in the company of Bunny Lee and Larry Lawrence, Perry caught I Roy's performance at Battersea Town Hall, where the toaster was backed by upcoming London reggae act Matumbi. According to the group's guitarist and producer, Dennis Bovell, Pauline Morrison introduced I Roy onstage as U Roy, causing an uproar until she rectified the mistake, and midway through the concert, Perry made his way to the stage, but when he asked for a song that the band was unfamiliar with, he pushed their keyboard player out of sight and made a mighty noise by running an arm up and down the keyboard, much to the delight of the audience.

Lawrence was helping him to equip the studio: 'When he was building that studio, all those equipment that you saw in there, both of us bought them together with his money. Trojan gave him the cheque, but we drive around and look for those JBL speakers and all that was in there, we bought them and shipped them down there. We would drive down to Charing Cross Road to look for bass drum mikes and all that.'

There was Perry's first mixing desk, an Alice AD62, which had six channels and limited capabilities. Ted Fletcher, who designed the board, said only fifty or so were manufactured (unlike their later 828 model, which was mass-produced), and Perry said he picked his up cheaply from a shop on Edgware Road.

'I don't think my mixer, the Alice, cost me even thirty-five pounds. It was for radio station balancing or maybe like a PA system. You couldn't start a studio with that, but we were using them. Those were domestic machines, not professional machines – they were only toys.'

Somewhere along the way Perry purchased a drum kit that had reportedly been Ringo Starr's, and some other equipment is said to have been liberated from a London studio that had recently closed, though the exact circumstances remain unclear.

In a spate of press interviews arranged by Trojan, Perry spoke of the plans for his new studio, telling Chris Lane of *Blues & Soul* that he would be launching a new label called Black Ark and that he was bored by reggae's standardisation.

'I want to change the beat. The people are getting tired of hearing the same thing over and over again, and the musicians are getting bored with playing the same rhythms all the time. At the moment, I'm thinking of ways to make the beat more demanding, more powerful, more new.'[4]

He told *Melody Maker* that, instead of bringing rhythms from Jamaica to overdub in Britain, his new concept involved the reverse.

'I've seen so many artists from the UK coming to Jamaica to record backing tracks and bringing them back over here, so I wanna know what the difference is. If the studios are any problem or if the backing groups are any problem, I wanna test something. All being well, I plan to spend three or four days in Chalk Farm studios with Greyhound and the Cimarons recording the backing tracks for some original and standard items. Then I'll add girlie choirs in New York because they can give me a much more soulful black sound there. The lead vocals will come last, when I get back home to JA. I shall use Annette Clarke and the Silvertones, a fresh group that I think will make it. They already did a good version of Wilson Pickett's "In The Midnight Hour" and my record for being right about artists is pretty good.'[5]

The Cimarons and Greyhound were then the premier reggae backing bands in England and Perry ran some sessions with members of both groups at Chalk Farm as planned, while Larry Lawrence remembered sessions with a Black band based in High Wycombe, and keyboardist Earl 'Wire' Lindo spoke of a jam session he recorded for Perry in Cambridge around the same time. Some of the Chalk Farm material was used for singles voiced by the Twinkle Brothers and D. D. Dennis (including alternate takes of 'Woman And Money', written by Perry), but Perry laid the rhythm tracks for the Silvertones' work in Kingston instead, according to members of the group.

The Silvertones started in the ska years when Keith Coley

and Gilmore Grant began singing together in east Kingston. Delroy Denton became the leader in the mid-1960s, and their debut for Duke Reid, a cover of Brook Benton's 'My True Confession', was an instant success, followed by their hit cover of Wilson Pickett's 'In The Midnight Hour'. Further hits followed for Reid and for Sonia Pottinger, the original 'Blam Blam Fever (Guns Fever)' a popular rude boy anthem (credited to the Valentines). Then, after their sparse recordings for Perry in 1968 and '69, the Silvertones reconnected with him just as he was preparing his studio.

'We know Perry from the record shop he had on Charles Street,' said Gilmore Grant. 'That time he have an album named *Cloak And Dagger* and it sell in a plain plastic, he couldn't make the jacket fast enough to sell that album. We check him as Scratch, said we'd like to make a few songs for him. In that time we had "Early In The Morning", "Sweet And Loving Baby", "Rock Me In Your Soul". Scratch said, "Let's do an album", and we voiced that album in Tubby's studio, just a small little place. Each time we do a song, we would have to come outside and get some breeze and go back again.'

According to Grant and Coley, Perry laid the album's rhythm tracks on a few different sessions, using old hands like Hux Brown and Ansel Collins for the melodies, along with younger musicians like Ranchie McLean and drummer Basil 'Benbow' Creary; Benbow remembered working on the material at Dynamic and Harry J, and said that Hugh Malcolm played on a few of the tracks.

As with most of Perry's previous LPs, the resulting Silvertones album, *Silver Bullets*, reflects the inherent duality of Perry's output, as well as the Silvertones' general oeuvre, in that it mixes cover tunes and originals that are seemingly at odds with each other. Although popular songs like Ben E. King's 'That's

When It Hurts' and 'Souvenir Of Mexico', Jerry Butler's 'He'll Break Your Heart' and the Archies' bubble-gum hit 'Sugar Sugar' are covered credibly enough, the group really shines on the Denton originals, such as the ardent 'Soul Sister', while the spiritual 'Rejoice Jah Jah Children' was strikingly different (and followed by a fine reverberating version, 'Rejoicing Skank', with snatches of fast delay on UK pressings), the song, a definite high point that was written by Pauline, according to Perry: 'She write it and ask me to make them sing it.'

Intriguingly, Denton's 'Rock Me In Your Soul' was issued in Jamaica as the sole 45 on the Pilot label, funded by insurance salesman Cecil Ramanand, with Pauline Morrison named as producer; contemplative non-album tracks 'Take Time Out' and 'Just Like A Log' surfaced on Bullet, credited to the Three Tops with Pauline again as producer, and to further complicate matters, the final song on the Silvertones album is a dub mix of Dave Barker's rendition of the Staple Singers' 'Are You Sure', recorded at Dynamic and tacked on to *Silver Bullets* at a Chalk Farm session (where Larry Lawrence was adding Moog overdubs), when Perry found that his album was too short.

'I was in the studio putting some crazy noise on top of it and Scratch was editing *Silver Bullets* the same day, and he said to me that he's only got something like nine tracks, so he would take that one and finish the album,' said Lawrence. 'He had to go to the record company to do his business the next day and he needed a track, and that's the way we live. He mixed that cut himself off of my tape in Chalk Farm studio.'

This add-on seems an odd choice, especially as Perry recorded other material with the group that he left unreleased, including a Gilmore Grant composition called 'I've Got This Feeling'. That said, the presence of 'Rejoicing Skank' meant

191

that another dub did not seem entirely out of place on what was already a diverse collection of styles pointing in several directions.

Unlike the Trojan issue, when the Silvertones album was released in Jamaica it was mixed in split stereo, with the vocals in one channel and the rhythm in the other, and some songs featured alternate vocal takes or other musical variations. Instead of issuing it on the Black Ark label as suggested by his summer press interviews, the new label was called Black Art, its hand-drawn motif showing a grinning golden sun facing a smiling black crescent moon, with a blue sky full of twinkling stars in between them; once up and running, the studio would eventually be known as the Black Ark but was typically credited as the Black Art studio on Perry's output throughout 1974 and '75, though there was some interchange between the terms in this early phase.

Annette Clarke began her career in the early 1960s through Vere Johns' talent shows, cutting rhythm and blues duets with Shenley Duffus and Roy Panton. Her rendition of Doris Troy's 'Just One Look' was another early single on Black Art, issued in Jamaica with a sparse instrumental called 'Dub Power' on the flip (which played at 33RPM), and Trojan's issue, on their Techniques subsidiary, had a soulful original called 'Sinner Man' on the B-side instead, marked out by a bluesy guitar line. Blank label pre-releases of 'Just One Look' also surfaced with Clarke's adaptation of Ed Robinson's 'I Just Wanna Be There' on the B-side, which somehow got faster and faster as the runout groove approached – a very strange listening experience.

More Leo Graham singles from this transitional phase drew out the best of his abilities, mostly voiced over sparse rhythms with shining guitar work by Hux Brown. Early Black Art pre-release 'Dig Pit' warned a false Rasta of coming retribution, and B-side 'Double Attack' showed the singer's relentless determination to succeed; 'Black Candle' counselled Obeah workers that Jah would render them powerless; the suggestive 'Want A Wine' (issued on Upset) lamented the lack of a partner for intimate dancing; and 'Revelation Time' sang of present suffering, as foretold in the Bible.

The rhythm of 'Revelation Time' was reused for 'Labrish', a grudgeful, gossiping duet voiced by Perry and Bunny Lee at Tubby's. Bemoaning the trials and tribulations of independent producers, they take passing swipes at Rupie Edwards, Niney and Clancy Eccles, who is dissed for having supported Manley's election campaign, only to be left without a vehicle in the aftermath, sparking 'answer' tunes that were never released.

'Financially, I went broke,' said Eccles. 'I mashed up my two vehicles in the bandwagon for the People's National Party, a brand new van and a brand new car. At the end of the exercise I neither had car nor van, while some singers who went with me had an old car and got a better car, but it's just one of those things – it happens to the best of us. Then I made songs that I didn't publish. I call one "Big Gut Striker" and the other one "Bangbelly Chicken Scratch", and I told them some most derogatory things about their life, but I thought it would be bad for me to put out things like that and I only did it to get them off my back.'

Other early Black Art releases include U Roy's 'Stick Together', a deejay cut of 'Want A Wine', backed by '006' (aka 'Double Six'), voiced on a cut of 'Auntie Lulu'; some pressings appeared on the Black Ark label, the first to bear its name, and there was a Black Art single with a song contemplating natural wonders called 'Nobody Knows', credited to Ken McKay, with '006' on the flip.

By the end of 1973, Perry had compiled two further albums as his evolving studio was taking shape. The first was *Double Seven*, which would be the final of his mixed collections issued by Trojan, notable for Moog overdubs by Ken Elliott at Chalk Farm and a sophisticated stereophonic mix with much cross-channel fading, especially of vocals and percussive effects. There was Perry's relaxed version of Sam and Dave's 'Soul Man', David Isaacs' spirited take of the Chi-Lites' 'We Are Neighbours', and 'In The Iaah', which sounds like a Wailers outtake. U Roy's 'Double Six' and 'Stick Together' contrast with I Roy's delivery on 'High Fashion' and 'Hail Stone', both riding sped-up organ instrumentals. Then, using a continuous rain sound in the left channel, Perry's 'Cold Weather' finds him trying to get to grips with the English climate, while Ken Elliott's Moog makes 'Ironside' even more dramatic than the vocal cut. The odd one out is 'Just Enough', David Isaacs' emotive 1971 cover tune, sounding somewhat out of place, while dub cuts of 'Jungle Lion' and 'Justice To The People' (the latter titled 'Waap You Waa') exposed the funky, soulful base of Perry's contemporary beat. Best of all is 'Kentucky Skank', an ironic celebration of Colonel Sanders' secret recipe with the sounds of a frying chicken in the mix, as Perry references earlier works, adapts Bible verses and throws in a line of Amharic for good measure.

Perry reused the latter rhythm for various other cuts, including 'Bathroom Skank', a sensual duet voiced with Pauline at King Tubby's studio, with hilarious instructions for the rhythmic scrubbing of body parts, as Tubby drops custom effects.

If *Double Seven* continued the natural progression shown on his Trojan collections, the other late 1973 album release was far more divergent and important. Released in very limited quantities on the Upsetter label in Jamaica, *Upsetters 14 Dub Blackboard Jungle* – later known as *Blackboard Jungle Dub* – was a true landmark, presenting the hardest of Perry's contemporary rhythms in their purest dub form.

Among the first dub albums ever issued, there is magic in *Blackboard Jungle Dub* as it bears traces of collaborative work between Lee Perry and King Tubby, using rhythms that were originally voiced and mixed at Tubby's, but the exact nature of the collaboration is difficult to pinpoint, and Perry has sometimes tried to downplay or negate Tubby's role.

'Tubby was there, like in what was happening,' said Perry. 'He was a part of it, and he was the engineer, but he didn't have anything to do with the effects. It was I did all the effects as well. I make a lot of effects there, I create it, and it was like a joke.'

Blackboard Jungle Dub highlighted dub's transformative power and its ability to radically alter any given composition through creative mixing and spatial representation. The first Jamaican issue of the LP collected fourteen of the hardest Upsetter dubs of recent months, mixed in split stereo with definite channel separation; subsequent issues had twelve of these tracks, usually with a monophonic mix.

The original opened with 'Black Panta', an awesome dub of 'Bucky Skank' with flute and horn overdubs atop a phenomenal mix that gave Tin Legs' pounding drums a disproportionate sense-surround dimension, while roaring sirens and the overamplified scraping of a guitar string increased the overriding tension. 'Black Panta' was liberally bathed in echo and delay, adding a surreal quality of timelessness and an otherworldly feel; 'Version Panta Rock' was a slightly faster trombone take with dark jazz leanings. 'Kasha Macka' gave 'Hot Tip' a stop-and-go makeover, and while the rhythm bumped jerkily along, hidden piano and percussion were uncovered. The Hurricanes' 'You Can Run' was recast in drum and bass mode as 'Elephant Rock', with a smattering of bright horns left in for a treble dimension. 'Place Called Africa' was stripped down to drum and bass as 'African Skank', with bursts of guitar and keyboard sneaking into one channel at odd intervals; 'Dreamland' got similar treatment on 'Dreamland Skank', and 'Jungle Jim' was a swirling dub of 'Black Man's Time' that emphasised the 'Pop Goes The Weasel' horn refrain. After a roaring introduction from Scratch, side two begins with 'Drum Rock', an eerie cut of 'Fever' punctuated by screeching sirens, a squeaking toy hammer, and odd percussive and vocal effects. 'Dub Organiser' left in enough of Dillinger's toast to salute the greatness of King Tubby as a dub creator, placing emphasis on clicking wooden sticks and rock-solid bass. 'To Be A Lover' was stripped to its drum and bass core for 'Lover's Skank', with Tommy McCook's keyboard springing in to vary the texture. 'Keep On Moving' was dropped down to bass and drum for 'Moving Skank', with enhanced emphasis on cymbals and high-hat, while 'Apeman Skank' reworked 'Caveman Skank' to place bass, drum and percussion at centre stage. 'Jungle Skank' was 'Water Pump' purged of its rude vocals, with only the bassline hinting at its former lasciviousness, and 'Kaya' became 'Kaya Skank' through a fast drum and bass mix that fed in keyboard and guitar at random intervals.

Blackboard Jungle Dub had a continuity that previous Upsetter albums lacked, yielding a sense of wholeness. Dub albums would later find a ready market overseas, its practices slowly filtering into other forms of popular music, but *Blackboard Jungle Dub* shows Perry again as an innovator in his field. The original edition remains a stone-cold classic of the genre and a masterpiece of engineering ingenuity. It also emphasises the highly skilled musicianship of the Upsetters and shows just how creative Perry's approach to rhythm could be.

In the half-decade that had passed since he first became an independent producer, Lee Perry had progressed dramatically. His skills as a hit-maker were renowned in Jamaica, and his unconventional outlook and odd musical sensibilities were already legendary. He was known overall for his experimentation, for fearlessness in the aural realm and for a willingness to try what his peers and competitors would not. But if albums like *Cloak And Dagger*, *Rhythm Shower* and *Blackboard Jungle Dub* seemed bizarre and excessively experimental, they merely pointed to the further innovations that Perry would unleash once his studio was fully operational.

CHAPTER SEVEN

Hurt So Good:
Early Fruits of the Black Ark

The creation of the Black Ark studio initiated a period of optimism and enthusiasm for Lee Perry, allowing greater agency in his work and heightening the sense that he was finally exercising some control over the fulfilment of his destiny. Its location at the home compound made the studio a part of everyday life, enabling him to better tune in to his guiding spirit to channel creative ideas more readily, but the division between work and domestic life was inevitably less defined.

Though recordings were made there in the latter weeks of 1973, the studio was a rudimentary facility and the early works are marked by the limitations of its minimal equipment. Much of the material made use of older rhythm tracks recorded elsewhere to which new vocals and instruments would be overdubbed through the practice of 'bouncing'; as most Jamaican recordings of the 1960s and '70s have the vocals isolated in one channel of the master tape when played on a two-track machine, it was easy to bounce the rhythm track onto one or two tracks of a blank four-track tape and then overdub additional instrumentation or voice onto the remaining tracks.

Perry's studio had an unusual split-level design to make optimum use of limited space. On the ground floor, there was the main recording room for musicians and singers with an adjacent rehearsal room, and just by the front door, a passageway with a short staircase led to a tiny elevated control room, where a large Perspex window allowed Perry to view the proceedings below; as there was no audio link between the two spaces, Perry would pound on the Perspex and shout instructions to the assembled singers and players, running down the stairs when really necessary – a situation that would remain constant throughout all its years of operation.

At this point, Perry had a quarter-inch four-track Teac 3340 for the recording of new material and a quarter-inch two-track Teac, fed through a Teac AX-300 line mixer, on which to mix down. He had the Alice board, a Marantz amplifier and speaker for guitar or keyboard use and the small drum kit, placed on a riser. Short of microphones, he initially tried using an AKG drum mike to voice, without much success. There was a Grampian spring reverb unit that used a tensed reverberating spring to generate sonic reflection, providing the illusion of greater dimensional space, and, according to Perry, an Echoplex tape echo that allowed instruments or voice to be subjected to echoes of different length and speed, each of which would significantly impact the sound once the studio was fully operational. A copy of the Bible was another permanent fixture to consecrate the studio as holy ground, as well as being a ready source for missing lyrics.

The studio wiring was installed by Errol Thompson, but Perry said he alone could make it function.

'Errol Thompson, who build the studio, can't do nothing in there. Even the great Tubby come in there and don't know what to do.'

There was a Vox Continental organ, known for its thinner sound, and an Italian-made Elkapiano 88, a fairly new model on the market that had clavichord, steel guitar and 'jingle piano' settings, as well as a standard electric piano preset, which could be used independently or in different combinations; if checking for the sound of the early Black Ark, the inexpensive keyboards and an overamplified kick drum with a squeaky hinge are often the most obvious giveaways, especially when the Elka was in clavichord mode.

The world oil crisis brought on by conflict in the Middle East drastically increased the cost of vinyl, making a further drain on Perry's limited finances, so the reuse of old rhythms helped reduce overheads, the practice especially handy during the slow months of December and January that were affected by the Christmas and New Year holiday period, though 'version' always held a fascination that went far beyond mere economics.

Early in 1974, a new label design for Black Art reminded that the name represented more than just the celebration of African-Jamaican creativity, for now a scowling, hooded figure lurked behind stylised blood-red lettering, again suggesting the black art of Obeah, as alluded to on the early Upsetter and Upset designs.

Some say Perry was involved in Obeah, though the accusations are vague and contradictory. It is claimed that he visited the Revivalist preacher and intuitive artist Mallica 'Kapo' Reynolds at his home in Waterhouse, the artist's work supposedly indicative of Obeah practice, though the allegations against Reynolds are questionable. There are alternate suggestions that Perry regularly visited an Obeah man based on a backstreet near Bob Marley's uptown headquarters at 56 Hope Road, or another somewhere in St Thomas, and others claim Perry was even practising it himself, with one colleague suggesting he painted his Jaguar purple – a colour associated with Obeah – to demonstrate the fact. Some of those closest to Perry claimed that Val Bennett first introduced him to an Obeah man in the late 1960s and that the meeting marked the start of all of Perry's problems, though others say he, like Duke Reid, wanted to cultivate the myth to ward off enemies and potential foes.

Yet, ultimately, the label's symbolic equation of Black Art with Obeah made a mockery of mainstream Jamaica's perception of the Rastafari as 'Black Heart men', subverting the notion that followers of the faith were godless Devil worshippers who performed human sacrifices, and Perry has always denied involvement in Obeah himself.

'The whole of them things them say, like me deal with Obeah, that cannot be true because how could I deal with good *and* evil?' said Perry. 'I never have no contact with Obeah man, the person who say that are a goddamned liar. The only people I have contact with is righteous, spiritual people who know about God. Me want to know about things that happen in Africa, long time before we reach Jamaica, not idiot Obeah man, for me no need curse.'

In later years, he would speak of his music as part of a magical process, naming his creations as the only 'science' he employs: 'I don't have no other Obeah but the music.'

Perry has also given many contradictory statements regarding why he named his studio the Black Ark. Sometimes symbolically likened to the Ark of the Covenant that housed the Ten Commandments, though the appellation was transposed by Perry to describe the Ark of the biblical Flood, it was conceived as as a sanctuary for Black Rastafari and an antidote to the Caucasian myth of Noah's Ark, a place where joyful music could be made unto the Lord on unmitigated terms.

'The Ark itself is like some heroism, some mystic and mystery of the prophecy about the Ark that save some people,' said Perry. 'So at that time, me did see it like how the dread them see it, like I and I know we are Black, so I said, the Ark is the saviour, and the message was, we're going to save all the people who Black.'

At the new studio, Perry began using the talents of the bassist and musical arranger Boris Gardiner, a gifted bandleader and session musician who was equally adept at cover tunes and original material, and who would play an increasingly important role in Perry's productions.

One of the first groups to record at the space was harmony quartet Time Unlimited, formed in nearby Duhaney Park in 1972. Brought for an audition by future producer Trevor 'Leggo Beast' Douglas and his friend Vill, the group was comprised of lead singer Junior Delgado (Oscar Hibbert Junior, nephew of vibraphonist Lennie Hibbert, who was bandleader at Alpha), with harmony singers Orville Smith, Hugh Marshall and Glasford Manning, whose brothers were in the Abyssinians and Carlton and the Shoes.

'The first song I sang was "Why Did She Cry", we play it R&B style,' said Delgado. 'Then I sing "Warrior No Tarry Yah", he was the first person I record that song for, but it didn't release, and Glasford Manning sing "African Sound". When we do the audition, Scratch wanted to record us right there, same night, because he's a genius. In the morning, we turn up early with our guitars and well-polished voice because in those days they have to hear talent. You're facing the mastermind like Upsetter.'

According to Delgado, Perry worked closely with the group for some considerable time, coaching their vocal deliveries and changing their overall sound, just as he had done with the Wailers.

'Scratch taught me how he want me to sing the songs because I used to have a more R&B type of singing, and he changed that. I was kind of polished and he want me to do this native singing.'

'Reaction', co-written by Delgado and Smith, had a deceptive pop arrangement with soaring soul harmonies, complimented by Wire Lindo's curious keyboard melody, but Delgado sang of the harshness of ghetto life. It was one of a few early Black Ark creations issued on Joe Gibbs' Reflections label, another being Gregory Isaacs' middling cover of Skeeter Davis' 'End Of The World', mixed with an overly loud horn section.

Time Unlimited's more unfettered 'African Sound' had a wild vocal arrangement that fit its repatriation subject, again with an unusual keyboard accompaniment, but for reasons not entirely clear, the song was issued on Upsetter bearing the labels of Leo Graham's 'Black Candle', rendering it unduly obscure.

'23rd Psalm' was an alternate of 'Reaction', with Manning speaking portions of its verses and Delgado singing them after, but this song did not surface for some considerable time and the bulk of their Black Ark recordings were held back, causing the group to begin working with Rupie Edwards, the song 'Rasta Dreadlocks' issued under an alias.

'Scratch have some real wicked songs, over two albums' worth,' said Delgado. 'I can remember "No Need To Buy A Newspaper Anymore", Boris Gardiner wrote that one, and I can remember "Lying Lips". People really admired Time Unlimited, and we couldn't leave Scratch at that time. If we even want to go and do a song, it would get some argument, so we decided to record for Rupie, and on one song they put the Heavenly Singers because they don't want Scratch to know it's Time Unlimited.'

In late December 1973, Chris Lane of *Blues & Soul* came to stay at Cardiff Crescent, Perry having extended an invitation when the pair met in London in July, but a lack of street signs in Washington Gardens made it difficult to locate Perry's place in the dark, so after spending a costly night at an uptown hotel, Lane went down to Orange Street to enlist Bunny Lee's help in reaching Perry, Lee drafting his production assistant, Rodguel 'Blackbeard' Sinclair, to smooth rocky relations.

'What I didn't realise was they were at war,' said Lane. 'They'd fallen out big time. Bunny Lee had just taken me out and fed me, taken me around town and introduced me to a few faces, then he's taken me up to Scratch's and he won't come in the house. Pauline's slagging him off something terrible, they were all having a row. Blackbeard came in with me to act as mediator between Scratch and Bunny Lee because Bunny Lee wanted his microphones back that he'd lent Lee Perry and I'm caught up in the middle of all this, but by the time I'd left Jamaica they were the best of friends again.'

Arriving just before his eighteenth birthday, Lane stayed at the Perry household for about a month, witnessing the voicing of some of the earliest material to emerge from the Ark, most of it marked by minimal instrumentation,

The release of the moment was Leo Graham's 'Black Candle', which reportedly sold 15,000 copies in Jamaica, its popularity triggering further cuts on the rhythm, including Graham's alternate vocal 'Doctor Demand' (aka 'Doctor Demon' or 'Pampas Judas'), with hefty doses of reverb, wah-wah guitar from Chinna Smith, an uncredited toast from Prince Jazzbo, and characteristic keyboard overdubs.

Bob Marley turned up one afternoon with Bunny Wailer to sink a few beers and soak up the vibes, voicing another alternate on the rhythm as 'Keep On Skanking', co-written by

Lane, and returning the next day to record the improvised 'Turn Me Loose' on the 'Kaya' rhythm.

'They seemed like good mates,' said Lane, of Marley and Perry. 'They definitely had something, you could see there was a little spark between them, and I didn't see that between Scratch and Bunny. Bunny Wailer was sitting in the corner, smoking this little pipe, looking miserable.'

During Lane's visit, Delroy Denton voiced the spiritual 'Give Thanks' (credited on release to Delroy Butler, after Jerry Butler of the Impressions), one of the last songs he recorded before emigrating. Perry dug up an old rhythm to suit the lyrics and had Ansel Collins and Horsemouth blow melodica riffs, before Horsemouth voiced an impromptu toast for the 'Herb Vendor' B-side, a relaxed rap about his dealer's super-strength weed, though Lane said Perry was smoking herb infrequently himself.

'He said now and again he'd stop smoking for months, and I think he'd just done three months without it. He was smoking some, but not continually.'

'He used to smoke a lot of cigarettes,' said P-Son. 'I think Pauline is the one who smoke lots of herbs.'

A couple of other Prince Jazzbo tracks were voiced around the same time, ostensibly because Lane requested an interview, though Perry was motivated to work with the toaster because of the lasting success of his breakthrough hit, 'Crab Walking', recorded for Studio One in 1972.

'Me know Lee Perry from me a little boy and me was a street boy,' said Jazzbo, born Linval Carty. 'Me have parents, but they call them rude boy them time there. Him just see me one day and respect me because them big man there love youth, so as a youth where at Coxsone's studio I mash up the place, him just say, "Jazzbo, I want you to come do something for me."'

Jazzbo's 'Penny Reel' was a slow-motion reworking of a bawdy folk tune laid on the 'Hail Stone' rhythm, embellished by melodica and percussion overdubs, while 'Good Things' was a cut of 'Retail Love', Jazzbo warning listeners to disregard Dennis Alcapone's message of dancehall ribaldry and go to school instead, though his toast peters out halfway through.

Leo Graham's 'We Have Got A Date' (aka 'Jump It') also made use of 'Retail Love' for a smooth love song with a prominent wooden fish emphasising the sensuality of the lyrics. It was issued as a limited edition single on Graham's short-lived label, Blue Jay, which also handled rude number 'Greedy Gal'.

During Lane's visit, the song shaking up Jamaica was Delroy Wilson's 'Have Some Mercy', which aspiring producer Ainsley Folder had voiced on the rhythm of 'To Be A Lover', having gotten a cut from Niney, and it became a longstanding favourite in Britain too. As the hit edged closer to the Jamaican top ten, which it would permeate in April, Perry revisited the original rhythm for a new version of 'To Be A Lover' with Earl George (born Earl George Lawrence), a singer from Rae Town in southeast Kingston who was known for soul and rhythm and blues covers. George had entered into self-production from premises on Charles Street in 1973, but his rendition of the Temptations' 'Gonna Give Her All The Love I Got' was issued in London without his permission, so eventually, he agreed to record for Perry.

'When I had my little thing going down by Charles Street, he checked me there and asked me to do some work with him, but I didn't begin working with him right away,' said George. 'It was about a year or two after, and first with Lee Perry I did "To Be A Lover" as George Earl.'

Though his deep tenor had plenty of soul, and despite the addition of a prominent keyboard overdub, this attempt at 'To

Be A Lover' made little impact. Instead, 'Have Some Mercy' continued to reign, spawning Folder's further cuts with Big Youth, Augustus Pablo and Tommy McCook.

As rivalries mounted, Perry voiced some playful material aimed at competitors who had versioned his rhythms. For instance, Augustus Pablo recreated 'Dub Organiser' with Family Man and Tin Legs for Clive Chin at Randy's, leading Perry to voice the dub plate 'The Rightful Organiser', taunting Pablo as a miser and Chin as a blood-sucking vampire for copying his tune – all stated in jest, though the sting of the lyrics betrayed the bitterness.

Clancy Eccles also cut the folksy 'Mi Muma Yard' at the Ark with the Barrett brothers, Lloyd 'Gitsy' Willis, Gladdy Anderson and percussionist Larry McDonald, and although Rupie Edwards sensed a hit and offered a significant sum to release it, Clancy left it unissued for decades.

Meanwhile, Perry's record salesman Pat Francis began recording deejay tunes as Jah Lloyd (using his middle name), taking inspiration from Perry's deejay productions.

'One day I hear a song on the Bob Marley "Keep On Moving" rhythm and Big Youth do the toasting, and Dillinger do a few songs like "Bring The Kuchy Come",' said Francis. 'When I hear them voice, I say, "Looks like I could deejay instead of sing now" because I sound like Big Youth too.'

'That was one of the best deejays in Jamaica,' said Perry. 'Him look simple and was really a little lion. He had the best deejay voice so far. Better than Jazzbo, better than Big Youth, better than all of them. He used to sell records for me and want to deejay, and when me listen, the voice was sounding very, very good.'

Francis launched a label called Teem with his brother Vincent, which was based at the Upsetter Record Shop, beginning with some recuts of Bill Withers' 'Ain't No Sunshine' following Ken Boothe's popular cover version; Pauline wanted to licence 'Sunshine Girl' as an Upsetter single, but Francis issued it himself, along with related instrumentals.

When Perry voiced Francis' 'The Lama' (aka 'Flashing Whip'), a portentous cut of 'Kentucky Skank', Francis opted for a cut of 'To Be A Lover' as payment, voicing the popular 'Soldier Round The Corner' on it to comment on the increased presence of soldiers in the street during curfews aimed at curtailing gun violence. Further Jah Lloyd cuts included 'Zion Gate', 'Ganja Crop' and courtroom drama 'Judge Natty', as well as his vocal cover, credited to Jah Ali.

Perry was also collaborating more concretely with Winston Blake of Merritone sound system, now running the Turntable Club on Red Hills Road, which was such a hip spot that Marvin Gaye would make a guest appearance there in May 1974, though Blake's creative collaboration with Perry failed to achieve much commercial success.

'Lee Perry used to produce and sing for Coxsone and I met him through that, but our friendship didn't blossom at that time,' said Blake. 'When I really became close to Lee Perry was in the '60s, when we become so popular that we were the musical statement for the whole middle class and everybody wanted Merritone. When Scratch used to operate downtown at Charles Street, my aunt used to run a business in front of him, that was a little after the Tuff Gong period, when everybody knew of my work. If you wanted to get a record to hit, you knew that Merritone was a showplace. I used to go to his shop and get anything I want, so we developed a working relationship there and became friends.'

In the spring of 1974, Blake issued a four-song EP on his The Turntable label, with instrumental mixes of 'Cloak And

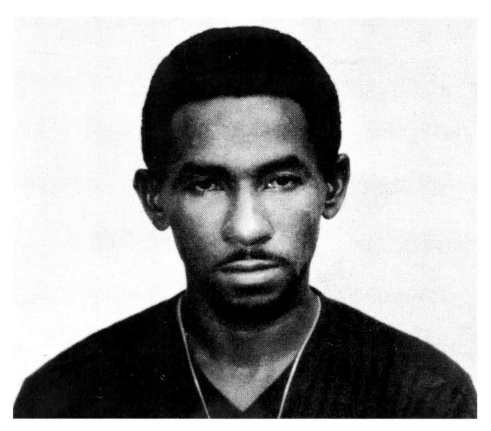

WIRL publicity photo, circa 1968

The Upsetters at Randy's studio, 1969 (L to R: Aston 'Family Man' Barrett, Carlton 'Carly' Barrett, Alva 'Reggie' Lewis, Glen 'Capo' Adams)

Return of Django

Written by LEE PERRY

LEE PERRY leader of The Upsetters

TROJAN

ISLAND-B & C MUSIC LIMITED,
REMO HOUSE, 310/312 Regent Street. London, W.1. 3/-
sole selling agents:
SOUTHERN MUSIC PUBLISHING CO., LTD. 8 Denmark Street. London W.C.2.

Publicity photo, 1969

Above: *Cloak And Dagger* LP cover, with Pauline Morrison

Left: Photomontage from the home of Perry's mother, Ina Blythe. Main photo: publicity still, circa 1972; photo strip: publicity stills taken in London, 1987; small centre photo: Ina Blythe (centre), her sister (right) and daughter Lorna 'Miss Nell' Blythe (left)

Inside the Black Ark with the Alice mixing desk, circa 1974

Bob Marley at the Black Ark, January 1974

Above: Inside the Black Ark with Max Romeo and friend, 1975

Left: Outside the Black Ark, 1975

Outside the Black Ark with Max Romeo (left, in white), Clancy Eccles (right) and Earl 'Chinna' Smith (with guitar), 1975

Above: With Omar and Marsha, 1977

Left: Outside the Black Ark, 1977

Below: Inside the Black Ark, 1977

With Omar, 1977

Left: Outside the Black Ark, 1978

Below: The Black Ark players, circa 1978, including Herman Marquis, Richard 'Dirty Harry' Hall, Lee Perry, Errol 'Tarzan' Nelson, Boris Gardiner, 'Deadly' Headley Bennett, Winston Wright, Robert 'Billy' Johnson, George Faith, Junior Murvin and Cedric Myton

Left: George Faith, Sean and Omar, 1978

Below: With Seke Molenga and Kalo Kawongolo, 1978

Above and left: Pipecock Jackson, 1979

Black Ark graffiti, 1979

Dagger', 'Jungle Lion', 'Caveman Skank' and a version of 'Rude Walking' titled 'Table Turning', evidencing the collaborative works that were happening organically.

'He moved into Washington Gardens with his family, and we became very, very close. I'd be in the studio and while nothing was going on, we'd do little things together, fooling around. Lee Perry is one of the most brilliant minds in terms of percussive productions, he could put things in productions and really excite it – he was really a master at that. How those records came is that we had the rhythms and people would come up with their different experimentations, so we would be in the studio and he would say, "Winston, try this", and we would produce. Some of the stuff we did, we'd just put it on a track and then we'd just put that track out.'

Credited to Judge Winchester, 'Public Jestering' was a courtroom drama on the 'Rude Walking' rhythm, in which the harsh judge sentences Sylvester the Public Jesterer from Manchester and his son Chester (both played by Perry) to indefinite detention for being disrespectful, continuing the 'Judge Dread' tradition that laid bare the inability of harsh sentences to deter violent crime, pointing to the social injustice that was at the root of delinquency.

In March 1974, Michael Manley introduced two brutal acts of repression in the face of escalating gun violence: the Suppression of Crime Act and the Gun Court Act. The former granted the security forces new powers to arrest and detain, the latter saw the notorious Gun Court established on Kingston's South Camp Road, where those caught with an unlicenced firearm or even the shell of a bullet could be sentenced to indefinite detention with hard labour through trials that took place without a jury – draconian measures from a Leftist champion of human rights, and, when objections were raised by the British Privy Council, which holds the final say in Jamaican legal matters, the maximum sentence was changed to mandatory life behind bars.

The B-side of the single, 'Darkness On The City', was a grim slice of social realism voiced on the 'Sokup' rhythm, begging an end to the senseless violence that saw neighbours and even family members killing each other in the street. Also credited to Judge Winchester, it was sung by Jimmy Riley, who went on to record a spate of singles for Perry in 1975.

Blake also had a hand in some of the new rhythms Perry began building at the Ark, including Junior Byles' light-hearted 'Mumbling And Grumbling' and the Versatiles' take of Peter Tosh's 'Stepping Razor' (retitled 'Cutting Razor'), issued with Perry's surreal 'Black Belt Jones' on the flip, the rhythm now laden with karate grunts and whistling in homage to the Black martial arts movie hero. There was a reworking of Barbara Acklin's soul hit 'Lady, Lady, Lady' with Cynthia Webber (credited to Cynty and the Monkees), which spawned Perry's 'Enter The Dragon', another karate-themed dub cut, and upcoming singer Joy White voiced an alternate vocal take of Acklin's hit too.

In late May 1974, Perry and Blake were appointed to the assessing panel for entries to the Festival Song Competition, and although Blake had high hopes for the material he backed with Perry, the production partnership faded when the releases failed to reach very far.

'When he broke up with Bob he was going through a lot of trauma,' said Blake. 'A lot of stuff I did with him, I just give him some money as his friend. He's my brethren, so I helped him regardless, expecting nothing in return. With all good intentions, he said, "Winston, if things happen, me and you are brethren and brethren . . ." It just so happened that nothing really big happened in that time.'

Decorating the walls of his studio with blacklight kung-fu posters, album sleeves, artist photographs and some topless pics from girlie magazines, Perry continued working with unknown talent and established hitmakers, as well as voicing the odd track himself. There was a recut of the Versatiles' 'The Thanks We Get' issued on a blank label pre-release, with a xylophone version on the flip; 'Rebel's Train' was Perry's funky reggae take of MFSB's 'TSOP' (the *Soul Train* theme song), with chugging electric piano chords, a slide whistle and percussive effects all emphasising the railroad reference; a one-off single with the Ethiopians, 'Life Is A Funny Thing', explored life's cyclical nature, with the B-side, 'Prophecy', relating biblical wonders in visionary terms.

Watty Burnett was a regular presence at the studio, playing percussion on sessions and suggesting basslines for whichever player Perry was using at the time, and as his friendship with Perry strengthened, under the name King Burnett he recorded 'Babylon A Fall' about the victimisation of Rastafari, and later 'I Man Free', notable for its use of a roaring siren, contrasted by a trilling flute.

'We just sing all day, and I didn't even go home,' said Burnett. 'Junior Byles and I sleep in the studio – it's like we lived there. I'm with Scratch from around fourteen years old, so he's like my daddy.'

Other producers and artists were using the Black Ark for their own work too, sometimes with dazzling results. For instance, Doctor Alimantado recorded the dejected deejay piece 'Just The Other Day' on a cut of the Flames' 'Zion', lamenting Jamaica's rampant inflation, and the sung vocal 'Ride On', credited to Ital Winston, called for love and unity atop a particularly durable rhythm with wah-wah guitar, a bright horn line and a prominent wooden fish, the distinctive keyboard echoing a refrain from Barry White's 'I'm Gonna Love You Just A Little More Baby'.

The printer and record producer Lloyd F. Campbell, who supplied many of the record labels used by Perry and other producers at his premises at 135 Orange Street, produced Keeling Beckford's 'Samfy Girl' for his The Thing label, riding an odd recut of Busty Brown's 'You Inspire Me'.

Little Roy also began working at the Black Ark with Maurice 'Scorcher' Jackson and his brother Melvin 'Munchie' Jackson, who were also based in Washington Gardens, for material issued on the Tafari and Earth labels, as well as Munchie's Aires label in New York.

'I started Tafari with Scorcher and the first song that we did was "Prophecy",' said Little Roy. 'The rhythm was laid at Harry J's studio by Blacka Morwell, who sold us the rhythm, and Upsetter was the one who engineered my voice at Randy's, before Black Ark was running.'

In early 1974, Little Roy recorded 'Tribal War', a signature tune celebrating the peace treaty brokered between warring politically aligned gangs in east Kingston.

'It was the end of some war that usually be carrying on over east. It reach a time when the brethren say them stop the war and it came out in the newspaper, so it give me the idea. Dennis Brown played bass, Horsemouth played the drums, Pablove Black played keyboards and Roy Hamilton, a guitarist that usually be amongst Upsetters then, he played the guitar, and this song was between me and Munchie.'

Recorded at the same session, 'Black Bird' used a predatory metaphor to describe the European pillaging of Africa, here with Reggie Lewis on bass.

Munchie was affiliated with Bullwackie's Disco, a pioneering sound system established in the Bronx by Lloyd Barnes, a former Trench Town resident who recorded for Prince Buster in the ska years and who ultimately became one of the most important producers of reggae in America; Aires became a subsidiary of his Wackies label and Munchie took cuts of Perry's older rhythms to reuse for new Aires releases. There was the Heptones' powerful 'Revolution', which was voiced on 'Tight Spot' at a studio Winston Blake ran on Hagley Park Road, and deejay Jah Vill's pedestrian 'The Bump', voiced on 'Stand By Me', and more rhythms surfaced on the *Tribal War* album, released on Tafari in 1975, but Little Roy said the album was unfinished.

'Most of the songs on that LP was some rehearsals that we used to have in a packing house. If you notice, most of the songs don't sound that clean. Upsetters gave Munchie some rhythms and I'm rehearsing them in the packing house, so I don't even count that as an album.'

Both Munchie Jackson and Bullwackie would become important allies in New York, but now there were changes on the UK reggae scene that added to Perry's frustration: Trojan executives were being vague about the future of the company and it eventually became clear that the label was experiencing financial problems, while Pama had serious issues of their own after Harry Palmer returned to Jamaica to become a preacher and real estate agent, leaving brother Carl to take the reins.

With his ordinary British outlets seemingly blocked, Perry was now fielding his output through Larry Lawrence's Kilburn-based Ethnic label, distributed by EMI through Creole, beginning with Perry's 'Fist Of Fury', voiced on the 'Sokup' rhythm, issued with Jah Lloyd's fearsome deejay cut of 'Kentucky Skank' titled 'Spiritual Whip' (released as 'The Lama' in Jamaica), Perry bringing the master tapes to London to cut the stampers. 'To Be A Lover', 'Pampas Judas' and 'Mumbling And Grumbling' followed, while 'Give Thanks' was issued on Fight, Lawrence's independent imprint, and later material would surface on Ethnic Fight, launched when Lawrence broke with Creole.

Perry also voiced some slack stuff for Lawrence at Chalk Farm, using the rhythm of John Holt's 'My Heart Is Gone', which London-based Tony Sexton had covered for Lawrence. There was Jah Martin's deejay cut 'Kung Fu', and for the B-side (titled 'Part 2') Perry voiced a rude duet with an anonymous childminder from the Philippines, who rebuffed his sleazy pleas in no uncertain terms in her native Ilocano: 'I want to go home, they are going to look for me. I am going to die of shyness, I am shy in front of Mrs Brown. Don't be like that, I really don't like you. Even if you beg for it, I will go home. I don't like you, you aren't handsome, take me home! Even if you marry me, I don't like you!'

'Me and Scratch would always go way out to find different people to do different things,' said Lawrence. 'This girl, she don't know nothing about recording studio. Somebody introduce us to her at Chalk Farm studio and Scratch says, "Why don't we record her?" I put on "My Heart Is Gone" cos we were putting some horns on it with Vin Gordon, and Lee Perry was speaking to her and she was answering him with her language. Then I done another vocal with him and an English girl on the same track, we call it "69". It's Scratch speaking to her in a sexy voice, they're making love on the rhythm in other words.'

Joe Gibbs' cousin, Winston Edwards, was also working at Perry's studio during this phase. In the mid-1960s, Edwards was running the family hardware store on Beeston Street when Gibbs returned from Guantanamo Bay and opened his record shop a few doors down; Edwards' secret ambition was to become the JLP candidate for West Portland, where he hailed from, but as Gibbs began producing records with Perry's assistance, Edwards was intrigued.

'Scratch was a friend even when I was not involved in the music industry,' said Edwards. 'Scratch and Mr Gibson were very close friends because in those days Gibson wasn't the producer, Scratch was more or less the producer, as he would come around and lend his talent to Gibson, so I know Scratch from those days, but I really get involved with Scratch when I came to England.'

Edwards joined his parents in London in the late 1960s but spent most of the early '70s back in Kingston. By early 1974, he was preparing to emigrate permanently to further his education, making his first serious stab at record production in conjunction with Perry before he left, recording a rendition of Ben E. King's 'Don't Play That Song' with Dennis Walks at the Black Ark, leaving Perry to manage the production himself.

'I was not a producer then, I was the executive producer and Lee Perry was the man. I said, "I want this thing to be so and so and so", and he said, "Don't worry about it, I'll get some of the guys." I think it was Lloyd Parks, Geoffrey Chung and Gitsy.'

When Edwards returned to England to finish his A-levels, he issued the song on his Stop Point label, based in New Cross, southeast London, where he would later establish the Joe Gibbs Record Shop and distribution service. Although the song was not a strong seller, Edwards could see the potential for earnings and arranged to record more material in Jamaica, which he would issue on Fay Music, named after a girlfriend, licencing Leo Graham's 'Greedy Gal' for one of the first singles.

'I said to myself, the easiest way to do my A-levels was to continue in the music business, so I travelled back to Jamaica and had one or two recording sessions in Joe Gibbs' studio, but the atmosphere at Joe Gibbs' was not the one I like, though I could have had the studio time for nothing, and Scratch also gave me a lot of studio time for nothing too because of the connection with myself and Joe Gibbs, but the atmosphere of Scratch's was much more what I really liked. Joe Gibbs' studio was powerful. It was a bigger studio, it had a lot of sounds, it was probably even more equipped, but I wanted to record at Scratch's because the man was creative himself. I realised that he was more like twenty-four tracks going around, even if his studio was only four tracks at the time! I felt at all times he would assist me to give me that twenty-four tracks pleasure. So although Errol Thompson at Joe Gibbs' was again like a member of the family, Scratch was more like an uncle teaching a nephew, so I love the man. Upsetter's studio was more like a unique little place: when you go there, you're trying out things and the ideas was always coming.'

With Edwards between London and Kingston, much of his Black Ark work remained obscure. There was the broken-hearted 'Just Been Feeling Bad' by Tony Brevett of the Melodians, with an overpowering organ between its verses, Shelton Walker's mediocre cover of Patti Page's 'One Of Us (Will Weep Tonight)', 'Jah Jah De Pan Dem', a Rasta update of Hugh Godfrey's rude boy tune by one Sydney Smith, and a robust love song called 'You Are So Real', credited to Euslin Gregory and released on Fay Music in Jamaica in February 1975; U Roy's protégé, U Brown, would later voice deejay cuts on some of these rhythms at King Tubby's studio.

Dub cuts of 'Don't Play That Song' and 'Jah Jah De Pan Dem' appeared on Edwards' *Natty Locks Dub* in late 1974, an LP that straddled the divide between dub and instrumental jazz. It used diverse rhythm tracks, some supplied by Tony Brevett, some laid at Joe Gibbs' studio and others at the Black

Ark, with some voicing and remixing undertaken at Tubby's, and horn overdubs were later made at London's Berry Street studio with trumpeter Michael 'Bammie' Rose and a saxophonist named Brown.

Lloyd Brevett's presence at the Black Ark with Ras Michael and the Sons of Negus resulted in some intense self-produced work around the same time, as heard on the devotional 'Star Light'. Sonia Pottinger also began working on a Melodians album with Perry at the Ark, recording 'Survival Is The Game', 'Nuh Go Long So', 'Better Days Are Coming', 'Dry Up Your Tears' and recutting Tony Brevett's 'Don't Get Weary', but financial issues caused the project to falter, so the songs would be issued overseas without the group's knowledge as *Pre-Meditation* in 1978, padded out by earlier work.

'She was down there in the studio with Lee Perry and at that time she and Perry was really together,' said lead Melodian, Brent Dowe. 'They were grounded, but after we did all those songs for her, there was a breakup. We left because it wasn't too financially strong, and we didn't know that she would put out that album.'

Using the same rhythm as Dowe's original, Marcia Griffiths voiced an alternate 'Survival Is The Game' for Pottinger, which became a popular High Note single in 1975.

For his own productions, Perry was still recording with the Silvertones, their 'Financial Crisis' very topical and on point; Perry's 'Kill The Music', which drew on the children's ring game song 'Emmanuel Road', benefitted from their harmonies, as did his lewd alternate 'Dub The Pum Pum', saluting a woman's private parts in slang.

Perry's abstract scat vocal 'Kiss Me Neck' had startling phased horns (sadly missing on the Attack pressing issued by Trojan), the B-side another zany scat titled 'Da Ba Da'. It was the first of his singles handled by Micron Music, a record distribution service established by Pete Weston, Ronnie Burke and Mike Johnson, the latter distantly related to the family behind the Johnson and Johnson cosmetics company, with Winston Blake another early partner.

Upcoming singer Linval Thompson's 'Kung Fu Man' brought the obsession with martial arts into focus again, the lyrics referencing 'Fu Kung' in a typical Perry reversal. The singer had recently returned to Jamaica from New York and was brought to the Ark by Phil Pratt to record his Jamaican debut, 'Girl You've Got To Run', after Pratt discovered him outside Randy's at the area known as Idler's Rest; Roman Stewart's foreboding 'Fire At Your Heel' (aka 'Run Come Feel') was captured on tape at the same session.

Pratt had first used the Black Ark some weeks earlier to record Al Campbell, another singer whose delivery held a precursor of the dancehall style. Based at Three Mile, an industrial section of west Kingston along Spanish Town Road, Campbell had been active with the Thrillers and a number of other vocal groups at Studio One before recording for Pratt, the captivating 'Where Were You', engineered by Perry at the Black Ark, being one of the first.

'It is a true story,' said Campbell. 'I had this girlfriend, we broke up and she was coming back, and that session was good because Phil Pratt sing harmony on it.'

Pratt said Perry modulated the guitar on Campbell's hit by routing it through a four-band equaliser, resulting in another marked difference, but it was Pratt's use of lesser-known session musicians that partly contributed to the distinctive sound of his Black Ark recordings, overseen by the keyboardist and arranger Bobby Kalphat, who also blew melodica on the song; other players included underrated drummer Fish Clarke and future Gorillaz bassist Sydney Gussine (alias Junior Dan).

Phil Pratt enjoyed considerable local success with material he cut at the Ark, and 'Where Were You' impacted in England, but Lee Perry was still clamouring for a hit of his own, which ultimately came from unexpected quarters.

Controversial soul singer Millie Jackson's 'Hurt So Good' reached the Jamaican top ten in April 1974 following its appearance in the blaxploitation flick *Cleopatra Jones*, prompting Perry to cover it; written by the singer-songwriter Phillip Mitchell, the ambiguous love song that hinted at masochism was first recorded by Muscle Shoals act Katie Love and the Four Shades of Black, without success.

Perry built the rhythm of his rendition with Boris Gardiner, drummer Paul Douglas and guitarist Dougie Bryan, and from the Zap Pow band, trumpeter David Madden and saxophonist Glen DaCosta. Joy White tried voicing it but Perry was displeased by the result, so the rhythm languished for a time, until Anne Cadogan arrived.

Cadogan's father Claude was a prominent Methodist minister from Belize, where Cadogan spent part of her childhood, and after her parents moved to Antigua in 1970, her father became president of the Conference of the Methodist Church in the Caribbean and Americas, while she remained in Jamaica working as a librarian at the University of the West Indies. Although long inspired by the Platters, the Supremes and Ben E. King, she never considered singing professionally until a schoolfriend that worked as a record librarian at JBC brought her to the Black Ark.

'I had a friend named Theresa Bryan, and her boyfriend, Jerry Lewis, was this disc jockey at JBC,' said Cadogan. 'He asked her to sing this song he had written called "Love My Life", so she said, "Ask Anne because Anne loves to sing", so both of us were to do it. One Sunday we went down there and in the end I sang Jerry's song myself alone, and Jerry played some of the instruments. When I finished voicing, Lee Scratch said, "Jerry, lend me your singer now?" He didn't even know my name.'

Perry felt Joy White's delivery was not sensual enough, but Cadogan sang 'Hurt So Good' just as he wanted, in a sultry, suggestive voice that retained a slight hint of innocence, captured on tape in just one take.

'After I sang "Hurt So Good", he said, "What's your name, Anne? No, man! You mean *Susan*, that sound sexy!" Then he said he wanted me to try some other songs. He gave me some tapes to learn, and I took them home.'

Cadogan returned to the Ark the following Sunday and every subsequent Sunday for the next few months, so by Christmas they had recorded over a dozen songs with Benbow Creary and Ansel Collins, sometimes assisted by the visiting Glen Adams, with whom she became romantically involved.

'Hurt So Good' avoided undue tawdriness though a sublime musical arrangement that made the most of the reconfigured rhythm and original horn parts. Cadogan emulated the drawl of a southern soul singer, and harmony from the Mighty Diamonds made the production more well-rounded, the group having been championed by Pat Francis.

'It was the first harmony for Perry and the first harmony we did 'pon a music, but we did start do harmony before we start doing any recording of our own,' said lead Diamond, Donald 'Tabby' Shaw. 'With Lee Perry, it was like a music college, and me glad to go through those vibes there with him because me learn 'nuff things towards the music.'

'Hurt So Good' was released in Jamaica to little fanfare. Cadogan suggested that Jamaican radio stations avoided playing it because Clement Dodd was promoting Elaine Montague's rendition at the same time, relegating Cadogan's superior effort to a batch of Perry productions that did not command the attention they deserved.

The other releases included the Diamonds' 'Talk About It', a song of unrequited love that showcased their fine harmonies, issued on some pressings with an absurd choral chant from Omar and Marsha on the B-side, titled 'Yama Khy', which became the platform for a further scat-vocal toasting cut by U Roy. There was a follow-up single from Cadogan, too, this time a slow reggae version of Doris Duke's 'Congratulations Baby', led by Glen Adams' keyboard, which was issued on Buttercup, another short-lived label backed by Cecil Ramanand. Buttercup also released a Perry-produced single by the Twinkle Brothers, an upcoming group from Falmouth on Jamaica's north coast that had been working with Bunny Lee, namely the soul-influenced 'Pretty Baby', backed by the censorious 'Woman And Money', both using rhythm tracks that Perry cut with the Cimarons and Greyhound at Chalk Farm.

None of this material achieved much by way of sales in Jamaica, least of all 'Hurt So Good', but pre-release copies delivered to Larry Lawrence saw an enthusiastic response in London in the summer of 1974, particularly at the Notting Hill Carnival, the annual celebration of Caribbean culture held at the end of August. Lawrence thus prepared to release the record, until Perry licenced it to a rival company.

'He phoned me and says Boris Gardiner has arranged it and it sounds good, so he send me up 2,000 copies of it, I play it and distribute it through the Carnival,' said Lawrence. 'Then I went to press the record, got the label printed, stamper and everything, and then he sold it to Dip, so I wipe it from my catalogue and then it goes on to be a hit record. That's not to say that I'm upset with him or anything – that's just business. Maybe the guy's offered him some money and I was giving him royalties, so maybe he needed to take the advance.'

Dip was established in southeast London by Clarendon native Dennis Harris, with assistance from Winston Edwards, who brought Harris back to Jamaica in 1974 in the hopes of making Dip an outlet for Joe Gibbs' product, but according to Edwards, Gibbs was mistrustful of Harris, who began working with Perry instead.

'Dip was trying to launch himself in the music industry, trying to get some records and labels to start signing up, and we both were living in southeast London. I was doing some work for Dip part-time and both myself and Dip went down to Jamaica. At that time, Joe Gibbs more or less appointed me to represent him in England, but somewhere down the line, Gibson did not hit it off with Dip. Dennis Harris was a highly intelligent man, very articulate. He's an old student of Clarendon College and went to Manchester University. Dennis was an engineer, very clever academically, and Gibson never trust any man who is too sharp. Gibson didn't like Dennis' fast-talking, but Scratch and Dennis hit it off. Scratch is such a man that he trusts every man. He thought, "This guy can't damage me", so Dennis and Scratch agree that Dip would control some of Scratch's things.'

Perry travelled to London in September 1974 to deliver his first batch of singles to Dip, tinkering with the mixes to better suit overseas ears. There was 'Hurt So Good', 'Enter The Dragon', Joy White's 'Lady Lady', 'Rebel's Train' and a new single from Junior Byles called 'Curly Locks', a heartfelt love song with a difference.

Riding an unusual rhythm courtesy of Benbow, Sydney Gussine, Theophilus Beckford, and Augustus Pablo on organ, accompanied by Desmond Minott's plaintive trumpet refrain, 'Curly Locks' described conflict between the Rastafari and mainstream Jamaica in the form of a disapproving father who does not want a dread courting his daughter, so Byles refutes him as a 'rum head', a 'walking dead' and a 'pork chop' – that is, an amoral conformist that drinks to excess and eats meat deemed unclean in the Bible.

On the same trip to London, Perry had D. D. Dennis voice a new rendition of 'Woman And Money', leaving in the screamed introduction from the Twinkle Brothers' take and updating the rhythm with a Moog overdub at Chalk Farm. One of the last Perry-produced singles issued by Pama, it was released on Pama Supreme, with production credited to Pauline, along with a bass-heavy mix of 'The Thanks We Get', backed by a moving Delroy Denton protest song, 'Oppression', both miscredited to the Heptones.

Then, on the night of 13 October 1974, Perry attended a three-way sound clash that took place at the Carib Club, located above a tailor's called Burton's in Cricklewood, northwest London, pitting Dennis Bovell's Sufferer sound against Lord Koos and Count Nick's. On the day of the clash, to counter Koos' supply of exclusive Bunny Lee dubs, Bovell went to the offices of Ethnic Fight in Kilburn to arm himself with some fresh Perry dub plates, including a trombone recut of the 'Real Rock' rhythm, which helped him to dominate, but then spectators clashed with the police, who stormed into the venue, supposedly in pursuit of a suspect. According to Bovell, the strains of 'Beat Down Babylon' were playing on a rival's record deck, another mike man spurring hostility towards the cops, and when things turned ugly, Perry turned up his collar, announced 'I am the Upsetter!' and fled the premises. A total of twelve were arrested, with the most serious charge of Incitement to Cause Affray reserved for Bovell himself. His infamous trial, which lasted nine months, saw him unjustly sentenced to three years' imprisonment, though he would serve six months in Wormwood Scrubs before being freed on appeal.

Back in Jamaica, 'Curly Locks' revealed itself to be the follow-up to 'Beat Down Babylon' that everyone was waiting for, despite being its antithesis in form. Byles had reverted to driving Kingston buses for a living, but 'Curly Locks' brought him back on top, leading to an opening slot for the Dells and Erma Franklin at the National Arena in early November, Sonia Pottinger's distribution of the song helping it to hit.

Then the Dip connection bore unexpected fruit in Britain early in 1975, once the disc jockey and former record shop proprietor Pete Waterman brought 'Hurt So Good' and 'Curly Locks' onto Magnet, the independent pop label established by accountant Michael Levy and the singer-songwriter Peter Shelley, then enjoying commercial success with glam rocker Alvin Stardust and fabricated boy/girl group, Guys and Dolls.

According to Susan Cadogan, Waterman first heard 'Hurt So Good' in Brixton Market.

'Pete Waterman had discovered "Hurt So Good". He said he heard it playing in a shop and took it to Magnet.'

However, Cadogan never knew that 'Hurt So Good' had been released in England until Dip's single topped the reggae charts in late 1974.

'I heard this rumour, "Your song doing good in England". My uncle is a lawyer and I remember him saying I should have something in writing, so I went to Perry and I remember he drafted up some funny-worded thing.'

Magnet re-released 'Hurt So Good' in February 1975 and 'Curly Locks' in March, and 'Hurt So Good' reached the UK top fifty in April. Then Cadogan got a call from Dennis Harris, saying that Magnet was summoning her to London, since 'Hurt So Good' was rapidly rising in the pop charts.

'I was met at the airport by the PR from Magnet and Dennis Harris and his wife, and they zoomed me off to the Holiday Inn like a big star. That was Tuesday, and Thursday I had to go on *Top of the Pops*, so they got me a wig and contact lenses. After I did *Top of the Pops*, the thing jumped right to number twenty-five. The next week it jumped to eleven, then to four!'

When Perry learned that Cadogan had flown the coop, he travelled to London in mid-May to confront her, the fluid nature of the working relationships and the convoluted sublicencing proving difficult to untangle.

'My mother told me that Perry came up there the weekend and was very annoyed to hear that I had gone. When I got the call from Magnet, I asked them, "Should I tell Mr Perry?" and they said, no, they had bought out the record, it's theirs. I think he had an inkling that something was going on, but Perry knew that he was signed to Trojan and yet he made dealings with Dip, who went and sold out the rights of the record to Magnet. So it started a big confusion. Magnet said that they need me to sign this contract and they put me in a hotel, they did everything for me. I remember Perry coming to my hotel room, he walk up and down and ask if I sign anything with these people. I say, "No, I haven't, but I *have* to sign something with them, they say they own the record." He said, no, I'm not to sign it. I remember he held my wrist and said, "If you sign that thing I'm going to make sure you never get a cent!"'

As Magnet had paid for her flight and living expenses, Cadogan felt she had no option but to sign with the company, and being young and inexperienced, the contract was definitely not in her favour.

'I got £3,000 on signing with Magnet and every statement I ever got from them, they excluded "Hurt So Good" from it. That one money I got, that was it, and out of all the royalties they were getting, they [deducted] my airfare, my hotel bills, my clothes, food and everything, so I was always in debt. I remember Magnet bought Pete Waterman a Jaguar for finding "Hurt So Good" and they said that I couldn't drive, so they wouldn't bother give me one.'

In June 1975, with 'Hurt So Good' still in the UK charts, things really came to a head when Cadogan was summoned to Magnet's offices for a legal battle over who had rights to the hit. It would mark the end of her working relationship with Perry and the waning of her stardom, though the Waterman-produced 'Love Me Baby' briefly skirted the lower regions of the top twenty-five.

'Magnet called me one day and said that they had to speak to me, and when I went, Magnet was there with their lawyers, Perry with his lawyer, Dip with his lawyer, even Warner Brothers was there, cos it was written by Phillip Mitchell at Warner Brothers. So it was one big table of lawyers and me alone! By that time I had signed Magnet's thing and because of all the trouble they got into with "Hurt So Good", they froze all the money and didn't want Lee Perry's other stuff, and I believe if they had released his stuff, I wouldn't have faded away as quickly as I did. At that point, they got Pete Waterman to produce me, and the material was just too light-weight in comparison to "Hurt So Good". On the Magnet album [*Doing It Her Way*], it didn't have the genuine "Hurt So Good", it was a re-recorded version and they'll never get back Perry's own again. Pete Waterman sings on "Would You Like To Swing On A Star With Me" in this chipmunk voice and they had the London Symphony Orchestra . . . they just didn't have the bass beat. One thing I liked with Perry, in all the recordings I have done, and I have done so many, he just let me sing the way I want. He don't stop and correct me, he just let me sing.'

Although Perry recorded an album's worth of material with Cadogan by the spring of 1975, the album was held back because of the Magnet furore, and the imminent collapse of Trojan caused further delays, ultimately diluting its appeal. Meanwhile, every time Magnet issued another Cadogan single, Perry made sure to let off one of his own, though all failed to find the same success as 'Hurt So Good'. Just as 'Congratulations Baby' aroused little interest, her take of Doris Duke's 'Feeling Is Right' was totally overlooked, her sultry version of 'Fever' and tantalising take of the Miracles' 'Do It Baby' did not achieve the chart position they were due, and her rendition of Elvis' 'In The Ghetto' attracted little interest.

In November 1975, Susan Cadogan received a silver disc for 'Hurt So Good', sales of Magnet's single having reached 250,000 copies, and the record reportedly went gold in South Africa. Cadogan spent nine months in London working with Waterman, but the second album she recorded for Magnet was never released and she returned to Jamaica, broke, to resume her career as a librarian. According to Cadogan, her first royalty payment for 'Hurt So Good' arrived in 1998, when the song was reissued on CD.

Perry also said he made no direct financial gain from Magnet's issue of 'Hurt So Good', nor of 'Curly Locks'. Instead, the true benefit of Dip's arrangements with Magnet came in the equipment that Harris shipped to Jamaica.

'What me make from "Curly Locks" is what me sell in Jamaica and Dip was supposed to have it in England, but after everything go caput with "Hurt So Good", he never organise himself proper and I lose everything,' said Perry. 'What I get from it was those equipment me could get for the studio, like the Soundcraft mixer.'

In late 1974, Soundcraft launched a 'twelve into four' and 'sixteen into four' series of mixing desks, the latter with sixteen inputs and four output busses, allowing effects to be applied with greater precision, either to one instrument or a group of them. The series was augmented by a second edition in the spring of 1975 (the later configuration placing the four output VUs on the same horizontal line), and it was this later configuration of the 'sixteen into four' that Perry installed at his studio.[1] A far more sophisticated board than the Alice, the Soundcraft enabled Perry to construct a broader sound that was richer, fuller, more complex, and resonant with deeper textures. Describing it as the first mixer he ever encountered with presence, Perry was amazed by the vocal clarity the desk allowed and its ability to aid spatial placement.

'It was just a little domestic set that make "Curly Locks" and all those hit songs, and after Dip give me some advance to put out "Hurt So Good", we buy instruments instead with it and he ship them down to Jamaica for me,' said Perry. 'That's how me get to change the Alice mixer to the Soundcraft mixer – he do that for me.'

As the studio upgraded, Perry was gearing himself up to face another transitional phase in which he would again test the limits of his creative abilities. Though always hoping for a hit, Perry was less concerned with the conventional vocal than his peers, his chief obsession remaining a song's overall sound. While his competitors trod firmly established commercial ground, the Upsetter thus continued to experiment, issuing unconventional vocal work and a series of minimal instrumental albums in 1975.

CHAPTER EIGHT
Enter the Dragon:
Black Ark Album Abstractions

Lee Perry upgraded his studio during a time of seismic shifts in Jamaican politics. In May 1974, Michael Manley nationalised most of the bauxite industry and tripled the fees due from multinational corporations, which displeased the Nixon administration in the United States. Relations remained frosty after Gerald Ford took office in August following Nixon's resignation over Watergate, and in November, just as Edward Seaga assumed leadership of the JLP, Michael Manley's implementation of democratic socialism swung the country further to the Left, setting off alarm bells in Washington.

Implementing ambitious new policies and sweeping reforms, Manley spearheaded free education and launched a large-scale literacy drive, improving public access to employment, housing and rural development schemes, as well as subsidies for the poor, but Washington was dismayed by Manley's strengthened ties with the communist government of Fidel Castro in neighbouring Cuba, especially after his five-day visit to the country in July 1975. The JLP began a vociferous campaign equating democratic socialism with communism, which Manley denied, and the broader Cold War politics at play in the region exerted a toxic influence, resulting in an escalation of internecine violence as Jamaica became increasingly polarised.

Simultaneously, Perry found himself in another transitory phase as he sought to stabilise his upgraded studio and re-establish his reputation as a pioneer. In addition to the Soundcraft board, other key bits of kit were gradually added and mastered, greatly changing the overall sound, one of the most important being a Roland Space Echo RE-201, a more advanced analogue tape delay unit, with an integrated reverb component, that gave a limitless quality to sound. From the spring of 1975, the Space Echo's gritty modulation was commonly applied to the vocal snippets on Perry's dub B-sides, allowing a message or certain words or syllables to echo seemingly to infinity. He had an MXR Phase 90 guitar pedal effects unit that subjected electronic signals to applied filtering to create audible peaks and troughs, lending an aural sweeping effect to whatever instrument it was applied, a spatial sense of rise and fall, or forward and back, depending on the application, and a portable Pignose amp for use as needed. There was also a Gibson Maestro Rhythm N Sound G2 guitar effects unit, made in the late 1960s, which in addition to bass octave, fuzzbox, tremolo, wah-wah, echo, wow wow and color tone settings, could trigger with a guitar or other input a range of rudimentary accompanying percussive sounds, though Perry typically operated this unit in an uncommon pairing with the spring reverb rather than simply running a guitar through it.

Perry upped his production schedule again, but oversaturating the market was counterproductive, especially with output that was far less commercially minded than that of his rivals.

'These guys just put out record after record with no business acumen, so one thing kills the other and then one day the bottom drops out,' said Winston Blake. 'Scratch would put out too much things at one time and that's where a lot of producers lose their material because if you put out five or six things, only one or two sell.'

But as Perry was continually bursting with ideas, he was compelled to commit as many songs to tape as possible. His studio allowed a greater creative unbridling, and although he was not scoring many major hits, Perry's unique approach often yielded extraordinary output.

Recycling rhythms was still a frequent preoccupation, executed with varying results. For instance, Jah Lloyd's 'Bad Luck Natty' was a talking tale of ghetto hardships, voiced on the 'Dub Organiser' rhythm, and later, Perry's 'Cane River Rock' updated the 'Tighten Up' rhythm as a dread motorcycle ride to Cane River Falls, a natural wonder in Bull Bay where Rastafari often bathed their locks, the mix cluttered by engine-revving sound effects, thick patois dialogue and Perry's wordless scat vocal.

'Three Blind Mice' was given multiple makeovers, too, first for Max Romeo's updated take, voiced at King Tubby's, relating a police raid on a sound system dance, with a beautiful Tubby's dub on the flip that had judicious use of his trademark high-pass filter, Tubby's promotion of the song on his sound system helping it to hit, according to Romeo.

I Roy's deejay version, 'Dread In The West', produced by Micron's Pete Weston, viewed Psalm 23 through red Rastafari spectacles:

> If the Capitalist is I and I shepherd,
> The higher high shall always want
> They maketh I and I to lie down
> Inna the sidewalk . . .

Then, with Leonard Dillon of the Ethiopians, Perry voiced the ironic alternate 'I'm A Dreadlocks', haranguing an auditioning hopeful, 'Bald Chin', for proclaiming himself a dreadlocks in song, despite being a baldhead, hinting at tensions between 'combsome' Rastafari, such as Perry and Dillon, and those who wore dreadlocks, including 'fashion dreads' that jumped on the Rastafari bandwagon despite not adhering to the faith.

'In those days, the majority of the Rastas were not dread and the Ethiopian Centre that we originate from, the Rastas did not dread, they are combsome,' said Leonard Dillon, an acolyte of the Ethiopian Reorganisation Centre in Waterhouse. 'So we say, "How come you no have a beard and say you're dread?" To what we were defending, you could assume that the spirit was moving within.'

'I'm A Dreadlocks' surfaced in an extended run of singles handled by Micron in 1975, the others including Pat Simpson's 'Two Bad Bull', warning a lover of Simpson's inherent dominance on a 'Skokian' adaptation, with plenty of Space Echo on the B-side, and Bobby Ellis' trumpet instrumental, 'Ska Baby', issued with echoing spatial effects on both sides.

Perry engineered much work for Micron at the Black Ark too, acting as an uncredited co-producer. For instance, Max Romeo's 'Revelation Time', co-written by Weston, was one of the first songs Weston produced at Perry's studio. Romeo had already recorded 'Socialism Is Love' for Michael Manley's public relations office, relaying the doctrine of democratic socialism in layman's terms, and now he used the imagery of the hammer and sickle to underline his commitment to the cause on a song that spoke out against capital punishment, police corruption and the forced shearing of dreadlocked prisoners.

Easton Clarke, an upcoming singer from Lucea, recorded 'Bike No License' for Micron at the Ark, recounting a drug bust during a curfew, and Clarke's 'Mr Phang, Mr Wong, Mr Chin' addressed the discrimination facing dreadlocks in the workplace (with Burning Spear and Tyrone Taylor credited as songwriters), both singles utilising prominent melodica parts and hefty Perry Space Echo B-sides.

Weston's own 'Revolution Is For The Chinaman', backed by Winston Jarrett and Junior Byles at the Ark, emphasised that Black people faced undue hardship worldwide, its version B-side jokingly titled 'Straight To Scratch Head', and in a lighter vein, on Byles' tongue-in-cheek alternate, 'Lorna Banana', Perry used delay to render a constant, double-tracked vocal. Byles also recorded a self-produced rendition of Ray Charles' 'Girl Next Door' at the Ark, which Micron issued, and Perry's 'Mighty Cloud Of Joy' rhythm become 'Psalm 53' on Prince Fari's *Psalms For I*, a fascinating religious concept album.

With so much interaction between Perry and Micron, there was confusing label allocation in this phase, with some of Perry's work issued on Micron and some Micron material released on his Upsetter and Black Art imprints, including singles he had nothing to do with, such as U Roy's 'The Right To Live', Jackie Brown's 'Bang Bang Lulu', I Roy's 'Jazzbo Have Fe Run', Jazzbo's 'Straight To I Roy's Head', Johnny Clarke's 'I Need Someone', Enos McLeod's 'All I Have' and Roman Stewart's 'Man Of Dignity'.

Furthermore, according to drummer Paul Douglas, Micron's high-profile fusion album *Negril*, featuring jazz guitarist Eric Gale, was partly recorded at the Black Ark, though Perry and his studio are not credited on the release and it remains unclear if his work made the final cut.

'Scratch had a particular sound, and everybody was fascinated by his sound,' said Douglas. 'He had this way of putting things together. It was just *his* sound, and it influenced a lot of people. I've even gone to the Black Ark with Eric Gale for that *Negril* album. Myself and Val Douglas, we laid some tracks there, and Eric Gale overdubbed stuff there, but I don't remember what happened to it.'

In the same time frame, Max Romeo's *Revelation Time* album, produced by Geoffrey Chung with Clive Hunt's assistance, was recorded at the Ark for Sound Tracks Limited, whose chief label executive, Pat Cooper, was one of Michael Manley's public relations assistants; their British distribution through the Tropical label was channelled via President Records, though the parent label in Jamaica would soon fold, due largely to production overspends.

'The entire thing was recorded at Black Ark in a day and a half for all the tracks, with live recording,' said Romeo. 'Clive Hunt and all the guys came in and bam! All tracks laid, and we mix it on two track at Black Ark.'

First tentatively entitled *Strictly Roots*, *Revelation Time* was released in Jamaica in the summer of 1975, and in the UK soon after, and it remains something of a landmark as the first Jamaican concept album rather than a collection of unrelated material.

'The songs may not necessarily sound alike,' said Romeo, 'but if you listen to the words, it's like reading the Bible and just turning the pages.'

Along with the opening title track and 'Three Blind Mice', Romeo recorded six new songs at the Ark, commenting on the shortcomings of Jamaican society from a Rastafari standpoint. 'No Peace', written by Hunt, spoke to the divisions of political allegiance and social class that made Jamaica a tinderbox, and 'A Quarter Pound Of I'Cense' declared that herb was a necessary solace in such chaos. Hunt's 'Tackoo' (mistitled 'Tacko') used pejorative patois for 'a slave who wasn't all that smart', according to Romeo, to send a message to Rastas whose faith was dwindling after news reports that Haile Selassie had been deposed in a military coup; the grave 'Warning Warning' commented on the growing chasm between rich and poor in Jamaica, reminding how Marcus Garvey prophesised that social inequalities and labour exploitation would bring bloodshed to Kingston's streets. Both sides of the LP were closed 'showcase' style, with a standard vocal immediately followed by a dub: the epic 'Blood Of The Prophet', co-written by Hunt, used verses from the Book of Jeremiah and the Book of Kings to proclaim that the Rastafari would be spared in the coming apocalypse, the dub making good use of the kick drum, rhythm guitar, synthesiser and Perry's percussion; 'Open The Iron Gate' was a call for repatriation over an updated 'Iron Gate' from *Cloak And Dagger*, now with prominent harmonica from Tyrone Downie.

'I deliberately did that rhythm over because I liked it: it had a thing to it that catch you,' said Romeo. 'We know that Babylon have an iron gate locked upon us as Black people, locked in the form of inhibition: freedom of movement is not in the West for Black people. You need visas for here, you're being deported from there, so I'm saying, "Open the iron gate, let us go back to Africa. Free us!"'

Pablo Moses' debut recording, 'I Man A Grasshopper', was one of the summer's most popular reggae releases, both in Jamaica and Britain, its symbolic lyrics and rock music leanings pointing to reggae's potential for crossover hits. The young dread from Vineyard Town, east Kingston, born Pablito Henry, began playing informally with Geoffrey Chung's brother Mikey while attending the Jamaica School of Music, which is how Geoffrey became aware of 'I Man A

Grasshopper'; sensing that the song would hit, he took Moses
to the Black Ark to record it. The song was inspired by conflict
with a lodger at Moses' mother's house.

'He was some captain in the army and he has this funny
attitude,' said Moses. 'I'm always in my room practising my
guitar, burning my spliff, but I don't go where he is. I heard
one day he went to the police station, reporting that I'm
smoking herb and blowing it into these kids' faces and I
thought, "Why would a guy do something like that, and I don't
trouble him yet?" so that's why I wrote that song. I said, "That
man saw I-man smoking I-man collie weed, that man should
never call Babylon to spoil I-man irie." He was a drunkard
too, so that's expressing, "That man loves sea and fish bowl
and that man loves to keep I-and-I soul" because a drunkard
is like a fish in the fish bowl.'

Recorded with Clive Hunt on bass, Mikey Chung on rhythm
and Michael Murray from the In Crowd on lead guitar, plus
Robbie Lyn and Geoffrey Chung on keyboards, the superior
musicianship of 'I Man A Grasshopper' paved the way for
Moses' individual vocal delivery, scoring an immediate and
lasting impact, its issue on Jigsaw one of the first to credit
Perry's studio as the Black Ark rather than the Black Art of
earlier releases.

Other less commercially successful Sound Tracks productions recorded at the Black Ark include 'Ethiopian Lament',
a mournful Clive Hunt melodica instrumental with a minimal
drum and bass rhythm, and the Black Traps' 'Kiss Me In The
Rain', a slow love song with a choppy keyboard line produced
and arranged by Tesfa McDonald.

One of the most intriguing Black Ark songs of the era was
'Concrete Castle King', sung by saxophonist Dean Fraser and
produced by Lloyd 'Gitsy' Willis, though a pressing fault

stopped it from hitting. After contributing to Perry's Wailers material, Willis lived in the Cayman Islands, and on returning to Jamaica began playing in Sonny Bradshaw's band, where Fraser sang the reggae numbers they covered, so when Willis wrote 'Concrete Castle King' about Jamaica's social divides, he thus asked Fraser to sing it.

'Gitsy decided that he wanted me to sing this song, so one day we just went round to Scratch,' said Fraser. 'It was me, Gitsy, Family Man and Robert Stevenson, who was the drummer for Sonny's band at the time. I'm playing tenor and Calvin Cameron is playing trombone. It came out on one of Gitsy's little labels that he had [Black Explosion], but the quality of the press was poor, and we never got much airplay, and years later, when I was at Joe Gibbs, I taught Dennis Brown the song.'

For Perry's own productions, after the Melodians temporarily broke up, Brent Dowe cut the excellent 'Down Here in Babylon' over a characteristically rugged rhythm provided by Boris Gardiner, Glen Adams and Winston Grennan, with vocal backing from fellow Melodian Trevor McNaughton and Max Romeo, plus B. B. Seaton and Maurice Roberts of the Gaylads.

Val Bennett's daughter Fay challenged the male hegemony of the deejay world with the censorious 'Back Weh', and Perry's 'Bury The Razor' showed his growing maturity as a lyricist, sending a warning from a Rastafari perspective and sympathising with the plight of the dreads, but the song was playfully constructed, with spongy wah-wah guitar, tinkling percussion and strangely muted bass, its version side 'Cheat Weston Head' returning the dig of 'Straight To Scratch Head'.

Jimmy Riley recorded a compelling sequence of covers and originals for Perry, beginning with an excellent rendition of Bobby Womack's 'Woman's Gotta Have It' (as 'Woman Gotta Have Love'), the rhythm reconfigured for reggae ears with a more languid and dislocated rhythm. Perry and Riley recut Ken Boothe's 'Train Is Coming' as 'Rasta Train', here done in the popular 'flying cymbal' style, with an open-and-closed high-hat pattern modelled after that of 'TSOP'; 'Stay Dread' saluted the dreads and dissed the baldheads, its rhythm used for Riley's alternate, 'Sons Of Negus', and 'Yagga Yagga' was an abstract concept record with nonsense scat vocals and a refrain from the 'Some Like It Hot' nursery rhyme (the platform for a rival hit by Dennis Brown). There was Riley's credible version of the Uniques' 'Give Me A Love', a domino saga called 'Key Card' and a take of Pluto Shervington's humorous 'Ram Goat Liver', with another Omar and Marsha version B-side, which deteriorates fairly quickly; the desultory 'Hypocrites' revisited the Reggae Boys' 'Mama Look Deh' for a jibe aimed at Niney and Jerry Lewis, and 'I Man Stand Still' had greater gravity, addressing Riley's frustration with the music business.

The presence of Glen Adams brought a creative edge to Perry's output, their long years of close association lending communicative ease, as heard on an outrageous new cut of 'The Thanks We Get' with thudding drums and a choppy keyboard, Byles' chastising vocal now bolstered by Omar and Marsha's yelping echoes.

After upcoming producer Prince Tony Robinson scored a big hit with Big Youth's 'House Of Dread', riding an adapted 'Curly Locks', Perry and Byles struck back with 'Dreader Locks', haphazardly attacking Babylon, the Vatican and Prince Tony himself, denounced as a phoney for copying Byles' hit, the single one of the first Perry productions issued on Brad Osbourne's Clocktower label in the Bronx, along with 'Golden Locks', Chinna's acoustic guitar interpretation, and 'Ital Locks', a further deejay cut by Johnny Lover, who had recorded for Joe Gibbs and Tuff Gong before moving to New York.

Adams also helped shape Byles' 'The Long Way', a lover's lament that referenced the television series *Kung Fu*, which found favour with Black audiences in Britain, and before everything went pear-shaped with Susan Cadogan, Adams introduced the upcoming singers William Clarke, alias Bunny Rugs, and Errol Kong, alias Ricky Storm (later known as I Kong), yielding impressive collaborative work.

'I was in a group with Bunny Rugs in the States called Bluegrass Experience,' said Adams. 'I took Bunny Rugs to Scratch, and Ricky, Leslie Kong's nephew, when we made "Bushweed Corntrash". Bunny was not on the roots side because he was with Inner Circle, so I took him around in a ghetto style, get him rootsy with Scratch, alongside Susan Cadogan.'

The son of an Anglican preacher from Mandeville, south-west Jamaica, Clarke was raised in the heart of downtown Kingston, his church background yielding a deep and power-fully expressive singing voice that was particularly suited to soul. He led prominent uptown nightclub act Inner Circle from 1969, and after moving to New York in 1971, performed with expatriate group Hugh Hendricks and the Buccaneers, as well as Bluegrass Experience. Back in Jamaica in late 1974, Clarke visited various studios in search of a piece of the action, until Adams brought him to the Black Ark.

'I walk to all the recording studios throughout Kingston, check out the vibes to see what was going on, and the one that I fell in love with the most was Lee Perry's,' said Clarke. 'For some strange reason I end up spending a year and a half there, [late] 1974 to [early] 1976.'

'He didn't have a song to sing, but he did have a good voice and he wanted to sing like a Jamaican, so I give him some tracks, find him somewhere to live, feed him, give him clothes to wear,' said Perry. 'Me would have to treat him like me son, buy him herb and everything to get him cool.'

Perry first had Clarke provide backing on Cadogan's take of Shirley & Company's disco hit 'Shame, Shame, Shame', though the harmony he attempted on her 'I Keep On Loving You' was rejected. Recording solo as Bunny Clarke, his rendition of William deVaughn's 'Be Thankful For What You Got', issued as an Orchid single (as 'Be Thankful'), showed how strong and soulful he could be; 'Bushweed Corntrash', the first duet with Ricky Storm, which Storm wrote, lamented the difficulty in finding decent weed to smoke, and their follow-up, 'Freedom Fighter', revived the 'Beat Down Babylon' rhythm to fine effect, now addressing gang warfare in Tivoli Gardens, denouncing the corrupt politicians behind the violence and essentially calling for change.

Clarke cut a range of material during his time with Perry. There were average covers of Neil Diamond's 'Sweet Caroline' and 'I Am I Said', plus new takes of 'To Love Somebody' and 'Sick And Tired' (the latter as 'Big May'), as well as a likeable rendition of Bill Withers' 'Use Me' and a very individual reading of Art Garfunkel's 'Second Avenue', made more outstanding by the horn section of the Chi-Lites, who recorded for Perry after delivering a series of concerts in Jamaica.

The Chi-Lites horns are also present on 'Kinky Fly', an original collaboration between Clarke and Perry, obviously inspired by *Superfly*, its ghostly pulsing tick provided by a Univox Super Rhythmer 55, one of the bulky drum machine prototypes manufactured by Korg in Japan. The unit had ten preset rhythms, such as rumba, mambo, foxtrot and rock, which could be used independently or in various combinations, allowing up to fifty-four different rhythms in all, as well as variation toggles and tempo and tone controls, and

Perry would use the machine sparingly, almost always with excellent results.

But much of the work Perry recorded in this era did not achieve its full commercial potential, especially with overseas audiences, since the collapse of Trojan Records in the summer of 1975 had dramatic repercussions. Perry had delivered a master tape to Trojan with 'Move Out Of My Way', a song attacking obstructive politicians that was one of Clarke's strongest; there was Junior Byles' 'Pretty Fe True', voiced on the same rhythm as 'Second Avenue', plus Byles' 'Fun And Games', another tale of conflict between an adolescent and her father, each with resplendent Perry dubs, but these all fell through the cracks of Trojan's voluntary liquidation and would not be released until the late 1980s. Similarly, the official release of Susan Cadogan's self-titled album was delayed until 1976 following Marcel Rodd's controversial acquisition and repurposing of the stricken company, though white label Upsetter pre-releases were briefly available, titled *Sexy Suzy*.

With Trojan no longer an option, Pauline helped broker deals with new outlets, including Klik and its Angen subsidiary, established by former Trojan staffers Joe Sinclair and Desmond Bryan with their associate, Larry Sevitt (which is why the UK issue of the Untouchables' 'Many Are Called' credited Pauline as producer), as well as the Black Wax, Mango and Locks labels, run by Keith Thornton and Brian Harris in Birmingham.

In late 1975, Klik issued Clarke's 'To Love Somebody'/'Second Avenue' as a single under the confusing alias Bunny Scott, and would release his album *To Love Somebody* under the same name early in 1976, but as with *Prisoner Of Love*, Clarke said the album was released without his knowledge or consent.

'I say, "Why the hell you go to England and name me Bunny Scott?" He said, "English people like English names." And it's not really an album, you know. I used to go to Lee Perry every day and hang out, and then I'd do a little voicing and he eventually put the whole thing together and I didn't know anything about it. He later told me that I have to start coming to the studio a little earlier in the morning, and I have to start dusting off the console, clean the instruments, sweep out the studio, and I wasn't prepared to do that, so I moved on.'

Clarke returned to New York to cut demos for Atlantic and ended up joining his old Inner Circle bandmates in Third World, but despite the problematic circumstances of *To Love Somebody*, Clarke said he learned much from Perry's unique working methods.

'Lee Perry wasn't any great instrumentalist, but he would mess around the keyboards and get some sounds. He have a sound that he call the "conk": he would take his finger and knock it on your forehead and say, "This is what I want to hear, the conk." Lee Perry's music has that keyboard sound that has a phaser sound on it. Sometimes it's in the distance, sometimes it's upfront. The approach he has to music and to recording, I think the music nowadays lack that kind of intuition. He's somebody that would use a pliers and a screwdriver to create a percussion sound. He wouldn't hesitate to experiment and that was really good. He was a little . . . not crazy, but somebody with that kind of thinking must be somewhere else, in another zone sometimes. Even the early Bob Marley works that Lee Perry was involved with, you can hear so much of Lee Perry in the lyrical formation. The way Perry writes and the way Bob writes is similar, so simple that it becomes so fucking complex! That is what I learn from Lee Perry at the Black Ark.'

At 5 Cardiff Crescent, running a home recording studio was more than just a full-time occupation. Sessions started early and stretched late into the night, with activity more often than not taking place all day, every day. Perry was completely consumed by his aural creations, and with so much pugnacious disorder in the downtown area, it made sense to vacate the premises at 36 Charles Street. The Upsetter Record Shop was no more, and the Upsetter sound system gone with it. Perry distributed his output from his home for a brief period, before making Lloyd F. Campbell's premises at 135 Orange Street his distribution base.

By then the Black Ark had become a magnet for underground creatives with a Rastafari orientation. For instance, the singer and producer Bobby Melody's Hi-Rock label was based off Washington Boulevard in Drewsland, so Perry's studio was a natural choice; his group, the Divine Brothers, recorded some exceptional singles there in 1975, including the self-issued 'Perception', which proclaimed unwavering commitment to Rastafari, and their stunning 'Warrior', which counselled against violence, was issued first on Upsetter, but when it failed to hit, Perry gave the stamper to Melody, who issued further copies on Hi-Rock. There was also the romantic 'Best Dress', which appeared on Pisces, with production credited to Pauline Morrison and a certain J Malcolm; Pisces also released the unity call 'Brother Man' by uptown university student Sam Carty, a Clarendon native of part-Indian extraction whose voice had a fragile, breathless quality.

The visionary singer and producer Vivian 'Yabby You' Jackson recorded a handful of singles at the Black Ark, his work among the most individual and outstanding to emerge from Perry's studio. Raised in an impoverished household in western Kingston, his father a follower of Marcus Garvey and mother a devout Christian, Jackson wandered the land from the age of twelve in emulation of Jesus, eventually settling with the Ites People, a radical Rastafari subgroup producing cast-iron pots at their metal foundry on the gully bank in Waterhouse to survive. After experiencing malnutrition, pneumonia, an ulcerated stomach and brain fever, he was hospitalised, emerging with an arthritic condition that rendered him unable to walk without assistance, forcing him to scrape a living by giving betting tips at the racetrack. Because of his individual religious beliefs, he experienced a complicated social isolation too: wearing locks and living among the Rastafari, he was already on the margins of society, but his worshipping of Jesus and denial of Selassie's divinity made him ostracised by many Rastas as well.

The rhythm of his fearsome 'Jah Vengeance' was recorded at the Black Ark and voiced at King Tubby's with Alric Forbes and Milton Henry on backing vocals, and the anthem-like 'Run Come Rally' was recorded at the Ark with Family Man and vocal harmony from the Royals. Then, Jackson's production of Wayne Wade's 'Black Is Our Colour', an affirmation of Blackness set to a lilting lover's rock rhythm, became an enduring underground hit with Black audiences in Britain in late 1975.

'Yabby You was trying to do something that him hear from the spiritual world,' said Perry. 'All the producers who was listening from the spiritual world and creating words what them hear from the spiritual world will have a chance. They will be saved in what world them think them believe in.'

The recording of 'Jah Vengeance' brought the Gladiators into Perry's orbit, making them his backing musicians for a time and yielding some impressive work of their own. The group formed in the rock steady era, hitting with 'Train Is Coming Back' for lesser producer Leebert Robinson and topping the charts with 'Hello Carol' at Studio One, where they were based during the early 1970s. Lead singer Albert Griffiths' distinctive tenor and use of proverbs marked out much of their best-known work, with Clinton Fearon's deeper tones a strong harmonic counterbalance, and Gallimore Sutherland joined in 1970, sealing the group's most lasting and popular incarnation.

Griffiths said he was inspired by Elvis and Tom Paxton in younger days, before Bob Marley became his favourite singer and most significant role model, though the trio always strove for something unique.

'We don't just sing to follow the metre,' said Griffiths. 'We all create a little sound in the group.'

At Studio One, in addition to recording a number of weighty Rastafari classics, riddled with proverbs and religious references, the Gladiators also worked as session musicians backing artists such as Burning Spear, with Griffiths typically on guitar and Fearon on bass. They came to know Yabby You through an acclaimed repeater player, Brother Joe of the Rightful Brothers, which led them to back his first recording at the Black Ark.

'Yabby You took the Gladiators to Black Ark and we did "Jah Vengeance" for Yabby,' said Clinton Fearon. 'Scratch ask Yabby if he workin' Obeah, cos no one supposed to come into Scratch's studio and get them sounds except Scratch! Scratch liked the sound he heard, and we came back later and did "Time", which is Albert's song, and one I wrote called "Untrue Girl". Me and Albert played guitar and bass and Audley Taylor was on keys. The session was a great one, although Scratch and Albert didn't hit it off – they were two strong personalities and obviously didn't see eye to eye on things – their spirits just didn't blend. Back then Scratch used to drink Tia Maria and he would get right into it! It was a treat watching Scratch mix.'

'Time' shows the overarching tightness of the Gladiators in this period, their formidable harmony a fitting vehicle for Griffiths' reverent lyrics, and Perry's non-standard production draws out the best from them, the subtle use of a xylophone providing unusual accents. 'Untrue Girl' was a song of romantic disappointment, and for its version B-side, Perry creatively looped a snippet of Fearon's muted vocal, its presence a repeated murmur of regret.

The musicianship of the Gladiators brought an unpolished beauty to Perry's productions, and Fearon had fond memories of working at the Black Ark, despite a lack of proper credit and financial recompense.

'I worked with all kinds of different musicians there and learned quite a bit about percussion from Scratch. Overall, it was like doing a day job: wake up and go to the studio, reach there ten o'clock and sometimes you don't leave till twelve or one the next night. I did that for about six months and sometimes we'd lay a whole LP, like twelve tracks a day! Scratch is one producer that get a lot of my bass work and I didn't get much money for it, but I don't feel anyway bad about doing those works as they were great works. The only thing I'm sad about is that I got no credit for any of them.'

Doctor Alimantado returned to Perry's studio to voice 'Can't Conquer Natty Dreadlocks' (an adaptation of Delroy Wilson's 'Never Conquer') and the landmark 'Best Dressed Chicken In Town', the latter voiced on the 'Ain't No Sunshine' rhythm, which Tado had used for 'Oil Crisis' in 1973; utilising a continuous new toast throughout the rhythm, with echoing vocal fragments of his earlier recording drifting in and out of the mix, 'Best Dressed Chicken' became an overnight sensation on the Jamaican sound system circuit, making an initial impact in the UK when released on Birmingham's short-lived Sun

& Stars label in May 1975, though the song would propel Alimantado to proper international stardom once Greensleeves reissued it in 1978.

'Where the "Best Dressed Chicken In Town" is concerned, I was in Randy's studio making a master and I played the tape and the idea flash in my head,' said Alimantado. 'I went to Perry, we work and develop up and add different voices filtering in to make it very exciting. Junior Byles wanted to do a song on the rhythm and later on, we let him do a voice on the rhythm and maybe a year or so after, I gave it to him.'

Alimantado said Perry was generous with studio time and always got involved in the creative process.

'If you go to him with an idea, he doesn't just handle it as though he's an engineer, he handles it as though it's his thing, so he puts his initiative behind it. Working in other studios like King Tubby's, there's always so much running after time, but with Mr Perry, if you book an hour or two hours, sometimes he will give you three or four hours on top just making sure you get the music right. With King Tubby, you go in for an hour and you have to come out within the hour because there's always someone else who's coming in.'

Upcoming producer Lloyd A. 'Spiderman' Campbell recorded the Viceroys' 'Freedom' at Perry's studio, during the time when they were working as the Interns, and group member Norris Reid provided backing vocals on Mike Brooks' 'The Earth Is The Fullness' as part of a short-lived group called the Tates, the minimal rhythm recorded with Fams, Carly and a trumpeter, according to Brooks, who was brought to the Black Ark by Jah Lloyd. Ronnie Davis and Pat 'Scabba' Sutherland also recorded Davis' excellent 'You Are The Fool' at the Ark, issued with a spacious, echoing Perry dub on the flip. Unusually, Perry also gave a helping hand to the Grace

Thrillers' gospel album *I've Got A Love,* though the release bears little evidence of his involvement.

During his extended stay in London, Perry assisted upcoming producer Clem Bushay, producing a version of Donny Elbert's 'What Can I Do' for Bushay with falsetto singer Locksley Green (alias Locks Lee, who would later release disco records as Jesse Green); the song became one of the records of the year on the lover's rock scene in Britain, ubiquitous in late 1975. A cover of War's 'Slipping Into Darkness' recorded with the Cimarons for Bushay, with lead singer Carl Levy credited as Carl Bradney, also found its way onto Perry's Orchid label through the partnership.

The seven-inch 45RPM single had always reigned supreme in Jamaica, but in Britain, albums held greater currency. Winston Edwards' *King Tubby Meets The Upsetter At The Grass Roots Of Dub* was one of the first to establish the dub album as a popular reggae subgenre, and it really peaked in the summer of 1975, when it spent eight weeks at the top of *Black Music*'s reggae album chart and eleven weeks crowning Capital Radio's.

Presented as a mixing contest pitting the Upsetter against the Dub Organiser, Tubby's mixes were allegedly on side one and Perry's supposedly on side two, though just as the back cover showed incorrect models of the mixing desks used at their respective studios, Edwards conceded that the mixes did not necessarily reflect the stated concept.

'Five of the tracks were mixed by Scratch and five were mixed by Tubby, or maybe four tracks is Scratch and the other six were Tubby, but Scratch did a lot of work on that album,' Edwards suggested. 'How that album comes about, I lay down some tracks in Scratch's place and a few tracks at Joe Gibbs' studio. I had some of the tracks mixed at Scratch's and some mixed at Tubby's, some of them were also over-dubbed at Scratch's and some overdubbed at Tubby's. In those days I have sound systems like Jah Shaka and Fatman who I have to supply with dub plates, so I was coming back on the airplane and I thought, "What should I name this album? Some of the tracks were done at Upsetter's studio and some were done at King Tubby's, so I'm going to name this album *King Tubby Meets The Upsetter*", and that was the birth of one of the best-selling dub albums in the UK.'

Several tracks featured Vin Gordon's trombone overdubs, adding a jazz subtext to the dubs, and the song 'Natty Roots' has vibrant conga drumming, overdubbed by Morwells member Eric 'Bingy Bunny' Lamont at the Black Ark. Most of the rhythms are originals, adding to the pervasive abstract-ness, though a recut of 'Born To Love' and a version of the Melodians' 'Come On Little Girl' are instantly familiar; 'Crime Wave' used the same Black Ark rhythm as 'You Are So Real'.

The mix is subdued throughout, concentrating on pure rhythm, and the supposed Upsetter side has little of the panache and zest typically associated with Perry's dub works, but the concept was original and compelling, the meshing of the two approaches making for pleasant listening, even if the difference between the sides is not so noticeable, except for more reverb on what is meant to be Tubby's side and more delay on the so-called Upsetter side.

Dip Presents The Upsetter, the first of Perry's albums for the company, which surfaced in the spring of 1975, collected twelve of his productions, mixing vocals and instrumentals. There was 'Enter The Dragon', 'Cane River Rock', 'I Man Free', 'Dub The Pum Pum' and 'Kung Fu Man' (credited to Linval Spencer), as well as Leo Graham's 'Jump It', the Gladiators' 'Time', a new Gaylads track called 'Nature Man' and a medley of their hits, 'Have Some Fun', plus a laughable guitar rendition of Ken Boothe's 'Everything I Own' (originally a pop hit for Bread), along with two peculiar Sam Carty efforts: 'I Don't Mind' pondered the tenuousness of human existence, and 'Life Is A Flower' used the imagery of nature to relate feelings of love.

A trio of abstract albums followed, but two of them were issued in minute quantities as blank label pre-releases, relegating them to obscurity, the first being *Musical Bones*, featuring trombonist Vin Gordon, an Alpha graduate who knew Perry from Studio One.

'Scratch used to be the second guy to Mr Dodd, give the introduction to the songs, set up the mike and everything,' said Gordon. 'After a while, Scratch start his own studio called Black Ark and said he want an album, so I just go up there and do an album for him. He had some of the rhythms already and some of the rhythms we put down live. I put down some Don Drummond solo track, like "Far East", and some other songs that I make in Studio One – my own instrumentals – I just change them over, cos it's not hard to do with the right musicians. Wire was the keyboard player and Wire was the one who arrange. It was musicians who play one instrument, but Scratch would say, "Try a next instrument" to see if it could work. He got Dougie on bass, Ansel Collins on keyboards and some of the tracks mix up different musicians.'

By adapting ska classics, Gordon recalled the spirit of his mentor, Don Drummond, with opener 'Coco-Macca' drawing on 'Green Island', 'Fly Away' transforming 'Real Rock' and 'Raw Chaw' riffing on 'Addis Ababa' and 'Eastern Standard Time'; originals such as 'Labrish' and 'Quinge Up' dissolved into free-form jams, and 'Licky Licky' finds Wire channelling Booker T as Gordon drifts in and out of the bass-heavy mix.

Over subdued wah-wah guitar, relaxed jazz drumming and didactic electric piano, Gordon's lead reminded how expressive the trombone could be in reggae.

There were also some examples of Perry's new mixing idiosyncrasy, the false ending: after fading down to silence, the rhythm returns again, repeating the process a number of times before the actual finish.

Only 300 copies of *Musical Bones* are said to have been pressed, rendering the LP instantly unavailable, and the lack of accompanying information did not help, but Gordon said his greatest disappointment was not being properly paid or credited for the work.

'I had a royalty arrangement with Scratch and believe you me, that thing go to England and sold. Scratch came back from England with a book, looking on it, saying that it's some royalty thing, and Scratch took out one pound and give me and say it's royalty! From that day till now, one pound!'

'That's stupid, man,' countered Perry. 'You have to laugh, you can't even be vexed with them. If I would give a pound, that is totally rubbish – even a beggar on the street I give more than a pound. The money I was getting from all the music I sell, me pay back to the musicians at weekends and as this was the start of the album, he's going to get an extra advance over the rest of the musicians that play and when me go to London, if me give them maybe two albums' worth of songs, the record company give you something like £600 if you're lucky; Harry J was getting big money from Trojan, but the smaller guys, it's small advance we get, so some go bankrupt. What advance we get, we have to pay musicians and give them advance out of it, but they eat it off. They're not fair enough to say, "We were taking money all the time."'

Return Of Wax – another album issued only as a blank label pre-release – had ten sparse Black Ark dubs largely void of reference points, some of which may never have been issued in vocal form, though 'Samurai Swordsman' was a subtle drum and bass cut of 'Curly Locks' with ringing xylophone notes, choppy piano chords and prominent percussion; 'Final Weapon' was a bass-heavy cut of 'Observe Life', one of the first recordings by future Black Uhuru frontman Michael Rose, and 'Big Boss' was a dub of 'Different Experience' (unreleased until 1980 and credited to Brother Roy).

Largely gimmick-free, *Return Of Wax* presented the raw rhythms of these early Ark recordings in their simplest form. Bass and drum have prominence and percussion is one of the few embellishments to make momentary appearances in the mix. The emphasis remains continually on rhythm, with slices of rhythm guitar and harsh electric piano chords shifting up and back, with barely a lead lick in earshot, and in keeping with Perry's latest mixing peculiarity, the trombone-led 'Big Boss' had a series of false endings.

The final Dip album, *Kung Fu Meets The Dragon*, with its classic cartoon cover showing the Mighty Upsetter in karate combat with a three-headed dragon, was a less abstract collection edging towards the instrumental side of dub, incorporating complex instrumentation and an array of sound effects. Aside from a quasi-dub of 'Kung Fu Man' and an odd recut of Roy Shirley's 'Hold Them' with a phased melodica (titled 'Hold Them Kung Fu'), the album was again based on dubs of fresh instrumentals, most of which were never issued in vocal form, but *Kung Fu Meets The Dragon* had far more melody than *Return Of Wax*. 'Theme From Hong Kong' and 'Scorching Iron' were led by a bright melodica; 'Fungaa', 'Black Belt Jones' and 'Iron Fist' had harsh synthesiser overdubs, and 'Skango' made use of a full horn section led by a swinging sax. The extremities were 'Heart Of The Dragon' and 'Flames Of The Dragon', both manic attempts to transpose the visual imagery of kung fu films to the aural dimension, their frightful forms heightening Perry's relentless experimental urges.

Winston Edwards remembered visiting Perry at rented accommodation Dennis Harris arranged for him in the southeast London suburb of Crystal Palace, where it was clear that Perry's cinematic obsessions were influencing more than just his music.

'I remember he went into a coffin to sleep,' said Edwards. 'He actually made a mattress like a coffin and went over to the West End, bought all these black clothes, looking like a vampire with his teeth like Dracula.'

Back in Jamaica, regardless of their ups and downs, Lee Perry and Bob Marley retained a special bond. Following problematic overseas tours that sparked insurmountable tensions, Marley had broken away from Peter Tosh and Bunny Wailer to establish himself as a solo artist, now working with the I-Threes for vocal harmony, the trio composed of Rita Marley, Marcia Griffiths and Judy Mowatt.

Perry had attended some of the *Natty Dread* sessions at Harry J in late 1974, influencing the outcome of certain tracks, the single 'Talking Blues'/'Bend Down Low', which surfaced in limited number on Black Art, attesting to his presence.

Then, in May 1975, Marley and Perry joined forces more concretely for *Escape From Babylon*, an album by the Puerto Rican-American singer Martha Veléz. Based in the hippie haven of Woodstock, New York, Veléz was signed to Sire, Warner Brothers' cutting-edge rock subsidiary, and when she wanted to cover Marley's 'Stir It Up', her A&R manager Craig Leon offered Marley the producer's role. The sessions were executed at Harry J over the course of three weeks, with Sylvan Morris engineering and Perry on hand to assist as necessary; the Wailers band provided the rhythms and the I-Threes the harmonies, supplemented by the Zap Pow horn section of David Madden, Glen DaCosta and Vin Gordon. Marley was in charge of artistic direction and Perry a vital, enabling production force, while Leon supervised later over-dubs and mixing in New York.

The result was a subdued Wailers band at their most commercial bubbling beneath Veléz's expressively melan-choly vocals, the absence of foreign musicianship lodging the music closer to its reggae roots than standard rock 'n' roll. Wailers numbers such as 'Bend Down Low', 'Get Up, Stand Up', 'Stand Alone' (as 'There You Are') and 'Hurting Inside' (as 'Happiness') were presented as the middle ground, and originals 'Money Man', 'Wild Bird' and 'Come On In' worked surprisingly well in reggae. The I-Threes comple-mented Veléz's deep timbre, Chinna's bluesy guitar enhanced some of the best numbers, and the percussion added by Marley and Perry gave the album extra African-Caribbean flavour.

Between 5 June and 20 July 1975, Bob Marley and the Wailers executed an extensive high-profile tour of North America, followed by four noteworthy concerts in England, one of which was issued as the album *Live! At The Lyceum*. Soon after their return to Jamaica, the group began working on *Rastaman Vibration* at Harry J, drafting Chinna Smith to make sure the sound was roots enough.

Chris Blackwell said that Perry produced some of the better tracks on the album, albeit uncredited, and Perry, Chinna Smith and Roy Cousins all said he played a big part in the creation of 'Rat Race', one of the album's most exceptional and distinctive entries. Additionally, Perry later adapted 'Crazy

Baldhead', while 'Who The Cap Fit' reworked 'Man To Man', 'Night Shift' was an update of 'It's Alright', and 'Cry To Me' was first cut at Studio One during Perry's tenure, but according to Blackwell, those songs were re-recorded simply because Marley was not earning from the originals.

'Bob told me a problem that he had was songs that he wasn't getting any royalties for, and I said, "The best thing you can do is just re-record those songs and the others will drop away", but of course they didn't drop away because they were great recordings,' said Blackwell. 'The rhythm tracks that Scratch did for Bob were the best and still *are* the best. He was very strong, just brilliant really, and he's the only person that I saw Bob a little anxious or nervous of when he was in the studio.'

At some point during the summer, Marley and Perry collaborated on a couple of drum machine-driven experiments at the Black Ark. The minimalist 'Rainbow Country' was recorded as a dub plate for Jack Ruby's sound system in Ocho Rios (though select sound systems in London also obtained copies), the song a free and breezy affirmation toying with the themes that would underpin 'Roots Rock Reggae' on *Rastaman Vibration*, the minimal rhythm driven by Family Man's powerful bassline, embellished by blasts from the Zap Pow horns and subtle conga drumming. Similar instrumentation was used for an early take of 'Natural Mystic', this rendition benefitting from a haunting male chorus that Perry overdubbed later with the Meditations.

When news reports reached Jamaica that Haile Selassie had died on 27 August, the Rastafari community was thrown into crisis. Many would lose their commitment to the faith, and for others the news brought unbearable turmoil: unable to reconcile his belief of Selassie's divinity with the physical death of his

255

earthly form, Junior Byles tried to take his own life, resulting in a long stay at Bellevue, Kingston's notorious psychiatric hospital, and subsequent battles with emotional instability.

Others were less troubled, interpreting the reports as the false propaganda of Babylon or an opportunity to strengthen their conviction. Bob Marley was one whose faith could not be shaken, and he was compelled to demonstrate this to the world in song, summoning Lee Perry to Harry J's to record one of his most outstanding works.

An unabashed affirmation of Selassie's divinity and the belief in everlasting life, 'Jah Live' was supported by the very foundation of Marley's faith. It remains a stunning testament to his spiritual beliefs and a triumphant expression of the positive, unifying power of religious conviction.

'Bob was partially sad, concerned and questioning, so that was one of the most serious sessions that we did,' said Marcia Griffiths. 'Bob does every single one of his songs with such conviction, but he was more forceful and firm that night than we have ever seen him. Whatever was being said, he knew Jah was alive, His Majesty was alive, come what may. That was the conviction that he did that song with.'

The version side, 'Concrete', is a finely balanced dub that shows off the tightness of the Wailers rhythm section, with Fams and Carly providing a solid rhythmic wall beneath Chinna's wah-wah and Touter Harvey's keyboards. The song begins with a vibrating yelp from Marley, apparently in a joking imitation of the manner in which Martha Veléz would clear her throat before recording.

'Jah Live' found instant favour with the Jamaican public, though its international release, like Martha Veléz's album, was delayed until 1976. As evidenced by these intense collaborations, Marley and Perry maintained an exceptional connection based on mutual respect. Marley knew that he could rely on Perry to raise the bar whenever something extra special was needed sonically, and Perry was always happy to oblige. Retaining a unique friendship that even their closest peers could not always fathom, they kept in regular contact, both on and off the island.

Towards the end of the year, Perry had another significant album release in Britain that again aimed for previously uncharted territory. *Revolution Dub*, issued on Creole's Cactus subsidiary in November, was a dub album with a difference: the obtrusive sound of television reared its ugly head over much of the record through overdubbed dialogue from an episode of television comedy *Doctor On The Go*. There was also drastic cross-channel stereophonic fading, heightening the separation of the bass and treble elements, and many vocal snippets were trapped in a kind of a freeze-frame echoing action, so that a word or individual syllable appeared from nowhere to echo over a dub's muted form. Such techniques emphasised the potentially menacing qualities lying beneath a seemingly innocuous rhythm, such as 'Woman Gotta Have Love' (here as 'Woman's Dub'), the most dramatic instance being 'Kojak', a transformed 'Move Out Of My Way'; over the barest of drum and bass rhythms, Perry becomes the bald, lollipop-sucking detective as Bunny Clarke's echoing voice is repeatedly frozen on the command 'move', a startling reconfiguration of disassociated brilliance. Byles' 'The Long Way' became a platform for TV slapstick (naturally titled 'Doctor On The Go'), and the title track another dub drum machine experiment; for the dub of 'Bushweed Corntrash' (titled 'Bush Weed'), Perry adds an element of fluidity by humming the absent melody line, positioning the track between a conventional dub and non-standard vocal.

Side two has Perry singing over several fresh dubs, further blurring the distinctions. 'Dreadlocks Talking' hinted that rude boy habits were influencing dread behaviour, as someone with a heavy French accent mirrors Perry's voice; the autobiographical 'Own Man' had a double-tracked Perry proclaiming his personal ethos; 'Dub The Rhythm', a slow and ghostly dub recut of 'Feel The Rhythm', was punctuated by Perry's belches, and 'Rain Drops' a Perry soul tearjerker.

Revolution Dub is another of Perry's long-playing oddities, lying somewhere between the extremities of dub and standard sung vocals. It emphasised Perry's inability to keep his work in any given static form, but the release was just another largely overlooked creation, its overreliance on television audio drawing protestations of gimmickry from the purists.

Lee Perry had spent 1974 and '75 building the reputation of his studio, refining his techniques within the new space, and giving input to the creations of others. But aside from the problematic success of 'Hurt So Good', the hits had not been forthcoming, his rivals regularly upstaging him during this transitory phase by updating classic Studio One and Treasure Isle rhythms for popular new dance tracks. Laying his rhythms at Channel One and voicing at King Tubby's, Bunny Lee scored a seemingly endless run of hits with singers such as Cornel Campbell, Johnny Clarke, Horace Andy and Linval Thompson, as well as deejay Jah Stitch from the Upsetter sound system; at Channel One, the Hoo-Kim brothers achieved far more with the Diamonds and Dillinger than Perry ever did, and Joe Gibbs was scoring with Jacob Miller and Leo Graham. Yet, Perry had no interest in replicating the formula of others. Sticking to his individual path, he was an outlier whose kinky sounds were in a zone of their own, a respected figure with a proven track record that was somehow still underground.

The big change came when Perry entered into an agreement with Chris Blackwell of Island Records, bringing his work to a whole new audience. In the early 1970s, Blackwell had largely turned away from reggae, dissolving his partnership with Lee Gopthal and turning Island into the premier independent label for progressive rock and folk music. After finding far more commercial success with acts like Traffic, Free, Cat Stevens and Jethro Tull, it seemed unlikely that Island would return to reggae until Bob Marley and the Wailers rose to international prominence after signing to the label in 1972. The progression from *Natty Dread* to *Rastaman Vibration* saw Marley emerging as an international superstar, bolstered by Eric Clapton's cover of 'I Shot The Sheriff' and the tremendous success of the 'No Woman, No Cry' single from *Live! At The Lyceum*, and by late 1975, Blackwell renewed his commitment to reggae in a broader sense by signing Burning Spear with the *Marcus Garvey* album, along with Toots and the Maytals, Third World and the Heptones, as well as Spear's producer, Jack Ruby.

Island built its reputation on music that was out of the ordinary, and although Blackwell was mindful that reggae could be difficult to market in its purest form, he had been bowled over by the music Perry produced with the Wailers. Blackwell rejected Perry's 'Dub Revolution', delivered as a prospective 45 in 1975, but the clincher came in Max Romeo's 'War In A Babylon', which Island released in February 1976 following its initial Jamaican issue under the title 'Sipple Out Deh'.

'I have a feeling the first thing that brought us together was "War In A Babylon" with Max Romeo,' said Blackwell. 'I can't remember how we initially got together. All I remember is spending a lot of time with him in the Black Ark studio.'

'He was hearing about me and want to meet me, and finally it happened,' said Perry.

Sipple means slippery and 'Sipple Out Deh' captured the
mounting anxiety as partisan vigilantes, police and soldiers
literally went to war in the street, with many a dread caught
in the crossfire:

> War inna Babylon
> Tribal war inna Babylon
> It sipple out deh
> The police man no like the dreadlocks man
> The dreadlocks man no like the policeman, no . . .
> Marcus Garvey prophecise, say
> One must live ten miles away in this time
> I man satta 'pon a mountain top
> Watching Babylon burning red hot . . .

Political violence was definitely on the increase, turning flashpoint communities into no-go areas, especially in western
Kingston, where the Payneland ghetto, off a middling stretch
of Spanish Town Road near the Three Mile roundabout, was
the site of repeated clashes, and the St Mary by-election of
October 1975 had been marred by factional attacks, showing
that partisan violence was not exclusive to the capital. Then,
relations with the United States sunk to an all-time low when
secretary of state Henry Kissinger held talks with Manley in
Kingston on 3 January 1976, pressuring him to renounce the
Cuban troops helping the MPLA to rout CIA-backed South
African forces in Angola, Manley's refusal to kowtow subsequently nullifying a billion-dollar trade agreement.

'Sipple Out Deh' used coded language to comment on
the slipperiness of these situations and their impact on
the common citizenry, the musical arrangement suitably
laden, especially in the intrusive lead guitar from Michael
Williams of the Zap Pow band, the percussion from Clinton

Fearon and Perry's wooden fish mirroring the tension in the streets.

Romeo said he brought the idea to Perry, who inserted the 'sipple' phrasing. Barry Llewellyn and Earl Morgan of the Heptones were recruited for harmony, the first of many records they would back at the Black Ark, and Bob Marley was so impressed by the song that he wanted to record it himself, borrowing the bassline for 'Three Little Birds' when Perry refused him the opportunity, according to Romeo.

Romeo also cut the scathing alternate 'Fire Fe The Vatican', and there was Jah Lloyd's taking cut, titled 'Leggo', as well as 'Stop The War In A Babylon' by baritone deejay James Brown, but the most important after-effect of 'Sipple Out Deh' was Blackwell's request for an album.

'Chris Blackwell came to the studio one day and Scratch played the song for him,' said Romeo. 'He said, "Yeah, we can do an album with this artist."'

The song would become an anthem for Romeo, though the economics were less straightforward.

'Scratch got [JMD] $15,000 for producing the song,' said Romeo. 'After production costs, he gave me $2,500, and that's the only money I get to date.'

Blackwell said Perry's studio was very orderly then, a reflection of his disciplined work ethic.

'It changed a lot over the years but when I first went there the place was absolutely pristine. You waited at the gate and it was usually one of his children that would go and call him. He'd come out of the studio, walk you down, show you where to sit. He was very precise and clean, very meticulous in everything he was doing. If somebody was smoking a cigarette he would instantly put an ashtray under them to make it clear what they were to do with it. On the back wall of the studio was a whole shelf of tapes and if you asked him about something that you'd listened to ages ago, he would be able to put his hand on it immediately.'

Both Blackwell and Perry remembered the working relationship as a loose one, based more on the spoken word than written contracts, leaving him free to work with other companies, similar to his arrangement with Trojan.

'There would always be an advance agreement and basically we had a royalty structure in Island,' said Blackwell. 'We had no Jamaican contract.'

Perry expressed a positive view of the bureaucracy-free relationship at the time.

'It's loose, working man to man. We a do it with words and words are the greatest contract – you can tell me the truth with words, face to face, and I believe you. And when you feel me a squeeze you, you say "watch out man, you squeeze me" and it done. We don't have to fight and shout out and chain down one another like slave, cos slavery days over.'[1]

Perhaps most importantly, the Island connection enabled another studio upgrade.

'Scratch came to England and was here for quite a few months,' said Bunny Clarke. 'He eventually made connection with Chris Blackwell, who I think gave him some money or some new equipment for the studio.'

The new gear included a Mu-Tron Bi-Phase, which made a dramatic impact on the Black Ark sound. Far more sophisticated than most other units on the market, the Bi-Phase had two integrated phasers that could be applied independently or jointly in various configurations. Each phaser could be allocated a standard smooth sine wave shape (as typically used by guitarists), or a square wave that oscillated between its high and low extremities, and there was also a reverse mode option for each phaser, allowing the frequency to phase downwards instead of up. Preset modes such as 'super phasing', 'stereo phasing' and 'double depth phasing' allowed for the synchronising of the phasers in various configurations, giving the kit near limitless parameters.

In Perry's hands, the Mu-Tron was a thing of wonder, a signature component that made his creations much more distinctive. It typically imparted a dense, spongy quality to whatever instrument or set of instruments it was applied, and when used in conjunction with the Space Echo, lent an otherworldly quality to his music.

The acquisition of a Pultec equaliser allowed Perry to draw out the best of the high and low frequencies without sacrificing the midrange, lending extra warmth and clarity to his work in the post-production phase, and the greater prominence of an acoustic Gerhard piano instilled a sense of timelessness to subsequent work, the upgraded equipment taking the edge off the cheap keyboards, rendering a sound that was ironically less dated than before, despite the obsolescence of the Vox and the Elka.

Once Perry reached an agreement with Island, he began working with a drive and determination that resulted in some of the finest work of his career. The new diligence made his studio a constant hive of activity, resulting in a series of superb albums with widespread international appeal.

CHAPTER NINE

Police and Thieves: The Golden Years of the Black Ark

The slower, heavier sounds that Lee Perry began to conjure at the Black Ark in 1976 had the quality of aural molasses, his rhythms holding subdued urgency, the deep dubs often undercut by a seething tension. These were dread echoes of what would prove to be a terribly turbulent period in Jamaican history, since both sides had much at stake in this election year, when the people would decide whether to continue with democratic socialism. As Perry's productions gained new depth and enhanced textural dimensions, so was his religious conviction deepening during a time of critical upheaval.

On 5–6 January, sustained episodes of violence erupted between the neighbouring communities of Concrete Jungle and Rema in Trench Town, where Seventh Street formed a boundary line. Jungle, officially Arnett Gardens, was a housing scheme established by the PNP in the early 1970s to counter the influence of Tivoli Gardens, and Rema, officially Wilton Gardens, a longstanding JLP stronghold. As the violence intensified, Rema was set ablaze, with twenty-two homes razed by firebombs, and a gunfight raged throughout the night, leaving one dead and dozens homeless.

As the disturbances spread to other areas such as neighbouring Jones Town, a Joint Committee meeting of the IMF and World Bank was underway at the Pegasus Hotel in New Kingston, where a noisy anti-apartheid demonstration was staged outside in protest of South Africa's attendance, and in the afternoon, the protestors marched to the US Consulate at Cross Roads, which was stoned, a shattered glass panel injuring visa applicants and staff inside. Later that night, in separate incidents, a special constable guarding the Consulate was shot dead, his colleague wounded, and two members of the Mobile Reserve guarding a construction site on Marcus Garvey Drive were killed by gunmen, who stole their firearms, sparking anti-government demonstrations by other members of the Mobile Reserve and a sick-out at the Cross Roads police station.

At the same time, acute cases of food poisoning were cropping up in St Thomas, with fifteen dead by the end of the month, the source eventually traced to a consignment of contaminated flour imported from Germany. Violence continued to flare in inner-city areas such as Waterhouse and Tivoli Gardens, and the PNP claimed that land earmarked for the Cooreville Gardens housing scheme, just west of Washington Gardens, was being used as a training ground for armed vigilantes intent on overthrowing the government.

Then, in February, when a Cuban contingent arrived on the island to begin building a donated school in Clarendon, Manley was accused of allowing Jamaica to become a pawn of Castro and the Soviet Union, met by counter-charges that the CIA was orchestrating a campaign to discredit him, allegedly assisted by the JLP, the *Gleaner* newspaper and foreign media.

Against this escalating backdrop, Pauline Morrison travelled to England with the first batch of Perry productions for the year. At the reggae emporium Daddy Kool, located on a backstreet in London's fashionable West End, Morrison delivered Jamaican pressings of Lord Creator's lewd calypso 'Big Pussy Sally', Fay Bennett's lewder alternate, 'Big Cockey Wally', and two singles by west Kingston harmony group Winston Heywood and the Hombres, namely 'Back Biting', a song against aggression and greed, and 'Long Long Time', lamenting the absent good times, which Morrison would subsequently licence to Mango in Birmingham.

The Blue Bells' 'Come Along' was one of the most noteworthy of the year's early crop. The duo was formed by Hector Wright and Raphael Martin, who first recorded at the Ark with the Gladiators band in 1975 for a song Martin led, 'Call Me Teacher' (released on Alvin Ranglin's Typhoon label); 'Come Along' featured a double-tracked Wright alone, imploring the listener to flee Babylon with heavy doses of delay on the vocal, the musical backing consisting of just drum, bass and keyboards.

Perry's 'Roast Fish And Cornbread' made a bigger splash, especially when Island released it in July, the song a playful celebration of Perry's favourite sustenance voiced on an unhurried rhythm from the Gladiators, laid down gratis, according to Clinton Fearon: 'We did eight rhythms that day but didn't get paid for the last one, which was "Roast Fish And Cornbread".'

There was Horace Smart's 'Ruffer Ruff', describing the upcoming singer's impoverished youth, its dub deconstructing the vocal, with heavy phasing on the piano and guitar; 'Four And Twenty Dreadlocks' was an adaptation of 'Four And Twenty Blackbirds' by one Evan Jones, and the lyrics of

'Babylon Deh Pon Fire', credited to Truth Fact and Correct, betrayed the influence of the Nation of Islam over a charging rhythm driven by Nyabinghi-styled conga drumming.

Keith Rowe of harmony duo Keith and Tex cut a few songs at the Black Ark during his brief visit to Jamaica early in 1976. He and Perry had become acquainted in Washington Gardens, where Rowe was based before moving to New York in 1972, and he returned after having won the first Festival Song Competition held in New York in 1975, the prize a first-class flight to Jamaica.

'It was January or February 1976,' said Rowe. 'He said, "Well, you're here, so let's work", though I'd never worked with him before. He called up Robbie Lyn and some other guys and we went in the studio and start working. I did three or four songs: "Groovy Situation", "Living My Life" and another one. Those songs that I did for Scratch had a feel I've never had. There was a real down-to-earthness that permeated the entire session. The feeling was right, and the mood was right, especially with "Groovy Situation". I left Jamaica a couple of days later.'

A laidback love song, 'Groovy Situation' obviously had hit potential, so Perry fielded it to Clocktower in New York, frustrating Rowe, who intended to release it there himself.

'Scratch was supposed to deal with Jamaica and England, and I would deal with America,' said Rowe. 'He gave me a master tape, but my friend had it in his Volkswagen that got broken into and it got stolen. Then Scratch reneged on the agreement: he sent tapes to Brad Osborne in the Bronx who put "Groovy Situation" out. That was the way the business went.'

Back in Jamaica, Devon Irons' fiery 'When Jah Come' surfaced in May, a stern warning to wrongdoers of coming retribution on another hard-hitting Upsetter rhythm with

Nyabinghi conga drumming, responding to the rising tide of partisan violence.

'When me check Scratch and sing the first line of "When Jah Come", him line up the musicians and lay the rhythm same time and we voice it the next day,' said Irons, an uncredited co-writer of Johnny Clarke's spectacular hit, 'None Shall Escape The Judgement', who was told of Perry's studio by a friend in the neighbourhood.

Although concentrating on his own productions, Perry was still engineering sporadic work for others at the Black Ark, including a couple of fine Cimarons tracks laid early in 1976. The group arrived in Jamaica in December 1975 for a series of concerts arranged by Tommy Cowan, who had issued their hit cover of Bob Marley's 'Talking Blues' on his Talent Corporation label. Remaining on the island for three and a half months, they played before a massive crowd at the National Arena on New Year's Eve, and in February gave a well-received performance at the Roots nightclub in Chela Bay, adjacent to the Playboy Club-Hotel, constructing their album *On The Rock* mostly at Joe Gibbs and Channel One, though the song 'Paul Bogle', saluting the Jamaican hero, was recorded at the Black Ark, along with 'Greedy Man', about the priceless nature of love (it would surface on the B-side of an extended twelve-inch of 'Bogle' issued by the group considerably later).

Rupie Edwards, then living in nearby Duhaney Park, recorded 'Three Pan One A Murder' with drummer Eric 'Fish' Clarke and bassist Errol 'Flabba' Holt at the Ark, addressing the political violence in Rema, Concrete Jungle and Tivoli Gardens; minimalist love song 'Baby It's You' was recorded at the same session and dubs of both tracks were issued as a separate single, Edwards later returning to voice 'Rise And Fall' on 'Three Pan One', overdubbing a new piano part he played himself.

Deejay Tappa Zukie, born David Sinclair, also produced inspiring work at the Ark in the same period, much of it in the predominate 'rockers' style that revolved around aggressive drum patterns and meaty basslines. He and his brother Blackbeard had longstanding association with Bunny Lee, and after a terribly disrupted youth, Tappa acted as a bodyguard for Lee, who helped him launch his career with Clem Bushay in England after he got caught up in the partisan violence of the early 1970s. Prince Allah's 'Bosrah' was voiced on a durable new cut of the 'He Prayed' rhythm, redone in rockers mode; the sure-fire team of Sly Dunbar and Robbie Shakespeare gave the song its rhythmic anchor and there was a brilliant horn fanfare worthy of the lyrics, which relay portions of the Book of Isaiah on the coming of the Lord from a Rastafari perspective, with Roy 'Soft' Palmer of the Spears and Tony Brevett on harmonies. The song would make an impact in Britain in the summer on pre-release.

'Lee "Scratch" Perry really did the arrangements,' said Prince Allah, born Keith Blake. 'He is a man weh in the spirit when him in the studio, so him just hold the spirit and give the brother the bassline and get it nice. Lee "Scratch" Perry did a great part because he was a more advanced man – he know about music.'

'Lee Perry was not just an engineer, he also add to the production that was going on,' said Tappa Zukie. 'I was a young producer then, but Lee Perry helped me structure that song, that's how my education start to expand from Bunny Lee's classroom. When I went to record that tune I didn't go there to just record, I go there to take in a lesson from Lee Perry.'

Trench Town harmony quintet Knowledge also worked with Zukie at the Black Ark, their 'What's Yours' addressing factional violence; 'Make Faith' emphasised the need for committed devotion and 'Everyone Have Their Works' warned against shirking and theft, while the devotional 'Zion' was initiated at the Ark and finished at Chalk Farm.

Gregory Isaacs' 'Mister Cop' was a popular single issued in Jamaica by Micron, who arranged distribution in Canada, with subsequent sublicencing helping it reach other territories. The song was co-produced by Isaacs, whose lyrics demanded that overzealous police cease their harassment of peaceful, weed-smoking dreads, the music enveloped by Perry's swirling phaser effects.

Except for 'Big Pussy Sally', virtually all of the singles Perry produced in early 1976 had tough, mind-bending dubs, the Roland Space Echo greatly influencing their overall shape. 'Say A Prayer', the version side of 'Three Pan One', was one of the more extreme examples, heightened by skilful freeze-frame mixing.

While working in earnest with Max Romeo on the *War Ina Babylon* album, Perry delivered Pat Francis' deejay LP, *Colombia Colly*, released by Island in May under his new alias, Jah Lion.

'It's kind of complicated, so much names,' said Francis. 'When I do as Jah Lloyd, Upsetter say, "You seem like a lion, so I'm going to call you Jah Lion", and *Colombia Colly* take about two weeks, recording three or four tracks a day.'

Most of the album made use of older rhythms, updated in keeping with Perry's contemporary style, and Francis' toasting is relaxed and confident, his charged yet understated delivery perfectly suited for Perry's complex musical stew. Most of the songs dealt with Rastafari spirituality, though there were glimpses of the lighter sides of life too.

Opening track 'Wisdom' set the tone by affirming Jah's ever-lasting life and limitless powers, delivered in drawling patois on a forceful cut of 'Words', with spring-reverb thunderclaps and plenty of vocal delay; 'Dread In A Jamdong' rode a fresh rhythm, the enhanced keyboard sound one of the benefits of Blackwell's cash injection; 'Hay Fever' was a clever recasting of the 'Fever' rhythm, a squeaking door emphasising its ironic new form, and 'Flashing Whip' a remixed cut of 'The Lama' with percussion moved to the fore.

In the mid-to-late 1970s, Colombia was a major exporter of marijuana, especially to the United States. Colombian weed had a reputation for being strong and pleasant to smoke, becoming the contraband of choice for many potheads, so the title track had Perry and Francis debating the merits of this imported weed on a modulated mix of 'Rejoicing Skank'.

Side two began with another new rhythm, a reverse adaptation of Carl Malcolm's hit ballad 'Fatty Bum Bum' as the censorious 'Fat Man', built around a disappearing bassline and again making good use of the Ark's new keyboard sound. There was the 'Bad Luck Natty' single, Francis bemoaning his poor lot over the 'Dub Organiser' rhythm with new percussion and keyboard overdubs, while the autobiographical 'Black Lion' double-tracked the toaster's interpretation of biblical events over an organ-led cut of 'What Can I Do'. 'Little Sally Daughter' (mistitled 'Little Sally Dater') referenced a children's ring game song on a cut of 'To Be A Lover', Perry multi-tracking Francis' voice to include frozen, echoing fragments beneath his toast. The closing 'Satta' rode Augustus Pablo's sterling recut of the Abyssinians' anthem 'Satta Amassa Gana', again with disjointed vocal fragments.

Colombia Colly failed to make much impact, and Francis was disappointed financially. Nevertheless, he praised Perry's instructive command.

'Me enjoy working with Lee Perry because he knows everything about the music. Forget about the money part of it, but he's a genius – me and him do some nice work.'

DAVID KATZ

Between the release of *Colombia Colly* and the completion of *War Ina Babylon*, local violence had drastically intensified. On the night of 19 May, following the tit-for-tat killings of partisan gang members near National Heroes Park in an area of Fletcher's Land then with mixed party support, a large tenement on Orange Lane was set alight by fifty men, who obstructed the exits and prevented police and firefighters from attending the blaze, leaving eleven dead and hundreds homeless. Then, after the Peruvian ambassador Fernando Rodriguez was stabbed to death, Manley implemented a State of Emergency on 20 June for an initial period of one month, ultimately extended to a full year. During that time, nearly 600 citizens would be detained, including Senator Pearnel Charles, deputy leader of the JLP, who would spend eleven months at Up-Park Camp (headquarters of the Jamaica Defence Force), allegedly suspected of plotting to overthrow the government; parliamentarian Olivia 'Babsy' Grange was held for seven months, purportedly for 'issuing firearms to unauthorised persons', according to the *Gleaner*, and freed only on the condition that she go into 'voluntary exile' overseas.

War Ina Babylon was completed amidst the chaos of the impending State of Emergency. Following the title track's issue in the UK in February, Island released it in the US in the spring (prompting Perry to reissue the single in Jamaica), and when the song took off in New York in May, they scrambled to release the follow-up, 'One Step Forward', holding back the album until mid-September.

According to Romeo, the incendiary second single was aimed at Michael Manley, urging him not to abandon his principles.

'I said, "We're taking one step forward and two steps backward because you don't know whether to suit Uncle Sam or

272

to suit the people. One day you're a dreadlocks to hold up the Rod of Correction and the next day you're a baldhead. Onward, forward and don't step backward, make we step out of Babylon!" That was straight to Manley's head.'

The rest of the album mixed broad social protest with a particular Rastafari worldview. For instance, 'Uptown Babies' portrayed the impact of Jamaica's vast social divide on her children, while 'I Chase The Devil' had Romeo donning an 'iron shirt' to rid the world of Satan's influence, responding to one of Perry's recurring preoccupations.

'Lee Perry is a man who have some contention with the Devil,' said Romeo. 'He come up with this song about hanging the Devil or cutting the Devil's throat and throwing him in the fire, so I said, "Let's just chase him out of earth and send him to outer space to find another race", and right away I go into writing the song.'[1]

According to Romeo, Perry reworked his lyrics, as usual.

'In those days, you write a song, and you take it to Scratch, no matter how good your song is, it's never good enough. You've got to debate it and then take out that, put that in, and at the end of the day, you give him 50 per cent of the publishing.'

'Norman' depicted gambling buddy Norman Elliot, brother of JBC disc jockey Desmond Elliot, the song's ominous quality imparted by the horn section of Richard 'Dirty Harry' Hall, Herman Marquis, Bobby Ellis and Vin Gordon. 'Stealin'' was aimed at devious preachers who used the cloak of religion to feed off the poor, while 'Tan And See' revived the 'Dub Revolution' rhythm for a Romeo sermon laden with proverbs and biblical symbolism, enhanced by harmonies from Marcia Griffiths, Earl Morgan, Barry Llewellyn and Winston Blake's future wife, Cynthia Schloss. 'Smokey Room' reworked 'Feel The Rhythm' for a song about strong weed, and 'Smile Out

Of Style' revived the Untouchables' 'Time' rhythm to bemoan the pervasive pessimism resulting from Jamaica's rampant inflation.

War Ina Babylon was the best-selling album of Max Romeo's long career, though he claimed never to have received proper financial recompense for it, and the uncredited presence of the innovative folk-rock artist John Martyn guesting on guitar added to the appeal for overseas audiences, as *Melody Maker*'s Ray Coleman discovered when he was treated to a sneak preview of the album at Perry's studio shortly before the State of Emergency was declared.

Chris Blackwell had sent Martyn to Jamaica on an extended holiday, hoping to avert burnout and for him to dry out following the tragic death of touring bandmate Paul Kossoff, who, like Martyn, had long battled substance misuse; Mandrax and heroin contributed to Kossoff's premature demise, and although cocaine and other hard drugs were part of the problem, alcohol was Martyn's chief vice. Nevertheless, during the months that he and his family spent at Blackwell's Strawberry Hill retreat in the Blue Mountains, Martyn took the opportunity to record at the Black Ark a handful of times, armed with a vintage Gibson SG and an Electro-Harmonix phaser, an attractive piece of kit that several players tried to cadge off him. Like Perry, Martyn had embraced the Echoplex and was an early experimenter with phasers and rhythm boxes, so they enjoyed a certain affinity, despite the vastly different spheres in which they worked, and hit it off when Blackwell brought them together, sharing plenty of rum during their studio collaborations.

'John Martyn was my personal friend,' said Perry. 'We write some songs, and it was great fun to work together. He was willing to try anything.'

Junior Murvin appeared at the Black Ark in May 1976 at the tail end of *War Ina Babylon*. A schoolfriend of Watty Burnett from Port Antonio (born Mervin Smith Junior), Murvin had a broad range, though was best known for his soaring falsetto. After passing through an early incarnation of the Hippy Boys, he wrote the chart-topping 'Solomon' for Derrick Harriott and cut a number of hits as Junior Soul before joining popular live band, the Falcons; then, after returning to Port Antonio, he began fronting Young Experience with trumpeter Bobby Ellis, performing in Cuba as part of a Jamaican delegation, and at high-profile events in Jamaica, including a birthday party for Michael Manley's wife, Beverley.

When Young Experience showed signs of faltering in the spring of 1976, Murvin concentrated on songwriting, composing much of his strongest material at Folly Ruins, the remains of a grandiose mansion on a peninsula east of Port Antonio, addressing Jamaica's political and social upheavals.

'While I was singing in Young Experience, I took time out from rehearsals, so sometimes I go by Folly Ruins, sit by the sea, punch my tape and sing what is happening, and when I come home, I put verses to it,' said Murvin. 'When the band break up, I get a vision to carry me to Lee Perry in Kingston because he was a very hardcore producer. I just get a vision and I went straight in with it.'

They had already met in the rock steady years when Perry was supervising auditions for Clement Dodd.

'I auditioned at Studio One with a song by Lloyd Price named "I've Got The Blues", and he told me all I needed was one more verse, so he sent me to sit under a mango tree and I got hungry and went away.'

This time around, one particular song caught Perry's ear: 'Police And Thieves', which spoke to the threat posed by both entities, armed to the teeth and using their weaponry indiscriminately:

> Police and thieves in the street
> Fighting the nation with their guns and ammunition
> Police and thieves in the street
> Scaring the nation with their guns and ammunition
> From Genesis to Revelation
> The next generation will be, hear me . . .

Though Perry felt the lyrics needed slight amendments, he began to build the rhythm track straight away.

'He said he needed a little more words, so we put in a couple more words and Boris Gardiner lay the rhythm along with Ernest Ranglin and Sly Dunbar, Keith Sterling on keyboards and Joe Cooper, an old friend from Port Antonio, a very good organist who usually play with the Mighty Vikings.'

There was harmony from Barry Llewellyn and Earl Morgan, too, their wordless chorus a hooking counterbalance, but the song's unusual lyrics really made it stand out, the imagistic commentary striking a note with listeners far and wide.

Everyone present knew that 'Police And Thieves' would hit, so Perry arranged for the single to be handled by Federal, who issued the song on their Wildflower subsidiary in May. Backed by the appropriately named 'Grumbling Dub', which reduced the vocal to stabs of echoed murmuring, the single was an instant success in Jamaica, despite being banned for 'saying the truth', according to Perry.

Chris Blackwell was struck by the topical nature of 'Police And Thieves', having first heard the song after passing through a roadblock.

'I remember going down to his studio one time and we just got stopped for no reason on the way, have an M16 shoved in our face by a young police guy,' said Blackwell. 'And when I went in the studio, they were doing "Police And Thieves".'

Released by Island in July, 'Police And Thieves' received widespread airplay and became the unofficial theme song of the Notting Hill Carnival, where it boomed from countless sound systems, since the police had increased their presence tenfold that year; after officers tried to arrest a pickpocket and the public intervened, pitched battles were waged between police and revellers over the course of several hours, leading to sixty-six arrests and dozens injured on both sides. Transposed surprisingly easily from Kingston to London, the unfortunate reality of police aggression made 'Police And Thieves' hit home for many in Britain. Remaining in *Melody Maker*'s top ten for twenty-three weeks, it was dubbed 'Reggae Single of the Year' in *Echoes* and the sixth-best single in any category on *NME*'s end-of-year chart.

The widespread popularity of 'Police And Thieves' inevitably spawned other versions on the same rhythm, including Jah Lion's 'Soldier And Police War', which began with Bongo Herman's laboured breathing in imitation of someone who had been chased; Jamaican B-side 'Dub Of Justice' had Herman's scattered conga drumming, and Island's overseas issue, backed by Glen DaCosta's saxophone instrumental, 'Magic Touch', was released in the UK in October and the US the following spring.

Just after Island released 'Police And Thieves', Perry's incredible *Scratch The Super Ape* appeared as a Jamaican pre-release, followed by Island's issue as *Super Ape* in early August (the UK pressings with sides one and two reversed). The album was a tour de force of Black Ark wizardry, weaving musical streams through the various pies Perry had his fingers in to form a startling organic whole of dub unity, with a smattering of standard vocals and an experimental jazz underpinning throughout.

The cover of *Scratch The Super Ape* had an elaborate illustration of an ape-like human with a leonine dreadlocked mane, painted by Ras Daniel Heartman's protégé, Anthony Witter (alias Witter Dread), while on Island's issue, Tony Wright's equally imaginative cover placed the Super Ape in a comic-book jungle, striding with authority through the mists of creation, uprooting trees and flattening all in his wake, powered by the fat spliff protruding from his hairy palm and the roast fish and cornbread in his stomach.

The rhythmic bedrock was laid by drummers Mikey 'Boo' Richards and Benbow Creary, with Boris Gardiner, Chinna Smith and keyboardist Keith Sterling, as well as Bobby Ellis, Dirty Harry, Vin Gordon and flautist Egbert Evens, with the Heptones handling the vocals on several key tracks. For 'Zion's Blood', the trio affirmed their African heritage on a modulated 'When Jah Come', now laden with searing horns and atmospheric keyboards atop its driving African beats. 'Croaking Lizard' edged closer to dub proper, Prince Jazzbo's esoteric toast on the 'I Chase The Devil' rhythm only partway intact, and the title referenced another Perry persona, this one a nocturnal gecko that makes an uncanny croaking sound during the mating season. 'Black Vest' was a 'War In A Babylon' dub with snatches of its alternate vocals, 'Underground Root' placed a female chorus atop one of Perry's most mysterious and bass-heavy rhythms, namely Clive Hylton's 'From Creation' (cut as a dub plate for Lloyd Coxsone's sound system in London), here with emphasis on Chinna Smith's wah-wah guitar and Boris Gardiner's rock-solid bass. 'Curly Dub' was a spiritual Perry scat, the jazz element heightened by the heady flute and trombone melodies.

On side two, 'Dread Lion' was a Heptones choral vocal chant on the 'Concrete Castle King' rhythm, lifted higher by melodica and flute overdubs, and made trippier by Perry's growling roars and shouted interjections, as well as spring-reverb thunderclaps. 'Three In One' was another spacey vocal chant with vibrant congas from Scully and freaky keyboard licks, while 'Patience' was a fresh instrumental with processed funky blues guitar from Chinna, the horn riffs hinting at jazz, but a ghostly toast from an uncredited deejay grounded it all in dub. 'Dub Along' replaced the male voice of the Blue Bells with snatches of a female chorus, and the closing title track used the Heptones' deep harmonies to emphasise the album's overriding theme on a rhythm punctuated by toy whistle blasts: 'This is the ape man, trodding through creation, are you ready to step with I-man?'

If *Revelation Time* and *War Ina Babylon* were reggae concept albums for Max Romeo, then *Super Ape* was Perry's dub concept album, using the rhythms to express his broader ideas about nature's powers of endurance. Perry grew up in the depths of the countryside, where the spirit world was readily acknowledged and Ettu part of the community's shared African heritage, and as Perry entered his forties, such buried influences began to re-emerge, here even reaching back to the primordial dawning of mankind to celebrate a naturalistic era free of greed and senseless divisions.

According to Romeo, Blackwell loved the album but was perplexed by Perry's lackadaisical approach.

'The tape was hanging an inch and a half from the reel. Chris Blackwell walked into the studio and said, "Holy shit! I've never seen anything like this! That tape's hanging from the reel! Come on Scratch, what's that?" Scratch said, "Man, this album is *Super Ape*, so it's got to be on a *super tape*."'

To celebrate his successes with Island and to emphasise his spiritual beliefs, Perry had Jah Wise, the selector of Tippertone, decorate the studio's exterior walls with huge, multicoloured murals: a portrait of Selassie was above the door, so that all would have to 'bow' to Jah upon entering or leaving; to the left was Selassie in his feline form as the Conquering Lion of Judah. Another wall had a life-size Super Ape, tree and spliff in hand, while interior images depicted African ancestors in chains and Rastafari tri-colour flags. Such images would be altered and recast as Perry sought to express alternate concepts; like the music that was made at the studio, its illustrated walls would seldom remain static. Perry also erected a 'Management Order' by the front gate, proclaiming that the premises were on the site of a private house where women and children lived, so all who sought to enter should wait for official permission and, once inside, were to refrain from using indecent language.

As *Super Ape* got its finishing touches, Perry began working solidly with the Heptones, who had endured a period of inactivity following Leroy Sibbles' migration to Canada in 1973, only to return to prominence with the *Night Food* album, a commercial success recorded at Harry J and issued by Island in March 1976, leading to their new work with Perry.

'I like the Heptones voices and how they sing harmony,' said Perry. 'Leroy is really something special. He's one of the best bass man and he can sing falsetto, he can sing natural, so he's very unique.'

The first single to surface from the partnership was 'Sufferer's Time', a protest song led by Barry Llewellyn, proclaiming that ghetto dwellers had as much right to own a decent house and car as the elite; a slow, roots-oriented rendition was issued first, the faster and lighter alternate that followed aimed at the foreign market, according to Earl Morgan.

'Lee Perry is a man who swap everything. He say, "That one there's a little slow, give me a faster one, upbeat, cos this one is for the foreign, that one is for local", so we do a foreign version and a local version.'

However, Island declined to issue the faster vocal, somehow placing the fast dub on the B-side of the slow vocal, but in any case, more impressive material would soon follow, as the album they were working on with Perry took shape.

On 28 August, Perry received a special award for continuous services in the field of record production at the inaugural Jamaica Arts Awards Committee Show Ball, held by Clancy Eccles at the National Arena. Island's concerted publicity effort brought several leading British and American journalists to town in time for the event, a steady stream of visitors witnessing key moments at the Black Ark.

NME's Neil Spencer arrived in time to catch Perry adapting a Hindi film song, 'Milte Hi Aankhein' (or 'As Soon As Our Eyes Met') with Sam Carty, who proposed it to Perry; the song was first performed by Talat Mahmood and Shamshad Begum in S. U. Sunny's 1950 Bollywood epic *Babul* (aka *Father's House*), about two women, one poor and one rich, vying for the attentions of a postmaster, though Carty was unfamiliar with the film.

'I learned the song "Milte Hi Aankhen" by chance as a young teacher on staff with some Indian expatriate teachers in Jamaica,' said Carty. 'I felt the reggae pulse on two songs I learned from them right away, tested them on my guitar, then went to share the idea with Scratch.'

For the Black Ark rendition, Perry built a dramatic rhythm with a hefty bassline, unusual percussion and dramatic sound treatments. Spencer was amazed by Perry's working methods, constantly dancing as he mixed and dropping instruments in and out without warning, but, noting that the Teac four-track was feeding the two-track, he could not fathom how many tracks were in use.

'We only have use fe three tracks here,' quipped Perry. 'That's the Father, the Son and The Holy Ghost.'[2]

When *Sounds'* reggae specialist Vivien Goldman arrived, she was astounded by the volume of material being captured on tape, likening the studio to a 'conveyor belt for harmony groups'. She found Perry very focused and serious about his work, and though his temper could be short when musicians failed to muster what he was searching for, Perry would dance non-stop in the control room, driven by the force of the music. Studio idlers were a bothersome presence that drew his bile from time to time, and when the work was done, sometimes Perry would screen kung fu films for respite in the evening.

Later, Perry's 'White Belly Rat' single was a vindictive barb aimed at Bunny Lee, sparked by another fallout. It was based on a Jamaican proverb about dishonourable intentions, and Max Romeo said Perry wanted him to sing the song.

'I wouldn't because Bunny Lee is supposed to be the white belly rat. He and Scratch always have a feud. I don't know why, but even now, they are friends today and enemies tomorrow.'

Perry asked young singer Earl 'Sixteen' Daley to have a go, too, but was dissatisfied with the result. The teenaged tenor had been in showband the Boris Gardiner Happening but was fired for failing to observe the dress code at a socialite nurses' ball; preferring the company of Hugh Mundell and Augustus Pablo, he was often present at the Black Ark from late 1976, hoping that Perry would make use of his talents.

Then, Prince Jazzbo's 'Dreadlocks Corner' was a weighty number issued on a label called Truth and Rights, its illustration showing a member of the security forces with guns drawn, aimed at a dread with the butt of a spliff in his mouth; flipside 'Ital Corner' was a tough toast of 'One Step

Forward' and Jazzbo's 'Natty Pass Through Rome' single was even heavier, the anti-Catholic chant relating his journey through the hell of Babylon on the 'Concrete Castle King' rhythm. These singles and a handful of other tracks would surface later in the year as *Natty Passing Thru'*, released by Black Wax in Britain, the material recorded in less than an hour, according to Jazzbo.

'Inna them time there I just love the music. Him play about sixteen riddim tracks 'pon a tape and me just start deejay on top till me reach at the bottom.'

The bulk of the album was cut on fresh creations from Boris Gardiner, Mikey Boo, Chinna Smith and Keith Sterling, the few earlier rhythms still seeming in place, thanks to Jazzbo's consistent delivery. There was a powerful alternate take of 'Satta' titled 'Prophet Live', 'Blood Dunza' sounded like an outtake from *Revolution Dub* due to its television dialogue, and 'Story Come To Bump' reworked Winston Heywood's 'Long Long Time'; 'Weeping And Wailing' had Jazzbo chanting proverbs over one of Perry's brilliant organ workouts (as featured on the cut-up 'Operation'), while 'Live Good Today' and 'Life Is Gonna Easy' rode Sam Carty's 'I Don't Mind' and 'Life Is A Flower' respectively.

Lacking a strong distribution network, Black Wax could only achieve so much with *Natty Passing Thru'*. Nevertheless, its sustained appeal as a cult classic would see it repackaged as *Ital Corner*, released on Clocktower in December 1979, with later reissues in various formats.

Dennis Brown voiced some exceptional work for Niney the Observer at the Black Ark in the summer of 1976, using rhythms laid at Randy's, the hit 'Wolves And Leopards' one of the most enduring of Brown's consistently strong career, though the rhythm was earmarked for another singer.

'We voice and mix songs at Black Ark like "Wolves And Leopards",' said Niney. 'Me and Scratch and Dennis Brown write that song, but Scratch write the most of it. I made the rhythm for Sang Hugh but when he reach a certain part of the song, it wasn't quite right, so he said he want a different rhythm. Me and Scratch come up with the idea of "Wolves And Leopards" and we say Dennis Brown is the right one to sing it. I bring Dennis round Scratch, and then we write and voice the song, and one named "Broadway" [a version of the Drifters' 'On Broadway' titled 'In Zion'] and "Here I Come", which was my idea. I have that song from in my twenties and I sing harmonies 'pon it. Those rhythms do at Randy's, but we come to Scratch to mix it and Scratch's studio was four-track, but you could get a lot of tracks out of it – it's a Teac, but it's a different machine. If he hook it up a certain way he can get up to twelve tracks.'

Perry's skilful mixing greatly enhanced the songs, helping 'Wolves And Leopards' to hit in Jamaica, and its UK issue on the Third World label, run by sound system proprietor Count Shelley, was also highly successful. I Roy later voiced toasting cuts 'Step On The Dragon' and rude alternate 'Maggie Breast', the latter saluting Perry's insatiable libido in an opening limerick.

Then, 'Here I Come' was a stunning devotional song that Brown retained as a stage-entry piece for the rest of his career, its release delayed until January 1977, and I Roy's toasting cut 'Jah Come Here' related tales of everyday life amongst the Jamaican immigrant community in London.

Devon Irons returned to the Ark to record the compelling 'Ketch Vampire', the strongest commentary yet on the 'false Rasta' phenomena, denouncing impostors that wore locks as a cover for wickedness. Issued in September 1976, the song recounted an incident of political factionalism he witnessed

– ironically on Unity Lane in Waterhouse – where his Rasta friend Sapo was chased by a dreadlocked gunman into the drainage gully dividing Waterhouse from Maverley, during a time when being on the wrong side of the political divide could easily get you killed.

'The dreadlocks was from a set of youth weh only preach politics every day,' said Irons, who also issued copies of the single on his Cannon Ball label. 'Them youth there no work, them rob and scam and kill people through politics.'

'You never know when Scratch call you in those days, he have some different ideas,' said Clive Hunt. 'I went with my trumpet and he tell me to play bass and just moved everyone around: Robbie Lyn play keyboard, Mikey Boo play drums and Fil Callendar from In Crowd play guitar.'

Around the same time, Errol Hammond, alias Lion Zion, a Jamaican-American based in Oakland, California, produced the album *Reggae In America* at the Black Ark with Lloyd Parks, Benbow, Keith Sterling and Fil Callendar, plus Barry Llewellyn, Earl Morgan and the Zap Pow horns. Its outstanding single, 'Who Killed The Buffalo', about the historic slaughter of bison by Buffalo Bill, surfaced in Jamaica on the House of Natty label, distributed by Talent Corporation.

The album itself was released in Oakland as the sole LP on House of Natty, with tracks like 'American Revolution', 'Arise America' and 'Gas Guzzler' criticising the self-centred greed of the 'Me generation' and the inherent hypocrisy at the nation's root. The album had rock-solid rhythms, though the singer's double-tracked vocals were not always so strong; choral over-dubs by the National Dance Theatre Singers of Jamaica and the Oakland Black Ensemble hinted at crossover potential, but Lion Zion distributed much of the stock himself on his bicycle, the album soon relegated to record shop bargain bins.

Back in Jamaica, Junior Murvin's 'False Teaching' was issued on Wildflower in November, followed by the Heptones' 'Crying Over You', reworking an early Caltone single. The Meditations harmony trio was also recording parts of debut album *Message From The Meditations* at the Black Ark for the singer-turned-producer Dobby Dobson, including the evocative 'Rastaman Prayer', led by Danny Clarke from the Flames, the contemplative 'There Must Be A First Time', led by soprano youngblood Winston Watson, and the outstanding hit 'Running From Jamaica', led by Ansel Cridland (formerly a member of the Hombres), which lambasted the wealthy elite that had abandoned the country for exile in Miami.

'"Running From Jamaica" is from election time in '76,' said Cridland. 'I no believe in *politricks*, cos politricks is what them use to overthrow Jah. One party say, "Plant food", trying to enlighten the people so that the people could read and write, but some want to keep people in the same runnings, so it cause a conflict. Now election coming up and people start to sell out and run away. I sorry I didn't have two shillings because I see some nice houses that sell out for little or nothing because them never want to stand up to the struggle. To run left Jamaica and come in any foreign land come live, it's slavery again, and this is torment more than anything for your mind. In Jamaica you can plant food in your backyard, and you can live, but [overseas] you have nowhere fe plant nothing and everything you buy is a tax 'pon you.'

Bob Marley also continued frequenting the Black Ark in late 1976, working with Perry on an alternate of 'Smile Jamaica', a song he wrote for the Jamaican Tourist Board to counter falling visitor numbers, according to Judy Mowatt. The better-known version, recorded at Harry J, was slower and more rounded with the full Zap Pow horn section and a broader vocal arrangement; it received widespread radio airplay in Jamaica, unlike much of the Wailers' more militant work, and in contrast, the uptempo Black Ark version was driven by phased keyboards and modulated guitar, with some fine Nyabinghi congas peppering Carly's quick beats, Marley scatting midway through over the punchy I-Threes harmonies.

'Bob did a version of "Smile Jamaica" at Harry J, but him come to me and say, "Boy, me want to change it up,"' said Sangie Davis, who knew Marley through the Twelve Tribes of Israel. 'Me and him go down to Scratch with the idea and did the next one.'

'The two songs sound different and I think the different recordings are two great recordings in themselves,' said Mowatt. 'You can't say you like this one and you don't like that one, you just love both of them.'

'We respect Scratch for his expertise and his talent,' said Rita Marley. 'It was always exciting at his studio.'

'Smile Jamaica' became the theme song of a free concert the Wailers would stage on 5 December, but the circumstances of the event yielded grave consequences. The idea was sparked the year before, when the Wailers shared the bill with Stevie Wonder at the National Stadium for the Wonder Dream Concert, a benefit for the Jamaican Institute for the Blind, and after Wonder donated half his fee, Marley conceived a free concert in Jamaica as a way of giving something back to the nation.

Nothing was organised until October 1976, when an event was proposed that would be sponsored by the cultural section of the prime minister's office, and some say Marley pitched the concept, others that PNP heavyweights approached him first. The mini festival, with Third World, the Light of Saba Drummers, and keyboardist Richard Ace and his son on the bill, was scheduled to take place on the grounds of Jamaica House, where the prime minister's office was situated, but quickly moved to National Heroes Park to make the event seem impartial.

Even though Marley had participated in the bandwagons that helped Manley come to power, he professed an apolitical outlook through Rastafari and had longstanding links with activists on both sides of the political divide, making a neutral stance mandatory, regardless of where his sympathies lay. But two and a half weeks after the concert was first announced in the press, Manley finally set the election date for 15 December, a mere ten days after Marley's free show, so the public was bound to equate the two events and see the concert as an expression of support for Manley.

'We were asked for a day to give our people a nice show because we usually spend most of the time touring,' said Family Man. 'Shortly after we get our date, the campaign was set for the same time, so people been looking at the thing differently.'

When anonymous threatening telephone calls began to be made to Marley's headquarters at 56 Hope Road, the government dispatched a couple of cops to guard the premises for the week preceding the event, but their attendance was sketchy. Many close to the group were suggesting that they perform after the election, but Marley insisted the Wailers appear as scheduled, so the group thus continued to rehearse as usual, with the exception of Marcia Griffiths, who used the pretext of a non-existent overseas engagement to exit the island after Mowatt spoke of an ominous dream of a rooster and three hens; shots were fired at the rooster, and a ricocheted bullet hit two of the hens, disgorging one's entrails.

On the evening of 3 December, Chris Blackwell passed through the Black Ark on his way to 56 Hope Road, where he was to meet a director to discuss the filming of the 'Smile Jamaica' concert. He found Perry working on a commanding new song called 'Dreadlocks In Moonlight', which Perry had written for Marley; using a rhythm patterned after 'Police And Thieves', Perry sang in symbolic terms of a policeman sent to intimidate him, but Jah is on his side, so the plan must fail, as devious acts cannot deter the faithful from their chosen course of right-eousness, with Perry's delivery holding much emotion. The title referenced the regrettable practice of prison staff shearing a new inmate's locks: you arrived at the prison a dreadlocks in the moonlight but arose the next morning a baldhead.

A time to sow, why not time to reap? Yes, my friend
The seed you sow, that's what you shall reap
You light a fire to burn this nyah, but it no work out
You're just a weak heart
You send your big neck police friend fe come cool I up
But it no work
For Jah-Jah walk right in and cool up the scene
You get a jerk
For they that put their trust in Jah
Shall be like Mount Zion high
That shall never removeth but abideth forever
The knife that stick the sheep ah go stick the goat
Do you hear?
How you gonna feel when the knife is at your throat?
For sowing bring reaping, and reaping is harvest
The seed that you sow, that's what you shall reap
Jah is I light and salvation, whom shall I fear?
Jah the protector, Jah a firelight
Of whom shall I be afraid?
Hypocrite in a broad day light, parasite in a dim light

Dreadlocks in moonlight, baldhead at sunrise . . .

Perry's performance was meant as a guide vocal for Marley, but Blackwell felt it strong enough to release on its own.

'I sat in a lot with him on sessions and that particular one was a major event in my life,' said Blackwell. 'He said it was a demo for Bob, and I said, "You should do it yourself. I just love the way you sing it as it is. I think it's great, but I don't want to take it because I have to go to a rehearsal at Hope Road." For him to do a few mixes, they take hours.'

In the end, Blackwell decided to stay while Perry mixed the song, possibly saving his life in the process, for after Blackwell went off into the night, Perry returned to working on a Junior Murvin track with Earl Morgan and Barry Llewellyn, but the session was interrupted when a friend burst in with shocking news.

'Somebody come in and tell we, "Them just shot Bob Marley",' said Morgan. 'We had just finished voicing the tune and me and Lee Perry and Barry drive up to UC [where the University Hospital is situated], look 'pon the man and say, "Wha'ppen?" and him say, "Jah Live". It was an experience.'

Seven gunmen said to be from JLP strongholds snuck into Hope Road around nine o'clock, during a break in rehearsals. They emptied an array of homemade bullets from assorted weaponry, critically wounding Marley's manager, Don Taylor, and a bullet grazed Bob's chest to lodge in his arm, another in Rita Marley's skull.

When Perry and his Black Ark entourage arrived at the hospital that night, they found Bob Marley seated upright on a bench, wrapped in bandages and covered in blood, before Michael Manley placed him in the care of security forces as Perry and other friends took their leave.

No one has ever been charged with the attack and the background remains hazy. It is generally believed that JLP gunmen carried out the shooting, either on direct orders from a top-ranking party official or operating under their own initiative. Some have suggested the incident was meant to be a warning rather than a murder attempt, as the assailants wounded several but killed none. Others linked it to a racetrack scam involving Tuff Gong associates, including Skill Cole.

Whatever the case, the Wailers showed extraordinary courage by playing 'Smile Jamaica' a mere two days after the shooting, especially Bob, who as the main target was most vulnerable, and Rita, who appeared onstage in her hospital gown (though Family Man somehow missed the event). The message of defiance was powerful: Marley would not be manipulated by politics, even if the refusal would kill him. He was born a man of the people and a free spirit, and so he would remain. And if the attempt on Marley's life was indeed a JLP ambush, it backfired badly: ten days after the event, the PNP won by a confident majority, ending a prolonged and bloody election battle that had seen over 200 killed.

Then the Wailers fled the country. After a month in the Bahamas, they travelled to London in January 1977 to begin working on *Exodus*, initiating a long period of self-imposed exile for Marley in Britain, and the move was entirely understandable, since Manley's re-election did not bring an end to Kingston's internecine battles: in February, around one thousand JLP supporters were expelled from Fletcher's Land to make way for a similar amount of PNP supporters, this bitter aftermath to the Orange Lane fire swinging the district's allegiance, and there was ongoing violence in western Kingston and at Wareika Hills in the east, as well as in St James, Clarendon and elsewhere.

Nevertheless, Perry maintained a hectic recording schedule in the spring and summer of 1977. It was the year that the twelve-inch extended-play format gripped Jamaica – confusingly known as the 'disco mix' in emulation of American dance music EPs – and while Perry was testing the limitations of the format at the Black Ark, Island was staggering his album releases overseas.

Perry was still squeezing in sessions for other producers, often with scintillating results. For instance, Earl Sixteen's rousing 'Freedom' was a popular self-produced song written by future engineer Clive Jeffries and arranged by guitarist Dalton Browne, which surfaced in Jamaica on a Federal 45 in February.

Island released the Heptones' *Party Time* in March, mixing recuts of Studio One hits and inspired originals, with a couple of ballads between the charged protest songs. The musical backing veered beyond the rockers style, aiming for an upbeat, guitar-based sound, with Willie Lindo's searing lead atop Fil Callendar's regulated rhythm (occasionally replaced by Tony Chin), and the recently returned Ronnie Bop gave further augmentation on 'phased guitar'. Drummers Mikey Boo and Sly Dunbar kept the pace upbeat, Boris Gardiner and Michael Williams from Zap Pow kept the basslines heavy, while the keyboard interplay between Keith Sterling and Winston Wright was virtually buried in the mix. There was the Zap Pow horn section and Scully's vibrant percussion at select moments, too, and the vocal arrangements gave a passing nod to the funkier side of Philly soul.

Along with the slow version of 'Sufferer's Time' and the tormented 'Crying Over You', the thunderous opening title track made excellent use of all three Heptones' voices, Mikey Boo's pounding rolls raising the tempo to fever pitch. Bob Dylan's

'I Shall Be Released' was given the Upsetter treatment with a rousing horn fanfare and the verses shared between each singer in turn, while Sibbles' 'Why Must I' and 'Now Generation' were totally reconfigured, with crashing cymbals, unrestrained vocals, fuzzy guitar and intricate percussion. Of the new material, the affirmative 'Road Of Life' spoke of determination and compassion as key components of success, while 'Serious Time' and 'Storm Clouds' pointed to the gravity of the age, 'Mr President' reminding listeners that the actions of a distant foreign leader had very real consequences for ordinary Jamaicans.

Later that month, Perry received an unexpected gift from Chris Blackwell: an eight-track Teac Tascam 80-8 recorder, which used half-inch tape reels, since Blackwell hoped to broaden Perry's musical horizons by doubling his recording capabilities.

'Chris Blackwell bought me an eight-track, it was like a birthday present,' said Perry. 'He never tell me what was happening, but he send down a surprise for me: an eight-track Teac from Island. He say, "If four-track sound so good, image eight-track" because me experiment and him hear the songs me do on the Teac four-track, it let him know that if that was sounding so good, and now they have another advanced machine, him think this would be fun. Him have a surprise for me and him send it, but I didn't ready for using it yet.'

Very little would actually be recorded on the new machine. Perry said he did not use it for any of his work with Junior Murvin, the Heptones or George Faith, and only sporadically engaged it in later years, the four-track remaining his backbone.

Despite Blackwell's patronage, funds were still somehow in short supply, so the house was remortgaged in late March, freeing up another JMD$8,000, enabling Perry to continue recording at an incredible pace in the spring of 1977, resulting in a slew of impressive material.

On twelve-inch, there was an Upsetters disco mix with an extended version of Max Romeo's 'Norman', here with added domino game audio, and another Jah Lion toast; 'Sexy Natty' was a boastful song portraying Romeo's ethos towards romantic conquests, with a brief toast from Prince Jazzbo. There was also a four-song Heptones 'Disco Dub' EP that had extended mixes of 'Mr President' and 'Crying Over You' with forceful toasts by Jah Lion, plus dubbed-out mixes of 'Why Must I' and 'I Shall Be Released'.

More Junior Murvin singles were issued in Jamaica too. 'Tedious' expressed symbolic support for Manley's vision over a thunderous rhythm, Murvin imploring Jamaicans to stand firm in the face of adversity rather than fleeing the country. And since 'Police And Thieves' was still popular, Murvin voiced alternate cut 'Philistines On The Land', attacking unscrupulous arms dealers trading in nuclear weapons, its version side 'Bingo Kid' led by Chinna's meandering blues guitar. Another alternate, 'Bad Weed', called for the weeding out of thieves, Murvin handling the baritone backing as well as the falsetto lead, released on a twelve-inch with 'Closer Together', merging lines from the Impressions' 'Grow Closer Together' and 'Gypsy Woman' in a sweeping roots reggae arrangement. 'Roots Train' was a hard bop with horns and keyboards emulating railroad sounds, the twelve-inch edition coming with a tough pro-marijuana Dillinger toast.

Murvin's *Police And Thieves* LP was issued by Island in April 1977, the material recorded with slow determination.

'We was working, so we take we time, and Scratch don't rush,' said Murvin. 'We voice some songs today, tomorrow we don't feel good, so we leave that day. It was really a *work* more than a rush.'

Along with the ranking title track, 'Tedious' and 'Roots Train', 'Rescue Jah Children' referenced liberation struggles in Rhodesia and Mozambique, demanding the cessation of Black-on-Black violence and calling for more equality at home over a deliciously slow rhythm with phased horns, guitar and Nyabinghi conga drumming. 'Solomon' was recut in roots reggae mode, with echoing guitar lines ringing throughout, with 'False Teaching' striking against the educational brainwashing that perturbed Perry as a child. 'Easy Task' reminded listeners that life is a struggle, and 'Lucifer' was a hard-hitting update of the 'Ketch Vampire' rhythm, calling for the collective death of the perpetrators of the slave trade. 'Workin' In The Cornfield' also emphasised the legacy of slavery in contemporary Jamaica, and 'I Was Appointed' attacked hypocritical parsons as well as doctors peddling abortion and birth control pills.

The album is ultimately a testament to the close working relationship that had grown between Murvin and Perry, their mutual appreciation yielding work of a consistently high standard.

'To work with Scratch is a great thing: he's the greatest producer I've ever worked with,' said Murvin. 'He is a genius, you know, he feel the vibes. Sometimes he used to tell me, "Junior, you remind me of Bob Marley . . . Junior, 'Police And Thieves' will never die. Your talent, they can't stop you." He keep on guiding me, like, "Some of them guys, them no like you – watch them." He was a true man. When Perry sees a great talent, he don't like it to be destroyed, he love to push it to the fullest. That's how he is, spiritually.'

Augustus Pablo was also working at the Black Ark in the spring and summer of 1977, blowing melodica and playing keyboards on Perry's rhythms in exchange for studio time. 'Vibrate On' was a dense instrumental groove probing the outer reaches of reggae jazz, with a subdued vocal chorus; Pablo reworked 'Java' for his 'Ethiopia' single, and there was Perry's 'Java' update, 'Lama Lava', which remained unreleased for some years, until Pauline Morrison unearthed the master tape.

'You could listen to Augustus Pablo for a long time and not get bored,' said Perry. 'He always have some good ideas and he play the piano different from everybody else. He was very, very talented, a very good musician and very good composer, and he is humble and honest. You won't get any problem from Augustus Pablo.'

Pablo also recorded Hugh Mundell's 'Let's All Unite' at the Ark, driven by solid beats from Benbow, and the frustrated 'Why Do Black Man Fuss And Fight', with Chinna on bass; 'Me Breda You A Go Feel It' by vocal duo Hands and Heart was arranged by Pablo for Everton Da Silva's Hungry Town label. Bassist Sydney Gussine recorded the rhythm of 'Look Out For The Devil' at the Black Ark, too, and it was voiced and mixed at Tubby's, the single on his Hi-Try label aimed at devious politicians and unscrupulous producers.

Of Perry's own productions, there was Lloyd Robinson and Devon Russell's defiant 'Wolf Out Deh', which warned of treacherous predators, and Errol 'Bagga' Walker recorded the optimistic 'Better Future' (mistitled 'Better Feature'), though 'In These Times', his adaptation of show tune 'Summertime', was held back, along with the foreboding original, 'John Public'.

Junior Delgado's 'Sons Of Slaves', issued on seven-inch and twelve-inch formats, was one of the greatest songs of his solo career. Giving voice to the lowly status bestowed on Jamaica's African descendants, Delgado's agonised lead was complemented by forceful harmony from the Heptones and Dennis Brown.

Carlton Jackson's 'History' surfaced on the back of the 'Sons Of Slaves' twelve-inch, one of the EPs issued in an Upsetters Disco Bum sleeve (the 'Bum' a misspelled 'Boom', meaning explosive). Jackson was a civil engineer who had recorded some dub plates for a small sound system called Ethiopian Hi-Fi in the early 1970s, and he had written 'History' in 1973 during a lunch break in the woods, but it was not until his friend Bunny Wailer released *Blackheart Man* that Jackson considered recording the song. He made his way to the Black Ark in the spring of 1977, where Perry had the Diamonds add a wordless chorus to his restrained monologue.

'Scratch is a teacher and he wanted me to do an LP, so I did a few more tracks for him, but because I knew nothing of the release of "History" until after it was published, I decided not to do any more tracks,' said Jackson. 'Chinna Smith told me, "You have this nice tune", and when Scratch came back to Jamaica he told me about it, and I was a little upset.'

To compensate, Perry gave Jackson a cut of 'History' to release himself, the alternate mix surfacing as 'History Of Captivity' on Jackson's Ital International label.

Perry was also working with Earl George on deep roots covers of American soul and pop hits, redone in a thick syrup of Black Ark rhythm marked by Perry's individual sound treatments.

'Scratch gave me these songs to do because I do covers so good and Scratch gave the musicians a lot of work because he's a very technical guy,' he explained. 'You can be playing a drum pattern and he say, "Play that upside down." His way of working is very unique: his rhythms have a different sound, as the mix is totally different from everybody else and he does percussion different from everybody else too. He might bring the garbage pail, play a few instruments, then in a certain spot, he just kick that dirt bin. When he mix all the sounds together, you get some way-out kind of sound. You see, Scratch is a genius. Working with Scratch, you learn a lot of things too. Scratch is really the type of producer who was deep into the music.'

As usual, there was the required Perry name change for the singer.

'It take maybe about eight months, voicing it and the background vocals and the mixing take a long time too. It was taking so much time that he said to me, "Boy, you have a lot of faith. You should change your name to George Faith." I said, "That sound all right" because faith move mountain. From there I just stick with that name.'

One of the first songs captured on tape was Faith's driving version of the O'Jays' 'I've Got The Groove', marked by Headley Bennett's echoing sax and subtle phased guitar and keyboards, Faith's subdued phrasing helped along by wordless harmonies from the Diamonds.

In the midst of the production peak that generated this material, Chris Lane returned to Kingston in mid-April 1977, this time with John MacGillivray, with whom he had founded the Dub Vendor record shop in south London, and photographer Dave Hendley, who had taken over Lane's *Blues & Soul* column. During their month in Kingston, these reggae aficionados made several visits to the Black Ark, now a flurry of constant activity, with plenty of rhythms being laid but very little voicing; Perry ran off cuts of 'History' for them and was finishing the Heptones' 'Mystery Babylon', which the group would issue on their own Hep Hep label.

Perry's sound treatments were becoming more striking and outré, but on one of their visits to the Black Ark, the three Brits found Perry to be behaving oddly, his excessive intake of booze and weed yielding unpredictable results.

'That was the time when he was starting to act a little bit peculiar,' said Lane. 'He was drinking white rum, smoking and laughing maniacally, but no one could work out what he was laughing at. He was talking nonsense, being odder than usual.'

'When you drink rum, you want to fight everything for any reason at all,' said Perry. 'When me start to drink rum, it have a lot to do with the Devil, as rum and cigarettes have a lot to do with evil spirits.'

Though the troublesome behaviour waxed and waned in response to various stimuli, including booze, spliff and Kingston's continued unrest, the eccentricity was but a precursor to the baffling personae of the future.

Perry's work with the Congos is among the most mythical of the Black Ark. Lead singer Cedric Myton first met Perry at Studio One when he was working with fellow Tartan, Devon Russell, and although inactive for much of the early 1970s, he passed through the Royal Rasses, led by another former Tartan, Prince Lincoln Thompson.

Roydel Johnson's tenor was a fitting counterbalance to Myton's falsetto, his calmer demeanour offsetting Myton's skittishness, and although Johnson's vocal range was not so wide, his interpretation of biblical imagery rendered some of their best lyrics, and Johnson's youthful connection to Perry helped convince him to work with the group.

'I and Lee Perry is from the same district and we used to dance together,' said Johnson, later known as Congo Ashanti Roy. 'Both of us would go out to the sound system dances for contests in Hanover and Westmoreland.'

At sixteen, Johnson moved to Kingston to live with an aunt. He began hanging around recording studios in the ska years and was taught to play guitar by Ernest Ranglin, with further coaching from Gladdy Anderson and Winston Wright. He was also among the Jamaicans recruited by the US Peace Corps to work at the US naval base in Guantanamo Bay, where he was stationed for five and a half years from 1964, though in 1966 he arranged his holidays to spend time in Jamaica during Selassie's visit.

After the abortive recording of 'Standing On The Hill' that Johnson made for Perry at Channel One, he concentrated on playing the guitar and later passed through the Rightful Brothers, before crossing paths with Perry by chance in the spring of 1977.

'After I did that first song, I didn't see Scratch for about six years,' said Johnson. 'One day I was at my home over Independence City, playing my guitar, and I see this guy walk in through the gate and it was Scratch, who told me he was looking for a breadfruit tree to plant at his house. I said, "Yeah, man, you can get a breadfruit tree, but what's going on in the music business?" He said, "I have a studio now", so I picked my guitar up and start to sing "Row Fisherman". Scratch said, "You should come to the studio, make we record the song."'

Roy Johnson knew Cedric Myton through their shared involvement in the Nyabinghi Theocracy (officially the Issembly of Patriarchs of the Churchical Order of the Nyabinghi), the militant branch of Rastafari that evolved from the Youth Black Faith, as well as through mutual acquaintances such as independent producer Leggo Beast and top-ranking toaster, Big Youth. After selling their hand-knit tams and belts on the street, the pair began singing together, so when Perry extended his invitation to Johnson, they arrived at his studio as a duo.

The first song the Congos put together at the Ark was the same 'Row Fisherman' that Johnson had sung for Perry, about fishing to feed his growing family. Neither Perry nor the Congos thought the first take realised their potential, so the duo returned the next day to recut the song with a different set of musicians, including drummer Paul Douglas and Geoffrey Chung on bass. Once 'Row Fisherman' was in shape, they cut the follow-up, 'Ark Of The Covenant', retelling the tale of Noah from a Rastafari perspective, although the Ark of the Covenant connotes the gold-plated chest that houses the Ten Commandments, said to rest in Axum, Ethiopia, rather than Noah's Ark, whose journey in the Flood is recounted in the song.

When Island reactivated their Black Swan subsidiary, the first twelve-inch release, issued in May, was the Congos' arresting 'Congo Man', a lengthy, sombre chant over a skeletal beat-box rhythm with a free-form bass pattern skilfully executed by Winston Wright, its version side punctuated by ominous, echoing vocal fragments. Chris Blackwell was particularly struck by the song and expressed interest in an album by the group, though the single received a mixed reaction in the British music press.

The first George Faith twelve-inch on Black Swan, issued in late May, was a slower, heavier rendition of 'To Be A Lover' powered by modulated horns and sliding bass grooves, and although the Jamaican edition was nearly twelve minutes long, with Perry soliloquies on Rastafari rejection of funerals towards the end, the Black Swan pressing inadvertently went one step further by leaving in portions of Dillinger's 'Roots Train' toast, which bled through one channel of the tape, highly distorted and out of sync. Similarly, on the Black Swan B-side, 'Rastaman Shuffle', which revised the Skatalites' 'Beardman Feast' (based on Ernie Freeman's 'Live It Up'), there were two different strands of the same Dillinger toast at the front of the song, somewhat out of sync with the rhythm.

While 'To Be A Lover' was holding strong in Europe, Island issued 'I've Got The Groove' backed by an unlikely adaptation of Paul Anka's 'Diana' that somehow worked well, Faith's voice floating above a virtual river of delay and reverb. There was also a dreamlike take of 'Midnight Hour' issued with a reggae rendition of Tyrone Davis' 'Turn Back The Hands Of Time'. These pleasantly palatable cuts of psychedelic Jamaican soul were subsequently shortened for George Faith's debut album, together with the slow and smoky 'Opportunity' and an updated version of the Temptations' 'Gonna Give Her All The Love I've Got' (titled 'There's A Train'), issued in Jamaica as *Super Eight*; Perry delivered the master tapes to Island in early July, their overseas edition, released in mid-September, naming the album *To Be A Lover* after the most successful hit.

'I've Got The Groove' impacted in the summer, as did a remixed 'Groovy Situation' issued on Black Swan, now with a cooing female voice added to the mix, and something similar could be heard on Junior Murvin's 'Memories', melodically patterned after the Impressions' 'Minstrel And Queen' (adapted countless times in Jamaica as 'Queen Majesty'), which was the B-side to Island's thunderous extended twelve-inch mix of 'Tedious' issued in July.

As Lee Perry's profile was raised abroad through well-publicised records released and promoted by Island, the more forward-thinking members of the rock aristocracy began clamouring to work with him, including Paul and Linda McCartney, who were introduced to Perry by Chris Blackwell. In June 1977, the McCartneys sent Perry a demo tape of songs they wanted him to recreate at the Black Ark, which Linda would voice in Scotland the following August, including the Maguire Sisters' 'Sugartime' and the Chordettes' 'Sandman'. Perry thus spent a week building some rhythms with Boris

Gardiner, Mikey Boo, Winston Wright and guitarist Robert 'Billy' Johnson, brother of keyboardist Tony Johnson from Burning Spear's band.

'Me meet Paul in London at this studio in Wembley and lots of other places, but he didn't come to my studio to do the songs,' said Perry. 'Chris Blackwell tell me that they want me to do something, so they send the music like it was originally, and said they want it in my style. Me have my musicians make it, me send it back to them and they voiced it somewhere else.'

Somehow the project was abandoned for nearly twenty years, the couple only returning to the Jamaican creations in July 1998, when Linda was battling cancer, and both songs would be issued on *Wide Prairie*, a posthumous collection issued shortly after her death.

Back in Jamaica, Perry continued working closely with the Congos, laying the foundations of an exemplary roots album of the highest order titled *Heart Of The Congos*. It was the greatest album the Congos would ever record and arguably the strongest album Perry ever produced with a vocal group, though it was also one of the most contentious. Part of its strength lay in the songwriting: on 'Can't Come In', 'Open Up The Gate', 'The Wrong Thing' and 'Solid Foundation', Myton imparted a visual quality to his words, celebrating their African heritage while condemning the workings of Babylon and the divisive destructiveness of Christianity; on 'La La Bam Bam', 'Sodom And Gomorrow' and 'Ark Of The Covenant', Johnson related religious allegory in a way that was never stale or ordinary, recasting Bible tales the Rastafari way.

As Myton and Johnson were testing their abilities, Perry was reaching his artistic apex, applying unknown techniques to render his output different from the rest. With the help of Ernest Ranglin, Boris Gardiner, Keith Sterling and Winston Wright, Perry made sure the Congos had the inspired backing their devotional songs deserved, with Perry's bursts of African-inspired percussion adding another dimension.

Though the two Congos were both competent songwriters, Perry felt their voices were not strong enough as a duo and thus recruited Watty Burnett's deep baritone, the combination working so well that he became a full-fledged member of the group by the time the album was completed.

Burnett had cut a few recent singles at the Black Ark, including 'Rise And Shine' with Clinton Fearon (as Watty and Tony), a Rasta recasting of an old spiritual, which had little impact. Burnett's big hit came with a cover of Brook Benton's 'Rainy Night In Georgia', adapted at the Ark as 'Rainy Night In Portland', issued as the B-side of the thoughtful 'Know Love' by harmony duo Twin Roots (first issued on seven-inch in 1976), and there was a fearsome repatriation original, 'Open The Gate', with a rousing horn fanfare and spine-tingling cymbal crashes.

'When "Rainy Night In Portland" hit, everybody's telling me I should stay solo, and Scratch is saying, "You can still go solo, but I would like you to join this group Congos", so from there, I didn't do any more solo, I just involved in the group,' said Burnett. 'I sung on seven songs on the album but my photograph wasn't on it because I took a week off and went to Grand Cayman when the photograph shoot was happening.'

To further round out the vocals, Perry later added the Meditations on certain songs, along with Barry Llewellyn and Earl Morgan on 'Children Crying' and Gregory Isaacs on 'La La Bam Bam', while Roy Cousins and the Royals had some input, too, according to Cousins.

As Perry was helping to structure their music, the Congos were also influencing his lifestyle. They would begin most days with a run out at Hellshire Beach at the tail end of the morning, getting physically charged and clearing their minds for the tasks that lay ahead. Myton and Johnson spoke disparagingly of Perry's rum drinking and encouraged him to cultivate herb in the yard instead. They conducted lengthy reasoning sessions about the wonders of Rastafari and brought Watty Burnett fully into the faith, as well as eliciting a greater outward commitment from Perry. It was the Congos who largely convinced him to 'locks up', resulting in the presence of the short nubs of dreadlocks growing on his head for the first time in his life.

After 'Row Fisherman', 'Ark Of The Covenant' and Island's 'Congo Man', there was a stunning Upsetter 'Disco Cork' twelve-inch issued in June, with Johnson's 'Nicodemus' recounting the tale of a Pharisee that visited Jesus in the gospel of St John, and Myton's devotional 'Solid Foundation' attested to his faith in Rastafari, both with extended dub portions.

During Perry's work with the Congos, British film-maker Jeremy Marre appeared at the Ark gathering footage for *Roots Rock Reggae*, a documentary broadcast on BBC television in September. Marre's three-man film team captured a fully charged Perry bouncing around the elevated control room in boxer shorts and a sleeveless tank top, pounding on the Perspex and governing the session in his incomparable fashion. The eight-track Tascam is visible in the background, but still not in use; instead, Perry relies on the Teac four-track and two-track machines, using a screwdriver to reset the counter on the four-track each time he winds back the tape. The Congos and the Heptones were in the voicing area, creating a delightful impromptu reggae jam with Boris Gardiner, Mikey

Boo, Keith Sterling and Robbie Lyn, Junior Murvin picking out a guitar riff on the floor. The resultant 'Play On Mr Music' was created especially for the documentary, the footage of its spontaneous creation ultimately emphasising the fluid nature of Perry's work at the Black Ark.

'It wasn't a thing that we really arranged,' said Earl Morgan. 'We just go in and play the rhythm and Barry just start singing, "Play on Mr Music, play on." Rhythm ah play, something just happen – it's a groove.'

Lee Perry returned to London in July 1977, ostensibly on his way to Nigeria to produce an album for Island with Ghanaian highlife trumpeter Eddie Quansah, but problems obtaining a visa delayed the project to the point of abandonment. Perry wanted Island to release *Heart Of The Congos*, but Chris Blackwell felt the master tape Perry delivered was not strong enough in its current form, forcing Perry to rethink its sonic structure.

Staying in the flat above Island's Basing Street studio in Ladbroke Grove, west London, Perry spent much of his time in the company of Bob Marley, renewing their bond and hatching plans for fresh creations. This was at the height of punk's ascendancy, as the mutinous music of disaffected youth stimulated a serious shake-up of the self-indulgent excesses of stadium rock and caused British society to take another look at its conformist tendencies.

'Punks loved the basslines, they loved the anti-establishment focus, they liked the weed, and they liked the musical reportage quality of the music, songs that were about something,' said Don Letts, the 'Rebel Dread' disc jockey who introduced many punk fans to reggae at pioneering punk club the Roxy. 'What the reggae community got from punk was exposure.'

Letts had already experienced Marley's disapproval of punk's heretical dress code, underlining that Jamaican artists took time to warm to the punk aesthetic.

'I used to sell Bob herb when he was living in Oakley Street and one time I go round to Bob's place to get my money and Bob says, "You look like one of them nasty punk rockers." He'd obviously been reading about nihilism and swastikas in the tabloid press, but I stood my ground, and I said to him, "These are like-minded people and they're my friends." And in the coming months, as the whole punk thing was unfolding, he's talking to journalists like Vivien Goldman and Chris Salewicz, and he tunes into the depths and the spirit of punk and he realises they are like-minded rebels.'

Shortly after Perry's arrival in London, Vivien Goldman met Perry and Marley at the flat above Basing Street, where she played them the Clash's cover of 'Police And Thieves'. Marley was still grappling with punk's shocking imagery, but in the ensuing conversation the Jamaicans made it clear they understood that the punks and the dreadlocks were on the same page, both outcasts that rebelled against society.

'The whole idea was absolutely novel to them of a link between punks and Rastas because, at that time, they just thought punks were weird,' said Goldman. 'Bob grimaced slightly and said, "Look at them with their safety pins through their mouths", and after I was explaining that it was a manifestation of people feeling oppressed within society, Bob said, "I get it. I like to see a man who can suffer pain without crying." There was definitely a bit of resistance to the idea, but when I'd say things like, "They're the same groups of community, they're the dispossessed, they're the downtrodden", then they would say something back to me in a similar vein.'

As noted in Goldman's *The Book of Exodus*, Perry then revealed that he had already written a song called 'Punk Rock Reggae', which he and Marley would soon record as 'Punky Reggae Party', an assertion supported by Perry's northwest London link, Tony Owens, who claimed that Perry wrote the lyrics on the way into London from Heathrow Airport.

'I picked Lee Perry up at the airport about three o'clock in the afternoon and we were talking about the big explosion of punk in London,' said Owens. 'By the time we got to the flat, he already wrote the song called "Punky Reggae Party". Bob Marley was staying in Earl's Court. Scratch phoned him and said, "Bob, I've got a song for you, come now", and Bob was there in about twenty minutes with his guitar.'

The song saluted punk's defiant energy and its commonalities with reggae's insubordination, placing the Damned, the Jam, the Clash, the Slits and Doctor Feelgood on an even footing with the Wailers and the Maytals, but the 'boring old farts' of rock's old guard were barred.

Perry was already acquainted with Aswad, who had visited his studio earlier in the year when they were in Jamaica working with Burning Spear, so he phoned up drummer Angus Gaye and asked him to bring his drums to Basing Street. Thus, on the night of 25 July, Marley and Perry began recording a new rendition of 'Keep On Moving', followed by 'Punky Reggae Party', with Gaye, bassist Richard Daley and guitarist Steven 'Cat' Coore of Third World, as well as session keyboardist Phil Ramacon; Candy McKenzie, a singer of Guyanese parentage from nearby Cricklewood was on backing vocals, together with her brother Bunny and Michael 'Ibo' Cooper of Third World, joined midway through by Aurelia Msimang (Aura Lewis), a South African exile who had just completed a tour of West Africa with Jimmy Cliff.

Candy, born Annette McKenzie, came from a prominent musical family: her father Sonny was a noted jazz contrabassist, her uncle Mike a popular pianist and arranger, her brother Bunny an expressive guitarist and vocalist, and brother Binky a gifted bassist for whom Miles Davis wrote 'Binky's Beam'. However, following Binky and Bunny's incarceration on drugs charges, an incomprehensible tragedy occurred in July 1971 when Binky stabbed his parents to death at the family home, along with Candy's husband, Richard Sims. The eighteen-year-old Candy sustained knife wounds in the attack, the harrowing ordeal inevitably causing lasting psychological damage. Yet, Candy and Bunny did not give up on music. Instead, they became part of the bourgeoning northwest London reggae scene, forming a group called Rebel with Delroy Washington, appearing on Aswad's sterling debut for Island in 1975 and in '76 on Rico's reggae-jazz odyssey, *Man From Wareika*. Aware of Candy's talent and photogenic looks, Island made plans for a solo LP to be produced by Perry at the Black Ark.

Aura Lewis' father, an agronomist, was of Khoi, German and Madagascan Malay origins; her mother, a schoolteacher and women's rights activist, was considered Hlubi as the offspring of a Zulu and Khoi-San. After the family fled South Africa and were expelled from Rhodesia, Aura made her singing debut in Sierra Leone with Sierra Success, arriving in New York on a tuition scholarship to study at Hunter College in 1968, and after marrying jazz drummer Art 'Shakti' Lewis, she caught the Wailers at Max's Kansas City, embedding reggae in her consciousness.

As Lewis' awareness of Black issues intensified, she joined the Caribbean American Repertory Theatre (CART) in Brooklyn, which brought her to Jamaica in July 1976 to study drama at the Jamaica School of Art on a scholarship obtained through

CART. Once in Jamaica, she met Pamela Reid, an African-American dance and drama student from North Carolina who had been recording with Harold Butler and Beres Hammond through keyboardist Peter Ashbourne, with whom Reid had been romantically involved the year before, while he was a student at the Berklee College of Music.

Lewis and Reid began singing together in September 1976, when Reid was working on a Festival Song Competition entry called 'Irie Jamaica'. It was recorded with members of Zap Pow and Augustus Pablo for aspiring producer Philip 'Tuffy' Robinson, who would soon become Reid's long-term partner, during a time when Reid was preparing to appear in *Masqueraders*, written by emerging playwright Stafford Harrison, with Lewis part of the technical crew. Once they became properly acquainted, Lewis introduced the concept of a female harmony trio called Full Experience, with an African, an African-American and a woman from the Caribbean, but after trying local singers such as Sabrina Williams without success, they were unsure who should represent the Caribbean element.

Then, in the spring of 1977, a chance meeting with Jimmy Cliff on the veranda of his uptown home on Lady Musgrave Road brought Lewis and Reid into his backing band.

'I told him where I'm from and he says, "I've just been invited to go to South Africa", and I said, "I wouldn't suggest that you go because of the cultural boycott",' said Lewis. 'After class we told him that we were busy putting music together, that we wanted to do an album, shared this whole vision that we had with him, and he was excited about that. He says, "Maybe I can use the two of you to back me because I also will be going to West Africa."'

Pamela Reid missed the tour because she chose to visit her

family in North Carolina during term break, but Aura Lewis was there for the entirety, and when she and Cliff reached London at the end of the tour, they went to Basing Street in search of percussionist Rebop Kwaku Baah (then working on Steve Winwood's eponymous solo album), only to find Marley and Perry at work with McKenzie.

'One day Jimmy took me to Island Records. It was during the time when Bob and Lee were doing "Punky Reggae Party" and "Keep On Moving", and when I went in the studio, Lee Perry says, "I'm looking for a singer. We're doing something downstairs, and we've got Candy McKenzie and we need another vocalist." Jimmy Cliff said, "Here's Aura, she sings with me and we just came back from Africa." The first time I saw him, he said, "You look just like my daughter", and it's true, we have the same face. He had the Congos' *Heart Of The Congos* album, he had just been trying to make a deal with Island Records, and I think I met the Clash at the same time because Lee was co-producing their album or something. It was a very exciting period.'

In addition to cooing choral vocals in the verses, Perry had McKenzie and Lewis add ascending and descending sol-fa scales. 'Keep On Moving' had a couple of new bridges too, penned on the spot, in which Marley sang salutations to his children and spoke of increasing African unity; left unfinished, the song would surface on the B-side of an extended mix of 'One Love' in 1984. According to Lewis, a third song was also recorded at these sessions, and Tony Owens said that Marley and Perry were working on the lyrics of Marley's 'Babylon System' at the same time.

Before these sessions concluded, Lewis told Perry about the material she was preparing with Pamela Reid and her concept for Full Experience, so they made plans to meet in Jamaica.

Marley asked Lewis to join his forthcoming tour as a backing singer, but she opted to remain with Cliff.

When the Clash got wind that Perry was working with Marley in London, they dispatched their manager and former reggae record shop proprietor Bernie Rhodes to ask Perry to produce their third single, 'Complete Control'. He may have seemed an unlikely choice of producer for a band then basing their songs around three chords, but the request came with respect and admiration.

Bassist Paul Simonon was heavily influenced by reggae. Raised in Brixton, where Jamaican music was ever-present, he was inundated with rock steady in his teens and used the *Tighten Up* album series to teach himself bass melodies, Perry's 'People Funny Boy' and 'All Combine' making a strong impression during his youth.

'I see Lee Perry as the Ennio Morricone of Jamaican music,' said Simonon. 'His music is like the soundtrack to my childhood.'

Though Perry told the group they had ruined 'Police And Thieves' with their musically inferior cover version, he felt enough of a connection in spirit to consider working with them, and the financial arrangements persuaded him to consent.

Recorded at Sarm East studio in Whitechapel, 'Complete Control' was a quick-fire blast against corporate manipulation and a dig at Rhodes' dictatorial tendencies, though by all accounts the session was a bit of a mismatch: Perry thought their instruments were turned up too loud and the band disliked Perry's overuse of echo, which they removed after he left the studio, leaving soundman/co-producer Mickey Foote to sort out the mix. Simonon said Perry made little concrete difference but remembered him saying that Jones played his guitar 'with an iron fist', and Perry later demonstrated his approval of the collaboration by giving a Clash group photo a place of prominence at the Black Ark.

'They was really loving reggae music, really want to get involved with it, but they did not know how to do it,' said Perry. 'They're playing the drum and the guitar too loud and turn up the bass too high till it's distorted, so me had to take them back down to normal. But with punk, that's why reggae music extend to the heights where it reach because it wasn't just me and my Black people that make the reggae music live, it was the people who believe in hairstyle . . . we call them punk and if you want to know the truth, I am really a punk, that's why I cannot be controlled.'

Perry also crossed paths with John Martyn at one of Chris Blackwell's properties, located a few miles outside Reading, where Martyn was working on *One World* in a converted horse barn. According to Martyn, the morning after his arrival, Perry pontificated about the art of sex before Blackwell's assembled guests at the breakfast table, using coffee mugs to illustrate his point, the wacky depiction of sexual union inspiring Martyn's 'Big Muff', which Perry helped him record during the visit.

With plenty of downtime during the three weeks he spent in London, Perry appeared on BBC Radio London's *Reggae Time* show and gave interviews to *Sounds*, *Black Music* and other publications, the articles focusing on the punk-reggae connection, and if Perry was tight-lipped about his working methods and special effects, he was happy to weave esoteric rings of Rastafari reasoning.

When *NME*'s Neil Spencer commented on the staggering volume of material that was emanating from the Black Ark, suggesting that some of it was not necessarily up to standard,

Perry said he was perpetually compelled to create, whether anyone was pleased by the result or not.

'I have to let it out. So whether you love it or not, you have to sympathise with me, I have to put it out so something else can happen.'[3]

There was an uncommon mix of kinship and divergence when Perry was interviewed by Linton Kwesi Johnson, the Jamaican-born poet, playwright, journalist and activist whose melding of poetry and dub was shortly to instigate the inventive reggae subgenre that became known as 'dub poetry' after Johnson's description of the verbal artistry of Jamaican toasters; Johnson was a longstanding admirer of Perry's work, though Perry's cryptic speech remained open to interpretation.

'The first Lee Perry tune I was aware of was "Doctor Dick" by King Perry, a version of Kitchener's very risqué calypso,' said Johnson. 'I think the first record by Scratch that I bought was "People Funny Boy" around 1968, when the music was changing from rock steady to reggae; in fact, it was one of the prototypes of the early reggae, and what I found extraordinary about the tune was this baby crying in the background, it was the first time I'd heard anything like that. Later on, Scratch used cows mooing and broken bottles and all kinds of weird sounds, so after he started putting out those Black Ark records, I realised he is a special guy, and I began to see him like the Salvador Dalí of reggae music with an unorthodox approach. I met Lee "Scratch" Perry in 1977 at the offices of Island Records, and at that time he was producing the *Heart Of The Congos* album. I remember saying to him, "You have a unique sound, you use the flanger and phaser", but he didn't want to let out his trade secrets. Most of the time he spoke in parables, about things like "the shadow that walketh underneath a man". It was an experience. The other thing that struck me about Scratch at that time was his shamanistic approach to music-making: he thinks like an Obeah man and I think, to him, music is a kind of magical act, an act of conjuring up things, whether they be evocative of Africa, judgement, Armageddon, or whatever.'

Perry returned to Kingston in August to embellish the hollow shell of 'Punky Reggae Party', which he felt had not been voiced properly, its musicianship under par, as heard on an early take from the London sessions that was issued on the compilation *This Is Reggae Music 2*, released by Island in Holland through Ariola Benelux in 1977, sounding decidedly dry and unfinished.

'Me write the song in England and think it could record at Chris Blackwell's studio but there was no life in Blackwell's studio to do it, neither Third World didn't have any energy to do it,' said Perry. 'So me take it back to Jamaica and remake it in Joe Gibbs' studio with my musicians.'

Perry was particularly dissatisfied with the rhythm's bass and drums, recruiting Val Douglas and Sly Dunbar to overdub new parts at Joe Gibbs', adding further instrumentation in the form of bright blasts from the Zap Pow horns and keyboard riffs from Tyrone Downey, but the icing on the cake came in further backing vocals from Watty Burnett and the Meditations: Burnett boomed out a *basso profundo* refrain of 'punky, punky, punk' as the Meditations made incredulous oinking noises over Sly's thunderous beat. Perry's trademark bursts of crashing cymbals gave the rhythm further demarcation and Glen DaCosta's tenor sax injected an essence of swing.

All the song needed now was a proper lead vocal from Bob Marley, but the Tuff Gong was in Miami, so Perry joined him there, the song successfully voiced in one take at Criteria studio (the new vocal removing the reference to the Slits).

The resulting track was released in Jamaica as an extended twelve-inch single on Perry's Black Art label and also on a Tuff Gong maxi, both featuring long scat-vocal sections from Bob, and in November, Island released the song on the back of 'Jamming', a single from the *Exodus* album issued in both seven and twelve-inch formats, helping a whole new generation of fans to tune in to Perry's creations.

Though the Criteria recording session went smoothly, Marley confronted Perry with shocking news in Miami: doctors planned to amputate the big toe of his right foot, or the foot itself, as a form of pre-existing skin cancer had been detected underneath the toenail following a troublesome football injury.

'He call me over and they were going to cut off him foot,' said Perry. 'If not, it was going to kill him long time, but before he die, they say if him lose a foot him would live longer. Me write "Punky Reggae Party" and make him sing it and that's how I heal him – me fly back to do it in Criteria studio in Miami and that was the power that heal him from the foot. After the session, him feel a different vibration.'

Various suggestions have been made about Bob Marley's toe. He reportedly left London on 23 August to have surgery in Miami, overseen by Dr William Bacon, the surgeon that had earlier repaired Don Taylor after the ambush at Hope Road, but instead of agreeing to the proposed amputation, Marley opted for a lesser operation in which a portion of his toenail was removed; after many weeks of recuperation, he was given a clean bill of health and plans were made to reactivate a thrice-postponed American tour.

Back in Jamaica, Perry arranged a meeting with Aura Lewis and Pamela Reid, with fellow aspiring singer Dhaima Matthews along for the ride.

'We went to a private beach somewhere and Aura and I sang those songs for Scratch, *a cappella*,' said Reid. 'He said, "Can you come to the studio tomorrow?"'

Since Jimmy Cliff had gone to Ghana with Rebob Kwaku Baah and still had outstanding issues to resolve with Warner Brothers, the timing was fortuitous for Lewis and Reid. The first Black Ark song to benefit from their harmonies was 'Disco Devil', an inspired reworking of Max Romeo's 'I Chase The Devil' that Perry sang himself to repel the negative aspects of the disco dance craze, suggesting that the fashion-conscious 'hustlers' give their unwanted cocaine to the Pope, instead of seeking to corrupt the natty dreads through licentiousness.

'Disco Devil' was issued in a plain white sleeve, illustrated by a ghoulish disco phantom, and hidden away on the B-side was an extended mix of the Wailers' 'Keep On Moving', no doubt inspired by Marley's London recut, which began innocuously enough: aside from a few honking bars of Headley Bennett's sax, nothing much seems amiss until halfway through the song, when the rhythm is stopped and abruptly restarted. Then, out of nowhere, deejay Wong Chu, a selector of Tippertone sound, bursts in through a wild haze of delay to deliver a bewildering toast about all things straight and twisted. When the rhythm runs out, Perry starts it up for a third time, to segue into a dub punctuated by echoing vocal stabs and horn blasts frozen by the infinite reaches of the Space Echo. This excessive release provided a rare glimpse of just how challenging the Wailers rhythms could sound when attacked by a talented toaster, though as ever, Perry's boundless mixing really made the song outstanding.

Lewis and Reid are also present on an extended twelve-inch of 'Ketch Vampire', which segued into a fearsome Alimantado toast; an extended cut of 'Words' graced the A-side, which rolled straight into a disturbed alternate that Perry voiced himself, based on the repeated phrase 'Lion A The Winner'. Reid and Lewis also retroactively added a chorus to 'Dreadlocks In Moonlight', which Perry later retitled 'Big Neck Police'.

Other noteworthy EPs surfacing in the latter months of 1977 included an 'Upsetter Disco Jam' twelve-inch with 'Rasta Train', a bouncing recut of Desmond Dekker's 'Rude Boy Train' by former Time Unlimited vocalist Hugo Blackwood, together with Doctor Alimantado, backed by an extended reworking of 'Vibrate On' titled 'Reggae Music', extolling the virtues of 'the music of the dispensation of time'. There was also an extended post-rockers cut of Eric Donaldson's 'Cherry Oh Baby', with the devotional 'Say A Little Prayer' on the B-side, and on seven-inch was Donaldson's 'Freedom Street', about dehumanising incarceration, and the defiant 'Stand Up', with Donaldson urging the people to fight for their rights, its dub a swathe of distorted echo that repeatedly proclaimed the word 'I'.

One of the clearest indications of Perry's increasingly troubled frame of mind came in 'City Too Hot', an Upsetter twelve-inch from the same period on which his psychological anguish was all too evident. Though Perry sounded light-hearted and fully in control on the flipside, 'Bionic Rats', recorded with Lewis and Reid, on 'City Too Hot' he was close to tears and clearly desperate. Lamenting the oppressive forces that were actively weighing against him, Perry alluded to the political gang wars, harassment by police and soldiers, divisive Rasta in-fighting and the 'tit for tat' mentality that made Kingston so perilous; the lyrics had Perry heading for the hills to find some relief, though he never managed a retreat to the countryside.

'It was war, gunshot and fighting, roadblock and problem, everything getting upside down, a rum-head problem and all that,' said Perry. 'Sometimes in Kingston you hear that another set of politicians send gunman to cause havoc, then soldiers come out to back up the police, to make themselves stronger, so places have to close down, and shops have to lock. Police in full control, so business have to close down. It's always happening in Kingston.'

Perry's overburdened work schedule added to the stress. He would typically begin his sessions at one o'clock in the afternoon and work straight through to five or six in the morning, then sleep until ten and be on the beach by eleven, the cycle endlessly repeating itself. Sometimes people were already at his gates by nine o'clock in the morning, and still the sessions would stretch right through to the following dawn.

The Black Ark was in constant use in this period, with many peers seeking out the facility since no one else was capable of creating such an intense and unique sound. For instance, lesser-known producer Sean De Laire recorded noteworthy work for his Grass Roots label at Perry's studio, the most successful being the Roots' 'Mash Down', a moving song of harmonic brilliance that spoke of the inequalities, fostered in slavery days, that still condition Jamaican society, Greensleeves' overseas issue especially popular in the UK.

Zap Pow's instrumental 'River' was exceptional too, a self-produced jazz-dub experiment that benefitted from Perry's intensive mixing treatments, resulting from his inability to pay the horn section for session work.

'Me and Glen DaCosta and Vin Gordon were doing some things for Lee "Scratch" Perry over a two-week span, when he was putting on horns for some Bob Marley songs,' said trumpeter David Madden. 'When we were supposed to get paid, Scratch didn't have any money, so he said to us, "The most I can do is give you some time to do something." I told the group that I had this song, "River", so we rehearsed it and went to the studio. At that time we had the keyboard player Tony Johnson, but he didn't come, so I called Geoffrey Chung, and I got Noel Seal to play the congas and the lead guitarist was called Roy. When we started to do it, Scratch said, "Wait, ah no so my music go, man. This kind of music, whoa!" I said, "Scratch, I don't care about *your* kind of music, this is *my* song! I do my song in your studio." Then he eventually started to say, "*Rahtid!* It sound good!"

'We did about three takes of it. When he was mixing, he had a phaser that you hear running through it and him say, "This is my latest sound, do you want me to put it in?" I said, "If you feel that it could go in there, put it!" So he put the phaser in there. I really wanted to call it "Mamee River", after the place that I was born up in Gordon Town: the song gives me the feeling of where I was as a little baby boy, but we just say "River", though the guys were singing "reggae river". It was Dwight, Mikey and one other guy that used to hang out round the studio that was singing.'

'That was the mastery of Lee Perry, the Noah of the Ark,' said Michael Williams. 'He was involved as a co-producer and he give us ideas. When we recorded that at Lee Perry's Black Ark studio, that session was heavenly vibes because we had the great Leslie Butler on keyboards. That made the session very interesting because he got in that sweet flow, into the reggae river.'

Of all the songs created at the Ark by bartering associates, 'River' is among the most remarkable for the way its heavy phasing pushed the music into the realm of abstract jazz. A song that instrumentally alluded to the wonders of nature, 'River' is one of the finest instrumentals to ever emerge from the Ark.

Sometime after 'Disco Devil', Robert Palmer travelled to Jamaica to undertake some ill-fated work at Perry's studio. Long inspired by soul and having already released *Pressure Drop*, influenced by reggae and other Caribbean forms, Palmer now sought a more cosmopolitan feel for his brand of rock 'n' roll and was already aware of Perry's other-worldly productions, having been struck by the flushing toilet on *Cloak And Dagger*. In arranging for Palmer to record at the Ark, Chris Blackwell hoped to get viable crossover material for Palmer's upcoming album, *Double Fun*.

Palmer said Perry's status at the Ark went far beyond that of an ordinary producer, and the man was now seen as a mystical leader: 'His studio seemed to be the spiritual and political centre of the island. It was heavy, and it was all about getting this magic on the tracks.'[6]

Despite the rapport that developed between Palmer and Perry, the week he spent at the Ark was marked by hostile confrontation. Perry was continually testing the singer, though he accepted Palmer as an ally once his seriousness and ability were clear; musicians like Sly and Robbie were more obstructive, though Ernest Ranglin and Boris Gardiner were friendly and well-mannered, but the harshest negativity emanated from the assembled dread idlers, intent on disturbing his concentration.

'These guys come around wearing robes and they've got magic wands and shit. I'm doing vocals and one stands in front of the mike and starts doing this weird dance. I thought it was fucking ridiculous, but I couldn't laugh because it would have been an insult. That didn't work, so they brought in another guy who stood with his back to me and pushed me with his shoulder blades into the microphone while this other guy did the magic wand shit. It was very strange, and Lee didn't do a thing to try and stop it. He was very amused by my reaction. When that didn't work, they brought all these friends who were dressed like military. They gave me the white boy routine: *What're you doing here?* And Lee's looking at me, grinning . . . he was like, *I can't do anything about these hangers-on. I'm sorry, I think it's ridiculous too.*'[7]

'Chris send him to do an album but him was a little nervous singer, a bit scared of Black people,' said Perry. 'We could get more from him, but he was scared when he see too much people around and some of the dreads wanted to push him around. Him see one come in the corner and whisper to the other one, "What that white boy doing here?" So him get nervous, very nervous.'

Regardless of the antagonism, Palmer had nothing but praise for Perry's techniques.

'I've been asked who was my favourite producer and it's definitely him. He used to do amazing things that were hard to accept unless you witnessed what he did. He used to record on a Teac four-track and mix as he went, occasionally cleaning the head with his T-shirt . . . he was just this magnet for a scene that was the real musical cutting edge.'[8]

Somehow, none of the songs he recorded at the Black Ark would make it onto *Double Fun*; instead, Palmer re-recorded the material under more controlled circumstances in New York. Perry provided Island with a single mix of the track he felt was the strongest, 'Best Of Both Worlds', complete with dub version, but the 45 was rejected. The only song to surface from the sessions was the calmly emotional 'Love Can Run Faster', which was bolstered by a sweet chorus from Lewis and Reid, incompatibly issued on the back of Palmer's hard-rocking commercial cover of Moon Martin's 'Bad Case Of Loving You' in 1979.

At one of Robert Palmer's sessions, circa late August 1977, Perry met Wayne Jobson, an aspiring singer and guitarist based in Golden Grove in the hills of St Ann, brought to the Ark by Boris Gardiner. Jobson was from a prominent family that had close links with the Wailers: cousin Diane was Bob Marley's lawyer and one of his closest confidants, while cousin Dickie acted as the group's manager circa 1973–74, and also managed Joe Higgs.

According to Jobson, Perry pushed Palmer hard, striving for original results: 'Scratch made him redo a song for about eight hours straight until Robert Palmer was losing his voice.'

Jobson experienced the Black Ark as a unique space driven by Perry's idiosyncrasies: 'I remember he was producing, and he wanted a female vocalist, so he called Pauline; she was in the kitchen mixing some dumplings with flour all over her hands, so she brush off the flour and come in the studio and sing the line, then go back in and mix up the dumplings again. In the studio he put a pineapple in front of the fan – it was like scented air conditioning. On the walls was all these X-rated pictures out of *Hustler*, and I'm thinking, "Is this a Rastaman with all this pornographic stuff?" It was wild. At the time, you could sense his genius, but it was this kind of madness that just changes every day.'

Jobson's English and Scottish forebears established plantations in St Ann, and he was of mixed Spanish and African heritage too, but when Jobson sang a few songs with his acoustic guitar, Perry said he was happy to work with him because Jobson was an Arawak – that is, an indigenous Amerindian whose population was decimated by the Spanish in the 1600s. A baffled Jobson thus returned a few days later with his brother Brian to record a five-song demo with the nucleus of their band, Native: bassist Sydney Bennett, drummer Ray Levy and keyboardist Peter Couch, plus Joe Higgs on percussion. The day-long session yielded the melancholy 'Late September In May', 'Rockstone', which used a proverb to diss a high-society hypocrite, 'Meet Mr Nobody', exploring alienation, 'In A Strange Land', about the ongoing legacies of slavery, and 'In The Land Of Make Believe', a hazy tale of fallen empires foretold in ancient scripts.

Jobson was departing for England the morning after the session, where he would spend a year completing a law degree. Though he only paid Perry fifty dollars upfront, promising to cut him in on any ensuing record deal, the producer stayed up all night mixing the material, striving to get the best out of what had been rapidly captured on tape; in London, the demo would be championed by former Sex Pistol John Lydon and Vivien Goldman, tipping Native as the next big thing.

Then the Jolly Boys appeared at the Black Ark. Composed of Winston 'Shine' Edwards, Lennox Miller and Willis Gordon, and based in the Edgewater area of Portmore (halfway between Perry's studio and Hellshire Beach), the group was brought to the Black Ark by their friend and musical coach Mattis, who oversaw the recording of two originals: the song 'Colour', which dealt with racial discrimination, was released in small numbers on the group's Jolly Records label, and the song 'Conscious Man', which became a sleeper hit overseas.

Using biblical allegory to advise how to avoid being hurt in romance, 'Conscious Man' had an infectious harmonic chorus and hooking guitar line that hinted at commercial potential, so when Tony Owens came to Jamaica seeking material to release in Britain, Perry let Owens deal with 'Conscious Man' and an arresting Black Ark recut of Lord Creator's 'Such Is Life' (credited to Prodigal Creator), which took time to surface.

Owens would launch the Seven Leaves record shop and label in Kensal Rise, northwest London, in 1979, but since he did not yet have a label of his own, Owens arranged for 'Conscious Man' to be issued on the newly formed Magnum label, run by former Creole employee Mo Claridge, who also ran a record distribution service called Mojo, and Claridge would enjoy considerable success with the song in due course.

The years 1976 and '77 had seen Lee Perry at what many would describe as his creative peak, seemingly destined for greater future rewards by way of his escalating ingenuity. The material he made for Island would stand the test of time, the albums remaining classic representations of the broad and complex sound he was capable of mastering in such a small and technically limited studio, and the product he was fashioning with Jamaican ears in mind also saw him progressing by leaps and bounds, as he continually sought to expand his sonic horizons.

Though another set of stunning innovations would emerge from the Black Ark in 1978, many projects were abortive, counter-productive enterprises that would fill him with unbearable frustration, ultimately pushing him over the edge.

CHAPTER TEN

City Too Hot:
The Excessive Apex and
Sudden Fall of the Ark

After the furious production schedule of 1977, Lee Perry continued to release remarkable material in the early months of 1978, though most of his Jamaican singles remained underground and several overseas album projects were stymied. So much was going on that it was hard to keep track of everything during another phase of turbulence and confusion.

Through Perry's collaboration with the Congos, he began to have greater contact with the Nyabinghi Theocracy, the strict Rastafari subsect whose adherents now formed a habitual presence at his studio. Leader Pa-Ashanti was a founding member of the Youth Black Faith and a major figure in the development of Nyabinghi drumming; twenty-two years older than Perry, he came from Mount Moriah in the hills of St Ann and was then based in Trench Town with Ma-Ashanti, his common-law wife. Other prominent members included Bongo Chef, Jah Stone, Bongo Tawny, Jah Lion from Clarendon, and the elder Bongo Wake-I, but it was Jah Ned Willacy, the group's funde specialist and youngest member, with whom Perry forged the strongest connection.

Jah Ned's father Seebert was a bassist in Val Bennett's band, and as a teenager, Ned's knowledge of Kingston's dancehalls landed him a job as informal talent scout for Celebrity Concerts, suggesting local support acts for Jamaican performances by the Impressions, Sam Cooke and James Brown. He also worked as a silkscreen printer in downtown premises shared with the Sheiks, making labels for stage outfits worn by the Blues Busters, Byron Lee and Clancy Eccles, and in the ska years often saw Perry playing percussion with the Skatalites, his work in the downtown Kingston area bringing him closer to Perry and other industry personnel.

The Nyabinghi taught Jah Ned how to drum in Back-O-Wall, and when it was bulldozed to make way for Tivoli Gardens, the order moved their base to Marcus Garvey's former head-quarters at Liberty Hall on King Street, and later established an office and permanent base on nearby Church Street. The group made their first devotional recordings in 1970, but the project was abandoned through a lack of funds; then, during the 1976 State of Emergency, they were galvanised into taking serious action, using their music to help bring positive change to Jamaican society.

The Black Ark thus gradually became a focal point and meeting place for the Nyabinghi Theocracy. Lee Perry was the most prominent producer making music that was relevant to the Rastafari cause; his records were consistently radical and uncompromising, and he was never afraid to express his religious beliefs. The brethren thus appointed him their 'Minister of Music', heightening his role within the movement.

'Scratch is instrumentally a representative of the Rastafari government, and his musical contribution was enough weaponry for him to do his part,' said Jah Ned. 'Scratch was responsible for the musical development within the movement of Rastafari itself, so Scratch was generally responsible for the music ministry of our movement and everyone was looking forward to Scratch.'

Influenced by the Congos and the Nyabinghi brethren, Perry turned away from worldly things to enact a more religiose lifestyle, but Jamaica was still in the midst of ongoing political and social upheaval, as evidenced by the Green Bay Massacre, one of the most notorious incidents in Jamaica's fractious history. The backstory involved tensions that had been mounting between residents of the JLP-affiliated Southside neighbourhood, centred on High Holborn Street and Gold Street, and the PNP-affiliated Tel Aviv, a few blocks further west, where a government-backed housing project on Barry Street was a particular source of friction regarding employment opportunities. After repeated conflict with JLP activists at the site that was not addressed by the police, covert operations were carried out by the Military Intelligence Unit (MIU) of the Jamaica Defence Force, identifying a number of Southside JLP activists who were deemed a threat to national security.

Through an intermediary known as Junior Star, who had recorded a few tunes as a deejay, the men were offered access to automatic weaponry and employment as construction-site guards, the lure of firepower and money too hard to resist. A rendezvous was arranged in Southside at daybreak on 5 January, but some baulked at the sight of a German Red Cross ambulance that had been sent to collect them. In the end, ten Southside men were driven to the Green Bay shooting range near Port Henderson, midway to Hellshire Beach, where they were fired on by MIU snipers that had lain in wait with submachine guns, the five dead including reggae singer Glenroy Richards, former professional footballer Norman 'Gutto' Thompson, and an area leader known as Saddlehead.

The JDF line was supposed to be that the Southside men had ambushed the soldiers, who were at the range to conduct target practice, but leaked photographs and the testimony of survivors cast doubt on these assertions and a public furore erupted as facts about the case came to light, especially after the Minister of National Security, Dudley Thompson, infamously remarked that 'No angels died at Green Bay', suggesting that the MIU had uncovered a plot to smuggle guns into the country. An inquest launched in March would not conclude until late May, since the conspiracy was so obscure and contentious.

Thankfully, positive changes were afoot in the immediate Green Bay aftermath, when the Nyabinghi Theocracy played a crucial role in bringing a year's worth of tranquillity to the streets of Kingston in conjunction with Bob Marley, Lee Perry and their confederates, helping to instigate a peace treaty on the war-torn streets of the capital.

The unexpected truce was called by two of the highest-ranking political activists, Claudie Massop and Bucky Marshall. Massop spent a long period in England after being acquitted of murder charges in Jamaica in 1973 but had returned to the island to resume fronting the JLP stronghold of Tivoli Gardens, only to be detained at the Red Fence section of Up Park Camp during the State of Emergency. Marshall, born Aston Thompson, his opposite number in PNP-affiliated Matthews Lane, had been jailed on a murder charge before the Green Bay Massacre.

During their incarceration, both men had reconsidered relations with their political masters, Massop reportedly clashing with Edward Seaga in recent times, and as each had connections on the other side of the political divide, they came to the slow realisation that they were pawns in a politicians' game in

329

which common ghetto folk would never be the winners; much like the gunmen that had been rounded up and obliterated at Green Bay, they were expendable in their role as 'enforcers' of party loyalty, regardless of political patronage. They thus began to conceive of unity as the only alternative to Jamaica's seemingly endless spiral of self-destruction.

Upon his release, Marshall put the word out that he wanted to see Massop and a number of meetings were arranged with the help of intermediaries such as Bunny Goodison, an old schoolfriend of Massop's who was affiliated with Clement Dodd, Glen Brown and other music figures. The final summit took place at the Sheraton Hotel in New Kingston with PNP general secretary D. K. Duncan, Minister of Youth and Sports Hugh Small, and Manley's trusted advisor Howard Aris, as well as Concrete Jungle's top PNP activist Tony Welch, just as the Nyabinghi Theocracy held a lengthy Nyabinghi to pacify Tel Aviv, helping to demonstrate that Kingston's flashpoint communities were ready to embrace togetherness.

On 10 January, Massop and Marshall officially declared their truce before a gathered crowd of hundreds at the corner of Beeston Street and Oxford Street, the accepted boundary between JLP- and PNP-affiliated areas, with barely a member of the security forces in sight, enacting the first ceasefire since 1967.

A telephone call was subsequently made to Bob Marley from the offices of the Nyabinghi Theocracy, proposing the One Love Peace Concert to help publicly cement the peace and raise money for the impoverished communities that had been destroyed by the sustained factionalism. Members of the Twelve Tribes of Israel visited Marley in Miami to obtain his consent, but Marley requested clarification from Massop that he would no longer be a target for JLP bullets; Massop and Marshall offered to come to

Miami, but Marley did not want gunmen around his family, so a meeting in London was scheduled for February, when Marley would be there filming a promotional video for 'Is This Love'. Massop, Marshall, Welch and Marley thus spent a week in London negotiating, and after Marley was assured of his safety, the concert was set for 22 April.

Meanwhile, Perry continued reworking *Heart Of The Congos* at Island's request. The first import copies of the album appeared in scarce quantities in Britain early in 1978, some sleeves adorned with yellow stripes in the margins, hand-painted by resident artist Jah Wise, but as with the early mix of 'Punky Reggae Party' that surfaced in Holland, the first Congos pressing was restrained, with few effects or technical embellishments. The vocals were dry, with scant delay or reverb, Keith Sterling's piano placed to the fore, and there was little of the phasing that defined Perry's previous Island albums.

In February, Chris Blackwell travelled to Jamaica with his lawyer, Tom Hayes, to negotiate the terms of *Heart Of The Congos*; contracts were signed, and everything seemed set for Island's overseas edition, so Perry devoted untold hours to completely restructuring the album, rendering subsequent pressings radically different. He bathed the vocals, keyboards and guitar in high doses of delay, the piano was made fainter, upfront percussion and manic crashing cymbals were added, several songs rolled into extended dub portions, and now there was a mooing cow sound on some tracks too, made by Watty Burnett's voice resonating through the cardboard centre of a tinfoil roll.

'People sometimes say Scratch take a cow into the studio — well, the cow is me,' said Burnett. 'We went around with a microphone in Duhaney Park, but whenever the cow see us, the cow ran, so it's an aluminum foil roll: I put my mouth in the cardboard part and I make a sound with a music in my throat. I won't tell nobody how I get that effect, but it's natural to me. I make the sound, "Moo", and Scratch say, "Wow! Sample that". We did the first sample, Scratch have it on a quarter-inch tape. Scratch think it was funny and he use it on a lot of stuff.'

Perry and the Congos conducted their business meetings with Blackwell at the Sheraton, where John Lydon was holding court in the aftermath of the Sex Pistols' disintegration, acting as an A&R consultant for Virgin Records, who were in the process of establishing their Front Line subsidiary as a reggae concern that would rival Island's. On the run from the paparazzi, Lydon arrived on the island in early February with Don Letts, Vivien Goldman and photographer Dennis Morris, staying for the better part of a month.

As a longstanding reggae head whose love for the music ran deep, Lydon was in his element in Kingston, hanging out with Big Youth, Jah Lion, Culture, Tappa Zukie, Prince Fari and other acts that Virgin signed, although the Pistols were almost entirely unknown in Jamaica. The Congos even took him to an isolated cave with a body of water in its interior.

'Punk made no impression on the island,' said Letts. 'They just knew that John was some crazy white rock singer from the UK and what impressed them is that he was public enemy number one. Jamaicans love a bad man, so that's all they needed to know.'

Virgin hatched a plan for Perry to produce some reggae covers of Sex Pistols songs at the Black Ark, but Lydon felt the results unworthy of voicing.

'That day could have started at U Roy's yard at seven in the morning, with a pipe and a Red Stripe for breakfast,' said

Letts. '[Virgin co-founders] Simon Draper and Richard Branson had an idea of doing reggae versions of some Pistols tracks, and they got Lee "Scratch" Perry to get a bunch of studio musicians together, but it was nothing to do with John. I think Chinna was in the mix and Horsemouth was around, but Lee Perry was in control and all I remember about that session was me and John being in the control room, stoned out of our heads, laughing at the absurdity of the whole thing while they put together these rather lame versions of "God Save The Queen" and "Holidays In The Sun". The musicians didn't know us from Adam – they're getting paid to do some kind of hotel reggae.'

NME's Chris Salewicz flew to Kingston on 10 February when he got wind that Lydon was there. At the Black Ark, he found Perry in the company of Cedric Myton, JBC disc jockey John Wakeling, and an array of onlookers, working with a rookie five-piece from the countryside called Quake-In Vibrations, and fleshing out ideas with the newly arrived Candy McKenzie, who was reading from the Book of Revelations. Amongst the publicity photos of Bob Marley and the Clash, Max Romeo's had 'Judas' scrawled over it, the result of some perceived slight that had him momentarily in Perry's bad books.

Perry told Salewicz he was working on new albums with Junior Murvin and George Faith, as well as a *Super Ape* sequel, *Return Of The Super Ape*. He had been negotiating with Island for a planned 'Upsetter Revue' tour that would bring Murvin, Faith, the Congos and Perry's ace session players to British audiences in the summer, but it was already clear that the package was another utopian project unlikely to be realised.

Murvin's 'Cross Over' was then impacting the Jamaican charts, placing Rastafari teachings above the failings of the 'white man philosophy' and calling for an abandonment of violence; at the ever-evolving Black Ark, where a mural dubbed Perry 'the Mad Scientist' and painted handprints now adorned the outer walls, Salewicz found Perry echoing the sentiments of 'Cross Over' in rapid-fire, declamatory pronouncements. His music resulted from an ordained calling, Perry explained, and would pacify Jamaica and the world at large, challenging power imbalances.

'I and I is to warn them that the bomb going to blow up on them that makes it! I and I is here to warn them that if they use it then them *dead* by it too. So our part is to make sure that reggae music take the message across to the warriors in the war zone whom you can't reach by the telephone. If it gets to him on a gramophone him must hear it. And *this* am the message of reggae music! *We* turn the world around *now*! We talk – man listen. See me! Because the word is it, y'know. The army of Jah Rastafari set sail on a ship on a mission that can never fail. With all his militant soldier, armed to the teeth, the word of Jah Rastafari has come to kill the wicked.

'Equal rights and justice! We take reggae and bring it forth to the earth. We no deal with the whiteman philosophy. We go deal with His Majesty. Too long we have had to kill a brother for his money. *Don't sell your soul for silver and gold!* Dig me, man, Babylon is a con trick and me going to lick it with a brick.'[1]

Perry said he had no choice in making records; he was *appointed* to make them and could not refuse. Voicing a trope he would often return to in future, he pontificated on the veracity of excrement; since the Truth was surely in 'all the good food that you eat,' Perry reasoned, 'when you shit that food out, the Truth is in there too.'[2]

During Salewicz's visit, Augustus Pablo was working at the Ark, the bartering arrangements yielding some of his most timeless work. Portions of *East Of The River Nile* were recorded or remixed there, with Perry's trademark phasing giving tracks like 'Upfull Living' a very special sound, also heard on the single 'One In The Spirit', credited to Sister Frica. Further unreleased melodica-based instrumentals were also cut in this period, enough to make up an album, according to Perry, track titles listed on tape boxes including 'Soul Too' and 'Colombia Gold Dust'.

Two of the year's early singles had vibrant Nyabinghi drumming: the Meditations' 'House Of Parliament' called for the replacement of the traditional seat of government with a Rastafari firmament, and 'Forward With The Orthodox' by vocal trio Mystic I, based at a Rasta camp in western Kingston, invited the listener to stone the Devil and called for the abolition of income tax.

Led by furnituremaker Lesburn Clarke, with Trench Town resident Anthony Johnson and Maxfield Avenue nightclub chef Balvin Fials on harmony, Mystic I were brought to the Ark by Johnson's cousin Cleveland, who had known Perry since the ska days; 'Feeling Happy' (aka 'Forward With Love') and love song 'Elaine' would surface the following year.

Both Lloyd Robinson's 'Peace And Love', credited to Shaumark and Robinson, and the Meditations' 'No Peace', spoke to the volatility of the time, the latter, written by Ansel Cridland, naming wealth disparity as the main cause of violence.

'Scratch start tell we he would like to do an album, but I didn't want to sing an album for anyone at that time because my experience with the two albums that I did before didn't give us any satisfaction,' said Cridland. 'But I love Scratch. I see the way that he was producing, so we decided to do "No Peace" for him, "Much Smarter" and "House Of Parliament", and he wrote another song for us named "Time For Police To Go To Jail" or "Babylon Arrest".'

Issued in Jamaica as 'Think So', 'Much Smarter' was written by Danny Clarke, decrying the discrimination facing the Rastafari, with conga drumming to drive the message home, and Island would release it on the B-side of the extended 'Life Is Not Easy', a self-produced song the group recorded at Channel One.

Debra Keise's 'Travelling' (miscredited to Debra Keese) was one of the spontaneous creations that came together at the Black Ark from time to time, another song that saluted the Nyabinghi, although Keise was not a disciple herself.

'Lee Perry was a Nyabinghi and most of my friends were trying to recruit me to join Twelve Tribes,' said Keise, 'but I was an uptown fly girl who didn't want to give up her flyness in order to be Rasta.'

Born in Birmingham, England, and adopted by Jamaican parents, Keise moved to Kingston at the age of six in 1964, her family one of the first to occupy a house on Cardiff Crescent. In her teens, Keise began hanging out at Aquarius Records and got acquainted with uptown artists such as Third World; according to Kiese, her friend Althea Forrest was dating Inner Circle's frontman Jacob Miller, and after Keise wrote the song 'Top Ranking Girls' in 1977, Forrest convinced Inner Circle to allow them to record it, along with Forrest's friend, Donna Reid, but the song was released in Florida without their knowledge, credited to the Cordets. Then, when Keise became pregnant, she and Reid fell out, which is why Keise was absent when Forrest and Reid re-recorded the song as 'Uptown Top Ranking', which became a massive hit overseas, topping the British pop charts for the first three months of 1978, just as Keise began frequenting the Black Ark.

'My daughter was born in December 1977 and I started going to Scratch's studio in the spring of 1978, but I never really tell Scratch that I was a singer; the Congos and Junior Murvin used to always be down there and there was always an artist painting some biblical stuff on the walls,' said Keise. 'One day I had some good weed, and I took it down cause I know Scratch love a smoke, and when I got there he was recording the Black Five, which was three guys, singing something about travelling, and I said, "You're really recording *that*? It sounds awful!" Him say, "You can do better?" So me just start rhyme, "Travelling, travelling, travelling, travelling to Rastafari, Nyabinghi ah weh we ah deal with, come make we chant we way through." I gave them the lyrics and I was singing it for them, but when they went back in, they couldn't do it, and when I go in there and sing the verse, I see Scratch jumping up and carrying on. He give it to the radio announcer that was there the day, and the song was out the following week. Keith Sterling played on it, and I remember being there when Ernie Ranglin was putting a guitar riff on it.'

Keise began joining Perry and the Black Ark crew for the daily jogging sessions on Hellshire Beach, which is how the song 'Sweat Suit' came about. Patterned after 'Uptown Top Ranking' and credited to Sonny and Debbie, it paired Keise with Winston Watson of the Meditations, with lacklustre results.

'We used to meet at Hellshire Beach to run the beach every morning with Dhaima and Dennis Brown, and I think "Sweat Suit" was written on the beach, but it's Scratch who write that song and when Scratch put out "Sweat Suit", Bob Marley said, "No make Scratch make you do them little fool-fool tune." He said he didn't like the song that Perry want me to sing, just like him never like "Punky Reggae Party".'

Waterhouse-based deejay Lord Sassafrass used to ride his bicycle to Perry's studio on a regular basis, hoping for a chance to record, and Perry finally gave him the opportunity in response to the ongoing investigations into the Green Bay Massacre, first on a cut of 'Big Neck Police' for the condemning 'Green Bay Incident', with the follow-up, 'Green Bay Inquest', voiced on the 'Travelling' rhythm.

Bob Marley returned to Jamaica on 26 February, ending his fourteen-month exile. Around two thousand people are estimated to have pushed past police barricades to swarm the airplane when it came to a halt on the runway, the largest public gathering at the airport since Selassie's visit in 1966. Several functions had been organised for Marley's return, including a Rastafari rally at National Heroes Park, where Marley gave an informal performance, followed by dub poets such as Mutabaruka, Oku Onuora and Mikey Smith. Flanked by bodyguards, Marley went on to join Perry and the rest of the inner-city's most devout brethren for a night-long groundation held by the Nyabinghi Theocracy in Matthews Lane, one of a series of historic events they staged to motivate the people to embrace peace, their government sanction allowing the brethren to chant, drum and smoke without fear of police harassment.

After Jah Ned had a vision that the city was decorated in red, green and gold, the brethren made tri-colour sashes to mark off the area of the Nyabinghi, draping the former streets of bloodshed with the divine presence of His Majesty. Marley was overcome with emotion at seeing former foes gathered in the spirit of oneness, and midway through the proceedings, Kingston was shaken by an earthquake as though in acknowledgment of the magnanimity of the event; in the coming weeks, Marley would spend many days visiting ghetto areas to help bolster the peace.

Kiddus I's 'Security In The Streets' was one of the most impressive songs applauding the peace treaty, the singer a member of the committee that helped broker the truce. Born Frank Dowding in rural St Mary, he took the name Kiddus, which means Blessed One in Amharic, after embracing Rastafari. Since 1971, this quiet, thin and thoughtful dread had been operating a communal Rastafari crafts centre and café at 1C Oxford Road in New Kingston, with the goal of establishing a self-sufficient community; at the juncture of uptown and downtown, it allowed persons from all social strata to meet in a harmonious atmosphere, making the compound unique in a city starkly divided by class. As some of the best *ital* food could be found there, and Rastafari was the main focus, it naturally became a congregation point for musicians, with the Zap Pow band building a rehearsal space on the premises, which was also the base for Tommy Cowan's Talent Corporation.

Issued on seven- and twelve-inch formats on Kiddus' Shepherd label and recorded at the Black Ark once the peace treaty was in full swing, 'Security In The Streets' praised the efforts of 'Brother Claudie, Brother Bucky and Brother Tony', with clavinet bursts from Tyrone Downie, bright brass timbres from saxophonist Cedric Brooks and trumpeter Mike Hanson, plus a smooth lead guitar from Chinna over Robbie Shakespeare's throbbing bass and Horsemouth's understated drumming, augmented by kette drumming from I Jack of the Sons of Negus and Kiddus himself on funde; flipside 'Too Fat' pointed a guilty finger at the greedy, its unusual line-up including Santa, Michael Williams, guitarist 'X' Sweeney Williams of Zap Pow and multiple keyboard players. Kiddus I also recorded the politically censorious 'Crying Wolf' at the Ark in this period, and each of the songs had an air of majesty and seriousness, complimented by Perry's lush production.

'Economic Crisis' by former Kingstonians frontman Jackie Bernard (credited as Jack Lord) had an emotionally laden delivery emphasising the desperation of the times as the bottom dropped out of the economy; an inability to repay outstanding IMF loans brought protracted negotiations to put an Extended Fund Facility agreement in place, its punitive conditions exacerbated by rampant inflation and a series of local strikes.

'Captive' was another double-tracked Perry proclamation, attacking the continual enslavement of Black people in Jamaica's post-colonial present, calling for mental and spiritual liberation.

In contrast, Earl Sixteen's 'Cheating' was a song of romantic disappointment, issued with two different mixes in quick succession, and the second would skirt the Jamaican charts in late September, but never quite reach the top ten. There was also the atmospheric 'Land Of Love' by the otherwise unknown Sons of Light, and a beautiful repatriation song called 'Ethiopian Land', recorded by Waterhouse duo Peter and Paul Lewis, its dub complete with plenty of cow sounds.

Perry mixed a wild dub for the B-side of pre-teen heart-throb Junior Tucker's 'Look Into Your Heart' (a cover of Aretha Franklin's hit, written by Curtis Mayfield), which was released by Talent Corporation, though he had little to do with the A-side, which entered the Jamaican top ten in late March, remaining there right through to August.

In the midst of so much other material, Candy McKenzie's album was one of Perry's main preoccupations during February and March, another hectic period that saw the studio in near-constant use. The bulk of the rhythms were constructed with Boris Gardiner, Mikey Boo, Ernest Ranglin, Billy Johnson, Geoffrey Chung, Keith Sterling, Winston Wright and Headley

Bennett, along with Zap Pow's drummer Cornel Marshall for certain songs, and on a couple of tracks, Cat Coore, Ibo Cooper, Richie Daley and percussionist Irvin 'Carrot' Jarrett from Third World.

McKenzie found the recording sessions chaotic and Perry inflexible; he would thrash out the rhythm tracks with the players by day and get her to voice the material late into the night. McKenzie said that working with Third World was 'fabulous' and the connection was not only musical: her romantic liaison with Ibo Cooper would produce a daughter named Adeama, born in London in December 1978.

But there were disagreements with Perry about the music. McKenzie felt he wanted to steer her in certain directions as a female, just as he had done with Susan Cadogan. You can hear it in her sultry take of Baby Washington's 'Breakfast In Bed' and in the less successful attempts at covering Sami Jo Cole's 'Tell Me A Lie' and Jeff Barry's sentimental 'Walking In The Sun', though Boris Gardiner's 'Someone To Love Me' was heartfelt lover's rock. Much of the rest of the album deviated from that script: Perry's 'Disco Fits' was a playful beatbox number ostensibly about the allure of funky reggae with some cool harmony from Bunny Rugs and his Third World compatriots; Perry's 'Ice Cream' spoke of the joy brought by the neighbourhood ice-cream seller over one of his off-kilter Ark creations, though McKenzie's soul-tinged high notes are somewhat at odds with the reverberating percussion and heavily treated aural effects. Similarly, on McKenzie's original material, her voice does not always fit easily with Perry's complex musical creations; 'Jah Knows' spoke of the hardships she had faced over a surprisingly easy-going rhythm, and on the dejected 'When The Big Day Came', McKenzie clashes with the dense dub textures behind her, including the mooing cow sound, especially when incongruously appropriating phrases from Barbara Lewis' 'Hello Stranger'. The contemplative 'Sky At Night' was pleasingly optimistic, McKenzie's double-tracked voice locking nicely into the spongy reggae groove, and 'Keep Him Strong' appealed to God for guidance and protection, the bubbling rhythm punctuated by Perry's primitive drum machine. Yet, even if the tracks sound a bit raw in places and the album thematically incohesive, there is no doubting the strength of McKenzie's voice nor the emotive honesty with which she delivered her lyrics.

As the album slowly came together, Perry drafted McKenzie into Full Experience, providing the missing voice they had long searched for, though bad blood with Aura made her presence brief.

'None of them wasn't strong enough to be an individual star,' said Perry. 'Candy didn't strong enough, Aura didn't strong enough, and Pam was good looking and sexy, but she didn't have a strong voice to help the sexiness, so the best thing was to use them to do something together – that would be very sensible.'

'Scratch was working simultaneously with Candy and us and the Meditations, and he was just rotating,' said Pamela Reid. 'Like in the afternoon maybe the Meditations would be there and then eight o'clock, here comes me and Aura, but we know that we were the prize because we would work until two or three in the morning. We'd voice stuff, but then he'd work with Candy, and I don't know if it worked out the way that she or he wanted, because once he started working with Full Experience, he was giving us the most time.'

According to Aura Lewis, Full Experience recorded eleven or twelve songs with Perry and his musicians in the spring of 1978, incorporating traditional South African elements and

African-American soul into the pervasive roots reggae of the Black Ark. Aside from an extended reggae arrangement of Nina Simone's 'To Be Young, Gifted And Black' (as 'Young, Gifted And Broke'), the songs were mostly written by Lewis and arranged by Reid, included broken-hearted ballad 'Can't See You' and the patois-infused 'Nar Soh, So It Stay'; the playful 'At Midnight' was semi-improvised in the studio, and the pick of the bunch was the self-titled 'Full Experience', a bass-heavy groove with a rousing horn fanfare and striking vocal harmony, the lyrics explaining the concept behind the group. There was also a funky excursion called 'Let's Move', led by Reid, and a ballad called 'Love Song', written by Lewis, which Reid remembered as the best song of all, as well as reggae versions of the traditional Swahili songs 'Malaika' and 'Haposamane'. The music was coming together forcefully, though Lewis and Reid said trouble soon arose.

'We did this album in a wonderful environment, but in the middle of all this work little aspects started coming in to create confusion,' said Lewis. 'First there was Lee Perry's crush on Pamela. Black Ark was in the same yard as his house and Pauline and the kids were there . . . Pauline would say stuff like, "That Full Experience album will never see the light of day." Then it turns out that Candy was having an affair with Ibo, so sometimes at night, Ibo's wife used to come up to Stony Hill where Candy and I were staying and make a scandal. Also, Candy didn't want to do her songs with us because Island was going to back her to do an album of her own. So a lot of bad vibes started coming on the scene.'

'Aura and Candy didn't vibe too well,' said Reid. 'One day we were recording something for Geoffrey Chung at Harry J's and Geoffrey said, "Somebody is off", and Candy said, "I know it's not me because I have perfect pitch." They had a little exchange of words and I remember Candy saying to Aura, "You're going to bust a blood vessel, you might want to cool down." And that was it for Candy as far as Full Experience was concerned. The next time we saw Scratch, Aura said, "No, I don't want Candy." There was a personality clash for sure.'

McKenzie appeared on I Kong's stunning 'Take A Hold' twelve-inch, co-produced by Chung, its equally arresting B-side, the devotional 'Zion's Pathway', having been initiated at the Black Ark in late 1977 but finished off elsewhere.

Perry pressed copies of McKenzie's 'Disco Fits' and 'Breakfast In Bed' on an Upsetter twelve-inch, though McKenzie was unaware of it. He would deliver a completed master of her album to Island in mid-May, but Blackwell opted not to release it, one of several Perry-produced LPs he would reject. And then, conflict with the Congos had a knock-on effect with Full Experience.

'Lee told us to come and do this little patch-patch work in the Congos album that Chris Blackwell had asked him to fix before he would accept the product,' said Lewis. 'So while this was going on, Cedric's wife went to the States and heard a track from the album in one of the record shops in Brooklyn. So she comes back to Jamaica with the album, and all hell broke loose because here we are, doing these little things that Scratch said Island wanted, meanwhile he's already pressed the album and he didn't tell Congos that. So this scared me because I said to myself, "If I leave this stuff of mine in the studio, it might never see the light of day." And just at that time, Jimmy's problem was getting solved with the record label to do *Bongo Man*.'

With the atmosphere worsening and no sign of the album's release after so many months, Lewis began to get cold feet. Reid said Perry planned to introduce Full Experience at the forthcoming One Love Peace Concert, even taking her to meet Marley during preparations for the event, but before anything solid was in place, Lewis asked Jimmy Cliff to intervene.

'Jimmy convinced Aura that Sunpower, his company, would produce the album because she was starting to have second thoughts about Scratch and she should not have,' said Reid. 'Scratch heard us and took us right into the studio. It didn't cost us nothing but our time, our talent and our sweat, and Jimmy is not as committed as Scratch.'

According to Lewis, Cliff was infuriated when he heard about the project and ultimately buried it. Though a Sunpower single purporting to be Full Experience's 'Strictly Roots' (aka 'Full Experience') was issued when Cliff got involved, the music on the mislabelled disc was actually a cover of the Drifters' 'Up On The Roof' by male harmony group Heat Inc, and Cliff somehow never got around to releasing the Full Experience LP, both Cliff and Perry avoiding Lewis thereafter.

'I told Jimmy that I had been in the studio with Scratch, Pamela and Candy and we had done this album called *Full Experience* and that I was afraid of leaving it in the studio, so what I needed him to do was help me pay for it because Lee had already paid the musicians, so I needed to refund him that, pay for the studio time and pay for Lee's time, for us to get the masters from him. And Jimmy was shocked. I don't know what he thought we had been doing all those weeks that we were waiting for him, but he wasn't very impressed that we had done this thing with Lee. Lee thought that I'd sold him out to a baldhead, and Jimmy Cliff was wondering what's happening because the last time I'd worked with Lee, we were working with Bob, so what's my story? Lee gave

Jimmy a quarter-inch tape of some of the tracks and from that moment, both of them wouldn't talk to me again. It was like I didn't exist. And I went crazy. I went off for about a year in Jamaica, walking barefoot in the streets, until my friends sent me back to the States.'

'Jimmy Cliff bring Aura to Jamaica and would not record her,' said Perry. 'She finally come to me and Jimmy Cliff did not like the idea. Him get mad about it and me say, "You no have to get mad, just pay me back for the studio time and for the musicians." He was plainly vexed, so me just give the four-track tape that me have to Jimmy Cliff and me didn't mix it neither and I don't know what happened after that.'

Aura would retrieve a remixed five-song master tape from Cliff's office in 1981, released in France as *Full Experience: Aura Meets Lee "Scratch" Perry At Black Ark Studio* in 1987, but the rest of the material has never been released, and according to Lewis, the album master tape probably perished in a fire at Cliff's recording studio in Montego Bay. McKenzie's LP would languish in Island's vaults much longer, finally surfacing in 2011.

During all this confusion, in the spring of 1978, Perry was approached by Rastafari cooperative 100 Drums Incorporated, one of the groups lobbying the government to decriminalise marijuana (along with the Nyabinghi Theocracy and the Mystic Revelation of Rastafari), for funding towards their proposed stage play *Imojah: The Journey Of One-Hundred Drums From Africa*, scheduled to open at the Jamaica House Garden Theatre in April, directed by Stafford Harrison and featuring Ras Michael and the Sons of Negus, United Africa and Fred Locks; Perry reportedly gave hundreds of dollars to the group, but the production descended into chaos and its opening was indefinitely postponed.

Marley, Perry and other associates were then attending weekly services at the Ethiopian Orthodox Church, also known as the Holy Trinity Tewahedo, located a short distance from Channel One studio at 89 Maxfield Avenue.

'Scratch used to carry we there every Sunday,' said Sean. 'Bob Marley used to be there and Tommy Cowan, cos more artists used to go to the church then. We learn a different religion by going to church and the main concept was that we are in oneness.'

The services were presided over by Abba Mandefro (later Archbishop Abuna Yesehaq), who was sent to Jamaica by Haile Selassie to spread the Ethiopian Orthodox form of Christianity and to quell the belief that Selassie was God, but official denials could not shake the faith of the Rastafari, and though baptism into the Church was technically dependent on a denounce-ment of Selassie's divinity, many believers attended services there and Mandefro often found himself at police stations and prisons trying to secure the release of Rastafari innocents whose only crime had been to wear dreadlocks.

According to Chinna Smith, in the run-up to the One Love Peace Concert, Marley found the time to lay the foundations of a couple of new scorchers with Perry one Sunday at Dynamic. Recorded in front of an array of onlookers that included Claudie Massop and Bucky Marshall, 'Blackman Redemption' and 'Rastaman Live Up' were optimistic proclamations of right-eousness that drew on biblical imagery, the former celebrating Selassie's Solomonic lineage, the latter rounding on the Rasta faithful to stand firm in their belief, both songs harder than the bulk of the *Kaya* album. The rhythm of an early take of the historical 'Buffalo Soldier', about Black US cavalry regiments that fought in the Indian Wars of the 1860s, was also laid at the same session and Perry's influence is readily apparent, particularly on 'Rastaman Live Up', which incorporates a favourite refrain from the Book of Judges about Samson slaying the Philistines with a donkey jawbone.

'Me used to go to the Orthodox Church,' said Chinna. 'Me see Scratch one Sunday and him say, "Bob just come in now, we need fe go clap them tunes," and we clap "Buffalo Soldier", "Blackman Redemption" and "Rastaman Live Up", them three tunes we clap that day at Dynamics.'

After the basic rhythm tracks had been laid, Marley and Perry set about voicing and restructuring the material at Aquarius with engineer Mervyn Williams, plus Bunny Wailer as a silent observer, and to give the songs an added harmonic difference, Perry then sent for the Meditations, who arrived at the studio around seven o'clock. Though Perry had retro-actively placed their backing vocals on some of Marley's earlier material, Bob had never actually met the trio and now happily informed them of the strong impression their song 'Woman Is Like A Shadow' made on him in London, though Cridland said Perry was not satisfied with Marley's delivery until well after midnight.

Bob Marley's mother, Cedella Booker, underwent an offi-cial conversion to Rastafari around the time of the One Love Peace Concert, so to further express her newfound faith, Bob suggested she record an album of reggae hymns at the Black Ark, but the few songs they recorded probably never passed the demo stage.

'Bob told me he want me to do a gospel album, so he make arrangements with Scratch and send me there,' said Booker. 'We did "Enter The Lord's Anointed" and about three other gospel songs, and Scratch was a good director. He tell the musicians what they're doing wrong and how they are to work with me.'

'Blackman Redemption' would enter the Jamaican top ten in late July and remain there to the end of the year, by which time Marley and Perry would join forces on another couple of impressive efforts, but for the moment, Marley had other commitments to fulfil.

On 22 April, the One Love Peace Concert was a truly historic event. The National Stadium was filled to capacity, the unusually low entry price allowing the common citizenry to witness some of Jamaica's top acts at their peak of form (including Dennis Brown, Bunny Wailer, the Mighty Diamonds, the Meditations, U Roy, Dillinger, and Ras Michael and the Sons of Negus), with Perry's Soundcraft mixer, keyboards and other equipment helping to enable its execution. Peter Tosh delivered an expletive-strewn lecture aimed at the wealthy few, imploring Seaga and Manley to take up the principles of the peace movement and stop victimising the poor, but by far the most incredible moment came at the climax of the Wailers' triumphant performance, when Marley had Manley and Seaga join hands onstage, a gesture that would have been unthinkable until Marley precipitated it.

Perry's *Roast Fish Collie Weed And Cornbread*, his first solo album as a vocalist, was released in Jamaica towards the end of the month on the new Lion of Judah label. In addition to the remixed title track (now with added cow sounds), 'Big Neck Police' and a recut of Junior Byles' 'Curly Locks' with crashing cymbals, the album had seven originals, driven by plenty of humour: 'Soul Fire' had a double-tracked Perry wailing the lingo of soul over a thick Upsetter mix of mooing cows, echoing percussion, funky guitar and mournful sax; 'Throw Some Water In' used automobile upkeep as a metaphor for taking care of the human body over a militant rockers drum line; 'Mr DJ Man' asked radio jockeys to help his new material to hit so that his family could eat properly, and 'Favourite Dish' used promi- nent sound effects to bring home its message, with bawling babies, mooing cows and out-of-time percussion as Perry sang of the food he loved, which kept his manhood in shape without the need for artificial stimulants. Social protest number 'Ghetto Sidewalk' spoke of absent streetlights in underprivileged areas and 'Free Up The Weed' was an optimistic plea for the legalisa- tion of herb. Yet, the track that most indicated Perry's predom- inant frame of mind was 'Evil Tongues', an ominous, vindictive number that verges on the paranoid:

> There are some hypocrites around me
> Who pretending to be my friend
> Little did they know that I saw them coming
> Saw them coming around the bend
> Evil eyes and wicked heart
> I saw them coming from afar
> Coming, coming to play their part
> You want the lion's share, but Jah Jah know that no fair
> Wicked tongue and evil heart
> By the sweat of your brow you shall eat bread
> Then how you want to live off the next man head?
> You're too lazy, you can't leave your bed . . .

Perry later said the song was about the Congos, though they are shown on the album's back cover, along with Full Experience, one of Perry's young sons and Perry himself – a harmonic image of happy times, before Perry fell out with everyone.

The more experimental *Return Of The Super Ape* was completed by July, a mixed bag that transcended category. Though most of the songs had lead vocals of some sort, the jazz experimentation placed everything in dub territory, the vocal tracks far removed from the typical reggae hits of the day.

Opening number 'Dyon Anaswa' was roughly based on Roy Richards' 'Freedom Blues' (adapted from a Little Richard hit) but was restructured so drastically as to be barely recognisable: a Full Experience chorus, seemingly in African language, formed the only words, with echoing, out-of-time percussion pushed to the fore. The title track was a mutation of U Roy's 'OK Corral', sounding entirely in place through new percussion and jazzy sax breaks, incongruously followed by a laughable scat version of Rufus' 'Tell Me Something Good'. 'Bird In Hand' was a dub mix of Sam Carty's 'Milte Hi Aankhen', followed by the dub-jazz hybrid instrumental 'Crab Yars', with magnified percussive effects at centre stage.

Most of the songs on side two had lead vocals by Perry, though the subject matter is difficult to follow. 'Jah Jah Ah Natty Dread' denounced the Pope as a baldhead, with a Perry sneeze its uncommon centrepiece; 'Psyche & Trim' dismissed godless 'top ranking' gang members with a spanking, and 'The Lion' recycled the rhythm of the Hombres' 1976 single 'Africa' to elevate the righteous dreads above the heathen. 'Huzza A Hana' was a mumbled scat vocal over a jazzy dance riff driven by a rousing sax line, and the closing 'High Rankin Sammy' was a slow skank with a double-tracked Perry vocal that saluted its unknown protagonist.

Roast Fish and *Return Of The Super Ape* are fine achievements, marking a high point of Lee Perry's career as a self-produced solo artist. They are complex and dense experimental works on which Perry's individual personality shines through and are equally indicative of how far his creations were from reggae's mainstream. Perry still largely eschewed the Studio One and Treasure Isle remakes that were yielding so many hits for Bunny Lee, Channel One, Joe Gibbs and Studio One itself, preferring to stick with originals or mutate an American standard, and on the few occasions that he adopted the practice, he would completely transform a Jamaican adaptation, rendering it beyond recognition. But the price of such uncompromising originality was that Perry's work was not achieving much mainstream popularity in his native land; though he maintained a fierce reputation as a sound originator and was noted as the most vocal of producers espousing the Rastafari cause, his productions were not ramming the dance halls or generating the sales of his competitors, which brought increasing frustration. Island Records was beginning to give Perry mixed messages about his unconventional material too; their policy seemed to be shifting, though no official declaration had been made.

The album that the Congolese artists Seke Molenga and Kalo Kawongolo recorded with Perry in 1978 is one of the most mysterious and misrepresented of Black Ark projects. During the 1960s and '70s, Molenga Mosukola, better known as Seskain Molenga, was a key member of some of Congolese music's most iconic groups and esteemed for his sterling drum work, though he was also a singer-songwriter, guitarist and percussionist. Conga Success, African Fiesta and Empire Bakuba all benefitted from his talents, and he released material under the name Surboum Seke-Seke on his own Molenga label too, but the introduction of the 'Zaireinization' policy by the dictator Mobutu Sese Seko in late 1973 brought a dramatic decline to the local economy, so Molenga was part of a growing exodus of musical performers that emigrated to Paris.

After conducting a lengthy tour of France with Afrisa International in 1976, Molenga was recruited to an experimental fusion project by the Congolese bassist Toni M'Batchi (alias Toni Batchi), who had been playing with Senegalese guitarist Wasis Diop in the Afro-jazz fusion band West

African Cosmos, which had folded following the release of a self-titled debut album by CBS France. At the core of the new group, which Diop said may have been called Autocar, was singer/guitarist Lucien 'Zabu' Zabuski, who had recorded blues and psychedelia, and saxophonist/vocalist Laurent Grangier of Gilbert Artman's Urban Sax ensemble. The intention was to record a rock album with African undercurrents in Jamaica, the project overseen by Nadette Duget, a complex and mysterious figure who was by all accounts a stunning beauty.

The child of a Vietnamese father and a French mother, Duget was raised in Dakar, Senegal, and later moved to France with her family. In September 1977, while working on a documentary series on the castles of the Loire Valley for public television channel FR3, she began dating Corsican bass player Philippe Quilichini, and when Quilichini and his close friend, the photographer Antoine Giacomoni, decided to move to Jamaica in January 1978, Duget was motivated to head to Jamaica too, leading to the proposed fusion project.

'Toni Batchi was in Paris and knew Bernadette Duget,' said Molenga. 'We saw Bernadette and had a drink together, then we went to the rehearsal room and I saw Zabu and Laurent and, four days after, Wasis Diop came too. The heart of the group was Zabu and Laurent.'

'Bernadette is a Cleopatra, half French and half Asian,' said Diop, who first met Duget in Dakar in the early 1970s, when she often visited his older brother, Djibril Diop Mambety, director of the trailblazing film, *Touki Bouki*. 'My big brother was very much a playboy and I think Bernadette loved visiting my brother. Djibril presented me to Bernadette, and I think five years after, in an incredible situation, I met her in Montparnasse in Paris.'

353

As the line-up solidified and M'Batchi was removed, Molenga recruited the saxophonist and percussionist Kawongolo 'Buffalo' Kimwanga, alias Kalo Kawongolo, who had played with him on the Afrisa International tour.

'I called Kalo Kawongolo just before we went to Jamaica,' said Molenga. 'We were doing rehearsals with Philippe, Wasis, another guitarist and Laurent and Zabu, and we wanted to strengthen the band with another saxophonist who could take the saxophone when Laurent sang. At the rehearsals, we were playing rock music, but when we arrived in Kingston the situation changed.'

Perry was open to the project from the outset, but as the weeks rolled by, things simply did not go according to plan, the anticipated album becoming another of the many disputatious, aborted projects.

'Duget arranged the airplane tickets and had reserved a large apartment with ten rooms,' said Molenga. 'She invited the Wailers and Lee Perry to meet us and when they came in the evening, we had a Jamaican soiree: we ate and drank champagne together and had a jam session to get to know each other. The intention was to record the songs we rehearsed in Paris, so when we went to the Black Ark, we recorded the music first, and Laurent and Zabu recorded their voices afterwards, but they had trouble getting their voices to fit the music. So there was discord between Zabu and Duget. She began to rail, "I spent all my money, but you cannot sing properly." Jimmy Cliff was there, and he encouraged Zabu. He said, "Take some rum with lemon so that the voice improves", but it was even worse after that – the voice was totally broken.'

After having made painfully slow progress on eight songs, which Duget felt were not of sufficient standard, the project splintered. Perry had noted the skills of Molenga and

354

Kawongolo and bonded with them as kindred spirits of Africa; indeed, the Congos had been trying to recreate an ancestral link with the Congo, yet here were a pair of musicians from the Congo itself, with its very language on their lips and its rhythms and melodies in their music. He thus recruited their services alone, leading Molenga and Kawongolo to begin working at the Black Ark for Island.

'We were waiting for the singers to remake the songs, and later, Lee Perry called and said, "I wanted to ask him to help us during the sessions",' said Molenga. 'When Duget took me and Kalo to the studio, I saw that there was a fight between Carlton Barrett and Bob Marley, but Lee Perry wanted us to continue to record, so I mounted the drums. We all played and then we went home and after that, Lee Perry called again and said that he wanted to see me and Kalo alone, so we went out to talk, eat and drink. He began to explain that he wanted us to stay in Kingston to work together. He said, "Since you're from Congo, this is perfect. This is our root, the Congo." After that, he called Tom Hayes of Island Records. Hayes was in the US and called his assistant in Kingston and said, "Prepare the contract." Kalo and I stated our conditions and when Tom Hayes arrived, we met at Strawberry Hill to make the contract. Tom Hayes then put us in a suite [at the Sheraton] and we lived there with a driver. We were like studio musicians in the Black Ark, with a three-year contract from Island and after, we asked to make an album with Lee Perry. With the original project, it was not us who gave up, but Bernadette felt that the band was not able to do what she wanted and Zabu failed to accept his responsibility as a singer, so Bernadette lost a lot of money. Since we were in France, she paid for food, drinks, rehearsal rooms, flights and the ten-room apartment with a pool and a car. Bernadette had unknown incomes – very complex – but this was her own money and Philippe was heir to a rich family, so Philippe also financed this project, but she lost a lot, so things have gone bad because of that. Bernadette was forced to arrange something with the Congos because the record she intended to make with us was a failure.'

Duget brought Zabuski, Grangier and Quilichini to Dynamic to record the twelve-inch single 'Ghetto Child', credited to Immigration Act, and poached the Congos away from the Black Ark to produce the *Congo Ashanti* album at Harry J and Aquarius with Quilichini on bass, mixed at Dynamic in February 1979 and released by CBS France at the end of Duget's year-long Jamaican sojourn.

'Some white people working for CBS France came down to Jamaica and they was recording these African guys in Scratch's place,' said Roy Johnson. 'They see us do three or four tracks a day, and when those guys come, they can't finish one track for a day, so one day they say, "Shanti, you know where we can get some congo drums?" So I took the lady to get some drums and she asked me, "Would you like to do something with us? We would like to do some business."'

As Perry continued working with the Congolese performers, his connection with the Congos was severed. Lured by the promise of a lucrative contract, they left Perry's camp to work with Duget after a bitter parting in late 1978. It was at this point that Perry trimmed off his budding locks, rejecting the notion that an inward belief in Rastafari must be manifest through visible dreadlocks on his head.

Though conflicting views have been put forward on the circumstances of the rupture, all agreed that it stemmed from Island's failure to issue *Heart Of The Congos*, and although the company publicised its upcoming release in April, they ultimately chose to keep it on the shelf. The master tape of the first mix Perry provided had been recorded at slow speed on a reused four-track master tape that had 'Big Cockey Wally' still present in another two channels at a faster speed – hardly an ideal format for mastering. Yet, as the album would never cease to be in demand and would be re-pressed on at least a dozen labels in eight nations, achieving a high volume of sales when lovingly reissued by Blood and Fire Records in 1996, Island's refusal to release the Congos' debut is difficult to understand in retrospect.

Johnson suggested that Island feared the album would potentially damage sales of Bob Marley's work.

'Leslie Palmer used to work in the A&R Department in Island, so he know what's going on,' said Johnson. 'He said to me, "When that album come from Jamaica, we have meeting for a month straight about who we was to put the promotion on, Bob Marley or the Congos."'

Max Romeo made similar claims about *Reconstruction*, his self-produced follow-up to *War Ina Babylon*.

'I realised that they sign all the artists that was a threat to Bob Marley and put them on the shelf so they can send the King ahead and crown the King. We were all victims, all sacrificed to make the Marley empire, but we thank God for it because the world would hear reggae music.'

Johnson said tension had already been growing between Perry and the group after Cedric Myton's son started a rumour that Perry deliberately fed him pork, a taboo meat for the faithful as stated in Leviticus. However, his suggestion that Perry asked Blackwell to block the album is clearly misguided, as Perry was greatly angered by Island's refusal to release it.

'Cedric's little boy go and tell a lie that Scratch cook pork and give him to eat,' said Johnson. 'Scratch get vexed and maybe he tell Chris, "Just keep that on the shelf." When we did *Heart Of The Congos*, it stay so long to surface, for Chris Blackwell have it there doing nothing with it, Scratch have it there doing nothing with it.'

Watty Burnett recalled the pork incident but said the real friction stemmed from Perry's view of Johnson's vocal abilities.

'There was no pork cook in that house, but Roy and Scratch had a feud because Scratch always say Roy couldn't sing, and Roy knew he didn't have a great vocals, so he take it offensive,' said Burnett. 'It start from that, and Cedric is easily led. When they had the feud I was very upset because I didn't want to leave Scratch. It really fuck my head up until now. I sleep and dream about it. When CBS took us, I didn't want to leave Scratch. Scratch feel a way badly. Scratch take it very hard too.'

When asked about Island's decision not to issue *Heart Of The Congos*, Chris Blackwell hesitantly stated, 'I remember at the time thinking that there was one great track and the rest of it was weak.'

However, he was quick to deflect claims that he venerated Marley at the expense of other artists.

'People think a guy like me does an incredible job to make and break artists, but you don't at all. You're around to try and help the artists you're working with make it. The main role is to help guide, to try and be a friend, help develop choices and open doors. I didn't push Bob above anybody else, Bob just had more going for him than anybody else. I honestly believe that is the case. I pushed Burning Spear, I pushed Toots — I love Toots, I've known Toots much longer than Bob — but I just wasn't able to get him across. Lee Perry, like most reggae artists, was more embraced by the press than the radio. The press gives you credibility, but radio is really what sells records, so Lee Perry never sold a lot of records in the same way how Bob sold a lot of records. Songs like "Roast Fish And Cornbread", these are absolute masterpieces, but we weren't able to make them hit singles at that time.'

By the time that Island rejected the Congos album, Perry had cut the second mix in Jamaica, and when the split happened, the Congos were given tapes of this second mix, which they would use to re-press and sublicence the album on a number of occasions. Burnett was also given master tapes of his material, including a partially completed ballad called 'Chances', which he would later revoice and issue in New York, and Burnett purchased a cut of Earl Sixteen's 'Freedom', which he intended to issue on his own label but never got around to releasing in vocal form.

Molenga and Kawongolo's proposed album title was *Monama*, a Lingala term meaning still in good spirits. According to Molenga, unlike the material attempted with Duget, the album he and Kawongolo created at the Black Ark was completed in just a couple of weeks, since they had already written some songs in Paris, though others were created ad hoc in the studio with Perry and his Black Ark players.

Molenga's 'Africa Roots' established the mood as an Afro-reggae hybrid sung in English of the connection between Africa and Jamaica being forged at the Black Ark; in contrast, his 'Moto Ya Motema' is sung in Lingala, the title roughly translating to 'Fire In The Heart', while his 'Nakoya' or 'I'm Coming' expressed commitment to fidelity with his wife.

Kawongolo's 'Bad Food' drifted between pidgin English and his native Yanzi language. It speaks of the food poisoning the pair experienced during their time in Kingston, but Molenga said that contrary to what has been written elsewhere, the duo were never made homeless and did not scrounge food on the streets; it was simply a case of choosing the wrong dish on a certain occasion. Kawongolo's 'Mengieb' or 'Pity Me' had a sorrowful melody behind his tear-jerking delivery, and 'Guipimbu Gienu', which switched between Yanzi and English, roughly translates as 'Hello Everyone', a salutary number that celebrated the connections made at the Black Ark and the unique experience of creating the album there; four other songs were recorded for a slated twelve-inch single that was never released.

When the album was finished, Molenga and Kawongolo were summoned to London by Island staff, who placed them in a fancy hotel and arranged a photoshoot with Dennis Morris. Expectations were high, but unexpected problems arose when they surrendered the master tape: instead of the stunning result that had been captured at the sessions in Jamaica, the master was heavily distorted and highly muffled, not only marred by excessive doses of echo and delay, but by the poor sound that results from the repeated reuse of magnetic audio tape. Molenga believed this to be intentional sabotage by Perry, though since *Heart Of The Congos* had been rejected by Island for similar reasons, and as other material was also delivered on poor quality reused master tapes, Perry may simply have suffered from a lack of ready materials since tape was often hard to come by in Jamaica. On the other hand, his output was generally becoming denser, more layered, and highly abstract, and as various pressures came to bear, the state of the material mirrored the general unravelling that would soon see Perry shut the Black Ark doors. In any case, despite Molenga's fielding of the album to another label, Island's rejection blighted the otherwise ground-breaking enterprise.

'When the album was finished, I wanted to go back to Kinshasa, but Lee Perry was not happy,' said Molenga. 'He wanted me to stay in Jamaica, so that's when Lee Perry started to mess with the recordings. He put a lot of echo and messed it up – very complicated – but I did not know this. When we listened to the mix in the Black Ark, the record was impeccable, but when we handed the tape to the executives at the headquarters of Island Records in London, it was different. They heard that the sound was not good, and they were very mad at Lee Perry. The version he kept was better than the one he gave us – it was not the same. Island said, "We do not want that", so we went to Paris to see Sonodisc and their sub-label Sonafric released our record. It was the wrong mix, so we tried to arrange it a bit before they released it. After that, Island were looking for us to get back to work, but I was so angry with the whole story, I did not like it anymore. So I returned to the Congo and we set up a band in Kinshasa called Show Machine and I never went back to Jamaica.'

Before Molenga and Kawongolo travelled to London, the Jolly Brothers returned to the Black Ark to record an album for Tony Owens, since 'Conscious Man' was getting hot in England after Mo Claridge re-released it in mid-July on Ballistic, a United Artists subsidiary, and UA soon issued pressings in other territories, including Holland and South Africa, widening the demand. Molenga and Kawongolo were thus enlisted to play guitar, congas and saxophone on some of the Jolly Brothers' new material.

Eight topical Jolly Brothers songs were laid at these sessions, the group often singing in unison over Perry's spongy rhythms, and they backed their friend Henrick Nicholson on a song called 'Brotherly Love', released on a Seven Leaves twelve-inch, but conflict between Owens and Ballistic derailed the Jolly Brothers' album project. Claridge thus enlisted King Tubby's protégé, Prince Jammy, to record an album of love songs with the group at Channel One and Harry J, released as *Consciousness* in 1979; the material they cut for Owens was shelved until the early 1980s, when a few twelve-inches were released on Seven Leaves, though most of the work would not arrive until 1993, when the *Conscious Man* album finally surfaced on Owens' Roots Records imprint.

But the biggest problem was that Island Records was no longer issuing Perry's material. Aside from the Meditations' 'Much Smarter' B-side, there was a notable absence of Perry's work in Island's 1978 release schedule. Island had yielded the greatest exposure for Perry outside Jamaica, helping to establish him as a revered cult figure with an entirely new audience, and Perry was especially proud of *Roast Fish* and *Return Of The Super Ape*, but when Island chose not to issue either of them, the relationship was indelibly strained.

'Chris did not like that album and I didn't too happy that he didn't like the album,' said Perry of *Roast Fish*. 'He didn't pay it much mind because of the lyrics. It wasn't with what was happening at the moment, it was just something about exercise and different views, how to live good, what to eat and what not to eat, and I don't think they were ready for anything like that. I forgive him, but I was really upset about it, that he didn't like an album like that.'

'I think he got pissed off with us because we didn't issue some of his records,' said Blackwell, 'and it must be that I didn't think they were great.'

To redress the balance, Pauline Morrison launched PM Records in London to house some of the work Island rejected. There was a Jah Lion toast of 'White Belly Rat' with a dub of 'Ketch Vampire' on the B-side, Junior Delgado's 'Sons Of

Slaves', backed by the Congos' previously unreleased 'At The Feast', about the Feast of Passover, and a twelve-inch of Leo Graham's love song 'My Little Sandra', but these independent releases could never achieve anything close to the kind of sales stimulated by Island's ample promotional budgets and far-reaching distribution network.

In Jamaica, Perry made the bill of the 'Reggae Family Day' event, held at Fort Clarence on 7 August as part of independence celebrations; Derrick Harriott, Winston McAnuff, Junior Tucker, Sugar Minott, Little Roy and Ian Rock, Dhaima and Ras Michael and the Sons of Negus were also featured, with Lloyd Parks' We The People supplying the backing. It had been years since Perry graced the stage, yet the return went largely unnoticed; for now, the studio was a more appropriate environment for creative expression.

Despite the conflict with Island, Perry continued to issue noteworthy one-off singles in the latter half of 1978. 'Free Up The Prisoners' was a vocal magnum opus, a 'Disco Prisoner' twelve-inch that played at 33RPM, released on the retitled Conquering Lion of Judah label. Over a hesitant recut of 'Feel The Rhythm' that unfolded for some thirteen minutes, Perry listed the many reasons why Babylon should send the prisoners home 'to chant the Nyabinghi', and as the song progressed, there was an overpowering crescendo of sound effects, with sine waves and electric seesaw sounds gradually overpowering the mix, while the sobering B-side 'Chase Them' spoke of unkosher elements that needed to be chased away, including income tax and birth control.

Perry was introduced to Michael Campbell, alias Mikey Dread, before the rupture with the Congos. An old friend of Watty Burnett from Portland whose late-night *Dread At The Controls* radio programme on JBC was then the only show on the island to feature home-grown Jamaican music exclusively, Campbell had revolutionised Jamaican broadcasting overnight and Perry's work was often featured on the show.

'Watty Burnett brought me to Lee Perry when he was singing in the Congos and I was on the radio by then,' said Campbell. 'Scratch was a man who was really into his music and into his mixing in his studio. He's magical at what he does, and Scratch is not an engineer that sit down on the left-hand side of the board, stretching towards the right-hand side, Scratch is *all over* the board, skanking and doing him echo and extra special effects. Then Scratch give me some jingles and some specials, like "Row Fisherman" and most of the Congos tunes, so after a while me just start play a whole heap of Lee Perry every time.'

Getting Campbell to voice some toasts for him was a natural next step, beginning with a cut of 'Big Neck Police' logically titled 'Dread At The Control' (or 'Mantrol', as the lyrics had it), followed by 'School Girls', which was voiced on Mystic I's 'Elaine', and 'Home Guard', which sarcastically attacked the recruitment of volunteers to help the police fight crime over an abridged cut of 'Free The Prisoners'.

'Me go to Scratch to get fi him tune them on the air. After that, Scratch check me one time and say that him want me to do a tune, and I think I did "Dread At The Mantrol" first. Me do nuff more rhythms for Scratch. Every morning when me leave JBC and reach home by six o'clock, Lee Perry's there, and him gone with me for the whole day until it's time for me to go back and work the night. Him get a lot of good things because him always have some great ideas, and me and him never had a problem because the man is a genius and I could recognise it, because I come from a different academic school.'

'Dread At The Control' entered the Jamaican top ten in mid-October and remained there for two months straight, being one of the year's biggest hits for Perry (along with 'Blackman Redemption', released on Tuff Gong).

There was also the condemning 'Mr Money Man' by a certain Danny Hensworth, and 'Brother Noah', a harmonic retelling of the Great Flood by the Shadows, three singers apparently named Sam, Don and Errol.

But the overly long hours of work were beginning to take their toll on Perry, the endless disappointments heightening his perplexity, and his behaviour was becoming increasingly extreme, especially when fuelled by rum and weed, but still the tapes kept rolling. Though many of his creations from this period would never be released, the music that sprang forth evidenced an overloaded genius at the peak of his powers.

For instance, Junior Murvin's follow-up to *Police And Thieves* was recorded with the nucleus of the band now known as Axx of Jahpostles, based in Norwich on the Portland coast, just before Perry severed his ties with the Congos.

'Scratch told me to get a band and these young kids were living in Norwich, so I started training them as Junior Murvin and the Apostles Band,' said Murvin. 'I carry them to town, and we did an album which wasn't released. Scratch still have it there. The second album, we rehearse it for two weeks straight, just went straight in and do it. That was Leslie Mowatt on organ, Lynford Richards on guitar, Devon Bradshaw on bass and Tony Bradshaw on guitar, Rocky on drums, and I think Roy from the Congos is playing congos. When Lee Perry was supposed to start the album, he put the Congos in my space. I don't know if that caused Chris Blackwell and him to fall out, because when Chris wanted the second album he didn't get it.'

George Faith also recorded a second Black Ark album, completed by the end of 1978, of which precious little has surfaced.

'*Working On The Guideline*, that's another album for Lee Perry, but I don't know what happened to that one,' said Faith. 'It was ten songs, took maybe about nine months or a year to finish. He use musicians like Robbie Lyn, Winston Wright, Sly and Mikey Boo, but he switch around the musicians along the way.'

In late 1978, Perry issued the arresting single 'Guideline', which was meant to be the title track of the album; a twelve-inch version was later released in New York by Munchie Jackson on a label called Andre, named after his son. Driven by a highly modulated keyboard line from Winston Wright, the vocal performance on 'Guideline' showed that Faith could be just as successful with original material as with the cover versions that were always foisted on him.

Somewhere along the way, an American punk group called Scratch contacted Perry, asking their namesake to produce them. Perry was pleased by the album they sent and agreed to work with the group, but the project was yet another that would not be realised. However, Pauline Morrison was sufficiently inspired by their rendition of Dusty Springfield's 'I Only Want To Be With You' to cut a version of her own at the Black Ark, ironically recorded just before the betrayal that ended their relationship.

As on previous occasions, some of the year's best work was created with Bob Marley and the Wailers, though the creations themselves were ultimately a source of friction. When the Wailers returned to Jamaica in August after their extensive *Kaya* tour, Marley came to the Black Ark to record two monumental numbers that would not be issued for over twenty years: 'Who Colt The Game' and 'I Know A Place'. Details of the recording sessions remain obscure, though lead guitarist Chinna Smith supplied the following: 'I think it was Mikey Boo, Scratch's resident drummer. I don't think it was Family Man on bass, if it's not Boris Gardiner it would have to be Winston Wright because Winston Wright used to play a wicked bass too, and Billy Johnson might be the next guitarist.'

According to Clancy Eccles, Perry had written the lyrics of 'Who Colt The Game' in the late 1960s, though certain adaptations were made when Bob Marley recorded the song.

'"Who Colt The Game" was written at West Indies Records, some years before Bob Marley sing on Scratch's own productions. Friday night everybody meet and gamble, play twenty-one, and one Friday night Scratch, Linford Anderson and Bill Garnett was playing dominos down by WIRL and the song come up. Ten years later he give that song to Marley.'

'Who Colt The Game' used domino metaphors to query the injustices of Babylon; Natty Dread was revealed as the innocent victim and Baldhead the guilty party who cheated. The rhythm was a slow, shuffling, one-drop skank, spiced up by plenty of wah-wah riffs from Chinna, plus piano and organ licks that Chinna said were overdubbed later. Perry added male harmony vocals at a later session, though who sang them is unclear: the Meditations would have been likely candidates, but each member stated plainly that they did not sing harmony on the song. Though never properly finished, the symbolic humour of 'Who Colt The Game' certainly equals the best of Marley's metaphoric deliveries.

'I Know A Place' was the other unfinished masterpiece to emerge from these sessions, Marley's depiction of a utopian sanctuary in which to escape from the hypocrisy and hatred of the world. Over a tightly wound, distinctive rhythm with a distorted guitar line and accentuated drumming that emphasised the urgency of the lyrics, Marley and the I-Threes sang with an intense passion, present on only their finest works.

At the same time, Perry was deepening his commitment to the Nyabinghi Theocracy, who held a month-long Nyabinghi in National Heroes Park from Emancipation Day on 1 August, where they demanded to meet cabinet ministers to discuss the legalisation of ganja, the removal of Queen Elizabeth II as head of state, and a proposed repatriation programme. Rastafari attended from across the island, setting up a massive camp in the park.

On 6 August, in the midst of the Nyabinghi, Pope Paul VI died – a consequence of the energies released at the Nyabinghi, according to the more radical members of the Theocracy. During the papal conclave on 26 August, the presence of white smoke from the chimney of the Sistine Chapel should have indicated that a new Pope had been chosen in John Paul I, but the smoke reportedly changed from white to greyish black, flummoxing those assembled in St Peter's Square, inspiring Perry's tongue-in-cheek response on 'Baffling Smoke Signal', an incendiary single with mirthful lyrics, double-tracked vocals and distorted guitar, recounting the occurrence from Perry's particular Rastafari perspective, its title lifted from a *Gleaner* headline.

The Nyabinghi Theocracy was forcibly evicted from National Heroes Park on 5 September, during which an oak tree that had been planted by the Queen in 1953 was burned, and then Perry funded another forty-day Nyabinghi to maintain the momentum of the movement.

As Perry's priorities shifted and Nyabinghi came to the fore, he produced an album at the Black Ark with Ras Michael and the Sons of Negus, one of the most important proponents of Nyabinghi music.

Ras Michael knew Lee Perry from his early days in Kingston, but aside from 'Earth's Rightful Ruler' the two never really worked together until Ras Michael played percussion on some Junior Murvin material at the Black Ark, and the presence of the Sons of Negus at Bob Marley's 1978 session led to the recording of the exquisite *Love Thy Neighbour*.

'That album was done by Lee Perry and it's a funny thing, an adventure,' said bass drummer Sidney Wolfe. 'Same time Bob was doing "Who Colt the Game", we were there and then we came to agreement with Scratch to do that album at Black Ark.'

'Ras Michael and everybody come around and they always have a big reasoning right there,' said P-Son. 'They sit and reason about God.'

The Sons of Negus completed over ten songs at the Black Ark, the resultant *Love Thy Neighbour* a high point of their career. The application of extreme levels of reverb and delay gave *Love Thy Neighbour* an apocalyptic aura; fragments of instruments and voice burst forward at unexpected moments, heightening the menacing quality of these serious works. 'Don't Sell Daddy No Whisky', 'Wicked Got To Go' and 'Hear River Jordan' are among the most extraordinary songs Ras Michael ever recorded, while 'Little David', 'Perfect Love' and a recasting of the nursery rhyme 'London Bridge Has Fallen Down' are optimistic visions for the present and future of the Rastafari community; 'Time Is Drawing Nigh' reworked the Studio One classic 'Darker Shade Of Black' (which drew on the Beatles' 'Norwegian Wood'). There was also 'Long Time Ago', which spoke of the injustices of slavery days, and repatriation cry 'Do You Know', as well as praise song

'Jesus Christus Is The King'. Boris Gardiner, Santa Davis and Mikey Boo supplied the rhythmic bedrock and Hux Brown's expressive blues licks greatly enhanced the work.

Brown had just completed a tour of West Africa with Toots and the Maytals, and his time in Jamaica would be brief. The harshness of life had affected him badly in the mid-1970s, culminating in a low period where he often sought solace in drink, resulting in his emigration to Oakland, California, in 1976, in an effort to straighten out.

Fellow guitarist Alva 'Reggie' Lewis also developed an alcohol dependency from which he would never fully recover, and after his halcyon days with the Wailers, Lewis became a vagabond, later saved from a life of destitution by Rita Marley, who gave him an informal job as gatekeeper at Tuff Gong, the studio Bob Marley opened in 1979.

Leo Graham was also feeling distressed, the repeated financial frustration and other pressures causing an emotional breakdown, effectively ending a long and brilliant singing career.

And then there was the troubled mind of Lee Perry himself. During the completion of the *Love Thy Neighbour* album, Perry's behaviour became resolutely drastic; he entered a new phase that centred on graffiti, painting cryptic proclamations on the walls of his studio. Then he began placing the letter X over certain letters of his proclamations, as though to erase or blot out the cipher and, later still, whole words would be covered with Xs. In time, entire walls would be carpeted with nothing but the letter X, or completely overwritten by a series of words or statements scrawled in paint or magic marker.

'During that period of time, he got a little bit upset, or probably got mad some people would say,' said Sidney Wolfe. 'He was writing up a lot of Xs and shit like that around his place and refuse to do any more recording. That was about the time that Black Ark studio started to get demoralised.'

Fortunately for the Sons of Negus, Perry allowed them to retrieve their master tapes before things totally disintegrated. On their emigration to Washington DC, they arranged for *Love Thy Neighbour* to be issued on the Jah Life label, and contrary to the track listing, its original issue substituted 'Long Time Ago', 'Do You Know' and 'Jesus Christus Is The King' for 'Perfect Love' and 'London Bridge', unlike all future pressings. Further incomplete and partially mixed tracks from the sessions were also included on Ras Michael's 1981 release, *Disarmament*.

Though a few Black Ark works would trickle out in 1979, Perry turned his attention away from producing conventional music in late 1978, since the Nyabinghi Theocracy had become his main focus.

'Me decide that me want to close the reggae factory because reggae is a dog – a monster dog,' said Perry. 'Me decide to close the reggae shop and open the ears, close the reggae campaign. The reggae people didn't have nobody else to live off of. Vampire always want something, so me decide to close it, then Nyabinghi is a church me start now.'

Perry demonstrated his commitment to the movement in a *Gleaner* notice that appeared in late November:

'He that have an ear let him hear
And he that have eyes let him see this day.'
Lee 'Scratch' Perry from the Black Ark Studio
In co-ordination with the Issemble of Patriarchs of the
Nyabinghi Order
Of the Haile Selassie I Theocracy Govt (Black Supremacy)
69 Church St, Kgn,

'Calling the nation to Repentance now (Churches and All) by the order of His Royal Majesty King Selassie I, King of Kings and Lord of Lords, the Conquering Lion of the Tribe of Judah, the Elect of Himself and the Light of the Iniverse. Selah.'

Another notice appeared on Christmas Eve:

REPENT EVILDOERS
TO THE WORLD COUNCIL OF CHURCHES AND STATES
Now hear this as the truth liveth
I and I Ras Tafari – Issemble of Patriarchs and Elders of the
Nyabinghi Order King Alpha Selassie I
RIGHTEOUS THEOCRACY GOVT.
Black Supremacy
69 Church Street
Kingston, Ja
Demanding that the Governwrong of the World TRANSFER all authority to
His Majesty's Righteous Theocracy Govt. for the GUIDELINES of all Suffering Humanity
Says LEE SCRATCH PERRY
Repentance is a capital order from His Majesty Haile Selassie I
The first King of Kings and Laws of Laws
Conquering Lion from Mount Zion.
Selah I Pyramid.

Perry had been strengthening his bond with the sect after they increased their visible displays of musical and social activism. In truth, they were planning a revolution together that would usher in a new era of theocratic government, and the declamatory graffiti erupted from his intensified involvement with the group. The Nyabinghi are said to have taken the linguistic code of Rastafari I-words to even more radical heights, placing great importance on letters and sounds as well as on the more standard Rastafari word usage, and Perry adopted their methods with an incessant fervour, seeking another means of expression.

'Even now, in Jamaica, certain words to the Rastaman don't right,' said P-Son. 'I think in his mind he was back to school studies. I think it was just inspiration and the good from the bad, like X stands for the Devil, D for Death.'

'The realisation came to Scratch that certain words did not belong to His Majesty,' said Jah Ned. 'Some words really belong to Satan.'

Perry began working on an album with members of the Nyabinghi Theocracy, tentatively entitled *Nyabinghi Slaughters The Dragon*, using both the four-track and eight-track machines.

'Scratch was the one who had changed the whole phenomenon of the music, because Scratch was the one that brought everyone to the path of singing about His Majesty,' said Jah Ned. 'We were doing some live recording at the Nyabinghi that we had in the city, and then we decided to add a portion of studio recordings. Scratch was responsible because he was the general responsible for the music ministry for the movement. After the One Love concert, I had taken full duty with Scratch strictly for doing recordings now to make funds to help do what we want to do. We did quite a number of recordings, but Scratch never release – it was an ongoing thing. Sometimes we were here, and other musicians came, and we go in the studio and we did something, sometimes an instrumental, sometimes a vocal. We had Santa on drums and P-Son sometimes, Mikey Chung on bass, Gladstone Anderson, Headley Bennett, Cedric Brooks.'

But the project was never completed, since the Nyabinghi Theocracy fell foul of Perry, along with all the other dreadlocked

Black Ark regulars. Everyone was castigated and rebuffed in a series of hostile confrontations, Perry reaching a breaking point by January 1979 after experiencing overwhelming pressures. The Black Ark gates were then generally closed to visitors and its premises increasingly marked by declamatory words.

'After "Blackman Redemption" came out, a lot of people used to be down there during the day, asking for money from Scratch,' said Ansel Cridland. 'Musicians, people that work for him, everybody come for money.'

'I hung out in the studio all the time,' said Earl Sixteen. 'Heptones come and did *Party Time* album and Bob Marley did "Blackman Redemption", until Perry started drinking too much rum and smoking at the same time. Then there was this elder dreadlocks who used to come across and preach a lot, and he used to get on Perry's nerves. I don't know what happened, Perry went on this trip. He was getting focally rich, really rich: companies used to come from America and would want to film the studio and Perry would take their money and kick them out, literally. Then there was the bad boys called Spanglers, who was coming up for money every day. They wanted weekly paid protection money and Perry didn't need that. He was building up the studio, Jah Wise came and painted up the studio all nice. Perry just tripped out and started making X on all the As and Es.'

'Spanglers and all the guys from town who follow music used to come and beg money, lots of people from each side,' said P-Son. 'Scratch would talk to them. He'd say, "Put down your gun, cool off", try to stop them from the bad ways they're doing, killing people. And they would listen to him – he do a lot of work.'

Furthermore, Perry's extended family continued to look to him as the breadwinner. In addition to Pauline, the children and P-Son, Perry's mother, and sister Girlie depended on him for financial support, and there were occasional demands from the family of Delano, his alleged offspring.

The financial pressure was an ongoing source of worry, but spiritual conflict had a more decisive impact. As a faithful servant of His Majesty, Perry was chiefly concerned with using his music to elevate Rastafari but took issue with the wearing of dreadlocks following his rupture with the Congos. His anti-dread sentiments were shortly to intensify, remaining a negative focal point for decades to come.

Achieving peace of mind was a necessity, but also an impossibility, in Kingston. If he had followed the direction of his spirit guide and gone to the tranquillity of the Blue Mountains or some other unspoiled country retreat, he may have been able to clear his head and find a practical solution to his troubles. Unfortunately, Lee Perry did no such thing. As he had regularly done for the last five years, Perry remained deep in the bunker of the Black Ark, immersed in his creations day and night, hardly stopping to eat or sleep, the most regular forms of sustenance herb and alcohol.

As Perry's behaviour became less predictable, Pauline Morrison began to feel the strain. When Perry had been earning good money from Island, he had spoken of buying a house for her in the tranquillity of Beverley Hills in uptown Kingston, but she is said to have feared isolation and never followed through with the idea. Fissures had formed in their relationship that were now widening.

'A lot of women who is mixed up with men in the music business have a terrible experience through their lives, so it's not easy to talk about,' said Pauline. 'Scratch was so wild. He had so many women when I was with him, and I beat up some, I broke up some and I broke him up too. It's kind of disturbing, so I said I want to leave that part of my life behind.'

They also clashed over her decision to keep the dreadlocks she began growing in 1977, but it was Perry's extreme behaviour that finally became unbearable.

'Even now, it kind of marvels me. If you see our house, this guy write all kind of shit on the wall, on the fence . . . he used to build sculpture into the wall! I spent years of that, wondering if I'm going to go insane, until I finally just went, "Rah!" It just take me by surprise, and I couldn't be a prey to Scratch's stupidness. If I was, probably I would be in the asylum.'

Pauline was preparing a meal one afternoon when she noticed an odd smell coming from the kitchen, and when she checked the pot, she found that Perry had emptied the simmering contents in the garden, substituting rocks in their place on the stove. He had also taken a week's worth of newly purchased groceries out of the refrigerator and thrown them to perish in the dirt. As Kingston was hit by harsh flood rains towards the end of 1978, Pauline knew that she had to make a change to retain her sanity and thus began spending nights away from Cardiff Crescent, beginning an affair with Danny Clarke of the Meditations.

'Scratch was going out of his head,' said Clarke. 'I don't really know what happened. He was all right, and the next thing I know, he start marking up the walls and making all kinds of Xs. I used to live over by Central Village, up near Sufferer's Heights. When Meditations were working on the *Guidance* album, Pauline came up by Three Mile Market and we spent the whole day in the studio. Pauline said she couldn't take it anymore, she was finding some way to get out because if she stayed, she might go crazy too. After two weeks I hadn't seen her, so Ansel takes her by my house one night. Buses stop running so she have to spend the night. That's how we really get hooked up. I was just coming out of a relationship of two years, so I was all by myself then. After that, I stay away from Cardiff Crescent because there was a lot of vibes going around: people saying I take away from Scratch and I drove Scratch crazy and all that shit.'

As the affair began under such difficult circumstances, their problematic relationship would take time to blossom, and despite efforts to keep it secret, the grapevine that is the Kingston music scene soon spread the news as Pauline was more frequently away from Washington Gardens. She eventually rented a room of her own in the uptown suburb of Cherry Gardens and then settled into a larger space in the same neighbourhood, sending for her children shortly thereafter.

But Lee Perry and Pauline Morrison found it hard to make a clean break. The kids were back and forth between both addresses, as was Pauline, she and Perry doing their best to keep their conflicts under wraps. Sean, who greatly idolised his father, was worried that Perry was not caring for himself properly, so he and Omar gradually began to spend more time at Cardiff Crescent to keep an eye on him; as the weeks passed, their sisters followed suit and all four children moved back by the end of the summer, by which time Pauline had gone to New York to visit her mother, seeking advice on how to repair her ruptured life.

As Pauline was in and out of the Ark, Perry's grasp of the line between reality and fantasy deteriorated. He told certain key people that he was not really crazy, that he was just enacting an elaborate charade to rid himself of unwanted attention, but the charade superseded his control. Many close to him have testified that he underwent a breakdown, though even this is disputed; others insist his behaviour is simply an act. There are also tales of Perry ingesting hallucinogenic mushrooms, or an unknown substance that caused permanent change.

'When Scratch become mad, it wasn't him mind,' said Roy Cousins. 'Scratch did have a lot of hangers-on round him at the time and I remember on one occasion they were mixing something, give Scratch to drink, and that's what bust Scratch's head up. If a man get mad by natural causes, it can be cured, but when a man get damaged by chemicals or false ways, it cannot be cured and that's what happened to Scratch.'

In any event, a tumultuous new persona emerged to take charge of his actions, and though his perceived 'madness' would wax and wane from this point onwards, he would never be the same again.

Though he did not want to admit it, Pauline's departure greatly affected Perry. She had long handled much of his business affairs and provided some badly needed stability in his life. That she would take up with one of the musicians whose career he had helped build hit him hard, and that the man was a dreadlocks was worse still.

Perry soon found fault with almost everyone around him and enacted drastic measures to shake them off.

'Scratch was a Rastaman from way back,' said Danny Clarke. 'At the time you have Ras Michael and the Sons of Negus used to go by Scratch, you have the Nyabinghi people used to come and sit down, and everybody come want money – everybody always looking money, money, money, money! So them drive Scratch to zero, take Scratch to country, say they're going to kill the Pope and them shit, so all those things just kind of get to Scratch and because Scratch is a scientist, Scratch just come with something to get rid of these people.'

'He had a Rastafarian church he started with a bunch of dreads, and I don't know what happened, but these dreads fall out of grace, so he wanted to keep them off him,' said Max Romeo. 'He put a pound of pork on his antennae and rode around town until it rotted, and maggots were falling from it, claiming that he don't want no Rasta round him because Rasta come give his kids lice. After he put the pork on the antennae, the dreads was still coming, so he wrote on his car back, "I am a batty man".[3] That's when the dreads run in all different directions! His situation continue a little further with the game: he took the bonnet off, planted flowers in and was driving around – the dirt lodges in his carburettor, so the car can't go no further.'

'I don't remember doing anything like that, but definitely I did have too much dread around me anyhow,' said Perry. 'Me would have to support the dread and support the dread family, so me did want to make different changes that could drive them away. Them think me mad and some of them would disappear.'

'Scratch started to change, and people were saying that he was going crazy,' said Debra Kiese. 'I remember going down there and somebody saying that he put how much thousand dollars out in the street, and somebody take it, and I remember him pasting money on the walls.'

'At one stage, I was supposed to go on a tour and Scratch was supposed to make the arrangements with Island, but he went away and when he came back he was a changed person,' said George Faith. 'He started to deal with something else. For instance, equipment or anything in the studio that had the letter R, he would throw it outside because it represent Rome, and he begin his routine of making X all over the place. I didn't think anything was happening to him. I think, "That is just Lee Perry" because when you're working with him, he do some strange things too.'

By the end of January 1979, the Black Ark was entirely devoid of visitors. Though the mixing desk and tape recorders were still connected, the studio became little more than an abandoned shell covered in words; despite retaining basic functionality, it had virtually ceased to exist.

CHAPTER ELEVEN

The Return of Pipecock Jackxon: The Partial Rebirth and Ultimate Destruction of the Ark

While Pauline was seeking perspective on the chaos of Cardiff Crescent, Lee Perry ensconced himself in lonely solitude. He spent his days rearranging items in the compound, building abstract sculptures and painting declamatory graffiti. Though dread outsiders had been barred, he was still occasionally voicing previously recorded rhythm tracks, but severed ties left few outlets for his work and he was not actively seeking new avenues.

In late January 1979, Mo Claridge, Dave Hendley and broadcaster David Rodigan appeared at the Black Ark gates, along with Prince Lincoln Thompson of the Royal Rasses.

'By this time, Scratch was totally transformed,' said Hendley, then working as a Trojan A&R. 'We went up once and there was no one around, so we peered through the railings and you could see he had covered the place, scrawled absolutely everywhere and that's the first thing that hit you, all the little crosses on the walls and all the elemental stuff. When we eventually linked, he was just talking virtually non-stop, even if he was talking to himself a lot. I thought he looked in really bad shape, and there was a certain tragedy about it. I remember him saying, "No one comes by anymore, they've taken everything they can off of me." The board was still set up, he had the Teac, and it could still play tapes, but all the tape boxes were scribbled over and were just laying around everywhere. There wasn't one surface that he'd not written on, and the amount of time that he must have spent just writing that stuff is phenomenal. He must have been so alone when he was doing that. It's very solitary stuff and the tiniest of things like the staplegun had been written on. Even the little Polaroids had writing everywhere, and eyes were crossed out on people's pictures.'

Though Perry seemed in no mood to do business, he was secretly waiting for divine intervention to show him the way forward, and the next foreigner to appear helped initiate another creative phase.

The son of Polish immigrants who met in England during World War II, Henk Targowski was raised in Joliet, southwest of Chicago, where his father, a former cinema projectionist, worked in electronics. Hopping freight trains to San Francisco in 1967, he became involved in the Diggers collective and other underground groups before relocating to Amsterdam to join a growing community of bohemian expatriates. In 1978, he formed the Black Star Liner distribution company and record label with the express purpose of issuing product by the best Jamaican producers, and Lee Perry was top of the list. Financial backing was provided by Billy Bradford, an African-American from Northern California who made a fortune through international imports, and there were silent partners, including Sicilian friends Santo and Fred.

Targowski made his first trip to Jamaica in the spring of 1979, some weeks after Claudie Massop was killed by police, his body riddled with dozens of bullet wounds, bringing an abrupt end to the peace treaty. The Jamaican economy had become more precarious too, with unemployment and inflation gone through the roof as further faltering IMF recovery plans brought increasingly stringent conditions.

'I was staying at the Terranova Hotel, where all the politicians and secret agents used to eat,' said Targowski. 'So, there were a lot of CIA and Cuban spies there.'

As he later recounted in the Dutch magazine *Vinyl*, Targowski received an ominous reception at the dilapidated Black Ark: 'No dreads in the yard, only children playing. At the end [of the driveway] stood Lee "Scratch" Perry, the Upsetter himself. You can imagine my great surprise when Scratch greeted me with the words "I've been expecting you." How that could be was a mystery since I had neither previous contact with Scratch, nor had I told anyone of my visit who could have warned him. Scratch made it seem like a foreordained event – apparently, Scratch had anticipated someone showing up from outside of Jamaica, someone to help him with some master scheme . . . Scratch invited me to follow him into the inner sanctum of the Black Ark. The colourful paintings which had decorated the outer wall of his studio were all gone. Scratch had covered them over with splotches of ugly green and shit-brown paint. Black graffiti had been scribbled in felt-tip over everything. When I entered the studio, the inside décor proved to be an even greater shock: the place was a disaster area. Bits of equipment lay scattered around the room, shelves had been torn down. Boxes of recording tape lay strewn in a jumbled heap in the middle of the floor . . . tape ends, unravelled from their reels, had spilled out in a tangle of confusion. The mouldy rug onto which they had been carelessly thrown was soggy wet from rainwater which leaked through holes in the roof. The inside walls had become a wild montage: the previous art had been painted over with the same green and brown as outside. Scratch had also glued records, metal stampers, tapes and other assorted objects to the walls – layers upon layers of paint and posters and book pages, a chronological history of Scratch's mental state. The overall atmosphere of the place was oppressive . . . the horrible smell coming from an over-flowing septic tank added to the feeling of discomfort. After carefully noting my reactions to all this, Scratch proceeded to give me his rap: he was the "Lord Thunder Black" and his black footprints of Time trod upon the Rainbow. Scratch went on about his mission on Earth, how he had been entrusted with the job of protecting the "original Jah Soundtrack", guarding it from violation by the profane. Scratch was fond of using props to illustrate his conversation: an upright piano stood in the room, painted entirely yellow including the keyboard. Scratch explained that it represented the Golden Harp of David. A bass guitar symbolised the female element, while the drums stood for the male. Scratch had developed a metaphysics which linked nature to music. Every so often he would ask me a direct question like, "Do you know who Jesse the Hammer is?" When I inevitably answered no, he responded with some revelatory statement like, "Jesse the Christ, get it?", then burst into a mad cackle of laughter – the mad professor instructing a neophyte, asking test questions to ascertain if his teaching was penetrated. The thought that Scratch had gone off the deep end was hard to suppress, yet I sensed a method in Scratch's madness.

'Somehow, Scratch created a feeling of conspiracy. He was weaving spells and forming a vast cosmology – and all of it was directed towards the accomplishment of some clandestine goal. In the beginning was the Word, which is sound. Thunder crashes and lightning strikes the earth, causing an X-shaped crack in the surface, out of which life forms emerge – Mother Earth giving birth. Scratch applies the alchemical elements of Earth, Air, Fire and Water into his music – he balances these into a nature track. Symbols of these elements are seen in the three nature trees: Coconut, Banana and Marijuana. The coconut contains distilled water, which is necessary to operate a battery . . . it is the medium which allows the spark to form. Black banana water is a tonic rich in iron, it represents the earth and also the ink used to write the words. Marijuana smoke is air, the medium through which sound travels. Lee Perry was releasing the product of his explorations through "King Solomon's Mind"; By tapping into the "Stone Age Skull Cap of Wisdom", Scratch hoped to unravel the secrets of Jesse the Hammer, who is Love, thereby creating a philosophy of "Love Universal Automatic Vibrations". The console wizard had become the magician of words, operating out of his "Raja Faith Sound Magnetic Power Station". His aim was to bring tidings of Great Joy by loosing the "Seven Seals of Love" with sound power. "Target 9" was to Hijack the Earth with music . . . But I was still confused. Why was there no music? And why were his tapes, those magnetic archives of Upsetter music, getting irreparably damaged on the floor? I ended my first meeting by asking Scratch if he could use my help in straightening out the tapes. He accepted my offer and I agreed to come by the following morning.

'Bright and early the next day, I arrived to find Scratch walking around outside. When I announced my readiness to begin the day's work, he told me to wait a while until he was finished with what he was doing: Scratch was performing his ritual. He'd pick up an object, hold it in the sun, walk with it, touch it to other objects or to certain words, wave it through the air with a brisk movement of his arm, then do a tornado spin so fast that the eye only caught a blur, and walk off again. The same actions were repeated many times. Scratch would suddenly grab a felt-tip pen, hold it in front of him, then go and scribble some cryptic words and phrases on any available surface – casting a magic spell, tuning into the ethers, establishing contact with the elemental forces. When I asked him what he was doing, he said that he was "Declarating the Rights and Executing the Wrongs".

'The recurrent phrases which appeared on walls, tape boxes, instruments, mixing panel, pieces of paper and whatnot were mantras. Scratch felt that his studio had been used by negative people; he was performing an Exorcism to remove the bad vibes . . . As part of his Declarating ritual, he re-cemented the walkway in front of the Black Ark so that only new clean footsteps should pass through . . . Eventually we went into the studio to start clearing up. We carefully rewound all the loose ends back onto the tape reels, and then stacked the boxes into neat piles.'[1]

Targowski briefly explained that he wanted to distribute some of Perry's back catalogue in Europe through Black Star Liner, and with money in seriously short supply, Perry was pleased. For the remainder of the six weeks Targowski spent in Jamaica, he travelled to the Ark most evenings after conducting business with other producers, including Augustus Pablo and Yabby You, and gradually won Perry's confidence, the friendship developing through metaphysical conversations.

'After cleaning the place up, Scratch was still "declarating", but it started to get more colourful, more creative, more artistic,' said Targowski. 'The whole place started becoming an artwork: the garden, his house, the studio. It was quite an exhibition in more ways than one.'

Perry offered Black Star Liner *Roast Fish Collie Weed And Cornbread* and *Return Of The Super Ape*, the masterworks that Island scorned, but as copies were already available in Europe on import, Targowski asked for older material. Perry thus supplied the master tapes of *Cloak And Dagger* when Billy Bradford came to Jamaica towards the end of Targowski's stay, and also delivered 'Cane River Rock', 'Different Experience', 'Disco Devil', 'Leggo' (issued as 'The Earth Is The Lord'), 'Norman The Gambler', 'Sexy Natty', an alternate mix of 'Dread Lion' and the Heptones 'Disco Dub' EP, plus 'Baffling Smoke Signal' and 'Captive'.

'He also played me about nine tracks in various stages of completion, but he had sort of given up on them because he needed new equipment,' said Targowski. 'There were some technical flaws, but I still quite liked the stuff and asked him if we could put some of it out. "Babylon Cookie Jar A Crumble" was one of them and there was one called "Black Cinderella". He had a song about the seventy-two names for the Almighty where he rattles off quite a few of them, and another song was "Jesse The Hammer", his name for Jesus Christ. So we made arrangements to work on the most finished pieces.'

Plans were made to refurbish the Black Ark to Perry's specification, the expenses to be covered by Black Star Liner. Unusually, the company offered no advance for Perry's material; according to Targowski, there was to be a 50/50 profit share for the releases, the money paid in cash on subsequent visits.

In Amsterdam, Black Star Liner thus re-released *Cloak And Dagger*, followed swiftly by the other tracks on four disco 45s that would surface later in the year, various members of the crew travelling to Kingston at regular intervals to further the refurbishment of Perry's studio.

Wayne Jobson reappeared in May, ready to record an album with his band Native, having scored a contract with Arista on the strength of the Black Ark demos, but Perry was in a different headspace.

'At this stage, he was saying that bananas were God,' said Jobson. 'Every time I went to see him, I had to carry a big bunch of green bananas and he would kneel down and pray to the bananas. Then he would say that he had to X a wall, so he would take a whole day just to X maybe three feet square.'

Perry told Jobson he would be happy to record the album once the studio had been renovated, so Jobson returned every few weeks to see how things were progressing, but Perry was too preoccupied to work.

'One week I went there, and the equipment had arrived two or three weeks before, but the car battery had died, and it was an omen from Jah, he was not going to get the equipment until the car battery came back to life by itself. So, I bought a new car battery, and he gets the equipment, but the equipment is just thrown down there. He's X-ing the walls, painting things red and worshipping bananas, and he doesn't get the studio together. He says, "I'm going to be ready for you next week. Bring the band and we'll record it next Wednesday", so I get the truck, bring the band and all the gear, and the day we arrive, the equipment is still thrown down in the studio. So, I had to go to Dynamics, and Scratch didn't produce the album. He had just gone too crazy, and he couldn't co-ordinate.'

In mid-July, the I-Threes' 'Many Are Called' entered the Jamaican top ten, the Tuff Gong single enhanced by a reverberating Perry mix, but when Vivien Goldman and photographer Adrian Boot arrived that month, they found Perry hitting poles with a hammer and speaking of a plan to 'hijack Earth' with music, referring to his daughter Marsha as 'the reincarnation of the Queen of Sheba'. The week before, Bob Marley told Goldman that Perry was a genius who he was willing to work with at any time, but Perry said he could not work with Marley because of his dreadlocks: 'I love him as a brethren but I wouldn't agree with the dread situation he's portraying.'[2] He further explained that the dreads had placed a 'dread lock' on the Earth, which Perry himself would undo with the assistance of Pipecock Jackxon, apparently a new name for the Almighty, and Perry's dramatic new persona, as demonstrated on a newly recorded song he played for his visitors. From this point, Perry would blur the line between being a servant of God and being a component or extension of the Almighty himself; after all, it was Pipecock Jackxon who was 'X-ecuting the wrongs' in his human form as Lee 'Scratch' Perry.

With Pipecock Jackxon otherwise engaged, precious little Black Ark material was released in 1979, and what did surface was largely handled by Pauline. In addition to her cover of 'Be With You' (credited to Isha Morrison), there was an extended twelve-inch of Mikey Dread's 'School Girls', backed by Keith Rowe's 'Living My Life' (credited to Keith Texon), as well as an Orchid twelve-inch with Winston Watson's 'Dispensation', which implored all races to embrace Rastafari, and Dillinger's enigmatic toasting cut titled 'Lion Rock', which saluted Perry's new complex personage.

'The last one I recorded at Black Ark studio goes, "This is the dispensation lion rock, the power of the pipe, the power of the cock, the power of the Lord Rajah", me and Scratch write the lyrics,' said Dillinger. 'These times he was marking

389

up the studio and do all kind of crazy things, so people was afraid of him. One day Bob Marley come round there for some of his tracks and Scratch was there marking up all the walls with paint.'

Then, Leroy Sibbles' utopian 'Garden Of Life' featured a weighty Boris Gardiner bassline and imagistic lyrics; B-side 'Jah Far I On A Pinnacle', written by Perry, playfully saluted Jah's almighty powers, this twelve-inch single the sole issue on the Big Spanner Ajax label, again alluding to the cleansing powers of the letter X.

A few stray Heptones Black Ark gems would also surface abroad on releases they organised, including an extended mix of 'Party Time' backed by the ballad 'Come On Into My World', as well as the seven-inch 'Babylon Falling', which adapted 'Na Na Hey Hey', both handled by VP in New York (the new company established by Vincent and Patricia Chin), and an extended 'Mystery Babylon' was issued by Third World in London.

Similarly, sound system proprietor Ken 'Fatman' Gordon fielded Dad Brown and the Fantails' 'Stand And Look' to Trojan, the song addressing the stigmatisation of Rastafari, and Clarendon-born singer Thomas Whyte's 'Ivory Girl' used the rhythm of Jah Lion's 'Dread In A Jamdong', which Perry gave to producer Carl 'Stereo' Fletcher, who lived on Weymouth Drive in Washington Gardens before emigrating to New York, while portions of the Slickers' *Breakthrough* LP, released in New York by Tad Dawkins in October 1979, had been recorded at the Black Ark, but were embellished and remixed elsewhere.

Back in Jamaica, Dave Hendley and Mo Claridge returned to the Ark in July, again with Prince Lincoln, just as the Jolly Brothers' re-released 'Conscious Man' was breaking the top fifty in Britain, though communicating with Perry was insufferable.

'Mo was trying to get a couple of tracks for disco 45s, like Leroy Sibbles' "Rastafari",' said Hendley. 'Scratch seemed to be having a kind of three-way conversation with Pipecock Jackxon. At times he *was* Pipecock Jackxon and at other times Pipecock Jackxon was over there with some other character. He told us to come back tomorrow and we'll talk about it, but when we turned up at the gates he just ignored us altogether. I remember later driving around Kingston with Scratch in our hired car. Nobody wanted to sit next to him, and I got lumbered with it. He had a large stone and a piece of wood and I was thinking, "I hope he's not going to hit me." He was just talking complete nonsense and you had to humour him. Whatever you asked him, he'd come back with something that was totally somewhere else. In the main studio room where the musicians would play, there was nothing in there but half a drum kit, and he'd dug a hole under the drum about three foot square with water in it, but it was boarded over, and that was back to this thing with the elements, to get the sound of water. When it came down to working out the deal with Mo, I remember being in the control room and Scratch had been talking complete bollocks for about an hour, but he was able to land back on earth to work a deal out with Mo for "Rastafari" for £300.'

Claridge also successfully licenced 'Forward With Love', 'Elaine', 'Don't Be Afraid', 'What's The Use', 'School Girls' and Jimmy Riley's 'I Never Had It So Good' (miscredited to Bunny Scott), all released on Warrior twelve-inches in the autumn of 1979, just as Island released *Scratch On The Wire*, a hodgepodge compilation mixing tracks from *Roast Fish* and *Return Of The Super Ape* with Jah Lion, Max Romeo and George Faith singles, as well as Augustus Pablo's 'Vibrate On', the Meditations' 'No Peace', and Errol Walker's 'John Public' and 'In These Times.'

During one of Henk Targowski's return visits to Jamaica, Pauline Morrison was back at Cardiff Crescent and offered to supply him with whichever tracks he wanted, but Targowski made it clear that he would only licence material directly from Perry, especially as the couple's relations were visibly strained.

Nevertheless, the Black Ark remained a place of wonder, where unfathomable things happened on a regular basis.

'One time I heard a bass sound coming out of the studio and Scratch said, "It's the heart of the palm" – he had stuck wires into the soil of a palm tree and somehow got this pumping bass sound out of it,' said Targowski. 'Then he got into this whole philosophy about how the bass and the drum is Mother Earth and the sky and everything else. He still had that old drum machine of his, and there was a funky drum set and a keyboard, but everything was slightly out of tune. It wasn't really prime equipment for a studio, and it wasn't working very well because he'd been pouring baby oil on it, but it did work because a young set of kids came in to do a record, they weren't professional in any way and they asked Scratch if he would let them record this song and it sounded lousy until he started fiddling with the knobs, he added some effects and corrected when things were out of tune by adding reverb with this strange connection that he had. When I first heard it, just the way it was played, it was dreadful, but when he played it tuned-up and effected, it had possibilities.'

Targowski and Bradford returned in the autumn to arrange new recordings, so Perry spoke to Errol Thompson and Winston Wright, but no sessions actually took place. Perry then declared that he wanted to work with white musicians, which Targowski and Bradford vetoed, their suggested compromise placing non-dread Black Jamaicans into the proposed rhythm section, leading Perry to recruit guitarist

Dwight Pinkney and drummer Cornel Marshall of Zap Pow along with Don Grant on bass and keyboardist Tony Johnson, since Winston Wright refused to take part. In a three-week period, these musicians thus laid a number of rhythms on the eight-track Tascam, the very last material to be recorded on the machine according to Perry.

Targowski and Bradford sensed that Perry would benefit from a break from the stresses of Kingston, so they took him to Negril for a few days, where Perry let off steam with some local beauties and spent an afternoon gathering boulders in a duffel bag, requiring the purchase of an extra seat on the light aircraft to accommodate the boulders on the flight back to Kingston.

Perry had an idea for a feature film, provisionally entitled *Nature Survival*, later known as *Sea Bath Cloud 9*, starring Perry as Doctor Sea Bath, a 'nature defender' related to Pipecock Jackxon, so Bradford arranged for a Canadian film crew to spend a week in Ocho Rios capturing Perry's ideas on 16mm celluloid.

'We was going to make a movie,' said Perry. 'It was sunshine and moon and stars, and we base part of it in Ocho Rios with the waterfalls. It would look like everything would be with the Ark, the Flood, the Judgement.'

As Pauline Morrison made her first trip to Africa, visiting Ghana with a friend, Black Star Liner brought Perry to Amsterdam in late December 1979 in anticipation of a proposed European tour, billed as 'The African Jungle Safari'. Word of his arrival had circulated, so Perry was greeted at the airport by a large contingent of followers whose enthusiasm generated an impromptu reception at the Black Star Liner offices, located near the Vondelpark.

'I think he had about five or so vanloads of people come to meet me at the airport, so it was like a festival,' said Perry.

393

'That time reggae just coming, and people hear about me and it was so much people – people like nothing.'

One of the first European recruits for Perry's backing band was the gifted British guitarist G. T. Moore, who had played in the folk-rock act Heron before fronting white reggae band the Reggae Guitars, who signed to Charisma in 1973. Moore went on to play in Curved Air with Stuart Copeland, and when Copeland quit to join the Police, Moore assembled the Rhythm Tramps with some London-based Texans, building a strong following in Amsterdam.

'When I did the audition, he'd written something like, "White bloodsuckers, stop sucking the Black man", and he'd smeared his own shit on the wall,' said Moore. 'Basically, the whole media gang were waiting to meet him, so he did a little number to shock everybody. He also said that Europe was the antithesis of his culture, but what was good about Europe was that you could have peace and quiet compared to Jamaica.'

'I don't pay police protection, I don't pay gunmen protection, I believe in my shit, so why shouldn't I plant my shit on the wall in Amsterdam?' said Perry, suggesting the faeces were present for ritual defence. 'My shit is my lawyer, my barrister, my attorney, my scientist and my Obeah man, so anyone fuck with me, why should I hire a gunman when I have my shit?'

Moore roped in Rhythm Tramps keyboardist James Lascelles and saxophonist Bud Beadle from Geno Washington's Ram Jam Band, a newspaper advertisement brought German backing vocalist Jutta Eichhorn, who invited her Martinican friend Jocelyn Béroard (later to find fame with zouk group Kassav'), and an American, Karen Harvey, was drafted from Sail, the house band of the Melkweg arts centre. Once assembled, to familiarise them with Perry's material, the new recruits were played a rehearsal tape of Perry working with the Jamaican musicians, which included 'Soul Fire', 'Big Neck Police' and 'Baffling Smoke Signal'.

In the midst of the rehearsals, Perry learned that the Japanese government had imprisoned Paul McCartney after the singer was caught bringing a half-pound of weed into the notoriously strict nation at the beginning of a tour with Wings, which was cancelled upon his arrest. McCartney faced a seven-year prison sentence for drug smuggling, so Perry had Black Star Liner dispatch the following telegram to the Minister of Justice in Tokyo on 21 January 1980:

> I Lee Pipecock Jackxon Perry would love to express my concern over your consideration of one quarter kilo to be an excessive amount of herbs in the case as it pertains to master Paul McCartney. As a creator of nature's love, light, life and all things under the creation sun, positive feelings through songs, good times and no problems, I find the herbal powers of marijuana in its widely recognized abilities to relax, calm and generate positive feelings a must. Herbs is his Majesty's. All singers' positive directions and liberty i-rations; please do not consider the amount of herbs involved excessive. Master Paul McCartney's intentions are positive.
>
> [Signed] Baby Blue Green Star Pipecock Jackxon Lee 'Scratch' Perry, Banana Eye I Pen, Jamaica, Nature's Love Defender

In February, Perry travelled to London to reclaim the master tapes of *Revolution Dub* from Creole, and reconnected with Tony Owens, conceiving future archive reissues on Seven Leaves. Perry caught up with Paul and Linda McCartney too – now freed from their Japanese caper – discussing Paul's proposed participation in the Jungle Safari tour, and mooting plans for future collaboration. Perry also appeared on the *Roots Rockers* show on Capital Radio, blasting David Rodigan with confusing statements about his frame of mind and motivations.

'It is a pleasure being for one to say that I am mad, because it mean that the individual are doing something different from the massive crowd. I am glad to be mad because I am the son of William Shakespeare, Marcus Garvey, Rajah the Conquering Lion of Judah. He order me to rest and leave all the hypocrites out of the studio, which is the moon base, the Black Ark, the painted bird . . . I am clean crystal, I am Crystal Chris, Jesse the Hammer, the Royal Iron Fist . . . I am the rootsman of creation, I am the dust of Marcus Garvey's ashes . . .'[3]

Back in Amsterdam, Perry delivered the master tapes of *Revolution Dub* and made further arrangements for the refurbishment of his studio. Perry had been staying in a spare room at Billy Bradford's place and was later housed by associates Bert and Eleanor in their apartment on Churchill-laan in the southern outskirts of the city, but was moved to a nearby hotel after defacing their apartment with graffiti.

Perry voiced some of the fresh rhythms he had brought from Jamaica at Ballad Sound studio in the country town of Vuren, which appealed to him as it was surrounded by water, his ad-libbed lyrics based on notes he had written or dictated for others to transcribe, the sparse rhythms embellished by G. T. Moore's effervescent guitar lines. An eleven-minute jam that he recorded with Zap Pow was thus shaped into the rude 'Bed Jammin', with a catchy, lustful chorus from Jocelyn Béroard, Jutta Eichhorn and Karen Harvey, and a slower, spooky rhythm became the inscrutable 'Easy Knocking', one of his first associative poems, both songs among the only works initiated on the eight-track Tascam to find release.

'When I start to use the Tascam, making some tracks with

musicians, it sound extremely good, excellent,' said Perry. 'The Teac was in there as well, it never move out yet, and on some sessions I was using the Teac and the Tascam, but I don't think I used the Tascam for long and I haven't put out any record off it, except those rhythms we done on it and carry to Amsterdam to voice, like "Easy Knocking". All the other songs that record on that Tascam machine, I don't see them, like we have a whole Nyabinghi session, can't find one of the tapes even now.'

G. T. Moore said the musicians were tripping on psilo-cybin mushrooms on the day of the Ballad Sound session, which Perry avoided, though the guitarist would later hear widespread rumours in Jamaica that Perry lost his senses after drinking mushroom tea brewed in Negril. A related tale put Perry's subsequently agitated behaviour down to his having taken LSD in Amsterdam, but Perry denied ever taking hard drugs.

'In Jamaica, somebody was trying to say me was taking cocaine with Bob Marley, but if I was taking coke or LSD I would get addicted to it,' said Perry. 'It's like with the herbs: I was trying not to smoke it so much and I was smoking too much. I love it so much that I don't want to be without it. I did want to smoke for knowledge, for a spiritual vibra-tion, and I get to the point that I was smoking one spliff after another. Then it get to a next point where Pauline was making my spliff, and when I discover what was going on, I wonder what was she putting in my spliff? At that point, I stopped it before it can go further. The only thing I was getting addicted to is herbs, Wincarnis wine and beer. That's what I was getting addicted to that is really destruction, but not LSD, cos once you start you can't stop.'

'I don't think it ever happened, and we were with him

all the time,' said Targowski. 'He was smoking a lot like he usually does and when he drank he was impossible to deal with, but to the best of my knowledge, he never took LSD or other hallucinogens – not intentionally nor unintentionally.'

In later years, Perry would variously be debated as schizophrenic, bipolar, with a personality disorder, or an acute sufferer of Tourette's Syndrome, though none of these terms adequately explain the reality he experienced nor the behaviour he exhibited on a daily basis.

Upon Perry's return to Jamaica, Black Star Liner sent American expatriate Dave Sampson, a houseboat restorer known as Sampson the Iron Man, to begin repairing the studio, housing Perry and his children in apartments at the luxurious Casa Monte Hotel in Stony Hill while the work was undertaken, though Perry was quick to return to Cardiff Crescent. Pauline Morrison wrangled a hotel room, sometimes with Danny Clarke in tow, enjoying a long stay at the company's expense, and once the majority of the work had been completed, the kids moved back to Cardiff Crescent, but continued to have their meals at the Casa Monte.

In late March, G. T. Moore, James Lascelles and Bud Beadle arrived at the Casa Monte, the latter two with their wives and children, to supplement Perry's core of Jamaican musicians. Black Star Liner's commitment was instigating a new renaissance at the Black Ark, but Perry was still angry with most of his dread peers and according to G. T. Moore, the very day that the European musicians arrived, Perry ejected a carload of Rastas from his compound – members of the Nyabinghi Theocracy, presumably – which would ultimately delay the recording schedule.

'He had this commune of dreads that he was using as a band, they had something to do with the Congos and when I arrived, they had just got the sack and were all moving out, piling their gear into this Volkswagen Bug,' said Moore. 'There was a lot of talk of Rastafari, so you got the feeling that Scratch did his ravings to get rid of them. They'd had an argument and Scratch had told them that he had the greatest players in the world that he had flown out to play for him and he didn't need these Rastafari yagga-yaggas. So when I told Black Star Liner that there was no band, they told us to get into the vibes and go on holiday, so we went to Negril for two weeks.'

But when the European players returned to Kingston, replacement musicians still had not been recruited.

'Nothing was really happening,' said Moore. 'He had this guy called Artist [Jah Wise], so he would say, "Artist, paint me the Pope", and Artist would come running up with his little natty dreads and he'd start painting a classic picture of the Pope with a golden papal hat. Then Scratch would prognosticate, enact some quasi-ritual where he would expound something like, "Rastafari, the sun, the earth, my mother, Lee Perry", and then Artist would write those words on the artwork. The studio was all set up. It had this incredible rainbow carpet that was deep and full of fleas and there was a painted ledge that went all the way around the top and pigeons and doves would fly up there. It was a really happening place, but he didn't have any musicians. Everything was painted, and he had minimal equipment, but it all worked. In the control room he had the Teac, the reverb out of a Fender amp and a bio-phase analogue tin effects unit that had phase and tremolo – it's marvellous and a lot of his sounds were coming from it. He had the old, out-of-tune upright piano which he'd painted red, gold and green, an Ampeg bass amp and an old Gibson semi-acoustic bass guitar which had the deepest, wickedest sound, and he had some kind of drum kit and drum booth, but they couldn't get a drummer. For weeks they were talking about Mikey [Boo], "Mikey's going to come", but what I didn't know was that Scratch had more or less got it that no one would play with him anymore, that's why he was getting people to fly from Amsterdam. One day we went up to Tuff Gong because [Wailers guitarist] Al Anderson is from Texas and he moved a bit with my Texan band, and James Lascelles knew [guitarist] Junior Marvin, so we went up to see them and the I-Threes said, "We heard that you were coming, how's it going with Scratch?" They were taking the piss, but I didn't realise it at the time.'

Eventually, a drummer who lived near Roosevelt Avenue was conscripted, and Moore arranged for bassist Colin Gibson, who had played in Ginger Baker's Air Force, to be flown in from England, before Jutta Eichhorn and Jocelyn Béroard arrived.

It was a chaotic start to six weeks of anarchic mayhem, as work on the album began in earnest; Gibson only lasted three weeks and was replaced by Eichhorn's American boyfriend, who had little command of the instrument.

'We were recording every day, all day and there was no real organisation, but there was a great order in the chaos,' says Moore. 'What we had to do was come down and start a rhythm, and Scratch would be around the house and more or less ignore us. He'd be walking around declaring, and when the rhythm was irie, Scratch would come in and toast, but sometimes we would play a rhythm for forty-five minutes and he wouldn't come in. It was an effective way of controlling the band without saying a word, while also leaving us with the freedom to play as we wanted. Dwight Pinkney and the keyboard player, "Snapping" [Theophilus Beckford], they played all the time, and a lot of people were hanging around just for mealtimes, like Dillinger. Joe Higgs was there, he sang one time and Scratch said they were going to arrange something, and Max Romeo used to hang out and check the vibes, when Scratch was holding court, they were his buddies. Rico came round and Pauline went off with his car to Negril and did some kind of herb deal: she got forty dollars from me, some money from Bob Marley, some from Danny and some from another guy called Teeny Bop, said she'd be an hour and was gone five hours and Rico was cursing her. Scratch said, "Me have him in a dunce cap" because Blackwell had signed Rico and put him on ice. Scratch said, "Why does he have the Island on the record label? Because every time the record goes round, he can control the island." Scratch also had a cardboard box of these reel-to-reel tapes of rhythms from the '60s or '70s. Sometimes he would just stick a tape on the Teac and then do dubs on top of it. A typical thing was "Disco Devil" on Max Romeo's "Chase The Devil": he would take it out, whack it on and voice it up with a cowbell or something, or then he'd want the horns to do something on it or the singers to do it with him, so sometimes we'd lay a track and sometimes we'd just dub over these tapes. The best tune we did was "Baffling Smoke Signal". I played a new guitar line through all of it, and we learned the bassline of "Disco Devil", turned it around and he did a new version of it. Another tune we did was "Pipecock Jackxon". I don't know if that ever came out but that was one of the tunes that he'd written and was into at the time.'

The eight-track Tascam was still connected, but Moore said Perry showed no interest in using it.

'He still had the four-track, and he didn't like the eight-track. He'd got a system of mixing where he put the bass and drums on track one – sometimes the bass and drums on track two as well but with a lot more bass – and all the music like the chops, the brass and the vocals on track two, and then he'll use tracks three and four to dub. So if he's got something he wants to voice, he'll just keep the bass and drums on, have a rap with a cowbell or something, and because he's using a percussion instrument with his voice, that makes an acoustic link with the drums. You can't do that with eight tracks because it's a different mentality, I would say a Western mentality: every track is separate and almost equal.'

Perry wanted the group to be billed as Pipecock Jackxon and the Cornerstones on the forthcoming tour, but Moore said rehearsals remained chaotic.

'He had herb plants growing in the front garden, the police came one day and pulled them up and Scratch started cursing them in the middle of the sessions, and it produced a hitherto unfelt solidarity in the camp, and then I got sacked by Scratch because he got drunk and knocked over my amp. One night I was going to go out with Poppa Son to a disco in New Kingston. Like most of the people hanging out there, he hardly had a penny to rub together, they were impotent socially, and Scratch was a despot – everything that they ate and drank came from him, so no one challenged him. Poppa Son got all dressed up in a pastel green outfit and as we were about to go, Scratch said that Poppa Son had to dig the garden. He was so humiliated, and he got his green disco clothes dirty, and I went right off Scratch then.'

As April turned to May, the chaos wore on and the album seemed no nearer to completion, though the band was getting tighter despite the personnel changes. G. T. Moore began moonlighting, playing on a session with Sly and Robbie at Channel One, and cutting some songs of his own at Harry J with the musicians of Perry's album project; Bud Beadle played flute on the Majesterians' 'So Many Times', mixed at the Black Ark for producer Phil Matthias, and added flute to the Silvertones' 'Rejoice' for Pauline (who retitled it 'Give Praise').

Concurrently, Sampson the Iron Man continued to fix the Black Ark roof and make whatever structural alterations Perry deemed necessary, constructing the drum booth to allow for the presence of water birds.

'Billy said, "David's going to build you a drum booth, Scratch, how do you want it built?" and Scratch started to prognosticate,' said Moore. 'The first thing he said was "Egg", and then something like "Aqua", then we got "the Earth", "Rastafari" and "Metal", David looked at it for a while and said, "Egg – could you make that out of concrete?" and Scratch says, "Irie". Then David went, "Aqua is water. Earth – can you have sand? And metal, what do you think of chicken wire, Scratch?" and Scratch said, "Irie". So he built this booth that had a fantastic sound. It took three or four days and in the end it had a wooden floor and underneath was sand. There was a large hole in the wooden floor in the shape of a Star of David and there was water in the hole. Above it was wood up to the halfway mark and then glass, and there was chicken wire on the top. It made all the high sounds have this metallic ring that was partly the glass and partly the wire, slightly vibrating, and the bass drum and low toms had this dull thud, which was a combination of the wood and the sand. It had an incredible sound, and it was very much the Scratch sound, very punchy and psychedelic.'

'The heat itself and the energy that was coming, the heat was so strong that we were going to need water to cool it,' Perry later explained. 'It get too powerful and might be exploding, so then I need birds, because the birds is the power of the air, and the water . . . it work because when you're not playing drums, then ducks would be swimming around and having fun, and when you're playing drums, then the ducks could go outside and rip up plants.'[4]

One evening, Perry and his children were in his Thunderbird, travelling back to town from Billy Bradford's apartment in Red Hills, and when Perry made a sharp turn, the vehicle careened into a ditch. Miraculously, no one was injured and even the Thunderbird required only minor repairs, though Perry wondered whether a faulty front end was really to blame, or intentional sabotage.

Finally, Black Star Liner installed new tape recorders, a state-of-the-art Allen & Heath Modular III mixing desk and top-of-the-range Quad amplifiers, but the machinery would never be made fully operational, its abortive installation severing Perry's relationship with the company and ending any hope of the Black Ark's rebirth.

'Billy buy up-to-date machines and was ready for every-thing to go but it couldn't happen,' said Perry. 'Billy buy tape recorders and Sampson bring me two transformers from the ship, specially made. We had a new booth from Amsterdam and a new mixer, but after we turn on, it was an explosion. The engineer set up things wrong – maybe he was an amateur, and he blew up the machine. Then me say, "No, leave it. Take everything back." We just set up and it go, "Whoosh!" and that was it. I just get mad and say, "No, forget the whole thing", and that's when Billy crashed the tour. Musicians stayed for weeks and nothing happened, so I didn't want to go on the tour. I tell Billy, "Take back the things them, because I don't really ready to rebuild and I don't want to do it." I just didn't want to replace the studio when he want to replace it.'

The musicians returned to Europe around 9 May, and after

the tour was cancelled, Perry withdrew again, though he retained respect and appreciation for Billy Bradford, whose support he readily acknowledged.

'Me and Billy never had no problem. Don't care what happened, I will never say nothing bad about Billy as I am sure Billy somebody really fucking special. If I said, "Billy, we need this", Billy said, "Choose all you want." If I say, "Billy, give me $10,000", him give you instantly without any argument. He would give me every fucking thing. Even what Chris Blackwell wouldn't do, Billy would do everything to see that you were comfortable. I can take Billy for his word: if Billy's saying he's going to do something then he's fucking going to do it. Him get into some trouble and when I see him again, he said, "Lee, I bring back some tapes from Amsterdam and leave them at your house." Billy did have so much tapes, and after things go bad, him bring them back to my house, like "Bed Jammin" and "Easy Knocking". Nothing him ever said to me him didn't do.'

Without financial backing and a concrete goal to work towards, Perry was overcome by depression and mental anguish. He continued to shun outsiders and kept the studio in a state of unfinished chaos, though some of the gear remained in place in bareboned, semi-functional configurations, including the Allen & Heath mixing desk and a Teac.

The saving grace for Perry and his family came in Vicky Nelson, an impressionable young singer with a big heart. Raised in the town of Grantham in the hills of northwest Clarendon, one of ten children born to a farmer and tailor who was also a minister at the local Church of God, she moved to Kingston as a teenager to complete her schooling and began performing on talent contests. By the early 1970s, she sang gospel and pop in hotels on the north coast, and in 1979, as she sought greater exposure, Dennis Brown suggested she approach Perry as a potential producer, but when he brought her to Cardiff Crescent one afternoon, Perry was nowhere to be found.

Then, after experiencing a vision at her home in nearby Duhaney Park, Nelson made her way to the Black Ark to meet Perry for the first time, and although he seemed to be expecting her, she was struck by the foreboding emptiness that permeated the place.

'At that time he wasn't hardly seeing anyone, like when somebody gone into exile,' Vicky explained. 'He welcomes me very good, and the kids were there and then my heart reach out, definitely. I told him I'm a singer and I did a 45 with him, "Black People You've Got To Know Yourself", with musicians like Family Man and Easy Snapping, but I don't know what happened to that song.'

Perry never got around to releasing Vicky Nelson's song, or anything else he was working on, but she became a frequent visitor to Cardiff Crescent, forming a lasting bond with Perry's children. A few months after the tour was cancelled, Perry asked Vicky to move in, and although she had to break up with her boyfriend and faced ostracism by her family for doing so, she felt unable to refuse. The children thus gained a stepmother and Perry a new partner, during a time of increased instability.

'I was a part of whatever he was doing. My foot would be in paint, I would get rocks and all those nature things, and I remember we go about three days with no sleep. Whatever he was going through, I would be there.'

Pauline Morrison briefly returned to Jamaica, voicing Carol Cole's 'Ethiopia' at King Tubby's studio over the rhythm of 'Dispensation', but finally left the island for a new life in

New York, where she planned to launch a career as a record producer. Danny Clarke was in New York too, but their relationship had its ups and downs.

While passing through London, Morrison delivered some material to Starlight Records, established by former Trojan staffer Desmond Bryan and his cousin Popsy in Harlesden. *Black Ark In Dub*, released towards the end of the year on the new Black Ark International subsidiary, had a somewhat misleading title as some of the material was not recorded at the Ark and most of the tracks had obtrusive synthesiser overdubs added in London, but there were excellent dub versions of 'Jah Love Is Sweeter' and 'Ethiopia', a reverberating dub of Perry's 'Lion A De Winner', a bass-heavy mix of 'Open The Gate', a groovy dub of 'Guideline' and a sparse, spooky deconstruction of 'Mr Money Man', as well as a dub version of the song 'Dreadlocks I', first voiced for Family Man by Ras Keatus I (former footballer Milton Samuels), its Black Ark rendition recorded in May 1978.

In Amsterdam, Black Star Liner released *The Return Of Pipecock Jackxon*, trying to earn back some of the estimated US$65,000 they spent, but the album was still in its unfinished state. Along with 'Bed Jammin', 'Easy Knocking' and the skeletal 'Untitled Rhythm', there were unreleased works from the late 1970s, including 'Who Killed The Chicken', with its playful cow sounds, and 'Some Have Fe Halla', about sycophantic beggars, which both sounded like *Roast Fish* outtakes, while 'Babylon Cookie Jar A Crumble' and the devotional 'Give Thanx To Jah' probably dated from around the time of 'Baffling Smoke Signal'. However, what was released had not been mixed by Perry and the combination of old and new material was decidedly uneven.

'They were in a haste to catch a flight which isn't ready,'

said Perry of Black Star Liner, 'so it's a bad spell me a cast 'pon them – them fall into the twilight zone.'[5]

At Cardiff Crescent, Perry remained in tumultuous solitude as he enacted his rituals, and the dramatic outbursts and self-destructive episodes mirrored the state of the nation, since Jamaica was tearing itself to pieces in the most violent election campaign it had ever known. After the abolition of the peace treaty, political violence had rocketed, and firebombs and automatic weaponry were increasingly used in partisan attacks. In March, just as Bucky Marshall met his death in New York, violence erupted in Waterhouse, Tower Hill and Greenwich Farm, and an attack by PNP activists in Majesty Gardens caused 500 to flee their homes, leading to counter-attacks by JLP activists in Lizard Town, bordering Tivoli Gardens. On 21 April, PNP-affiliated gunmen used M16s to kill five people at a dance held by JLP supporters in Gold Street, and throughout April and May, repeated gang incursions blasted Waterhouse, causing hundreds to flee their homes, some of which were firebombed. Then, on 20 May, 153 elderly residents of the Eventide Home were killed in a fire that may have been politically motivated arson. In further incidents of domestic terrorism, police stations were attacked by gunmen and MPs from both parties were shot at on the campaign trail, including former prime minister Hugh Shearer, as well as both Manley and Seaga. The election battle was nothing short of a civil war, and by the time Michael Manley and the PNP suffered a crushing defeat in late October, the orgy of violence had resulted in over 800 deaths.

During such a perilous election year, in which Kingston became a hellish inferno, friction inevitably grew between Lee Perry and his closest peers, and everything escalated during Bob Marley's *Uprising* tour, which was delivered in two legs, the European dates between 30 May and 13 July, and the US engagements beginning in mid-September, including two nights opening for the Commodores at Madison Square Gardens.

'Bob was going on a tour with the Commodores and Scratch say him mustn't go, him must stay in Jamaica and build a stadium and make the people all over foreign come here and see Bob,' said P-Son, with a reminder that Perry and Marley were on good terms before the tour. 'They were talking about how the music was changing and how they're going to change it to chanting, keep it on a reggae level, and Bob say him is like Selassie-I and Scratch is like Marcus Garvey.'

'We decide to take over everything as Marcus Garvey and Emperor Haile Selassie, and that was something very big of an African culture,' said Perry. 'I was playing the part of the Prophet and Bob playing the other part of the King to establish the music, to bring the music from the ghetto to a higher standard of King and Prophet. I did have total respect for him, but I don't know where he lost his respect. Maybe it's because he didn't want to go back to his past.'

An unhealable rift formed when Marley failed to provide some promised small change to get Perry's car back on the road; Perry, P-Son and Jah Ned all dated the conflict to late August, just before the US leg, but set designer Neville Garrick and other Wailers associates said that Marley stayed in Miami after the European performances, dating the conflict to May.

'Bob Marley promised to lend me one thousand Jamaican dollars to buy a car part, which wasn't expensive,' said Perry. 'When I have money, Bob Marley couldn't want. He didn't have nowhere to live and I give him my house and I didn't charge him any rent, but when my car did caput, money wasn't in sight. I only need a thousand Jamaican dollars to get the new parts for it, and somebody go to America and bring it back for me, so I was invited to come [to Marley's] at one o'clock, but [Marley] tell me a lie, because when I come at one o'clock, him gone. He didn't tell me he was going on a tour and he didn't have it in mind to give to me. Those times he have all those rude boys, too much money to give them, so I said, "That stupid idiot, they didn't tell me never to come, fuck this." I couldn't get the parts that was here for me car, and the next thing you hear is that Bob dropped down onstage.'

'Scratch went to Bob to ask for Bob's assistance, which Bob did not give him,' said Jah Ned. 'Scratch said that Bob is going to die cos him ears hard.'

When the Wailers arrived in New York, Ansel Cridland was there, and Marley asked him to retrieve the tapes of 'Who Colt The Game' and 'I Know A Place' from Perry when he returned to Jamaica, but Perry refused him.

'When he held on to "Who Colt The Game", Bob send me to him,' said Cridland. 'At the time, the board was giving him problems and Scratch throw paint in the board and start acting a way to get people off of him, and when I go, Scratch said, "No, I nah let off nothing" cos something was wrong with him car and him go to Bob and say him want some money to fix the car and Bob never give him. So Bob never get back the song.'

Perry later said that masked gunmen demanded Wailers master tapes from him, though he never discovered who was behind the attack.

'One night me was there sleeping and three guys come in the house front, thieves trying to rob me, say them come for the Wailers tape,' said Perry. 'I don't know if he was involved, cos I don't think he would send no bad man to me for tapes, and even if he was involved, that doesn't matter to me, because me don't see Bob would really want to hurt me. He is a person me really love, and it is my belief that when you love a person, they can't hurt you, don't care what they do.'

On 21 September, Bob Marley collapsed in Central Park as a consequence of the melanoma skin cancer that had first been identified beneath his toenail in 1977; gravely ill, his time on earth was drawing short. He gave a final performance in Pittsburgh two days later and then travelled to Bavaria for experimental treatment.

During this time of drastic actions, Marley was not the only one to experience irreversible conflict with Perry.

'Bunny Lee, Tubby and I went to Scratch's when Marley was on tour, and Scratch went for a hammer to bust up Bunny Lee's and Tubby's head – they jump in the car and left me,' said Clancy Eccles. 'Bunny Lee is a friend, but anything you do, tomorrow morning Bunny Lee say it's him do it, and Tubby is another copy man again, so Scratch didn't like none of them.'

Yet, despite the unresolved issues and his dramatic behaviour, Perry was still held in high regard by the Marley family, so much so that Rita Marley had Perry mix a dub of her spiritual groove 'That's The Way' at Tuff Gong in December 1980, shortly before Perry travelled to New York, leaving his children in the care of Vicky Nelson and uncle P-Son.

David Last and Jay Chernow of the Brooklyn-based San Juan Music Group arranged Perry's airfare, having written to him earlier in the year requesting his pre-Island Bob Marley and the Wailers material, so Perry brokered a number of licencing deals with the company, prompting the widespread dissemination of the work on cheaply made compilations. Although the advances were relatively small, with Perry receiving US$4,500 for *Soul Revolution* in April, the 50/50 profit share was potentially lucrative, especially as the company provided regular accounting.

Perry began his New York sojourn at the low-budget Howard Johnson's Motel on Eighth Avenue, near Times Square in Manhattan, where Tommy Cowan's ex-wife Valerie, who was now working for Island, often visited. Then, after manager Gary Kurfirst got in touch, Chris Frantz and Tina Weymouth of the Talking Heads had a meeting with Perry in his hotel room to ask if he would consider producing what would become the first Tom Tom Club album for Island.

'We were always fans of Lee Perry, ever since the early Wailers albums,' said Tina Weymouth. 'Chris and I loved to put *Super Ape*, *Roast Fish And Cornbread* and *Police And Thieves* on the turntable to transport us out of the grimy poverty of our New York lives throughout the 1970s and into the early 1980s, and we still live under his spell.'

Although Perry's esoteric patois was hard to follow, the meeting yielded a positive response, so the work was scheduled to begin in March 1981 at Chris Blackwell's Compass Point studio in the Bahamas. Yet, at the appointed start date, Perry was still in New York. He then threw another spanner by telephone, stating that his required fee would be $1,000 per hour, paid in cash in advance, and when met with resistance, he told Kurfirst not to worry since he would produce the album in eight hours maximum. Weymouth and Frantz suspected this was Perry's way of issuing a polite refusal, but in any case, that amount of cash was not at their disposal and they had no intention of rushing the work.

Eventually, Blackwell arranged for Perry to stay at an apartment his friend Arthur Gorson kept on Irving Place, near Union Square, which Perry shared for a time with Kiddus I, one of the artists whose eyes had been X'd out of portraits at the Black Ark once the singer began recording at Tuff Gong, and before long, Perry continued his compulsion of writing declamatory graffiti on the Irving Place walls.

Max Romeo was in town, having moved to the city to work on the problematic Broadway musical *Reggae*, and upon their reconnection, Romeo took Perry to Brad Osborne's headquarters on White Plains Road in the Riverdale area of the north Bronx, leading to the twelve-song re-release of *Blackboard Jungle Dub* in April. According to Romeo, Perry took a large pirate's chest with him, which he said would kill anyone who looked in it, and when the chest was finally opened, there was a stone the size of a television set inside, as well as bags of dirt, bottles of unidentifiable liquids and children's toys.

Influenced by punk, Perry began wearing studded bracelets and an SS cap, and on each subsequent visit to Irving Place, Romeo found more graffiti on the walls, as well as the ceiling, bathroom tiles, shower, toilet and fire escape.

Perry's new surroundings stimulated a more positive outlook, especially after he forged a romantic liaison with stunning blonde model Brynn Lacey, who had been dating Stevie Wonder's brother, Larry Hardaway, shortly before.

'She said she love me because I have an unusual face,' said Perry, who remembered her with fondness.

The new wave independent Stiff Records had recently released an album by Desmond Dekker, and after Perry visited their New York office seeking a deal, staff salesman Phil Fox took him to see Roland Alphonso perform at a club called Isaiah's on 7 March. Alphonso played a set with Jah Malla, led by his son Noel, followed by another with white reggae band the Terrorists, who also played a warm-up segment of their original material. Inspired by the band's blend of reggae and new wave, Perry leapt onstage midway through their performance, grabbing Alphonso's microphone while unceremoniously kicking him backstage, the impromptu rap beginning a brief collaborative period.

The group was formed in November 1977 by drummer David 'Dro' Ostrowe and bassist Gary Schiess (alias Gary Buildings), with singer John Collins and guitarist Mark 'Steady' Levi joining after, and Perry had met Dro and Schiess at Brad's Record Den a few months before the band's formation, when they were playing in Tribesman with saxophonist Baba Leslie, helping to cement their reconnection in 1981. Despite the recent departure of their rhythm guitarist, Dro and Schiess proposed a recording session, and as the Terrorists were already booked to open for Culture at Irving Plaza on 27 March, they rehearsed with Perry a few days before, reconstructing 'Soul Fire', 'Roast Fish And Cornbread', 'Babylon Cookie Jar' and 'Pipecock Jackxon'.

At Irving Plaza, where Christine Church of White Plains reggae-rock outfit Beast filled in on rhythm guitar, Perry appeared in an outlandish space costume, his performance drifting between ad-libbed spontaneity and semi-faithful versions of what had been rehearsed. The three Congos watched the entire set from one side of the stage, along with Cedric Myton's brother Patrick, who was soon to establish the Electric Dread studio on Tenth Street, but their backstage greeting barely drew any response.

During the weeks that Perry worked with the Terrorists, Dro would go to his apartment to wake Perry most mornings, witnessing the daily ritual of heating the rings he wore on each finger over the gas burners of the kitchen stove. In the pirate's trunk, there were five or six 16mm reels from the unfinished *Sea Bath Cloud 9*, and later, the apartment housed an antique silverware set, the unlikely result of revenue from

Island Records.

'I loved doing music with Scratch and the main impetus was for me to learn, to touch his genius so to speak,' said Dro. 'The other half of the story, which I barely even saw, was the sideshow that was his personal life, and every day was some kind of a trip. One day Scratch said he needed to see Chris Blackwell because Blackwell owed him back money. Island was selling all kinds of Perry productions and he was collecting his quarterlies or whatever, so we went to the offices of Mango Records on Madison Avenue, where he did a graffiti design on the wall with a black magic marker. It was around that time Scratch got the check for $20,000 and spent most of it on a beautiful antique silver serving set that would serve ten people, which he brought into his apartment, and I think he wanted to get the money so he could buy it.'

'It was $25,000,' said Blackwell. 'I knew the studio was rebuilding and I figured he wanted to start back, but he wasn't asking me for money. I might have been encouraging him to get something back together again and I heard all kinds of stories, like he took the money and bought silverware, that kind of thing. All I know is it didn't happen. It was a long shot, and I don't regret it.'

'They give me an advance on some royalty, and I don't know which of the songs they give me off of, but when me say that me didn't have no money, they make sure that they give me money for some of the Marley tunes that they were taking away, like "Blackman Redemption" or "Kaya",' said Perry. 'They give me that $25,000 and I buy some material and cloth and sterling silver. When you go on a treasure hunt, you must want silver and gold to make sure, because when paper money won't value anymore, the silver and gold will. So I wanted to have a selection of silver because silver represent immortality.'

Phil Fox arranged for Perry to make a second appearance with the Terrorists in April at a blues joint called Tramps, but as the band played their rendition of the Silvertones' 'Rejoice' to usher him onto the stage, Perry was AWOL, so Dro rushed to Irving Place during an unscheduled break, only to find Perry administering harsh discipline to Fox.

'Scratch was repeatedly slapping Phil Fox's face because Fox didn't come together with the money,' said Dro. 'Scratch thought he was trying to make a fool of everybody, and he was fucked up on drugs, so I told Fox to take a hike and got Scratch to come back to the club with me to finish the gig.'

Later in the month, a recording session was proposed at a twenty-four-track studio, but Perry insisted the Terrorists use Munchie Jackson's Sunshine Studio in the Bronx's Baychester district, a rudimentary eight-track facility lacking basic components such as reverb, where Perry was already working on material of his own with Tyrone Downie and Jah T on keyboards, and Bahamas-born Ronnie Burke on guitar.

Although three rhythms were built at the Terrorists session, only the rollicking 'Love Is Better Now' was voiced, which Perry versioned as the rambling 'Guerrilla Priest', a 'white smoke signal' seemingly about God's many powers, delivered by Perry in the form of 'Smokin' Joe, Joseph the Hammer'. The songs were released in May as the sole issue on Fox's Splif Rockers label, a twelve-inch single that became *Black Music*'s 'Pick of the Month' in September, peaking at number eight on *NME*'s Reggae Hit Parade.

Perry's own Sunshine sessions yielded largely ad-libbed metaphysical diatribes and rambling declamatory rants, firmly in the mode of *The Return Of Pipecock Jackxon*. Songs such as 'Hi-Jack', 'Atlas Road Map' and 'Calamooch' all evidenced the optimism stimulated in New York, and 'Cockroach Motel', inspired by his Howard Johnson stay, somehow also sounded upbeat, though other songs conjured a darker mood, particularly the black magic declarations of 'Seven'. Two albums' worth of material was rapidly captured on tape, scheduled for release as a double album in the summer, though Jackson's involvement in music quickly waned and he sadly perished in a tragic domestic incident during the mid-1980s, keeping Perry's material unreleased until 1994, when eight songs were issued as the album *Smokin'*.

Cocaine was an insidious presence on the New York music scene and its destructive powers would soon come to bear in Jamaica, much to Perry's chagrin. According to Dro, when Fox offered cocaine to Perry, he rubbed a fistful all over his body in defiance and denigrated drug abusers.

As Perry continued working with the Terrorists, Pauline Morrison made a brief reappearance in his life, spending time with him at Irving Place, despite his bitterness at her liaison with Danny Clarke, and he even gave her a substantial portion of the Island payout.

'She was going to buy a car in New Jersey,' said Perry. 'Me see the car and everything, but I never knew she was taking coke, so I give her $6,000 and they coke it out.'

On another trip to Brad's Record Den, Perry was incensed to discover that Brad Osbourne had released a compilation, *Scratch And Company – Chapter 1*, without permission.

'Brad idolised Scratch and was really happy to see him, but Scratch got real angry when he saw *Scratch And Company – Chapter 1* for the first time,' said Dro. '*Chapter 1* is the result of Brad going through tapes that Scratch sent him over different periods of time and I think that's what pissed him off, that Brad compiled it without asking. Brad was making excuses and gave him some money, but only small change, so Scratch drew all over the cover and ripped it up. He took a bunch of them with him and a bunch of the *Blackboard Jungle Dub* and *Ital Corner* albums, and later, at his apartment, he had drawn something like "I hate Brad" or "This is the Devil" on a picture of Brad.'

Perry's third gig with the Terrorists took place at the Mudd Club on 1 May, with Jah T and Ronnie Burke in the band and Munchie Jackson mixing. Backstage, Perry told *NME*'s Richard Grabell that he wanted to work with white musicians and would relaunch his studio, but with certain new conditions.

'I want to change my life. I work with the black so long and they give me a hard fight. I want to live a cool life, no problem . . . the studio, it's being remodelled for a new future with some cleaner people, honest people worthy to step into the Ark of the Covenant to sing. I have locked it away from parasites and vampires. All I see in the business is singing parasites, singing lies, singing something which they don't mean. It really bothers me, it really get me mad . . . they kill you, the vampires and bloodsuckers, take away your diamond, stab you in the back and take away your girl. They kill the prophets, one by one, because every prophet come to tell the truth. But tell them they can't kill *this* bloodclot because him can't dead.'[6]

Things were looking up for the Terrorists until an ill-fated concert with Perry at Boston's Spit club on 11 May, organised by promoter Mike Cacia through Phil Fox. According to Dro, the Terrorists pulled out at short notice because of unclear financial particulars but were pressurised into fulfilling the engagement by the well-connected Cacia, who suggested their popularity in Boston would suffer should they fail to appear. The band thus drove to Boston while Perry and Brynn Lacey were flown in, with vocalist John Collins drafted as rhythm guitarist – an unfortunate choice since he could barely play a note.

At soundcheck, a laughing Cacia broke the news that Bob Marley had died.

'Cacia looked at Scratch and said, "Well, what do you think?" and Scratch said, "I am the teacher, Bob Marley was the student." That was his first verbal reaction,' said Dro, who noted that the news cast a pall over the evening, culminating in the Terrorists' all-time worst performance.

Though Perry made disparaging comments about Marley on a radio broadcast recorded after soundcheck, the news clearly upset him. He would thereafter continue to be haunted by Bob's absence and the lack of closure afforded by their final dispute.

'When Bob Marley die I was in Boston and there was an instant telephone call saying he dead,' said Perry. 'So I said, "OK, he got away. When he was alive he had problems, now he has no problems." Me love him still, and me still see him at night. But he dead because he would not repent.'

After the gig, the band sulked back to New York with saddened spirits, while Perry went to Cacia's home to receive his pay and spent the night in a spare room, but in the wee hours Cacia was awakened by a commotion on the doorstep.

'Do you know this guy?' asked an incredulous policeman, pointing at Perry. 'Some of the neighbours called, he was dancing around with butcher knives on the street. Do me a favour and just keep him inside.'

The next day, Stephen Davis and Peter Simon came to Cacia's to interview Perry for their *Reggae Bloodlines* book, and Cacia played Perry a video of Bahama Mama, a white band from his hometown of Rochester, near Lake Ontario, that played a mixture of reggae and new wave. Core members had recently regrouped as the Majestics with Ron Stackman on keyboards and guitar, Jim Schwarz on bass and Louis LaVilla on drums, and Perry was sufficiently inspired by the video to make them his new backing band, but guitarist Jim Kraut had left before the name change, so Cacia temporarily drafted I-Tones guitarist Chris Wilson, a white American who spent much of his youth in Kingston, where his British father, a market researcher, promoted sports matches with Byron Lee during the 1960s.

Towards the end of the month, Perry travelled to the town of Victor, southeast of Rochester, where he spent a couple of weeks rehearsing with the band at an isolated farmhouse, surrounded by fields. Pauline Morrison joined him there after the first couple of days and would return to Manhattan with him when everything was finished.

The rehearsals were largely unstructured, involving long free-form jams more than anything else. After a guarded start, Perry slowly built a rapport with the group, though his actions were often puzzling; there was graffiti galore at the farmhouse, even on the electrical sockets, and any cockroaches he obliterated were taped to the walls, but when someone pilfered a rock he had decorated with words, Perry became withdrawn for a couple of days and refused to partake in the rehearsals.

One night the Majestics went to play at a club called the Haunt in Ithaca, and although Perry insisted that he would not perform with them, the band ultimately fired his inspiration.

'About 1 a.m. he came on a killed everyone,' said Ron Stackman. 'I don't think the crowd had any idea what they were witnessing, but they knew it was something special. Lee was awesome, and the people went wild.'

'They are very good artists, very good musicians, very

obedient, very normal and very simple people,' said Perry. 'They live on the mountain, out of pollution, like rich people's pickney.'

The Clash were then arranging a series of June performances at Bond International Casino, a historic Broadway nightclub, and offered Perry and the Majestics the prime opening slot on the Friday and Saturday night shows of 5 and 6 June. Jim Kraut was back in the fold, but the first performance began on the wrong foot: as the band vamped on 'Give Thanx To Jah', Perry was in the dressing room putting on his stage outfit (a tracksuit, studded bracelets, and a Yankees baseball cap, topped by a feather), but an automatic door somehow rolled up to expose him in the midst of changing his pants.

'When he finally came out, he spent several minutes placing artefacts around the stage, and then marching up to each musician and saluting, so we never got past "Give Thanx To Jah" that night, it went on for maybe forty-five minutes,' said Stackman. 'I recall a stagehand yelling at me from the wings to get off the stage, as if I was going to interrupt Scratch's thing, and they finally cut the power and we skulked off. So we impressed upon Lee the need to have endings for the tunes and to shorten them up a little, and we had an onstage rehearsal the next afternoon at Bond's and Lee devised his ending cue: he'd raise his outstretched arms perpendicular to his body and clench his fists, and the second night we got through the entire set.'

The second set included 'Give Thanx To Jah', 'Roast Fish', 'Pipecock Jackxon' and 'Soul Man', all strongly received by the capacity audience of 1,800 people, who were later treated to a duet between Perry and the Clash of 'Police And Thieves'.

By then, Perry had done so much damage to the Irving Place apartment that the manager of the restaurant downstairs threatened to sue, prompting Perry's eviction. An Island acquaintance put him up for a while, until Pauline arranged for him to stay with Danny Sims at his plush Fifth Avenue apartment, surreptitiously offering 'Rainbow Country' and 'Lama Lava' to San Juan in July, shortly before her own departure to Jamaica.

Sims was trying to gain control of the material Perry produced with Bob Marley and the Wailers before they signed to Island, convincing him to sign a contract on 20 June stating that Marley was under exclusive licence to JAD while working with Perry, the agreement allocating Perry a $10,000 advance against a future royalty of forty cents per album sold in the USA and twenty cents in other territories.

During their negotiations, Perry began painting the walls, marking them and Sims himself with crosses, and the pigeons Perry brought from Central Park got Sims in trouble with the building superintendent. Then Sims brought Perry back to Jamaica at short notice, scuppering a twenty-date tour with the Majestics, his departure hastened by domestic and financial complications.

Perry had been sending money regularly to his children through Joseph Hoo-Kim at Channel One and had given a large sum to Pauline on hearing she was travelling to Kingston; when Pauline was delayed, she sent the money to Channel One, where her firstborn son collected it, and when Vicky Nelson told Perry that he refused to share the funds with Perry's children, Perry hastened his return, only to find Pauline at Cardiff Crescent as well as Vicky, causing further upheaval in the disrupted household. Perry's stepfather, Granville Blythe, had recently passed away too, another serious matter he was swiftly forced to deal with.

Since Perry had overstayed his visa in New York, he was subsequently barred from performing in the USA for over fifteen years. Valuable items had been left behind, including the silver service set, placed in the care of Keith Chin of Keith's Records, who would later meet his death in Puerto Rico.

In the summer of 1981, the London-based Jamaican-American film-maker Howard Johnson was in Jamaica conducting interviews for *Deep Roots Music*, a Channel 4 television series. He filmed Perry at Cardiff Crescent ritualistically spinning in circles, wearing a straw hat with 'poop' written in black marker pen on the top (and plenty more words on the brim), banging a supporting pillar with a hammer in the compound as he bellowed, 'We, the Black people, must rule the universe – it is compulsory!'

In the last-known footage of the Black Ark when it was still essentially intact, Perry is shown inside the control room, which was messy and decrepit but still functional, with a Teac reel-to-reel, the Allen & Heath MOD III and the Roland Space Echo all still up and running, along with Perry's vintage drum machine, and in the main recording room on the ground floor, Sean, now renamed X-on, played the Vox Continental as Perry proclaimed himself 'the only man that can heal the world from cancer', naming music as 'the only comforter' and claiming to be the reincarnated Black Jesus. Pipecock Jackxon came up in the discourse, along with Meanie Meanie Tekel, another character of his evolving cosmology.

Johnson also filmed Perry recording at Joe Gibbs' studio, working on a bright and optimistic adaptation of the spiritual 'Daniel Saw The Stone' and a new version of 'I Am The Upsetter'; Perry would change the lyrics of the former for 'Jah Road Block', saluting 'Allah-Jah' at the expense of Pope Pious and the Council of Churches, which would be issued as a Joe Gibbs twelve-inch in 1982, the musicians commissioned by Gibbs, according to guitarist Andy Bassford.

But the most important problem in the summer of 1981 was

that 5 Cardiff Crescent faced repossession due to repayment defaults, Perry's mortgage lender, the Workers Savings and Loan Bank, briefly offering it for sale in late August until he managed to wrest back control.

Mike Cacia relocated to Kingston shortly thereafter and began taking Perry's children on frequent outings to video arcades and the zoo. By December, he arranged for the newly formed Heartbeat label to fund a new Perry album and thus summoned the Majestics to Jamaica for ten days of recording in January 1982, the group now a trio since Jim Kraut quit when the US tour was cancelled.

Perry and Cacia wanted to record at the Black Ark, but all of its contents had been moved inside the house because the studio roof was leaking again and water permeating the floor.

'Water was coming in when the rain falls, and from underneath the ground too,' said P-Son. 'So through it was leaking, he take out the equipment.'

'All the recording equipment had been removed,' said Jim Schwarz. 'Scratch still had the original Ampeg B-15 amp that he used on most of his recordings in his house. There was junk littering the control room and hundreds of Scratch album covers on the floor.'

'He wanted to record in his house, that's where a lot of instruments from the Ark were,' said Ron Stackman. 'Everything was painted: cymbals, piano keys, tubes, and there was a breezeway chock-full of master tapes, so we all convinced Lee that it'd be tough to get that stuff working and we'd better go over to Dynamics.'

The band thus laid the core of their rhythms at Dynamic with guitarist Don Grant and Perry on vocals and percussion, Gladdy Anderson later overdubbing piano on two songs, and other multi-track overdubs took place at Aquarius. The resultant *Mystic Miracle Star* was entirely conceived in the studio, with Perry gradually directing the band after scrawling the outlines of his lyrics on empty record sleeves (especially those of 'Free Up The Prisoners').

'He would have us play a few chords and then things would develop,' said Stackman. 'Sometimes he would ask for a specific bassline or guitar lick and we'd jam on each rhythm for quite a while. Most of the time Scratch would be singing, then we'd go back and add more keyboards and guitar. Don Grant was there for all the sessions, a very nice man and a great guitarist who had worked with Scratch plenty and knew the program. Scratch's sons Mark and Marvin and his daughter Marsha were around all the time, and in the studio, Mark sat next to me at the Hammond B-3, operating the Leslie speed control when I nodded to him. They were really nice kids.'

Though the music of the farmhouse rehearsals bordered on hard rock, the Jamaican recordings had a pervasive roots feel, with the exception of 'Chalice Ablaze' and 'Music Breeze', both at the rock end of the spectrum. Much of the album was driven by Perry's stream-of-consciousness raps: 'God Bless Pickney' related his magical powers between comments on the cosmos; 'Radication Squad' was a twelve-minute jam that saluted the latest special police unit tasked with reducing crime; and 'Pussy I Cocky I Water', which named sex as a vital force of nature, would later feature on the soundtrack of *Brother From Another Planet*, John Sayles' 1984 drama about a Black alien who visits earth.

As with *The Return Of Pipecock Jackxon* and his recent recordings with Munchie Jackson, Perry employed certain devices that would often be repeated in future works, including the recitation of the alphabet and the musical sol-fa scale, and double-tracked vocals gave the impression that he was having a conversation with himself. But the sessions themselves were not without friction, especially when Bunny Wailer was working in the same space.

'We arrived at Dynamics for a session and Bunny was still recording, so we had to wait till he finished,' said Schwarz. 'Scratch gathered pieces of wood and built a small fire on the ground outside, directly in front of the door, and when Bunny and his band were getting ready to leave, Scratch positioned himself behind the fire, facing the door, with his arms folded. So anyone who wanted to exit the studio had to negotiate both Scratch and his fire, and I remember being surprised at how small Bunny was and how timid he looked as he tried to get through the door without disturbing either Scratch or his fire.'

There was conflict with other industry figures too, according to Schwarz.

'One night Scratch took us to Federal studio to collect some money that was owed to him. I remember him knocking on the door and a small window opened, speakeasy style. Words were exchanged, with Scratch yelling, "What is this, a jail-house?" but no money. I guess that Scratch thought having three white guys backing him up would increase his chances of getting paid, but he was wrong.'

As part of the advance from Heartbeat, Perry asked for a video camera, which became a new fixation. He would set it up at any given opportunity and was obsessed with filming images reflected in mirrors, particularly when he was a passenger in a moving car, and according to Schwarz, when Perry ran out of blank videotapes, he filled the compartment with earth, though the camera somehow continued to function.

Then, after the Majestics left Jamaica, Cacia took Perry,

Sean, Omar and Marsha to Negril for some rest and relaxation, where Perry spent much of his time filming the sea and its environs; one evening, while trying to film something reflected in the bathroom mirror, he stood on the sink, which broke loose from the wall, flooding the condominium.

Back in Kingston, Perry turned his attention to a new album project, working at Joe Gibbs' studio with Errol Thompson and the Professionals house band, with his children often in attendance, recording adaptations of Bob Marley's 'Rainbow Country', 'Nice Time' and 'Keep On Moving', but the disordered sessions were halted halfway through, with Perry facing a large studio bill.

Life at Cardiff Crescent continued to be chaotic, prey to Perry's ever-changing whims. And then, in the early hours of a spring morning in 1982, the Black Ark control room received a literal baptism by fire, in which much of it was totally destroyed.

The cause of the fire is still disputed, and it remains unclear whether it burned by accident or intention, the rumours reaching epic proportions and contradictory statements by Perry and the family members who witnessed its destruction lodging the incident firmly in the realm of legend.

'One morning me wake up and see the studio catch a fire and when me fly out of the house, you can't out it because it burn fast,' said Sean. 'I was sleeping, so I couldn't tell you is a man light a fire there, but the alleyway, it's there the fire start, beneath the control room; it go into the rehearsal room, the [floor]boards catch fire, the whole place light up. Scratch say, "P-Son! Come fe the fire!" but the fire just build, never go away within the space of an hour and by the time the fire brigade come, the [roof]top just lick off, blown super high like volcano lava, so we couldn't out it because of the heat alone that come off of it, we couldn't go near it. Scratch call we to help him put out the fire and I couldn't tell you is him start it definitely cos I didn't see it and I don't tell lie.'

'I know for a fact that it was electrical problems because one time we was in the studio and saw smoke coming from the meter, so maybe the electrician did not drop the [electrical] cord [properly],' said Marsha. 'Whenever two negatives meet, you know you definitely have to have a negative – positive and negative clash, so we see smoke coming from there and everywhere. But this thing that they're saying that my dad burned it down, that's a lie. It was definitely electrical problems.'

'I don't really think that it was intentional, I think he make a fire inside there and somehow the fire just get out of control,' said Omar. 'He's having a connection with the elements and he feels alive when a little fire's blazing, and there's nothing wrong with that, but at that time he was writing on his walls, making different arts, because if you see how the house was, it was very museum-like, and normally nobody would never do that to their own place, so sometimes things might be normal for him, but for us, we don't understand. I was roughly thirteen by that time and it was quite a chaotic situation. All of a sudden things was just going downhill for us, so to tell you the truth, it's really not a memory that I hold onto.'

'I was in the room where Bob Marley used to stay and I wake up and see it, like six in the morning, and he tried to out it with water,' said P-Son. 'It start from the passage right against the control room and I don't think it was a deliberate thing that he want to burn it down. Like he was reasoning in the morning, say so much bad spirits in the studio, I think he did catch a little fire at the front in the passage to burn out the bad spirits, but it get out of hand right there through the padding on the walls and the carpet that was in there. When the fire brigade come, the fire done already. The roof did drop down at the control room and the padding on the walls and the carpet, they all burned off, but when it burned, the board and all the tapes was out because no work was going on in there.'

P-Son, Sean and Jah Ned emphasised that the fire did not obliterate the entire building. Instead, the control room was irreparably damaged, with its collapsed roof and melted Perspex, but aside from the destruction of the drum booth, in the main recording room on the ground floor and the attached rehearsal room, it was only the padding on the walls and the carpet that burned, leaving them otherwise intact.

'It was a good while after Bob's death and it wasn't really burned down,' said Jah Ned. 'It was only the carpet inside had burned and some of the wires, so it was no burning down thing, and the equipment wasn't burned because Scratch had moved out the equipment long before that.'

Perry has given conflicting accounts of the fire, and despite claiming responsibility most of the time, we are unlikely to ever be certain of its origins. The closest thing to a believable confession first came in the *NME* in November 1984.

'For weeks and months the pressure had been building up. I was getting no money, just pressure, pressure, pressure. I got up that morning with turmoil in my heart and went to the bottom of my garden, the studio y'know. I love kids' rubber balls. They are air, trapped. I love that and I collected many of these balls. Anyway, I have one favourite, it came from America and I kept it on the mixing desk. Someone had taken it when I got to the studio and I was just filled with anger. First all the pressure, the thievery, and then this . . . I destroyed the studio. I smashed it up and then I burnt it down. Over.'[7]

Could Perry really have destroyed his studio because someone took a child's rubber ball from it? On other occasions, Perry has strictly denied burning the Black Ark: 'If the government or whosoever try to find out if it's me who try to burn out my studio, they'd make a big mistake because it's not I who burn down my studio.'[8]

In May 1999, I hoped to clear up the situation once and for all by asking Perry directly what happened. Did he burn the studio in a deliberate act, or did the fire result from an accident or electrical fault?

'Of course it's me who burn it – who else could burn it?' said Perry, with absolute gravity. 'I was just working morning, noon and night for musicians and singers, and I did want to be a singer. And then that ball was there for concentration, and nobody should go inside the studio when I leave there. Somebody was messing with my energy, so it wouldn't be clean anymore, so I throw gas in there and light it. I didn't hold no insurance on my building, I only hold life insurance for me. I cannot get money from it, so it was mine to do what I want to do. When the fire light, the only time me try to put it out is when me see the light wires start to burn off. The fire was going out, so when it comes to those places, that's when I was trying to get it out.'

And how did Perry feel about it all those years later? 'Good thing I did that!' was his immediate reply.

After the fire, Perry was held for several days in the lock-up at Hunt's Bay Police Station while an investigation was launched into the cause of the blaze, only to be released without charge due to lack of evidence. Contrary to popular myth, he spent no time in Bellevue mental hospital or any other sanatorium, and as his master tapes were stored elsewhere, none perished in the fire.

'They thought I have insurance on the studio, then I become a prisoner, but they discover that there was no insurance neither, so I am free to do my own thing,' said Perry. 'Me did know one of the detectives, he used to come to me every weekend, and him vexed then because me was mixing with dreads, but they didn't treat me with no disrespect.'

Tony Owens returned to Jamaica to attend his grandmother's funeral as Perry languished in captivity, and when Perry was freed, they reconnected and made plans for future releases, drawn from Perry's back catalogue.

'I went to Jamaica in '82 and I hadn't seen him for a couple of years,' said Owens. 'When I went to Jamaica, he was in custody because they were saying he burnt his studio down and fire is an offence because you put lives at risk. But they had no evidence to substantiate, so they had to release him.'

When the actor Carl Bradshaw brought a small crew to film Perry in July 1982 for a proposed Marley documentary that Los Angeles-based director Gary Weis was assembling for Island, they found him at his most unhinged, vociferously pontificating on obscure concepts, spinning with boulders on his head and walking through a fire that was burning on the kitchen floor, every visible surface covered by impenetrable graffiti. The garden hose served as a baptismal font in the front yard, though the brick wall next to his front gates bore the painted message 'Satan the Devil live here', and there were hand-drawn diagrams, presented on camera, illustrating arcane truths.

The children were filmed singing Welton Irie's X-rated 'Cocks Man' in the ruined shell of the studio's main recording room, now home to piles of rubble, its bare walls covered with freshly scrawled graffiti, the remains of a drum set and partly ruined bass guitar the only visible instruments, and what was once the control room now a void. In the house, the unplugged Soundcraft was on its side in a corner, the Allen & Heath now heavily defaced by graffiti, and the Roland Space Echo, Vox organ and Gibson Maestro Rhythm N Sound were among the other disconnected items languishing in disuse, along with dozens of neatly stacked master tapes, safely in storage.

With Perry producing precious little in Jamaica, outdated bits and pieces were surfacing overseas. *Black Ark – Volume 2* was cobbled together from vocal material Pauline Morrison left with Starlight, and on Seven Leaves, Tony Owens issued the authorised compilation *Heart Of The Ark* in September, with *Megaton Dub* to surface the following year.

Then, in December 1982, Vicky Nelson left Jamaica to join her mother in Canada, where she would remain for nearly a year, her departure instigating another reign of turmoil and depression at Cardiff Crescent, returning bitterness and bile to the forefront of domestic life.

Pauline Morrison was overseas, soon to give birth to the first of two children fathered by Danny Clarke, and seventeen-year-old Michelle was heavily pregnant too, dropping out of school after having begun a relationship with a dancer named Wayne Campbell who worked at J. Wray and Nephew's Kingston facility. Their son Lasanno was born in February 1983, but Perry strongly expressed his disapproval, only then informing Michelle that he was not her father, which was hurtful, especially as no one would tell her who her biological father really was. Tension would increasingly grow between her and Perry, especially after Campbell moved in.

At this point, Perry was still planning to refurbish the Black Ark, as revealed in a *Jamaica Times* article dated 1 March, in which he proclaimed, 'Mek dem know mi a come strong again, mi soon open the studio',[9] but Perry could not square this desire with his bitterness about the past and nursed a festering mistrust of his peers. Afflicted by drastic mood swings, particularly when tanked up on rum, he lacked the concentration and ready cash to renew it, so the Black Ark remained in its vacant state and, most of the time, it was only the unproductive, anti-social Perry and his children at Cardiff Crescent, until Vicky Nelson returned, bringing some stability back into the picture.

'I didn't really want to go back, but I *have* to go back cos it's like my job wasn't finished,' Vicky explained. 'He was trying to hide away from the music business because of some rough times he had, the whole issue with Bob Marley and other musicians and people. He was very hurt deep down, so getting him back into music was very hard.'

On one of his return journeys to Jamaica, Tony Owens brought Perry to the recently opened Music Mountain studio in Stony Hill to lay some rhythms with the Sagittarius band, including an original song and a new version of Marley's 'One Drop', though Perry only laid guide vocals then.

Perry was largely inactive in the months that followed, until Vicky convinced him to approach Chris Blackwell, who flew him to Nassau on 29 November to begin recording the *History, Mystery, Prophecy* album at Compass Point.

Armed with the master tapes of the tracks he began at Joe Gibbs in 1981–82, Perry worked for a solid month at Blackwell's studio, adding synthesisers, drum programming and fresh vocals with the assistance of engineers Steven Stanley, Kendal Stubbs and Andy Lyden; he returned to Jamaica on New Year's Day, then went back to Nassau on 31 January 1984 to spend another couple of weeks refining the material.

John Martyn was at the studio working on *Sapphire*, and Robert Palmer on *Riptide*, so the trio had a jam together with the guitarist Barry Reynolds, leading Perry to ask Palmer to overdub bass on his album and Martyn to overdub guitar. Perry was a hard taskmaster, according to Martyn, who witnessed plenty of perplexing activity in Perry's apartment.

'The cooker was on all day,' said Martyn. 'He had metal coins on one burner, a dead fish and flowers on another, and it really stank.'

Martyn said he began cooking for Perry, who insisted on paying him for dishes of ackee and saltfish and curry goat, and intervened when Perry was robbed by a local hoodlum. 'People say you're fucking mad,' Martyn challenged when he found Perry cuddling trees one morning, the whispered response being, 'I'm keeping them away from me.'

Chris Frantz and Tina Weymouth were also on-site with their young son Robin, recovering from the Talking Heads' lengthy *Speaking In Tongues* tour, the casual atmosphere allowing for plenty of cordial interaction with Perry.

The recording sessions stimulated some new songs, including the rambling word association 'Funky Joe' and an alternate take of 'Bed Jammin' (as 'Bed Jamming'); 'Heads Of Government' was less frivolous, though Perry's favourite was 'The Ganja Man', the loose update of 'I Am The Upsetter' began at Joe Gibbs, and there was the melodious 'Mr Music', which loosely adapted themes of Marley's 'Roots Rock Reggae', as well as 'Nice Time' and the funky adaptation of 'Keep On Moving' titled 'Tiger Lion'. Perry also took another stab at 'Pipecock Jackxon' as 'Pipecock Jackstone', its rhythm drawing from Studio One classic 'Pressure And Slide', but as with earlier attempts, the song was left unissued.

History, Mystery, Prophesy ultimately occupied an uneasy space between commercial reggae influenced by disco and experimental language poetry, which may be why Island released the album only in North America that spring, aimed at younger new wave fans. Its most radio-friendly offering was 'Mr Music', and footage of Perry dancing around the control room at Compass Point as Kendal Stubbs tried to apply his instructions to a mix of it featured in an episode of Channel 4's *The Tube* profiling Island Records, the ever-driven Perry super-focused in the scene, his biceps inexplicably adorned by wedges of silver duct tape.

Perry returned from Nassau on 14 February, and the very next morning, former Squeeze pianist Jools Holland appeared at Cardiff Crescent with Valerie Cowan, gathering material for another special edition of *The Tube*, titled *Jools In Jamaica*; Perry did some ritual firewalking outside the front gate as Holland pondered the disused toaster impaled on it, and Perry used the baptismal hose in the courtyard to anoint the outer wall of what had been the main ground floor recording room, decorated by a cosmological image, as Cowan attempted some on-screen context for Perry's confounding conduct. Though not as manic as on *Deep Roots Music* or the Gary Weis footage, Perry still talked nineteen to the dozen, introducing himself as the Atomic Man, stating that Marcus Garvey/Moses painted the walls in the form of Pipecock Jackxon, and reminding that he only sought truthful people to work with, regardless of their skin colour.

'When you meet him, it's quite overwhelming, but I think he sensed that I was an admirer,' said Holland. 'In my diary, I wrote that we spent the first half of the day filming Lee "Scratch" Perry, who is charming, eccentric and sets light to things.'

'I remember him taking a quarter of an hour to position his trainers in a certain way before he walked in, and he put his feet in and out of the fire that he'd made,' said director Geoff Wonfor, who spliced some of the Compass Point footage into *Jools In Jamaica* since Perry's studio was out of action. 'We lit it the way I normally would, but he went, "Take all these lights down! I'm not coming back until I've got blue for heaven and red for hell!" So we lit it in red and blue, which sounds absolutely ridiculous, but it looked amazing.'

Jools In Jamaica captured something of the pervasive chaos still reigning at Cardiff Crescent. Vicky Nelson said that, on her return from Canada, she saw that some musical instruments and pieces of ruined equipment were still being stored at the house, but Perry soon dispatched them to the stinking depths of his septic tank, resolving to destroy them rather than allowing perceived foes to reap from his ongoing misfortunes.

'Me take out the instruments, like drum kit and guitars, and the eight-track Chris Blackwell bought me – all of those, I throw them in the toilet pit, just like that and they are there still now,' said Perry. 'Bunny Lee want me to sell the Tascam to his friend Jammy, that's when me decide me have to throw it in the pit. Him send somebody that wanted to buy and me don't have no money. The Tascam was there, and Bunny Lee come with something about Jammy want my mike to buy, and Bunny go into the studio and take my mike, so I throw them all in the pit, run it off before I have to send it to Bunny's friend Jammy. Those are bad vibrations.'

Perry said he eventually gave the Allen & Heath mixing desk to Errol Thompson, who may have passed it on to Bunny Lee, though the whole episode was hazy and hard to account for, the timeline muddled.

Lacking motivation and focus, it soon became apparent that there was little for Lee 'Scratch' Perry in Jamaica, the final destruction of the Black Ark denoting a definitive boundary line. He no longer had a facility in which to further his independent experiments and was wary of his former collaborators, so in April 1984, he obtained a multiple-entry non-immigrant visa, allowing admission to the US as a tourist, but Perry lacked the cash to make the journey and was mindful of his previous immigration problems, so went to Rita Marley, cap in hand.

'Scratch asked her for some funds because Scratch was not getting any royalties from the music he and Bob had done together,' said Jah Ned. 'Scratch had a lot of music to release and him wanted some new machines in the studio, so he say, "Rita, I want some money, five million Jamaican dollars would be a good start", and she told him he would have to go to England to see Chris Blackwell.'

When it became clear that Perry would remain stagnant in Jamaica, Vicky Nelson spoke to Tony Owens about sending him to London, inciting Perry's anger, since he had not devised the plan, but when Owens offered to pay for an airline ticket, Perry capitulated. Thus, on 26 September 1984, Sean, Omar, Marsha, P-Son, Vicky and Jah Ned accompanied Perry to the airport, beginning a long phase of life outside Jamaica.

CHAPTER TWELVE

I Am a Madman: Years in England

After so much turmoil, relocating to London was to herald a new beginning, but the transposition began another unsettled phase of short fuses, tangential culs-de-sac and self-sabotage, with alcohol a big part of the problem, exacerbating mood swings and flightiness.

On arrival, Tony Owens installed Perry in a spare room of the flat he occupied with his wife and children on the St Raphael's Estate, a low-income housing scheme squeezed between the North Circular Road and the end of the River Brent in peripheral Neasden, northwest London. *Megaton Dub 2* was impacting the reggae album charts and since Island only issued *History, Mystery, Prophecy* in the US and Canada, Owens helped Perry issue an alternate on the UK branch of his Lion of Judah label, though neither pressing sold well, despite decent reviews.

Perry soon learned that Joe Gibbs was in town, so Owens took Perry to meet him and Winston Edwards in the far reaches of southeast London, the entourage turning up en masse at Ariwa, the recording studio that Neil Fraser ran in Peckham.

Born in Georgetown, Guyana, Fraser was exposed to reggae through the radio in his youth, and after joining his parents in London in 1970, he worked as a technician for Soundcraft for a couple of years, before launching Ariwa in 1979 as a front-room studio at his Thornton Heath home, the name adapted from the word *ariwo*, which means communication in Yoruba. Producing reggae, lover's rock and dub under the alias Mad Professsor, he promoted local acts like Rockaway and Sister Audrey, and the studio became a focal point for visiting Jamaican artists after Congo Ashanti Roy and Mikey Dread recorded their own productions there in the early 1980s.

Using the rhythm tracks he and Owens laid at Music Mountain, the first songs Perry voiced at Ariwa were the startling 'Judgement In A Babylon' and an unremarkable version of Bob Marley's 'One Drop', with Valerie Skeete and Vyris Edghill of Akabu on backing vocals, the latter an old flame of Family Man. Mixed by Perry's Studio One associate Sid Bucknor, the songs would surface on a Lion of Judah twelve-inch in December 1984 and 'Judgement In A Babylon' was aimed straight at Chris Blackwell's head:

> I saw Chris Blackwell in Nassau
> Drinking the blood of a fowl from a rum glass
> At his new studio in Compass Point . . .
> He offer me a cup of fresh fowl blood . . .
> Chris Blackwell is a vampire
> And I am speaking the truth through electric wire,
>   Aba-Jah
> Tom Hayes his lawyer is a vampire . . .
> His secretary Denise is a witch
> Who claims to me she's the high priestess
> They believe in cult voodoo and Obeah . . .
> Chris Blackwell is a vampire
> Sucking the blood of the sufferers . . .

Chris Blackwell killed Bob Marley
And take away his royalty
Because Bob Marley was speaking the truth . . .
Chris Blackwell came to Jamaica
Want to sign up all the artists
Because he want to control Jamaican music
Then he can take the Black man's music
And promote his white artists
But Jehovah Jah Rastafari say it won't work . . .
He give Bob Marley cancer
He couldn't find the answer
He take away his riches, he take away his wealth
Chris Blackwell is a vampire . . .

Though many artists acknowledged a debt to Blackwell, others resented his control over the dissemination of Jamaican music and the wealth it afforded him. Yet, had Perry gone too far by calling Blackwell a vampire? Would the Island boss really have been sipping chicken's blood from a rum glass at the opening of Compass Point in 1977?

'Well, that's true,' said Blackwell. 'It's part of a custom in Jamaica, and I'm from Jamaica: when you build a building, you kill a chicken and mix the blood with rum in your mouth – just a little bit – and drop it on the four corners.'

However, Blackwell took exception to the claim that he was 'sucking the blood of the sufferers'.

'I don't agree with it, but if he felt that way at the time, that must have come across to him. Hopefully, what I do is introduce and help promote his stuff.'

'He always be a nice man to me and sometimes go over the border to do things for me, but when me call him a vampire, it was the truth,' said Perry. 'When me say the truth, me *have* to say it, don't care what it cause.'

After 'Judgement In A Babylon', Perry began voicing new material on rhythms Mad Professor made with his Robotics house band (also known as the Sane Inmates), then featuring the multi-instrumentalist Errol 'Black Steel' Nicholson and drummer Anthony 'Drumtan' Ward, Perry often turning up with a young Black woman named Martine, with whom he had a brief liaison. Dozens of songs were recorded over a few weeks, though nothing would surface until 1989, when Professor released the eight-song LP, *Mystic Warrior*.

'Scratch would come in from twelve o'clock and stay till midnight,' said Professor. 'When he finished his tracks, he ended up voicing a load of tracks for me as well and some of them came out on *Mystic Warrior*, but there was at least another two albums that never came out, with tracks like "Hippy John". Between Scratch and Sid Bucknor, I learnt a lot from them guys and soon after these sessions, I started making really good hits.'

Mystic Warrior drew on the Marley legacy with an updated 'Crazy Baldheads', 'Put It On' redone as 'Feel The Spirit', and 'Natural Mystic' adapted for the title track, but the most effective numbers were originals cut over disconcerting Ariwa rhythms, allowing Perry to unleash the anguish of his tortured soul, as heard on the extremities of '25 Years Ago':

> This is Madman Scratchy
> You better watch it
> He draw matches and the place go 'Boom!'
> I've been working for twenty-one years
> And I ain't got a cent
> I've been working in the studio all my life
> And I don't have no fucking money

This is Madman Scratchy with his episode
This is Madman Scratchy
Who is getting rid of his heavy load
Five years ago I-man bend down low
Bend down in the earth
I want to change my shirt
Bow down in the earth
I even eat the earth
Sometimes I eat my shit
Sometimes I drink my piss, why?
Because the food is the shit
And the water is the piss . . .
Twenty-one years ago
I been working night and day
Ain't got nothing to show
Because the wicked take it away . . .
Twenty-five years ago
I been working like a slave in the ghetto
Never earn a cent
Neither praises for the work that I have done so . . .

The ambiguous confession at the start alludes to the burning of the studio, and the middle shock-value lines are there as a reminder that excrement is part of the sacred cycle that sustains life. The overriding theme is frustration, with decades of work resulting in neither financial nor aesthetic reward.

Tony Owens arranged British tour dates in November and December, with Mad Professor as live engineer, backed by the Sounds Ultimate Sounds (S.U.S.) band, a reliable west London reggae outfit led by Hopeton McLean, with a two-piece horn section and two female backing singers. In preparation for the opening night at Dingwalls on 22 November, which would be Perry's debut performance as a vocalist outside Jamaica, Perry appeared on Tony Williams' *Rockers FM* show on BBC Radio London, along with Desmond Dekker, lambasting Chris Blackwell and lamenting the absence of Bob Marley.

The sold-out Dingwalls debut was well-received by a crowd of adoring fans, despite moments of hesitancy from Perry, the set including 'Mr Music', 'Nice Time', 'One Drop', 'Pipecock Jackstone', 'Soul Fire', 'Big Neck Police' and 'People Funny Boy', with rapturous requests for an encore at the finish.

Backstage, Perry was approached by twenty-one-year-old divorcee Sandra Cooley, who offered to share a spliff with him, prompting a request for her address.

'I said I lived in Middlesex, so that kind of tickled him,' said Sandra. 'Some other girl had given him her address and she lived in Surrey, so he said, "If I got to Surrey I'll be sorry, but in Middlesex I'll be OK."'

The daughter of a lorry driver from suburban Wealdstone, Sandra and her young daughter Sharon lived in a council house at 15 Waghorn Road in Kenton, outside Harrow, a few miles northwest of Tony Owens' place, and after Owens dropped them there, one thing led to another and Perry ended up spending the night.

'I thought it was going to be a one-night stand and that would be the end of it,' said Sandra. 'Then he come back again the next day.'

Perry would drift between Tony's and Sandra's for a time, and the same week as the Dingwalls gig, after the word of his appearance got out, some of Sandra's friends came round with copies of his records, including former boyfriend Richard Thomas, who played drums and saxophone in the instrumental post-punk quartet Dif Juz, then signed to independent label, 4AD.

'We were massive Lee Perry fans and there were all these mysterious stories about him shaving a mole on his head and calling it the third eye to God, so the reputation had well preceded him,' said Thomas. 'There was an electric bar fire in the middle of the room which we were all sitting round, trying to keep warm, and he opened the door and went, "Fire!" and threw this bottle of nail varnish remover onto the fire and the whole fucking thing went up and everybody's hair got singed. And then he started to draw on all the walls.'

When Thomas put Dif Juz's *Who Say So?* on the turntable, Perry expressed interest in collaboration. He wanted to record an adaptation of Bob Dylan's 'Mighty Quinn' as 'Mighty Scratch' and wondered if the band could manage it, so Thomas put the wheels in motion, arranging a rehearsal session a few days later, followed by a recording session at a studio near London Bridge, funded by 4AD.

'We went to Acton and rehearsed for a day and polished off his "Mighty Scratch" thing in about ten minutes, then we started jamming and he just started scatting on top of what we were doing, and he loved it because it was something new. So we ended up going to the studio and doing these four tracks and he was dancing all over the studio, putting a lot of energy in and just making up the words on the spot. There's a song we did with him called "Sweet Little Roses", and on others he was singing about the IMF and Stonehenge, it was all very futuristic. At the end of the day we thought we better get a little mix going, so I whipped out my Roland 201 Space Echo, which I used to put on my high-hat live, and I said, "Put this across the drums and the high-hat", and Lee said, "Take it off! I don't want that!" It really upset him, and I had a really strong feeling that he just wanted a break with the past.'

4AD co-founder Ivo Watts-Russell felt the material needed improvement and enlisted Robin Guthrie of the Cocteau Twins to improve the mix.

'A couple of weeks later, we went to Blackwing studio, near Blackfriars Bridge, and Robin made it sound really present, really in-your-face, and Lee really liked it,' said Thomas. 'It was better, but they didn't think it was right for 4AD. They were more about rose petals and frosted glass and some obscure abstract beauty, whereas Lee was very guttural, very punk.'

After travelling between Tony Owens' home and Waghorn Road for a few weeks, Perry brought boxes of his possessions over, including his video camera and a box of videotapes, full of ominous proclamations.

'He said, "I've got some videos of the sky", but they were videos of himself chatting and that's when I thought things were a bit strange,' said Sandra. 'Up until then, there were a couple of eccentricities that you'd allow, like writing on my wall. I was decorating, the upstairs had been done and the living room hadn't, and he started with one or two things on the top, just writing his name.'

Before Sandra knew what hit her, Lee Perry had moved into Waghorn Road and junk sculptures began to appear in her front and rear gardens, symptomatic of the great changes wrought by Perry's presence in her life.

Although Perry was unfazed by their differences in age, he was sensitive to growing old as he approached fifty. Ludicrously fit and with the boundless energy of a youngster, Perry took note when Sandra said that his glasses made him look older, so he subsequently abandoned them, preferring blurred vision to an elderly visage.

When Perry was living with Tony Owens he spoke to his children every Sunday on the telephone of their next-door neighbour in Cardiff Crescent, and since Sandra lacked a telephone line, he installed one, but began contacting his children more sporadically.

One day, a pair of immigration officers appeared at Waghorn Road, making it clear that Perry's movements would be monitored. The Thatcher government had increased restrictions on the citizens of its former colonies and Jamaicans were under special scrutiny, since the island had become a waystation for cocaine smuggling; many of the former politically aligned gangs were now involved in the international drugs trade and the presence of violent Jamaican criminals in Britain – the so-called 'Yardies' – gave rise to a pathological mistrust.

Following the Dingwalls debut, Perry and S.U.S. hit Sheffield's Leadmill and St Albans City Hall, and they were filmed in Newcastle performing 'Mr Music' and 'One Drop' for *The Tube*, with Perry in a crisp white two-piece and holding a mirrored talisman, but following an uneven set at Manchester's Hacienda, Perry fired the band after a concert at Leeds Polytechnic on 15 December.

'S.U.S. were doing their own set first, getting a very good response,' said Professor. 'Then Scratch come on and start to cuss the band, telling the people that the band's trying to steal the show.'

After the ugly backstage scenes that sent the band packing, Perry and Sandra Cooley travelled to the town of Clitheroe, near Blackburn, staying overnight at the home of BBC Radio Lancashire disc jockey Steve Barker, so that Perry could appear on Barker's *On The Wire* programme, co-hosted on this occasion by Roger Eagle, co-founder of the renowned Eric's nightclub in Liverpool. The three-hour session drew illuminating responses from Perry (some of which were later worked into the song 'Scratch On The Wire' on Barker's

Bugs On The Wire compilation), but Barker said Perry seemed rundown.

'Lee was like an old man with low energy levels. Through a lot of that period he was drinking horrible stuff, like bottles of sherry. At that time, he wasn't as obviously obstructive and quasi-mystical. When people started paying attention to him, he got more spooky.'

'It was usually sparkling perry, or Country Manor perry,' said Sandra of Perry's preferred tipple. 'When we first met I explained to him that I couldn't handle anyone around me drinking, so he curbed it for a while, but he still drank.'

After the rupture with S.U.S., Bad Manners' manager Ron Scorpio stepped into the fray, another in the long line of prospective administrators who would find out the hard way that Perry was virtually unmanageable. In late December, Scorpio brought Perry to community facility Pyramid Arts in Hackney, east London, introducing him to a mixed band called World Service, with guitarist Steve Marshall, who blended rock, funk, soul, blues, jazz and new wave, and since Perry was seeking to broaden his palate, they became his new backing band.

Perry and Sandra attended the New Year's Eve party that Bad Manners threw at their Hackney headquarters, since frontman Buster Bloodvessel wanted Perry to produce the ska revivalists, but Perry said they would have to change their name to Good Manners to benefit from his help.

Perry made his debut with World Service at Dingwalls on 31 January 1985, inviting Dif Juz to play an opening set with him, consisting of the four songs they cut for 4AD, and according to Marshall, the main concert was recorded for broadcast on Capital Radio, but Perry said such negative things about the station during the performance that it was never aired. Pop-reggae act Amazulu were in the audience and asked Perry to produce them too, the collaboration another potential hit that never happened.

Further gigs with World Service took place in February in Folkestone, Manchester, Portsmouth, Bournemouth and at the Albany Empire in Deptford, before Perry sacked the band, and Ron's management, after a final performance at Walthamstow Town Hall in late March, disappointed by the size of the venues they were playing and the poor press reviews. Steve Marshall kept in touch and, in December, persuaded Perry to mix the track 'Lightnin Strikes Twice' at Elephant Studio in Wapping, later released on Marshall's State of Emergency Records, though Perry's presence is hard to detect and the single garnered little interest.

Then came the unexpected news of Sandra's pregnancy, met with some initial trepidation on both sides, since it was unclear how long Perry would remain in the UK, and though the couple gradually embraced the notion of raising a family, Sandra suffered a miscarriage in May.

As the search for a new backing band continued, Perry was on Portobello Road with Tony Owens one day when he was approached by longstanding fan Mark Downie, a rhythm guitarist, songwriter and graphic artist from Stevenage then in a band called Studio Six. After hearing a demo tape at Waghorn Road, Perry travelled to Stevenage for some informal group rehearsals at the Pyramid pub, with inconsistent results, though Perry and Downie soon developed a friendship based on a love of nature and musical experimentation.

Perry appeared on a couple of low-key Hertfordshire gigs with Studio Six, first at a pub called The Bell in Codicote, outside Hitchin, the second before a larger crowd at Stevenage College, and when Downie and keyboardist Russ Cummings

In the Black Ark yard, April 1980

With Family Man and Wire Lindo, London 1987

Above: Live in Paris, 1987

Right: With Tyrone Downie, London, 1987

With Sid Bucknor, London, 1987

Above: With Adam Yauch (right) and Mario Caldato Jr, New York, 1997

Right: With Linton Kwesi Johnson, Jenins, Switzerland, 1990

Below: With Clement 'Coxsone' Dodd at Studio One, Kingston, 1998

5 Cardiff Crescent, 1998

5 Cardiff Crescent, 1998

Perry's mother, Ina Blythe, Hanover, Jamaica, 1998

Marsha Perry in the Blue Mountains, 1998

Sean Perry at Cardiff Crescent, 1998

Above: Omar Perry in London, 1997
Right: Sandra Cooley and Cleopatra Perry, Harrow, 1999

Above: With Mireille Campbell, 1989

Right: Shiva Perry, Switzerland, 2015

Below: With Gabriel Perry, Switzerland, 2016

Inside the Blue Ark, Switzerland, 2006

Above: With the author, London, 1995

Left: In London, 2019

formed Dub Factory with bassist Mark 'Spike' Kolodzinski, Anglo-Jamaican drummer Ken 'Peng' Smith and British-Asian guitarist Tarlok Mann, Perry fleshed out ideas with them during three days of rehearsals in November 1985, preparing to record a proposed dub album.

Trojan Records had recently changed hands and was now being run by the accountant Colin Newman and his associate Frank Lea (the brother of Jim Lea of Midlands rock group Slade), who furthered Marcel Rodd's policy of keeping Trojan largely a reissue label, and one of their first projects was the critically acclaimed *Upsetter Box Set*, reissuing *Africa's Blood*, *Double Seven* and the scarce *Rhythm Shower*, with extensive liner notes by reggae journalist and former Daddy Kool staff member Steve Barrow, released in the autumn of 1985.

While trying to straighten out his back catalogue royalties, Perry was persuaded to provide Trojan with two albums of new material, so in November, label manager Patrick Meads booked Perry and Dub Factory into Thameside, a small sixteen-track facility in Rotherhithe run by Jerry Tilley, a gifted engineer and musician that played with Bill Haley and Fats Domino, where the Pioneers and Boris Gardiner had recently been working. Fifteen songs were captured on tape during a three-day marathon, with the band even sleeping in the studio, laying the foundations for the *Battle Of Armagideon (Millionaire Liquidator)* LP.

With the album still unfinished, Trojan quickly released the 'Merry Christmas, Happy New Year' 45, featuring backing vocalist Sandra Robinson, incongruously pressed with the original 'Return Of Django'; the twelve-inch edition also had the anti-abortion alternate take of 'Happy Birthday', plus a 'Return Of Django' update titled 'All Things Are Possible', with Downie scatting in place of Val Bennett's saxophone.

449

Perry frequently returned to Thameside over the next four months to rework the material, sometimes with Downie and other band members in tow. Patrick Meads brought in trombonist Trevor Jones and saxophonist Lloyd Clarke of the Ipswich-based Jah Warrior to play on certain songs, and Perry added new vocal lines and other arrangements.

On one of his visits to Thameside, Perry found Max Romeo's London-born sister Jennifer recording 'You Can Wake Up With Me' for Sydney Crooks of the Pioneers, an answer to Boris Gardiner's hugely successful 'I Want To Wake Up With You' (an adaptation of Mac Davis' 'It's Hard To Be Humble'). Jennifer was there with her Barbados-born husband/manager Rudy Mascoll, then working as a baker and minicab driver to make ends meet, and when Perry learned that Jennifer was Max's sister, he was ecstatic, hailing Max as one of his key artists and earmarking Jennifer as a new star.

Battle of Armagideon was completed in March 1986 and released in late June. Along with 'Happy Birthday' and 'All Things Are Possible', 'Show Me That River' loosely adapted Prince Buster's 'Wash Wash' (based on Frankie Laine's 'That Lucky Old Son'); the rambling, double-tracked 'Drum Song' riffed on 'Dark End Of The Street' and borrowed a guitar refrain from the Beatles' 'Norwegian Wood'. Autobiographical opener 'Introducing Myself' was a strong point that spoke of formative years in Hanover and warned Thatcher, Reagan and the Queen that he was coming to right their wrongs; 'Grooving' placed a chant of international banking over references to Zodiac signs and heathen activity. There was a cockney meditation on the Devil called 'The Joker', built around the sol-fa scale, and the eerie 'Time Marches On' had Perry's percussive banging on an electric fire (pictured on the back cover atop his head); 'Sexy Lady' was a failed attempt at disco-funk that contrasted strongly with the album's most popular and notorious track, 'I Am A Madman', another auto-biographical song with a complicated history.

Like '25 Years Ago', 'I Am A Madman' ambiguously contemplated Perry's sanity, though the song was originally titled 'The Cuntist', his tribute to the female sex organs from which all humans are born and with which he was perpetually fixated.

'Obviously, you could never print "I Am A Cuntist" on a record,' said Mark Downie, 'so that's how "I Am A Madman" came about.'

Trojan's press release for *Battle Of Armagideon* claimed that Perry drank petrol while recording 'I Am A Madman' and Mark Downie said he witnessed it, though during the recording of 'Time Marches On'.

'Spike and I went to the studio with Lee one day, stopped at a garage and Scratch bought a container and filled it with petrol, and he was in the back of the motor, sniffing it. We thought, what's he doing? But being Lee Perry, you just accept that kind of thing. We got to the studio and he had some rum and blackcurrant, and he took the lid off the petrol, so the fumes were circulating. Then he ran out of rum, so he said, "I've got to try the petrol." So he was drinking petrol and blackcurrant – not very much, but how much could you drink? The fumes were all over the place, it was like sitting in a petrol station. We were trying to create the rhythm to go with "Time Marches On" and Spike fell asleep, and I was dozing but Lee was vibrant. Jerry was going, "Oh my God, what's happening to my studio?!"'

Since the late 1970s, when the spirits became more forthright in their communication, Perry continually set himself impossible tasks in keeping with their instruction, partly to try his own faith. The idea was that God was testing Perry to see whether he was a true believer, and Perry intimated that his actions stemmed from a need to demonstrate that his faith was such that God would never abandon him.

Battle Of Armagideon's striking front cover was designed and illustrated by Downie on Perry's instruction.

'Lee said to me, "I want a ghost smoking a spliff wearing a crown sitting on a Bible throne", and that's my interpretation.'

The album's popularity helped revive Perry's profile in the UK, and in the US it drew widespread airplay on the college radio network, largely through 'I Am A Madman'. A brief UK tour began on 10 July at Gaz's Rockin' Blues, the weekly club night hosted by Gary Mayall, son of blues guitarist John Mayall, at a venue called Gossip's in the West End, but Dub Factory, now billed as the Upsetters, was buckling. Without a contract, the musicians would never receive a penny for their work on the LP (except Downie, who received a nominal fee for his cover illustration), and when Trojan refused to pay the band, the rhythm section quit, forcing Downie to draft Gary and Mick Lewis of Studio Six for the Gossip's gig, the internal friction and disparaging reviews prompting Perry to fire the band.

Patrick Meads then recruited Jah Warrior to back Perry at the first 'Reggae Seasplash', held in St Austell, Cornwall, on 16 August, followed by a gig at London's Wag club, but Perry disliked Jah Warrior's approach and dismissed them too.

In the autumn, Trojan tried to string out the album buzz with further singles. 'Sexy Lady' and 'All Things Are Possible' were released in late November with little impact, followed by yet another cut of 'Merry Christmas, Happy New Year', remixed by Mad Professor. The latter was also issued as a Trojan twelve-inch with Professor's inspired cut-up mix of 'I Am A Madman' on the flipside; both songs had melodica parts overdubbed by Downie at Ariwa, the studio temporarily back in Professor's Thornton Heath front room following a break-in at the Peckham premises.

By then, Perry had begun recording a second album for Trojan at Thameside with members of the Southall-based Misty in Roots, including bassist Anthony 'Tsungirai' Henry, drummer Julian 'Bampy' Peters, guitarist Dennis 'Tendai' Augustine and keyboardist Delford 'Tawanda' Briscoe, and with that project in mid-air, he began collaborating with inventive British producer Adrian Sherwood, proprietor of On-U Sound.

After working for Pama during his teens, Sherwood distributed reggae in the northern and central regions of England through the J&A distribution service, formed in conjunction with Joe Farquarson, partner Anil Kanna and former Trojan employee Chips Richards. Carib Gems was launched in 1976 to house material by Black Uhuru, Dillinger and Trinity, as well as Prince Fari's *Psalms For I*, licenced from Pete Weston, and when Sherwood subsequently met Fari in Birmingham with bassist Flabba Holt and drummer Fish Clarke, a strong friendship developed, leading to significant collaboration.

By 1977, with J&A heavily in debt, Sherwood established the Creation Rebel imprint, operating from a backroom of Pama's record shop in Harlesden, voicing Jah Whoosh's *Marijuana World Tour* in an evening over pre-recorded dubs. Then, the Hit Run label was the home for some impressive Prince Fari productions and Sherwood mixed all four volumes of his *Cry Tuff Dub Encounter* series, working closely with the toaster on *Message From The King* and *Voice Of Thunder* too, and there was *Starship Africa*, a spacey dub set by London session players he named Creation Rebel. Hit Run morphed into the short-lived 4-D Rhythms label, which gave way to the more lasting On-U Sound, home to many adventurous hybrids. Early acts included the New Age Steppers, whose shifting line-up included Ari Up and Viv Albertine of the Slits, former Pop Group frontman Mark Stewart, former Aswad bassist George Oban, drummer Style Scott of the Roots Radics, and Vivien Goldman; the London Underground, a post-punk mix of Gaelic soul with rock and reggae hues; Singers and Players, an amalgam that backed visiting Jamaican artists such as Congo Ashanti Roy, Bim Sherman and Mikey Dread; and African Head Charge, centred on Jamaican percussionist Bonjo Iyabinghi Noah.

Perry was a major influence on Sherwood, especially the Black Ark recordings of 1973–77, and although Sherwood recalled a chance teenaged meeting with the maestro in Pama's shop, it was Steve Barker who suggested that Perry team with Sherwood, following Perry's Radio Lancashire broadcast. A meeting was thus arranged in the spring of 1986, beginning an abundant collaboration.

'Steve Barker said that Lee should be cutting with On-U Sound and working with me on a record,' said Sherwood. 'I was originally going to be working on some rhythms he'd built, like a recut of "One Drop" he'd done with a little crew south of the river, but when I played him a couple of Dub Syndicate rhythms that were heavily processed, he said, "This is great, give me a mike", so we parked what he'd been doing and flew straight into *Time Boom*.'

Dub Syndicate was another On-U conglomeration of Jamaican and British musicians that became a vehicle for drummer Lincoln 'Style' Scott, who would often recruit other Roots Radics members, including bassist Flabba Holt, guitarists Bingy Bunny and Dwight Pinkney, and keyboardist Anthony 'Steely' Johnson, as well as saxophonist Headley Bennett; for this project, the British contingent included guitarist Martin

'Frederix' Harrison of the London Underground, bassist Evar Wellington, percussionist Bonjo-I and Doctor Pablo on bass, guitar and keyboards, as well as Sherwood's then wife, Kishi Yamamoto, on keyboards.

Most of the voicing took place during the autumn and winter of 1986 at Berry Street Studio in Clerkenwell and Southern Studio in Wood Green, north London, the sessions proceeding smoothly despite Perry's eccentricities.

'I heard he was off his head and found him not to be,' said Sherwood. 'He's a lot more eccentric than your average, but he's very inspirational to work with, very talented with timing and he's got the energy of a kid. I wouldn't say it was difficult, but nothing that's good comes easy.'

In November, when the bulk of the album was finished, Perry appeared with Bim Sherman, Mark Stewart, drummer Keith LeBlanc and other On-U stalwarts aboard riverboat *The Elizabethan* for 'The On-U Sound Party Conference'. Floating down the Thames past the Houses of Parliament, Perry sang songs from the new album over pre-recorded backing tracks, accompanied by live conga drumming and percussion.

'We had 280 tickets which sold within hours at Rough Trade and about 500 other people were begging to be let on,' said Sherwood. 'I had just gotten back from Poland and Lee came over to our house in East Ham on the day of the gig, but we weren't watching him, and he drunk a whole bottle of Polish vodka, so he was trying to climb up this shelving unit in the front lounge, screaming. Then he got really ill and says we've got to get some weed and ended up comatose on the floor. We cleaned him up and got him to the gig and he was welcoming everybody onto the boat, then he got a mike and was doing karaoke, singing on his back on the floor. There was a lot of spliff and drugs on the boat and after about two and a half hours, the police were trying to stop us, so Scratch was hurling abuse at the police with a megaphone, saying, "Fire on your head in the river Thames! Back off Babylon!" and cursing "*Bloodclaat*!" It was the maddest night, great fun, and I'll remember that forever.'

There was shamanism in East Ham, too.

'We had a Prophet 2000 keyboard and Kishi said Lee had a cooking pan with three pebbles in it underneath the Prophet in the lounge, and he'd got the kiddies' watering can. So she said, "Lee, what are you doing?" and he looks up at her without blinking and goes, "I'm watering the stones at the foot of the prophet." He's always thinking of something that will cause some magic. He's a one-off completely, cut from a different cloth.'

Sherwood tried to master *Time Boom* in January 1987, but a couple of tracks had technical issues, so a last voicing session took place at Southern on 22 February and, once the final mixdown was executed, it was clear that *Time Boom* was easily the strongest work Perry had made since the Black Ark's demise. Perry responded brilliantly to Sherwood's complex rhythm tracks, since the Roots Radics core was familiar enough for him to feel comfortable singing over, the On-U augmentations and Sherwood's sonic treatments yielding the contemporary sound that Perry was seeking, both unique and broadly appealing.

As is typical of the post-Ark canon, Perry's lyrics were all over the map. 'SDI' caught him at his most critical, protesting Reagan's Strategic Defence Initiative as perpetuating a needless Cold War. 'Time Conquer' cursed liars and blessed truthtellers, proclaiming Black supremacy and reminding listeners that humanity was insignificant in the face of time; Perry spoke of his own supernatural powers on 'Kiss The Champion',

'Jungle' and the title track, and 'Blinkers' hailed 'the return of President Abraham Perry and his holy hands', saluting his shit over a rhythm filled with collapsing buildings, electric drills and breaking glass. 'Music & Science Lovers' was a rambling excursion on a spirited saxophone-led rhythm (used for Dub Syndicate's 'Night Train' twelve-inch), while the catchy 'Allergic To Lies' stuck in the mind despite being the song Perry was least pleased with.

The pre-recorded rhythms left plenty of space for Perry's verbiage, and Sherwood was adept at facilitating what Perry envisaged, helping him build the sol-fa vocal bridge at the end of 'Blinkers', for instance. Overall, *Time Boom* resulted from the powerful chemistry built between two independent thinkers, both with keen ears, fast hands and plenty of ideas.

In between the *Time Boom* sessions, Perry worked sporadically at Thameside on the tracks begun with Misty in Roots, and when *Time Boom* wrapped, he returned to the material in earnest. Thameside became his second home, much to the regret of Jerry Tilley, since Perry was covering the walls with paint and magic marker, placing champagne bottles filled with his urine at strategic points around the space, blowing reefer smoke onto the moving master tapes as he worked and treating the machines as though they were living beings. A Turkish fan became a regular fixture when Perry was in residence, typically ingesting magic mushrooms while observing Perry at work; sometimes he would sit quietly in the corner, other times dancing with reckless abandon as the music played.

Jerry's brother John became Lee's manager during these sessions, having previously handled heavy metal act Desolation Angels. John understood Perry's moneymaking abilities and spoke of schemes to fall back on if his music career failed, like painting abstract works on canvas to be sold at extortionate prices, but Perry had little confidence in him, John's chief duties being to ferry Perry between the studio and Waghorn Road, with Rudy Mascoll recruited as backup.

The Thameside sessions yielded an extended remake of Marley's 'Exodus' that lasted over thirteen minutes, with lyrics about 'flying Scratchy the flying Apache', changing 'Exodus' to the 'ashes and dust' of Marley's passing, and a random encounter with a dog-walking jogger brought an Alsatian into the studio for some ferocious barking overdubs. There was a new version of 'Duppy Conqueror' scolding his 'bad friends' for their wrongdoings, and he had another crack at 'The Ganja Man', this time proclaiming himself 'the King of Poop, Shit, Piss and Spit', while 'Seaside (Mystic Mirror)' was an esoteric contemplation bolstered by a fine female chorus.

At many of these sessions, Perry videotaped himself at work, sometimes placing stones inside the video monitor, and continued to film whatever he saw in the rearview mirror of any moving car, later overdubbing different sounds and spoken conversations onto the audio track. Photographs of himself became another obsession, Perry seizing every opportunity to be snapped in peculiar poses, as though each flicker of a camera shutter could freeze any of his limitless personae in time, capturing the momentary emergence of a fragment of his being, and prints were given talismanic function, pasted to the wall, worked into sculptures or glued to the surface of instruments.

As the album neared completion, circumstances spoiled Perry's mood. Unresolved issues with Trojan over royalties led Perry to hire music lawyer Tim Spencer, who began the torturous process of unravelling the particulars in conjunction with music publishers Westbury Music; a barrister was engaged and a lawsuit pending, but Perry changed his mind at the eleventh hour by refusing to acknowledge their representation.

Patrick Meads was also getting up Perry's nose by meddling with the Thameside material, bringing rock musicians for over-dubs without prior consultation and sometimes mixing Perry's work without permission. Perry would generally disappear when Meads arrived, taking barefoot walks in the snow along the river or building sculptures in the kitchen until Meads left, and would then work late into the night, sometimes spending hours undoing the changes.

Then came the news that Sandra was pregnant once more, with some uncertainty in the air since the pregnancy was again unplanned, though both parents would be delighted when the baby arrived in the summer.

John Tilley arranged another Dingwalls performance for late February, misprinted in the music press as 22 January, so despite later corrections, Perry dutifully appeared at the venue in January to apologise to any fans and ended up performing three impromptu numbers with British funk band, the Nomadiks.

As with many of his public appearances in Britain, Perry was drunk by the time he hit the stage, the booze bringing on strange behaviour. He spent much of that evening grabbing electric lightbulbs with his bare hands while ritualistically sounding a whistle, blowing weed smoke through a wooden recorder placed in alternate nostrils while standing on the corresponding leg.

To prepare for the Dingwalls performance on 23 February, Perry began rehearsing at Thameside with a new band of London-based Jamaicans, led by bassist Larry 'Professor' Silvera, along with Jennifer Romeo, who would open the show.

At Dingwalls, Perry appeared in a homemade hat, covered

in silver foil, with yew sprigs poking out of the top, singing through his own personal microphone, which had talismans attached to its handle, hidden behind a wall of silver duct tape. The setlist was largely drawn from *Time Boom* and *Battle Of Armagideon*, and there were versions of 'One Drop' and 'Exodus', Adrian Sherwood augmenting the mix with an Echoplex.

After the performance, publicity agent Jenni Francis offered to represent Perry, the working relationship leading to a brief romantic diversion in the spring, despite the child he was expecting with Sandra.

At the end of February, Rudy Mascoll brought Perry and Adrian Sherwood to BBC Radio Lancashire for another broadcast with Steve Barker, Perry staying overnight at Barker's home in Blackburn. Singer Mick Hucknell of white soul band Simply Red wanted Sherwood and Perry to remix some tracks, and when they met, the singer made a positive impression, so Perry agreed to the project and a mixing session was scheduled for March.

Other groups to approach Perry in early 1987 were not so fortunate. New York hip-hopper Mantronick failed to impress Perry with his 'technotronik' sound, and Californian heavy metal experimentalists Faith No More were turned down, as was Big Audio Dynamite, which former Clash guitarist Mick Jones formed with Don Letts, possibly because the group had barred Perry from joining them onstage during a performance at the Brixton Academy.

Nevertheless, Perry maintained a busy schedule for the rest of the year. Much of his time was spent in recording studios, creating dozens of tracks, many of which remain unreleased. There were frequent rehearsals for live performances with various short-lived backing bands and sometimes industry functions to attend, such as the Radio London Reggae Awards on 7

March, with Rudy Mascoll now assuming management duties.

Towards the end of the month, Perry and Sherwood remixed a dub of Simply Red's rendition of Bunny Wailer's 'Love Fire' at Southern, where Hucknell overdubbed some vocal lines that Perry thought could be improved, before Perry added his own introduction, imitating a wailing baby and improvising a western showdown theme.

Time Boom was released by On-U Sound on export for Europe and North America on April Fool's Day (its British release scheduled for July, which would be further delayed as Sherwood negotiated with EMI), and two days later, Perry performed at Manchester's International club with Larry Professor's band and Jennifer Romeo, with Sherwood mixing and Sandra along for the ride. Perry appeared onstage in a tracksuit, holding a bare electric bulb on an extension lead, and Roger Eagle was the support deejay, the appreciative crowd including a large skinhead contingent in Ben Sherman shirts and bovver boots.

Max Romeo arrived for a family visit, his presence greatly lifting Perry's spirits, the revitalisation stimulating new ideas. Conceiving a shared 'confrontation' album, they recorded some collaborative work at Thameside, reusing rhythms from *Battle Of Armagideon*, though the work was left unfinished and remains unreleased.

Summer live dates were pending for Austria, Germany and Zimbabwe, and after Perry fired Professor Larry's band, he rehearsed with other expatriate Jamaicans, drafting two Australian women for the horn section, but fired these musicians when they demanded upfront payment for rehearsals; the keyboardist, packing a pistol, insisted on fifty pounds for his expenses, so Rudy Mascoll duly issued a rubber cheque. Then Perry drafted rhythm guitarist Locksley Gichi and keyboardist

Sonny Binns from the Cimarons, along with lead guitarist Trevor Brown (alias Trevor Starr), who had worked with Perry in Jamaica on some Wailers material, circa 1970.

At the end of May, Perry began working with Jennifer Romeo and the Cimarons at Southern with resident engineer Trigger, running twelve-hour sessions, three days in a row. After executing Romeo's 'Music', he reworked 'Drum Song', first as 'King Of the Punks' and later as 'Poor People Rights', which remain unreleased. As the final session wore on, Perry became increasingly energised, despite never taking a break; continually anointing himself with baby oil before a portable heater, he eventually poured the oil directly onto the heater, releasing a cloud of sickly sweet smoke, so everyone fled in terror, except for Perry, who was somehow further energised by inhaling the noxious gasses.

In June, Perry began working at the Brent Black Music Co-op, an expansive community arts facility in Willesden, northwest London. With engineer Sid Bucknor, Perry put the finishing touches to Jennifer Romeo's 'Music' and began mixing the second Trojan LP, but as Perry's dissatisfaction amplified, he began making disgruntled noises, vowing to let the company only have the less-appealing tracks, before deciding they deserved none of them.

The album was scheduled for release in the summer, and after Patrick Meads left Trojan, Enzo Hamilton began overseeing the project. Since his father was one of EMI's top European executives, the Italian-born Hamilton got his start at the Barcelona branch of EMI's Odeon subsidiary before founding experimental jazz label IRI in France in the late 1970s; later, he worked for nebulous catalogue label Charly Records and reggae imprint Vista Sounds, though Perry distrusted him, dubbing Hamilton 'the vampire from Notre Dame' since he had licenced 'Rainbow Country' from Pauline, released on a Daddy Kool twelve-inch.

Hamilton asked why the album was taking so long, and demanded that Perry surrender the master tapes, so two reels were eventually supplied with the following song titles:

- I Am The Upsetter
- Yes Me Friends
- Boom Cannibals
- Fire Wankers
- I Win The Revenge
- Pal Bad Breath
- This Time It Is Different
- Eye For Eye
- Tooth For Tooth
- Surprise

The tapes were blank, and, with Trojan momentarily thrown off his scent, Perry continued altering the material, recording and mixing at Matrix in the West End and BBMC in June and July, getting Winston Grennan to overdub new drum parts on select tracks when Grennan turned up at BBMC.

Despite the excesses of 'Judgement In A Babylon', Perry attended Island's twenty-fifth anniversary celebrations at Pinewood film studios on 4 July, toasting live on a John Martyn jam with Andy Shepherd on saxophone, in the company of Millie Small, Robert Palmer, Aswad and other luminaries, though Blackwell seemed unsettled by his presence, according to Perry: 'He approach for a handshake and it's body-shake he get.'

On an early August afternoon, as striking bus drivers again paralysed the London transport network, Perry should have been at the Townhouse in Shepherd's Bush, where *Time Boom* material was being mastered for EMI, but was dropped off in error at the Roundhouse in Camden, where a chance encounter with members of indie dance-rock band the Woodentops led to an impromptu collaboration.

'I had gone in to work on the song "Wheels Turning", which was still in nappies with just a basic arrangement template, working with Scott Litt who was over from New York,' said singer/bassist Rolo McGinty. 'I went to the kitchen to make a coffee and in walks Lee "Scratch" Perry, who had mirrors in pieces strapped all around him, held on by elasticated bungies, a human lighthouse putting reflections randomly on the ceiling and walls, sometimes dazzling your eyes with a full-on Scratch beam.'

While waiting for a replacement cab, Perry got involved in the session and ended up staying until the wee hours, spliffs and flowing red wine easing the comradery. Keyboardist Sonya Waters was directed to an ancient pipe organ, but what she played was rejected, and after drummer Benny Staples arrived Perry ended up voicing an alternate of 'Wheels Turning', a phrase about 'wooden-foot cops on the highway' ultimately becoming the title of the album in progress, the term referring to the stiff-legged walk of an arresting officer, which Perry demonstrated to hilarious effect.

'I remember Rolo and I working on "Wheels Turning" and inviting him in to hear it, and at the end of the track, hoping for a bit of feedback, Lee says, "Alright, I go and do a vocal", and he did a toast about wheels,' said Staples.

'Hearing my lines cut up and mentally remixed was incredible,' said McGinty. 'He jammed with my thing and added humour and a kaleidoscope of meaning. His way with words is another super-strong aspect of his talent, and his performance of them too. Proper clever maniac!'

The rudiments of a new track were also laid as the platform for an original Perry vocal reacting to the bus strike, provisionally entitled 'Get Back To Work (You Lazy Bastards)', and both songs remain unreleased, though the 'Wheels Turning' variant is accessible on YouTube.

'Unfortunately, he asked for more than Rough Trade were prepared to pay, even more so Columbia Records USA, who had control of the budget,' McGinty lamented. 'But I know he really enjoyed himself, and we did too.'

On 13 August, Sandra gave birth to Cleopatra Perry, delighting both parents, the baby's arrival marking a shift away from the Black supremacy Perry championed in the latter days of the Ark and strengthening his resolve to remain in Britain, though Sandra's postnatal depression would bring unexpected challenges.

At the end of the month, Perry performed on a float at the Notting Hill Carnival with Adrian Sherwood, Keith LeBlanc and Akabu, promoting *Time Boom*'s forthcoming EMI release. Clad in SS regalia, a spiked wristband and masses of rings and necklaces, with a hammer in one hand and microphone in the other, Perry toasted continually over the backing tracks, and broke into 'Wooden Foot Cops On The Highway' when Benny Staples appeared.

Jennifer Romeo's 'Music' was released on a new label called Arkwell, established by Perry and Rudy Mascoll, and distributed by Jet Star (the new name for Pama Records), and hidden on the B-side was a new version of 'Keep On Moving' (mistitled 'Music Well'), built on Tawanda's melodic keyboard riffs. Displeased with the result of the A-side, Perry remixed 'Music' for a second pressing that made his toasted interjections more prominent, this time with Romeo's 'Dance' on the B-side, recorded without Perry's involvement, though both pressings were soon deleted.

The next Arkwell release hinted at occasional tension with Adrian Sherwood, Perry's pervasive mistrust again resurfacing, spurred on by disgruntled members of the entourage and exacerbated by factors of race.

'Adrian is a white man who wants to steal my power,' said Perry, as he awaited *Time Boom*'s UK release. 'Would I give my power to a white man? I would never do that. I would rather die than do that.'

Perry became impatient as EMI stalled, and when he learned that Black Ark singles were changing hands at high prices, he repressed Devon Irons' 'When Jah Come' (retitled 'First Judgement') on an Arkwell/Upsetter twelve-inch, its label designed by Sandra, depicting Perry as a monkey with wings. The other three songs – titled 'Water Genesis', 'Second Judgement' and 'Fire Revelation 22', credited to Jesus Rainford Perry – were actually the first three songs from *Time Boom*, with mumbled interjections such as 'I give and I take what is rightfully mine' overdubbed when blotto on booze.

Such impertinent reactions turned out to be a little premature. In September, just before Peter Tosh's tragic murder at his Jamaican home, EMI released the single 'Jungle' on seven-inch ('Radio Plate'), ten-inch ('Disco Plate') and twelve-inch ('Big Hot Plate') formats on their new Syncopate subsidiary, boosted by a substantial publicity campaign using zany posters of Perry, co-ordinated by Paul Smith, head of Mute Records' sub-label Blast First, and his colleague, Amrik Rai, through an outfit they ran called Daisy Sounds.

As the hype escalated, Perry quickly assembled a pick-up band of Harlesden-based musicians (with Locksley Gichi, Trevor Starr and saxophonist Lascelles James, a reggae session musician who had played in Boney M and Spear of Destiny) for a sold-out performance at London's Town and Country club on

22 September, with Adrian Sherwood mixing. Taking the stage in a cat mask and flanked by Anglo-Caribbean dancers Eve and Christine, who Perry recruited from Kensington Market, Perry did four songs from *Time Boom*, as well as 'Nice Time', 'Roast Fish And Cornbread' and a version of 'Mr DJ Man' dedicated to David Rodigan, all receiving a strong audience response.

The following week, Perry performed at Kensington Town Hall at a benefit gig for the family of Michael Galvin, the victim of a stabbing at Carnival, with the Trinidadian rapso artist Brother Resistance and former Osibisa bassist Spartacus R, though the lack of publicity rendered the event low-key.

In late September, young French promoter Patrick Jammes proposed a concert in November at L'Élysée Montmartre in Paris, which would be filmed for a home video release, meeting Perry in London to negotiate his fee in person. Then Perry began rehearsing an expanded band with keyboardist Caroline 'Rhythm Queen' Williams and Valerie and Vyris of Akabu, preparing to perform the best *Time Boom* tracks, along with Perry staples, and on 10 October, they recorded a new version of 'Small Axe' at Ariwa, now permanently situated at Whitehorse Lane in Thornton Heath, though the song was left unfinished.

Time Boom's critical acclaim helped introduce Perry's work to a new audience, with sales in excess of 50,000 copies, but Perry was still mistrustful of the industry personnel behind EMI's release, prompting an angry confrontation with Daisy Sounds at Mute's offices and negative statements about Sherwood.

'Who is Adrian Sherwood? He is one of the past, he is not one of the future and I don't want to hear about him anymore! He is finished, totally finished, he is wiped out! He asked me to do him a favour, I didn't ask him to do me any. I don't need Adrian Sherwood, he is copying Lee "Scratch" Perry, he is doing what Lee "Scratch" Perry used to do twenty-five years ago. Adrian Sherwood needs Lee "Scratch" Perry, but Lee "Scratch" Perry does not need Adrian Sherwood . . . He is a good copy artist, but I like people original . . . I see him as a pagan, next to a vampire. Bloodsucker. Trying to steal other people's birthright . . .'[1]

'Well, he's not called the Upsetter for nothing,' said Sherwood. 'It was my turn then, but Neil Fraser also got slagged off for several years, and so did Chris Blackwell. It's not confined to us either – it's like producers, and everybody else.'

Time Boom's ascent prompted other collaborations, the first a Perry remix of subversive pop-rocker Zodiac Mindwarp's 'Backseat Education' for PolyGram, executed in a daylong session at Matrix on 3 November for £500, where Perry added keyboards, Syndrums, water sounds and vocals as co-producers Bill Drummond and David Balfe shared a bottle of whiskey, but the remix was never released since the original single dropped from the charts.

Hungover and preoccupied, Perry began the next day in a foul mood, haunted by bitter memories of the past. On the way to a rehearsal with Akabu in Stonebridge Park, he bought a bottle of overproof rum and began drinking it as though it was water, but each swig only intensified his acrimony. Using a portable sampling keyboard with a built-in microphone, he formed a minimal, mechanised rhythm, repeatedly sampling the words, 'I don't like dreadlocks' until the rhythm was permeated with multiple layers of the phrase.

Drunk and angry, he snapped at the musicians, who failed to muster a plausible version of 'Duppy Conqueror', until Family Man and Wire Lindo appeared, the pair in town for an upcoming Wailers Band show at the Astoria, and at Perry's request, Wire stepped up to the piano and banged out the melody of the song, which immediately brightened the mood. Then Perry wiped the caustic phrases from the sampling keyboard to replace them with a new spell: 'I love dreadlocks!'

Family Man visited Perry at Waghorn Road, receiving some cash from Perry to deliver to his children at Cardiff Crescent, and although Carlton Barrett had been murdered by his wife and her lover only five months earlier, Fams was still trying to stay positive, and thus made plans to finish the project that Perry had initiated with the brothers three years before.

'After we finished the *Legend* tour in 1984, I and my brother were supposed to meet back with Scratch in Europe to do something, cos I help him to finish an album at Harry J and we start an album together at Tuff Gong,' said Family Man. 'All the rhythm tracks are just there, unfinished, waiting on Scratch.'

With Perry's Parisian debut sold out in advance, a second show was added at the same venue, the new date announced a few weeks before Perry's arrival at considerable risk. Then, mere days before the event, Perry fired Akabu, drafting Locksley Gichi and bassist Franklyn Dunn from the Cimarons, as well as drummer Gary Duncan, rhythm guitarist Vassel, keyboardist Stefan Lumsden and saxophonist Lascelles James, with female harmony trio African Pearl on backing vocals.

Shortly before heading to Paris, Perry spent three days at Matrix remixing songs by Terence Trent D'Arby, whose debut album had topped the British pop charts on release in July. The androgynous, mixed-heritage soul singer's star was clearly still on the rise, so Perry brokered the fee of £1,000 per day to embellish future hit 'Sign Your Name' and album tracks 'If You All Get To Heaven' and 'Rain'. At the sessions, Perry added baby Cleopatra's pre-recorded cries and used a

Chinese novelty toy for cow sounds, as well as the sampling keyboard and a cabasa, turning crowd-pleasing pop into Dada excess, but drank so much rum on the first day that he could barely stand; magic-marker graffiti and other studio damage brought additional costs for CBS. After further tinkering, the songs were issued on ten-inch and twelve-inch EPs in Britain and Europe at the end of the year, followed six months later by a white label twelve-inch Stateside, D'Arby voicing his approval by suggesting that, in a past life, Perry 'had to have been one of the twelve disciples'.

Perry and his band hit Paris on 18 November after only two rehearsals, heading straight to Radio Nova on arrival, where Perry toasted live over his vintage works for a couple of hours, breaking for an interview with station co-founder Jean-François Bizot, who had visited the Black Ark a decade earlier. Because the opening night's show had been added late, it was somewhat undersold, and despite the usual pre-gig nerves, Perry waited until after the show to get drunk, so gave an excellent performance, the *Time Boom* material and a version of 'Duppy Conqueror' as 'Yuppie Conqueror' drawing a particularly potent audience response.

The second night's set before a sold-out crowd was truly outstanding, the best performance since he left Jamaica. Too hungover to drink, he was stone-cold sober in a black cape and top hat, looking like a cross between a chimney sweep and an undertaker, and kept the capacity crowd hanging on every note, the musicians going the extra mile to keep things memorable, climaxing with the spontaneous encore of 'Put It On', delivered as a frantic ska duet between Perry and Jennifer Romeo.

Because of the undersold extra gig, promoter Patrick Jammes lost money, though Perry took pity and returned some of his fee. Then, the band was stranded at Charles de Gaulle Airport for several hours due to an incident on the incoming plane, and when finally allowed to board, Perry, decked out in military garb, set off the metal detector with an electric guitar in one hand and a duffel bag of magic objects and master tapes in the other, a magnifying make-up mirror hanging from his neck, plastered with an Ethiopian decal, prompting perplexed airline staff to keep their distance.

On arrival at Gatwick, immigration pointed out that Perry had overstayed his visa and when asked how long he intended to stay this time, Perry said, 'Don't know – could be a day, could be a thousand years.'

Rudy Mascoll swiftly intervened, explaining that Perry lived in London with his common-law wife and their newborn child, displaying the working visa obtained for the Paris performances. In the end, Perry was granted restricted entry on the condition that he return to Gatwick the next day to discuss the situation further, and when Perry complied, he was ordered to leave the country and to obtain the necessary paperwork in order to be granted the correct status upon re-entry; the immigration officials suggested he return to France, as it was the country he had last entered Britain from, but Perry had no desire to linger there while waiting on bureaucratic red tape. On 30 November, he thus boarded a flight to Kingston, where he planned to stay for less than a week, since he was due to perform at the Mean Fiddler in Harlesden on 6 December.

Although his children, P-Son and Vicky were pleasantly surprised, Perry's return to Jamaica was stressful.

'Early in the morning I saw this big coach drive up,' said Vicky, of Perry's unexpected appearance. 'When I looked it was just Scratch alone in this big bus and we were all glad

471

to see him. I wasn't hearing from him all this time and I was worried and depressed not knowing if anything happens to him, but we were all glad to see him and just welcome him right there.'

Sean and Omar had been attending St Joseph's, a private high school near Cross Roads, but had dropped out as they could not afford the fees. Marsha remained at Fitz-Henley's Secretarial Institute in New Kingston and was set to graduate the following June, but Michelle kept her distance, since she was living at the home of the boyfriend Perry disapproved of.

A few days later, when Perry said he would be returning to England, Vicky Nelson was vexed.

'I told him that my time is up, and I don't think I can stay there anymore because I want to get my life together. I didn't hear anything for all this time and to be honest, I was pissed off. He was saying that Marsha, which is his little queen, if she as a girl-child is to be left all alone, what is going to happen? Then he tell me that everything will be fine after a while and we would be all OK, and he's just going up there to make the way, but that wasn't so. Anyway, I promise him I'll stay until Marsha graduated from school, and I did keep that promise.'

According to Vicky, Perry's actual departure was as unexpected as his arrival.

'He send me to get something and when I ask where he is, he's gone to the airport and went back to England, he leave me just like that.'

Nevertheless, a mix-up with the airline tickets meant that Perry returned to London two days after his Mean Fiddler gig, greatly disappointing the expectant crowd on the night, and Perry was given the most minimal of entry clearances on arrival, allowed to remain in the UK only until the end of January 1988.

Rudy Mascoll thus approached Tim Spencer, who was reluctant to represent Perry again due to unpaid fees for previous work, though an application was eventually submitted to the Home Office, beginning a phase of uncertain limbo as Perry's particulars were scrutinised.

Perry appeared at Dingwalls on 6 January, but pre-gig drinking rendered a sloppy performance, with band members insulted onstage, and afterwards, Perry harangued Mascoll and Jennifer Romeo in the dressing room.

The Mascolls were already peeved with Perry for taking numerous liberties. He had destroyed their fish tank and relieved them of an electric organ which he plastered with photographs of himself, only to sink it in the mud of his back garden, where it was ruined by rain, and several master tapes were also placed beneath the earth in the period. Rudy and Jennifer were normally spared Perry's ire, but the alcohol took over at Dingwalls, his tirade triggering a period of mutual avoidance.

With his leave to remain expiring and paperwork still unsecured, Perry travelled to New York on 5 February to spend a month working with Max Romeo and Lloyd 'Bullwackie' Barnes at Wackies' new studio in Englewood, New Jersey, across the Hudson from his old Bronx base. Perry also recorded material at Clement Dodd's studio in Brooklyn's Cypress Hills, but the work with Max was the main focus.

'The whole idea was to do an album, Max Romeo meets Lee Perry, I'm going to do one side of the album and he's going to do the other, but when he flew over, the plans change,' said Romeo. 'He ended up doing two albums for the company and I end up doing one, which is *Transition*, and he didn't really do anything else on *Transition* other than be in the studio. By the time that session was done, that studio had to be re-painted – he was scrawling all over the bloody ceiling!'

Perry and Romeo recorded a couple of duets before diverging. A new version of 'Keep On Moving' was the most artistically successful combination, so Bullwackie quickly issued it on a twelve-inch, complete with a toast by a certain Major Irie, who also acted as recording engineer. Perry and Romeo reworked 'Maccabee Version' too, which was included on *Transition* along with an alternate 'Keep On Moving' edit.

By the end of the month, the bulk of Perry's *Satan Kicked The Bucket* was complete, the album released in July by Wackies in the USA and Overheat in Japan, the latter through executive producer Sonny Ochiai, who was based in Wackies' basement. Although not as memorable as *Time Boom*, *Satan Kicked The Bucket* was competent and contemporary, the synthesiser-driven rhythms edging it closer to the predominant Jamaican dancehall style, but with greater textural depth from the Wackies musicians, the exception being 'Ooh La La', a money-summoning chant that resurrected the 'Tight Spot' rhythm.

Along with 'Keep On Moving', a few other songs revisited past hits, Perry grafting a refrain from the Wailers' 'It's Alright' onto an unrelated rhythm, turning the Techniques' 'Love Is Not A Gamble' into 'One Horse Race' and revisiting themes of 'Grooving' on 'Bank To Bank', but the strongest tracks were pure originals, such as the title track, which took another swipe at Island, as well as the discomfiting 'Sweet Dreams' and freaky 'Bat Bat', on which Perry targeted Margaret Thatcher with his bowels.

The pioneering Japanese dub band Mute Beat, who were managed by Sonny Ochiai's older brother, Shizuo Ishii, sent over three songs for Perry to remix for their *Dub Wise* album, and when Perry heard the material, he immediately began to sing along, so their jazzy hit 'After The Rain' was transformed into 'Day Should Turn To Night', a meditation on Curtis Mayfield, Otis Redding, Michael Jackson, the Bar-Kays and Simply Red, which became the closing track on *Satan Kicked The Bucket*. The other two songs appeared on *Dub Wise*, issued by Overheat in May 1989, where the slow skank of 'Beat A Way' became the autobiographical 'Thread Mill Of Life' and 'Frozen Sun' (based on Gershwin's 'Summertime') became 'Yackety', which channelled 'Yakety Yak', Marley's 'Talking Blues' and 'Coming In From The Cold', along with ad-libbed warbling aimed at Lionel Ritchie, the Clash and 'Michael Jackstone', Perry throwing in a request for Munchie Jackson to resurrect himself from the dead.

Perry accomplished a lot during his brief time at Wackies, but as he returned to London before *Satan Kicked The Bucket* was completed, he had little control over the LP's end result and was absent for the creation of dub companion *Satan's Dub*, released by cassette label ROIR in the US and Danceteria in Europe.

In 1990, the New Jersey-based soca and reggae label Rohit Records would reissue *Satan Kicked The Bucket* on CD and cassette, and unfinished outtakes with off-key, out-of-time vocals would be cobbled together with alternate takes of earlier tracks as *Message From Yard*, a poor excuse of a disc perhaps best summed up by the song 'Money Me A Deal With'. *Message From Yard* had a few agreeable moments, such as a multi-voiced recut of 'The Joker', and some lyrics were certainly amusing (with bold statements such as 'I am the President: if you don't like that, drop dead' retaining a stinging humour), but most of it was filler, marked by haste, sloppiness and a quick-buck ethos, and companion set *The Dub Messenger*, released on Rohit's Tassa subsidiary, made further use of the same lousy outtakes by placing more delay on Perry's substandard vocals.

Perry returned to London in early March, glad to be away from the New York area, which had 'too much poverty people' for his liking. He spent his fifty-second birthday at Matrix reworking 'Time Marches On' in the company of Sandra, her daughter Sharon and the sleeping Cleopatra, and a few days later, Adrian Sherwood joined him there for further work.

Sherwood would shortly include Perry's 'Train To Doomsville' on the second of his *Pay It All Back* compilations, voiced on Dub Syndicate's 'The Show Is Coming' rhythm, with Perry slating Trojan, Island, CBS and EMI; Rudy Mascoll and Jennifer Romeo's young daughters Emily and Zara are also featured, and an alternate voicing of the rhythm, 'Rolling Poland', was broadcast on Polish radio.

Perry spent much of May and June at Matrix reworking his partially completed album with engineer Tom-Tom, though Perry was dissatisfied with the mix and unpaid bills hampered him from finishing it. He also had no real outlet for his own work, and was wary of giving it to another company, despite lacking the funds and drive to issue it himself. An unfinished master tape was eventually dispatched to Trojan, but the album was virtually abandoned for the next ten years.

In June, Steve Marshall summoned Perry to Mark Angelo studios in Acton to remix 'A The Time (B The Inclination)' for funk-rock act the Neighbourhood, which was issued as a Parlophone twelve-inch, embellished by a touch of Perry's vocals, and once that mix was finished, Perry and Marshall began working on new material together.

On 16 July, Perry made a guest appearance with Marshall's new State of Emergency band at the Hackney Empire on a fundraiser for Pyramid Arts headlined by African Head Charge, where a tipsy Perry performed 'Train To Doomsville', accompanied by a dance troupe led by Marshall's partner,

Debbie Baddoo, and afterwards, he mumbled gibberish over a pre-recorded extended mix of 'War In A Babylon', enhanced at home with water sounds and other effects, until Empire staff escorted him offstage.

Perry returned to Mark Angelo in August to record some fast-paced, hard-rocking jams with Marshall and engineer/ bassist Lindel Lewis of the S.U.S. band. The lengthy 'Masters Of The Universe' reused the soundtrack of a read-along audio-book based on the campy sci-fi drama of the same name, its cluttered and heavily overdubbed beats a platform for Perry's baffling double-tracked commentary, which refuted the hero, He-Man. 'AD Vendetta' edged closer to straightforward rock, with Perry singing of 'Lady Upsetter' and an alligator; other titles recorded at the sessions include 'Teddy Bear', 'I Am God' and 'French Connection'.

Though Marshall and Perry met with major label executives in September, no deal was struck, prompting Marshall to cut 'Masters Of The Universe' and 'AD Vendetta' as an Arkwell twelve-inch, distributed by Jet Star in February 1989, to little response.

Hurricane Gilbert decimated Jamaica on 12 September, and once Perry got through to his children, who were thankfully unhurt despite damage to the roof at Cardiff Crescent, he dispatched a care package by airmail.

Much of the autumn months passed calmly in London, with Perry spending most of his time with Sandra, Cleo and Sharon, but there were times when he was beset by frustration, becoming incommunicable; pacing around the house, he would murmur darkly to himself or record cryptic statements on cassettes, sometimes voicing vindictive pronouncements aimed at perceived foes or revisiting grievances of the past. Sandra's postnatal depression made it increasingly difficult for her to cope with Perry's moods, and she was also too in awe of him to insist he curtail the mess he was making.

In this period at Waghorn Road, Lee Perry dictated the following proclamations for inclusion in this book, provisionally entitled *The End Of The Universe:*

I. HOT NEWS

This is an interview from Lee 'Scratch' Perry to the outerviewers of the modern world. The First World and the Second World live, but the Third World is finished because I, Lee 'Scratch' Perry, know the head of the IMF — the IMF big boss, the Bank of England big boss, the Midland Bank big boss, the International Giro Bank big boss.

Mr Lee 'Scratch Westminster Bank' Perry is my new name. IMF must see I, is a compulsory, cos is me got the world paper money book that is missed upon the future — I lock it away in the past.

Hot news! World news, international news; it's not the Hot Plate label; it's Hot News label this time. Hot news! I, Lee 'Scratch' Perry, is the King of the Jews. Hot news! Worldwide news message from Lee 'Scratch' Perry to the Third World: the First and Second World, King Alpha and Queen Omega, live, but the Third World finish, so them better start feed on spinach like Popeye, because I, Mr Rainford Hugh Perry, own the sky, and all the banks must come and see I, cos it is I who work the SDI and hide the world paper money book and zap the 100 cash index.

My stingray gun, sunshine super sun; sunshine super sun, my super gun; time boom, X29; the Devil dead on cloud nine. IMF must call I, the Bank of England must call I, the Bank of Egypt must call I, and the Bank of India must call I, and the Swiss Bank must call I, because I am the asset and I am the cassette, and I am the basket, and I am the boss kid Flash, the Sundance Kid; the Tree of Life, history life given, Mr Music.

Live and direct: rain check, air check, breeze check, lightning check, thunder check, brimstone check and fire check, and blood and fire. Confidence of Rastafari: burning fire in the bush; Kush Kush, push push. The Jungle Book, the Jungle King, the Jungle Lion, the Jungle Lord, the jungle yard; the graveyard, the cemetery, the grave; the box and the ghost in it. The death angels sing, angels flap their wings; the death angel sings the sweetest song I ever heard: Lee 'Scratch' Perry on the wire, Lee 'Scratch' Perry ball of fire.

The Devil dead, God live. The Devil Dead! God Live! God take and God give, God's son and God save. X29, Master of Time: X29, Master of Time, Isaiah 9 from the Holy Book of Life, calling all his 300 wives, 900 concubines to powder his behind, and 144,000,000 angels from the Bird Laws Squad, with the Sea Bird Squad, the Jungle Squad, and the Jungle God.

The Third World drawn in. The game blocked; the road blocked, the lane blocked, and the street blocked, so who can't see good better see them eye specialist and take a good look upon the road: the road blocked; all roads are blocked.

This is a supernatural black magic spell from Lee 'Scratch' Perry, the Upsetter, that is done, and it cannot be undone until Thy kingdom come, oh Lord, Rastafari.

I, Lee 'Scratch' Perry hold the key to the past, the present and the future, cos I don't use gunmen to fight my war. I am the Duppy Air Ace Marshall; I run a Duppy Squad and it is legal. I am the boy of the Royal Air Force. When I clap my hands, duppies appear to me from coast to coast, flying through the night post and through keyholes; sometimes they melt the key, if the key is in the keyhole, in a puff of smoke – Pffffff . . .

When I cut a stench, it's so loud that it brings up volcano lava, and is more dangerous than a hurricane, so beware: it liquidates cocaine, kills instantly and takes away pain – a painless killer.

I am a spirit, and I am a sleepwalker, a sleep-talker, a sleep-flyer,

479

and a sleep-swimmer; they call me Mr Grimmer, the Grim, Grim, Grim Reaper and his Desolation Angels of Destruction in a Babylon.

Mr Perry and his ganja gun that cannot be touched or conquered by the evil hand, cos my sword is Psalms 1, the holy hand and love fire, writing on the wall of Babylon; Meanie Meanie Tekel.

Behold! I conquer Hell with my Merry Christmas bells. I am Santa and my toys; me and my reindeer, my rainbow and my sledge, and my pledge, my sea and my bed, my box of fire on my head; I am Charles Atlas, with the world on my head, A to Zed.

Zebra say, 'The Devil dead'. Cobra say, 'The Devil dead'. Abba say, 'The Devil dead'; robbers, don't touch my head because I am the triple red, the massive red, and I'm a walking, talking time boom. Once I was dead, but now I'm alive, and the light of the world is Jesus: Sweet loving Jesus, massive Jesus, sexy Jesus: Cocksman Jesus, the Mighty Fucker; Jack Lightning, Pipecock Jackxon, President Abraham Lee 'Scratch' Perry.

Emperor Haile Selassie the overthrower, exterminator, dissolver, executioner, TNT H-boom, boom Hell with a bad, bad spell called 'Poor People Rights'.

I pen tax and I pen VATs. No more of that! No VATs, Third World rats! No more VAT and no more tax! Tax the rich, and tax the witch, Margaret Thatcher; they can afford it, poor people cannot afford it. Tax Reagan, behold pagan, who is a close resemblance to Satan, the old dragon from Hell bottom with his spell of dooms; Reagan the doom-maker, Thatcher the Queen-fighter. Thatcher who want to overthrow the Queen with her criminal government team . . . Ministers of crimes and governors of wrongs, killers of animals and eaters of flesh which is known as the cannibals (we call them the Cannibal Squad, name given unto them by God), scum of the Earth, bloodsuckers, cock-suckers, and motherfuckers; wankers and skankers; robbers and thieves. The big stealing from the small; the heathen face Paul. Paul John, the rougher don; Dandelion the King of Zion; Piss the Cramper, vampire slayer.

480

Vomit worm and shit maggot; old witch Margaret Thatcher, she vomits worm and shits maggots. I'll save the Queen and her country and see that you rot in Hell, old witch Margaret Thatcher from the FBI and the lady spy. I am the 'Spycatcher' the book write about; I catch spies with my eye and hand them over to the sky for a death sentence, life detention, an instant execution without mercy, without pity and without consideration. Instant execution of wrongs and declaration of rights.

Animal rights come first, not human rights, because we were all animals before we became humans on this planet Earth. If you don't believe me, ask the Earth, wind and fire, ice and snow, heat and cold weather, Mr P the weather bee.

God and the Seven Seas present the big breakdown; Hot Plate and Syncopate; cue plate and thumb plate, and tongue plate and hot plate; tongue fate, the fatal boom. I boom Death and I boom debts, and I bust bets and I win bets, and I sin Death, and I kill Death with my fate lock. I tick and I tock, and I open the lock, and I kill some cock with my Kryptonite rock.

X bank. Sell all you've got, Richie Rich, and give it to the poor, and take up your fuckin' ragged cross and follow me to Tombsville where I get my train, where I say, 'Be still!'

I am the Hebrew king, executor of sin; Super-Chin from Castle Gray Bed; spooky Scratchy on Blueberry Hill, where I get my thrills, saying 'Be still' by skill. Say 'Hi' to the lovers of Christ and 'Bye' to the lovers of the Devil, cos I kill the Devil with my spiritual level MXR Armageddon war; electric machine, computer man, the mighty Upsetter, the ghost in the machine; mad Perry, lightning headmaster, breaker of doom, Dr Fu Manchu. Boom! Boom! Boom! Boom! Boom! Boom! Boom! Boom! This is a musical curse: Blessed are the poor and cursed are the rich. Hick hick, hock hock, yak yak. It finish, yak yak.

II. THE RETURN OF THE GRIM REAPER

Back to our conversation with Mr President Abraham Rainford Hugh

Perry: at last, Lee 'Scratch' Perry the Upsetter saying in a loud voice: repent ministers of crimes, repent governors of wrongs, and this is my brand new song, coming from the sea and sun, Jamaica, the island in the sun. Emperor Haile Selassie I, lightning and thunder, hailstone, brimstone and fire, music whirlwind, hurricane, and tidal-wave judgement; mixed by Earthquake, the Ambassador, produced by Flood.

Jesus Christ's blood on the cross, while a piece of shit stuck in Moses' ass when he was writing the Ten Commandments, as well in transfiguration of Jesus Christ on Mount Sinai, lightning flashing out of his eye, riding his white horse. Lightning, thunder, ball of fire, 1980 and 8 future; Mosiah Zodiac, the weather interpreter, Pipecock Jackxon, Jack Lightning, Jesse the Hammer, Magnetic Abajah Perry.

Push Bush alight, cos it is Lee 'Scratch' Perry who controls all the American assets and world economic structure: the 100 Cash Index, all millions, trillions, zillions of dollars, and all millions, trillions, and billions in pounds hijacked and kidnapped by Jesus Christ – my sweet prick who piss, and rain come; shake his cock and lightning flash; fart, and thunder roll. God, the Upsetter, Him that sent I, music sceptre, Conquering Lion of the Tribe of Judah, Elect of God, Light of the World, Earth's Rightful Ruler, Evil Cooler, INRI.

I am the He that sent I to scorch with lightning and burn with ball of fire, through the heart of this world, Selah; Selassie-I All, Ali-Kali-Eye. Seven seas and seven seals, Neptune world, nose code. I am the future, and all who doubt it, go and ask Satan: Lucifer, the Devil, Phantom Pluto, Lex Luther, the arch-criminal from Krypton (Phantom Zone Jail), where he escape in a pail of shit by drinking acid and turning into mercury, in Oblivion, but I came, and I saw, and I conquer. I came to London, England, Britain, and conquered. I capture Lex Luthor with my Teddy Bear, my hair, and my invisible chair, and my 144,000 Mosquito Angels what sting with lightning, pssssst!

I am carrying a personal feeling for BBC Radio and BBC Television, because they fight against the truth, and that's why they don't want to

play my records for the public, because they know my words are the
truth that represent the true and living God's predictions of prophecy
and things that must happen on Earth, written from Heaven by Moses'
law: 'An eye for an eye and a tooth for a tooth.'

I, Pipecock Jackxon, Jack Lightning, Jesse the Hammer, Lee
'Scratch' Perry (Perry Lee: £ for pound, $ for Scratch, and 'D' for
Daniel Dandelion the Lion); Jah, Jehovah, Jah Rastafari the Crumbler;
black supremacy, black music; the ghost of King Arthur and his sword,
Excalibur (the oath of the King: 'Death before dishonour') put a curse
on BBC Radio and Television, and BBC government, that they can never
overcome or undo until they repent and start playing Mr Perry's records
morning, noon, night and day, and around the clock – tick tock.

Tick tick toe, Big Ben the timeclock is my headmaster. Together we
interpretate disaster for the popes, the deacons, and the pastor, for all
who don't piss, shit and poop, and spit and fuck (makin' love like it
is), hold up them hand and God will strike them with lightning, cos He
knows that they will be committing a sin, that their grandfather and
grandmother did in the beginning, tempted by sin.

'I am the flying fish,' says Scratch; prophecy by Bob Marley, the big
fish's crotch, in 'Trench Town Rock', his first hit when he leave Scratch
with Family Man and the lot. 'And the Lot's wife that turn a pillar of
salt,' says A to Zed. Heavy asphalt; aspects of dog mess, puss mess, all
mess; rats, roaches, flies and lizard, frogs and mosquitoes, birds and
bees, trees, dew water comes from the sky, and water, and flowers, and
plants by night.

Angels sing and God smile, for the angels sing the sweetest song
God ever heard: Lee 'Scratch' Perry legalise ganja. The devil dead.
Lee 'Scratch' Perry legalise collie, internationally. Lee 'Scratch' Perry
legalise ganja, universally. Lee 'Scratch' Perry legalise cannabis, and it
globally. The devil dead. Kill it with lightning head.

17 Million BC. Waterfall and water-rise. Tarzan and the Jungle
survive. The Master is in full control. God never lose a war, and from

the beginning, God was black like tar, and all who think God white, tell me what colour them think them shadow have. Stand up in the light, and they will see a shadow transfer from their body, and tell me what colour the shadow have, is it black or white?

Highty tighties, mighty mighties; Jah is mightier. Jah is wicked, wickeder than the wicked. Jah is strong, stronger than the strong. Jah is right, righter than the wrong. Jah is evil, eviler than the evils, cos it is He, Jah, who creates the good and evils, and it is He, Jah, who create the good and bad. Jah is cruel, crueller than the cruel. Jah is mean, meaner than the mean.

Jah Eenie Meanie Tekel nick hell riches, nick hell wealth, nick hell fortune, and nick hell fame; nick hell moneyum and cashum with opium, onion, garlics, scallion, and thyme. AD Vendetta, the Upsetter, riding the alligator as the Grim Reaper: Killer of thieves, butcherer of traitors, exterminator of vampires, liquidator of robbers, and the exterminator of the IMF, and the liquidator of the rich, and presenter of the poor, for the rich shall be poorer, and the poor shall be richer; it is a switch connection, coming from Buddha, from Oblivion, where He sits in Infinity.

The great Ball of Fire, volcano lava; Marcus Garvey, God's horse; Lightning and thunder, first class. The first aeroplane without engine, that President George Bush mentioned on television, this is it: it named Lightning and Thunder, God's riding horse; Garvey made it.

Black Moses, the Honourable Marcus Garvey the Prophet. Words that live forever, the God's incomparable words that bring rain from the sky, flash lightning, and roll thunder; that change the weather, and make the weather cry, whipping them from the sky with the Holy Mystic Eye. Thank God for Jesus Christ: Marijuana, collie, ganja, tampy, lambsbread, sinsemilla, black hash, rocky, time weed.

Tick cop, tut-tut cop; I am the mop who don't shoot; I chop, and who I don't run through with my sword, I slew them with my rod. At last, road map, A to Zed. Haile must kill the Son of Light, Tree of Life, Book of Rules,

Bag of Tools, Table of Stone. God on His throne in His rainwater rainbow crown: crowned by rights, crowned by nights, crowned by days, crowned by weeks, crowned by months, and crowned by years, crowned by breeze, and crowned by trees, crowned by air, and crowned by hair, and walking on an invisible chair.

Lee 'Scratch' Perry, the man who goes around with an invisible chair on his bottom (called Ethiopian Swastika); the man who stick Hitler's bomb and defuse it in them face, and defeat Hitler's race, and put them to disgrace, and wipe them out of space with his drum and bass, guitar, piano and organ, horns, trumpet and trombone, baritone, tenor sax and alto sax; cricket and bats, Peter Piper, and his pack of rats.

Washing machines, waterpipes, tops, mops, fridges, freezers, Caesars, geezers. Guilders, yen, German marks, sterling; pounds and dollars, pence and pences, cents and senses; munch and munches, dime and dimes, halves and quarters. Uncle Sam Sharp return with him harp, with ice and sickle, his hammer and pickle. Ashes to ashes, dust to dust; six foot six, and 666; mixiplix.

This is a magic potion named VoomVATa, and it have a name BoomTax-a. Voom VATers and boom Taxers, and as for you Locksers, repent, before I cut another stench and defuse thee with my shit-pipe, hot-pipe. Ha, ha, ha, ha, ha, ha, ha, ha, ha, ha, ha, ha, ha!

Voice of the Master, laughin' in the echo chamber. I repeat, I break the spell, and I undo what the wicked have done. I now turn the Table of Life and make the rich poor and the poor rich. All that a rich man have will be taken away and given to the poor, and if them argue about it, we will shoot them in this full-scale glorious revolution of our Lord and Saviour, Jesus Christ.

Super Ape firmament; Ten Commandments: Death to liars. Death to heathens. Death to pagans. Death to vampires. Death to thieves. Death to robbers. Death to rulers of sins and commanders of murders in cold blood. An eye for an eye, tooth for a tooth; that day gonna be a bloodbath soon.

485

Words from the Almighty: God in the Moon, Africa baboon, balloon man, Marcus Garvey (seven miles of Black Star Liners). Water and flood, blood fe blood, fire fe fire; Thunder vex and slew the Devil in his Echoplex.

'The time has come,' says Elijah. Time Boom presents the Return of the Grim Reaper: Death riding on a horse in the cloud with 144,000 Death Angels to conquer Egypt and slew the firstborn of every royal family. History repeats itself. The book is unfold, the mystery untold. Miracles by the score, with a natural mystic blowing through the air, and if you listen carefully, you will hear the news and you will see the news.

BIG NEWS FLASH

Lee 'Flash Gordon' Perry with the Kits of Life and the Key to the Future: heaven's galaxy of stars, and Saturn, Jupiter, and Mars; Atlas A to Zed, Lee 'Scratch' Perry and the electric fire on his head say Merry Christmas, Happy New Year, the Devil dead, amen.

III. THE RETURN OF THE GOD OF THUNDER

Lee 'Scratch' Perry on the wire, with the Hammer of Justice, re-changed from a record producer to a newspaper editor and magazine expert. To establish the life of Lee Perry in this magazine called Upsetter Magazine, *I resign from the recording business; I don't want no part of it anymore. It's filled with grief, thieves, robbers, scoundrels, heathens, pagans, vampires, and scum of the Earth.*

Record business now becomes a pain and headache, stinkard and stink, a positive waste of time, waste of energy, waste of knowledge and waste of wisdom. It stinker than shit; it ranker than piss. It's like dog vomit, a rat race and a cutthroat affair in the dog-eat-dog world.

Thinking of the future, education comes first, so this is where I see my magazine could be a second episode of the great and mighty William Shakespeare who write the Holy Bible, the Word of God that we are living on today, word of wisdom, knowledge and understanding. So I'd rather to waste my money in books, education to teach people knowledge than to waste it in recording industry to feed pagans and vampires and entertain bad manners people. I refuse to do so any longer in the Year of Our Lord Nineteen Hundred and X29, Selah.

Selassie-I, His Majesty the Emperor of Ethiopia; lightning teleportation, a positive education. Ha, ha, ha, ha, ha, ha, ha! Life guarantee, cat collateral and security is education, not in music. Music is good to cheer the spirit up, but too much of it could distort your mind, and make you live in a World of Dream, of negativity, next to madness and a low profile where there is no way out. The only way out is Boot Hill or madhouse, or poorhouse, graveyard, and cemetery. So see God before it's too late, or Judgement might catch up on you in the dancehall, or in the club, or in the pub (rubbin' dub where the mighty lightning flash and the mighty thunder roll), and all electric wire catch a fire, and the big blaze is on and the big panic start, and all the doors jammed – people runnin' to and fro, stampede in high speed; people climbin' over each other's backs, heading for an exit that is jam-packed. 'Where will they run to?' says the Rock, the God of Lightning, Pipecock.

This vision is for the wicked who deny God and say there is no God, and 'It won't be long, it will be soon,' says the moon, the stars, the sun, the clouds, the rain, the rainbow, the birds; and the animals from the jungle that speak through the wind say, 'Vengeance is ours to take revenge, and the cannibals that eat our flesh . . .' As for the bird hunters, it's worse, and as for the animal killers, they get a permanent curse.

Catch a fire, vampires, and burn yourself out, but there is no antidote to remove the poison of the animal flesh from the cannibal's throat. Conquer-worm from the Earth and maggot-flies soon sort them out and get even with them that kill the animals and shoot the birds for their selfish pleasures. 'Enjoy death,' say the dead birds and 'Enjoy death,' say the dead animals.

'The curse of the animals is on the cannibals, the curse that can be cured by no doctor, no scientists and no psychiatrists,' says Fire, Jehovah, Jah Rastafari on the wire; Blabba Blabba, Abba Abba. Death to all robbers.

TEA BREAK AND EARTHQUAKE, RATTLE AND SHAKE

Back to the truth, words from the root: reggae music finish and diminish. Reggae music is a curse. It breed death and hatch cancer, and I Lee 'Scratch' Perry say reggae music is no good. It breed bad men, it breed bad women, it hatch gunmen. It creates violence and encourages sin from deep within. It is the evilest music that ever come on the face of the planet Earth.

God turn his back on reggae music and said, 'I know it not, neither them that deal with it. It is a total destruction, and I have no lot that part with it.' The name itself is a doom, created by an evil scientist called Dr Doom, who lives in an iron coffin; Death himself, in person. Reggae breeds death, gangsters, gunmen, bad men, thieves, liars, hypocrites and parasites, liars, robbers and dumb skulls, nincompoops. It triggers off a violence so stink, stinker than stink-boom.

Jesus Christ, Son of God, see it and ban it out of Earth planet, so I wonder what all the reggae singers, reggae producers, and the reggae artists going to do now that reggae finish. God don't like reggae music; he tell me, Lee 'Scratch' Perry, that in a dream, so all reggae music producers and all reggae artists doomed with reggae music.

Reggae music is a curse, the ultimate destruction. The reggae artists and producers, them so ugly and horrible looking, that when decent people's children look upon the jacket sleeve, it give them nightmares for days and bad dreams to change the children them into horrible monsters and bad manners brats, look at that!

Logical fox, Solid State Logic. Words coming from my lip, words from my tongue of fire: Obadiah, the one and only chapter in the Bible; Obadiah I, who says reggae music is a curse, kill Bob Marley. It kill

Peter Touch, and Bunny Wailer is next to be wiped out by reggae music, according to History, Mystery and Prophecy from Jerusalem schoolroom.

Ancient King Solomon's tomb; Marcus Garvey, the man in the Moon. Seven Miles of Black Star Liner; Theocracy, Black Supremacy. Shit rules us all; Piss designed it. Pisces the King Fish; Jack Lightning. President Abraham Rainford Hugh Perry, His Imperial Majesty Haile Selassie-I in the skies as the executioner.

Battle Axe, Small Axe, Dr Syntax, Professor Pentax; Olympus, the Slayer of VAT, who says, 'No Poll Tax and no VAT for the Vaticans who kill them own white men and impersonate Jesus Christ.' I am sure Jesus Christ is Black, cos Jesus Christ is my sweet cock. Any girl I fuck, compulsory must say these words: 'Lord, Jesus Christ! Fuck me!' and when them discharge, them must say, 'Oh God!'

Lee Perry says his music represents God, the living air, in my interpretation of poop, fart (also called stench), the Most High Stinky-Poo. It have nothing to do with reggae. The only reggae music I ever make is 'Punky Reggae Party'. My music is spiritual background: heaven's churchical order, that bring rain and form flood, flash lightning, roll thunder, form earthquake, volcano lava, whirlwind, hurricane, tidal wave, heatwave, and bring hailstone from the sky, and form ice and snow at the wintertime.

My music represents Time, the Master Himself, cos I am the son of Mother Nature, and I can destroy anybody I don't like just by lifting a finger, just by casting my spirited tarts telepathically, or using my X-Ray vision, John I.

Repent and be Baptised by water or you shall be burned by fire. Fire gun and fire boom; fire bass and fire drum; fire guitar and fire organ, cos I am the fire gorgon, and I am the bull bucker, and I am the Duppy Conqueror. I wrote them all, and I am the same John Paul.

My Father is the Sea, and he is very salt and Peter, and dreader than dread, rougher than rough, tougher than tough, badder than bad, crueller than the cruel, wickeder than the wicked, eviler than the evil, madder than the mad, badder than the bad who slew King Pharaoh with the rod, who make Nebuchadnezzar the King of Babylon eat grass like a horse, and broke a stick in his ass, and kill the Devil with the iron cross.

Ha, ha, ha! We laugh. Everything wreck, everything finish, so we want to start over again. You have to start from Scratch, whether you like it or not. Who want to start have to start from Scratch, whether you like it or not, cos Scratch is the beginning and the end of all things, so I am lucky to have that name because I am Scratch, so who love Scratch will live, and who hate Scratch will die.

Words that fill the immortal sky, the Almighty Eye. Now as I live, I swear I will never tell a lie, neither lick molasses nor catch a fly, cos my eyes is the light, and the light is in my eye.

The moon, the stars, the sun, the clouds, the world, the globe, the universe, the equator, the galaxy, everything is in my eye. I kiss the Earth and thunder roll. This is the truth and nothing but the truth, so help me true and living God.

My bat-bat holy third eye, Cyclops: I've got three eyes, two on my face and one on my bottom: my bat-bat hole, the third eye, Cyclops. My head is the pillar of sky, and my two hands are fins that change into wings, because I am a Pisces, and I change into a bird and fly, change into an eagle, the flying fish.

* * *

In late October, Perry joined Mark Downie at a small north London studio called Second Sense to toast over some of Downie's new rhythms, but abandoned the project when Rudy Mascoll informed him of a pending gig at the larger Mutualité in Paris; Dennis Brown was on the bill, though Mascoll never mentioned it, fearful Perry would refuse to open for the dreadlocked singer. Another pick-up band was quickly assembled, with drummer Trevor Fagan, bassist Lenny Mead, a guitarist, two keyboardists and saxophonist Lascelles James.

A few days before the concert, Perry and Mascoll went to Jet Star to see about some business and met Mireille Campbell, a striking Swiss woman with Jamaican connections and a rather colourful past.

Born Mireille Rüegg in November 1959 to a couple that ran a guesthouse and restaurant, she intended to be become a psychiatrist when she finished secondary school at age eighteen but found the prospect of medical school too daunting, so obtained a counselling qualification by attending night classes, but never practiced. Instead, she delved into the paranormal, psychic phenomena and spiritualism, a love of reggae spawning her Fire Music record shop and booking agency in Zurich, which became Lion Star promotions.

She visited Jamaica for the first time in 1983 and became involved with a man from Montego Bay who returned to Switzerland with her to start a family, fathering a daughter named Collette, but the relationship broke down when Mireille had an affair with Max Romeo, whose Swiss concerts she had promoted. She later bought a house in Montego Bay and in 1987 married a certain Mr Campbell, who fathered her son Noel that same year, but the relationship faltered when Noel was still an infant.

In this period, Mireille began working with the author Michael Hesemann, a German UFO expert and publisher of the magazine *2000*, helping to distribute his publications and audio cassettes, co-ordinating international conferences and organising trips to Egypt for UFO enthusiasts, in addition to her music promotions. She also established the Institute for

Humanistic Therapies in Zurich, which employed a healer and specialists in rebirth therapy, massage and shiatsu.

When Lee Perry met Mireille at Jet Star, she was buying stock for her record shop and planning an upcoming tour with Dennis Brown, and she and Mascoll were already acquainted, since Jennifer Romeo had performed at Max's Swiss concerts, which Mireille organised with Mascoll's assistance.

'I always liked Lee "Scratch" Perry's voice, but I didn't really check who he is and *what* he is,' said Mireille. 'When my first two children were very small, there was this album *Time Boom* and they used to love the song "Jungle" and always used to sing along when I played that song in the car, and when I was in Jet Star to buy records wholesale and organise this Dennis Brown tour, I was with three Rasta friends who work with me and they introduced me to Lee. He was wearing a little red plastic coat with a black collar – something funny, like an imitation fur – and he had a little toy radio in his hand, so I said my name and he gave me his hand, and then he hold my hand by saying, "Hello" at least for about three minutes. I said, "Eh? What is this?" but that was it. They asked me if I was interested to book a tour with him, but I said I have to finish the other one first.'

Their meeting intoxicated Perry, though neither knew then the role that she would come to fulfil.

A few days later, heading to Paris, Perry was surprised to see Dennis Brown stepping onto the same aircraft at Heathrow, but quickly engaged in friendly banter, allaying Mascoll's fears. Perry's pre-performance nerves brought the usual excessive drinking, and his slurring Mutualité set contained the standard mix of *Time Boom* and *Roast Fish* material, plus versions of 'Duppy Conqueror', 'Keep On Moving' and a rendition of Millie Small's 'My Boy Lollipop' delivered in shrill shrieking tones.

On the return journey, Perry was interrogated by British immigration officers who reminded him of the procedures he had failed to comply with the last time and then denied him entry, forcing Sandra to plea for his release in person.

'I had to go and explain to them I needed him to come in because I was on antidepressants for postnatal depression as things were getting to me then,' Sandra explained. 'For a while, he got a reprieve, but he had to go back out. A friend of mine drove me up there and on the way back, Lee was saying to everybody how we were going to have a big wedding.'

With no right to remain in the UK, Lee Perry flew to Jamaica in late November 1988 with the intention of returning to London within a couple of weeks, but once on the island, other paths would be taken, this departure marking the end of his residence in Britain.

CHAPTER THIRTEEN
The Secret Laboratory:
A Base in Switzerland

Lee Perry returned to Jamaica while the island was on tenter-hooks about its forthcoming election, the date of which was still to be set. Seaga had precipitated a move to the Right and stronger ties with the Reagan administration, who made Jamaica a major recipient of aid, and he was credited with stabilising the economy, but hefty IMF loans came with puni-tive conditions and Jamaica was lumbered with crippling debt. The fallout from Hurricane Gilbert was palpable through the decimation of the agricultural sector and the loss of thou-sands of homes, and the JLP's alleviation effort was tarnished by scandals involving the partisan distribution of disaster relief. Yet, since the horrifying bloodbath of the 1980 general election, both parties had shifted from their ideological foun-dations to occupy more of a middle ground. Abandoning democratic socialism and toning down the rhetoric, Michael Manley adopted free-market policies, wooing the business sector and placating Washington, while Seaga pledged an ambitious social well-being programme, with improvements to health, education, jobs, housing and transportation, especially in neglected areas.

With the ideological divide less important, some former 'enforcers' of party loyalty were now involved in the distribution of crack cocaine, with terrible results for Jamaican society. Reggae was now driven by the harsh, aggressive beat of the dancehall style, with lyrics often glorifying the violence of drug 'posses' and the 'Dons' that headed them. After Seaga and Manley signed a peace accord, pledging an election free from violence, a cowed Michael Manley would return to power by a wide margin in February 1989, this time with a centrist agenda.

Once back on Jamaican soil, Perry experienced mixed emotions, since reuniting with his children was tremendous and Jamaica would always be his natural habitat, but home life was far from conflict-free and the electricity and water were disconnected for outstanding bills.

Sean and Omar were planning to break into the music business and had begun to videotape weddings and sound system dances with borrowed equipment; Sean's daughter Nakeesha was nearly two years old, and although his relationship with the child's mother did not last, they remained on good terms and in regular contact. Marsha was living with Vicky Nelson in Constant Spring and helping her to run a restaurant in nearby Half Way Tree, but on hearing that her father was back, Marsha returned to Cardiff Crescent for a few weeks to cook for him and ensure that his clothes were clean. A low grade in maths prevented her from graduating from Fitz-Henley's Institute, so she would later support herself through hairdressing, just like Michelle, who now had a second son, Lauren 'Buzz' Campbell, with her partner Wayne.

Relations with Michelle remained mutually problematic. She was bitter about her surrogate father's unfair treatment following his split with Pauline, but Michelle's very face reminded him of Pauline's betrayal, so he found it hard to be around her, and when Michelle visited, she was met with harsh treatment, with Perry demanding that she leave Cardiff Crescent since she was not of his flesh and blood.

Despite this disharmony, time somehow passed quickly in Kingston, where Perry found himself surprisingly content. Sandra Cooley spoke to him on his neighbour's telephone once a week to discuss the progress his legal representative was making with the paperwork, and after repeated delays, Perry suggested Sandra join him in Jamaica, but she refused due to a fear of flying, even when Perry offered to send airline tickets for her and a friend to travel together. Later, Perry's vagueness hinted at a growing indecisiveness as he fell back into the Jamaican way of life; as ever, he felt that he was merely living out his destiny and was watchful for signs of deliverance.

Clement Dodd was back on the island too, so Perry began voicing Studio One rhythms at Brentford Road with Sean, Omar and Jah Ned, possibly recording as many as forty songs in a short space of time.

'Myself and his two sons went to studio and they was supposed to do harmony,' said Jah Ned. 'At that time Mr Dodd and Perry decided they were going to revive the music business because it was going down and they wanted a new *lieges*, so we decided to use some old rhythms with new lyrics to make an uprising for the music. We did a number of songs for an All Star album, with Tony Brevett of the Melodians and a brother that was there with Scratch. "Mighty King Reveal Yourself", myself and Scratch did that as a duet, but it never came out.'

In February 1989, Mireille appeared at Cardiff Crescent after experiencing a powerful compulsion to visit Perry while she was in Jamaica to finalise Dennis Brown's forthcoming European tour.

'From the moment I heard he was in Jamaica I get a feeling I have to go to see him, but it took about ten days because everyone was afraid,' said Mireille. 'They were all saying he has broken bottles on his gate and a TV on the roof, and I should not go there because he is crazy. Finally I had my three Rasta friends from England in the car and Bongo Herman decided he's going to take us there, so we went to his house and he came out of the gates and said to the guys, "Oh, come out", and they said, "No, no!" and locked the car door! I came up and he said he was telling people in England to get in touch with me. He said he was waiting on me.'

After her friends drove off, Perry escorted Mireille to the inner courtyard of his home, where she took a seat on the low cement wall on the veranda, and although the disorder was startling, she enjoyed hanging out with Perry and his children.

'Those times he had a lot of pigeons in a cage. Everything was messy, and his shorts and T-shirt were full of holes. The three kids came and was very pleasant, but said they are suffering: they have nothing to eat, there was no water or electricity in the house, and their father doesn't give them no money.'

Within a short space of time, Perry said he had something to show her, which they both accorded mystical significance.

'He said, "What is your sign?" and I said, "Sagittarius". Then he said, "Look here", and on the bedroom wall was written "SOS Sagittarius". He said, "I was expecting a Sagittarius, but I never know it was a woman!" He had an iron bed in the middle of the room and under the bed was a poster of Princess Diana in white clothes with some yellow stars around the waist, neck and sleeves, and there was a bow and arrow on top of it. And I had a white miniskirt on and a belt, both with the same yellow stars on them.'

Before Mireille's friends returned to bring her back to the plush Pegasus Hotel in New Kingston, Perry asked her why she had come to see him.

'He said, "What do you really want?", and I said, "I just have a feeling I should come, and I don't know nothing about your life, but actually I want to be involved in everything that you do." He said, "Really? Sure, arrange it!" So I said, "I can make a management contract by my lawyer", and he said, "Write anything you want, and I'll sign it."'

The next day, Perry accompanied Mireille to the offices of noted music lawyer Lloyd Stanbury, who drew up a management and personal contract that would renew itself periodically, granting her 20 per cent of his business gains and allowing her to take charge of all proposed future projects and live engagements.

A few days later, once the contracts were signed, they returned to Cardiff Crescent to spend the evening smoking weed and engaging in intense conversation. Mireille was supposed to attend a party with popular dancehall deejay Yellowman, but changed her plans when Perry became amorous, so the couple retreated to the luxurious privacy of her room at the Pegasus, where they spent the first of many passionate nights together.

In the morning, Mireille bought Perry a new wardrobe, and after returning to Cardiff Crescent, she made a list of clothes to buy for his children. A few days later, she moved to her property in Montego Bay and Perry joined her there soon after, but when he found her in the company of a Barbadian musician that intended to marry her, Perry sequestered the man to the guest room and then ejected him from the property in no uncertain terms.

For the next few months, Lee Perry and Mireille Campbell

were inseparable. Towards the end of their time on the island, they went swimming with Mireille's children in the dramatic setting of Joseph's Cave in Negril, where a diver found a starfish while searching for her misplaced sunglasses. Perry took it as a sign and told her, 'You have to give something to get something, so let's make a baby.'

As hinted at in London, the chemistry between the couple was exceptional and immediate, and Perry was entirely smitten, the child they conceived in Negril solidifying what would prove to be his most lasting relationship of all. Basking in the glory of their newfound love, he accompanied her to Switzerland in May, beginning an enchanted existence.

Accustomed to extravagance, Mireille made a point of living life to the fullest, cruising in a Jeep with like-minded thrill-seekers. Her large home, overlooking the sunny side of Lake Zurich, was in an exclusive suburb known as the Goldcoast or Millionaire's Row, where her live-in servant, Weetus, looked after the kids, kept the place clean and made sure the family and dog, Schatzi, were well fed, her Jamaican assistant Bobby a toughie who ensured that her business ran smoothly.

As Perry turned the large cellar into his Secret Laboratory, dubbed the Blue Ark after he decorated it with blue paint, life in Switzerland brought distant dreams into focus: there was the wealth that had so long been denied him, the fiery sex that he could never get enough of, and the peace of mind that had been so elusive. In London, as in Kingston, he was surrounded by disrespectful greedy people who meddled in his affairs; the tense, unhealthy atmospheres brought destructive behaviour, the demons driving him to drink, but the Goldcoast was far removed from the urban centre, devoid of music industry personnel and their disheartening attitudes.

Mireille encouraged a vegetarian diet and, more importantly, managed to wean him off alcohol, stimulating dramatic changes. Though he missed his young daughter Cleopatra, there was no question of returning to Sandra in London, as life with Mireille was just too good to give up.

Despite seeming an odd couple outwardly, Lee and Mireille had a forceful connection, their temperaments and tastes overlapping. An ardent herb smoker who shared Perry's belief in UFOs and extraterrestrial life, Mireille was against taxation, rejected conformity and held individual spiritual views, and Perry adored her two children, referring to them as angels in the literal sense. He had long discussions with Collette about a 'money tree' that grew currency, and loved to chase young Noel around the garden, though the extent of his day-to-day parenting was minimal.

In the summer of 1989, Lee and Mireille came to London to wrap up some of his chaotic affairs. In late July, he was back at Ariwa with Akabu, having another go at 'Small Axe', and broached the topic of the earlier Peckham studio recordings, but Mad Professor was evasive and nothing concrete was arranged, and approaches to other record companies did not yield the desired results.

Then there was the inevitable confrontation with Sandra, who was shocked to find Mireille with Perry, collecting some of his possessions one evening at Waghorn Road.

'I got this call at my mum's saying he'd be arriving at about 7.30, so I thought, "He's coming home", so the house was clean and there was a meal under way,' said Sandra. 'The last couple of months I couldn't get a hold of him. They said he was at the studio, which was a way of being polite. The phone bill was nearly £800, so I said to one of the boys, "Tell your dad, if he isn't there on Friday, this is the last time I will ever be phoning because I'm not in that habit of chasing people." He was only meant to be gone two weeks, and I had said to him, "If you've met somebody, tell me." It turns out he was at Mireille's house, apparently they'd been together about three months. I said, "Come and see the child", as he hadn't seen her for eight months. Mireille come marching up the stairs like it was her house, and I said, "What the hell do you think you're doing? You're carrying on like you're his woman." That's when she dropped the bombshell: "I *am* his woman!" and my jaw hit the floor. I think he was a bit taken aback by my reaction, but I think he was also a bit shocked to come back and find that everything was exactly as he left it.'

Their business in London completed, Lee and Mireille returned to Switzerland just as Mad Professor was preparing to release *Mystic Warrior* and its obligatory dub companion, entirely mixed by Professor, who visited Perry a few months later, along with his wife Holly, on their way to a holiday in Neuchatel.

'By that time he had moved to Switzerland,' said Professor. 'I thought, "I'm sitting on this stuff, I need to change the direction", so I decided to put it out swift, and he hear about the album and gave me his address, so I went there with my wife to give him some money, and from then on, whenever I see him, I fix him up with more money. I think at that time we had sold a few thousand copies, and he got £1,500. We've got standard royalty rates – it works out about 8 per cent retail.'

Perry later said he was unhappy that Professor released the work before it was finished.

'He is another man who is trying to hustle as usual because we done [those tracks] when I was a little bit addicted to alcohol, so I didn't take advantage of it because I know that them tapes not ready to put out. I ask him to give me [them] back and him play sick the day and disappear. Him wait till me leave England and go and put it out. The people them love it, but it no done yet, but it's all right, him can't spoil my name.'[1]

Compilations of Perry's work were surfacing with greater frequency, though the question of rights was not always clear-cut. Along with several new Trojan retrospectives, Seven Leaves' *Excaliburman* mixed Black Ark work with earlier recordings, and on Henk Targowski's new Anachron label, *Turn And Fire* repackaged some Black Star Liner twelve-inches, but *Magnetic Mirror Master Mix* had Black Ark singles that Perry never licenced to the company. Worse still, Rohit's *All The Hits* had late 1960s and early '70s Perry material, courtesy of Bunny Lee, who had acquired some of Perry's master tapes.

Unauthorised collections were an increasing problem, issued without Perry's knowledge or consent, though occasionally money would be paid retroactively when Perry confronted those responsible in person. Such practices would continue unabated through the 1990s, often with product that beggared belief and sometimes repackaged and retitled by multiple labels, seeking to squeeze maximum financial gain by issuing material in Perry's name that had nothing to do with him.

Among the more questionable 1989 releases were Laurel Aitken's *Blood Vapour* and Jah Whoosh's *Sensi Dub 2*, both using Channel One rhythm tracks (the former mixed by Prince Jammy at King Tubby's), Whoosh's *Reminah Dub*, using Soul Syndicate rhythms produced by Pete Weston, as well as Phil Pratt's two-volume fake, *Lee Perry Meets The Mad Professor In Dub*.

'That is a fiction,' said Pratt. 'Scratch never have nothing to do with it, neither Professor. Those were the people who were selling, so in order to survive, that's what I did. I made them here at Easy Street with Drummie from Aswad, the bass from Aswad and [keyboardist] Bubblers. Professor was angry, but Scratch, we have an understanding: we have to survive.'

'He just shrug his shoulders and say, "People have to eat bread",' said Professor, who confronted Pratt to no avail. 'It's the kind of thing Pratt and Bunny Lee do to wind up the opposition.'

Unable to get Pratt to take his counterfeits off the market, Professor was forced to label *Mystic Warrior* 'The only genuine' release, and Pratt later issued *Lee Perry Meets King Tubby In Dub Confrontation*, supposedly recorded by Perry and Tubby at the Black Ark in Kingston between 1986–88 – an impossibility given that the Black Ark was ruined and Perry in the UK – one of the flood of questionable issues cut in Tubby's name following his senseless murder in February 1989.

In June, Perry discovered that Clement Dodd was planning to release some of the material he voiced in Jamaica and New York, but as the songs were unfinished and controlled by Dodd, Perry instructed Lloyd Stanbury to hold a press conference at the Pegasus, where Dodd was threatened with litigation, temporarily halting the release.

Once Perry was settled in Switzerland, he was hankering to record new music and to get back on the road, but had no studio to work in, nor musicians to draw from, so he and Mireille travelled to Neuchatel to discuss a proposed European tour with reggae promoter Marc 'Nof-Nof' Tourtchaninoff, who suggested Perry use the Zurich-based Ganglords, but he rejected them on artistic grounds. Tourtchaninoff then mentioned a friend named Victor, known as Fizzè, who had a recording studio in the village of Jenins, near the Liechtenstein border, his open-mindedness and left-field approach sparking

Perry's interest. Fizzè was duly summoned to Mireille's home in July, his easy-going manner propelling Perry to Jenins in early August.

Tutored by Mississippi-born blues pianist Eddie Boyd, Fizzè opened Neuchatel's Jazzland club and record shop in 1976 and began working with avant-garde group Débile Menthol in the early 1980s. Then, after launching the Mensch Records label in 1986, collaboration with Swiss reggae group the Heart Beat Band led Fizzè to Jamaica, where he worked with Dean Fraser, Robbie Shakespeare and Scully for the first of his projects titled *Peeni Waali* after the Jamaican term for fireflies, bringing Rico Rodriguez to Switzerland to collaborate with the Heart Beat Band. Fizzè also began working with Linton Kwesi Johnson and Dennis Bovell, developing a long working relationship and close friendship with Johnson.

Fizzè returned to Jamaica in April 1989 to rework the *Peeni Waali* material with Horsemouth, Headley Bennett and others, and when Lee and Mireille made the hour's drive to Mensch House at the beginning of August, Fizzè was still tinkering with it. Since he lived alone, there was plenty of space, and with Perry in the guest room, the pair spent most of the month in the studio, Perry breaking every few days to spend time with his new family and soon making his own way back by train, letting himself into the studio if Fizzè was elsewhere.

Ten stream-of-consciousness songs were on tape by the end of the month, delivered scattergun and largely unconnected.

'It was a rhythm box and a little percussion and loads of overdubs, with samples of animals and machine guns,' said Fizzè. 'It was one thirty-minute reel that just went on, and Scratch was not working on a concept.'

Though the sessions went smoothly, Perry's behaviour could be trying. He insisted that a microphone be placed outdoors to record the sounds of the countryside while they were working, and when Fizzè protested that it would get wet, Perry built a 'shaman's hut' for the device. He would roll around on the ground at random intervals too, and pissed in empty bottles, which he placed at strategic points around the studio.

'I think he's a big con man, a big jester,' said Fizzè. 'He would always take a probe at me and check out just how much I would go for it. Sometimes he would squeeze orange juice over the electric plugs, so I said, "Hey, I don't want no pop star fried in here." I was very provocative with him, so of course we got along.'

With Perry back at home, Linton Kwesi Johnson arrived at Fizzè's in January 1990 to spend some thoughtful days in tranquil surroundings, constructing rough demos for his *Tings An' Times* album, before Perry returned one afternoon at Fizzè's request.

'When I was reintroduced to him by Victor, he acted as if he didn't know who was,' said Johnson, 'so I started to sing "Jane Ann And The Pumpkin", and he said, "Oh, that's why them call you Crazy Johnson, you remember me before I do."'

By the end of the month, Perry felt the ten songs were finished, though they were nothing serious, more an outlet for his creative expression than anything else, so he took the master tapes with him when he returned home in September, only to bury them in the garden.

Before his departure from Jenins, Perry voiced a song for Fizzè after awakening one Sunday morning with a craving for weed.

'At six in the morning, he wake me and say, "Victor, give me something to smoke." Luckily, I knew someone right here, close to Liechtenstein, so we got a piece, and on the way back I explained what Liechtenstein is, the smallest country, and did a little detour just to show him the place. I explained that everyone's been stashing their money there, and when we came back, he said, "Let me voice a track for you now."'

Using 'C'est Loin?' from Dizzi Rieder's *Manoeuvres D'Automne*, 'Licht & Stein' was a comical, half-sung chant about Frankenstein stashing his cash in Liechtenstein, the rhythm stripped to the balafon patterns at its base. Fizzè would later reconstruct the song with Dennis Bovell for inclusion on *Peeni Waali*, released as a limited edition Mensch CD in 1991 and reissued in the US on Shanachie the following year.

By the autumn of 1989, Perry regarded music with great ambivalence. A performance was scheduled at the Mutualité for late November, which was cancelled, and then Perry began to speak of retiring from the business altogether, abandoning music for art. Then, early in the new year, he told Fizzè not to release any of his work, but not because of retirement: instead, he had signed a contract with Island and was mindful of its restrictions.

Perry had sworn vengeance on the company for several years and made defamatory statements against Adrian Sherwood after *Time Boom* but travelled to London to voice a new album with the producer for Island in a typical Perry reversal. He had eventually fallen out with most of his collaborators but would make amends if the offending party demonstrated their loyalty, had been known to swallow his pride if the price was right and had sometimes been swayed by public opinion, as in this instance, according to Perry, though Sherwood's upfront approach made the project less daunting.

From The Secret Laboratory had more complexity than *Time Boom*, melding the core of Jamaican rhythm tracks laid by Style Scott and the Roots Radics at Kingston's Mixing Lab with electronic programming integrated at Matrix by David

Harrow, who began working with On-U Sound in 1989 after playing in Jah Wobble's Invaders of the Heart; Tackhead guitarist Skip McDonald, keyboardist Carlton 'Bubblers' Ogilvie and Akabu were among the other Matrix contributors.

'Working at On-U Sound, I was thrown into the deep end,' said Harrow. 'I'd go up to Adrian's house, we'd have a cheeky quarter-tab of acid to start the day off, and whatever job was coming in, we would do it. Sometimes we were working rhythms from Jamaica, the drummer would come over with a suitcase full of two-inch tapes, and they were all pretty raw. One day Adrian said, "We're going to be doing this Lee Perry album", and Matrix studio was booked, which was the usual home from home, but a lot of the Jamaicans were not really into technology then. Using computers and keyboards sometimes created a bad vibe, so I was asked to come in early and set up a computer, keyboards and sampling stuff, get it comfortable in the room so it wasn't stressing people out. So I set up an Atari 1040, an emulator, an Akai sampler and some of my old Roland gear.'

The blend of computer technology and live instruments is used most effectively on songs such as the exceptionally executed 'Secret Laboratory (Scientific Dancehall)', the opening number that set the tone with its ironic chorus of 'Rocking and reeling and having a ball, swinging and singing, straightjacket and all', as well as 'Inspector Gadget', a playful homage to the animated cyborg that became a stage show mainstay, but there were less successful integrations, such as the techno-dub reconstruction of 'I've Got The Groove', which Island issued as a twelve-inch single, along with average updates of 'Vibrate On' and 'Party Time', to lukewarm reviews.

'I was always trying to bring a bit of techno into On-U, more of a dance attitude and there was a fine line,' said Harrow.

'I had to sneak those rhythms in because the Tackhead guys called it "butt music", but Mr Perry was all for the technology – he loved it.'

Harrow was very inspired by Perry's unorthodox working methods at the sessions.

'Lee Perry had a lightbulb above his head. I'm not a spiritual person at all, but there was this energy about him that I rarely came across. I remember some moments in the studio where it wasn't quite working – people lose interest and wander off, and I remember him coming over and saying, "Don't do it like that, do it like *this*", and the tune turned around and everybody got excited, and then he went back to building his little rock sculptures in the corner. We often had razor blades in the studio, officially for cutting tape, and I remember looking down at the keyboard one day and saw a couple of them placed upright in the keyboard, and he said, "I want to keep you sharp."'

Secret Laboratory definitely had its moments: 'African Head Charge In The Hackney Empire' referenced Perry's drunken performance of July 1988 and 'Seven Devils Dead' his first trip to the UK; he named himself an outer-space alien on 'African Hitch-Hiker', and on the rocky 'You Thought I Was Dead', he castigated Manley and Seaga for their disrespect, but the album's pervasive unevenness resulted from time constraints.

'We spent a year making *Time Boom*, but *Secret Laboratory* was made in ten days,' said Sherwood. 'Island were saying the budget is very small. I think it might have been ten grand and that was to pay Lee, pay Style Scott, pay for the studio and do everything. I didn't make anything on that album and Scratch was pissed off with me because we hadn't finished it. I'm getting all the gyp, but I actually only got paid a £2,200 Akai sampler for producing that album and David Harrow ended up getting the sampler! I really like songs like "Seven Devils Dead", which could have been so much better if we had more time.'

Nevertheless, Island managed to achieve relative commercial success, aided by a striking album cover depicting Perry as the King of Switzerland, though Perry still railed against the album when it was released.

'I am mad about this album because the album mix behind me back, singers singing where they shouldn't be singing, what wasn't my plan . . . Me have me destiny to fulfil, so me fulfil me destiny, but me have a better album than this that me do one year before . . . It won't have 'pon it no Adrian, it will only have mixed by Lee "Scratch" Perry written on it. I asked him if he get some white girls for me to sing with "Inspector Gadget" and he fuck around the plan before it finish, and I won't be pleased of it. I'm fucking mad about it, you understand?'[2]

When the sessions were finished, Perry visited Cleopatra at Waghorn Road and he and Sandra were briefly reconciled, though she chastised him for his abandonment.

Back in Switzerland, Perry made plans to record some new material, and although heavily pregnant, Mireille opened the Conoshimi Institute in Zurich, another centre for humanistic therapies.

Marsha travelled to Switzerland in late January to help with the birth, the daughter that arrived named Shiva Elaine Sharon Perry. Remaining at the household for three months, Marsha was pleased to spend time with her father, but the experience was trying, her difficulty with the language and dislike of cold weather exacerbating her perceived alienation. There was also growing tension with Mireille, who resented the financial support she continued to provide for Marsha and her brothers in Jamaica; a series of arguments caused Marsha to travel to England, where, after a brief visit to a penfriend, she stayed for a few months at Waghorn Road, bonding with Cleo, Sandra and Sharon.

Belgian music fan and executive producer Robert Kuypers, who helped Tony Owens with *Excaliburman*, came to Switzerland to arrange the reissue of Seke Molenga and Kalo Kawongolo's album, having met Kawongolo in Belgium. Kuypers made several return visits in 1990, sometimes bringing journalist Karel Michiels, and re-released the album as *From The Heart Of The Congo* as the sole issue on a label called Jolie Zaire.

Meanwhile, in the spring of 1990, Perry was recording the album *Spiritual Healing* at Powerplay studios, on Lake Zurich's western shore, with members of the band Legal Tender, plus keyboardist Andy Mueller and backing vocalists Myriam Russo and Claudia Boggio, most of the material layering a mutant collage of rock and disco over Black Ark rhythm tracks.

The first songs to surface from the sessions were issued as the *Moonwalk* EP on Black Cat, an independent label run by former Ocean bassist, Higi Heilinger. The A-side, Perry's poppy paean to the gliding steps Michael Jackson adapted from James Brown and Fred Astaire, used a rhythm Mireille built in Jamaica before she met Perry for dub plates voiced by Yellowman and other deejays (apparently inspired by 'Jungle' but sounding closer to J. C. Lodge's dancehall hit, 'Telephone Love').

On the B-side, 'Spiritual Healing' reused Jackie Bernard's 'Economic Crisis' for a contemporary Perry romp on all things spiritual (Collette and Noel helping out with the refrain, 'Lee's coming to save the world'), while 'Cross My Heart Babush' was a disco rant atop 'Lady Lady', relating magical events in England.

The *Spiritual Healing* album, showing a papal-garbed Perry before two Swiss banks on the back cover, had a restructured title track with an alternate vocal, and an alternate 'Babush' aiming powerful farts at the Pope. 'Sex Vibration' was another rocky cut of 'Vibrate On', here inspired by Mireille, as was the lusty excess of 'Sexy Boss', which recounted the history of their relationship. Pablo's 'Lama Lava' was turned into rocking dance number, 'Com'On And Dance'; another vintage rhythm became the scatological sexology of 'Mr Dobberman', and 'Vindetta' an alternate of 'AD Vendetta', created with Steve Marshall in London. Though divided between 'Spiritual' and 'Dance' sides, the true differentiation is the overabundance of pseudo-sexual groaning on side two.

In support of *Secret Laboratory*, Island booked an extensive European tour to commence in April, so Style Scott flew up for rehearsals and the On-U crew was all set to go, but conflict between Perry and Island forced a less costly rethink; Island executive Jumbo Vanrennen proposed an alternate backing band, the Revolution, with Jah Wobble and David Harrow, but in the end, Perry did his own thing, engaging a Black pick-up band and three female backing vocalists for low-key dates in France and Germany in May, the set mixing material from *Roast Fish*, *Mystic Miracle Star*, *Battle Of Armagideon*, *Mystic Warrior*, both On-U albums and *Spiritual Healing*. Further UK dates were secured for later that month, but Perry cancelled them without explanation and fired the band.

For an engagement at the mid-sized Bataclan in Paris on 1 June, following the suggestion of Higi Heilinger, Perry used teen-aged jazz-rock band the Limit, with drummer Lukas Bernays, keyboardist Jeannot Steck, bassist Robin Halley and guitarist Micha Lewinsky (supplemented by Myriam Russo and Claudia Boggio from *Spiritual Healing*), and at the couple of rehearsals they managed with Perry in late May, it was clear that the Limit knew little of reggae and nothing of Perry, which suited him fine, as he wanted to explore new avenues of pop and dance music.

The Bataclan performance almost did not happen because Lee and Mireille missed their flight after quarrelling with airline check-in staff; eventually, he was rushed to the stage to deliver lengthy funk adaptations of 'Introducing Myself', 'Sexy Lady', 'Happy Birthday', 'Jungle' and 'Bank To Bank' before the lights came on and the audience was ejected.

Karel Michiels returned to Switzerland with freelance writer/director Ludo Timmermans to film Perry at home for a documentary video, *The Unlimited Destruction*, released by Jet Star. Though too short and low-budget to capture the essence of Perry's story, his rambling commentary and surreal antics gave a glimpse of his daily life in Switzerland: Perry carries a boulder on his head and assembles abstract, reflective sculpture in the front yard as he declares that he cannot be managed, penalised nor poisoned; he defends Switzerland for its permissive marijuana laws and says that France and Britain will be wiped out through music as he enacts his duty in the Battle of Armageddon, and there is testimony from Doctor Alimantado, Carlton Jackson and Mad Professor.

Cultural theorist John Corbett shot more footage of Perry at home in early July, fuelling his lengthy examination of Perry's oeuvre in the 1994 book, *Sounding Off*.

In October 1990, Lee, Mireille and their children travelled to Montego Bay to relax, but on an excursion to Negril, the couple had their first significant rupture: she confronted him about an infidelity with Sandra earlier in the year, and Perry's denial was unnerving since Mireille believed she had concrete proof of the deed, so she left in a huff back to Switzerland, leaving Perry on his own in Jamaica.

Then Perry went to Kingston, where Niney the Observer proposed a collaborative album for Heartbeat; Chris Wilson, now the company's A&R, came to Jamaica to pay the advance, so the pair got work at Channel One in December, and although the rhythmic core was electronic, select live instrumentation ensured greater textural depth.

Perry painted new messages on the walls at Cardiff Crescent, where it was clear his children were finding it difficult to make ends meet; much of Heartbeat's money helped replace the roof of the house, badly damaged by Hurricane Gilbert.

Marsha had moved back home upon returning from Europe and was scraping a living through hairdressing, but all were short of clothing, with Sean and Omar particularly scruffy. Perry's sons had been trying to make a name for themselves as the Upsetter Juniors through the family link with Caveman sound system, videotaping Caveman dances and co-producing Geritol's anti-drug 'No Stocky Shop' and Nardo Ranks' 'Want Some Money' at Caveman's studio in east Kingston, though the singles failed to land, despite support from former Upsetter Hour radio host, Winston Williams; their own 'Positive Vibration', led by Sean, harmonised by Omar and backed by the Food, Clothes and Shelter band, was also neglected, as was Vicky Nelson's electro recut of 'Lady Lady'.

Perry tried to persuade Vicky to move back to Cardiff Crescent to keep an eye on his children, but this time she refused.

'He was trying to tell me I shouldn't leave the house,' she lamented, 'and then he tells me, "You are the only Black queen I have" and all this stuff, but I'm not in that crap.'

Nevertheless, Vicky agreed to sing backup on *Lord God Muzick*, together with the Upsetter Juniors.

The album's most controversial track was an associative rhyming recut of 'Who Colt The Game' aimed at Bunny Lee, mocking his recent marriage to Annette Wong, implicating him in Slim Smith's death and asking who murdered King Tubby; 'Hot Shit', riding a rhythm previously voiced by Augustus Pablo's protégé, Yami Bolo, was dedicated to Chris Blackwell. Songs like 'Free Us' and its alternate, 'Happy Birthday Marcus', 'Supersonic Man' and the autobiographical 'Angel Gabriel And The Space Boots' worked well enough, but 'Reggae Emperor' was inconsistent and 'Collie Ruler' an inferior 'Real Rock' remake; out-of-place adaptations of older songs broke the continuity, including an 'I Am The Upsetter' update titled 'Lee The Upsetter'.

The weaker tracks were affected by the uptake of booze and herb, as away from Mireille's watchful eyes, Perry got blitzed on Dragon Stout and an overabundance of spliffs. The album ultimately helped to heal their rift, though, especially when Perry gave Omar a cassette of the newly voiced 'Lightning And Thunder Flash', which he dispatched to Switzerland by express mail, its cryptic message cooling her anger and paving the way for Perry's return.

Heartbeat would issue several Perry albums in relatively quick succession: a few months after the release of *Lord God Muzick* in early 1991, the label released *Soundzs From The Hot Line*, an impressive compilation of rare Black Ark and Dynamic recordings taken from Perry master tapes obtained from Alvin Ranglin, who is said to have acquired them as surety for a loan that was never repaid.

Then, in 1992, Heartbeat issued *The Upsetter And The Beat*, twelve of the songs Perry voiced for Clement Dodd in New York and Jamaica, despite the earlier threat of litigation. The concept of Perry adding wit and wisdom to classic Studio One rhythms was an inspired one, but the album felt incomplete, his deliveries intermittently lacklustre. 'Welcome Aboard' kicked things off with Perry warbling atop the Wailers' 'Rudie', his disorienting, off-key ad-libbing at odds with the anthem; Wailing Souls standards 'Back Out With It' and 'Mr Fire Coal Man' fared little better as 'Don't Blame The Baldhead' and the stuttering 'Twiddle With Me', though mutations of 'Freedom Blues' as 'Love Power' and Ken Boothe's 'Just Another Girl' as 'Coming In From The Cold' are unobtrusive and Perry somehow sounded better on Dodd's synthesiser-driven dancehall rhythms, as heard on 'Big Apple Coconut' and 'There Is A Place For Us'.

With *Lord God Muzick* committed to tape, Perry returned to Switzerland, and for much of the coming decades, he and Mireille would divide their time between the two countries, hitting other parts of Europe and further afield when live dates or studio work beckoned, and there were also long periods when family life took precedence and music the backseat.

In the spring of 1991, Mireille attended a UFO conference in Tucson, Arizona, where Vitko Novi recounted the alien abductions that brought him from Peru to the planet Apu in 1960–61, naming Moses, Jesus, Pythagoras, Martin Luther, Karl Marx, Leonardo da Vinci and Robin Hood as among those that originated there; impressed by his story, Mireille licenced a German edition of his book, *170 Horas con Extreterrestres*,[3] published by Lion Star as *170 Stunden mit Ausserirdischen*.

In mid-September, Perry made his Belgian debut at the Leffingeleuren festival with Adrian Sherwood and On-U musicians, taking the stage with his eyes outlined in white paint and a white cross drawn on his forehead, clutching a small red electric guitar, which would soon be covered with glass and other objects, much like the crown on his head. Since Perry had cancelled every previous Belgian engagement during the past five years, the performance was greatly anticipated and the tight versions of 'Roast Fish' and 'Soul Fire' had the rapt audience hollering for more.

'That's one of the best gigs I've ever been to in my life,' said Sherwood. 'I saw about ten people crying at that gig, it was that good, and that band was only Bonjo-I, David Harrow with the computer, Reuben Junior Moses on bass and maybe one guitarist. I had all the sounds, so it sounded like a record, dubbing up exactly in time.'

'Aswad was on the same bill and we blew 'em off the fucking stage, even though Lee didn't rehearse with us,' said Harrow. 'I remember Aswad standing on the side of the stage, watching our little group just mash it.'

Then Lee and Mireille attended an annual spiritualism conference in Basel, where Michael Hesemann was a keynote speaker, at which strange events transpired: first, a healer with a divining rod said that Lee's energy gave her stomach aches and headaches due to the conflicting elements that were mixed up inside him; then, an onlooker approached Mireille to tell her that she had to marry Lee, and Hesemann, standing by a Krishna Consciousness exhibition, agreed: 'Yes, Mireille, marry Lee "Scratch" Perry. We're going to have a big party, Hare Krishna, Hare Krishna.'

Thus, on 30 November 1991, Rainford Hugh Perry and Mireille Rüegg Campbell were married before twelve guests in an intimate ceremony at a Hare Krishna temple in Zurich, Adrian Sherwood acting as Perry's witness.

'I was really honoured,' said Sherwood. 'It was a very spiritual wedding in a Krishna temple – it was incredible, and I had a brilliant time. We went round the lake in a boat with Mireille's friends, and we ended up in this hotel, having a party all night.'

The following months passed quietly, with Perry creating

little music and performing infrequently; spring 1992 live dates included a return to the Mutualité and a gig at Ghent's Vooruit club, using a pick-up band of London-based Jamaicans led by guitarist Renford Bailey, where 'Curly Locks', 'I Am The Upsetter' and 'White Belly Rat' were revived.

In June, Lee and Mireille travelled to Japan with Adrian Sherwood and Dub Syndicate for his first performances on the Asian continent, organised by Australian-born promoter Ray Hearn, with engagements in Tokyo, Osaka and Kyoto, where Lee and Mireille holidayed for one week.

'In Osaka, Lee Perry did the whole gig with a flowerpot on his head, standing on one leg,' said Skip McDonald. 'He had a mirror he'd taken off the wall and was shining the light in the audience, baptising everyone with water.'

After the Tokyo performance, Perry found Mute Beat trumpeter Kazufumi Kodama backstage with a demo tape of *Quiet Reggae*, the debut solo album he was working on for Sony; inspired by two of the songs, Perry agreed to voice them a few days later at a studio called Echo House, located in the thriving nightlife district, Roppongi.

'When he came into the studio, I said, "I am sorry that there is no herb" because I heard he wouldn't work without herb, but he said, "What are you talking about?" and ignored it,' said Kodama. 'He placed many candles around a microphone and lit them, put the Bible on a sheet-music stand, and made up the studio just like his own room, then asked his wife to write down the lyrics he had been preparing and sang them impressively. With the two songs, he produced his own world instantly and he looked happy and relaxed all the time, just like a great master of the art. During the rough mixing, he seemed to want to play the small strange electric guitar he brought along and asked if he could do dub mixing, but unfortunately it was impossible because the master tapes had been mixed in stereo. After finishing the session, he shook hands with me and all the staff and put guitar strings around a duct pipe in the studio before leaving.'

Most of *Quiet Reggae* had trumpet interpretations of mellow grooves popular in Jamaica, such as the traditional 'Greensleeves', Skeeter Davis' 'End Of The World' and Max Romeo's 'We Love Jamaica', but Perry chose to voice Kodama's original work. 'Open Up The Japanese Door' pitted the usual Perry meandering over a melancholy rhythm, and the dance-hall-oriented 'Japanese Rock' employed cheap devices, its simple refrain rhyming rock and clock, trumpet and crumpet; the time constraints rendered an unremarkable result, though Perry's presence was a major selling point in Japan, where his mystique had spawned a considerable following.

'A little crowd was stalking us,' said Harrow. 'They had bags of records and when he signed all their stuff, they were in tears.'

Conditions on the tour were good and Perry loved Japan, particularly the unusual approach to vegetarian cuisine and the respectfulness with which people approached him, though Harrow said keeping Perry off the booze was a challenge.

'I remember at dinner Lee getting a waiter to bring him alcohol and then somebody quietly moving it away and giving him an orange juice instead, and he just sighed and carried on.'

Back in Switzerland, Perry took a long break from music. The most momentous creation was a son named Gabriel Merlin Zay Perry, born in the winter of 1992, around the same time that Mireille opened the Alpha and Omega health and beauty clinic in Zurich. Maintaining a low profile in the months preceding and following Gabriel's birth (just as the Prodigy's 'Out Of Space' was rising in the British charts, riding a 'Chase

The Devil' sample), Perry refrained from making music until the summer of 1993, when he became involved in another problematic project that did not follow its intended course.

At a Zurich music shop that May, Perry recognised staff member Jeannot Steck, the former keyboardist of the Limit, who backed him at the Bataclan three years before. Steck told Perry that he was recording an album with a band called the Roundabouts with drummer Lukas Bernays, with whom he was also making electronic dance rhythms at a small studio called SHS. Perry thus rented SHS to collaborate with Steck, who brought Bernays in to add electronic drumbeats, the duo calling themselves X-Perrymental.

Perry returned to SHS every two or three weeks, voicing dozens of tracks over the summer, some of which would be issued in altered form as *Technomajikal*, an album plagued by miscommunication.

'He and Jeannot decided to make something because Lee was a bit bored and greedy of making new things with new people,' said Bernays. 'We made about twenty or thirty sessions, sometimes with people playing instruments, sometimes with keyboard programmes, and sometimes Scratch just had his microphone and was spelling out his fantasies on the machine.'

Bernays and Steck planned to form a label and booking agency with Lee and Mireille but were disappointed when the pair began their own negotiations with the CBF Management Agency, and X-Perrymental understood that they could not launch this enterprise on their own, so they wrote to former Yello frontman Dieter Meier with details of the project, leading Meier to meet with the pair.

In June 1994, X-Perrymental informed Perry they would rework some SHS material for a limited edition maxi-single, to be released on Meier's Solid Pleasure label, so Perry faxed his consent for three songs to be remixed. In October, Bernays and Steck thus travelled to Meier's Soundproof studio in Malibu, California, where the material was reworked with Austrian engineer/producer Martin Kloiber, gaining sitar, flute and didgeridoo overdubs, but as Meier was busy, the material was left in limbo.

Back in Switzerland, Perry was generally laying low. Besides a return to L'Élysée Montmartre in April with Mad Professor, Perry made few public appearances that year, though he and Mireille were guests on the *Daily Talk-Taglich* television programme, where Perry was uncharacteristically subdued.

Lee and Mireille returned to Jamaica for a few weeks in June, where Don Letts, Rick Elgood and Steve Barrow filmed an esoteric interview with him at Cardiff Crescent for the *Reggae Xplosion* archive project funded by Chris Blackwell, but his brief time in Kingston was far from tranquil.

Marsha was still keeping herself together best and retained the strongest bond with her father. She had recently moved in with her fiancé, a custom auto-builder she met in Canada, at his home on a low-income housing scheme in Portmore, located a bit further west.

In Washington Gardens, P-Son had moved around the corner after his girlfriend became pregnant with their first child and was working sporadically as a road technician for Lloyd Parks' We the People Band, though he still spent much of his time at Cardiff Crescent.

Michelle, who now had a young daughter named Leticia, had moved back home, but Perry demanded she leave Cardiff Crescent after another angry confrontation, so she subsequently moved to Forest Hills during a particularly unsettled period, since Wayne Campbell then emigrated to America, leaving her with three children to care for and little chance of earning enough to support them.

Perry's sons also felt the force of his censure on this brief trip. Although Sean still idolised his father, he was singled out for particular criticism as he was intermittently using crack cocaine. Busted for drugs towards the end of the year, he was rescued from jail by his mother, who returned to Jamaica for the first time in many years just at the moment to make the necessary intervention.

Pauline had long lived apart from Danny Clarke, who had moved to Arizona in 1987. After spending some time in Los Angeles, where she performed as a singer and imported African fabrics, Pauline returned to Jamaica in 1994 to arrange schooling for her two daughters by Clarke, before making London her home in 1995–96, where she made deals with an array of record labels with Perry's material, sometimes providing one label with DAT or cassette copies of master tapes she had previously sold to another, sanctioning unauthorised collections culled from vinyl, and occasionally pressing her own productions using Black Ark rhythms altered abroad.

Although Omar avoided the pitfalls of hard drugs, the tensions that arose during Perry's 1994 visit drew him closer to his mother. He would subsequently obtain engineering experience through an apprenticeship at the eight-track Track Star studio, gaining skills in equalisation working at Boris Gardiner's small sixteen-track facility, and by 1995, he was working at Junior Reid's twenty-four-track studio engineering veterans such as Big Youth and Tyrone Taylor, as well as upcoming artist like Terry Ganzie.

During Perry's mid-1990s dormancy, product continued surfacing in Britain and Europe at an escalating pace, with varying degrees of authenticity. For instance, Dub Syndicate's

1993 release *Echomania* had 'Dubbing Psycho Thriller' and 'Dub Addisababa', grafting previously recorded *a cappella* statements onto new On-U Sound creations.

'The samples we used, they date from the late '80s or early '90s,' said Adrian Sherwood. 'We paid him a bit of money for the usage, and he said, "Cool". Sometimes he says better stuff away from a record than he does on a record, so I'd pick up on ideas, write down things he was talking about, almost interview him and make him enlarge on the idea. I actually have a couple of reels of tape, just *a cappella*.'

VP's *Smokin'* was genuine Perry but omitted that the work dated from 1981. Earl Sixteen's *Phoenix Of Peace*, released by Seven Leaves/Roots Records, was more misleading, as it claimed to be a Black Ark album produced by Perry, but failed to mention that all but one of the rhythms were voiced in London in 1993, without Perry's involvement. Then, Lagoon's grossly mistitled *Lee Perry Meets Mafia And Fluxy In Jamaica* was downright ridiculous; despite its contemporary sound, the album claimed to have been recorded at Bunny Lee's studio in 1976, a decade before the England-based rhythm team ever set foot on the island, at a time when Lee had no studio of his own. Equally absurd was Rhino's *Lee Scratch Perry And The Upsetters Meet At King Tubby's*, which had King Tubby and Prince Jammy dubs produced by Bunny Lee; *Guitar Boogie Dub* was a reissue of Aggrovators guitarist Carl Harvey's *Ecstasy Of Mind* album, which Perry had nothing to do with, and *Lee Perry Presents Gregory Isaacs* reissued *Extra Classic* with retitled tracks.

Creole's Rhino subsidiary continued the onslaught in 1995 with *Lee Perry The Upsetter Presenting Dub*, comprised of Aggrovators dubs and Augustus Pablo material, while *Bunny Lee & The Aggrovators Aggrovate Lee Perry & The Upsetters* had twelve Perry dubs and fourteen Aggrovators dubs, but the Perry tracks were lifted from a badly scratched copy of *Blackboard Jungle Dub*, retitled to suit the release.

As such dubious product continued to flood the market, Perry was anxious to create something new, and when Mad Professor got in touch towards the end of 1994, proposing another Ariwa album, Perry was keen, especially as Prof offered 'a huge advance of several thousand pounds – the biggest I've ever paid anyone.'

Mindful of Professor's penchant for brandy and pretty things, Mireille had a couple of stipulations: no alcohol and no girls.

'Before I came, Professor could give Lee a bottle of brandy, have him sing for many hours and Lee would not even remember, but Professor would just put out things,' said Mireille. 'But suddenly those things couldn't work because I was there observing his plans.'

Lee and Mireille came to London just before Christmas, booking into a Hilton hotel for a long weekend, during which a volume of material was created with Professor and assistants Nolan Irie and William the Conqueror, some of which would be released as *Black Ark Experryments*.

'He come Thursday, finish by Monday,' said Professor. 'Myself, William and Nolan, we put together the basics of those tracks – three guys, none of us you would say are musicians. We sequenced some tracks, and some were played live and then afterwards overdubbed.'

Despite the great haste, *Black Ark Experryments* was the most coherent album in years, arguably better than anything since *Time Boom*, the multi-dimensional rhythms part-computer durability and part-organic roots, a diverse grounding for Perry's flights of fancy.

The outstanding 'Open Door', which became a stage show staple and was issued as a twelve-inch single, spoke of the doors he had opened for many collaborators but closed on insulting upstarts like Bunny Wailer; 'Heads Of Government', which was also often performed live, blasted politicians with shit from Jupiter's toilet pit, and the title track, with its lilting flute, spoke of miraculous phases, from early days crushing boulders in Negril to the Secret Laboratory in Switzerland. Some studio dialogue was audible on the introduction of 'Super Ape In A Good Shape', though potentially libellous insults levelled at a range of former peers was thankfully edited out.

There was plenty of time to graffiti Professor's studio during the sessions, and when everything was done, Perry made a fleeting visit to Cleopatra. Yet, by the time he returned to Switzerland, Professor had already mixed most of dub companion *Experryments At The Grassroots Of Dub*, and though Perry 'turned a few knobs' during the initial mixes, his involvement was minimal. Professor also threw together outtakes for the largely unlistenable *Super Ape Inna Jungle*, an opportunistic collection of unused Perry vocals remixed in the hyper-mechanical 'jungle' style then sweeping London, and further snippets appeared on *Rupununi Safari (Steaming Jungle – The Jungle Dub Experience 2)*.

Then, in January 1995, Perry met with X-Perrymental and Dieter Meier at Meier's Zurich home to discuss their collaborative work. According to Perry, nothing concrete was decided as he and Meier merely exchanged ideas over tea after listening to the reconstructed material, though Meier was struck by Perry's forceful vision.

'It was an extraordinary meeting with a man who had a clear vision of who he was and what he wanted to do,' said Meier. 'He had a hat with various antennae to tune in to the artistic and spiritual vibrations. He seemed to listen but was very involved in his personae and it was as though he was listening from another world. I've never met a guy who seemed to operate on this planet but was so very involved in his own artistic vision.'

Meier later asked X-Perrymental to send further rough mixes made in Switzerland, which were duly provided some weeks later, though Perry was never informed. Martin Kloiber then had Los Angeles-based remix artist Rich Sihilling rework selected tracks, aimed at the hardcore trance and ambient crowd, again without Perry's knowledge, and after a deal with dance label Eye-Q Music fell through, the project was seemingly abandoned again. Kloiber and Sihilling later licenced the unfinished material to ROIR, who released it as *Technomajikal* in June 1997, without authorisation from Perry nor X-Perrymental.

Meanwhile, Mad Professor was putting the finishing touches to *Black Ark Experryments*, and after securing live dates in France and Britain for the spring, he brought Lee and Mireille back to London in late February for rehearsals and for Lee to revoice a few tracks, but the couple's relationship was shaken by a dramatic domestic incident.

After working at Ariwa for a couple of days straight, Perry went out on the town with Nolan and William on a Saturday night, angering Mireille when he returned to the hotel very late. The next day, their argument escalated, until Lee assaulted Mireille in their hotel room.

'He licked me on the head with these long, hard, exercising sticks,' said Mireille. 'You know why? Anytime somebody else come around, Lee wants to play important. He change completely. He's not the same as when he is with me alone, so this argument started. When Lee came back to the hotel, he hit me on the head, and it burst – blood was all over.'

A traumatised, angry Mireille telephoned Professor, but when he arrived at the hotel with assistant Eddie Brown, Mireille had already been taken to hospital by hotel staff, so while Brown went to check on her, Professor took an agitated Perry to Ariwa to calm him down.

Accustomed to high Swiss standards, Mireille was displeased by the overcrowded, rundown hospital, so once she was no longer bleeding, she returned to the hotel to collect her things, taking Lee's passport with her, and after staying overnight in another hotel, flew back to Switzerland the next day.

After a private surgeon assured her the wound was likely to heal itself in time, Mireille sent a fax to Ariwa with a list of harsh personal demands Lee would have to fulfil should he wish to retrieve his passport.

'He was essentially stuck here,' said Professor. 'I put him up in a house I've got at Thirsk Road, across from Ariwa, and ended up babysitting him for about a month.'

Perry continued rehearsing with the Robotics for the dozen French dates, despite his missing travel documents, and was voicing more rhythms with Professor, recording enough to fill two new albums, while slowly trashing his accommodation at Thirsk Road.

Crossing paths with Pauline Morrison, he took her to Sandra Cooley's home to meet Cleopatra, though he would later be furious to learn of Pauline's unauthorised releases, including *Black Ark Almighty Dub: Chapter Three*, which had a few Black Ark rhythms with synthesiser and guitar parts crassly overdubbed abroad.

As the French dates approached and Perry was still without his passport, Professor conceived a way to stealthily spirit him across the border.

'It comes back like a nightmare to me: how do you get

someone into France without a passport?' said Professor. 'We
got him into France, did about fifteen shows in March and
April and got him back into England. He was staying across
the road and I was giving him food and money.'

The French performances were more consistent than usual
due to a previously rehearsed set from which the band never
deviated: along with the Black Ark, Thameside and On-U
favourites, there was 'Open Door' and 'Heads Of Government',
as well as restructured versions of the Staple Singers' 'If You're
Ready (Come Go With Me)' (adapted as 'Come Go With Lee')
and 'Bucky Skank' (blended with 'Poppa Was A Rolling
Stone'); the show allowed for vocal improvisation, but the
revue-style presentation kept a lid on rambling excess, and
when Perry opted for scattered vocal interludes, Professor
would apply a 'doppelgänger' effect to heighten the otherworldly nature of his rants and chants.

After the French dates, Perry somehow made his way to
Switzerland by car with Eddie Brown, only to find that Mireille
had frozen the 30,000 Swiss Francs in his bank account.
Hoping to resolve the situation, they went in person to Perry's
former home, but were chastised and castigated by a ferocious
Mireille, who denied entry, demanding from a balcony that
they disappear immediately.

Once back in London, at the start of April, Perry voiced
a few songs with Akabu and Bubblers Ogilvie at the On-U
Manor, the studio Adrian Sherwood opened in Walthamstow,
east London, though Sherwood was largely absent from the
sessions, which were run by engineer Andy Montgomery and
his assistant, Maggie Apostolu; nothing was completed, and
the songs remain unreleased.

At the end of the month, Perry performed 'One Drop',
'Crazy Baldheads' and 'Roast Fish And Cornbread' with the

Robotics at the Town and Country Club as an unscheduled guest on a benefit concert for the family of D. Elmyna Davis, a Rastafarian film-maker who tragically contracted fatal malaria in Ghana, Perry's unusually sober, calm performance befitting the gravity of the event.

However, the weeks apart from Mireille had thoroughly depressed him, so he continued to destroy the Thirsk Road dwelling as the melancholy weeks dragged on.

'We later spent about £4,000 redecorating,' said Professor. 'Every possible surface was painted – even the light bulbs – with words, drawings, all kinds of things.'

In May, Perry went back on the road with the Robotics, hitting Belgium and Holland for a few live dates, including a performance at the Amsterdam Paradiso where he berated Mireille onstage for abandoning him, yet they were publicly reconciled the next day.

'Scratch was feeling lonely and pissed off, and I guess he missed her as well,' said Professor. 'One night we were in Amsterdam and she called me on my mobile. He was onstage saying not the most pleasant things, and then she called him and they're on the phone about half an hour, and he said, "I sort it out with Mireille." We arranged for her to reach the gig at Tilburg the next day and they had a reunion, and if you hear the two shows it's quite incredible: one night he's saying the worst things about his wife, then he's saying she's the best thing, the only one who could understand. We did another few gigs, and then they went home together, so I guess they resolved all the arguments.'

At the end of the month, Perry headlined the inaugural reggae day of Brighton's Essential Music Festival, receiving a strong audience response, though the presence of U Roy and Max Romeo backstage mildly unsettled him.

An American booking agent arranged US dates for August, which were all cancelled at the last minute because of his outstanding visa problems, the increasing demand showing that public attention was focusing on Perry as never before. The many retrospectives brought a thorough re-examination of his back catalogue, so the brilliance of his innovation was being belatedly acknowledged on a wider scale, and younger, more mainstream artists were referencing him. In July, 'prog-jungle' duo Spring Heel Jack even released a poppy jungle EP titled 'Lee Perry' in tribute to the man's dub techniques, sampling the Reggae Boys' 'Ba Ba', and Perry was increasingly lauded in print, with David Toop's *Oceans Of Sound* following John Corbett's *Extended Play* as notable music theory books to praise him. But the most noteworthy namecheck came on the Beastie Boys' 'Sure Shot', a track on their 1994 release *Ill Communication*: 'Like Lee Perry, I'm very on. I rock a microphone, then I'm gone.'

'All three of us are all really inspired and influenced by Lee Perry's music and production,' said co-founder Mike D. 'I think of it in terms of opening up truly infinite possibilities of sound and music. By manipulating sounds through using the mixing board and every outboard effect and every potential tape speed to achieve sounds you might have in your head, to make those a reality. More than anyone else, he was the example of that for us, though I would say I became aware of his music unwittingly, probably first through the early Bob Marley and the Wailers stuff he did, and in a way from the Clash. I was a big Clash fan when they had that cover of "Police And Thieves", and I later realised he was the guy behind all this stuff. Then Adam Horovitz really got into it and started making a lot of tapes, like "Best Dressed Chicken In Town", and our co-producer, Mario Caldato Junior, is a huge Lee Perry fan, so that of course had an influence.'

Caldato played the group some of Perry's more experimental material, including *Revolution Dub*, and introduced them to Mad Professor, who remixed some of their work in 1991, which remains unreleased.

As their albums became more musically varied, the white rappers diversified their creative activities to form the Grand Royal clothing line and record label, launching *Grand Royal* magazine in 1994 with a debut Bruce Lee cover story; the second issue, published in the summer of 1995, gave Lee 'Scratch' Perry a twenty-four-page spread, the most comprehensive magazine coverage devoted to the man to date, raising Perry's profile in America as never before, the Beasties' sanction of his genius instigating a wave of interest among their young fans.

In Switzerland, time passed uneventfully as Perry took another extended break from the music scene, though an appearance on Channel 4's *Baadasss TV* with rapper Ice-T kept him in the public eye, Perry now sporting punkish purple hair and pierced ears.

The year 1996 began with a renaissance of sorts, as Blood and Fire's lavish reissue of *Heart Of The Congos* placed Perry's Black Ark back in the spotlight, even as fake Perry albums surfaced increasingly (including *Lee Perry Meets Scientist At The Blackheart Studio*, *The Great Lee Perry King Of Dub* and *Scientist Upset The Upsetter*, to name but a few). High-profile performances would take place in Asia, though his personal life would clearly suffer for it.

In mid-January, Lee and Mireille travelled to Hong Kong to launch a tour with Adrian Sherwood and Dub Syndicate, their performance at the Sub Zero club part of series of events that anticipated the territory's control passing back to mainland China the following year. The concert was well received, and afterwards, Sherwood's birthday party was held at a large venue, attended by post-grunge stars the Foo Fighters as well as the Beastie Boys, who were introduced to the maestro for the first time in person, but the event was sullied by a dramatic quarrel that nearly split Lee and Mireille permanently.

Mireille was exhausted and fighting a bad cold, but Lee was reluctant to leave the party, especially since 'there was some girl sneaking around', according to Mireille. After their argument spiralled out of control, with cruel words exchanged, an enraged Mireille bolted, returning to Switzerland on the first available flight, where she filed for divorce and alimony payments.

Meanwhile, Perry flew to Japan to continue the tour with Dub Syndicate, travelling on the same aircraft as the Beastie Boys, for whom Perry would open at a stadium in Kawasaki; though some of the audience grew restless towards the end of his set, Perry returned to the stage to deliver an impromptu rap during the Beasties' 'Sabrosa', much to the delight of the crowd.

Perry played to capacity audiences at Osaka's Club Quattro and Tokyo's Liquidroom, and when the tour was over, Perry crashed at Adrian Sherwood's flat in Finsbury Park, north London, where he had recently moved after a change in personal circumstances, but when Perry buried his expensive television set in the garden, Sherwood suggested he return to Jamaica.

Once back at Cardiff Crescent, Perry was determined to rebuild the Black Ark, despite the mixed emotions he carried for what it came to represent and his acknowledgement that his days behind the mixing desk were over. Sherwood's encouragement acted as the strongest catalyst, prompting Perry to make amends with Omar and pledge to rebuild the studio with him.

In the following weeks, Perry installed new plumbing and had windows fitted, purchasing materials and drawing up concrete plans for the rebuilding of the facility, using revenue from various sources, including the Asian tour dates, as well as Clement Dodd, who had been reissuing his productions in New York.

'Him don't show me the list of the records that he press up, but somebody tell me Dodd was pressing my records in America, and him did get some money towards that and give me, so me take it and buy some materials as I was maybe going to replace the Black Ark studio,' said Perry. 'It was US$8,000 he get, but he have to take a certain percentage, so me take maybe $6,000 and buy materials, bring back money me get in Japan too, and me send to England for money.'

The English funds came from *Voodooism*, the first Black Ark retrospective on Pressure Sounds, which former London Underground frontman Pete Holdsworth began as an On-U subsidiary, a keen antidote to the flurry of bootlegs that continued to surface in Perry's name.

Towards the end of March, Perry flew to London via New York to prepare for more live engagements with Dub Syndicate but was detained on arrival at Heathrow when customs officers discovered some ganja glued to the toe of his boot and seeds in the battery compartment of his foot-long flashlight. This offence usually results in a nominal fine, but the officers decided to release Perry into the custody of Sherwood and Steve Barker after learning he had reached his sixtieth birthday a few days before.

Due to the television incident, Sherwood was reluctant to host Perry, so Mad Professor came after a few days to discuss how On-U and Ariwa could form an alliance to best cater for Perry's needs. Professor then housed Perry for a couple of days at one of his south London properties, but Perry was clearly in low spirits since he greatly missed his family in Switzerland and was resolved to return to them.

Perry was eventually reconciled with Mireille, who retracted her divorce proceedings and allowed him to return home, but she held Adrian Sherwood partly responsible for their domestic woes and made sure that links were severed, so they had no further communication for several years, but Sherwood continued to hold Perry in high regard.

'I understand I got stuck between Lee and Mireille and that's my stupid mistake, but that's neither here nor there. When me and him have worked together, we get on well. I love him, I actually think he's one of the most important music figures of the twentieth century. I can't speak highly enough of him as a talent, and as a man, he's great company, really good fun. I like working with him more than anybody, though he can be awkward as well – but who wouldn't be?'

Perry performed at the Essential Festival with the Robotics in late May, second on the bill below Burning Spear, where, dressed in lurid silver spandex, he shocked the crowd by equating his dick with Jesus, briefly flashing to emphasise the crudeness of the joke.

In the summer, Lee and Mireille returned to Jamaica, where he was filmed at the ruins of the Black Ark for the punk episode of BBC documentary series *Dancing In The Street*, but the earlier construction work had been undone, with many of the materials sold off or stolen, since Sean was feeding his crack habit by any means necessary.

Perry then visited his mother in Hanover, ending an extended period of silence that began when she told him he was crazy after the destruction of the Ark; mother and son had an emotional reunion and siblings Sonny, Sitta, Lloyd and Miss Nell were also pleased to see him. Though now over eighty, Miss Ina was still planting yams and working the bush with a machete, continuing her Ettu displays at the annual Mento Yard festivities, and had even travelled to the USA to perform at a televised event. Perry offered to install plumbing in his mother's home, but Miss Ina could see no need for running water, though she did eventually allow him to supply electricity.

Before leaving Jamaica, Perry again began rebuilding the Black Ark despite Mireille's warning that things were unlikely to proceed as planned if he was absent during the construction. Nevertheless, workmen were hired to clear the space and prepare to lay new foundations, before everything stalled for a lack of funds, leaving the Ark in limbo again.

'I was supposed to travel within that time frame, and when he came, I cancelled everything,' said Omar. 'He said that he's ready to build up the studio, so I decide that I'm gonna stay and give my input and involve myself, to make sure that I was a part of it. He bought some tools and some stuff for the windows, but after he start to build it up, he and his wife reconsulted. He went back to Switzerland and nothing was finished, and after a while, I was a little distraught.'

When several months passed and Perry failed to reappear, Omar decided he had waited long enough and joined his mother in London in November, helping her with *Upsetter Meets The Upsetress In Dub Around The World*, the first of several questionable releases handled by B. B. Seaton's Sprint label; like Fotofon's *Dub-Net Philosophy*, the album had a few Perry rhythms buried under recent guitar and synthesiser overdubs, and some songs would later be retitled for Graylan's *Lee Perry & The Upsetter Meet Scientist At Black Ark Studio*. Omar Perry subsequently accompanied Pauline to a new home in the Gambia, where she based herself after marrying a West African, and during his time there, Omar gained considerable local fame as presenter of the *Roots Rock Reggae Showcase* on Gambia's premier station, Radio One FM, stimulating the shift from singer to toaster as a performing artist.

'I take a trip to the Gambia and I really fell in love with the place as it remind me of Jamaica, so I spent about two or three years there, working on a radio station and organising sound systems,' said Omar. 'In Jamaica, I used to sing with my brother in a group named Upsetter Juniors and when I went to the Gambia it was a bit difficult to do singing, so I end up becoming a deejay.'

Meanwhile, Sean remained at Cardiff Crescent, still dreaming of his father's return. Unable to shake off his crack dependency, he would wander the streets at night like a duppy, begging for change outside nightclubs after smoking the proceeds of the rent collected from a stream of lodgers at the house.

In Switzerland, after a few non-eventful months, Perry proposed a new album with Mad Professor, and although Prof was sitting on plenty of Perry material, he brought Perry to London to set to work at his new twenty-four-track studio near Thornton Heath railway station, ambiguously titled Are We Mad, which was specifically designed for the recording of live instruments, housing much of Professor's older equipment.

'We ended up doing this album *Underground Roots* in about four days and having a bust-up,' said Professor. 'It was wicked roots tracks, all brand new, with a new version of "Curly Locks", but he wanted to take the tapes and finish them in Switzerland, and I didn't want him to take the tapes because it's my studio time and I paid for everything. So he stormed off angry and sent me some strong fax, tell me he's an Obeah man and he'll do this, so I tell him my father's an Obeah man, and I give him the same. I'm from the West Indies as well, so Obeah's not out of the question. I fired him back and then we didn't speak for months.'

To compensate, Professor issued *Who Put The Voodoo 'Pon Reggae*, voiced in the spring of 1995. Thematically similar to *Black Ark Experryments*, the album was another stream-of-consciousness experience, with Perry striving to express the minutiae of his world vision over electronic rhythms. He saluted his newfound Japanese popularity on 'Megaton Bomb', warned romantic rivals on 'Don't Touch My Shadow', spoke of his bad habits on 'Messy Apartment' (naming himself as Selassie's twin), and made oblique references to Mireille on several songs, notably 'Go And Come Back'. However, much of the rambling lacked focus and no song was truly outstanding, though the album evidenced a certain musical continuity, with several finely constructed rhythms.

Back in Switzerland, as the children were growing fast, in early 1997 the family moved to a larger property in a village atop a mountain in the middle of the country. The new home was spacious and warm, with fantastic views of the surrounding valleys, and as before, the expansive basement allowed Perry the space to exercise his artistic compulsions without fear of affecting anyone else with his mess.

Island was preparing its high-profile *Arkology* box set, the material taken from original master tapes, with many songs previously unreleased, and got in touch to request Perry's consent, so after some haggling over money, Perry travelled to London to conduct a high volume of press interviews. He was filmed by Don Letts and Rick Elgood for Island, who mixed the footage with archive material for their thirty-minute documentary, *The Return Of The Super Ape*, and made a guest appearance on the mike at Talvin Singh's Anokha club night, held at the fashionable Blue Note in Hoxton, east London. *Arkology* was released in July to critical acclaim and remains one of the finest Black Ark compilations.

Mad Professor was able to heal the rift by engaging a lawyer to sort out Perry's US visa problems, leading to his west coast debut at San Francisco's Maritime Hall in April, where Perry performed two nights in a row, backed by the Robotics, with Eddie Brown on bass, Black Steel on guitar, Sinclair Seales on drums and Noel 'Fish' Salmon on keyboards.

On the opening night, Perry mounted the stage at eleven, bearing candles and incense, full of energy and roaming the stage, and after a midnight break for a costume change, he returned for the better part of an hour, much to the delight of the crowd. The set included an extended 'Roast Fish And Cornbread' with Perry on bicycle horn, and an adaptation of 'I Shot The Sherriff', highlights from the second night later released as *Live At Maritime Hall*.

Back in Switzerland, Perry was anxious to cut new material, so he went to see Fizzè, who was now living with his wife and son in Weite, a few miles from his former home; at his twenty-four-track digital home studio, Fizzè was working on *The Return Of Peeni Waali*, with contributions from Horsemouth, Chinna, Studio One keyboardist Pablove Black, and the London-based Steve Gregory, John Kpiaye and Michael 'Bammie' Rose, as well as Georgie Fame and Taj Mahal. Determined not to repeat the folly of their earlier sessions, Fizzè supplied Perry with some opening lyrics for an oompah/ska hybrid called 'Nice Time', on which Perry narrated a firefly's journey 'from the cockpit of Peeni Waali', the rest of the lyrics improvised.

Perry returned to the Mensch studio several times over the ensuing month to work on his own material, experimenting with Fizzè's hip-hop rhythms, but when he asked Fizzè to construct something for a ballad, the note dispatched with a rough mix requesting 'sensible lyrics' from Perry caused offence, prompting him to abandon the project, Mireille later informing Fizzè that Perry was tired of collaborating with humans and wanted to only work with machines.

Nevertheless, in May, Mad Professor brought him back to London to voice *Dubfire* over a few days, released on Ariwa the following year, excavating chestnuts from Perry's back catalogue for mutative purpose. Though the listener could never predict where Perry's ramblings would lead, the album veered dangerously close to self-parody, as heard in his fake baby cries on the title track and the excessively filthy delivery that spoiled the new 'Doctor Dick'. Similarly, cracks at 'Place Called Africa', 'Soul Rebel', 'Satisfy My Soul' and 'Duppy Conqueror' were pale comparisons, though the new lyrics were certainly original, with 'Favourite Dish' here describing magic powers employed to Obeah the Devil.

In June, Perry and the Robotics travelled to New York to perform at the second Free Tibet benefit concert held at Randall's Island, staged by the Milarepa Fund, a non-profit organisation co-founded by Beastie Boy Adam Yauch, working to free Tibet from Chinese occupation, where Perry took the stage draped in an American flag with a hat made of currency, his hair a streaky pink-blond mix.

In late July, Perry performed at the Fuji Rock Festival with Mad Professor, held at a ski resort on the side of Mount Fuji in Japan; backstage, Perry and Horace Andy, who was there with Massive Attack, murmured dark prophecies on the wrathful nature of God as the elements unleashed their fury in the shape of Typhoon Rosie, giving such a battering that the second day's events were cancelled.

Perry and the Robotics then returned to London to headline the Roots Day at the first Essential London Weekender, held at Finsbury Park, where Perry was distracted and delivered a poor performance, followed by select European dates.

In the autumn, Perry and the Robotics began a month-long tour of North America, delivering nineteen performances, beginning at the 9:30 Club in Washington DC, followed by three nights at New York's Wetlands. The Beastie Boys were then working on a new album with Mario Caldato in a makeshift studio in the basement of Sean Lennon's office in Greenwich Village and asked Perry if he was willing to voice a rhythm they had built some years earlier, led by an Upsetters-style organ and peppered with Nyabinghi beats. Unlike anything else the group ever issued, the rhythm was reminiscent of 'Mr Brown' and perfectly suited for Perry.

After a brief meeting at the World Trade Centre Hilton, Perry was ready to roll, but as it was Adam Horovitz's birthday, Horovitz and Mike D were otherwise engaged, so Yauch and Caldato brought Lee and Mireille to the studio, where Lee transformed the rhythm into 'Dr Lee PhD'.

'It was great,' said Perry. 'Everything was good because they want to be a part of what I do, and they deal with me reasonable, like me dealing with myself, so me want to give them full support.'

According to Caldato, Perry got into his poetic flow as soon as the tape was rolling.

'Before we started he went to the mixing board, put his hands on top of it and banged his head on it a couple of times, blessing it. He had a poster of the gig in his pocket with his lyrics already written on it, and after about thirty seconds of listening to the track, he said, "OK, let's record this." Then he said, "Let's do it one more time", he did it better and that was it. Then he goes, "Give me a background track again", and he did two background tracks with cow sounds and coughs and they were great. Then I said, "Lee, I love the way you play percussion on your old recordings", so he got maracas, tambourine, cowbells, and chucked them on the floor in front of the mike and said, "OK, let's go." There was this picture of Bruce Lee in front of the console and after we finished the session, I said, "Can I post you up there? I'll put you up with Bruce Lee", but he said, "I-man no go next to a Chinee man, put me on top", so we put his picture on top. He said, "Make sure it doesn't come down for a long time."'

Perry needed to make a swift exit to deliver his final Wetlands performance, but the Greenwich Village Halloween Parade made it impossible for a taxi to reach him. Lee and Mireille thus headed to Wetlands with Caldato and Yauch by subway, the costumed revellers allowing Perry to blend naturally with the crowd.

'It was the one night of the year that Lee Perry could walk down the street and nobody would give him a second look,' said Mike D. 'His clothes had mirrors all over them, painted everywhere. Every potential surface was covered with something, but no one gave him a second look.'

Later, Perry made his Canadian debut at Toronto's Phoenix Concert Theatre, followed by Detroit's Majestic and a memorable evening at Chicago's Cubby Bear Lounge, where fans bowed down in prayer before the stage, and there were performances in Colorado and throughout the west coast, ending at San Francisco's Maritime Hall.

During the quiet period that followed the tour, Perry discovered the unofficial Lee Perry website Eternal Thunder, established by disc jockey Mick Sleeper of Edmonton, Canada, in August 1996. The site's engaging visual presentation and textual pizzazz made a strong impression on Perry, who contacted Sleeper through an intermediary to address the world via two telephone interviews. The first, conducted in December 1997, had Perry waxing lyrical about why he abandoned reggae, alluding to conflicts with Sean and industry associates of the past; he claimed to be building a White Ark and said he would no longer perform with Black musicians. Then, after Lee and Mireille decamped to Jamaica for the Christmas holidays, Sleeper conducted a second telephone interview in February 1998, elucidating candid comments on various artists.

Perry's extensive touring with the Robotics continued during the spring, beginning with live dates in France in April in support of *Dub Fire*, the highlight an appearance at the Spring Festival in Bourges, where Perry performed to a crowd of 5,000 on a bill shared with Linton Kwesi Johnson. Then he and the band headed to Eugene, Oregon, to kick off a fifteen-date US tour concentrating on the west coast, the highlights including returns to San Francisco's Maritime Hall and Cubby Bear in Chicago (again with praying fans before the stage), and two final nights at New York's Wetlands.

At Seattle's Fenix Underground on 25 April, Clinton Fearon came backstage to pay his respects.

'I reminded him who I was, and we were excited to see each other again, as it had been maybe fifteen years or more since I last saw Scratch,' said Fearon. 'Scratch said to everybody, "This is a bad bass player. He come from the hills, from nowhere, come play several hits like "Curly Locks", and I tried to correct him and say it's "Roast Fish And Cornbread", but he was still saying "Curly Locks". At one point him turn to his wife and say, "Give him fifty dollars for me", then him scratch him head a bit and said, "OK, give him a hundred." She wrap up some bills and put them in my hand and I thought it was a hundred bucks but found out later it was just fifty bucks, so now I can say I got fifty dollars in royalties from all those past works! I don't know what happened to Scratch, I heard all kinds of different stories. At one point he was actually walking around as though something had really happened to him in the head, which left everyone thinking that Scratch was mad. But in those same times, I happened to talk with Scratch and Scratch was sound to me. I thought maybe Scratch was covering something up, or intentionally fooling the public. I always think that Scratch is more of a genius than a madman.'

After the US tour, Perry played the Essential Roots All-Dayer on 25 May, this time at the Brixton Academy, which was overcrowded, dirty, dimly lit, with poor sound quality and so overbooked that many artists had their sets cut drastically short, most notably an ailing Augustus Pablo, who was dragged offstage after only a few songs, and Perry's performance was also lacking since he yelled more than sang on most numbers, though two 'trip-hop' styled rhythms proved popular with the audience.

In the summer, Perry and the Robotics returned to the US, giving a notable performance at San Francisco's famous Fillmore venue, where he told the audience that 'Jesus was a hippie', baptising the electrical wires onstage before 'War In A Babylon'. He appeared at the Reggae on the Rocks festival in Morrison, Colorado, before playing Reading Festival in England, sharing the bill with the Beastie Boys, who had just released *Hello Nasty*. After other summer performances in Holland, Perry and his family lingered for a brief vacation, as was often the case during tours of Europe and North America.

In September, Lee and Mireille returned to Montego Bay, and after relaxing for a time, Perry went on to Kingston where he renewed his links with Clement Dodd, who was back on the island following his mother's death. Dodd was in the process of refurbishing Studio One, so Perry frequently visited him at Brentford Road, where King Stitt, the Silvertones and Winston Jarrett were often present.

At the end of the month, Perry kicked the lodgers out of Cardiff Crescent. He had come to rebuild the Black Ark but understood the work could not be completed while Sean lived there and persuaded his errant son to move on.

Despite attending a drug treatment centre in Half Way Tree, Sean had not been able to break his addiction and continued to live a problematic life, his arm slashed by a tenant in a fracas at the house shortly before his father's arrival. To demonstrate his loyalty, Sean dyed his hair a similar shade of orange, but the gesture failed to impress Perry senior; nevertheless, a tenuous peace was established, so Perry again issued directions to construction workers once Sean vacated the premises, and Jah Ned was appointed guardian of the property.

Marsha had married her fiancé in March and was continuing her hairdressing, but when she visited her father at Cardiff Crescent one afternoon, he was guarded and reserved.

Michelle continued to avoid Perry because of all the past upheaval. Unable to support herself in Kingston, she had placed her children in the care of others – including Marsha, who took charge of Lassano – and travelled to Grand Cayman in 1996 to work as a hotel hairdresser, returning to Kingston a few months before Perry turned up at Cardiff Crescent, trying to raise enough money to travel to the Turks and Caicos Islands for work.

After engaging builders and issuing instructions, Perry returned to Switzerland, where he soon discovered that Jet

Star had released a box set of Black Ark rarities, *Lost Treasures Of The Ark*, the material obtained from Pauline, including Marley's 'Who Colt The Game' and 'I Know A Place'; a furious Perry confronted Carl Palmer by telephone, prompting Palmer to cut Pauline out of the deal and begin making payments to Perry.

In mid-February 1999, Perry spent a week relaxing in Orlando with his family before launching the 'Fat American Tour' with the Robotics, covering thirteen dates in two and a half weeks, mostly concentrating on the east coast. Notable engagements included gigs at Chicago's House of Blues, where Perry exposed himself onstage despite the cold weather, and a return to Irving Plaza. Then Perry went to Kingston for a few weeks to oversee the rebuilding of the Black Ark, though progress was at a snail's pace.

Back in Switzerland in April, Perry considered a new touring band with Family Man, but changed his mind after a CD Fams sent him jammed his CD player. In early May, Trojan executives arrived, proposing an 'all inclusive' contract that would give them control of the recordings he produced between 1967 and 1980, aside from material assigned to Island, as well as select 1980s material covered by an earlier agreement; in addition to a significant upfront payment and a monthly retainer, the deal appealed to Perry because the executives proposed to put an end to the ceaseless stream of illegitimate releases, so he would sign the paperwork in June, leading to a comprehensive reissue programme by the company.

In mid-May, Perry returned to Jamaica to spend another three weeks supervising construction at Cardiff Crescent, reportedly spending over US$30,000 on this last attempt, to little avail. P-Son installed some outdoor fish tanks and an area for turtles, but that was about it; although Perry insisted he was building a studio in which he would produce pop music, Mireille began suggesting that the space could be used for a museum or some kind of 'holy house'.

Perry later said the unfinished edifice was a 'seat of power' he was obliged to construct, due to his destruction of the original.

'I'm going to buy another house for myself, because what I rebuild, I won't be living there. Because I burn it down, I overstand that I was wrong. I couldn't take those people, what those guys want me to take, so I say I commit a sin and burn down the Ark, so I am out there now, working to rebuild back that Ark. It looking to a movie or film house because the film was filming from the beginning of time. God did make the original film and whosoever here to play the part, we play it now and me reach Revelation which is the Judgement. Me know me working for God, but other people working for money or working for the Devil. So it won't be a recording studio, it will be a government to rule the world, the universe, the globe, and the equator straight from there with rain, thunder and lightning, hailstone, brimstone and fire, hailstone and ice and smoke, with the blood of Jesus — with Jesus Christ's bloodbath.'

Back at home in Switzerland, Perry was visited by the Berlin-based director Volker Schaner, who had worked on Peter Fleischmann's award-winning documentary *Deutschland, Deutschland* (about Germany's reunification), and his Israeli counterpart Guy Leder, who had edited Sharon Shamir's *Peace By Piece* (about a Jordanian political satire). The idea was for Perry to appear as a messiah who triumphs over evil in a feature film the pair scripted, *The Revelation Of Lee 'Scratch' Perry*, and hours of footage was filmed for it during this initial meeting over the course of four days.

Then Perry embarked on a twelve-date North American tour with the Robotics, starting at Wetlands in mid-June. Highlights included a ninety-minute performance at Boston's Roxy, where Perry was clad in military garb, a prime slot at the Sierra Nevada World Music Festival, held in remote woodland, and an appearance at Vancouver's Sonar. There was also a triumphant return to Fuji Rock in late July, this time with Jerry Lyons on guitar.

For an appearance at the Hove Festival in September, Perry and Professor revamped the Robotics with Etienne 'Spider' Johnson on drums, Mark Downie on bass and Richard Doswell on keyboards and flute; initially dubbed 'the Robotics II', they were soon called the Silicon Squad and, ultimately, the Kill-a-con Squad. The band then backed Perry on his highly successful debut appearances in New Zealand and Australia, performing to capacity audiences at Auckland's Logan Campbell Centre and Wellington Town Hall, delivering two nights at Melbourne's Corner Bar and the closing set at Sydney's Metro. Then, in October and November, Perry and the band embarked on a twenty-one-date European tour that took in France, Holland, Switzerland and Scandinavia.

In December, Volker Schaner reappeared with a rough trailer of *The Revelation of Lee 'Scratch' Perry*, bearing the tragic news that Guy Leder suffered a fatal epileptic fit in July, and although *The Revelation* had been derailed, Schaner and Perry recorded an album together during this visit, which remains unreleased.

'I brought an eight-track Tascam, which we had discussed, and Lee had a Roland 808 or something similar and we recorded six songs during one intense night,' said Schaner. 'The most remarkable was "Cool Walk", a forty-five-minute epic about life and family, a really fantastic song that he especially liked, and there was a potential hit called "No Satan No".'

As the twentieth century drew to a close, Perry contemplated the future, and when asked about his intentions, issued the following statement: 'A message: I'm going to reorganise Africa with my music government. In England, I must caput the Queen, caput the taxes, rebuild African government, and show them in Jamaica who me responsible for. An eye for an eye and a tooth for a tooth, the law of Moses: You be good to me and I'll be good to you, you be bad to me and I'll be extremely bad to you – if you be wicked to me, I'll be wickeder to you. The Upsetter presents the end of the Heads of Government because the 2000 is here, and I represent the year 2000. I come before my time and they respect me. For the future, I see that Jesus Christ is Black and God is also Black, so the Pope and the Bishop wrong: Jesus Christ wasn't white, so I black the future of all the politicians and all the governments – black it with the Black Ark. I black the future as Superman, Super Ape. Me no have no mercy anymore, I'm cold as ice. When the children must exist, children don't exist in fear, so you have to upset them and when them rediscover the spaceship, they will see it is the Ark of the Covenant and the right solution. Let people know what is going on: I am here to prove that God is Black, and that Jesus Christ is Black, that's why I'm here with the Black Ark. The game blocked, cannot be opened after me. Lee "Scratch" Perry is in God's spaceship.'

CHAPTER FOURTEEN

Jamaican E.T.:
Belated Recognition in the
New Millennium

The year 2000 began in fine fashion with capacity performances in Osaka, Yokohama and Tokyo, the restructured Robotics comprising drummer Gary Williamson, bassist Earl 'Broadfinger' Francis and Spider on keyboards, mostly showcasing *Techno Party*, which Perry finished voicing in London soon after.

The album blended ancient and modern as Professor tastefully fused Perry's histrionics to trance, jungle and trip-hop rhythms, partly based on classic reggae, Perry returning to the mixing desk himself for the first time in aeons. The outstanding title track, a Goa-trance update of 'Punky Reggae Party', had an accompanying video of Perry in the Swiss mountains, which was aired on MTV and VH1; 'No Dreads' was a bass-heavy reconstruction of 'Who Colt The Game', and 'Having A Party' similarly reworked 'I Know A Place'; 'Mr Herbman' launched headlong into trip-hop, weaving reverberating drum-and-bass loops around Perry's menacing threats; 'Come In Dready' was a deep house number based on a James Brown sample, and rap-influenced 'Crooks In The Business' relegated unscrupulous industry personnel to the firing squad.

Other Ariwa voicings from this period would surface as 'Twisted' on ex-Prodigy member Leeroy Thornhill's *Flightcrank* EP, released in June, and Mission Control's 'The Last Trumpet', the latter on Alan McGee's post-Creation Poptones imprint the following February, the link stemming from Control member Kate Holmes (McGee's wife), who blew flute at Ariwa some years prior.

Being perpetually on the road with constant changes of scenery brought welcome distraction from the demons, and in live performance, Perry was repeatedly lifted by the crowd's youthful energy on any given night, the endless adoration a belated vindication of his talents, as well as a soothing ego-stroker. However, Perry's ire was frequently raised when things were not to his liking or when perceived slights caused undue offence, often precipitating dramatic outbursts. For instance, when Perry's brief US tour kicked off at Santa Cruz's Palookaville in February, he found that a dreadlocked Jamaican-American guitarist had joined the Robotics at the promoter's request, sparking an onstage Upsetter tongue-lashing the following night at Eureka's Club West, which forced his removal.

Of the ten other dates to fulfil on the west and east coasts, the last three were cancelled at short notice after conflict with the promoter, causing Perry to head to Jamaica on his own to decompress, following the latest mini-break-up with Mireille, though things were soon smoothed over.

Crossing the Atlantic at regular intervals allowed Perry to live contrasting realities, indulging his various compulsions in starkly different settings. Most of the time, Perry enjoyed the anonymity of living in a remote Swiss village, and the tranquil setting quieted the mind, his ultimate outsider status shielded by hermit-like tendencies, since he was often ensconced in his workspace on his own; being in Jamaica allowed him to reconnect with his roots and to reaffirm the essence of his being, so long as he could avoid the peers of the past who had disparaged him and taken him for granted.

Yet, flitting between two countries when not on the road gradually widened personal fissures, and proclamations of the period reveal a divided soul with a shattered identity. Perry was still duty-bound to inform the world that God was Black and Jesus too, but the former adherent of Black supremacy now called his very Blackness into question, since his adoring fans were almost exclusively white, and the perceived tormentors Black Jamaicans.

'Me no want to know those people anymore because me no owe Jamaica any favour,' Perry insisted. 'It remind me that when them fall in the pit, not to help them again. Honestly, I am having a black colour but I'm not Black, and if you want to put that in the book, you can put it. I have black skin, but I have a white heart. I don't owe Black people nothing at all whatsoever.'

In April, Trojan released *On The Wire*, the 'lost' follow-up to *Battle Of Armagideon*, which had moments of brilliance despite an unbalanced mix and several obviously unfinished tracks. There was the extended 'Exodus' with the barking dog, the long, baffling 'For Whom The Bell Tolls', a recut of 'I Am the Upsetter' and a new mix of the Arkwell 'Keep On Moving' with baby Cleopatra's bawls, but 'Seaside (Mystic Mirror)' sounded off-kilter and 'Buru Funky' half-baked. Worse still, the title track was the Arkwell 'Jungle' version with Perry's drunken overdub and 'The Grim Reaper' an alternate 'Train To Doomsville'.

Perry travelled to Finland in early July for a couple of performances with Spider, Gary and bassist Ted Collins, though Professor had conflicting engagements, so saxophonist Derek Litchmore tackled the mixing. The following week, they returned to Brighton's Essential Festival with Prof, where Perry's performance was lacklustre, and then delivered better sets at sold-out events in London, Bristol and Glasgow.

In September, shortly before the release of *Techno Party*, there were September dates in the American southwest with Prof and the band, including an appearance at Tucson's weed-themed Grassroots Affair, followed by an enchanting desert excursion with Mireille in search of UFOs, the professed interstellar communication granting another energy boost and mood lifter. And after a triumphant return to San Francisco's Maritime Hall, the gig at the John Anson Ford Theatre in East Hollywood, featuring Scientist, was attended by rock maverick Perry Farrell of Jane's Addiction, himself a long-standing Perry fan.

The tour rolled through Europe in October in live dub mode, beginning with a rapturous performance to a capacity crowd in Lisbon, where Perry offered a few confounding pearls, both onstage and at the press conference.

'If you look into the alphabet from A to Z, you will see L is for Lee, L is for light, L is for love, and L is for the Lord. S is for the sky, and S is for shit and for ships. P is for power and the pyramids, and I am the pyramid and the power.'

October performances in the UK and France were also sold-out, and after another revitalising sojourn in Jamaica, Perry played well-received gigs in France and Holland in December.

Then, at the live dub performance given at Berlin's Pfefferberg Theatre during the later European leg, Perry spotted Volker Schaner in the audience and summoned him backstage by repeatedly chanting, 'Volker, come to me, I need help!' during his performance.

'At first, I didn't realize what he was saying, cos I was standing in the crowd with a girl,' said Schaner. 'But then I understood, so I went backstage, where we even gave an interview together. So I kept going to Switzerland every six months, and sometimes more often, and always I filmed, mostly alone with him in his studio there.'

The film project was thus reactivated in a new form, with Schaner slowly gathering footage (often capturing the maestro at work on material that would never be issued), and ultimately giving him another platform on which to express himself.

The 2001 touring schedule continued in much the same vein, with international engagements interspersed with relaxation in Jamaica and Switzerland. In March, there were ten band-less US dates, Professor's dub backing utilising custom DATs, keeping costs to an absolute minimum. More performances took place in Scotland in April and Switzerland in May, the Robotics backing a riveting set at London's Ocean, with Black Steel now in the band, and later that month, Perry made his debut in Israel at a Tel Aviv warehouse with the three-piece Robotics/Sane Inmates, promoted by reggae specialist Guil Bonstein, who enhanced Perry's visitor experience through guided tours of local sights.

After more live dates in Europe in June, Perry travelled to Dublin to appear in six Guinness commercials, directed by Zak Ové (son of pioneering Trinidadian-British film-maker, Horace Ové), pontificating on alien abduction, telepathic meditation, time travel and world peace. But did endorsement of an alcoholic beverage equate to selling out? Dalí comparisons seemed increasingly appropriate.

Perry then travelled to California for select dates, including a glorious headline performance at the Sierra Nevada World Music Festival, held in a Gold Rush town in the Sierra Foothills, and he was photographed backstage at the Galaxy Theatre in Santa Ana wearing only stars-and-stripes socks, ankle bracelets and a wicked grin for *Vanity Fair*, the front-cover placement indicative of his growing mainstream kudos.

In August, Perry wowed the 50,000-strong crowd at the Witnness festival, held at a Dublin racecourse, and topped the One Festival at San Francisco's Maritime Hall, where he shared the bill with guitar comrade Ernest Ranglin, dancehall star Buju Banton, and Senegalese reggae stalwarts, Toure Kunda.

Then came the horrific destruction of the World Trade Centre on 11 September, which wreaked havoc on the Western world, just as Perry was set to begin another American tour. He performed at SOB's in Manhattan not long after the attack, as New York was gripped by drastic tensions; air travel within the US became noticeably more problematic and the few live dub performances given were largely unfocused, resulting in refund demands.

Things had improved by the time Perry reached the west coast in October. He sold out venues in San Francisco and Los Angeles, where Scientist and Errol Dunkley visited backstage, and headlined the opening of the Island Revolution exhibition at the Experience Music Project in Seattle with Scientist, the Fully Fullwood Band, Mikey Dread and Adrian Sherwood, though backstage bickering soured the atmosphere, rendering his performance under par.

Perry returned to London in November to conduct publicity for *Jamaican E.T.*, released by Trojan the following February. The previous June, Trojan had been acquired by Sanctuary, the world's largest independent label, for a record-breaking £10.4 million, so Perry's back catalogue was now controlled by the company, who retained links with Trojan's former administrators during a lengthy changeover period,[1] the former

Trojan head continuing to provide administrative support to Perry through limited company, Lee Perry Productions.

Jamaican E.T. was produced by Coventry-based Roger Lomas, who cut the Selector's 'On My Radio' and other hits by 2Tone artists such as Bad Manners and the Bodysnatchers. He drafted ex-Style Council guitarist Anthony Harty, Fresh For Lulu drummer Al Fletcher, Hammond specialist Justin Dodsworth and session saxophonist Leigh Malin, along with Sharron and Michelle Naylor (who had worked with Roy Wood and Fairport Convention) on backing vocals. The album makes for challenging listening: though the rock-oriented backing is competent, the music is incidental wrapping to layers of impenetrable Perry vocals, in places so thickly encrusted as to be incomprehensible. A disjointed recut of the Staples Singers' 'I'll Take You There', ersatz reggae 'Babylon Fall' and funky numbers 'Holyness, Righteousness, Light' and 'Love Sunshine, Blue Sky' suggest bright optimism, yet Perry's multi-tracked vocals cast a long shadow. 'Hip Hop Reggae' featured neither genre, with funk leanings beneath Perry's ironic rap, while 'Telepathic Jah A Rize' and 'Evil Brain Rejector' are soups of Perry platitudes. Two and three-star reviews were the norm.

In the midst of the recording sessions, Perry was detained under anti-terrorism legislation. He always transformed his environment through sculpture, elaborate totemic objects often incorporating electrical equipment, but these were potentially dangerous to display in the aftermath of the World Trade Centre attacks, especially as the British government under Tony Blair was helping George W. Bush to pressure Saddam Hussein. Perry had placed a 'Do Not Disturb' sign outside the door of his room at the Hilton before travelling to Lomas' studio, but police were called when a cleaner found her face displayed on the television screen, the wires from

Perry's video camera wrapped around a plastic gun, causing the hotel's evacuation.

'The police sent four armed SWAT officers to the studio,' said Justin Dodsworth. 'There was quite a bit of hashish being consumed, and literally the second a large plume of smoke was exhaled, and the bong pipe placed on my keyboard, the door got kicked in and the officers burst through, pointing guns at us. They barged past me and said, "Mr Perry, I'm arresting you under the Terrorism Act", or words to that effect.'

'There was one big commotion about it, but it nah hurt me,' said Perry. 'You should know, if you listen to the CD, not to blame Saddam Hussein – they're looking in the wrong direction. All the facts are on the CD and them solve it in England with the police at the Hilton hotel. Them take me to the station and lock me up, take away me money and think I have a boom, say we's terrorists, but them couldn't take me to court. I have my work to do here, and I don't want to be disturbed.'

Touring recommenced in December 2001 with a rocky start as Perry, decked out in a Superman suit, was denied entry to Slovenia with no visa. The Sane Inmates then backed him on four shows in Germany and a return to London's Ocean, and the following month, Perry played Lucerne and Neuchatel with his children in tow, along with Wendy, the family au pair, but their presence did not stop him from exposing himself onstage, now an embarrassingly regular occurrence.

The Neuchatel gig took place at the Case à Chocs night-club, where DJ Startrek, a musician, disc jockey and osteo-path otherwise known as Thomas Lautenbacher, was resident engineer. Startrek mentioned an electronic rhythm he thought Perry could voice, which he unveiled on a laptop at Perry's hotel the next day, and Perry suggested he get back in touch once there was enough for an album.

In mid-February, Perry was summoned to Brighton by the executives behind *Jamaican E.T.*, now running a revitalised Secret Records, for a one-off performance at Concord 2, backed by the album's featured musicians, which would be issued on DVD the following year as *The Ultimate Alien* (with a bonus Perry interview, conducted by Dave Hendley).

Then, with Black Steel back in the Sane Inmates/Robotics, Perry hit France and Italy in April, sharing the bill with Mikey Dread and Max Romeo at a huge venue in Annecy, though Romeo was snubbed when duetting 'War In A Babylon', Perry totally ignoring him onstage. Mad Professor issued *The Truth As It Happens*, a live album culled from the best recent performances, as new bookings brought Perry to Greece and Yugoslavia in May, and in the middle of the month, DJ Startrek travelled to Perry's home to conduct his first voicing session.

Perry spent most of the summer of 2002 in Jamaica, his weeks in Kingston reigniting old grudges with Clement Dodd. He was given a Lifetime Achievement Award at the annual 'Tribute To The Greats' on 10 August, but as Dodd's associates were behind the event, which was sponsored by a liquor company, Perry boycotted it, leaving P-Son to collect the award on his behalf.

'I don't know what it means, but it don't mean anything to me,' said Perry. 'It seems like it was a trap, like them want to use me, and why didn't they give me an award before? If you look 'pon it you will see "J. Wray and Nephew", a white rum affair. Them give me an award from the death squad, a present from the people who worship dead, but I am worshipping the living. I used to drink rum and eat meat, but I put those things away. Then I see myself reincarnate and if people are eating dead meat, the present that them give me, what kind of present that? A dead present!'

After a quick return to London for the first of many appearances at the Jazz Café with the three-piece Robotics, then came a greatly anticipated return to Australia and New Zealand for live dub shows in September, the Melbourne performance the best of the bunch, with Perry exhorting the audience to join him in a rousing opening chant of 'Down with Evil! Up with Good!'

Once Perry was back in Switzerland, DJ Startrek returned to Perry's home for more voicing sessions in September and October, the pair taking frequent strolling breaks together to a nearby village, where Perry would gather inspiration for lyrics and song titles.

He flew back to Jamaica in November for another extended stay, much of it spent at Cardiff Crescent on his own while Mireille partied in Negril, and here he felt the full force of the island's pull on his psyche, suggesting that permanent relocation made the most long-term sense.

'I will move because this country is the best country, and the country cannot take the jinx anymore,' Perry explained. 'Jamaica is the best country in the world. That's where the sun is shining, that's where the sun is coming from. Touring, I'm going to quit that too. But me didn't have enough of Switzerland, me just go out there to prove that me nah need Jamaica, and me no want to hear the music anymore.'

Above all, he wanted the world to know that his latest studio album, *Jamaican E.T.*, was anything but reggae.

'It's not reggae, it's commercial, and I'm not defending the reggae because where the reggae is coming from is the roots of real evil. I take the album like a prayer meeting, and me don't know if it's really dancehall. My fans don't like me to have contact with those people anymore, so I ban them forever. It's my voice now, my voice and the words. In the beginning, there wasn't any musicians, there wasn't any music, there was the Word, and the Word is God, and the words are earthlier than human beings.'

In late February 2003, Mr Perry received the unexpected news that *Jamaican E.T.* had been awarded a Grammy, beating Bounty Killer's *Ghetto Dictionary*, Capleton's *Still Blazin*, Freddie McGregor's *Anything For You* and Alpha Blondy's *Merci* in the 'Best Reggae Album' category of 2002. In Jamaica, there was outrage: Perry's music received little airplay and the album was totally unknown, and overseas, the most positive reviews only granted two or three stars, while respected writers derided it as unremarkable gibberish; some suggested the award acknowledged achievements of decades earlier rather than the album itself. Yet to Perry, everything made perfect sense. Indeed, he predicted a Grammy win on 'Good Lucky Perry' some twenty years earlier.

'On the CD, I was mixing styles,' said Perry. 'I call it reggae hip-hop or hip-hop reggae. There was a spirit telling me that the hip-hop is coming like another version of reggae, but everything is coming from the one God, through the one aim and the one destiny.'

Nevertheless, Perry refused to travel to the awards ceremony in New York due to the imminent US invasion of Iraq, stating that any action taken by George W. Bush would be 'reversed'.

Just as news of Perry's Grammy win surfaced, along with his abandonment of reggae for a new form he termed 'eggae', so did his curation of the annual Meltdown festival, to be held at London's prestigious Southbank Centre in June. The organiser, former New York club promoter Glenn Rechler (known as Glenn Max), travelled to Switzerland in preparation, and once an understanding was established, a potential shortlist of artists was put together, Perry publicly declaring his intention to 'celebrate with the music makers from all over the world, melting down sweet songs and evil beats . . . to save the human being world.'

But first came another round of tour dates in March, with Spider, Kirk and Sinclair Seales, including a shared bill with Sly and Robbie and Michael Rose at Landernau in Brittany and three uneventful nights at London's Jazz Café.

The tour coincided with the public announcement that Lee Perry was now herb free, but could the perpetual ganja venerator really no longer be partaking of the 'wisdom weed'? As so much of his oeuvre had depended on his relationship with the substance, it was incomprehensible that Perry was no longer smoking marijuana. And yet, Perry had gradually removed harmful ingredients from his diet, rejecting alcohol and becoming a strict vegetarian, so the abandonment of herb was not necessarily such a giant leap, especially for a man in his late sixties. In any case, the purge gave the tour a shaky start, as Perry experienced withdrawal symptoms, though in time, less cryptic interviews were among the unexpected benefits.

'I save myself from the corruptive smoking and save myself from the rum, because rum is a demon and nicotine is death, and smoking the herbs eat out your brain cells, take out your brain and sit on top of you and turn you into a zombie,' said Perry. 'I was drinking rum and smoking, so at the time I didn't have no reason to care, but now that people listen to what me said, and many people try what me say and it work for them, it give me more reason to live and make me don't want to smoke or drink anymore. Me want to live to see some of the people who take my word, how far them reach in life. It make me feel very happy because they follow my education and my education becomes their *livication*, and my education didn't come from the school, it come from nature and the earth, wind and fire, and me tell it to lots of people and them follow it, and it make some rich and make some happy and heal some hearts and heal some brains. So now me know me have reason for living.'

Perry flew to Kingston in late April and began voicing new lyrics on old rhythms with Errol Thompson at Joe Gibbs' studio, but little was completed and the tracks remain unreleased. He returned to Switzerland in early May for live dates in Scandinavia and Germany, followed by a debut live dub show with Mad Professor in Mexico City on 7 June (on a shared bill with the Orb's Alex Paterson, Dreadzone's Greg Roberts, and Earl Sixteen), leaving no time for reflection before the Meltdown began.

Perry wanted heroes such as James Brown, Ray Charles and Stevie Wonder to perform, but they were unavailable and unaffordable, so the varied programme wound up with Ivorian reggae superstar Alpha Blondy, progressive funk-rock group Spearhead, dub poets Mutabaruka and Linton Kwesi Johnson, British trip-hop/rap maverick Tricky and rock-oriented R&B singer Macy Gray, along with Susan Cadogan and Sly and Robbie. The Royal Festival Hall lobby became a 'Black Ark Study Centre' with a mini-recreation of the studio for public use, and there were dance workshops, deejay nights and contextual lectures.

Perry's first Meltdown performance was an unrehearsed cameo with electronic duo Coldcut on 11 June that fell flat, Perry murmuring nonsense to the vague melody of the nursery rhyme 'This Old Man' as a cameraman filmed, the voice and image heavily manipulated. An even less successful guest spot followed with Tortoise, the dub-influenced avant-garde act from Seattle, the result decidedly unintegrated. Three days later, an evening of Marley and Perry tribute songs hosted by Brinsley Forde of Aswad featured former Jazz Warrior

Cleveland Watkiss, Neville Staple of the Specials, Rankin Roger of the Beat, Michael Rose and Finley Quaye, all backed by Sly and Robbie, the event scuppered by a very late start and jaded participation.

The next night, headlined by Mutabaruka, was devoted to dub poetry and the unsuspecting audience treated to an unscheduled 'spoken word' opening by Perry, making a David Icke-style reference to George Bush as a member of the 'reptiles family' and castigating Rita Marley for having travelled to Ethiopia to witness the reburial of Haile Selassie, the diatribe lasting nearly fifty minutes before Perry was finally escorted offstage.

Thankfully, the guest spot with Tricky the following night was surprisingly excellent, Perry a ray of light on a couple of impromptu duets after half an hour of the hoarse vocalist's murmured dark groans, and later in the month, Perry's brief appearance with Macy Gray was decent, if seemingly incongruous.

Despite top performances by Linton Kwesi Johnson, Michael Rose, the Sun Ra Arkestra and DJ Spooky (whose recent album, *Dubtometry*, featured snippets of Perry's voice), the Meltdown often fell short of its dynamic potential, though Perry enjoyed the stylistic mixture of the 'mystery show'.

Just as the Meltdown was drawing to a close, Secret issued their follow-up to *Jamaican E.T.*, the desultory *Alien Starman*, featuring the same set of musicians. The company was hoping for another Grammy, but the overly slick album was a commercial failure, typically meriting one-star reviews. 'Sound Of The Underground' proclaimed the music 'eggae', but most of the disc was dated fodder, and Perry was off-key on a rendition of the Temptations' 'My Girl', though a bouncy recut of 'Duppy Conqueror' fared marginally better. One review described it as 'a nadir of pointlessness', another 'entirely missable'.

Apart from a few scattered festival appearances with Mad Professor, the rest of the year was quiet, though in October, Perry began rehearsing at Case à Chocs with the White Belly Rats, which DJ Startrek formed with drummer Daniel Spahni of Dennis Bovell's Dub Band and experimental guitarist Lorenzo 'Lax Delux' Viennet, filling out the sound with previously recorded horns and electronic programming. The musicians added new overdubs to the album tracks too, along with some trombone from Rico, and everything was eventually given a final mixdown by Startrek and group manager/keyboardist Pascal Brunkow, a noted house music remixer with a penchant for archaic equipment.

Meanwhile, the appearance of a prominent 'Chase The Devil' sample on the song 'Lucifer', released on Jay Z's acclaimed *Black Album* in November, was further evidence of Perry's ever-growing influence on younger non-reggae practitioners.

The year 2004 began with a return to Australia with Mad Professor for the Good Vibes tour, again without a band, though the first scheduled appearance in Perth took place without Perry, who missed his flight, along with Mireille, despite having checked in at Heathrow on time. Catching up with Professor in Brisbane, Perry performed before 20,000 people at Sydney's Centenary Park, finishing off the mini-tour in Melbourne.

At the end of February, Perry delivered a strong debut performance with the White Belly Rats before a receptive capacity audience at Lausanne's Moulin à Danses, with Spahni and Viennet making live accompaniment to Startrek's pre-recorded backing tracks.

Then, in mid-April, Perry was booked to perform at London's Ocean with Steve Marshall's Megatonics, to show-case forthcoming album *The End Of An American Dream*, which drew on hip-hop, funk and other contemporary urban styles, but unforeseen logistical difficulties saw Marshall's group removed at the last moment, the White Belly Rats an emergency replacement. There were more gigs with the Rats in Switzerland in June, and a headlining spot at Köln Summerjam before 12,000 people (with Spahni now replaced by Nicolas Pittet, drummer of the semi-acoustic techno group Kera). Slowly but surely, the White Belly Rats became more prominent, alternating with the Robotics on European dates.

Perry and Mad Professor played a few gigs in Ireland, followed by four dub dates in Australia in August and another two in Japan, capped by an appearance in September at Bestival, the massive festival on the Isle of Wight staged by Rob Da Bank, who had recently voiced Perry for his Lazyboy project, the song 'Penguin' lambasting George W. Bush, Tony Blair, the Queen of England, Trojan Records, Niney the Observer and the late Clement Dodd, who had died in May of a heart attack.

In September, *Panic In Babylon* surfaced on the White Belly Rats' Damp Music label (with an alternate double-vinyl edition handled by German label, Moll Selekta), 'the perfect proof that any dream, as crazy as it may seem, can become reality', according to the sleeve. By this point, a new Lee Perry disc could be a gift or a curse, and even if Perry sometimes sang off-key, the Rats' reggae was tight and buoyant, driving the music forward even as Perry threatened to derail it, the tasteful mixing by Brunkow and Startrek and a powerful horn section raising the quality. On bass-heavy groove 'Purity Rock', Perry chanted against the Devil; the single 'Panic In Babylon', with a hot horn solo from Rico, mutated 'I Am The Upsetter' with sly digs at Mad Professor, Island Records and Tuff Gong; the repulsively titled 'Pussy Man' had Perry castigating the

563

rapper and record producer, Dr Dre; 'Voodoo' was bathed in swathes of swirling synths and 'Perry Ballad' full of delightfully incomprehensible Perry-speak. The second half is less enticing: though 'Baby Krishna' and 'Greetings' had imaginative backing, 'I Am A Psychiatrist' never really gets going and 'Inspector Gadget 2004' paled against the original; 'Are You Coming Home' was unconvincing sleaze and three live bonus tracks gratuitous filler. Nevertheless, it was stronger than the bulk of releases since *Who Put The Voodoo 'Pon Reggae*.

A mid-sized venue tour in support of the album began in December at Manchester University, with Horace Andy on the bill. Then, after the performance at Melkweg on 6 December, Perry was invited to the studio by Amsterdam-based electronic jazz-samba act Zuco 103 to voice two songs for their *Whaa!* album, released by Crammed a few months later. The single 'It's A Woman's World', heavily promoted on Dutch radio, commanded men to look after their families, and 'Love Is Queen Omega' spoke of the greatness of God over a bouncing neo-samba rhythm.

Perry and the Rats went back on the road for more dates in France in February 2005, notably performing with Dillinger and the Abyssinians in Annecy. Then, once back in Switzerland, Perry received an invitation from British artist Peter Harris to appear in a film called *Higher Powers*.

'I wanted different sorts of people who represented different kinds of higher powers, almost archetypal people,' said Harris. 'It might be a powerful gangster outside the law or a police chief, someone with a spiritual higher power, or someone who totally doesn't believe in higher powers, and for the visionary people, I thought of Ken Russell and Lee Perry. There was a set list of questions that I asked everyone in the film and a lot of the questions connected with his interests, things about luck and destiny, and faith and redemption through creation, so he responded really well.'

Filming began at Perry's home on Valentine's Day, where Harris recorded Perry's impromptu theme song using 'Black Vest' from *Super Ape* as backing.

After a quiet spring, Perry guested with Zuco 103 at the Cabaret Sauvage in Paris on 10 June, with positive audience response, and went back on the road with the Rats in July, playing Dresden's Back To The Roots Festival and at the Festi Val de Roots near Neuchatel. The rest of the summer was spent in harmony with his family, and after an exultant return to Bestival in September, Perry delivered the 'Truth As It Happens' tour with Mad Professor in Australia and New Zealand, followed by live dub shows in the north of England at the end of the month. Then, for Ariwa's twenty-fifth anniversary celebrations, Professor assembled a classic band with Fish Salmon, Sinclair Seales, Kirk Service and Black Steel, for three electrifying performances at the Jazz Café in early October, where Perry was accompanied by Mireille, Gabriel, Shiva and Wendy, the family au pair. With the band tight and Perry in high spirits, these were some of the most focused and captivating performances of recent years, attracting Adrian Sherwood, Rudy Mascoll and Jennifer Romeo in the audience, as well as former Pogues frontman Shane McGowan, who made a semi-inebriated backstage request for assistance with his next album. However, tension was clearly rising between the Perrys and Mad Professor.

After one of these gigs, over a late-night meal in Chinatown, I introduced Perry to Ethan Higbee, an NYU film studies graduate based in the boutique town of Ojai, outside Los Angeles, who had made a few music videos and produced electronic music with Sebastian Demian as International Friends (as well as solo work, credited to Nahte). Higbee proposed a documentary, titled *The Upsetter*, to be made jointly with Adam Bhala Lough, director of graffiti-art action drama *Bomb The System*, so tentative plans were made for winter filming in Switzerland.

Following the Jazz Café gigs, Peter Harris scheduled more thematic filming for *Higher Powers*, including a 'protest to God' at a church near Ariwa. Then, after a few White Belly Rats gigs were delivered in Spain and France in October, and more filming at home by Volker Schaner, Perry retreated to Jamaica, where he recorded an album of Marley covers with Flabba Holt, Dwight Pinckney, Robbie Lyn and engineer Errol Brown at Tuff Gong (plus a few numbers at Shaggy's Big Yard studio with Clive Hunt), the project overseen by Michel Jovanovic, whose Reims-based Mediacom agency had booked many previous Perry tours. Versions of 'Duppy Conqueror', 'Exodus', 'Kaya', 'Sun Is Shining', 'Punky Reggae Party', 'Blackman Redemption', 'Fussing And Fighting' and 'Heathen' were tastefully re-recorded, marked by the high musicianship and familiarity of the players; conceived as the platform for another European tour, the album remains unreleased, as does material voiced that year for producer Bobby Digital and his son, Cali Bud, as well as work cut for Dennis Bovell in London.

While in Jamaica, Perry was filmed at Cardiff Crescent by TVJ, Jamaica's most respected commercial television station, which helped raise his profile on the island through repeated screenings, the footage dubbed 'Interview of the year' as Perry was named one of the 100 Greatest Artists of All Time (or 'Immortals') by *Rolling Stone*.

Back in Europe, Perry performed in Berlin with the Rats in December before delivering three performances in Israel with Mad Professor and Earl Sixteen, notably joining De La

Soul for an event at Tel Aviv's massive Hangar 11. Then the Perrys distanced themselves from Mad Professor, beginning a long phase of mutual avoidance.

After spending the winter holidays with his family in Switzerland, there were five days of filming at home in late January 2006 with Higbee and Bhala Lough; off camera, I put some of the interview questions to Perry, who was characteristically playful with his answers, switching Day-Glo wigs for elaborate headdresses and lighting fearsome kerosene bonfires in the snow, his hair and beard now coloured by oil paints, regardless of the obvious toxicity.

Meanwhile, Volker Schaner's film was taking a different direction with plans to bring Perry to Ethiopia, Tibet and Jerusalem for an 'original sound movie'.

Instead, Perry returned to the USA in mid-February for a handful of dates, backed by Brooklyn-based Dub Is A Weapon, which guitarist/engineer Dave Hahn formed with veteran Jamaican percussionist Larry McDonald in 2003. Al Davis, road manager and engineer for funk pioneer George Clinton, organised the mini-tour in conjunction with alternative rock label Narnack Records, who later issued *Panic In Babylon* in the USA; advance publicity suggested a bonus disc of remixes featuring Clinton, Sinead O'Connor and Moby, along with TV On The Radio and DJ Spooky, but when the release finally surfaced in the summer, only the latter two were present and the live events postponed until May.

On 20 March 2006, Perry reached another milestone with the celebration of his seventieth birthday, just as he was named as a headliner at the Western Consciousness festival to be held in Savanna La Mar in late April; although still in Switzerland, Perry was feted at the press launch, held at the Pegasus in Kingston, where organiser Worrell King said that the festival would acknowledge his important contributions and celebrate his seventieth, the tributary performances including 'Words Of My Mouth' by Sangie Davis, young singer Nateesha 'Stream' Irving's rendition of 'Rastaman Live Up', and the S.A.N.E Band's take of 'Police And Thieves'.

To prepare for his first Jamaican performance since the late 1970s, Perry travelled to the island in mid-April, staying in Negril with Mireille, Gabriel, Shiva and Wendy, the family au pair. As Jamaican audiences are notoriously hard to please, Perry rehearsed with Flabba Holt's band from the Marley covers album, preparing a tight set for a triumphant homecoming. However, a solid day of torrential rain rendered the festival grounds a sea of mud, nearly causing the event's cancellation, and when the appointed hour arrived, the backing band was nowhere to be found, so the organisers had to scrabble together a pick-up band of available players loitering backstage, forcing Perry to appear with a loose set of musicians he had never rehearsed with, though as all were familiar with the originals, they pulled off a passable performance.

Relaxed and confident onstage during the opening number, dubbed 'Respect To Jamaica', it soon became clear that Perry was displeased, especially as his microphone, and its attached talismans, did not appear until midway through the set. Most of the audience was too young to be familiar with Perry and many were baffled by his individual renditions of 'Duppy Conqueror', 'Small Axe', 'Who The Cap Fits', 'Exodus' and 'Curly Locks', though appreciation slowly warmed. At the end of it all, emcee Cordel Green explained to the crowd why Perry was so important, and then Worrell King presented him with an award for his outstanding contributions to the Jamaican music industry, which he received onstage with Mireille by his side.

Though it would have been tighter with Flabba and company behind him, Western Consciousness was still a historic return to the Jamaican stage, and after his performance, in the company of Jimmy Riley, Tinga Stewart and Vicky Nelson, Perry granted interviews to various Jamaican television stations.

Then Perry's travelling schedule became more gruelling. The delayed tour with Dub Is A Weapon took place in May and June, including four nights at New York's Knitting Factory, and there were dates at CBGB in September. Lee and Mireille then spent some time in Jamaica, where he began working at Chinna Smith's home studio on another unfinished album that remains unreleased, and in late October, he hit Japan for a handful of live dub shows, mixed by Adrian Sherwood, painting artwork on a Perspex screen throughout the performances. Then came eight dates in the western US, the rapper Eve and bassist Tony Kanal of No Doubt making backstage appearances at the House of Blues in Los Angeles in November, and a few days after the tour came to an end in Boulder, Colorado, Perry played the Boss Sounds Reggae Festival in Newcastle, England, along with Prince Buster and Jimmy Cliff.

In February 2007, the live engagements picked up again, Perry performing to appreciative audiences at Budapest's floating A38 concert hall, Warsaw's Proxima and Moscow's trendy Bl club. In March, he played a well-received all-ages show at the Lonestar Lounge in Austin, Texas, for the South by Southwest festival, backed by Dub Is A Weapon, and was interviewed backstage for DirecTV by the eclectic alternative rock artist and 'New Age motivational speaker' Andrew W. K., beginning a connection that would later yield collaborative work.

At the end of the month, Perry was back at London's Jazz Café for a trio of gigs with Sinclair, Kirk, Fish and expressive guitarist Steven 'Marley' Wright, Secret Records filming the performance on 25 March for the future release, *Live At The Jazz Café*. Perry also spent considerable time voicing new material at Adrian Sherwood's tiny home studio in Hornsey, north London, assisted by young engineer Brendan Harding, before another 'protest to God' attempt for *Higher Powers*.

'We went to Hyde Park, which was good because there was one of those huge concerts on, so there were thousands of people walking around,' said Peter Harris. 'I wanted him to send a message to heaven, so I got one of those stupid helium balloons and he wrote this great message on it and sent it to outer space.'

At the end of March, Perry nipped over to Australia for three dates with the usual London-based backing band, followed by his Brazilian debut in April at Rio's Circo Voador, where Perry appeared before an enthusiastic crowd in a white Merlin hat, changing 'War In A Babylon' into 'War In A Iraq'. The show at São Paolo's Via Funchal also went down well, and while in Brazil, Perry dispensed words of wisdom on the genesis of dub for the superb documentary, *Dub Echoes*.

Following Perry's appearance at Italy's Tavagnasco Rock Festival at the end of the month, Adrian Sherwood joined him in Switzerland for more concerted work on the new album. Then there were summer US tour dates with Dub Is A Weapon (with Sebastian Demian acting as tour manager and designated driver), and in New York, where Perry played at B. B. King's, there was another interview with Andrew W. K., this time for his TV series in development, *Smokeshow*, where a collaborative album was proposed. Then came more gigs in Britain and Italy with the usual London-based band, though the performance at the Endorse-It-In-Dorset Festival in August used four local musicians at the last minute, a van breakdown preventing the arrival of the regular players. Furthermore, a performance at a New York boat party was cancelled when Perry's false teeth went missing.

Perry then spent a week in Los Angeles voicing experimental rhythm tracks with Andrew W. K. in chaotic sessions that yielded a new adaptation of 'Jah Live' and skeletal songs drawing on jazz and rock influences. The work continued at New York's Headgear Studio in October, after which Perry took a badly needed rest break in Negril.

Perry's MySpace page was the first inkling of a presence on social media that allowed fans and potential collaborators to directly engage. There would soon be all manner of dramatic proclamations on the page, and later incarnations on Facebook and Twitter ('I am Eloha-ha-ha, the only saver of the human race' and 'Governments lost hell doom' being fragments of early examples), though the shape of each site depended largely on who helped Perry to manage it, the task variously falling to Sebastian Demian, DJ Startrek, Volker Schaner and Noel Campbell, among others, with Mireille ultimately taking charge.

The End Of An American Dream was issued by Michigan's Megawave Records as the first of a trilogy created with Steve Marshall (working under the alias John Saxon). As was increasingly the case, the lyrics were driven by whatever came into Perry's head while recording, the lack of cohesion heightening the music's uncertain genre. For instance, opening track 'Disarm' had funk guitar and 'I Will Be There' vague reggae shadings, while 'I Am New Yorker' employed the scratch 'n' mix sampling of hip-hop, and both 'One God Rain' and 'Teddy Bear' rode techno beats. Furthermore, four 'songs' were fragments under thirty seconds long, but the album still had moments of appeal, the title track detailing America's imperial decline in multiple voices.

Higher Powers debuted at a small art gallery in Lüneberg, near Hamburg, on 1 October, placing Perry in the cinematic company of Boris Johnson, Peter Tatchell, Uri Geller and David Icke. Before making the film, Peter Harris had already approached David Bowie, Siouxsie Sioux and members of the Stranglers, using their ideas to create original artwork, and thus returned to Switzerland in November to collaborate with Perry, inducting him into the world of fine art.

'I'd done a *Self-Portraits by Proxy* series before, but with Lee it was a bit different,' said Harris. 'I said, "I've got these themes from the film, and I want you to give me the first image that comes into your head." I'd say, "Luck", or whatever, and he would come up with some mad image and I'd make it a drawing. Then I took all the drawings to his place in Switzerland, and he said we should cut them up. He was remixing them, like a record, taking something from one drawing and placing it with another and it was more like a ceremony or an Obeah ritual, so he spent a lot of time trying on different hats and costumes, as if he was getting into character. We started at seven and worked right through till four in the morning, and he had one CD that was just on repeat the whole time.'

After performances in France, Ireland and the UK in October and November, just as *The End Of An American Dream* was nominated for a Grammy, Perry and his family enjoyed a week's holiday in Egypt in late December; Shiva was fast approaching her eighteenth birthday and anxious to fly the coop, just as older sister Collette had been, soon moving to her own place in Zurich as a means of gaining some distance from the chaos.

The Upsetter premiered at South By Southwest in March, though Perry was unable to attend. Bearing the subtitle *The Life And Music Of Lee Scratch Perry* and narrated by actor Benicio Del Toro, the ninety-minute film's stronger points came in Perry's testimony, giving a sense of his view of himself, his approach to music and his unique vision. There were nice visual touches contrasting scenes of frozen Switzerland with tropical Jamaica, as well as a heated exchange with a hostile Canadian in a San Francisco gift shop, detracted by a few factual errors, a lack of context for some archive footage and patois subtitles far off the mark, the soundtrack alternating Perry's vintage reggae with Higbee's electronic background sounds, to mixed effect. If budgetary constraints and Higbee's relative lack of experience yielded an irregular, jagged-edged documentary that emphasised Perry's cult status rather than the definitive life story of a mainstream star, it was still miles ahead of anything previously attempted and Perry was certainly pleased with it.

Then Japanese fans were treated to the most momentous Perry album to surface in decades: *The Mighty Upsetter*, produced with Adrian Sherwood, a masterpiece that was easily the most impressive release since *Time Boom*.

'We want to try to capture back the fun and mischief,' said Sherwood when the album was still in production. 'I'm going to try to merge all his ideas to get a cohesive, contemporary album, and what we're doing now, it's almost like a point to prove. It's probably going to take all year, but I think it's better to nurture it and get it beautiful, as I want it to sound intense in the ears.'

So many recent albums were hasty, but Sherwood spent the necessary time, energy and money building complex rhythms, many of which playfully drew on great works of the past in a forward-facing way, instead of 'retro'. Paul 'Jazzwad' Yebuah, one of the more creative practitioners in contemporary reggae, built most of the basic rhythms, and quality players such as Steven 'Lenky' Marsden, Dennis Bovell and Skip McDonald added subtle touches. Refusing anything substandard, Sherwood was mindful of quality control, an element often sorely lacking, yielding an exceptional and unexpected return to form.

Meditative opener 'Exercising', co-produced by Swedish/ Portuguese duo Zilversurf, had Indian classical elements and a lyre; 'International Broadcaster' updated 'Bucky Skank' in hip-hop with Roots Manuva (and the lesser-known LSK); the anti-crack 'Rockhead' was an augmented 'Africa's Blood' that masterfully incorporated a snippet of Sam Carty's Hindi vocal from 'Bird In Hand'; 'Yellow Tongue' updated the 'Fever' rhythm to duet Perry with Tunisian-born Samia Farah (then Sherwood's flame); 'Lee's Garden' revisited 'Garden Of Life' with Valerie Skeete and Vyris Edghill's daughter Madeline, while 'Kilimanjaro' referenced 'Station Underground News' on a horn-driven cut of the Silvertones' 'Rejoice'; 'Everything Start From Scratch' made 'Kiss Me Neck' a platform for 'Pipecock in his dubwise character'. Additionally, 'Political Confusion' reminded that Tony Blair is a liar who will pay for his sins, while George Bush Junior was derided as a 'pussy hole' who will lose his soul for terrible misdeeds; 'God Smiled' has portions of the proclamations from Chapter Twelve of this book, allowing the music to infuse the messages with greater intensity. Furthermore, the Japanese edition of the album included raw bonus track 'Queen Elizabeth's Pum Pum', which radically reworked 'Jungle' to indecent effect.

'Most of them are some old-time tracks that we bring some reality to,' said Perry. 'Adrian bring it back to the reality of what it was, the original vibration of the music. I'm singing about governments and stupid people who cannot see the truth, show them a vision that, if them listen to your words, can understand it.'

As ever, when Sherwood mixed Perry's performances at WOMAD in July and the Big Chill in August, he added greater sonic dimensions to the live experience, paralleling the recent studio work.

At the same time, the hype surrounding the Andrew W. K. venture, *Repentance*, was intensifying through the trashy 'Pum-Pum' video directed by Jamaican-born film-maker Jay Will, with Perry appearing as an ageing, second-rate gangsta rapper in a Jamaican strip club. When the album surfaced in August, it was decidedly uneven, reflecting the difficult melding of backing musicians from disparate spheres, pairing 'noise rock' drummer Brian Chippendale with bassist Josh Werner from Orthodox Jewish reggae star Matisyahu's band. The gentle 'Heart Doctor' (updating rock steady classic 'Pressure And Slide') and devotional 'God Save His King' were pleasant enough, while 'Fire', 'Reggae Man' and 'War Dance' were driving dance tracks castigating foes as usual, but 'Baby Sucker' and 'Crazy Pimp' had objectionable, X-rated content.

Muddying the waters was *Scratch Came Scratch Saw Scratch Conquered*, issued in late September by Megawave, hot on the tail of *Repentance*. In opener 'Having A Party', Marcus Garvey's skeleton drops in from outer space, brandishing a jazz gun, along with eternal Saint Selassie, but quavering international bankers, politicians, police, church leaders and other 'sinful fuckers' are lined up for liquidation, their heads rolled off by Papa Perry, a handful of bagpipes and guest contributors Keith Richards and George Clinton, roped in for a major sonic coup, much to Perry's delight.

'Keith Richards play voodoo guitar, it is magic,' said Perry. 'He's a magician, a wise guy. He deal with a positive rhythm, and he play positive guitar, but his guitar is not just normal, it's real magic. He play singing guitar, talking guitar, magic guitar.'

Steve Marshall/John Saxon kept the backing melodic and minimal, allowing ample room for Scratch's demented warbling; Richards' bluesy guitar spices up 'Heavy Voodoo' and 'There's A Way', though Clinton's emailed contribution to the vengeful hip-hop of 'Headz Gonna Roll' made less impact. More focused than *The End Of An American Dream* and more artistically cohesive than *Repentance*, neither album managed to bag a Grammy, regardless of Narnack's major publicity offensive.

Somehow, *The Mighty Upsetter* was never even nominated, despite being the worthiest, the overcrowded market delaying its UK release until the following summer. Adrian Sherwood later issued the enthralling *Dubsetter*, a brilliant dub reconstruction every bit as good as the original. There were limited edition twelve-inch dubstep remixes too, including Kode 9's sparse take of 'Yellow Tongue' and the Moody Boyz' reworking of 'God Smiled' and 'International Broadcaster'; an obtuse outtake also surfaced on an On-U disco with Pempi's dubstep remix, the track a wacky cover of Black Sabbath's 'Iron Man' featuring Perry and Dennis Bovell on vocals, and further dubstep mixes would be issued in November 2011 as *Nu Sound & Version*, all pointing to Perry's endorsement of the latest dub offshoot.

'I am glad that people are creating on it because the word dub mean you can do anything,' said Perry of dubstep. 'So if people can find a different name for it, I say congratulations for the second generation of the now creation that is paying more attention to dub.'

With so much new material surfacing, small wonder that *The Mighty Upsetter* could be overlooked. For instance, Orange Street's *Lee Perry Vs The Observer* was a fast-buck release of below-par *Lord God Muzick* outtakes, 'Land Of Sex' and 'Rock Well' riding vintage Dennis Brown rhythms and 'I Am Craft' an exemplary self-referential free-word association, the album probably produced in an hour or two. It surfaced just as a twenty-date North American tour with Dub Is A Weapon was cancelled, but Perry made good use of the time off, voicing the album *Return From Planet Dub* in August and September with the Vienna-based dub crew Dubblestandart.

Formed in 1988 as a reaction to the stagnant Austrian pop scene, Dubblestandart fused dub reggae with new wave. After backing Dillinger and dub poet Lilian Allen onstage and working with Ken Boothe, Sly and Robbie, and Mad Professor, they first performed with Perry in 1991 and the album project began after bassist Paul 'Zasky' Zawilensky brought Perry to their Go! East studios to voice a couple of rhythm tracks, which were soon augmented by other voicings Perry undertook at home.

'As it was a dub concept album, we added the best of his vocal inspirations, which means that we, or he, might release a fuller version of some of the tracks in the future,' said Zasky. 'We spent almost a year working on the music. Lee was really open and gave us several vocal tracks for the same riddim and called me several times to discuss how we wanted it and how far he could go lyric-wise. The only answer: No boundaries, Mr President.'

As Dubblestandart began the long process of editing, Perry travelled to Jamaica in September, this time with Volker Schaner, who filmed him and Jah Ned staging a groundation ceremony at the ruins of the Black Ark. In Hanover, they found a housebound Miss Ina gravely ill and in constant arthritic pain at the family home, where Perry urged her not to worry, nor to feel obliged to remain in this life; he would get her a lovely coffin, he insisted, when the transition to the next life finally eased her suffering.

Just as Dubblestandart's New York cohorts Subatomic Sound System issued a limited edition twelve-inch dubstep remix of 'Chase The Devil' as 'Iron Devil', Perry was billed on a Narnack/College Music Journal showcase in New York at the end of October, but failed to appear. In January 2009, he was back in London for a few dates at the Jazz Café as usual, and shortly thereafter, fleshed out some ideas for a new album with Steve Marshall, who made a brief visit to Perry's basement studio in Switzerland.

After being approached via MySpace, Perry was visited at home on April Fool's Day by Ivan Diaz Mathé of Argentinian dub band Nairobi, voicing single B-side 'Paraiso Islamico', which referenced fears of Islam in the West, and the shaman-themed 'Agave Dub', the latter issued on debut album *Wu Wei* (credited to Nairobi Meets Mad Professor).

Later in the month there were performances in Germany with the White Belly Rats and dub shows in Italy with Adrian Sherwood, Perry again painting canvases onstage, which were auctioned to benefit Amnesty International. Perry, Sherwood and the London-based backing band then travelled to Australia in June to play the Luminous Festival at the Sydney Opera House, whose curator, Brian Eno, conceived it as an outlier event.

'I wanted everything in this festival to be something that was positioned on the outside of music, something that was a magnetic attractor which I knew music was being pulled towards, so I didn't want anything that came from the settled centre,' said Eno. 'I just thought, it'd be nice to have a whole festival of experimental popular music, so he came with Adrian Sherwood, but the show was the loudest thing I'd ever been to – agonisingly loud, with the hugest sound system.'

Shortly thereafter, *Return From Planet Dub* was released on Collision, a subsidiary of German independent, Echo Beach. Atop cavernous excursions into deep dub, chilling house and double-tough dubstep, Perry dispenses generic wisdom, referencing his magic genie and musical wars on a reworked 'Chase The Devil', Natty's dreadlock on 'Let 'Em Take It', Mister Rich and Mistress Bitch on a reconfigured 'Blackboard Jungle', the lowness of Hell and extreme heights of Heaven on 'Deadly Funny', plus the voodoo magic of blessed shit, emanating from the rumbling basslines that reach him when he sits on his toilet pit. As well as the Black Ark references, 'I Foo China' reminds of the halcyon days of 'Jungle' at On-U Sound, but 'Fungus Rock' is contemporary repulsiveness, with graphic warnings of venereal disease. Ari Up from the Slits has a fragmented presence, along with snippets of a lecture by David Lynch, and disc two has dub remixes by G-Corp, Rob Smith and Subatomic Sound System, who also issued twelve-inch vinyl dubstep remixes of 'Blackboard Jungle' (as 'Respect The Foundation'/'Respect My Shit'), and later, 'I Do Voodoo' and 'Deadly Funny'.

Following performances in Spain with the White Belly Rats and a live appearance at Berlin's House of World Cultures, Perry travelled to New York in July to blitz a gung-ho audience at Central Park's SummerStage with Dubblestandart and Subatomic Sound System, and after a rousing set at the Reggae Geel festival in Belgium, hit stages across America, backed by Maryland-based Lionize.

Then, on 10 September, Perry performed a special live dub set in elaborate papal garb at London's Tabernacle, with

Adrian Sherwood at the mixing desk and live video animation behind him, as the climax of the 'Higher Powers' art exhibition arranged by Peter Harris, which showcased drawings the pair had produced in 2007 as well as collaborative paintings made in Switzerland in August. The artwork, available for purchase via Harris' website, dealt with typical Perry themes such as social injustice, the unequal distribution of wealth, religious dogma, sex and personal vengeance; some paintings bore the man's handprints and footprints, and everything was marked by declamatory graffiti.

After voicing new material for Steve Marshall at home in Switzerland in late September, Perry enjoyed some fruitful days in Jamaica, where an unexpected reunion with the Congos was brokered by Michel Jovanovic of Mediacom.

'Michel asked me to do it, so me just said, "No problem, make it *gwaan*" because if it helps make the music survive, then that's good,' said Perry. 'If me was going to be funny to block the music, then it would be worse, so for the music's sake and the people's sake, let bygones be bygones.'

Video footage soon surfaced of Perry working on new material with the group (now a quartet with Kenroy 'Tallash' Fyffe of the Eternals), including 'Spider Woman', led by Congo Ashanti Roy, and 'Garden Of Life', led by Cedric Myton. Perry also had a hand in a recut of 'Rainy Night In Georgia' and gave input to Myton's 'Forever Young'. Material from the sessions, arranged by Clive Hunt, surfaced in March 2010 as the confusingly titled *Back In The Black Ark* despite being recorded at Mixing Lab and the Congos' home studio, Lion's Den, though many Ark stalwarts do feature.

'When I look in the studio and see man like Boris Gardiner, Dwight Pinkney, Robbie Lyn, Horsemouth Wallace, and Scratch, Cedric, Shanti and I, it's really coming like the days of old,' said Watty Burnett. 'It makes me happier more than words can say.'

'It's a new revelation working with Lee "Scratch" Perry right now,' said Myton during the album's construction. 'Him in a different focus, a different frame of mind.'

On the same trip, a random meeting in Negril with French art history teacher Nicolas Exertier yielded 'Hemperor Lee', one of the many incidental projects he somehow gave his blessing to, voiced at Lazeme Sound Studio on an electronic rhythm Exertier built with his brother, Perry renaming the duo Nicolas X and George Wanking Kebab.

Perry returned to Europe in November for an appearance at the Metropop Festival in Lucerne and other engagements in Holland, followed by six dates on the US east and west coasts in December, organised by Narnack. But before he left Jamaica, Perry was briefly reunited with his long-estranged and now rehabilitated son Sean, who was relaunching his singing career under the name Rum Roy following a long period of homelessness, during which rum was the crutch. Promoter Danny Champagne helped get him back on track, the poignant 'Story Of My Life' the most popular recording to emerge from the partnership.

As Lee 'Scratch' Perry contemplated the end of the first decade of the new millennium, openness was the key to everything. Mending fences with the Congos and reaching rapprochement with Sean would have been unthinkable even in the recent past, the new receptiveness pointing to a better frame of mind and greater flexibility. Live touring provided reasonably steady income and with further music, film and art projects pending, the future continued to be bright.

'What people can expect from me is happiness,' said Perry. 'I don't have any message but happiness and facts and reality.

You can show them a movie in the music and tell them a story in the music to cheer them up, let them be happy and give them something to laugh about.'

CHAPTER FIFTEEN

Heavy Rainford:
Planet Perry in the 2010s

The 2010s would be characterised by a near-constant flying regime, Perry crossing the Atlantic at the drop of a hat to deliver live sets in diffuse locations; increased recorded output yielded an inverse quality/quantity ratio, and there were various art and commercial side projects. The whirlwind was so all-engulfing that there was rarely time to pause for thought, save for the intermittent periods of relaxation in Jamaica and Switzerland, and the twin bugbears of booze and spliff rendered a quiet mind near unobtainable.

The first performances of 2010 comprised two nights at London's Jazz Café in late January, the opening set released by Secret as *Sun Is Shining*; then, Mediacom scheduled special European performances to mark the release of *Back In The Black Ark* and to celebrate Perry's seventy-fourth birthday. With Adrian Sherwood at the mixing desk, the unbeatable triple bill had Perry, the Congos and Max Romeo, the backing band with Horsemouth, Dennis Bovell and Black Steel considerably raising the standard, and collaborative encores of 'War In A Babylon' and 'Spider Woman' firing the response as grand finales.

Horsemouth was absent from the opening night in Dublin, but the show still went down a treat, and on Perry's birthday, the capacity crowd at L'Élysée Montmartre erupted when he received a birthday cake onstage. Omar had settled in Belgium early in the new millennium after Earl Sixteen introduced him to a promoter who became the mother of his first child, and since he was gaining ground as a recording and performing artist, he joined Perry onstage at the following night's show in Ghent to dispense an impromptu toast during 'Inspector Gadget'. Two other hot package performances were delivered in Athens, and a final collaborative concert with Perry and the Congos took place in July at London's Barbican.

CD releases were still coming thick and fast, Pressure Sounds' bespoke collection of unknown dubplates, *Sound System Scratch*, the most impressive of the retrospectives. Then, released in August, *Revelation* was the final instalment of Steve Marshall's Megawave trilogy, its contents typically harum-scarum: 'Holy Angels' and 'Revelation, Revolution & Evolution' retained old-school reggae orientation, while 'Weatherman' and 'Books Of Moses' strayed into blues, the latter thanks to Keith Richards' percolating guitar, overdubbed in New York the previous December. George Clinton returned for the hip-hop structured 'Scary Politicians', 'Freaky Michael' swiped at the recently deceased Michael Jackson, and 'An Eye For An Eye' had ill-fitting porno moans (footage from the sessions would be released in 2018 as *The Revelation of Lee 'Scratch' Perry*).

During a brief US tour in August with Lionize, bookended New York dates enabled Perry to voice *Rise Again* in a day-long session at Bill Laswell's Orange Music studio in New Jersey, the link made by bassist/co-producer, Josh Werner.

'Scratch commissioned some people to go out and get things, so there were balloons, toys, all kinds of weird stuff that put him in a surrealist environment,' said Laswell, best known for his inventive hybrid productions. 'The session was unusual because he's just improvising, not having anything prepared, so I edited the vocal heavily and did some overdubs later. We were able to pay him well and everything was smooth.'

Then, in November, *Secret Education* was the first Lee Perry solo exhibition, staged for a month at Dem Passwords, Ethan Higbee and Sebastian Demian's gallery and music space located on Santa Monica Boulevard. Large-format pieces echoed the Peter Harris collaborations, with Perry's paint-dipped handprints and £$P initials surrounding magazine cut-outs, another bearing a huge phallus with eyes on its hood, adorned by lewd graffiti, and there were idiosyncratic self-portraits and hand-drawn proclamations, blasting governments, taxes and other evils. The exhibition gave credence to Perry as an artist in his own right, generating another welcome income stream.

Then came the bittersweet news that Miss Ina had died on 13 December at the age of ninety-five. Afflicted by arthritis and housebound with reduced mobility, her passing brought relief as much as anything, since she had often expressed a wish to die, though the effect was still shattering; even if Perry perceived the event as preordained, nothing could have really prepared him for it.

'She did want to die and could not die until the right time come,' said Perry. 'Me never feel too good because me didn't know the meaning, and I was coming through the line of my mother. So me was just like a kid who love something straight, and I was her favourite son.'

Lee and Mireille reached Jamaica in time for the wake, and much of the extended family was there for the burial, including all of Miss Ina's children, as well as Marsha, but at the reception there was conflict between some of the older offspring and their younger half-siblings, mainly regarding the US$500 Perry had been sending every couple of months. Eldest daughter Dulcie was approaching eighty, with health problems of her own and numerous offspring with little livelihood; Sonny suggested Perry establish a foundation to benefit Miss Ina's grandchildren, in accordance with her wishes, but the squabbling caused Perry to withdraw, ultimately widening the gap.

Hanover had poignant memories, yet Perry said Cardiff Crescent remained the chief sanctuary, regardless of whether he was physically present.

'I have my house and me in deep communication all the time,' Perry explained. 'Wherever in the world, me still remember my house.'

Perry had a few weeks in which to process his grief before returning to London in late January 2011 for performances at the Jazz Café with the four-piece band, the set now including 'Heathen', 'Have Some Mercy', 'Crazy Baldheads', 'Secret Laboratory', 'God Smiled', 'Curly Locks' and 'Bucky Skank'/'Poppa Was A Rolling Stone'.

Patching up differences with Mad Professor, there were joint European performances in February, allowing Lee and Mireille to visit Disneyland Paris on Valentine's Day, the backing band now featuring Black Steel on bass and French guitarist Hugues Valot.

Then, *The Upsetter* was finally given a limited cinematic release, beginning with a week-long run in late March at Los Angeles' Downtown Independent. Self-distributed by the directors, it languished on the festival circuit for a couple of years and would enjoy short-duration screenings in fifteen cities in April and May, followed by limited overseas screenings.

Rise Again was released on Bill Laswell's MOD Technologies in May, handled by P-Vine in Japan. The multifaceted cast included Funkadelic keyboardist Bernie Worrell, Ethiopian vocalist Gigi Shibabaw (Laswell's wife) and Tunde Adebimpe from TV On The Radio, the psychedelic global stew a pleasant backdrop, though Perry's ad-hoc meandering was layered on top, a distracting presence rather than central focus. Tracks with an Ethio-jazz framework, such as 'Orthodox', 'Wake The Dead' and 'African Revolution' were the most musically appealing, thematically emphasising spiritual and historical bonds, and 'E.T.' had otherworldly charm, its chanted hook chorus referencing a new alien race, but Perry added little to the mishmash of 'Dancehall Kung Fu' and the title track lacked energy.

On 13 May, Perry dispensed an outstanding set at All Tomorrow's Parties, held at a Somerset holiday camp, proving that he could still deliver the goods onstage under certain conditions, retaining broad audience appeal when the mood was right.

Then Lee and Mireille flew to Argentina, where there were four performances to deliver with Nairobi, who took good care of the pair on their home turf.

During the 2011 summer festival season, after a triumphant set headlining Glastonbury's Glade stage, the Congos and Max Romeo joined him for a bubbly 'War In A Babylon' at Summerjam, though Perry's ire was unleashed at the post-gig press conference when a hapless journalist professed Catholic orientation. Perry was also a highlight of the Black na Cena Music Festival in São Paulo, backed by RotoRoots, a local groove band with a bright horn section and Black Steel guesting on bass, Mad Professor injecting a hefty dub element at the mixing desk.

Then, in September, Perry and Volker Schaner decamped to Sternhagen Gut, an artist's sanctuary located on a historic country estate some sixty-five miles north of Berlin, for a six-day marathon session with the Orb; Mireille dropped by briefly but opted not to stick around due to the remote location.

According to collaborator Martin 'Youth' Glover, who supplied bass parts remotely at his Space Mountain studio in Andalusia, and who later did some remixes for the album, the sessions got off to a rocky start due to an absence of traditional basslines.

'On the first day I got this really anxious phone call from Alex Paterson, saying, "You've got to put some bass on the tracks. Lee Perry won't do them until he hears the bass!" So, I laid down four or five different basslines and sent them over, and the next day Perry carried on.'

As Perry preferred to work nocturnally, Paterson and his longstanding co-conspirator Thomas Fehlmann tinkered with their electronic rhythms during the day while Perry absorbed Bollywood epics and Nollywood crime dramas, reeling off whatever came into his head once he was ready to address the microphone, offering changes to keyboard basslines and other direction. Schaner's footage reveals a playful camaraderie and spontaneity the order of the day, with four preassembled rhythms quickly abandoned, the trio revelling in mutual moribundity and shared outsider status.

At the end of the month, there were above-average Californian gigs, backed by a tight group of Jamaican players based in Los Angeles, the lengthy set at San Francisco's Independent allowing Perry to commune with his audience, who showered him with talismans and positive energy.

Then came another extended winter break in Jamaica, the visits becoming longer and more frequent since Gabriel had turned eighteen; still his father's favourite and now towering over him, they retained a strong bond with mutual prankster tendencies.

As a couple, Lee and Mireille remained exceedingly close, and despite the inevitable ups and downs of their unique relationship, he was grateful for her stabilising presence.

'I'm living with her maybe twenty-one years now, and I don't know if she Obeah me or what, but she is a nice person that carry me out of my hard times when I wanted to leave Jamaica,' said Perry. 'She gave me a place to live and save me from lots of problems, hard time and suffering, so maybe that's why we did last so long. And I like living in Switzerland very much. You don't see much people to beg you and depress you.'

Once back in Switzerland, the seeds of several fan-based projects began to germinate, the first instigated by Daniel Boyle, whose Rolling Lion studio in London's Crouch End had a Roland Space Echo, Grampian spring reverb and Mu-Tron bi-phase, as well as more modern equipment, following his apprenticeship at Norfolk's Purple Studios and a day-job with a City headhunting firm. An email to Perry went unanswered for two or three years but a reply from Mireille finally came in late January 2012, just as the studio was finally operational: Mr Perry was in town for two Jazz Café gigs, could they meet?

'I'm not replicating the Black Ark, but I'm hugely influenced by it and the idea was, by using some modern equipment and some old equipment, we'd be doing something different,' said Boyle. 'He picked up information for what he was going to sing about from the papers, like he's reading something about the royal family and then destroys them in a song, and he defaced my tree in the garden, so there's a line about the eucalyptus tree. He uses a lot of what's around him to fill the gaps.'

'I think he's a good person and him have a good idea, so we put the tracks together, make them work,' said Perry. 'We have some ganja trees around, so most of the inspiration were coming from ganja, but me only worship ganja now, me no smoke it anymore.'

Perry left the sessions with rough mixes of a song called 'Repent' and the project gradually took shape whenever Perry passed through London, though it would take time for the pair to understand each other's working methods.

In part due to geographical closeness, Easy Riddim Maker yielded swifter, more fleeting results. Drummer/multi-instrumentalist Olivier 'Piment' Gangloff of experimental rock band Yeallow formed ERM with sound engineer Romain 'EasyMode' Ferrey, and once Perry approved a demo, Gangloff prepared ten instrumentals, which Perry voiced in a day-long session in February 2012, the duo arriving at his home with a Neave console and manager, Amina Martin.

'It was like a ceremony: Lee burned incense, walked on the table and did a lot of different things,' said Gangloff. 'For every song, we just had a little conversation and then he went to the mike and boom! One take.'

Then Perry went back on the road for twenty-four European performances with Mad Professor and the Robotics, billed as the 'Roots of Dubstep' tour, followed by ten cross-country US dates in May with Subatomic Sound System, billed as 'Black Ark classics remixed live, from dub to dubstep'. As Perry mutated the lyrics of his Black Ark repertoire, Subatomic co-founder John Emch tackled the live dub mixing and pre-recorded backing tracks, blowing occasional melodica, with Dubblestandart bassist Paul Zasky, saxophonist Troy Simms and trumpeter Omar Little performing live alongside percussionist Larry McDonald, whose forceful rhythmic accents helped ground the work with its roots, even as Emch's mix propelled it towards the future. The much-touted shows helped to cement the connection between Perry and Subatomic, rendering them his official backing band for North America.

In August, it was announced that Perry had finally made the Honours list at home, granted the Order of Distinction (Commander class) by the Jamaican government, now headed by Portia Simpson-Miller of the PNP, who had been re-elected in January, though Perry opted not to attend the awards ceremony in October, sending P-Son in his place. Bunny Wailer, Toots Hibbert, Jackie Jackson and Peter Tosh were also honoured, the belated recognition speaking volumes about Jamaica's delayed acknowledgement of its musical heroes and the lingering notion of affiliation.

Perry's collaboration with the Orb, titled *The Orbserver In The Star House*, was released by Cooking Vinyl in late August. Lacking an overriding theme, the understated, downtempo tracks were a platform for circuitous rambles: 'Golden Clouds' revisited 'Little Fluffy Clouds' from the ambient house heyday of the early 1990s, here with a passing nod to the skies of Perry's childhood that devolved into rhyming free-word association; 'Soulman' repurposed Sam and Dave's 'Soul Man' to divine interventions of Jesus; and there was an ill-advised cut 'n' mix version of 'Police And Thieves' with Perry woefully off-key. It all reminded that the Orb were decades past their best, and Perry too, though at least the lyrics were unobjectionable (outtakes were released the following June as the less-cohesive *More Tales From The Orbservatory*).

Perry nipped back to New York in late September to perform at Subatomic's second Dub Champions festival; in

October, there was a one-off at Tokyo's Tsutaya O-Nest and the headlining spot at a special dub night at Motion, Bristol's fabled DJ warehouse complex, followed by top billing at the techno-themed Dublime event at the Electric Brixton in early November, plus more recording with Daniel Boyle.

Then came a performance at Oslo's Rockefeller Music Hall with an expanded Easy Riddim Maker, Yeallow guitarist Fred Tavernier and bassist Bill Ottomo joining Gangloff on drums and pre-recorded keyboards, with live mixing by Ferrey, in support of *Humanicity*, released the previous month. As heard on the album's buoyant opener 'Capricorn', ERM used electronics to modernise their reggae-influenced rock. Perry's stream-of-consciousness dominated, though was cheerier and more melodic than usual; the self-important 'Jesus Perry' saluted his 'reggae reincarnation' and '4th Dimension' updated 'Blackboard Jungle Dub', but 'In The Bathroom' was a borderline offender fantasy ('I pull them by the hair to the bedroom and jook my victim . . .') and 'Rastafari' boasted of killing Satan 'with my electric cock'.

Eventually, Volker Schaner decided that filming had been completed, the work in progress now titled *Lee Scratch Perry's Vision Of Paradise*. A crowdfunding campaign brought US$22,000 in early 2013, enabling him to begin the editing process and to commission animated sequences.

After a badly needed extended winter break in Jamaica, Perry's live schedule picked up again in February as usual, beginning with the headlining spot at the first Vienna edition of Dub Champions. Then, after another one-off with ERM in Hamburg, there were seven UK dates with the four-piece ex-Robotics and more recording with Boyle.

In March, Perry was summoned to Vernasca, between Milan and Bologna, to take part in a crowdfunded cinematic art project instigated by Simone Bertuzzi and Simone Trabucchi, alias Invernomuto. *Negus* referenced the burning of an effigy of Haile Selassie in Vernasca's town square in 1936, in celebration of the return of a wounded local soldier who participated in the fascist occupation of Ethiopia. To invert what they saw as 'a dark and simultaneously festive ritual which put colonial rhetoric under a different perspective', Invernomuto had Perry enact a 'cleansing counter-ritual' with fire, the resultant footage screened at an exhibition the following year and later incorporated into a full-length conceptual documentary.

A west coast US tour with Subatomic kicked off in April, now with backing singers Chezeré Brathwaite and Amanda Bauman, bookended by two sets at Coachella that were one week apart, allowing Perry to appear at the opening of his *Repent Americans* exhibition at Dem Passwords, where he created new artwork on the spot.

That same month, Perry shared the stage with Omar at the Free Music Festival in France, and after capacity sets in Moscow and St Petersburg with the four-piece Upsetters and a gig with ERM at the Dour Festival in July, Perry and Max Romeo played the main stage at WOMAD, backed by Romeo's Charmax Band, but with Mireille increasingly relegating tour duties to stepson Noel, booze and weed were back on the menu, leading to onstage outbursts and general moodiness. Nevertheless, at the Garance Reggae Festival, Omar and children Alexandra, Faya and Isaiah provided spirit-raising backing vocals during 'Soul Fire'. Then, in late September, Perry hit New York for the latest edition of Dub Champions, visiting the Dubspot music production and DJ school and voicing 'Black Ark Vampires' with Emch and Adrian Sherwood at Hook Studio in Brooklyn, riding a reconfigured 'Underground Root' cut-up.

During the New York sojourn, a chance encounter at Macy's department store with French percussionist Tony Freebird (Anthony Naudet) was another path to impromptu collaboration.

'I was going to buy some underwear, Lee popped up from the lift and we banged into each other,' said Freebird. 'I said, "Oh, Jah bless, this is destiny! I was trying to contact you for ten years!" Then he said, "Come with me, son, help me to choose my clothes."'

Playing a reggae-themed track on his phone from an album he was working on called *Magic Dancing Hands*, Freebird asked if Perry would consider a guest vocal, and believing that the meeting was not accidental, Perry said, 'Send me the material and I'll see what we can do.'

After Perry delivered sporadic European dates in the autumn, Daniel Boyle launched a slick crowdfunding campaign in November for his album project, titled *Back On The Controls* since Perry was also helping to mix the material, manipulating the bi-phase with variable results. Evocative photos of Perry at work helped raise £14,000, allowing for quality mastering and a double-LP vinyl format.

During the winter break in Jamaica, where Perry voiced the prayerful 'Happy Birthday Starlight' for Tony Freebird at the small Song Embassy in Papine, east Kingston, Mireille was scouting for land in the northwest countryside on which to establish a permaculture and 'alternative energy' project, known as the 'LSP Paradise Eyeland Community', complete with an 'LSP magic healing house' as well as private accommodation.

However, Perry stayed far from Cardiff Crescent to avoid confrontation with Sean, an unwanted guest who was still grappling with substance misuse, Perry's time in Negril largely spent typing obscure proclamations on his computer.

'I'm only writing my destiny,' Perry explained. 'There are so many versions of the holy Bible, but me gonna make another Bible, so my next destination will be writing the other Bible, stuck to the laptop.'

Back in Europe, as the finishing touches were given to *Back On The Controls*, Perry began working with Bregt De Boever, a singer, multi-instrumentalist and painter, known as Puraman, who had fronted Belgian reggae band Pura Vida for over a decade. Based in Maria-Aalter, between Ghent and Bruges, Puraman's Lost Ark studio paid homage to the Black Ark with similar vintage gear; he had produced the Congos' *We Nah Give Up* in 2011 and Congo Ashanti Roy later suggested he paint Perry's portrait, delivered with contact details at the Dour event, subsequent work inspired by LSP Paradise helping to pave the way for Puraman to send a rhythm track to Switzerland, which Perry voiced at home as 'Heaven Gate'. A sneak preview posted online in March 2014 revealed a dense roots production style reminiscent of the Black Ark heyday, with a chanted 'Super Ape' chorus atop a heavily processed rhythm that drew on the structure of 'Congo Man', as Perry spoke of returning to the Lost Ark in Jamaica.

Following Perry's inconsequential appearance on Jah Wobble and P. J. Higgins' 'Watch How You Walk' twelve-inch, *Back On The Controls* was released in May on a new Upsetter label, rightfully garnering positive press. Drummer Horseman and bassist Hughie Izachaar provided the rhythmic bedrock, trombonist Hornsman Coyote added brass accents, and there were other subtle instrumental enhancements, each vocal track followed by a cavernous corresponding dub. Opener 'Rastafari On Wall Street' was an oblique commentary on the lingering after-effects of the global financial crash; 'Blackboard Revision' was a horns-heavy remake of 'Blackboard Jungle

Dub'; 'Sound Of Jamaica' had ambient insect noise from Negril; 'Copy This & Copy That' attacked copycats; and there was the scathing 'Repent', voiced at the initial session. Everything hung together nicely, the extra effort yielding better-than-average results and a Grammy nomination.

'It was his idea about getting the instruments, what him knew me used to have,' said Perry. 'A lot of it I did in the spirit, where you don't remember what you do until you hear it again: Rastafari take over, come into the structure and put the body to sleep – it's a spiritual, telepathic transformation. We go into the future to do it. And it sounds 100 per cent perfect. I think Daniel is in the prophecy, one of the spirits that refuse to die, cos Daniel have an original vision that the Black Ark studio is forever and must continue. So God bless Daniel and his vision.'

To prepare for the late August opening of *The Death of Baphomet* at Dem Passwords, Perry painted declamatory words directly onto the walls and made new collage assemblages, a video installation and a 1,100-page volume of computer transcripts completing the show, which ran to early October. The title apparently referenced 'the death of the Illuminati and the doom of Egypt . . . the death of Baphomet and his puppet, Jay Z', though Perry's stated intention was 'to make all my fans in America laugh'.

In late September, Perry was back at Dub Champions in Brooklyn, shortly before Subatomic issued the 'Black Ark Vampires' 45. Then, in October, Perry performed a lengthy set with the seven-piece Pura Vida in Bergen-op-Zoom, southern Holland, featuring a live horn section and Puraman on backing vocals, melodica and percussion, giving extra textural dimension to an unusual set that included 'Catch Vampire', 'Play On Mr Music', 'Big Neck Police' and 'Heaven Gate'.

On the night of 23 November, former XL Recordings boss Richard Russell travelled to Switzerland for a record-jacket painting session in Perry's basement, the pair hand-painting 250 twelve-inch sleeves to house techno cut-up 'I Am Paint', which Russell produced using sampled audio from Gary Weis' film footage, Perry's green handprints and footprints featuring prominently, along with abstract circles and lines. Released the following April, the twelve-inch was only available in exchange for bartered artwork delivered to the headquarters of Russell's short-lived Residence La Revolution imprint.

After wintering in Jamaica, Perry played another Vienna edition of Dub Champions in February 2015, then went back to Jamaica for a few more weeks in the sun, where Mireille continued to search for land, hatching plans to turn 5 Cardiff Crescent into a museum, despite Sean's problematic presence, which would eventually be dealt with by a court order.

In March, Perry gave a live dub performance at Jake's, the boutique hotel in Treasure Beach, run by Perry Henzell's widow Sally and son Jason, who was an infant when Perry last encountered him. Jason housed Lee and Mireille in a sumptuous suite, provided excellent food and some choice weed, resulting in a relaxed and confident set from Perry, backed by selector Jah Wayne of Negril's Lazeme sound system.

Unfortunately, alcohol and herb caused recurrent problems since Mireille had gradually relaxed her policy of keeping Perry totally substance free; after all, she reasoned, was it really fair for everyone else to be drinking and smoking while Lee was forbidden to partake? But Perry never mastered the art of moderation. Drinking to excess, especially when smoking, precipitated dramatic mood swings and extreme outbursts, affecting the quality of performances and everyday life. Band members and an endless stream of tour assistants were thus lumbered with the unenviable task of trying to keep Perry within his limits.

In April, Perry delivered a week-long US tour with Subatomic, returning to Europe in time for another marathon with Pura Vida, delivered in the seaside town of Bredene, near Ostend.

'When he arrived it was pure magic: his eyes were painted with golden paint and he was in such a kind and inspired mood,' said Puraman. 'After the show, we had time to do some recordings for the album *The Super Ape Strikes Again* at the Lost Ark — a masterclass with great vibes and a very creative atmosphere. We recorded "Feeling So Good" and "Jesus Christ" that night, recording the vocals and bass together on the rudimental rhythms, and conga drums, percussion and all kind of sounds, even hitting the doors. We have a connection from the stars because we don't talk a lot, but we can create very smooth and easy together; the other tunes on the album Lee recorded in Switzerland.'

Lee 'Scratch' Perry's Vision of Paradise had its world premiere at the Chicago International Movies and Music Festival in April, followed by screenings at IndieLisboa and the San Francisco Black Film Festival, where it was awarded Best Documentary. Then, for its UK premiere at Whitechapel's Genesis Cinema in July, the East End Film Festival rolled out the red carpet, inviting Lee, Mireille, Adrian Sherwood, Volker Schaner and executive producer Daniela Schmid to participate in a chaotic pre-screening panel discussion, Perry's frayed-synapse commentary often lost on the audience, though an earlier interview with Channel 4's Krishnan Guru-Murthy boosted the profile, Perry memorably stating that he 'gave reggae to Bob Marley as a present'. The screening coincided with a one-day exhibition at the Red Gallery in Shoreditch, showcasing the work of Maria Sargarodschi, who did the paintings for the film's animated sequences, including a collaborative triptych with 'Africa in Danger' as its centrepiece, along with the joint Peter Harris work that featured in the film. Then, the late-night afterparty's rousing ninety-minute live set saw a highly charged Perry happily toasting over Upsetter B-sides spun by house producer, Ashley Beedle.

As for the film itself, Schaner had no intention of duplicating *The Upsetter* and no interest in a standard biopic. Instead, his 'fairy-tale documentary' opted for a personal arthouse approach, with Perry's unfiltered, contradictory testimony at its heart. Biographical information is thus thin on the ground, the soundtrack has more Wagner than Black Ark, and aside from sparse statements from Sherwood, Mad Professor and Dennis Bovell, much of the film is taken up with platitudinal Perry pronouncements, *ad infinitum*; whether working in his basement, performing onstage, conducting ceremonies in Jamaica or travelling to locations unknown, Perry comes across as a ritualistic eccentric who inhabits a world of his own, self-importance and impulsiveness the defaults, his childlike attention span constantly shifting. Jamaican footage adds context and contrast, as does shaky material from 1999, but the non-linear structure is confusing, and Ethiopian scenes feel unintegrated, budgetary constraints and a lack of external editing affecting the result. Yet, the segments with the Orb beautifully capture Perry's playful contemporary working method and propensity for punning, the animated sequences are strikingly different, and amongst the usual blasts against the Pope, Bob Marley and 'cannibal' meat-eaters, we learn that Perry ultimately does not care whether anyone understands him, preferring to bamboozle journalists, film-makers and the general public rather than resort to standard communication.

Despite its tagline as 'the one movie that explains it all', Schaner conceded that neither *Vision of Paradise* nor *The Upsetter* could 'completely, satisfyingly tell the story of this man', as he told the *San Francisco Bay View*. Nevertheless, Perry gave the film his unreserved endorsement.

In June, Perry voiced an album's worth of material at home for the singer, producer and painter Rankin' Alpha (Raffaele Ferro), who had assembled the rough electronic rhythms at his base near Pistoia, outside Florence, and after receiving the files remotely, Noel engineered Perry's vocal overdubs, the material later reworked by Alpha and fellow musicians of the group, Dubital.

Later that month, there were packed live dub shows in Mexico with Mad Professor, but Perry was distracted at Rototom in August, causing much of the audience to vote with their feet, and after capacity performances in Russia, Perry made his debut in autocratic Belarus, performing live dub sets at the White Mirror festival, where *Vision of Paradise* was screened. Then Perry crossed the Atlantic for a *Super Ape* fortieth anniversary Dub Champions tour, hitting thirteen US cities in September, accompanied onstage by a giant crowdfunded gorilla.

There were then live dub shows in Brazil, Chile and Argentina with Mad Professor, Perry voicing his portion of the song 'Estudando O Dub' for producer MPC of Digitaldubs while in São Paulo, later issued on a Muzamba 45 as a duet with fellow eccentric visionary, Tom Zé.

Perry returned to Europe for shows in Turnhout and Bruges with Pura Vida in late October and more voicing at Puraman's relocated studio (including a song called 'Good Spirit'), just before the release of *The Super Ape Strikes Again*.

Along with an extended 'Heaven Gate' as the album's opener, 'Mystic Morning' incorporated a subtle nod to the

Gatherers' 'Words' and Augustus Pablo's 'Ethiopia', the latter especially fitting since Pablo's son Addis played melodica on the song, with former Mothers of Invention keyboardist James Lascelles another noteworthy guest. Similarly, 'Jesus Christ' had a passing 'Underground Root' refrain and the title track naturally alluded to 'Super Ape', but Puraman opted not to recreate those rhythms. Instead, *Strikes Again* was entirely original, the tropes acting as musical signposts, and everything assembled with an ear for detail and good taste, with Perry keeping his lyrics positive and delivery more melodic than usual, Ernest Ranglin's guitar on 'Feeling So Good' another plus, though Perry sang on only four numbers, the rest of the album filled out by dubs and Congo Ashanti Roy's 'Treat Me Right'.

When not on the road, Perry continued to display a driven work ethic, crafting sculptures, painting, and drafting spells with his words, yielding temporary, shifting pieces that would remain unseen by the outside world. On 1 November, it was Mireille's birthday as well her wedding anniversary with Lee, but instead of going out to celebrate, they stayed at home, where Lee toiled in the basement late into the night as usual, and when he awoke in the morning, he was flabbergasted to discover that the basement was ablaze.

'When everything was happening, I didn't know what was going on. Then I realised it was time for me to recognise that this is the second judgement,' said Perry. 'I go to bed at about six o'clock in the morning, and when I come up from downstairs I forget to blow out the candle – it was on top of a Bible.'

'From the fire and the water, everything was like an earthquake,' said Mireille. 'After the firemen finished, everything was black and Lee's room completely burnt, everything gone. He didn't even have a pair of shoes to wear.'

Variously known as the Secret Laboratory, the Blue Ark or the White Ark, the basement was a solitary workplace visited by few outsiders, where Perry made music and abstract art every day, its walls heavily stratified by layers of paint and collage applied over the years. Perry also stored countless stage costumes in the basement, many of which were unique pieces handmade by fans. With so much music, art, clothing, magic microphones and other equipment now obliterated, Perry became dejected, though an outpouring of love from his fans on social media helped boost morale.

Before retreating to Negril to lick their wounds over the winter, Perry performed at the Tun It Up Reggae Night, held in the lakeside town of Zug, with Cookie the Herbalist, a Swiss reggae artist otherwise known as Stefano Raschi, who had recently collaborated with Perry on an upbeat song called 'Eaze!' The young dread's close proximity would see him engaged as tour assistant in future, particularly after Noel backed off from life on the road to concentrate on the CBD business he ran from home, just as Gabriel began working for a pest control firm.

Perry began his eightieth birthday tour with Mad Professor and the Robotics in March 2016, the new homemade costumes delivered at the opening night in Dublin helping Perry to regain his onstage character. To correspond with the nine British and Irish dates, Professor released the imprecisely titled *Black Ark Classic Songs*, with wobbly recuts of 'Zion's Blood', 'Voodooism' and 'Roast Fish', turning ska track 'Doctor Dick' into 'Doctor Shit' and morphing the Heptones' non-Ark 'Slipping Away' into 'Spirits Speak', off-key vocals a major detractor at times, the spoken-word moments less jarring.

There were nine further European dates that month with the White Belly Rats, a sold-out show with Pura Vida in

Antwerp and the birthday itself taking place at the Cabaret Sauvage in Paris with I Kong supporting, Perry receiving another massive cake onstage.

In April, just as *Vision of Paradise* was released on DVD by British independent Cadiz Music, Rankin' Alpha released the album *Science, Magic, Logic* on digital platforms. Despite the traditional roots reggae framework of 'Negril' and 'Show Me The Way To The Black Ark', much of the album's backing was electronic, edging towards house music, and 'Miserable Satan' had blues guitar. Atop the mishmash of styles, Perry's random proclamations were aimed at Geneva, Pauline, ragamuffins and the dreads, his voice an incidental addition sometimes at odds with the music, though the uptempo title track, issued as a single on Alpha's Jam Ra Records, was more cohesive, driven by Perry's cut-up vocal.

During the latest US mini-tour with Subatomic that included several dates in Texas in April, where their scheduled appearance at the Levitation festival was obliterated by a hailstorm that caused record damage in the state, Perry introduced a policy of silence on the road to better concentrate on his creative process.

'He didn't want any music in the car,' said Emch. 'Even if it was a three-hour drive, it would be silence and he would just type on his phone or his laptop, working on writing and getting lyrics for the shows, so it was Zen-like and peaceful. Sometimes he would break the silence with conversation and one time he said, "A woman wants you to build her a castle, but a man just needs a hut to be happy", and I think it says something about why Scratch is comfortable being on his own path, and his disdain for people chasing fame and fortune. This also struck me as very telling because as much as Scratch loved the shows and the energy of the fans kept him alive, the tours had a rocky schedule, especially for someone his age.'

Perry had long requested recordings of the shows on USB sticks, which he typically glued to the inside of his mosaiced cap rather than listening to them; now he was placing them inside his socks, walking with them for protective purposes.

'They were lined up almost like bullets in a holster, all around his ankle,' said Emch. 'He said, "I put these as a ring of energy to defend me, to ward off the Devil coming up through the earth." So he was using them as an energy barrier.'

After one-offs with ERM and Dubblestandart in May and June, Perry headed to Los Angeles to mount *Judgement Repentance God Order* at Dem Passwords, then temporarily at the King Hing Theatre in Chinatown, where Perry created new large format works, then headed north to perform with Subatomic at the Sierra Nevada World Music Festival, now in the Anderson Valley, where Perry's drunken tirade caused the departure of his backing singers, before the elements scuppered the event.

'Lee started drinking while waiting and, as he often does when he is bored, started giving someone a hard time,' said Emch. 'In this case it was Chez, who told him she was just there to help make him sound good, so he fired her on the spot, and Amanda then quit in solidarity. Five minutes later, the show got cancelled due to rain.'

In mid-July, Perry hit Rotterdam's Expedition Festival with Mad Professor before heading to Tokyo to deliver a 'best of the Black Ark' set at Liquidroom, with live dub mixing by Naoyuki Uchida of Japanese dub band Dry & Heavy, followed by an appearance at Fuji Rock. He was on fine form for his live dub set at Reggae Geel in August, the lack of formal stage in the forested 18-Inch Corner allowing him to better connect with his audience, as Mad Professor and son Joe pushed their dub effects to the outer limits. And before an eleven-date coast-to-coast tour of North America with Subatomic, highlighting *Super Ape*'s fortieth, there was an exceptional appearance at the marijuana-themed High Vibes Festival in Montego Bay.

'High Vibes was amazing, as Lee hadn't done a proper show with his own band in Jamaica in ages,' said Emch. 'Lee went onstage unexpectedly during Beenie Man's set and Beenie put his arm around him and hailed him up as the originator, and Lee said, "This is the Beenie Man and I am the Genie Man." The crowd loved it, so Lee went back onstage again, but the third time Beenie's bodyguard knocked him to the ground because Lee had taunted him. And later that night, at 3.30 in the morning, when everyone was partying backstage, Scratch and this crazy homeless guy were playing soccer, kicking around a little ball of trash.'

Among the increasing low-level releases, in late September, Megawave issued *Must Be Free*, a piecemeal creation initiated by label boss John Palmer in 2012 and finally completed in July 2016. Perry's thickly layered vocals conducted internal conversation over pedestrian ambient rhythms, nuggets of wisdom amidst the piles of perplexity, tracks like 'Rat Race' and 'Isabel' upping the dub ante through stereo panning and delay, and Emch remixed 'House Of Sin' for the CD bonus track (companion album *Space Dubs* would surface in 2017).

Perry was back in the UK for more dates in early October, then hit Berlin's fabled Funkhaus studio complex for the Loop festival in early November, where he, Emch and Volker Schaner took part in a panel discussion, the Perry/Sargarodschi tryptic behind them.

'Before we born, God make us off a map, say you go there and you must do this,' Perry told bemused moderator, Frances

Morgan, his spliff tail burning ever shorter. 'So I am a gift from God to my fans.'

After performing with Pura Vida in Wrocław, Poland, and headlining the electronic Subsonic Music Festival with Mad Professor, held at a mountain resort in an Australian national park, Perry overwintered in Jamaica as usual, where there was time for over-the-top online endorsements of Lindor chocolate on social media (Perry unsuccessfully angling to become a Lindt global ambassador), and in mid-December, Perry helped local charity One Love Brigade to distribute bicycles to underprivileged children in Negril, alongside Cookie the Herbalist, the pair also putting in a joint appearance with Yellowman at the beachside Boat Bar in early February.

Perry's spring 2017 engagements began with Dubblestandart at the electronic Geometry of Now festival, held at a former power station in Moscow, then back to the UK for a mini-tour in March, and a collaborative Perry/Harris art show, *The Higher Powers Bible: From Genesis To Revelation*, was staged for three weeks at London's Horse Hospital, casting Perry as modernised Bible characters, such as Jesus tempted by crack, money and sex; as Jonah, he emerged from the mouth of a sea beast surrounded by smashed computers, and elsewhere he was Daniel, the lion's den reconfigured as the burning Black Ark.

After more downtime in Negril in April, where Perry snuck in a performance at Roots Bamboo with the Hurricane Band, Chris Blackwell got in touch to request a live dub set, executed with Gabre Selassie of the Kingston Dub Club at Blackwell's exclusive Caves Hotel in Negril for the inaugural Tmrw. Tday Festival of yoga and techno music. Then a refreshed Perry toured North America with Subatomic (just as Emch was putting the finishing touches to *Super Ape Returns To*

Conquer), including a greatly anticipated performance at the Sierra Nevada World Music Festival.

'We did a press conference before the gig and I remember Lee almost getting crushed by the crowd,' said Emch. 'It was crazy. I had never seen something like that before.'

After the festival, Paul Zasky was supposed to accompany Perry back to Europe to begin the first leg of the *Electro Dubclubbing* tour with Mad Professor, but when Zasky opted out of chaperone duties, Perry missed his departure from San Francisco, as well as a connecting flight when he finally reached Heathrow, Noel eventually dispatched to collect an exhausted and frustrated Perry at Amsterdam's Schipol Airport, landing Zasky in the doghouse for a few years. Nevertheless, Perry managed to deliver performances to appreciative audiences in Russia, Scandinavia and Western Europe, including a gig in Ghent with Pura Vida.

After more British festival dates in July, Lee and Mireille returned to South America in late August for more gigs with Nairobi, this time in Brazil, Uruguay and Argentina. During some downtime in Buenos Aires in early September, an email arrived from the inventive producer and environmental activist Hernan 'Don Camel' Sforzini, who had just laid some rhythms with Sly and Robbie for a conceived *Final Battle* project that would pit the Rhythm Twins against the Roots Radics.

'I will go to bless the album,' Perry responded, 'pick me up at the hotel.'

As ever, Perry took Sforzini's appearance as a sign, telling the producer, 'I was searching for you for a long time' when they met at his Afro Studio, located in Lanús, south of the capital, where initial track 'Full Moon, Plant A Tree' was voiced after the duo planted a tree nearby at Sforzini's suggestion.

'I told him that I plant trees in my neighbourhood since 2000 and that I lead a project called *Planta & Canta*,' said Sforzini, 'so at ten o'clock at night we were planting a tree in an obscure place under the moonlight.'

Then it was back to Europe for the second leg of *Electro Dubclubbing*, before Perry enjoyed a headline spot with the local Homegrown Band at the Philharmonie de Paris, complimenting *Jamaica Jamaica!*, an extensive exhibition on Jamaican music that included a Perry shrine room, with vintage gear, clothing and a 1970s painting by another artist, bearing his handprints.

Perry enjoyed the extended night-long voicing session held at Abbey Road in late September for Daniel Boyle's new project, *The Black Album*, whose basic rhythms had been laid with bassist Hughie Izachaar, drummer Ed West of pop-reggae act the Drop and keyboardist Calvin Bennion, before Black Ark veteran Robbie Lyn overdubbed keyboards remotely at Anchor Studios in Kingston, considerably enhancing the work.

'We decided to do a new project, taking inspiration from the Roots Radics era, when the Jamaican studios had upgraded equipment, so things were a little less low-fi,' said Boyle. 'Lee asked for a roots reggae sound, but he wanted clarity and punch. I had been sharing the rhythm tracks and getting feedback, then at the vocal session he gave more direction, like adding digital beats or noises in certain songs, adding penny whistle to a track too. Then he added various ad-libbed vocal tracks that he wanted used for the dub versions and explained how he wants them mixed with effects.'

At a one-off gig in October in Istres, southwest France, Perry proclaimed ERM 'the best band in the world', signalling them as his main European backing band. Then Perry headed back to the USA for another coast-to-coast tour in support of the newly released *Super Ape Returns To Conquer*.

'As sound system culture continues to expand globally, I wanted to create DJ-friendly, heavyweight versions of Scratch material that makes sense in the twenty-first century and represents what we have successfully been building with him live, so it sounds like the classic Black Ark vibes in the high frequencies, but in the low end, it has the weight and punch of electronic music, dubstep and hip-hop,' said Emch, who had moved to Los Angeles. 'I also wanted to show that Scratch was forty years ahead of his time with *Super Ape*, and at eighty-one, more relevant to youth culture than ever.'

Super Ape Returns To Conquer was based on fairly faithful reconstructions of the original album, with Perry's magic spells and spoken-word content appearing as accompanying spices rather than linear centrepiece; even 'Curly Dub', led so compellingly by Perry on the original, had fragmented vocal input, and 'Zion's Blood' limited Perry to a chanted meditation on 'Emperor Rain and Emperor Fire', the format requiring repeated close listening to really absorb Perry's pronouncements. A studio counterpart to the Subatomic stage shows, you can hear the care that went into the backing tracks, tastefully reworked for a younger audience, with Screechy Dan and Jahdan Blakkamoore modernising 'Chase The Devil' and 'Three In One', the ghostly chorus of 'Underground Roots' chanted by Ari Up of the Slits, Troy Simms and Omar Little blowing the augmented horn fanfares and Larry McDonald's congas providing an organic roots underpinning, as Emch guides the project deeper into contemporary techno-dub. There were bonus 'dubstrumental' mixes, and outro 'So It Conquer' cleverly incorporated live concert audio, plus seashore sounds from Negril, and Emch went the extra mile with mastering too, ensuring maximum audio quality on all fronts.

'Monkey win, and it's not about Black Ark anymore,' said Perry, on the album's completion. 'Times change, and evil get squeezed. Too much singers. Too much vanity. But God don't have no confusion.'

Early in the tour, at François K's Deep Space night at Output in Brooklyn, it was evident that Perry was clashing with the latest personal assistant, a Swiss dread known as Sanka Fyah, who failed to keep Perry's drinking in check.

'Sanka just couldn't keep Lee under control,' said Emch. 'Lee had a lot of drinks before and after the show, and he was supposed to do an interview for *Billboard*, but it ended up being a really bad vibe. After trying to convince him to do the interview, he was shouting, "Fuck you Emch! You can't control the rain!" at the top of his lungs, repeatedly, as somebody was shoving him into a taxicab. The next night we played upstate at Daryl Hall's club, but Lee just wouldn't come out from backstage because he didn't want Sanka near him.'

According to Emch, things really erupted in Chicago, where a physical altercation resulted in Sanka's dismissal.

'We're checking into our hotel and Lee dipped into the bar and ordered a drink, so Sanka runs to the bar and tries to grab his arm, and it's like a kung-fu movie, with the sound of boards slapping, as Lee's fist is connecting with Sanka's face.'

'Normally when I sleep, I fly in my dream, but when this guy's around me, I'm chained down, pinned under a rock, and there's darkness,' Perry told Emch. 'I can't have his spirit around me.'

'Lee was a lot happier after Sanka was gone, but he was boozing at those shows, so he was having fun, but getting a little sloppy,' said Emch. 'When he's boozing, his energy is different. It's not as positive, and lyrically he can be more rambling, so we felt the difference.'

After the customary extended winter break in Negril, Perry was back in the US at the start of 2018 for another coast-to-coast tour with Subatomic, hitting thirty venues in the space of a month, but he returned to Jamaica thinner, weakened and with loss of appetite, the badly needed rest and reintroduction of fish to his diet firming him up for another series of gigs at mid-sized British venues with the four-piece Upsetters in March. Then, in April, there was a live dub show with Mad Professor at Yaam Berlin and a four-date mini-tour of Belgium and Holland with Pura Vida, followed by further festival gigs with Prof in the summer, a September appearance at Alexandra Palace allowing for more voicing with Adrian Sherwood at On-U's new headquarters in Ramsgate.

In mid-October, Daniel Boyle released *The Black Album*, again with every vocal followed by a dub. Boyle managed to keep Perry buoyant and melodic throughout, his lyrics better integrated and more the central focus, despite the brevity of the voicing session; you can almost hear Perry grinning as he delivers the boastful 'Trendsetter' and rhyming opener 'Mr Brown In Town', which revamps the 'Duppy Conqueror' theme; 'Dead Meat' gives carnivores a roasting and 'Killing Dancehall Softly' playfully refutes Jamaican music's predominant form. Subtle musical touches elevate the material, such as the lilting flute gracing 'Your Shadow Is Black' and the droning hurdy-gurdy on 'Captain Perry'.

'He has a clear idea of what he wants, but at his age I prefer to take his direction and realise those ideas,' Boyle emphasised. 'I'm not a fan of these albums where someone writes everything, then Lee pops in and sings and doesn't hear it again until its released. Lee asked me to produce another solo album, and my job is to produce it, so it is Lee's album, not mine.'

In late October, Perry began another extensive North American tour with Subatomic, this time celebrating *Blackboard Jungle Dub*'s forty-fifth anniversary, where close scrutiny of live recordings of each concert while on the road drew strengthening guidance from Perry.

'Once we started listening to the shows in the car together, Scratch's feedback made Larry and Troy play more in a dialogue with him, or do more of what they knew Scratch liked, and he often talked about bees or butterflies when describing sounds he wanted, as he thought fluttering wings sounded like trilling notes. He once told Larry that he played congas like a piano, which Larry told me was his greatest compliment.'

As a fortieth anniversary edition of Bob Marley's *Kaya* album was released to great fanfare, Perry expressed enduring regret over the circumstances of Marley's death.

'He kept talking to Larry on the drives between shows about whether he was guilty of not intervening more with Bob to change his lifestyle so that he would still be alive,' said Emch. 'He said, "Maybe I should have done something. I could have stopped it and Bob would still be here." I think it might have been triggered by a question from a radio interview, but he seemed very upset about it during that tour. He felt Bob had been lured to the dark side and succumbed to ego and fame. He always said that Bob was his greatest student.'

In Los Angeles, Perry conducted another painting session at Dem Passwords, now located in Santa Paula on the outskirts of Ojai, and reconnected with former Nairobi frontman Ivan Diaz Mathé (now working as Ivan Lee), for a thematic electro-dub mini-album titled *Life Of The Plants*, executed with husband-and-wife production duo Peaking Lights.

'I came up with the concept of a party on a spaceship that is a greenhouse,' said Diaz Mathé. 'When I moved to New York I found devices that translate the electromagnetic impulses of plants into MIDI language, enabling plants to play synthesisers freely, so I've been recording plants everywhere I go, and I was going to be in Los Angeles at the same time that Lee was passing by on tour, so I called Aaron Coynes from Peaking Lights and told him that the three of us should do something together. Stones Throw gave us their studio to work on the tunes, so we built the music tracks in two days, where Indra Dunis played keyboards and Aaron brought a percussionist friend, Onochie Chukwura, who did some overdubs. Then we had Lee come to voice, a very fun day at the studio, and I added the plant parts and mixed it at my studio in New York. Lee loved the concept and made it a call to saving the planet, an invocation of conscience and unity.'

Back in Switzerland, Noel's partner Geraldine gave birth to a daughter named Tea, brightening the household, the new arrival a stabilising presence and the couple entirely devoted to her.

After performing at mid-sized British venues with the four-piece Upsetters, Perry made a dissentious installation at Haus zur Liebe, a non-commercial exhibition space in Schaffhausen, outside Zurich. Running from early December to mid-January, it inverted traditional Swiss *Weihnachtsausstellung* Christmas exhibitions through sculpture, collage and free-word poetry, all replete with magic spells, Obeah references and wrathful proclamations as an individual recasting of Christian cosmology with antipathy to the perceived falsehoods of religious doctrine and those who misuse faith for nefarious ends. Beneath large-format mixed-media collages, a computer keyboard was held down by stones and empty drinks containers, a crown of thorns surrounding a collage of elephants and a dragon marked 'Lion-cap Perry and Egghead Adrian' referencing works in progress at On-U Sound. The exhibition was curated by Swiss artist Lorenzo Bernet, who had attended kindergarten with Noel, and who was in the process of arranging a larger Perry exhibition at the Swiss Institute in New York.

Then, one fateful day in late December, Perry received an unexpected telephone call from Marsha, out of the blue, with the shocking news that Sean was facing a dire medical crisis. A few days after his arrival in Belgium on a visit to Omar and his family, Sean was rushed to hospital for emergency surgery on a ruptured splenic vein. Diagnosed with leukaemia, he faced an uncertain future and mounting medical bills, which a crowdfunding campaign did little to alleviate.

Sean tragically died on 31 January 2019, aged fifty-one, a terrible end for someone who had endured long battles with substance misuse, though at least Omar and his family were with him when he passed, and Marsha in contact by telephone.

When he heard of Sean's death, Perry was distraught. Sorrowfully withdrawing into himself for several days, he was wracked by shame, guilt and regret, since he had never fully reconciled with his firstborn. It made the grieving process especially problematic, the crestfallen Perry inevitably pondering what might have been.

The extensive US tour he undertook with Subatomic in February helped keep Perry's mind off such difficult matters, though he was more up and down than usual in the aftermath. Twenty-three European performances followed with ERM in March and April, Olivier Gangloff handling the pre-recorded elements and dub effects, as well as live drums.

At the same time, Daniel Boyle issued *Back To The Ark* for Record Store Day, reworking 'Babylon Cookie Jar A Crumble',

'Who Killed The Chicken', 'Give Thanx To Jah' and 'Who Colt The Game' with Dennis Bovell and Vin Gordon to mixed effect, the new voicings by Perry and comrades lacking the cohesive ease of the Jamaican originals. Megawave also released *Rootz Reggae Dub*, grafting Perry's free-word pronouncements atop mediocre reggae-inspired rhythms made by a band called Speak Easy, voiced in Negril in 2017, the ska-paced 'Like A Megawave' and a loose reworking of 'Punky Reggae Party' offering momentary amusement value.

Then Perry flew to New York to mount the ambitious *Mirror Master Futures Yard* exhibition at the Swiss Institute, staged for six weeks from 19 April. For his first show in an institutional setting, there were specially commissioned sculptures using mirrors, stones and water from the Hudson and Harlem rivers, as well as customised paintings, original drawings and a Teac four-track adorned with collages beneath a lump of charcoaled wood topped by one of Perry's caps, black Madonna reliquary figurines and computer floppy discs the basis for another mixed-media piece, plus notebooks and ephemera from Cardiff Crescent.

In addition to Perry's presence at the opening, there was a reasoning session between the actor, poet and No-Maddz band co-founder Sheldon Shepherd and the poet and essayist Ishion Hutchinson, whose evocative 'The Ark by "Scratch"' brilliantly relayed the inspiration behind the building of the Black Ark, giving context to Perry's artistic output. The movers and shakers in attendance included Jeremy Tepper, a programme director at satellite radio giant Sirius XM, who secured Perry's participation at the next edition of the Outlaw Country Cruise, a country music festival held aboard the Norwegian Pearl, which would sail between Florida and Jamaica in the new year.

615

Perry went straight from the exhibition to Switzerland and reached Jamaica in time to perform at Shango Fest in Port Antonio, backed by the Uprising Roots band, then headlined the inaugural Food Art Music Environment Festival in Barbados with Mad Professor, just as Mireille, a self-described 'expert on conspiracies', launched an Instagram account to 'expose deceptions and lies and share hidden truths', the New World Order, yoga and vaccines among her favourite targets.

Back in Jamaica, in addition to collaborative recordings, there was time to film a video with the eclectic singer and actress Ebony Bones for her downtempo youth choir remake of 'Police And Thieves', before Perry delivered another European mini-tour with Mad Professor, just as On-U Sound released *Rainford*, Perry's long-awaited new album.

'Lee and the family said, "Why don't we do another record together?" And I just wanted to prove a point and make a really good record, so I got him involved,' said Adrian Sherwood. 'I think it's an album that people will have to play quite a few times before they get it.'

Several years in the making and adorned with Perry/Harris artwork casting Perry as the Horsemen of the Apocalypse, *Rainford* was assembled through far-flung recording sessions undertaken in Jamaica, the UK and Brazil, Sherwood continually striving for new audio textures.

'I'd been experimenting with stretched tuning, so it was stretched tuning and bent-up bits of noise on "Cricket On The Moon" and "African Starship", and it's live performance through the whole record, with Crucial Tony and George Oban, and some of the drums, bits are programmed and then readjusted. The beginning of the record is him and me at one o'clock in the morning after a thunderstorm in Negril, where all the crickets are making noise, and he starts off.'

Close listening reveals fine musical touches, such as an emotive cello on 'Let It Rain' and choral vocals from Sherwood's daughters Denise and Emily, most notably on 'Children Of The Light', though as 'Run Evil Spirit' rides a sparse recut of 'Bionic Rats', it was more in keeping with *The Mighty Upsetter*'s framework. In contrast, 'Makumba Rock' was propelled by a driving rhythm and fuzzy trumpet, a baritone voice intoning the title as a mantra while Perry shouts interjections on voodoo and zodiac dance moves, and there are his animal noises and cackling in another channel; released on a ten-inch with non-album track 'Heaven And Hell', it was the complex creation that kicked off the project.

'I started that ten years ago when I was working with percussionist Simone Soul in São Paulo, then I put Style Scott and Doug Wimbish on it in England,' said Sherwood. 'About four or five years after, I got Lee on the rhythm, so that became the starting point for the record and that set the yardstick for it, and I'd just got my hands on a Langevin equaliser, so I completely mangled it to make something leap out of the speakers.'

In addition to the anti-greed theme of 'Kill Them Dreams Money Worshippers', Sherwood suggested that references to the undead signified 'people who are dead in spirit' rather than zombie fantasies. Then, 'Autobiography Of The Upsetter' was the most personal number, recounting Perry's formative years in Hanover and glory Ark days, as well as its burning and Perry's dramatic transformation, plus the shift to London in the 1980s, echoing earlier On-U 'Autobiographies' voiced by Mikey Dread and Prince Fari, the latter given homage here, along with Bim Sherman (though calling his father a freemason was simply a joke, according to Perry).

'I wanted to try to get the serious side and the mischievous side of Lee, but not the *ridiculous* side,' said Sherwood. 'By going into the autobiography, I wanted it to sound like the most intimate and personal record, with Lee's voice right in your face, and all those little ear cookies, they're references for those who know. On the album in general, I just started morphing stuff together from Lee's background and then nicked bits of things to make an interesting sonic.'

If *Rainford*'s disparate composition felt incongruent in places, disallowing the riveting, brilliant whole of *The Mighty Upsetter*, it was still head and shoulders above anything issued in his name since then, testament to the unique working relationship the pair maintained and Sherwood's commitment to accepting nothing but the best.

'Adrian's a smart fellow,' said Perry. 'Him white, but him think Black, and he's not a bad-minded person, so me choose good-minded people to work with, people with scientifical mind, educational brain, arts and craft, because he's a scientist, doing music science and music Obeah. The album was a display of some magical vibration like curse and healing. I like the album because me speak my mind and speak the truth: I talk about how people funny, and we're supposed to love one another but we can't because we're too grudgeful. People don't want nothing else but what the other man have, and the Devil makes them because the Devil wants to be God.'

'Sometimes you can hear where somebody's trying for something magnificent and even if it fails a bit, you'll like the charm quality, but if it's just more of the same, I'd rather give up,' said Sherwood. 'All the people who made records with him are fans of his and I'm a fan as well, so I wanted to do this for me as much as for him. Hopefully, it will stand the test of time.'

Concurrently, diversionary material bearing Perry's name made an ever-growing slush pile, as heard on hip-hop producer

Mr Green's *Super Ape Vs Open Door*, which drew from Ariwa's stockpile, weaving incidental Perry murmuring into cut-up hip-hop beats. In contrast, 'Tongue Of Thunda', produced by Reuben Addis in the UK, was a more integrated ten-inch EP that rode a minimal electro-dub rhythm.

Summer festival highlights in 2019 included a live dub set with Sherwood at Seasplash Croatia and ERM gigs in Poland and the UK, including Moovin in Manchester, where Perry chewed the fat with rapper Big Daddy Kane. Then, more cross-country US dates with Subatomic in September, followed by four high-profile performances in Mexico.

Musically speaking, the most significant arrival was *Heavy Rain*, the excellent dub companion to *Rainford*. By deconstructing the rhythms and reassembling them with snippets of unheard Perry vocals, Sherwood explored the experimental potential not always realised on *Rainford*, a prime example being 'Here Come The Warm Dreads', a take of 'Makumba Rock' with Eno's ambient keyboards, as a Perry vocal fragment mentions a mental asylum; Vin Gordon blows the trombone centrepiece of 'Rattling Bones And Crowns' and 'Crickets In Moonlight', conjuring *Musical Bones* continuations. Similarly, 'Space Craft' turns 'African Starship' into a creepy melodica-and-harmonica duet and 'Heavy Rainford' brings forth snippets of Perry wisdom, wiping out racism and evilness on a reconfigured 'Autobiography' driven by trombone and mouth organ, while 'Hooligan Hank' is a cut-up associative poem over a looped 'Bucky Skank' fragment. It is the kind of album that reveals new layers with repeated listening, and rightfully reached number one on the *Billboard* charts – a first for a Perry album.

In late October, Perry fulfilled more west coast dates with Subatomic, then returned to Jamaica for just a few days before heading to Paris, where the scheduled gig was scuppered by his late arrival due to an airline strike, though UK performances with ERM were successfully delivered at the end of the month, and there was time to voice a couple of techno tracks at Rolling Lion in Suffolk.

Then Perry headed to Dubai with Subatomic for the Jamaican Sound System edition of Sole DXB, the Middle East's most prestigious street culture and lifestyle festival; at a round-table discussion chaired by Federation Sound's Max Glazer, Perry linked the burning of the Ark to Neptune's pitchfork, spoke of ups and downs with Marley and the angelic nature of his Swiss children, touching on myriad topics in the usual symbolic terms.

'Lee loved Dubai and was received very well there,' said Emch. 'He called it Dub-I and said that the people were very kind and smart.'

After returning to Switzerland, Perry spent a few inspiring days in Berlin voicing an unusual album with experimental duo Mouse On Mars and a range of guest collaborators, including house producer Eric D. Clark on keyboards and Sissi Rada on harp, as well as Elena Poulou of the Fall, who helped put the project in motion and who voiced a duet with Perry during the work, which evolved in a communal fashion once word of Perry's presence spread.

'There is so much love in this record, so much warmth and a passion that isn't driven by one spirit or one production team,' said Mouse On Mars co-founder, Jan St Werner. 'We had a beautifully varied and productive collective with musicians I have never seen before. It was so dense, yet so light-hearted, and we want to make this a virtual record in the sense that it's a headspace, something that is sensually possible, so the sound is around you and the sound is inside you, with physical resonance.'

Once back in Jamaica, Perry enjoyed the ganja-themed Rastafari Rootzfest in Negril, where he was reunited with Benbow Creary, now drumming with south Florida reggae band Jah Steve and the Counteract Crew, instigating future collaboration.

Then, over the winter months, Perry had time to reflect on his present direction, if only briefly. An off-grid LSP Paradise was still the long-term goal, though for the time being, he and Mireille would have to content themselves with Negril, where Russian producer Alexey Patsaev, alias Levsha Patsan or Lefty Rudeboy, arrived in January to gain Perry's vocal input on the crowdfunded *Aquarium In Dub* project, which reconfigured back catalogue highlights of controversial Russian alternative band Aquarium in an electro-reggae style, and although Perry was recovering from a bad cough, he added some incidental spoken-word accompaniment at Jah Wayne's studio in Negril, ad-libbing fragmented lines inspired by the translated song topics (500 copies of the CD would be pressed by Vygorod in October).

For his first performance of 2020, Perry returned to the Boat Bar at the end of the month on a low-key matinee with Cookie the Herbalist, backed by the resident One Love band, an inauspicious start to what would prove to be one of humanity's most challenging years in recent history.

On 1 February, an unsuspecting Perry boarded the Norwegian Pearl in nearby Falmouth to euphoric applause, performing messy versions of 'Curly Locks', 'War In A Babylon' and 'The Harder They Come' with alt-country act, the Waco Brothers. Later in the journey, he joined outspoken Texan rebel Jesse Dayton for a barely recognisable rendition of 'Police And Thieves', and gave a painting demonstration to baffled guests, hanging out with fellow icon Kris Kristofferson during downtime.

Despite not being an obvious choice for a floating country festival attended by a moneyed, aging clientele, the Outlaw Country Cruise attendees fully embraced Lee 'Scratch' Perry, who equally relished his time on board.

Yet, behind the scenes, strange things were happening. Chinese staff had reportedly been removed from the ship in Jamaica and sent home as a precautionary measure due to the rising spread of Covid-19, a debilitating virus first identified in Wuhan that was spreading to surrounding nations and other territories, with a handful of cases already reported in the US.

After docking in Miami, Perry zipped over to Los Angeles for a live dub set at One Love Cali Fest in Long Beach, then returned to Florida for five gigs with Jah Steve and the Counteract Crew, and, once back in Jamaica, he hit the Boat Bar for another matinee performance, just as he and Adrian Sherwood were announced as guest artists on the 2020 Meltdown, curated by Grace Jones.

A UK tour with ERM should have commenced in mid-March, but was postponed at short notice as Covid-19 lock-down restrictions kicked in. The rest of the year was essentially a write-off, and if social media posts of Perry chilling on the beach with local beauties suggested he and Mireille were unfazed by quarantine life, the inability to tour shut off the most reliable source of income in an era when earnings from music releases were at an all-time low.

Jamaica enacted an 11 p.m. curfew and gatherings of over twenty persons were banned. Nevertheless, Perry made the occasional late-night trip to micro-studio House Ah Knowledge at the beachside Drifter's Bar, allowing him to flex his creative muscles under the starlight by contributing to collaborative material when requested; Perry had sometimes complained about living out of a suitcase, yet as the months rolled by, he was frustrated by the carceral nature of lockdown, so recording always provided a vital form of release. One of the first to surface was the song 'Garvey Say', with his chanted embellishments, voiced for upstate New York band Mosaic Foundation in June, its backing inspired by the rhythm of a Haudenosaunee social dance.

Making the most of the Covid touring lull, Daniel Boyle booked Perry into a Negril studio for one solid week, sending more techno rhythms from his new base in southern Italy for Perry to voice remotely, the tracks becoming the platform for a forthcoming collaborative project featuring former Happy Mondays frontman Shaun Ryder, as well as Tricky, psyche-delic neo-soul singer Greentea Peng, and other guests.

Once restrictions had partially eased, Lee and Mireille flew to Switzerland in mid-August. The Meltdown and all other live engagements were postponed, but Perry remained active and focused, preparing new artworks for an exhibition proposed by Lorenzo Bernet, slated for spring 2021 at London's Cabinet Gallery, with another pending in Chicago, though both would be postponed.

ERM brought their mobile studio to Switzerland in September, banging out the rudiments of a new album with Perry in the space of a week, returning later to voice and adjust the material, and among the other releases still in the pipeline was an album for Youth that was voiced remotely over a longer period, a collaboration with Vancouver drone heads New Age Doom, and another collaboration with Rankin' Alpha, titled *My Name Is Pipecock Jackxon*.

Then, along with a spot of modelling for Gucci, Perry managed to take part in the Woerdz Festival in Lucerne in late October, delivering his lyrics over the backing of a local sound system before a socially distanced audience of fifty, though he looked drained at the post-gig interview, where he debated the merits of a crazy skull and a perfect heart, and proposed that God could be female.

Despite the total cessation of live events, Lee and Mireille were still staying up all night and eating dinner at seven in the morning, unable to break entrenched habits. Lee's room was now so cluttered that he avoided setting foot in it, so after being cooped up in their Swiss home for much of the winter, facing heavy snow and strict lockdowns, the couple returned to Jamaica in late January 2021, hoping to ride out the worst of the pandemic with warmer climes and more personal freedom. Thus, instead of being onstage somewhere, he spent his eighty-fifth birthday with Mireille and a few friends, the weeks in Negril stimulating a better frame of mind and a positive outlook for the future.

As humanity struggled to adapt to the new realities of a post-Covid world, collapsing airline travel, enforced quarantines and widespread local lockdowns pointed to a likely end to Perry's non-stop touring schedule, though, as ever, he was ready to comply with divine plans.

'Me discover that what happened is God do it, so nobody don't have to blame anybody anymore,' said Perry. 'Now we have to give Judgement what's due to Judgement, and if God said to rest and make him take over, then I must do that because me no know what God know.'

After an unusually quiet spring, Perry generated much creative output during the busy summer months and had positive interactions with notable visitors. In July, there was a happy reunion with Patricia Chin and her son Chris, who brought him copies of her autobiography, *Miss Pat: My Reggae Journey*, which featured his testimony. Then, a *Rolling Stone* film crew captured Perry at work at a recording studio in

Green Island and later interviewed him on the beach, an animated Perry revealing his plans 'to make different music with different beats'. Six of Perry's artworks were to feature at the delayed São Paulo Biennial in September too, including collages, marker-pen proclamations and a sculptured television set.

For much of the summer, a Negril studio acted as Perry's second home, since he was voicing new works for various overseas collaborators and rehearsing for British and European tour dates in October and November, which were supposed to be his last before retirement.

'He was going to the studio all the time, recording non-stop and rehearsing,' said Mireille. 'Sometimes he was also giving performances for free on the beach.'

Most importantly, Mireille finally found the ideal spot for LSP Paradise on a plot of land in Lucea with a river running through it. They began making plans for its construction, conceiving a new recording studio for Lee with an adjoining art house, the work scheduled to commence after the tour.

On 27 August, a post on social media titled 'What are your future plans?' announced that work on Perry's alternate community would begin in December, with a call for volunteers, including permaculture specialists, to join him.

'If any of you are looking for a way out and want to live with us independent from Babylon and are already ready for the change of life, you could become the foundation of my community,' the post proclaimed. 'Children [are] very welcome, as we'll do home schooling. Investment is not necessary, but [there will be the] possibility to build your own cottage or purchase one in the later stage.'

In the accompanying video, a grinning Perry delivered a blessing in his latest cryptic soliloquy, seeming his regular self. Yet, the very next day, on 28 August 2021, Lee 'Scratch' Perry departed our earthly plane with unexpected abruptness, his spirit leaving his body on his way to hospital, following attempted CPR.

'He spent his last moments at the doorway, right where he had his little magic garden,' said Mireille, adding that she will reveal more when the time is right. 'He wanted to leave his spirit right there, where he planted two *Lignum vitae* trees.'

During the preparations for his burial, Minister of Culture Babsy Grange provided support to the family, which was gratefully received.

'I really have to thank Ms Babsy Grange, who arranged everything,' said Mireille. 'From day one, she made herself available at all hours of the day and night and she really did a great job, from A to Z. I was still in shock and under stress, and I don't know how I would have done it without her.'

Grange presided over the brief, sparsely attended public viewing of Perry's body on 23 September. It was held at the funeral home run by the unrelated Peter Perry in the heart of Grange's Spanish Town constituency, where Perry's final outfit crowned him with a red studded baseball cap and oversized sunglasses. The body was then transported across the island in an eight-wheeled wagon with clear sides and top, displaying the coffin, amidst five Humvees with police escorts. During the three and a half hour journey, the massive speaker attached to the wagon repeatedly blared 'Jerusalema', the phenomenally successful South African house track with gospel leanings, produced by Master KG.

Perry's family plot is located on a patch of private land in the Francis Town district of Cauldwell, up a steep, muddy road that was largely neglected, so the vehicles struggled to reach their destination. Upon finally arriving, the music was changed to Perry's 'Stand in Love',[1] a bittersweet adaptation of Ken Boothe's 'When I Fall in Love' that spoke of love's eternal qualities and Perry's everlasting spiritual devotion. His sister Sitta had been interred at the plot just a few weeks earlier, and Miss Ina a decade before, as well as Miss Nell, who became the victim of a reckless driver about a year after Miss Ina's passing.

Covid-19 restrictions limited the permitted number of attendees; the core comprised of Mireille, their children and grandchildren, Lee's brother Sonny and a handful of other relatives and close friends, though a few local onlookers managed to join in. The occasion allowed Sonny to connect with the children, suggesting to them that he would 'come again, that their eyes can behold him'. Store assistant C.B. of Randy's Records was about the only industry personnel present.

Local MP Tamika Davis began the proceedings by reading a memorial statement prepared by Grange, highlighting the lasting impact of Perry's individual creativity and his mentoring role to Bob Marley and the Wailers, and pledging to erect a memorial bust of Perry in Hanover in 2022 as part of Jamaica's Diamond Jubilee Celebrations – another honour belatedly bestowed.

The rest of the service was presided over by Perry's friend Andre Johnson, a Seventh Day Adventist pastor from Lucea who had discussed spiritual matters with him on several occasions. Mireille delivered the heartfelt eulogy, speaking with feeling of their lasting bond, Lee's individual humour and his final earthly moments, emphasising that it was only his vessel that was being buried, since Lee still has more work to do in the spiritual plane.

'We didn't gather here to say goodbye to this extraordinary spirit that we knew under the name Lee "Scratch" Perry, we gather here to pay respect to his life on earth and to the vehicle he used in order to be able to exist in this realm,' she said in the eulogy, becoming overcome with emotion at times. 'It was impossible to accept that he suddenly disappeared out of our lives, but we know that his spirit is right here in Negril − the spirit never left . . . He could save people with laughter. He loved superheroes and Marvel comics, little toys and things that make people smile. It make them remember the joy of life . . . He was not an ordinary person, and he was not of this world. He was only a visitor here and he say it million times, over and over.'

Then American expat Steve Weinstein, who opened the Jah Freedom recording studio and guest house in Negril in 2003, gave a brief speech about the long friendship he enjoyed with Lee and Mireille, and the recordings Perry made at the facility.

As the casket was placed into the sepulchre, crashing lightning and rolling thunder scattered the crowd, bringing back the heavy rain that would continue unabated for the rest of the day, the elements in their firmamental chorus accentuating the finality of Perry's transition.

At the time of his unexpected passing, Lee 'Scratch' Perry's legacy was already assured. Remix culture is ubiquitous and taken for granted today, but never would have happened without the techniques Perry developed in the 1960s and '70s, reusing rhythm tracks for multiple purposes. The repercussions of this innovation found its greatest vein in the rap explosion that has made hip-hop culture predominant all over the world, which owes much to the pioneering procedures Perry developed in the 'version' phenomenon, the studio practice that evolved out of Jamaican sound system culture, and you can hear his version footprints beneath a broad rap spectrum, from the political treatises of Public Enemy to the lewd rhymes of Snoop Dogg and the stoned odes of Cypress Hill; Kanye West and Jay Z have made plain their debt to Perry through 'Lucifer'.

In a continuation of the punk/reggae crossover that began when the Clash covered 'Police And Thieves', during the late 1970s and early '80s, Perry's productions had strong influence on the work of post-punk's prime movers. For instance, Public Image Limited's *Metal Box* betrayed a deep love for the Black Ark sound as revered by John Lydon and Jah Wobble, and Perry's influence underpins work by the Slits, Talking Heads and A Certain Ratio, the latter especially when releasing music under their alter-ego, Sir Horatio.

In the realm of electronic dance music, of which he is considered a godfather, Perry's techniques have filtered through to diverse strands of house music, ambient, trance and other forms of techno, and a line can be drawn from the Black Ark and Perry's post-Ark works through jungle, drum and bass, garage, dubstep and grime, with further echoes arriving in the Afrobeats and kuduro of west and central Africa.

In the world of indie rock, artists as diverse as Khruangbin and LCD Sound System have acknowledged his influence, while Sun Araw and M Geddes Gengras have been highly inspired by his Black Ark heyday, as heard on their collaborative work with the Congos.

The sway of Perry's individual Afrocentrism and unique spirituality can arguably be traced to the contemporary jazz underground on both sides of the Atlantic, in addition to the many dub practitioners currently active in territories such as Japan, Brazil, Mexico and New Zealand, as well as in the work of contemporary Jamaican dubbers like Teflon and Yaadcore; Perry has also been venerated by many on the Jamaican dancehall scene, select stars such as Beenie Man,

Bounty Killer, Vybz Kartel, Spragga Benz and Jah Cure belatedly acknowledging the influence of his spiritual, carnal and sartorial individuality.

That the Jamaican Prime Minister, Andrew Holness, tweeted his condolences to Perry's family on hearing of his death is highly significant, especially as he went on to emphasise Perry's ground-breaking work in reggae and dub, and the Minister of Culture, Babsy Grange, equated him with Mozart. Echoing Linton Kwesi Johnson, Keith Richards was quoted as dubbing Perry the Salvador Dalí of music, and Chris Salewicz likened him to Picasso, reminding that Perry's creativity spanned different art forms, that he had complex relationships with the women in his life, and that he was often a volatile, unpredictable and contradictory man. Notably, painter Jean-Michel Basquiat had cited Perry as a significant influence on his Afrofuturist creations during the 1980s too.

In the aftermath of his death, Perry's production skills were ranked alongside those of African-American icons such as psychedelic soul producer Norman Whitfield, the jazz, pop and film score legend Quincy Jones, and the funk and new wave polymath Nile Rodgers, though in truth, much of Perry's work transcends the easy categorisation that can be applied to the work of others, his output more idiosyncratic and apart from the mainstream.

For many, Perry will always be best remembered as the man who mentored Bob Marley, bringing him to the attention of audiences outside Jamaica for the very first time and preparing him for the international stardom he would achieve with Island Records; when considering his career in retrospect, it is clear that we have much to be thankful for in Lee 'Scratch' Perry, his unique trajectory yielding exceptional creations during a singular life.

Yet, despite the topsy-turvy fairy tale he lived with his family, whether in Jamaica, Switzerland, or elsewhere, Perry remained a man apart who spent most of his days in solitude, building sculpture, writing declamatory graffiti, and typing magic words on his laptop or phone, displaying the drastic, individualistic behaviour that marked him since the demise of the Black Ark, and when asked about these ongoing compulsions, Perry reminded people that he was constantly directed by voices he heard in his head, who ultimately issued him with positive and negative commands.

During our last formal interview, Perry alluded to the impermanence of everything, and his looming retirement.

'Honestly, to where me reach now in my life, me just do entertainment until the time me feel to stop, but me no really have it in mind to get back in struggling and sufferation with anybody to prove anything, cos me already prove all that I have to prove already. I should live happy and live easy now, so I don't make no plan for anything.'

Instead of continuing to tour the world as a performing artist, he saw himself as returning to the Almighty, whom he had perpetually served.

'I see the future is like, I come from God and I'm going back to God. I did not come out of confusion, and I did not come out of illusion: I am coming from God's election and some people don't believe I am crazy, but craziness is a power.'

Looking back on his life and work, Perry offered the following reflections: he was mindful of significant mistakes, but everything happened for a reason; all things were still possible, and he was compelled to continue creating, right to the very end.

'When I leave 5 Cardiff Crescent, the studio was burned down. If I was looking on vanity, I would not do it because that was all my riches, and me could just make a hit song without trying, but if me keep it together, me wouldn't be here now, me would be dead and gone because of stupidness, so that is a part of death: you give away your riches and you born again, and you find a different set of people who wouldn't want to kill you for your riches. It's after me burn down the studio, me know that some of the people that me bring there, me should not bring there, because me was mixing righteousness and unrighteousness together and pollute the place.

'The things that I hear, I hear it and I don't know where it's coming from, but I think it's coming from God. He say, "Make that one play *this* and make that one play *that*", so we put it together and I think it's coming from some invisible spaceship. My music going to heal people by the ears, by the words that them hear, and it gonna heal them by the spirit vibration that I put into it, because there's no meat. I used to love meat very much and that was where I have to burn down the studio because most of it was creating off meat and cigarette and wine, but these set of music that I'm putting out now have no meat, no cigarette, no wine, no ganja, nothing, so it's pure – pure, clear spirit that whosoever believe in the word that I said, those are the chosen few that will be saved out of the world from 144,000 sins, and the rest belongs to the Devil. Sometimes I like to tease because I learn by practising with the words and the teacher was showing me that the words have two meanings, forward and backwards, so when you go forward, you can't do anything but come back, that means future and past.

'The Bible is another part of it: it's a door, an open door, and most of what happened, it's coming from the Bible but sometimes it takes long to manifest, and sometimes it manifest instantly, and if people going to show you the wisdom of God, they have to be very childish. I am the future teller,

I am the scientist, I am the miracle man and I'm living here because I don't have anywhere else to live at the moment, but I'm not coming from here.

'Any music cannot heal people, it's only God's music that can heal people, but my music is a space vibration, it's not coming from here. Art is life and God can do anything, so I want to keep on kicking forever.'

Notes to the Text

CHAPTER ONE
[1] Interview with Bruno Blum, Switzerland, May 1994.

CHAPTER TWO
[1] During the 1970s, Perry told journalists that he was already in Kingston in the late 1950s and a 1969 *Swing* magazine feature placed him in the capital from 1946–56, which Perry refuted; more recently, Perry said that he did not arrive in the capital until he was twenty-five years old.
[2] Jean-Francois Bizot, 'Jamaique: Reggae, Colts Et Cubans' in *Actuel Almanac Des Anee* (1980), page 256.

CHAPTER THREE
[1] Chris May, 'Starting From Scratch' in *Black Music*, Volume 4, Issue 47 (October 1977), page 13.

CHAPTER FIVE
[1] Blum, op. cit.
[2] Interview with Bruno Blum, Reims, 18 October 1997.
[3] May, op. cit.
[4] Interview with Steve Barrow for the Reggae Xplosion archive project, March 1994.

[5] May, op. cit.

[6] Carl Gayle, 'The Upsetter (Part 2)' in *Black Music*, Volume 2, Issue 15 (February 1975), pages 41–42.

[7] Ibid.

[8] Chris Lane, 'Scratch the Upsetter' in *Blues & Soul*, No. 112, 20 July 1973, page 27.

[9] Gayle, op. cit.

[10] Blum, op. cit.

CHAPTER SIX

[1] Balford Henry, 'The Man Who Gave Us "Beat Down Babylon" and "Place Called Africa"', in *The Star*, 21 January 1972, page 22.

[2] Gayle, op. cit.

[3] Ibid.

[4] Lane, op. cit.

[5] Rob Randall, 'Lee Perry: Reversing The Trend', in *Melody Maker*, 7 July 1973, page 52.

CHAPTER SEVEN

[1] A prototype of the Soundcraft Series II that would launch in December 1975, the desk was marketed in trade publications as 'Soundcraft Sixteen Into Four Series II' or 'Soundcraft Sixteen Into Four Mk II'.

CHAPTER EIGHT

[1] May, op. cit.

CHAPTER NINE

[1] Barrow, op. cit.

[2] Neil Spencer, 'The Rockers Uptown: Kingston Report Pt 2', in *New Musical Express*, 23 October 1976, page 35.

[3] Neil Spencer, 'Spikey Heads Meet Dreadlocks', in *New*

Musical Express, 1 October 1977, page 6.
⁴ Interview with Bob Mack, in *Grand Royal*, Issue 2, 1995, page 81.
⁵ Ibid.
⁶ Ibid.

CHAPTER TEN:
¹ Chris Salewicz, 'Jamaica: The Young Lion Roars', in *New Musical Express*, 27 May 1978, pages 37–8.
² Ibid.
³ That is, a homosexual.

CHAPTER ELEVEN:
¹ Henry W. Targowski, 'Lee Perry: Genius, Madman, Magician', in *Vinyl*, No. 7, 1981, pages 14–15.
² Vivien Goldman, 'Lee Perry Has Found God, And His Name Is Pipecock Jackxon', in *Melody Maker*, 21 July 1979.
³ Interview with David Rodigan, Capital Radio, London, *c.* 23 February 1980.
⁴ Interview with Pieter Franssen, VPRO Radio 3 broadcast, Holland, 4 April 1990.
⁵ Richard Grabell, 'Curse Of The Vampire', in *New Musical Express*, 25 July 1981, page 24.
⁶ Ibid.
⁷ Danny Kelly, 'Lee Perry' in *New Musical Express*, 17 November 1984, pages 6, 7 and 58. Kelly's article erroneously dates the fire to 1980, disproven by the *Deep Roots Music* footage of July 1981, with its intact control room. Anyone still under the illusion that the fire happened in 1978, '79 or '80 should take a closer look at *Deep Roots Music* and Gary Weis' footage of July 1982.
⁸ Tropic FM radio broadcast, Paris, 6 November 1988; interview

conducted November 1987 by Mary Nnankya and Florent Drouet.

[9] Bob West, 'The "Upsetter" To Return', in *Jamaica Times*, 1 March 1983, page 10.

CHAPTER TWELVE:

[1] Gordon C., *The Reggae Files*, Hansib, London, 1988, page 99; interview conducted 1 November 1987.

CHAPTER THIRTEEN:

[1] Interview with Robert Kuypers and Karel Michiels, Switzerland, 10 April 1990.

[2] Franssen, op. cit.

[3] That is, *170 Hours With Extraterrestrials*.

CHAPTER FOURTEEN:

[1] Sanctuary would issue plenty of Perry archive material for the next few years, until extreme financial difficulties led to its sale to Universal in August 2007; in 2013, the label was acquired by BMG.

CHAPTER FIFTEEN:

[1] 'Stand In Love' was released in 2014 on *Living Heart Vol I*, a compilation celebrating the 25th anniversary of the founding of Xterminator Records.

Further Reading

Barrow, Steve and Dalton, Peter. *The Rough Guide to Reggae* (Rough Guides, 2001)

Bradley, Lloyd. *Bass Culture: When Reggae Was King* (Viking, 2000)

Chang, Kevin O'Brien and Chen, Wayne. *Reggae Routes: The Story of Jamaican Music* (Temple University Press, 1998)

Clarke, Sebastian. *Jah Music: The Evolution of the Popular Jamaican Song* (Heinemann, 1980)

Davis, Stephen and Simon, Peter. *Reggae Bloodlines: In Search of the Music and Culture of Jamaica* (Anchor, 1977)

——— (eds.) *Reggae International* (R&B, 1982)

Davis, Stephen. *Bob Marley: Conquering Lion of Reggae* (Arthur Baker, 1983)

Foster, Chuck. *Roots Rock Reggae: An Oral History of Reggae Music, from Ska to Dancehall* (Billboard, 1999)

Goldman, Vivien. *The Book of Exodus: The Making and Meaning of Bob Marley & the Wailers' Album of the Century* (Aurum, 2006)

Goldman, Vivien and Boot, Adrian. *Bob Marley: Soul Rebel – Natural Mystic* (St Martin's, 1982)

Grant, Colin. *I & I: The Natural Mystics: Marley, Tosh and Wailer* (Jonathan Cape, 2011)

639

Masouri, John. *Wailing Blues: The Story of Bob Marley's Wailers* (Omnibus, 2008)

Murrell, Nathaniel; Spencer, William and McFarlane, Adrian (eds). *Chanting Down Babylon: The Rastafari Reader* (Ian Randle, 1998)

Salewicz, Chris and Boot, Adrian. *Songs of Freedom* (Bloomsbury, 1995)

———— (2001) *Reggae Explosion: The Story of Jamaican Music* (Virgin, 2001)

Salewicz, Chris. *Bob Marley: The Untold Story* (Harper Collins, 2009)

Schuler, Monica. *Alas, Alas, Kongo: A Social History of Indentured African Immigration into Jamaica 1841–1865* (John Hopkins University Press, 1980)

Small, Geoff. *Ruthless: The Global Rise of the Yardies* (Warner, 1995)

Steffens, Roger. *So Much Things to Say: The Oral History of Bob Marley* (WW Norton, 2017)

Steffens, Roger and Pierson, Leroy Jodie. *Bob Marley and the Wailers: The Definitive Discography* (Rounder Books, 2005)

Taylor, Don and Henry, Mike. *Marley and Me* (Barricade, 1995)

White, Timothy. *Catch a Fire* (Owl Books, 1998)

Picture Credits

Plate 1: Courtesy of Heartbeat Records, photographer unknown (*top*); courtesy of Trax On Wax, photographer unknown (*bottom*)

Plate 2: Courtesy of Trojan Records, photographer unknown

Plate 3: Courtesy of Ina Blythe, photographer unknown (*top left*); courtesy of Creole Music/BMG, photographers unknown (*top right, bottom left*); © Chris Lane (*bottom right*)

Plate 4: © Kim Gottlieb-Walker/www.lenswoman.com, from her book *Bob Marley and the Golden Age of Reggae* (*all*)

Plate 5: © Dave Hendley (*top left*); © Adrian Boot/urbanimage. tv (*top right, bottom*)

Plate 6: © Adrian Boot/urbanimage.tv

Plate 7: © Adrian Boot/urbanimage.tv (*top left, top right, bottom left*); courtesy of Robert Kuypers, photographer unknown (*bottom right*)

Plate 8: © Adrian Boot/urbanimage.tv (*all*)

Plate 9: © Jean-Bernard Sohiez/urbanimage.tv (*all*)

Plate 10: © David Katz (*all*)

Plate 11: © Ricky Powell (*top*); © Fizzè (*middle*); © David Katz (*bottom*)

Plate 12: © Adrian Thomas

Plate 13: © Adrian Thomas (*top*); © David Katz (*bottom*)

641

Plate 14: © Adrian Thomas (*top left, bottom right*); © David Katz (*top right, bottom left*)

Plate 15: © Robert Kuypers (*top left*); courtesy of Shiva Perry (*top right*); courtesy of Mireille Campbell-Perry (*bottom*)

Plate 16: © David Katz (*top, bottom left*); courtesy of David Katz (*bottom right*)

Acknowledgements

I am indebted to many for helping to shape specific aspects of this authorised biography. Lee Perry's family have been especially helpful in confronting the turmoil of the past; his mother, Ina Blythe, even insisted that I occupy her bedroom during my first few days in Hanover, while she shared the spare room with other relatives. Siblings Dulcie, Sonny, Sitta, Lloyd, Girlie and Miss Nell gave context to early days, and brother P-Son deserves special mention for locating musicians and family members, including Archie Moore of Caveman sound system, and for accompanying me around the northwest of Jamaica. Though adopted daughter Michelle and son Omar were initially hesitant, son Sean readily detailed his relationship with his father, as did daughter Marsha, who has my gratitude for hosting me on one of my trips to Jamaica, making me feel part of the family through home cooking and domino games. Former partner Pauline Morrison was also understandably reluctant at first, but opened up over time, and introduced me to the delights of the Blue Mountains in the process. Wife Mireille, now his widow, provided much frank information and enabled me to stay connected after Perry moved to Switzerland, while former girlfriends Vicky Nelson and Sandra Cooley also shared their memories, as did daughter Cleopatra and youngest children, Gabriel and Shiva.

ACKNOWLEDGEMENTS

Everyone else who agreed to be interviewed for this book has my utmost thanks, including the many musicians, singers, producers, executive producers and engineers that worked with Perry, and especially those no longer with us. Extra special thanks are due to my former neighbour, Doctor Alimantado, for friendship and for introducing me to the rigours of life on the road; to Rudy Mascoll and Jennifer Romeo, for making me feel that I had family in England; to Max Romeo for driving me all over Jamaica, introducing me to numerous musicians and for making sure I experienced aspects of the island that would otherwise have remained hidden; to Adrian Sherwood, for offering practical support and for providing sneak previews of important album works; and to Mad Professor for keeping me abreast of all things Perry, as well as for collaborating with me on live dub events.

Linton Kwesi Johnson has my heartfelt thanks for rising to the challenge of Perry's request by writing his incomparable foreword, shedding light on aspects of Perry's importance and the uniqueness of his vision, and I am grateful to Sharmilla Beezmohun for helping to instigate it.

The phenomenal Carolyn Cooper, Professor Emerita at the University of the West Indies, Mona, made useful contextual comments, hosted the Jamaican launch of the first edition of this book and introduced me to helpful colleagues, including Professor Clinton Hutton, Dr Sonjah Stanley Niaah and Dr Donna Hope at UWI, as well as Dr Dennis Howard of the Institute of Cultural Policy and Innovation and Herbie Miller of the Jamaica Music Museum at the Institute of Jamaica, all of whose input has informed this revised edition; I am also grateful to Maureen Warner-Lewis, Professor Emerita at the University of the West Indies, Mona, and Hazel McClune of the African-Caribbean Institute of Jamaica for clarifying particulars of Ettu. UWI alumnus Matthew J. Smith, currently Professor of History and Director of the Centre for the Study of the Legacies of British Slave-Ownership at UCL, also made many helpful comments on aspects of the music, culture, history and politics discussed in this book and engaged Sean Falconer to check elusive records.

Helpful interview co-ordination was provided by people in diverse locations, all of whom receive my gratitude, as do those who conducted joint interviews with me, including Lol Bell-Brown of *Boom Shacka Lacka*, Ray Hurford of *Small Axe,* Patricia Meschino of *Billboard*, Adrian Christani, formerly of Greensleeves, Bart Cattaert of Planet Ilunga, and Dave Hallworth, who also helped with French and German translations; John Sergeant assisted with video transfers and made helpful comments on an early draft, while Bethlehem Tekle and Tekle Alemu helped make sense of Amharic adaptations. I also thank photographer Adrian Thomas for his fine work in what were often very trying circumstances, as well as the other photographers whose work is included here.

Key industry personnel allowed access to their archives, including Steve Barrow of Blood and Fire, Marley authority Roger Steffens, Trevor Wyatt of Island, Chris Wilson of Heartbeat, Dana Smart of Hip-O, Laurence Cane-Honeysett of Trojan, Markus Vogel of Reggae Fever (who solved the mystery of Deltone) and broadcaster Doug Wendt, whose Midnight Dread radio programme on KTIM San Rafael was where I first heard Perry's music in my youth. Colin Leslie of Imani Music, Jeremy Collingwood of Lick It Back, James Dillon of Amoeba, Brandan Kearney of Nuf Sed, Kelly Maurice of Eight For Eight Music, Darren Mathers of Jamtone, Andrew Rush of UC Berkeley, Studio One researcher Carl Finlay, Clive Allick of Moa Anbessa/The Park Management, Daisuke

Sawa of Dub Siren, freelance producer Ayako 'Iyah' Knight, Professor Cat of Radio Centraal, Antwerp, and collectors Gary Simons, Jos Klijn, Ron de Groot, Ron Wittekoek, Al Kaatz, Rolf Cox and Todd Campbell are among the many who helped fill in the blanks. Extra special mention must be made of the late Jack Ruby, who introduced me to the mindboggling reality of the sound system experience through the 50,000 Watts of Dub Power tour of the US west coast in 1982, promoted by Lister Hewan-Lowe, who helped locate missing musicians. I am grateful to Ariel Tagar for particulars of Perry's burial.

I have quoted select interviews by other journalists, each of which is indicated by an endnote; Chris Salewicz of *NME*, Vivien Goldman of *Sounds*, Bruno Blum of *Best*, Carl Gayle of *Black Music* and Karel Michiels are due special thanks for providing unpublished work and other pertinent information. This book has also been informed by the work of writers such as Neil Spencer and Danny Kelly in *NME*, Chris Lane in *Blues & Soul*, Michael Turner, Richard Henderson and Leroy Pierson in the *Beat*, Penny Reel, John Masouri and John Williams in *Echoes* and Beth Kingston in *Reggae Quarterly*, and other useful sources appear in Further Reading. For this edition, I have also enjoyed visiting online resources including Upsetter.net, upsetter.smokeyroom.net, the Roots Knotty Roots and Reggae Matrix groups on Facebook and the Not Yet Upset pages on YouTube, as well as discogs.com.

I must also thank the many editors who have published my work on Perry and others, particularly Eric 'Black Dog' Cope of *Murder Dog,* who published my first Perry article in *Wiring Department* in 1986, as well as Peter Lilly and Ellen Koehlings of *Riddim*, with whom I have co-chaired many panel discussions with performing artists at Rototom

Sunsplash, together with our colleague Pier Tosi of Radio Città Fujiko in Bologna, yielding material for this revised edition.

For the first edition of this book, I will always be grateful to Jamie Byng at Canongate for recognising the need for a Lee Perry biography; he and editor Colin McLear achieved much under challenging circumstances, before Chris Charlesworth at Omnibus stimulated its rebirth. For this revised and expanded edition, massive thanks are due to Lee Brackstone at White Rabbit for recognising the worth of the book, his vision, experience and impeccable taste providing crucial guidance from start to finish. I also thank editors Ellie Freedman, Georgia Goodall and Jo Whitford, copy-editor Paul Baillie-Lane, proofreader Martha Sprackland and Anna Doble of Reviewed & Cleared, who all gave the text its proper due, working with admirable professionalism despite the stress of advanced deadlines, to Natalie Dawkins and Helen Ewing for facilitating the reproduction of the images to maximal quality, and to Tom Noble, Ellen Turner, Virginia Woolstencroft and the rest of the marketing team for bringing the book to the world. Fellow writers John Williams and Garth Cartwright helped make important connections, and I thank Cartwright, Angus Taylor, Chris Menist, and trumpeter Robin Hopcraft for helpful suggestions and for boosting morale. The provision and assistance of the Society of Authors is also gratefully acknowledged. Other less tangible support has been provided by family and friends, especially my longstanding partner, Claudia Bernard, whose love, patience and understanding means more to me than words can express.

My final thanks are to none other than Lee 'Scratch' Perry, the mighty Upsetter, who is easily the most original man I have ever met; the greatest debt is owed to Mr Perry himself, not only as he realised my potential for writing this book long before I was willing to accept it, but more importantly for providing the world with such exceptional music. The publication of the book made years of struggle in an alien land finally worthwhile, so I hope its realisation has also given something back to the man whose life it investigates.

About the Author

Born in San Francisco and long resident in London, David Katz is the author of *Solid Foundation: An Oral History of Reggae* and a contributor to *The Rough Guide to Reggae*, *A Tapestry of Jamaica*, *Keep On Running: The Story of Island Records* and *Mashup: The Birth of Modern Culture*, among other books. His writing and photographs have appeared in many international periodicals, including the *Guardian*, *Newsweek*, *Mojo*, *Wax Poetics*, *Caribbean Beat* and *Riddim* and he has compiled and annotated over 100 retrospective collections of Jamaican music. Katz has produced documentaries on the music and culture of Jamaica and Brazil for Public Radio International and contributed to documentaries and feature films for the BBC, Channel 4, Arte and other entities, and released original records. He has chaired panel discussions with performers and practitioners in diverse settings, performed as a deejay on four continents, and since 2004, his Dub Me Always vinyl nights have been a regular feature of London's musical landscape.

www.davidkatzreggae.com

INDEX